PRENTICE HALL

SCIENCE EXPLORER

Grade 8

Prentice
Hall

Needham, Massachusetts
Upper Saddle River, New Jersey
Glenview, Illinois

Grade 8

Program Resources

Student Edition
Annotated Teacher's Edition
Unit Resource Books, including:
- Chapter Project Support
- Lesson Plans
- Section Summaries
- Review and Reinforce Worksheets
- Enrich Worksheets
- Student Edition Lab Worksheets
- Answer Keys
Lesson Plans
Chapter and Unit Tests
Performance Assessments
Color Transparencies
Laboratory Manual, Student Edition
Laboratory Manual, Teacher's Edition
Guided Reading and Study Workbook
Guided Reading and Study Workbook, Teacher's Edition
Prentice Hall Assessment System

Program-Wide Components

Inquiry Skills Activity Book
Student-Centered Science Activity Book
    for the Southwest
Reading in the Content Area With
    Literature Connections
Probeware Laboratory Manual with
    CD-ROM
How to Assess Student Work
How to Manage Instruction in the Block
Teacher's ELL Handbook

Media/Technology

Science Explorer iText
Resource Pro CD-ROM
Science Explorer Web site
    at **www.phschool.com**
Computer Test Bank Book with CD-ROM
Student Edition on Audio CD
Student Edition on Audio CD—Spanish
Lab Activity Videotape Library
Science Explorer Videodiscs
Science Explorer Videotape Library
Science Explorer Videotape Library—Spanish

Acknowledgments

Acknowledgment for page 674: Excerpt from *James Herriot's Dog Stories*.
Copyright © 1986 by James Herriot. Published by St. Martin's Press.

ISBN 0-13-053480-3
1 2 3 4 5 6 7 8 9 10   05 04 03 02 01

This *Amphiprion percula,* or clown
fish, swims gracefully among the
tentacles of a sea anemone.

Program Authors

Michael J. Padilla, Ph.D.
Professor
Department of Science Education
University of Georgia
Athens, Georgia

Michael Padilla is a leader in middle school science education. He has served as an editor and elected officer for the National Science Teachers Association. He has been principal investigator of several National Science Foundation and Eisenhower grants and served as a writer of the National Science Education Standards.

As lead author of *Science Explorer,* Mike has inspired the team in developing a program that meets the needs of middle grades students, promotes science inquiry, and is aligned with the National Science Education Standards.

Ioannis Miaoulis, Ph.D.
Dean of Engineering
College of Engineering
Tufts University
Medford, Massachusetts

Martha Cyr, Ph.D.
Director, Engineering
 Educational Outreach
College of Engineering
Tufts University
Medford, Massachusetts

Science Explorer was created in collaboration with the College of Engineering at Tufts University. Tufts has an extensive engineering outreach program that uses engineering design and construction to excite and motivate students and teachers in science and technology education.

Faculty from Tufts University participated in the development of *Science Explorer* chapter projects, reviewed the student books for content accuracy, and helped coordinate field testing.

Book Authors

Elizabeth Coolidge-Stolz, M.D.
Medical Writer
North Reading, Massachusetts

Linda Cronin-Jones, Ph.D.
Professor, College of Education
University of Florida
Gainesville, Florida

Donald Cronkite, Ph.D.
Professor of Biology
Hope College
Holland, Michigan

Joseph D. Exline, M.A., Ed.D.
President
Exline Consulting Services, Inc.
Beaverdam, Virginia

David V. Frank, Ph.D.
Physical Science Department Head
Ferris State University
Big Rapids, Michigan

Fred Holtzclaw
Science Instructor
Oak Ridge High School
Oak Ridge, Tennessee

Jan Jenner, Ph.D.
Science Writer
Talladega, Alabama

Steve Miller
Science Writer
State College, Pennsylvania

Jay M. Pasachoff, Ph.D.
Professor of Astronomy
Williams College
Williamstown, Massachusetts

Barbara Brooks Simons
Science Writer
Boston, Massachusetts

Carole Garbuny Vogel, M.A.T.
Science Writer
Lexington, Massachusetts

iv

Jonathan Gitlin, M.D.
School of Medicine
Washington University
St. Louis, Missouri

Dawn Graff-Haight, Ph.D.,
Department of Health, Human
    Performance, and Athletics
Linfield College
McMinnville, Oregon

Deborah L. Gumucio, Ph.D.
Associate Professor
Department of Anatomy and
    Cell Biology
University of Michigan
Ann Arbor, Michigan

William S. Harwood, Ph.D.
Dean of University Division and
    Associate Professor of Education
Indiana University
Bloomington, Indiana

Cyndy Henzel, Ph.D.
Department of Geography
    and Regional Development
University of Arizona
Tucson, Arizona

Greg Hutton
Science and Health
    Curriculum Coordinator
School Board of Sarasota County
Sarasota, Florida

Susan K. Jacobson, Ph.D.
Department of Wildlife Ecology
    and Conservation
University of Florida
Gainesville, Florida

Judy Jernstedt, Ph.D.
Department of Agronomy and
    Range Science
University of California, Davis
Davis, California

John L. Kermond, Ph.D.
Office of Global Programs
National Oceanographic and
    Atmospheric Administration
Silver Spring, Maryland

David E. LaHart, Ph.D.
Institute of Science and
    Public Affairs
Florida State University
Tallahassee, Florida

Joe Leverich, Ph.D.
Department of Biology
St. Louis University
St. Louis, Missouri

Dennis K. Lieu, Ph.D.
Department of Mechanical
    Engineering
University of California
Berkeley, California

Desiree A. Jackson, Ph.D.
Department of Biology
Texas Southern University
Houston, Texas

Akhtar H. Mahmood, Ph.D.
Assistant Professor
University of Texas-Pan American
Edinburg, Texas

Cynthia J. Moore, Ph.D.
Science Outreach Coordinator
Washington University
St. Louis, Missouri

Joseph M. Moran, Ph.D.
Department of Earth Science
University of Wisconsin–Green Bay
Green Bay, Wisconsin

José L. Panero
Assistant Professor of Botany
University of Texas
Austin, Texas

Doris Rosenbaum, Ph.D.
Scholar in Residence, Physics
    Department
Southern Methodist University
Dallas, Texas

Ronald L. Sass, Ph.D.
Professor of Chemistry and Biology
Rice University
Houston, Texas

Eric S. Schmitt, Ph.D., M.S., C.G.C.
Genetic Counselor
Baylor College of Medicine
Houston, Texas

John M. Sharp, Jr., Ph.D.
Chevron Centennial Professor of
    Geology
University of Texas
Austin, Texas

Joseph Stukey, Ph.D.
Department of Biology
Hope College
Holland, Michigan

Seetha Subramanian
Lexington Community College
University of Kentucky
Lexington, Kentucky

Carl L. Thurman, Ph.D.
Department of Biology
University of Northern Iowa
Cedar Falls, Iowa

Edward D. Walton, Ph.D.
Department of Chemistry
California State Polytechnic
    University
Pomona, California

Susan D. Wiediger, Ph.D.
Research Associate
Department of Chemistry
Rice University
Houston, Texas

Aaron S. Yoshinobu, Ph.D.
Assistant Professor
Department of Geosciences
Texas Technical University
Lubbock, Texas

Robert S. Young, Ph.D.
Department of Geosciences and
    Natural Resource Management
Western Carolina University
Cullowhee, North Carolina

Edward J. Zalisko, Ph.D.
Department of Biology
Blackburn College
Carlinville, Illinois

Texas Consultants

Susan M. Cory, Senior Texas Consultant
Cypress Fairbanks ISD
Houston, Texas

Jill Bailer
Science Department Chairperson
Jane Long Middle School
Houston, Texas

Beverly Bowe
Comstock Middle School
Dallas ISD
Dallas, Texas

Sharon J. Delesbore
Olle Middle School
Alief ISD
Houston, Texas

Marcie Denton
Peterson Middle School
Peterson ISD
Kerrville, Texas

Cathy Harter
Mayde Creek Junior High
Katy ISD
Houston, Texas

David Hollis
Marsh Middle School
Dallas ISD
Dallas, Texas

Debra McCain
Science Department Chair
Bussey Middle School
Garland ISD
Garland, Texas

Candice Meyer
Hildebrandt Intermediate School
Klein ISD
Spring, Texas

Sharon Phillips-Watson
Science Department Chair
Rusk Middle School
Dallas ISD
Dallas, TX

Sarah Santos Montez
Science Specialist
Edgewood ISD
San Antonio, Texas

Paul Reyna
Lyles Middle School
Garland ISD
Garland, Texas

Eddie Rodriguez
Science Specialist
Edgewood ISD
San Antonio, Texas

C. Lorraine Thompson
Educator
Franklin Middle School
Dallas ISD
Dallas, Texas

Teacher Reviewers

José Luis Alvarez
Ysleta ISD
El Paso, Texas

Stephanie Anderson
Sierra Vista Junior High School
Canyon Country, California

John W. Anson
Mesa Intermediate School
Palmdale, California

Pamela Arline
Lake Taylor Middle School
Norfolk, Virginia

Lynn Beason
A & M Consolidated Middle School
College Station, Texas

Jennifer Becerra
Pease Middle School
San Antonio, Texas

Stacey L. Blair
Tivy Upper Elementary School
Kerrville, Texas

Richard Bothmer
Hollis School District
Hollis, New Hampshire

Jeffrey C. Callister
Newburgh Free Academy
Newburgh, New York

Judy D'Albert
Harvard Day School
Corona Del Mar, California

Betty Scott Dean
Guilford County Schools
McLeansville, North Carolina

Sarah C. Duff
Baltimore City Public Schools
Baltimore, Maryland

Patricia Durst
Handley Middle School
Fort Worth, Texas

Cecie Edwards
Sudan ISD
Sudan, Texas

Melody Law Ewey
Holmes Junior High School
Davis, California

Sherry L. Fisher
Lake Zurich Middle School North
Lake Zurich, Illinois

Melissa Gibbons
Dunbar Middle School
Fort Worth, Texas

Debra J. Goodding
Kraemer Middle School
Placentia, California

Jack Grande
Weber Middle School
Port Washington, New York

Carole W. Henry
Gus Garcia Middle School
San Antonio, Texas

Ross Ann Hill
Idalou Middle School
Idalou, Texas

Steve Hills
Riverside Middle School
Grand Rapids, Michigan

Sandra M. Justin
Swift Junior High School
Oakville, Connecticut

Rosie L. Leno
Krueger Middle School
San Antonio, Texas

Carol Ann Lionello
Kraemer Middle School
Placentia, California

Alison Minish-Ford
Ysleta Middle School
El Paso, Texas

Jaime A. Morales
Henry T. Gage Middle
School
Huntington Park,
California

Rebecca Morton
Wedgwood Sixth Grade
School
Fort Worth, Texas

Patsy Partin
Cameron Middle School
Fort Worth, Texas

Deedra H. Robinson
Newport News Public
Schools
Newport News, Virginia

Rick Robinson
Medina Valley Middle
School
San Antonio, Texas

Charles M. Sears
Belzer Middle School
Indianapolis, Indiana

Shirley Simon
South Park Middle
School
Beaumont, Texas

Barbara M. Strange
Ferndale Middle School
High Point, North
Carolina

Denzial Tittle
Thornton Middle
School
Katy, Texas

Kathy Usina
Belzer Middle School
Indianapolis, Indiana

Heidi M. von Oetinger
L'Anse Creuse Public
School
Harrison Township,
Michigan

Pam Watson
Hill Country Middle
School
Austin, Texas

Laurie Westphal
Thornton Middle School
Katy, Texas

Activity Field Testers

Nicki Bibbo
Russell Street School
Littleton, Massachusetts

Connie Boone
Fletcher Middle School
Jacksonville Beach,
Florida

Rose-Marie Botting
Broward County
School District
Fort Lauderdale, Florida

Colleen Campos
Laredo Middle School
Aurora, Colorado

Elizabeth Chait
W. L. Chenery Middle
School
Belmont, Massachusetts

Holly Estes
Hale Middle School
Stow, Massachusetts

Laura Hapgood
Plymouth Community
Intermediate School
Plymouth, Massachusetts

Sandra M. Harris
Winman Junior High
School
Warwick, Rhode Island

Jason Ho
Walter Reed Middle
School
Los Angeles, California

Joanne Jackson
Winman Junior High
School
Warwick, Rhode Island

Mary F. Lavin
Plymouth Community
Intermediate School
Plymouth, Massachusetts

James MacNeil, Ph.D.
Concord Public Schools
Concord, Massachusetts

Lauren Magruder
St. Michael's Country Day
School
Newport, Rhode Island

Warren Phillips
Plymouth Community
Intermediate School
Plymouth, Massachusetts

Carol Pirtle
Hale Middle School
Stow, Massachusetts

Kathleen M. Poe
Kirby-Smith Middle
School
Jacksonville, Florida

Cynthia B. Pope
Ruffner Middle School
Norfolk, Virginia

Anne Scammell
Geneva Middle School
Geneva, New York

Karen Riley Sievers
Callanan Middle School
Des Moines, Iowa

David M. Smith
Howard A. Eyer Middle
School
Macungie, Pennsylvania

Derek Strohschneider
Plymouth Community
Intermediate School
Plymouth, Massachusetts

Gene Vitale
Parkland Middle School
McHenry, Illinois

Zenovia Young
Meyer Levin Junior
High School (IS 285)
Brooklyn, New York

Contents

Grade 8

Unit 1 Physical Systems— Matter and Energy

Unit 2 Light and the Universe

Unit 3 Earth Systems

PRENTICE HALL
SCIENCE EXPLORER

Unit 4   Human Activities and Earth Systems

Unit 5 Genetics and Interdependence Among Living Systems

Reference Section

Activities

DISCOVER
Exploration and inquiry before reading

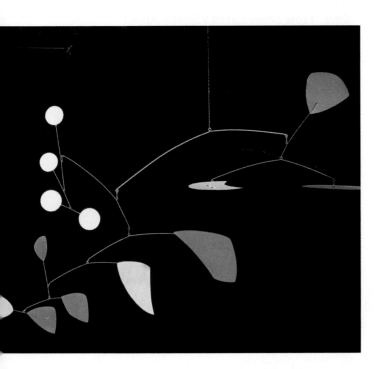

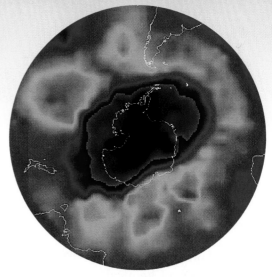

Sharpen your *Skills*

Practice of specific science inquiry skills

PRENTICE HALL
SCIENCE EXPLORER

TRY THIS

Reinforcement of key concepts

PRENTICE HALL
SCIENCE EXPLORER

Science at Home

EXPLORING
Visual exploration of concepts

Interdisciplinary Activities

Texas Essential Knowledge and Skills for Science

To Parents and Students:

The state of Texas has established standards describing science knowledge and skills for which students are responsible. These standards are known as the Texas Essential Knowledge and Skills, or TEKS. State assessments of student achievement in science are based on these TEKS. The Grade 8 TEKS are listed below. The chapter references show where the content and skills are addressed in this textbook. An individual TEKS may be addressed in more than one chapter. Some chapters address only part of a TEKS.

To check for mastery of the content and process TEKS, students may use the Chapter Assessments at the end of each chapter and the *Science Explorer* iText at: **www.phschool.com**

(8.1) Scientific processes. The student conducts field and laboratory investigations using safe, environmentally appropriate, and ethical practices.
(Chapters 1, 2, 5–8, 10–13, 17)
The student is expected to:
(A) demonstrate safe practices during field and laboratory investigations; and
(B) make wise choices in the use and conservation of resources and the disposal or recycling of materials.

(8.2) Scientific processes. The student uses scientific methods during field and laboratory investigations.
(Chapters 1, 2, 4–13, 16, 17)
The student is expected to:
(A) plan and implement investigative procedures including asking questions, formulating testable hypotheses, and selecting equipment and technology;
(B) collect data by observing and measuring;
(C) organize, analyze, evaluate, make inferences, and predict trends from direct and indirect evidence;
(D) communicate valid conclusions; and
(E) construct graphs, tables, maps, and charts using tools including computers to organize, examine, and evaluate data.

(8.3) Scientific processes. The student uses critical thinking and scientific problem solving to make informed decisions.
(Chapters 1, 2, 4–13, 16, 17)
The student is expected to:
(A) analyze, review, and critique scientific explanations, including hypotheses and theories, as to their strengths and weaknesses using scientific evidence and information;

(B) draw inferences based on data related to promotional materials for products and services;
(C) represent the natural world using models and identify their limitations;
(D) evaluate the impact of research on scientific thought, society, and the environment; and
(E) connect Grade 8 science concepts with the history of science and contributions of scientists.

(8.4) Scientific processes. The student knows how to use tools and methods to conduct scientific inquiry.
(Chapters 1, 4–13, 16, 17)
The student is expected to:
(A) collect, analyze and record information to explain a phenomenon using tools including beakers, petri dishes, meter sticks, graduated cylinders, weather instruments, hot plates, dissecting equipment, test tubes, safety goggles, spring scales, balances, microscopes, telescopes, thermometers, calculators, field equipment, computers, computer probes, timing devices, magnets, and compasses; and
(B) extrapolate from collected information to make predictions.

(8.5) Scientific processes. The student knows that relationships exist between science and technology.
(Chapters 5, 8)
The student is expected to:
(A) identify a design problem and propose a solution;
(B) design and test a model to solve the problem; and
(C) evaluate the model and make recommendations for improving the model.

(8.6) Science concepts. The student knows that interdependence occurs among living systems.
(Chapters 5, 7)
The student is expected to:
(A) describe interactions among systems in the human organism;
(B) identify feedback mechanisms that maintain equilibrium of systems such as body temperature, turgor pressure, and chemical reactions; and
(C) describe interactions within ecosystems.

(8.7) Science concepts. The student knows that there is a relationship between force and motion.
(Chapters 4–7, 9)
The student is expected to:
(A) demonstrate how unbalanced forces cause changes in the speed or direction of an object's motion; and
(B) recognize that waves are generated and can travel through different media.

(8.8) Science concepts. The student knows that matter is composed of atoms.
(Chapters 1, 2)
The student is expected to:
(A) describe the structure and parts of an atom; and
(B) identify the properties of an atom including mass and electrical charge.

(8.9) Science concepts. The student knows that substances have chemical and physical properties.
(Chapters 1, 2, 10)
The student is expected to:
(A) demonstrate that substances may react chemically to form new substances;
(B) interpret information on the periodic table to understand that physical properties are used to group elements;
(C) recognize the importance of formulas and equations to express what happens in a chemical reaction; and
(D) identify that physical and chemical properties influence the development and application of everyday materials such as cooking surfaces, insulation, adhesives, and plastics.

(8.10) Science concepts. The student knows that complex interactions occur between matter and energy.
(Chapters 4, 5, 6, 9)
The student is expected to:
(A) illustrate interactions between matter and energy including specific heat;
(B) describe interactions among solar, weather, and ocean systems; and
(C) identify and demonstrate that loss or gain of heat energy occurs during exothermic and endothermic chemical reactions.

(8.11) Science concepts. The student knows that traits of species can change through generations and that the instructions for traits are contained in the genetic material of the organisms.
(Chapter 17)
The student is expected to:
(A) identify that change in environmental conditions can affect the survival of individuals and of species;
(B) distinguish between inherited traits and other characteristics that result from interactions with the environment; and
(C) make predictions about possible outcomes of various genetic combinations of inherited characteristics.

(8.12) Science concepts. The student knows that cycles exist in Earth systems.
(Chapters 10, 11, 12)
The student is expected to:
(A) analyze and predict the sequence of events in the lunar and rock cycles;
(B) relate the role of oceans to climatic changes; and
(C) predict the results of modifying the Earth's nitrogen, water, and carbon cycles.

(8.13) Science concepts. The student knows characteristics of the universe.
(Chapter 8)
The student is expected to:
(A) describe characteristics of the universe such as stars and galaxies;
(B) explain the use of light years to describe distances in the universe; and
(C) research and describe historical scientific theories of the origin of the universe.

(8.14) Science concepts. The student knows that natural events and human activity can alter Earth systems.
(Chapters 8, 9, 12, 13)
The student is expected to:
(A) predict land features resulting from gradual changes such as mountain building, beach erosion, land subsidence, and continental drift;
(B) analyze how natural or human events may have contributed to the extinction of some species; and
(C) describe how human activities have modified soil, water, and air quality.

TEXAS *Field Trip*

IT'S A GO, HOUSTON!

Lift Off! The Space Shuttle Endeavor *thundered into space. After months of training at Lyndon B. Johnson Space Center in Houston, Texas, the astronauts were ready for their mission. Working as a team, they would connect the first two pieces of the International Space Station. The first piece, Zarya, had been built in Russia and was already in orbit. The second piece, Unity, built in the United States, was stowed in the shuttle's cargo bay.*

On the second day of the mission, Endeavor met up with Zarya for their rendezvous in space. Unity and Zarya were successfully connected. Astronauts then had to head out of the shuttle to connect electrical power cables between Zarya and Unity, and to set up communications equipment.

All of these activities were closely supervised by the Mission Control staff in Houston. Since 1961, every mission carried out by American astronauts has been monitored by the Johnson Space Center.

Astronauts train at Johnson Space Center. Mission Control, the operations center for United States space missions, is also housed here.

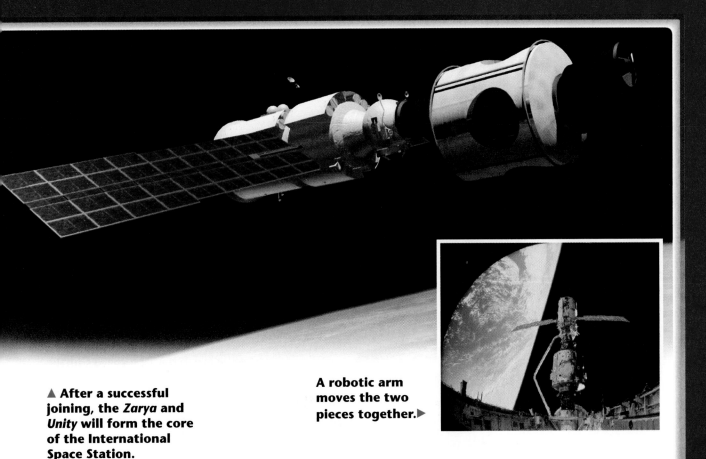

▲ **After a successful joining, the *Zarya* and *Unity* will form the core of the International Space Station.**

A robotic arm moves the two pieces together. ▶

An International Effort

Sixteen nations are working together to build the International Space Station (ISS), the largest space-based research center in history. The ISS will orbit Earth at an altitude of approximately 390 kilometers. The staff at Johnson Space Center monitors the contributions of the United States to the ISS.

A Huge Project When the ISS is complete, it will provide a crew of seven astronauts with about the same amount of living and working space as three average-sized American homes. Approximately 4,000 square meters of solar panels will power the labs on the station. These could cover a small soccer field.

Over 40 missions will be needed to assemble the space station and set up all the equipment. Officials at the National Aeronautics and Space Administration (NASA) expect the International Space Station to be completely operational by 2006. They predict that it will be a useful research lab for at least a decade.

Important Goals One of the main goals of the International Space Station project is to provide a space-based lab where scientists can carry out research in many fields of science, including medicine and ecology. But the project has other goals as well. For example, working in space may open up new business areas. It may be easier to manufacture some products in weightless conditions than under gravity.

Many people hope that working together to make the ISS will increase international cooperation among the 16 nations involved. In addition, people hope that the ISS can be used as a launching point to destinations across the solar system. Perhaps astronauts can travel from the space station to the moon to set up a base there. Or maybe they can journey all the way to Mars.

◄ **Diagram of what** *TransHab* **might look like once inflated.**

to get the space station crew back to Earth in an emergency. If something goes wrong in the space station, the crew will leave immediately on the X-38, instead of having to wait for a space shuttle to be sent up to rescue them.

Another new design being considered for the International Space Station is an unusual type of living quarters. While the rest of the space station is rigid metal, this component, called *TransHab*, would be inflatable. Before it is inflated, its diameter will be only 4.3 meters, a size that will fit easily into the cargo bay of a space shuttle. When it is inflated at the space station, *TransHab* will expand to a diameter of 8.2 meters.

NASA engineers imagine *TransHab* being put to other uses, too. If the design works out, they think it could be used as temporary living quarters for a crew landing on Mars. It would be a space traveler's version of a camper!

More Work to Do

Before the International Space Station can accomplish its goals, astronauts must assemble more than 100 separate pieces in space. Astronauts will spend nearly 2,000 hours latching, locking, wiring, and bolting the pieces together.

Planning and Practice To prepare for assembling and living on the ISS, work occurs in Houston. At Johnson Space Center, astronauts train for future space station missions. Every activity scheduled for a space mission is planned in advance. Astronauts use simulators to learn to fly the space shuttle and work its equipment, such as the robotic arm that lifted *Unity* out of *Endeavor*'s cargo bay. Scientists and engineers are testing a new spacesuit and a new life-support system that will be used by astronauts who live and work on the space station.

New Designs Engineers at Johnson Space Center have designed a new spacecraft to be used at the International Space Station. The X-38 Crew Return Vehicle will be used like a kind of lifeboat

This astronaut is using a simulator to prepare for an upcoming space mission ▼

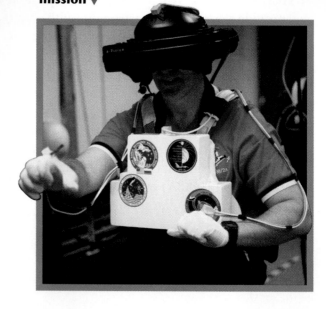

Other Research

While Johnson Space Center has a long history of developing spacecraft, training crews, and monitoring them during flights, not everyone there works on these projects. Some scientists contribute to the space program and other fields by conducting research in space.

Medical Research Working with Houston's Institute for Research, scientists at Johnson Space Center are experimenting with a new method for delivering drugs directly to a cancer-causing tumor. The drugs are packaged inside microscopic capsules that are similar to tiny water balloons. The microcapsules must be made under weightless conditions, and astronauts on board the space shuttle flights are currently doing the job.

Preparing for the Future Scientists at Johnson Space Center also work on programs to explore neighboring planets such as Mars. Before humans visit Mars, however, scientists must gather more information about the Red Planet, and engineers must design spacecraft to get there. It will take a long time for astronauts to make the journey to Mars. With no way to refuel or get new supplies, astronauts will have to carry their food and oxygen with them—or will they?

In one lab at the space center, a team of scientists has developed a device that can obtain oxygen from the chemicals in the cold, harsh Martian atmosphere. The equipment will be tested on Mars during an upcoming information-gathering mission.

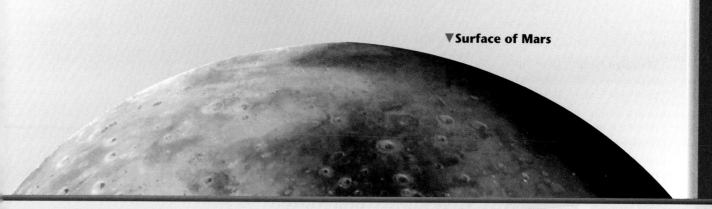

▼**Surface of Mars**

TEXAS
Field Trip

SCIENCE ROUND-UP
Find out more about what it takes to travel in space.

Creativity is an important skill in space travel. Enhance your own creativity. Use the following items to construct something that will float in a basin of water: a drinking straw, a 10 cm x 10 cm square of aluminum foil, a balloon, and an empty thread spool. If needed, use tape to assemble your creation. You must use all four items and nothing else.

If possible, pay a visit to Johnson Space Center in Houston. Find out more about the International Space Station and other space missions.

Write a list of all the things you need to survive each day on Earth. Now, suppose you are traveling to the International Space Station for several weeks. What items would be on your list of things needed there? How do your lists compare?

Write a detailed plan for an activity such as a camping trip. What preparations would you make for the activity, and what skills should you practice to ensure that your activity is a success?

ASSEMBLING THE INTERNATIONAL SPACE STATION

Madalyn Nelson grew up in Louisiana and attended Southern University in Baton Rouge, earning a degree in engineering. Madalyn recently moved to Houston where she works on projects for NASA.

When astronauts on the Space Shuttle *Endeavor* connected *Unity* and *Zarya*, all eyes were on them. But many other people were involved in the mission. Building the new International Space Station takes teamwork. Mission Control staff on the ground in Houston guided the astronauts through their tasks. Engineers and scientists created the vehicles and equipment used in space.

Madalyn Nelson is an electrical engineer who leads a team of engineers working on the International Space Station project. Madalyn thinks that contributing to a team is very rewarding. "I enjoy working with people and sharing ideas. It is really much easier to solve problems in teams. Someone else might come up with an idea that never would have occurred to me."

Keeping Everything in Its Place

Madalyn's first project for NASA was to develop the requirements for a barcode system that could be used to keep track of objects used in a spacecraft. "Astronauts have to be extremely organized up there," says Madalyn. "If they don't put a screwdriver away, it could float off and do some damage."

Madalyn did extensive research on barcode systems. After learning everything she could, she developed the requirements for a system that met NASA's specific needs. Under this plan, every tool and food item on a spacecraft has a barcode on it. When anything is removed from or returned to a drawer or rack where it is stored, an astronaut scans the barcode. A computer on board keeps track of this information.

Coordinating the Project

Madalyn's team of engineers oversees the integration of the International Space Station's many pieces. "We coordinate the whole process," she says. "We look at how parts made at different sites will fit together into one piece. Then we go over each step of the procedure used to attach the new piece to the rest of the space station. We think about exactly how the piece will be lifted out of the shuttle's cargo bay. We review every detail of how the astronauts will connect electrical and heating systems."

About two years before a piece is scheduled to head into space, Madalyn and her team conduct a review. This step helps people designing the equipment and planning the mission to spot potential problems. For example, some steps of the process may require electricity. Madalyn's team has to make sure that these steps are scheduled to occur after all the electrical cables have been hooked up to the station.

▲ Every item on a spacecraft has a barcode that helps astronauts keep an accurate inventory.

◄ Astronauts often have to work outside their spacecraft to make repairs or install new equipment.

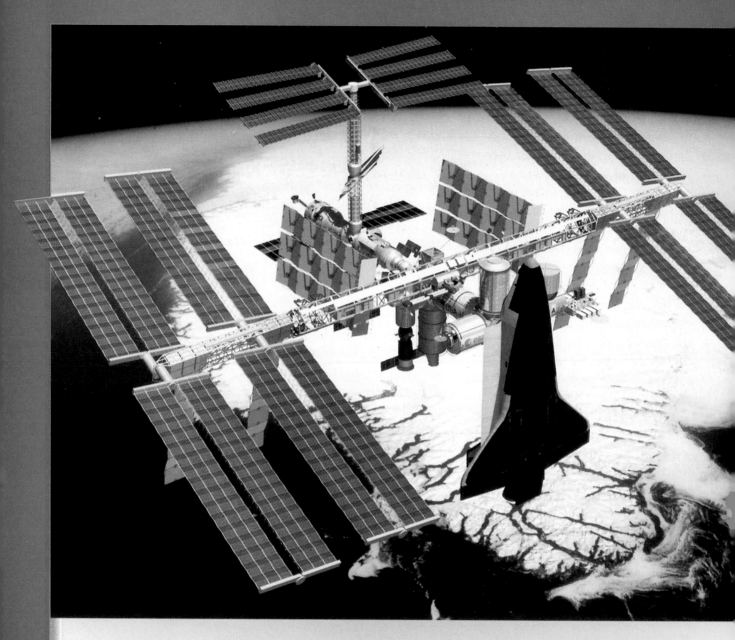

An artist's rendering of what the International Space Station will look like when complete.

Putting It All Together

Although the pieces of the International Space Station are being built all over the world, they will be launched and assembled by either the United States or Russia. Because the project is very complicated, everyone expects to encounter all kinds of surprises during the construction work in orbit. Madalyn's job is to make sure the astronauts know how to handle the surprises. "We look at all aspects of the project, but our priorities are always the safety of the crew and the safety of the vehicle," Madalyn notes.

Madalyn's team also needs to identify places where a broken part could stop the entire mission. For example, if a computer fails, is there another computer that could take over? If not, can the damaged part be identified and replaced? Spare parts have to be available on board, of course, because there's nowhere to get them in space!

The Importance of Teamwork

To do her job, Madalyn has to be creative and flexible. "I used to resist the idea of making changes," she recalls. "I thought, 'If it works, why change it?' But there are always better ways to do things. The technology is always changing, so there is always room for improvement."

Madalyn also finds it useful to tap into her co-workers' past experiences. "When a problem arises, we can go to a database that has information about 'lessons learned.'" she explains. The database describes the history of technical difficulties and outlines what was done to resolve each situation. Madalyn's team frequently updates the database to include what they have learned during their reviews. Madalyn became an engineer because she had always liked math and science. Engineering is a field that involves applying scientific principles to real-world situations.

According to Madalyn, there is no shortage of issues to consider and problems to solve when working on the space program. That's one of the reasons Madalyn likes her job. "Everyday is a new adventure," she says. "You never know what might come up."

In Your Journal

Madalyn Nelson mentioned NASA's database of "lessons learned." This resource is used to help teams to avoid repeating mistakes. Everyone has his or her own "database" of lessons learned. What lessons have you learned recently? How will these lessons shape your decision making in the future?

Teamwork is very important to the scientists who work on large projects. Here Madalyn reviews plans with members of her team. ▼

What Is SCIENCE?

GUIDE FOR READING

◆ What skills do scientists use in their work?

◆ Why are safe laboratory practices important?

Reading Tip Before you read, make a list of the boldfaced terms. As you read, write a definition in your own words for each term.

Key Terms science
• scientific inquiry
• observation
• inference
• hypothesis
• variable
• manipulated variable
• responding variable
• controlled experiment
• data
• scientific law
• scientific theory

Madalyn Nelson's road to NASA began with her interests in electricity and math. In her work as an engineer designing parts for the International Space Station, Madalyn applies the principles of science to real-world situations.

Science is both a way of learning about the natural world and the knowledge gained in that process. This body of knowledge is always growing and changing as scientists explore new ideas.

Another term for the many ways in which scientists study the world around them is **scientific inquiry.** Scientific inquiry is used every day by the engineers and scientists at NASA. You don't have to be an engineer or a scientist to use the methods of scientific inquiry. In fact, you have already used some kinds of scientific thinking. If you have ever tried to figure out why a radio has stopped working or decided on the best location for a garden, you have used scientific inquiry.

Thinking Like a Scientist

Madalyn Nelson and her team of engineers use scientific inquiry as they design and test parts of the International Space Station. In their work, they use a variety of skills.

Some of the skills that scientists use are posing questions, making observations and inferences, developing hypotheses, designing experiments, collecting data and making measurements, interpreting data, and drawing conclusions. Sometimes scientists make models of scientific events to help them solve problems. Scientists also must communicate their findings to others. Scientists may use only some or all of these skills in any single investigation.

You can use the skills of scientific inquiry as you make discoveries yourself. For example, look at the picture of the hang glider in Figure 1. How does the hang glider stay in the air? Where was his starting point? What will happen when he lands?

If you ask questions about things and events around you, you are thinking like a scientist. You have begun the process of scientific inquiry.

Posing Questions Are you curious? Curiosity drives scientific inquiry by leading people to think about a question or a problem. You may have questions about the natural world. Have you ever had a roll of film developed and seen shadows in your photos like the ones in Figure 2? Did you become curious about shadows? Perhaps it made you wonder, "What causes shadows to occur?" or "What makes shadows longer or shorter?"

Making Observations and Inferences In order to learn more about shadows, you use the skill of observation. **Observation** involves using one or more of the five senses— sight, hearing, touch, smell, and taste— to gather information. Using your sight, for example, you may observe, that shadows can change in length.

An observation is important, but it's only one part of a larger process. Observations usually lead to inferences. An **inference** is a logical interpretation based on observations or prior knowledge. You may infer, for example, that the length of an object's shadow depends on how near the object is to the light source.

It is important to remember that an inference is just one possible interpretation. Scientists must keep an open mind and consider many possible interpretations of their observations.

☑ *Checkpoint* *What senses can the skill of observation involve?*

Figure 1 How does this hang glider defy gravity and stay up in the air? Unusual sights or events often lead to questions.

Figure 2 Photographers make use of shadows to create interesting photos. *Posing Questions Think of some questions about light and shadows that a photographer might investigate in order to take photographs like these?*

Developing Hypotheses

Scientific inquiry moves forward when ideas are tested. In doing so, scientists often work from one or more hypotheses. A **hypothesis** is a possible explanation for a set of observations or an answer to a scientific question. In science, a hypothesis must be testable by observation or experimentation. In this way, information can be collected that may or may not support the hypothesis.

In your study of shadows, you might develop the following hypothesis: *The distance between an object and a light source affects the length of the object's shadow.* You could then design an experiment to test this idea. You might even predict the outcome of the experiment based on previous observations you have made. Perhaps you would predict that an object's shadow gets smaller as the light source is moved farther from it.

☑ *Checkpoint* **What is a hypothesis?**

Figure 3 The position of a light source can affect the size of an object's shadow. *Inferring How would you explain the length of the shadows in this photograph?*

Designing Controlled Experiments

To test a hypothesis, scientists examine all the factors that can change during an experiment. Such factors are called **variables.** The variable that a scientist changes is called the **manipulated variable,** or independent variable. The variable that is expected to change in response to the manipulated variable is the **responding variable,** or dependent variable.

The manipulated variable for the hypothesis being tested in Figure 4 is the distance between the light source and the object. The responding variable is the length of the shadow. To be sure that changes in the manipulated variable are causing the changes in the responding variable, scientists test, or change, only one variable at a time. All other variables must be controlled—that is, kept constant. In this example, some of the variables that must be controlled are the type of light source, the angle at which the light hits the object, and the distance between the object and the wall. An investigation in which all variables except one remain constant is called a **controlled experiment.**

Collecting Data and Making Measurements

The facts, figures, and other information that are collected during an experiment are called **data.** Scientists carefully record their data in order to have a permanent account of the results of their experiments.

Scientific data may include both qualitative and quantitative descriptions. Qualitative data are descriptions, such as color, odor, or sound, that don't involve measurements or numbers. Quantitative data are

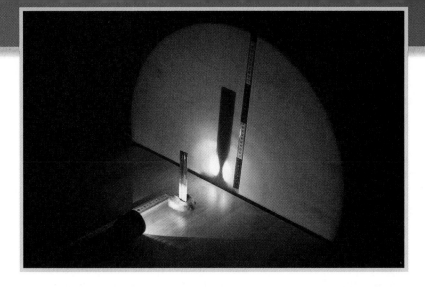

Figure 4 In this experiment, the distance between the flashlight and the ruler is the manipulated variable. *Applying Concepts Why is the length of the ruler's shadow the responding variable?*

measurements made using standard units, such as degrees Celsius (°C) for temperature or meters per second (m/s) for speed.

To make it easier to share data, scientists express measurements in a standard way. They use a system of measurement called the International System of Units. This measurement system is abbreviated as SI (for the French, *Système International d'Unités*). SI is based on the metric system used in many countries around the world. By using SI, scientists from all over the world can understand one another's data.

Notice that the data for the shadow experiment are measured in the metric unit known as centimeters. Before you conduct any experiments, learn more about making scientific measurements on pages 682–683 of the Skills Handbook.

Interpreting Data Scientists interpret data, or find out what the data mean, by identifying trends or patterns. Data are often organized in tables or graphs. Figure 5 shows a data table and graph for the shadow experiment. To learn more about data tables and graphs, see pages 694–696 in the Skills Handbook.

Distance Between Object and Light (cm)	Length of Shadow (cm)
10	32
15	27
20	25
25	23
30	22
35	21
40	20

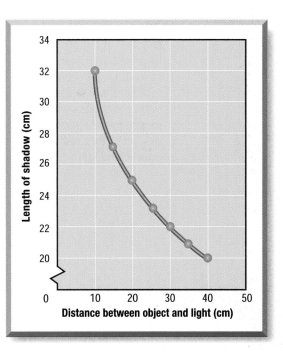

Figure 5 The distances and lengths recorded in this data table are examples of quantitative data. Notice that the heading for each column indicates the units used to make the measurements. When these data are graphed, the result is a curved line.

Drawing Conclusions After interpreting the data from an experiment, you are ready to draw a conclusion. A conclusion states whether or not the data support the hypothesis. For example, based on the data in Figure 5, you would conclude that the length of a shadow *does* decrease as the light source is moved farther away.

In this example, the data support the hypothesis. However, experimental data often do not support a hypothesis. Does this mean that the investigation was a failure? Quite the contrary. What may be most surprising to you is that failure is often an important step in the scientific process! What seems like a dead end can lead to new questions that need to be investigated further. Then the process of inquiry begins all over again. When answers come, they may increase scientific knowledge in small steps. Or, they may lead to a giant leap of understanding.

Making Models and Simulations Sometimes scientists cannot test a hypothesis by doing a controlled experiment. Another way to test a hypothesis is to use a model or simulation.

A scientific model can be a three-dimensional representation, or it can be a diagram such as a map. Many scientists today use computers to make models of complex objects or events.

A simulation is a model that imitates a real-world situation. For example, scientists who study weather may use computer simulations to predict the path that hurricanes will take. The computer uses data from past hurricanes as well as current conditions in its simulations.

Scientific models and simulations are important tools that help scientists understand complex events and make predictions about the future.

Figure 6 An understanding of light and shadows helps artists and performers create visual effects that delight and surprise the viewer. *Predicting If the photographer wanted to make the shadow of the musician look larger, how would the light source have to change?*

Figure 7 This scientist is standing behind a three-dimensional model of a disease-fighting molecule found in the human body.

But even the most sophisticated models have limitations because they are still only simplified versions of the real world. Scientists always work to improve the accuracy of the models and simulations they use. They do this by gathering new data and revising their models to reflect all of the latest information available to them.

Communicating Information

You may recall that parts of the International Space Station are being built in several different countries. The engineers designing these parts must communicate with each other frequently. Communication is the sharing of ideas and experimental findings with others through writing and speaking.

Scientists communicate directly with one another when they are working on the same project. They also communicate with the whole scientific community by writing articles in scientific journals, speaking at scientific meetings, and by using the Internet. In addition, scientists may communicate their findings to the public using nontechnical terms that most people can understand easily.

Checkpoint List three ways in which scientists communicate with one another.

Developing Scientific Laws and Theories

As a body of knowledge, science is built up cautiously. Scientists do not accept a new hypothesis with just a few successful experiments. Instead, it is tested repeatedly by different scientists. Some hypotheses have become so well established that they are called laws. A **scientific law** is a statement that describes what scientists expect to happen every time under a particular set of conditions. One law in science describes how objects fall toward Earth in a certain way.

Sometimes a large body of related information can be explained by a single major idea. If that idea is supported by many tests, it may develop into a scientific theory. A **scientific theory** is a well-tested idea that explains and connects a wide range of observations. For example, the theory that matter is made of atoms helps explain a huge number of observations related to changes in matter. It is possible, however, that a scientific theory will be contradicted by new evidence. If that happens, scientists will change the theory or abandon it.

Laboratory Safety

You will carry out experiments and other activities as you learn about science. During these investigations, be sure to observe safe laboratory practices. Always follow your teacher's instructions, and show respect and courtesy to your teacher and classmates. Before you begin an activity, make sure you understand every step of the procedure and the accompanying safety information. Handle all laboratory materials carefully.

Figure 8 Following laboratory safety rules keeps scientists safe and makes experiments run smoothly. *Observing* What steps has this student taken to protect himself while carrying out this experiment?

Before conducting any experiment or activity, read and learn the rules for laboratory safety and the meaning of each safety symbol in Appendix A: Laboratory Safety on pages 697–699. The safety symbols alert you to necessary precautions, such as wearing a lab apron or heat-resistant gloves. **Remember, safe laboratory practices will not only protect you and your classmates from injury but will also make your investigations run more smoothly.**

✓ *Checkpoint* What are three important safety rules to follow when performing a scientific investigation?

SWING TIME

You can study the movement of a pendulum by hanging an object—the bob—on a string.

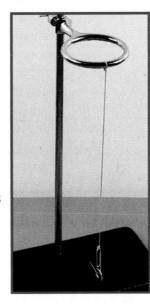

Problem

Does the swing of a pendulum take longer for an object of greater mass?

Materials

stand with clamp
large paper clip
ruler

string, 50 cm in length
5 metal washers
stopwatch

Procedure

1. Read the whole procedure. Write a hypothesis describing how the mass of the bob will affect the time of its swing. Then create a data table like the one shown.
2. Tie one end of a string to a clamp on a stand. Tie the other end to a large paper clip. Pull out one side of the paper clip to serve as a hook.
3. Place a metal washer on the hook, and let it hang down. If necessary, raise the clamp so that the bob swings freely.
4. Pull the bob back so that the string makes an angle of about 45° with the stand. Have your partner measure the height of the bob above the table top. Record this height as the starting position of the bob.
5. Release the bob gently, without pushing it. During a complete swing, the bob will move from its starting position and back again. Your partner should time 10 complete swings.
6. Record the time for 10 swings to the nearest tenth of a second. Then divide that time by 10 to find the average time for one swing.
7. Repeat Steps 5 and 6, increasing the mass of the bob each time by adding a washer. Make sure you always start the bob at the same height.

Analyze and Conclude

1. Graph your results. (*Hint:* Place the number of washers on the horizontal axis and the average time per swing on the vertical axis.)
2. Use the graph to decide if your data support your hypothesis.
3. What conclusion can you draw from this experiment?
4. **Think About It** How did this experiment enable you to test your hypothesis?

DATA TABLE

Number of washers	Time for 10 swings (s)	Average time per swing (s)
1		
2		

Design an Experiment

Design an experiment to test how the average time for a pendulum swing changes when the mass is constant but the length of the string changes. Obtain your teacher's approval before carrying out this experiment.

Branches of Science

There are four main branches of science—physical science, Earth science, life science, and environmental science. Physical science includes the study of motion and forces, sound and light, and electricity and magnetism. It also includes the study of the tiny particles that make up everything around you.

Earth science is the study of Earth and its place in the universe. Earth science includes the study of rivers, oceans, landforms, weather, climate, and the bodies that make up the solar system.

Life science is the study of living things, including plants, animals, and microscopic life forms. The study of the human body is a part of life science, too. Life scientists also study how living things interact with each other and with their surroundings.

Environmental science deals with the effects of human activities on Earth's land, air, water, and living things. Environmental scientists study problems, such as pollution, that result from human activities and the use of Earth's natural resources.

The branches of science are not really separate from one another. For example, the scientists and engineers working on the International Space Station use their knowledge of physical science as they design the parts of the space station. They use their knowledge of Earth science as they consider how the space station will function in space. And they use their knowledge of life science as they design life-support systems for the astronauts.

In Figure 9 you can see some of the diverse jobs that scientists perform. You can find scientists at work almost anywhere—from the depths of the oceans, to laboratories, mountains, and jungles on Earth, to space stations out in space. Wherever people are asking scientific questions and searching for answers, they are using the methods of science.

☑ *Checkpoint* *Name the four main branches of science.*

Technology and the Internet

Today, many scientists use the latest technology in their research. For example, life scientists today use powerful microscopes, some of which can magnify images up to one million times their size. Space scientists use telescopes that can detect objects in space more clearly than ever before. Most modern scientific equipment is connected to computers, which allow scientists to quickly record, store, and analyze the data they collect. You have already read how important computers are for creating models and running simulations of scientific events.

Technology also helps scientists communicate information to one another and to the public. You can find large amounts of information about discoveries and current research in science on the Internet. Many government agencies maintain Web sites. Hospitals and universities that have research centers often have Web sites, too. The publisher of this textbook maintains a Web site, **www.phschool.com**. This site includes links to other Web sites that may help you as you study science.

Figure 9 This is just a small sampling of the types of work that scientists do.
(A) Environmental chemists study the chemicals found in air, soil, and water.
(B) Botanists study plants. Some botanists investigate interactions between plants and other living things. Others help identify ways to increase crop yields.
(C) Audiologists test hearing ability through the use of specialized equipment.
(D) Structural engineers assess the safety of building designs, using their knowledge of building materials, loads, and the effects of weather and earthquakes.

Study Guide

Key Ideas

◆ Science is an organized way of learning about the natural world. Through observations and logical reasoning, scientists investigate problems and look for answers.

◆ Scientists use many specific skills, including posing questions, making observations and inferences, developing hypotheses, designing experiments, collecting data and making measurements, interpreting data, drawing conclusions, making models, and communicating information.

◆ A scientific hypothesis states a possible explanation for observations in a way that can be tested.

◆ In a controlled experiment, the manipulated variable is changed in order to determine its effect on the responding variable. All other variables are kept constant.

◆ Data from an experiment are analyzed to determine whether or not they support the hypothesis being tested.

◆ Safe laboratory practices prevent injuries and make lab investigations run more smoothly.

Key Terms

science	manipulated variable
scientific inquiry	responding variable
observation	controlled experiment
inference	data
hypothesis	scientific law
variable	scientific theory

Reviewing Content

 Review key concepts online using iText at **www.phschool.com**

Multiple Choice

Choose the letter of the best answer.

1. A logical interpretation based on observations or prior knowledge is called
   a. scientific inquiry.　**b.** an inference.
   c. communication.　**d.** an observation.

2. The scientific skill in which the senses are used to gather information is
   a. posing questions.
   b. drawing conclusions.
   c. observing.
   d. developing hypotheses.

3. A statement that is tested through scientific experiments is called a
   a. conclusion.　**b.** variable.
   c. law.　**d.** hypothesis.

4. In an experiment in which you change only the temperature, temperature is the
   a. responding variable.
   b. manipulated variable.
   c. hypothesis.
   d. controlled variable.

5. A well-tested idea that explains and connects a wide range of observations is a
   a. scientific law.
   b. scientific theory.
   c. hypothesis.
   d. conclusion.

True or False

If the statement is true, write true. If it is false, change the underlined word or words to make the statement true.

6. A <u>hypothesis</u> sums up what was learned from an experiment.

7. The facts and figures collected during an experiment are called <u>data</u>.

8. A factor that can change during an experiment is called a <u>variable</u>.

9. A <u>scientific theory</u> describes what is always expected to happen under a given set of conditions.

10. <u>Scientific inquiry</u> is the process of sharing information with other scientists.

Checking Concepts

11. Explain the difference between an observation and an inference.
12. Why is controlling variables an essential part of a scientific experiment?
13. How does a hypothesis guide a scientist in setting up an experiment?
14. Why is it an advantage for scientists to use one system of measurement when collecting data?
15. Explain how scientists use models and simulations.
16. Why is communication an important skill in science?
17. **Writing to Learn** The process of science usually begins with one or more questions. Write a question that you have about the natural world. Then write a plan describing how you might find an answer to your question.

Thinking Critically

18. **Making Generalizations** A friend tells you that science is all the information found in this textbook. Do you agree with that statement? Why or why not?
19. **Applying Concepts** You are about to conduct an experiment in which you drop a ball from different heights to find out how high the ball bounces at each height. Create a table to show your data. (You can refer to the Skills Handbook, pages 694–696.)
20. **Problem Solving** Suppose a company advertises a piece of sports equipment that's "guaranteed to improve your game." How could you use the idea of a controlled experiment to safely test that claim?
21. **Making Judgments** Why does everyone involved in science activities have to take responsibility for the class's safety?

Test Preparation
Use these questions to prepare for standardized tests.

Read the information below. Then answer Questions 22–25.

Three students wanted to find out whether the mass of an object affects how fast it falls. They designed an experiment in which different stacks of washers would be released from the same height. They tied the washers together and determined how long each stack took to reach the ground. Here is their data.

Number of Washers	Time (s)			
	Trial 1	Trial 2	Trial 3	Average
2	2.9	2.8	3.3	3.0
10	3.0	2.9	3.1	3.0
20	2.9	2.9	3.2	3.0

22. What is the manipulated variable?
  A number of trials B starting height
  C number of washers D time of the drop
23. What is the responding variable?
  F number of trials G starting height
  H number of washers J time of the drop

24. Which of the following could be the hypothesis for this experiment?
  A The height from which an object is dropped affects how fast it falls.
  B The mass of an object affects how fast it falls.
  C The mass of an object affects the force with which it hits the ground.
  D The height from which an object is dropped affects the force with which it hits the ground.
25. Based on the results of this experiment, what can you conclude about objects dropped from the same height?
  F Objects having greater mass will drop faster than objects with less mass.
  G Objects having less mass will drop faster than objects with greater mass.
  H All objects take 3 seconds to drop.
  J The mass of an object has no effect on the rate at which it falls.

The copper-covered Statue of Liberty has stood in Upper New York Bay for over 100 years.

www.phschool.com

Keep a Chemical Change Log

Look around. All sorts of changes are taking place. Some changes involve growth. For example, you and your classmates are growing. Other changes produce something that wasn't there before. A factory turns raw materials into desirable products, for instance. Rust coats the surface of a once-silvery fence. Even the green color of the Statue of Liberty comes from a change to the statue's copper metal covering. All of these changes are the result of chemical reactions, or changes in which substances react to form new substances.

In this chapter, you will learn more about the changes in matter that result from chemical reactions. Your project involves keeping a log of chemical changes occurring around you.

Your Goal To identify and observe chemical changes in your daily life and to record evidence for those changes.

To complete the project you must

◆ determine what evidence indicates that a chemical change has taken place
◆ record observations of the different chemical changes you notice in your life during one week
◆ classify the types of chemical changes you observe
◆ follow the safety guidelines in Appendix A

Get Started Begin by previewing the chapter to learn what a chemical change is. With a group, discuss some changes you observe regularly. Try to decide if each change is a chemical change.

Check Your Progress You'll be working on this project as you study this chapter. To keep your project on track, look for Check Your Progress boxes at the following points.

Section Review 3, page 43: List evidence of chemical changes.
Section Review 4, page 53: Construct a table for observations.

Present Your Project At the end of the chapter (page 65), you will compare your table of chemical changes with those of your classmates and classify the changes.

TEKS

In addition to process TEKS, this chapter addresses these concept TEKS as they relate to the chapter's topics.

(8.8) The student knows that matter is composed of atoms. The student is expected to:
(A) describe the structure and parts of an atom.
(B) identify the properties of an atom including mass and electrical charge.

(8.9) The student knows that substances have chemical and physical properties. The student is expected to:
(A) demonstrate that substances may react chemically to form new substances.
(B) interpret information on the periodic table to understand that physical properties are used to group elements.

(C) recognize the importance of formulas and equations to express what happens in a chemical reaction.

(8.10) The student knows that complex interactions occur between matter and energy. The student is expected to:
(C) identify and demonstrate that loss or gain of heat energy occurs during exothermic and endothermic chemical reactions.

DISCOVER ·· **ACTIVITY**····

How Far Away Is the Electron?

1. On a piece of paper, make a small circle no bigger than a dime. The circle represents the nucleus, or center, of a model atom.

2. Measure the diameter of the circle in centimeters.

3. Now predict where you think the outer edge of this model atom will be. For example, will the outer edge be within the edges of the paper? Your desk? The classroom? The school building?

Think It Over

Making Models The diameter of an actual atom can be 100,000 times the diameter of its nucleus. Calculate the diameter of your model atom. How close was your prediction in Step 3 to your calculation? (*Hint:* To compare your result to the real world, change the units of your prediction from centimeters to meters.)

GUIDE FOR READING

◆ What is the structure and composition of an atom?

◆ How can an atom be neutral?

◆ Why are valence electrons important?

Reading Tip As you read, make a table listing the particles found in an atom. Include the name of each particle, its charge, and where in an atom the particle is located.

Key Terms element • atom
• nucleus • proton • neutron
• electron • atomic number
• atomic mass unit (amu)
• valence electron
• chemical bond
• electron dot diagram

Clothes, rain, CDs, food, air, soil, gasoline, paper. Can you guess what all these things have in common? They are examples of matter—the "stuff" that makes up everything in the universe. Every kind of matter is made of one or more elements. An **element** is a substance that cannot be broken down into other substances by chemical or physical means. Carbon is an element. So are oxygen and hydrogen. These and all other elements are made of atoms. An **atom** is the smallest particle of an element.

Properties of an Atom

If you could look into an atom, what might you see? Theories about the shapes and structures of atoms have changed over the last 200 years and continue to change even now. But some properties of atoms are well understood.

Structure and Composition Although atoms are extremely small, they are made of even smaller parts. **An atom consists of a nucleus surrounded by one or more electrons.** The **nucleus** (NOO clee us) (plural *nuclei*) is the tiny, central core of an atom. Nuclei contain particles called protons and neutrons. **Protons** have a positive electric charge, which is indicated by a plus symbol (+). **Neutrons** have no charge. They are neutral. (Could you guess that from their name?) A third type of particle moves in the space around the outside of the nucleus. These are particles, called **electrons,** which move rapidly in all directions. Electrons carry a negative charge, which is indicated by a negative symbol (–).

The protons and electrons in an atom have opposite charges. **But, an atom is neutral because it contains equal numbers of protons and electrons.**

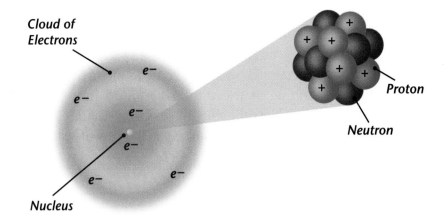

Cloud of Electrons

e−
e−
e−
e−
e−
e−

Nucleus

+ + + + + + +

Proton

Neutron

Figure 1 An atom's tiny nucleus contains protons and neutrons. The electrons move in the space around the nucleus.
Applying Concepts Is this carbon atom negatively charged, positively charged, or neutral overall?

Atomic Number

Every atom of a particular element contains the same number of protons. For example, every carbon atom contains six protons. Thus, an element's **atomic number**—the number of protons in its nucleus—is a unique property that identifies that element. And in an atom, the number of protons and the number of electrons are equal, making the atom neutral.

Atomic Mass

Atoms cannot be measured with everyday units of mass because they are so small. For this reason, scientists have created the **atomic mass unit (amu)** to measure the particles in atoms. The mass of a proton or a neutron is about 1 atomic mass unit. Electrons have a much smaller mass. It takes almost 2,000 electrons to equal 1 atomic mass unit. That means that most of an atom's mass is in its nucleus. An atom that contains 6 protons, 6 neutrons, and 6 electrons has a mass of about 12 atomic mass units.

Although atoms of any particular element always have the same number of protons, the number of neutrons they contain may vary. Carbon atoms, for instance, always have 6 protons. But they may have 5, 6, 7, or 8 neutrons. That means that the mass of atoms of an element can vary. However, the neutrons do not play a role in chemical reactions. The atoms of a particular element all have the same chemical properties despite their different masses.

Figure 2 When a fan is turned on, you see a blur instead of separate blades. A fan is a model for the way electrons fill the space around the nucleus of an atom.

☑ *Checkpoint Which particles in an atom are in the nucleus?*

The Role of Electrons

Electrons move around the nucleus so fast that it is impossible to know exactly where any electron is at a particular time. Think about the blades of a moving fan. They go too fast to be seen. As electrons move around the nucleus, the effect is like the fan blades, but in three dimensions. The space around the nucleus is like a spherical cloud of negatively charged electrons.

Little Particles, Big Spaces Most of an atom's mass comes from its protons and neutrons. But most of an atom's volume is the space in which the electrons move. That space is huge compared to the space occupied by the nucleus. To picture the difference, imagine standing at the pitcher's mound in a baseball stadium. If the nucleus were the size of a pencil eraser, the electrons could be in the outfield or as far away as the top row of seats!

☑ *Checkpoint* *Where are the electrons in an atom?*

SCIENCE & History

Models of Atoms

For over two centuries, scientists have worked on models of atoms in an effort to understand why matter behaves as it does. As scientists have learned more, the model of the atom has changed.

1808
Dalton Model

British chemist John Dalton published his *New System of Chemical Philosophy,* explaining that each element is made of small atoms and that different elements have atoms of different mass. Dalton imagined atoms as tiny, solid balls.

1897
Thomson Model

British scientist J. J. Thomson proposed a new model. He suggested that an atom is a positively charged sphere with electrons embedded in it. His model could be described as looking like a muffin with berries scattered through it.

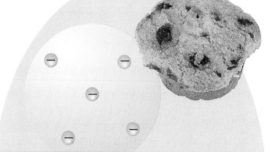

1800 ⚡ **1900**

For almost 100 years, not much ▲ new information was learned about atoms.

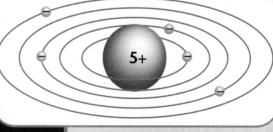

5+

1904 Nagaoka Model

Japanese physicist Hantaro Nagaoka proposed a model of the atom that had a large sphere in the center with a positive charge. His model showed the electrons revolving around this sphere like the planets around the sun.

Valence Electrons An atom's electrons are not all the same distance from the nucleus. Nor are they held to the atom with equal strength. Those farthest away or most loosely held are called **valence electrons** (VAY luns). **Many properties of the atom, and therefore of an element, are determined by the number of valence electrons.** For example, valence electrons can form chemical bonds. A **chemical bond** is a force that holds atoms together. When chemical bonds form, valence electrons are either transferred or shared between atoms.

In Your Journal

Find out more about one of the scientists who worked on models of the atom. Write an imaginary interview with this person in which you discuss his work with him.

1911
Rutherford Model

British physicist Ernest Rutherford concluded that the atom is mostly empty space. Electrons orbit randomly around a small, positively charged nucleus.

1932
Chadwick Model

British physicist James Chadwick discovered the neutron, a particle having about the same mass as the proton but with no electrical charge. The existence of the neutron explained why atoms were heavier than the total mass of their protons and electrons.

| 1910 | 1920 | 1930 | 1940 | 1950 |

1913
Bohr Model

Danish physicist Niels Bohr determined that electrons aren't randomly located around the nucleus. His model showed electrons moving in specific layers, or shells. He said that atoms absorb or give off energy when the electrons move from one shell to another.

Cloud of electrons

1920s to Present
Modern Model

The current model of the atom came from the work of many scientists from the 1920s to the present. It shows the electrons as forming a negatively charged cloud around the nucleus. It is impossible to determine exactly where an electron is at any given time.

Figure 3 In these electron dot diagrams, each dot represents a valence electron. The total number of dots around the symbol shows the number of valence electrons the element has.
Interpreting Diagrams Which two elements in this diagram have the same number of valence electrons? Which element has the largest number of valence electrons?

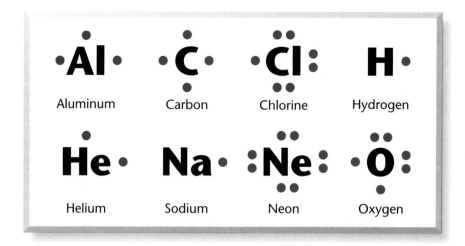

The number of valence electrons in an atom can range from one to eight. Each element has a typical number of valence electrons. Oxygen (O) has six valence electrons, for example. Carbon (C) has four. The single electron of hydrogen (H) is considered a valence electron.

Chemists often represent valence electrons with simple diagrams like those in Figure 3. An **electron dot diagram** is made up of the symbol for an element surrounded by dots. Each dot stands for one valence electron.

When an atom forms a chemical bond, one of two things usually happens. Either the number of valence electrons increases to a total of eight, or all the valence electrons are given up. When atoms end up with eight or zero valence electrons, the atoms become more stable—or less reactive—than they were before. In the next section of this chapter, you will learn which elements have atoms that are likely to give up electrons and which are likely to gain electrons.

 Section 1 Review

1. Describe the parts of an atom and tell where each is found.
2. Explain why the electrical charge on an atom is zero, or neutral.
3. What happens to valence electrons during the formation of chemical bonds?
4. Explain why electrons make up much of an atom's volume but not much of its mass.
5. **Thinking Critically Applying Concepts** What information can you get from an electron dot diagram?

Science at Home

Atoms on Display Draw sketches or construct models of atoms to show your family. The models can be made of clay, beads, string, and other simple materials. Explain what makes the atoms of different elements different from each other. Emphasize that everything in your home is made of about 100 different atoms. Explain how your models represent atoms accurately. Explain the limitations of your models.

SECTION
2 The Periodic Table

DISCOVER ●●● ACTIVITY

Can You Organize Your Desk Drawer?

2. Suppose you want to organize these objects into bins for a desk drawer. Separate the objects into three or four groups each containing at least two items that are similar.

3. Choose a short descriptive name for each group.

Think It Over

Classifying For each group, list the physical characteristics of the objects that caused you to place them together. What are the advantages of grouping the objects? Identify another item that could be added to each group.

1. Place the following objects on your desk: pen, paper clip, notebook, notebook paper, pencil, binder clip, thumb tack, pad of sticky notes, marker, clean unlined paper, index card.

Suppose you want to buy a pair of shoes. Do you need nylon, laces, and thick cushioning for sports? How about something calf-high and waterproof for rain or cold? Maybe you need shiny leather for a special occasion? These words describe characteristics, or properties, of different kinds of footwear. Chances are, you'll find that stores display shoes so that they are organized by these properties.

Matter has properties, too. A **physical property** can be observed without changing the substance into something else. Density and melting point are examples of physical properties. A **chemical property** is observed when a substance interacts with another substance. Flammability—whether or not a substance burns in the presence of oxygen—is a chemical property.

Scientists organize elements according to their physical and chemical properties. The periodic table of the elements is a tool that helps you study the properties of familiar elements and learn to predict the properties of other elements.

Using Properties to Group Elements

By 1830, 55 elements had been discovered. These elements displayed a wide variety of physical and chemical properties. A few were gases. Two were liquids. Most were metals. Some reacted explosively as they formed compounds. Others reacted more slowly. Still others did not form compounds at all.

GUIDE FOR READING

◆ How was the periodic table developed?

◆ What information does each square of the periodic table present?

◆ How does the overall organization of the periodic table relate to the physical and chemical properties of elements?

◆ How are valence electrons related to the periodic table?

Reading Tip As you read this section, refer to *Exploring the Periodic Table* on pages 32–33. Look for patterns.

Key Terms physical property
• chemical property
• atomic mass • periodic table
• symbol • group • period
• metal • nonmetal • metalloid

Figure 4 The shiny orange of this copper bowl will gradually turn to dull blue-green, like the tarnished copper sculpture. Mendeleev realized that several metals share with copper the property of tarnishing when exposed to air.
Classifying Is tarnishing a physical or chemical property?

Scientists of the 1800s did not know about atomic numbers. However, they suspected that the growing number of known elements could be organized in a useful way. One investigator found that some groups of elements, such as those in Figure 5, followed a pattern: The average of the atomic masses of the first and third elements roughly equaled the mass of the middle element. However, this system did not work for most elements.

By the 1860s, a Russian scientist had discovered a system that applied to almost all the elements. His name was Dimitri Mendeleev (men duh LAY ef). Like any good detective, Mendeleev studied the evidence, considered each clue, and looked for patterns.

Along with other scientists of his time, he observed that some elements have similar physical and chemical properties. Fluorine and chlorine, for example, are both gases that irritate your lungs if you breathe them. Silver and copper are both shiny metals that gradually tarnish if exposed to air. Mendeleev was convinced that these similarities were important clues to a hidden pattern.

To help him find that pattern, he wrote facts about the elements on individual cards. He noted all the properties he knew about an element, including its melting point, density, and color. He included two especially important properties: atomic mass and the number of chemical bonds an element could form. The **atomic mass** of an element is the average mass of one atom of the element. In Mendeleev's day, scientists figured out atomic masses in comparison to hydrogen, the lightest element. They found the number of bonds an element can form by studying the compound each element formed with oxygen.

The Periodic Table

Mendeleev liked to play a card game similar to solitaire, so he had practice in seeing patterns. He tried arranging his cards on the elements in various ways. **Mendeleev noticed that patterns appeared when the elements were arranged in order of one particular physical property—increasing atomic mass.**

Figure 5 In the 1800s, scientists tried different ways to organize the elements. They found that some groups of three elements displayed curious patterns.
Calculating When you average the atomic masses of calcium and barium, how closely does the result come to the atomic mass of strontium? Do the densities follow the same pattern?

Properties of Three Similar Elements				
Element	Description	Atomic Mass	Density (gm/cm³)	Chemical Properties
Calcium	silvery metal	40.1	1.55	Reacts readily with oxygen and water
Strontium	silvery metal	87.6	2.6	Reacts readily with oxygen and water
Barium	silvery metal	137	3.5	Reacts readily with oxygen and water

опытъ:

```
                                    Ti=50      Zr=90     ?=180.
                                    V=51       Nb=94     Ta=182.
                                    Cr=52      Mo=96     W=186.
                                    Mn=55      Rh=104,4  Pt=197,4
                                    Fe=56      Ru=104,4  Ir=198.
                              Ni=Co=59         Pl=106,6  Os=199.
                                    Cu=63,4     Ag=108   Hg=200.
H=1                        Mg=24    Zn=65,2     Cd=112
        Be=9,4            Al=27,4    ?=68        Ur=116   Au=197?
        B=11              Si=28      ?=70        Sn=118
        C=12              P=31      As=75        Sb=122   Bi=210
        N=14              S=32      Se=79,4      Te=128?
        O=16              Cl=35,5   Br=80         I=127
        F=19              K=39      Rb=85,4      Cs=133   Tl=204
Li=7    Na=23             Ca=40     Sr=87,6      Ba=137   Pb=207.
                          ?=45      Ce=92
                        ?Er=56      La=94
                        ?Yt=60      Di=95
                        ?In=75,6    Th=118?
```

Figure 6 Mendeleev (above) published this first periodic table in 1869. He left question marks in some places. Based on the properties of surrounding elements, he predicted that new elements with specific characteristics would be discovered.

Mendeleev's Periodic Table Mendeleev discovered a repetition of properties. After fluorine, for instance, the next heaviest element he knew about was sodium. Sodium (Na) bonded in the same way that lithium (Li) and potassium (K) did. So he placed the cards for these elements into a group. He did the same with other similar elements.

However, Mendeleev discovered that arranging the known elements strictly by increasing atomic mass did not always produce similar groups. So he moved his element cards into groups where they fit best. Doing this left three blank spaces. Mendeleev was confident enough of his discovery to predict that the blank spaces would be filled by elements that had not yet been discovered. He even predicted the properties of those new elements!

Mendeleev published the first periodic table, shown in Figure 6, in 1869. Within 16 years, chemists discovered the three missing elements, named scandium, gallium, and germanium. Their properties are close to what Mendeleev had predicted.

The Modern Periodic Table The word *periodic* means "a regular, repeated pattern." In the modern **periodic table,** the properties of the elements repeat in each period—or row—of the table. Since Mendeleev's time, discoveries have changed the periodic table. The most important came in the early 1900s, when scientists learned about atomic number. Also, elements were added as they were discovered. An up-to-date version of the table appears in *Exploring the Periodic Table* on the next two pages.

☑ *Checkpoint* What does "periodic" mean?

Sharpen your Skills

Classifying ACTIVITY

Choose any 10 elements and assign them letters *A* through *J*. On an index card for each element, write the letter for the element and list some of its physical and chemical properties. You may list properties that you have learned in this chapter, or properties presented in an encyclopedia or other reference source.

Exchange cards with a classmate. Can you identify each element? Which properties are the most helpful in identifying elements?

EXPLORING the Periodic Table

The periodic table has grown to include over 100 elements. Once you understand how the periodic table is organized, you can predict an element's properties from its position in the table.

C	Solid
Br	Liquid
H	Gas

Symbol
One- or two-letter symbols identify most elements. Some periodic tables also list the names of the elements.

Period
A row of the periodic table is called a period. Notice that the table becomes wider at periods 2, 4, and 6.

Group
Each column of the periodic table is called a group, or family. The elements in a group have similar properties, although the similarities are stronger in some groups than in others.

Atomic Mass
Atomic mass is the average mass of an element's atoms. Usually, atomic mass increases with atomic number.

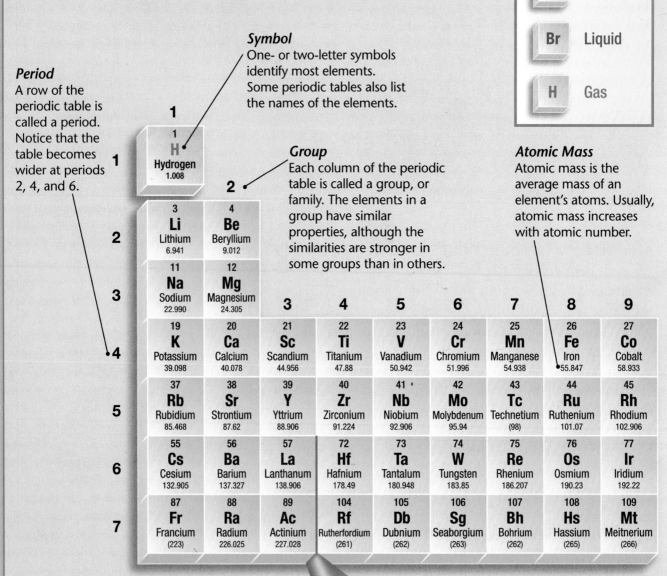

To make the table easier to read, elements 58–71 (the lanthanides) and elements 90–103 (the actinides) are printed below the rest of the table. Follow the blue line to see how they fit in the table.

Atomic Number

The atomic number is the number of protons in an atom's nucleus, for example, five for boron. In the modern periodic table, the elements are arranged according to their atomic numbers.

Elements 93 and higher have been created artificially. Elements with atomic numbers 114, 116, and 118 are the newest. Until chemists agree on permanent names, a few elements have Latin names that relate to their atomic numbers.

Metal

Metalloid

Nonmetal

Discovered recently

Many periodic tables include a zigzag line that separates the metals from the nonmetals.

18

13	14	15	16	17	18
					2 **He** Helium 4.003
5 **B** Boron 10.811	6 **C** Carbon 12.011	7 **N** Nitrogen 14.007	8 **O** Oxygen 15.999	9 **F** Fluorine 18.998	10 **Ne** Neon 20.180
13 **Al** Aluminum 26.982	14 **Si** Silicon 28.086	15 **P** Phosphorus 30.974	16 **S** Sulfur 32.066	17 **Cl** Chlorine 35.453	18 **Ar** Argon 39.948

10	11	12						
28 **Ni** Nickel 58.69	29 **Cu** Copper 63.546	30 **Zn** Zinc 65.39	31 **Ga** Gallium 69.723	32 **Ge** Germanium 72.61	33 **As** Arsenic 74.922	34 **Se** Selenium 78.96	35 **Br** Bromine 79.904	36 **Kr** Krypton 83.80
46 **Pd** Palladium 106.42	47 **Ag** Silver 107.868	48 **Cd** Cadmium 112.411	49 **In** Indium 114.818	50 **Sn** Tin 118.710	51 **Sb** Antimony 121.75	52 **Te** Tellurium 127.60	53 **I** Iodine 126.904	54 **Xe** Xenon 131.29
78 **Pt** Platinum 195.08	79 **Au** Gold 196.967	80 **Hg** Mercury 200.59	81 **Tl** Thallium 204.383	82 **Pb** Lead 207.2	83 **Bi** Bismuth 208.980	84 **Po** Polonium (209)	85 **At** Astatine (210)	86 **Rn** Radon (222)
110 **Uun** Ununnilium (269)	111 **Uuu** Unununium (272)	112 **Uub** Ununbium (272)	114 **Uuq** Ununquadium			116 **Uuh** Ununhexium		118 **Uuo** Ununoctium

63 **Eu** Europium 151.965	64 **Gd** Gadolinium 157.25	65 **Tb** Terbium 158.925	66 **Dy** Dysprosium 162.50	67 **Ho** Holmium 164.930	68 **Er** Erbium 167.26	69 **Tm** Thulium 168.934	70 **Yb** Ytterbium 173.04	71 **Lu** Lutetium 174.967
95 **Am** Americium (243)	96 **Cm** Curium (247)	97 **Bk** Berkelium (247)	98 **Cf** Californium (251)	99 **Es** Einsteinium (252)	100 **Fm** Fermium (257)	101 **Md** Mendelevium (258)	102 **No** Nobelium (259)	103 **Lr** Lawrencium (260)

Reading the Periodic Table

The periodic table is a useful tool for scientists. It contains over 100 squares, one separate square for each element. **Each square of the periodic table usually includes the element's atomic number, symbol, name, and atomic mass.**

Figure 7 Four important facts about an element are supplied in each square of the periodic table.

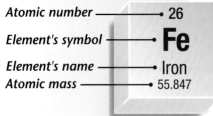

Atomic number ———————→ 26

Element's symbol ———————→ **Fe**

Element's name ———————→ Iron

Atomic mass ———————→ 55.847

Inside the Squares On the periodic table on the previous two pages, find the square for iron, located in the top position in column 8 in the center of the table. That square is reproduced in Figure 7. The first entry in the square is the number 26, the atomic number of iron. That tells you that every iron atom has 26 protons and 26 electrons.

Just below the atomic number are the letters Fe, which is the chemical symbol for iron. The **symbol** for an element usually contains either one or two letters. The last entry in the square is the atomic mass, which is 55.847 for iron. Remember that atomic mass is the average mass of an element's atoms. Some iron atoms have 29 neutrons in the nucleus, others have 30, and still others have 31. All of these atoms have different atomic masses. Despite the different masses, all iron atoms react the same way chemically.

Organization of the Periodic Table Remember that the periodic table is arranged by atomic number. Look over the entire table, starting at the top left with hydrogen (H), which has atomic number 1. Notice that the atomic numbers increase from left to right and from top to bottom.

Groups The main body of the periodic table is arranged into eighteen vertical columns and seven horizontal rows. The elements in a column are called a **group.** Groups are also sometimes known as families. Notice that each group is numbered, from Group 1 on the left of the table to Group 18 on the right. Typically, the group is given a family name based on the first element in the column. Group 14, for example, is the carbon family. Group 15 is the nitrogen family.

Periods Each horizontal row across the table is called a **period.** A period contains a series of different types of elements from different families, just as a week on a calendar has a series of different days.

As you can see, there are seven periods of elements. Periods have different numbers of elements. Period 1 has only two elements, hydrogen (H) and helium (He). You can see that Periods 2 and 3 each have 8 elements. Periods 4 and 5 each have 18 elements. You will also notice that some elements of Period 6 and some elements of Period 7 have been separated out of the table. These elements are part of the periodic table, even though

Language Arts
CONNECTION

You are learning science in the English language. But in other centuries, the language of science was Greek or Latin or Arabic. This is why the names and chemical symbols of many elements don't match modern names. For example, the symbol for copper (Cu) comes from the Latin *cuprum.*

In Your Journal

List some of the elements that have puzzling chemical symbols, such as tungsten (W), potassium (K), tin (Sn), antimony (Sb), and silver (Ag). Look up these names and symbols in the dictionary to learn the original names of these elements.

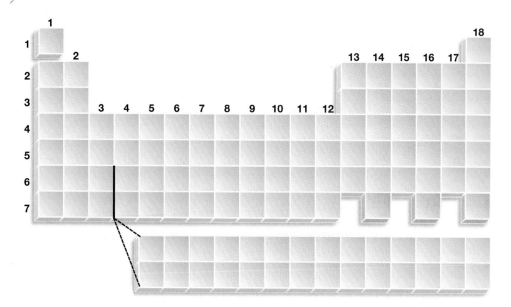

Figure 8 The columns in the periodic table are called groups or families. The rows are called periods.

they appear as rows below its main section. The elements are shown separately to keep the table from becoming too wide. Imagine what it would look like if Periods 6 and 7 were stretched out to show all 32 elements in a row!

☑ *Checkpoint* *What are the elements in a column called?*

Properties of Elements in the Periodic Table

An element's physical and chemical properties can be predicted from its location in the periodic table. Once you know a little about navigating the table, just a quick glance will tell you some basic information.

Metals Starting from the left side of the periodic table, you'll notice that most of the elements are metals. **Metals** usually give up their valence electrons in a chemical reaction. Elements are classified as metals based on their physical properties, including hardness, shininess, and ease with which they may be hammered into sheets (malleability) or drawn into wire (ductility). Most metals are also good conductors of heat and electricity. And some are attracted to magnets.

Nonmetals At the far right of the periodic table, you will see the nonmetals. **Nonmetals** usually gain or share valence electrons in a chemical reaction. Nonmetals have physical properties opposite those of metals. For example, nonmetals are dull, not shiny, and crumbly, not hard. They do not conduct electricity or heat very well, and they are not attracted by magnets.

You probably noticed that hydrogen is a nonmetal, but it is shown on the periodic table above the Group 1 metals. Hydrogen has unique properties. It may be classified as a metal or a nonmetal, depending on how it reacts with a given substance.

Figure 9 You can find the names of elements in the names of some common products, such as the ni-cad batteries in this camera. *Inferring What is one of the metals you would expect to find in a ni-cad battery?*

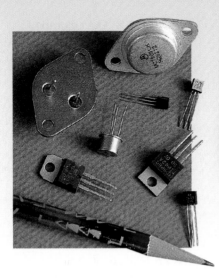

Figure 10 Places where metalloids are used include transistors (left), lasers (center), and computers (right).

Predicting ACTIVITY

1. Select an element from the periodic table to explore in depth. Use the table to identify the characteristics of atoms of that element, such as atomic number, atomic mass, and electrical charge.

2. From its position in the table, predict some of the element's properties by comparing it with its neighbors. Predict melting point, density, and how the element reacts. Would atoms of your element lose, gain, or share valence electrons?

Metalloids Between the metals and the nonmetals are elements known as metalloids. The **metalloids** have some properties of metals and some properties of nonmetals. The most useful property of the metalloids is their varying ability to conduct electricity. Temperature, exposure to light, and the presence of small amounts of impurities are some factors that affect the conductivity of metalloids. This varying ability is a necessary characteristic of the semiconductors used in computers, transistors, and lasers. Metalloids, such as silicon and germanium, work well as semiconductors.

Patterns Across and Down the Table As you look at elements across a row or down a column, many of the physical and chemical properties of the elements change in a predictable way. This predictability is the reason why the periodic table is so useful. For example, you can see that many nonmetals are gases, while almost all the metals and metalloids are solids.

Density and melting points are two other physical properties reflected in the organization of the elements. Density increases as you move down a group. Also as you move down, the melting points of metals decrease and those of nonmetals increase.

In addition to physical properties, the periodic table also tells you something about chemical properties. For example, the ease with which a metal reacts with other substances decreases from left to right across a period. The elements in Group 1 are all metals that react violently with water. The metals in Group 11, however, react with water slowly or not at all. For nonmetals, the opposite is true. Nonmetals in Groups 13 through 17 become more reactive from left to right. Group 18 elements are an exception. They almost never react.

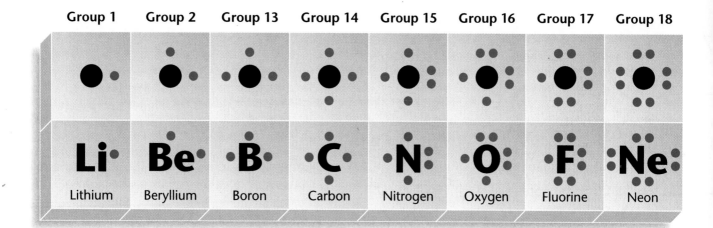

| Group 1 | Group 2 | Group 13 | Group 14 | Group 15 | Group 16 | Group 17 | Group 18 |

| Li | Be | B | C | N | O | F | Ne |
| Lithium | Beryllium | Boron | Carbon | Nitrogen | Oxygen | Fluorine | Neon |

Why the Periodic Table Works

Although Mendeleev successfully used the periodic table to predict new discoveries, he could not explain why the table works. **The periodic table works because it's based on the structures of atoms, especially the valence electrons.** Look at the electron dot diagrams in Figure 11 to see why.

Think of how atoms change from left to right across a period. You know that from one element to the next, the atomic number increases by one. That means that an element has one more valence electron than the element to its left. And since the first element in a period has one valence electron, the number of valence electrons in a row of eight increases from one to eight. As a result, the properties across a period change in a regular way.

By contrast, the elements in a family all have the same number of valence electrons. The elements in Group 1 have one valence electron. The elements in Group 2 have two. The elements in Group 17 have seven valence electrons, and Group 18 elements have eight. Because the valence electrons within a family are the same, the elements in that group have similar properties.

Figure 11 In a row of eight elements, the number of valence electrons follows the pattern shown in the first row of this diagram. The circle represents the inner part of the atom. *Predicting The atomic number of neon is 10. The atomic number of sodium (Na) is 11. What will the electron dot diagram of sodium look like?*

Section 2 Review

1. How did Mendeleev organize the elements into the periodic table?
2. What information is listed in each square of the periodic table?
3. Element A is in the same group as element B and the same period as element C. Which two of the three elements are likely to have similar properties? Explain your answer.
4. **Thinking Critically** **Relating Cause and Effect** Why do elements in a group have similar properties?

Science at Home

Cooking With Organization
With an adult family member, make a plan to organize the cooking utensils in your kitchen so that they are easy to find when needed. Describe your organizational scheme. Explain to your family how scientists organized elements in the periodic table.

SECTION 3 Observing Chemical Reactions

DISCOVER ·········· ACTIVITY····

What Happens When Chemicals React?

1. Put on your safety goggles.

2. Put 2 small spoonfuls of baking soda into a clear plastic cup.

3. Holding the cup over a large bowl or sink, add about 125 mL of vinegar. Swirl the cup gently.

4. Observe any changes to the material in the cup. Feel the outside of the cup. What do you notice about the temperature?

5. Carefully fan some air over the liquid toward you. What does the mixture smell like?

Think It Over

Observing Looking at an experiment is not the only way to get information. Your other senses can be equally useful in making observations. What changes did you detect using your senses of smell and touch?

GUIDE FOR READING

◆ What are the observable characteristics of a chemical reaction?

Reading Tip As you read, write one or two sentences to summarize the main ideas under each heading.

Key Terms chemical reaction
• precipitate
• endothermic reaction
• exothermic reaction
• molecule
• compound

Suppose you are a sculptor choosing the material for a new outdoor statue. You don't want your work destroyed by changes that can occur when your statue comes in contact with substances in the air. What material would you use? The artist who created the statue below chose bronze, a brownish yellow alloy of copper, tin, and other metals. Bronze is harder than iron and more resistant to chemical changes. However, its outer surface does react with oxygen, producing the dark color you see here. The new surface helps preserve the statue by acting as a protective layer for the unreacted metal atoms beneath it.

Evidence for Chemical Reactions

Picture yourself toasting marshmallows over a campfire. You use your senses to detect changes. You see the burning logs change from a hard solid to a soft pile of ash. You smell smoke. You feel the heat. You can even taste the results. The brown surface and gooey interior of the toasted marshmallow is a big change from the soft, white marshmallow just out of its bag. A **chemical reaction** is a change in matter that produces one or more new substances. Like the toasting of marshmallows, other chemical reactions involve two main kinds of observable changes.

◄ Bronze statue with a surface darkened by chemical reactions

Figure 12 Brilliant, glittering fireworks add excitement to many holidays. *Inferring What evidence tells you that fireworks involve chemical reactions?*

Changes in Properties One way to detect chemical reactions is to observe changes in the properties of the materials involved. Chemical properties change when new substances form. But what specific kinds of changes should you look for? First, a gas might be produced. If the reaction occurs in a liquid, you may see the gas as bubbles. Second, a color change may signal that a new substance has formed. Third, a solid may appear when two solutions are mixed. A solid that forms from solution during a chemical reaction is called a **precipitate** (pree SIP uh tayt). Finally, other kinds of observable changes in properties can also signal a chemical reaction. For example, hard marble forms a crumbly solid when it reacts with acid rain.

A single property change such as the formation of a gas may indicate that a chemical reaction has taken place, but it's not a guarantee. Sometimes physical changes give similar results. The sign of a chemical change is that one or more new substances are produced. When water changes physically, the resulting water vapor, ice, or liquid is made of the same particles as the starting substance. For example, when water boils, the gas bubbles you see are made of particles of H_2O, just as the original liquid was. When water changes chemically, however, the H_2O particles undergo a change. For example, when an electric current is passed through water during electrolysis, two gases are produced, hydrogen gas (H_2) and oxygen gas (O_2). **One observable characteristic of a chemical reaction is the formation of new substances with properties that are different from those of the starting substances.**

Mostly Cloudy

How can you tell if a chemical reaction is taking place?

1. Put on your safety goggles and apron.
2. Pour about 5 mL of lime-water into a plastic cup.
3. Pour an equal amount of plain water into another plastic cup.
4. Add about 5 mL of carbonated water to each of the cups.

Inferring In which cup do you think a chemical reaction occurred? What evidence supports your inference?

EXPLORING Evidence for Chemical Reactions

ubstances react chemically to form new substances. The signs of a reaction vary, but many reactions include one or more of the following types of evidence.

Precipitation Two clear solutions react when mixed, forming an opaque, red precipitate. The presence of the precipitate tells you a new substance has formed.

Color change Brightly colored chemical substances called pigments are produced by chemical reactions in the leaves of some plants. The reactions speed up in the fall season when the air temperature cools and the amount of daylight shortens.

Gas production Oxygen bubbles formed during photosynthesis collect on the leaves of this underwater plant. Oxygen is a product of the reaction between carbon dioxide and water inside the cells of the plant.

Changes in temperature The burning of natural gas (a chemical reaction) supplies heat to boil water (a physical change). A temperature change can result from the changes in energy during a chemical reaction.

Changes in properties Baking turns flour, water, and other ingredients into light, flaky bread. The loaf of bread with its crunchy crust has very different properties from the soft dough that went into the oven.

Changes in Energy From your everyday experience, you know about various types of energy, such as light and electricity. As matter changes, it can either absorb or release energy. **Another observable characteristic of a chemical reaction is a change in energy. Some reactions absorb energy, while others release energy.** One common indication that energy has been absorbed or released is a change in temperature.

If you did the Discover activity on page 38, you observed that the mixture became colder. When baking soda (sodium bicarbonate) reacts with vinegar, the reaction takes heat from the solution, making it feel cooler. This kind of reaction, which absorbs energy, is called an **endothermic reaction** (en doh THUR mik). The reaction that occurs in the cold pack in Figure 13 is another example of an endothermic reaction.

In contrast, the reaction in a barbecue grill between charcoal and oxygen in the air releases enough energy to cook a meal. This energy is given off as heat. A reaction that releases energy in the form of heat is called an **exothermic reaction** (eks oh THUR mik). You will learn more about energy and chemical changes in Section 5.

✓ *Checkpoint* *How are endothermic reactions different from exothermic reactions?*

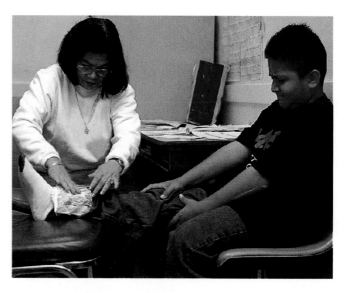

Figure 13 When this cold pack was squeezed, a reaction between water and another compound occurred and the temperature of the pack decreased. The resulting cooling effect reduces pain in the injured ankle and speeds up the healing process. *Classifying Is this reaction exothermic or endothermic? Explain.*

Figure 14 Foods sizzle and cook on a grill as thermal energy is given off by the burning charcoal.

Chemical Reactions on a Small Scale

If you walk along a beach, you leave footprints in the sand. Over time, the incoming tide erases them. A beach is constantly changing as each wave carries new sand in from the ocean and takes some of the shore sand back with it. Sometimes a violent storm can change the outline of a shore in just a few hours, but mostly the beach is changed by wind and water moving sand a little at a time.

Chemical reactions also occur one small step at a time. When you use your senses to observe evidence of a chemical change, you are detecting the combined effect of countless small, invisible changes. These changes involve the rearrangement of atoms. Recall that the force that holds atoms together is called a chemical bond. Often, individual atoms are bonded to other atoms in molecules. A **molecule** is a particle made of two or more atoms bonded together. If the bonds within a molecule break, its atoms may bond in with other atoms. The result of these changes among tiny particles is the formation of new substances.

Elements Forming Compounds

In the first two sections of this chapter, you read mostly about elements and their atoms. In this section, you have begun to look at chemical reactions. Suppose you put the two subjects together. What happens when elements react chemically with other elements?

A **compound** is a substance made of two or more elements that have been chemically combined. Water, carbon dioxide,

Figure 15 The sandy cliffs protecting this lighthouse from the ocean have been worn away as wind and water shifted sand one tiny grain at a time. Moving one piece of sand on a large beach doesn't make a change you can see, but moving billions of pieces changes the shoreline forever.

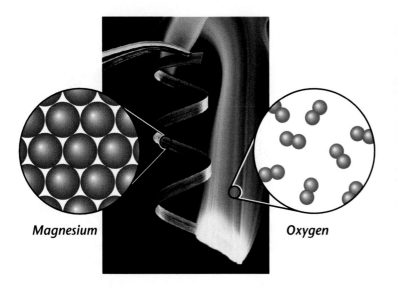

Magnesium

Oxygen

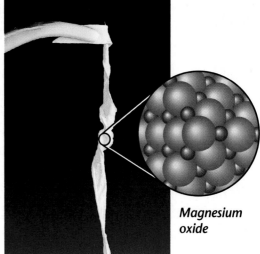

Magnesium oxide

table salt, and baking soda are familiar compounds. Indeed, you will find more compounds than elements in the world around you. Most elements exist in compounds in nature.

Figure 16 shows one example of elements combining to form a compound. In this case, magnesium (Mg) and oxygen (O) react when the magnesium burns. Before the reaction in the photograph, only magnesium atoms were present in the solid gray ribbon. Oxygen gas molecules were in the air. When the magnesium was ignited, the two elements reacted rapidly.

The result of the reaction was the compound magnesium oxide (MgO), which has properties that differ from those of both magnesium and oxygen. For example, the "ribbon" is no longer silver like the magnesium. Nor is it a gas, as is oxygen. While magnesium melts at about 650°C, temperatures of more than 2800°C are required to melt magnesium oxide!

Figure 16 When magnesium burns (left), its atoms give up electrons to oxygen atoms, forming magnesium oxide (right). Notice that the resulting particles of magnesium and oxygen are different in size compared to the original atoms.

Section 3 Review

1. How can you tell that a chemical reaction has occurred?
2. What two kinds of energy changes can take place during a chemical reaction?
3. When a solid forms as two solutions are mixed together, what is that solid called?
4. How is a molecule different from an atom?
5. **Thinking Critically** **Classifying** Classify the following as an endothermic or exothermic reaction: The temperature of two separate solutions is found to be 20°C. When the solutions are mixed, a precipitate forms and the temperature changes to 18°C. Explain your reasoning.

CHAPTER PROJECT

Check Your Progress
Use the information from the section to make a list of signs or evidence that a chemical reaction is taking place. Discuss your list with another classmate. (*Hint:* Look outside your home, think about reactions inside your body, and look for reactions that may occur either very slowly or very quickly.) Consider changes you might observe that shouldn't be classified as chemical reactions.

Where's the Evidence?

Chemical reactions occur all around you. In this lab you will observe different types of evidence of chemical reactions.

Problem

What are some signs that a chemical reaction has taken place?

Materials

4 small plastic cups   birthday candles
2 plastic spoons   sugar
tongs   clay
matches
sodium carbonate (powdered solid)
graduated cylinder, 10 mL
aluminum foil, about 10-cm square
dilute hydrochloric acid in a dropper bottle
copper sulfate solution
sodium carbonate solution
computer (optional)

Procedure

Preview the steps for each reaction. Copy the data table into your notebook or create a data table using your computer.

Part 1

1. Put a pea-sized pile of sodium carbonate into a clean plastic cup. Record the appearance of the sodium carbonate in the data table.

2. Observe a dropper containing hydrochloric acid. Record the appearance of the acid. **CAUTION:** *Hydrochloric acid can burn you or anything else it touches. Wash spills with water.*

3. Predict what you might observe when acid mixes with the powdered solid. Record your prediction.

4. Add about 10 drops of hydrochloric acid to the sodium carbonate. Swirl to mix the contents of the cup. Record your observations during and after the reaction.

Part 2

5. Fold up the sides of the aluminum foil square to make a small tray.

6. Use a plastic spoon to place a pea-sized pile of sugar into the tray.

7. Carefully describe the appearance of the sugar in your data table.

DATA TABLE				
Reaction	Observations Before Reaction	Predictions	Observations During Reaction	Observations After Reaction
1. Sodium carbonate (powder) + hydrochloric acid				
2. Sugar				
3. Copper sulfate + sodium carbonate solutions				

8. Secure a small candle on your desktop in a lump of clay. Carefully light the candle with a match only after being instructed to do so by your teacher. **CAUTION:** *Tie back long hair and loose clothing.*

9. Predict what you might observe when you heat the sugar. Record your prediction.

10. Use tongs to hold the aluminum tray. Heat the sugar slowly by moving the tray gently back and forth over the flame. Make observations while the sugar is heating.

11. When you think there is no longer a chemical reaction occurring, blow out the candle.

12. Allow the tray to cool for a few seconds and set it down on your desk. Record your observations of the material left in the tray.

Part 3

13. Put about 2 mL of copper sulfate solution in one cup. **CAUTION:** *Copper sulfate is poisonous and can stain your skin and clothes. Do not touch it or get it in your mouth.* Put an equal amount of sodium carbonate solution in another cup. Record the appearance of both liquids.

14. Predict what you might observe when the two solutions are mixed. Record your prediction.

15. Combine the two solutions and record your observations. **CAUTION:** *Dispose of the solutions as directed by your teacher.*

16. Wash your hands when you have finished working.

Analyze and Conclude

1. How do the results of each reaction compare with your predictions for that reaction?

2. How did you know when Reaction 1 was over?

3. Was the product of the reaction in Part 1 a solid, a liquid, or a gas? How do you know?

4. How are the properties of the material remaining after the reaction in Part 2 different from those of the sugar?

5. Was the product of the reaction in Part 3 a solid, a liquid, or a gas? How do you know?

6. How do you know if new substances were formed in each reaction?

7. **Think About It** What senses did you use to make observations during this lab? How might you use scientific instruments to extend your senses in order to make more observations?

More to Explore

Use your observation skills to find evidence of chemical reactions involving foods in your kitchen. Look for production of gases, color changes, and changes in properties. Share your findings with your classmates.

SECTION 4 Writing Chemical Equations

DISCOVER ·······················ACTIVITY····

Do You Lose Anything?

1. Place about two dozen coins on a table. Sort them into stacks of pennies, nickels, dimes, and quarters.

2. Count and record the number of coins in each stack. Calculate and record the value of each stack and the total of all stacks combined.

3. Mix all the coins together and then divide them randomly into four unsorted stacks.

4. Again calculate the value of each stack and the total amount of money. Count the total number of each type of coin.

5. Repeat Steps 3 and 4.

Think It Over

Making Models What happened to the total value and types of coins in this activity? Did rearranging the coins change any individual coin? If you think of the coins as representing different types of atoms, what does this model tell you about chemical reactions?

GUIDE FOR READING

◆ What does a chemical equation tell you?

◆ How does mass change during a chemical reaction?

◆ What are three categories of chemical reactions?

Reading Tip As you read, describe how each boldfaced vocabulary word relates to a chemical reaction.

Key Terms chemical equation
• formula • subscript
• reactants • product
• conservation of mass
• coefficient • synthesis
• decomposition • replacement

Suppose you were to take a walk in a foreign country where the language is unfamiliar to you. Think of the signs you might see—two doors with drawings of a man and a woman, the receiver of a telephone, a drawing of a bicycle, and a picture of a trash can with something dropping into it. You would have no trouble figuring out what these signs mean.

Symbols express a concept in a shorter form. "Hydrogen molecules react with oxygen molecules to form water molecules," is a sentence that describes the reaction between hydrogen and oxygen. But writing it is slow and awkward. A **chemical equation** is a shorter, easier way to show chemical reactions, using symbols instead of words.

Figure 17 Symbols are short and easy-to-recognize ways of saying something.

46

Formulas of Some Familiar Compounds			
Compound	**Formula**	**Compound**	**Formula**
Water	H_2O	Fool's gold (pyrite)	FeS_2
Hydrogen peroxide	H_2O_2	Propane	C_3H_8
Ammonia	NH_3	Rubbing alcohol	C_3H_8O
Aspirin	$C_9H_8O_4$	Rust	Fe_2O_3
Baking soda	$NaHCO_3$	Sodium chloride	$NaCl$
Bleach	$NaClO$	Sugar (sucrose)	$C_{12}H_{22}O_{11}$
Carbon dioxide	CO_2	Sulfur dioxide	SO_2
Carbon monoxide	CO	Washing soda	Na_2CO_3
Hemoglobin	$C_{3032}H_{4816}O_{780}N_{780}S_8Fe_4$		

Figure 18 Formulas for compounds tell you what elements as well as how many atoms of each element are present.
Observing How many oxygen atoms are present in water, carbon dioxide, and sugar?

The Importance of Chemical Equations

You may be surprised to learn that though chemical equations are shorter than sentences, they contain more information. That's partly because equations use chemical formulas and other symbols instead of the words. Also, equations follow a common structure that all chemists understand.

Writing Chemical Formulas You already know that most elements are represented by one-or two-letter symbols. (You can review those symbols in the periodic table shown in Section 2 of this chapter.) So, how do you represent a compound? If you've looked at Figure 18, you may already know the answer—formulas. In chemistry, a **formula** is a combination of symbols that represent the elements in a compound. For example, NaCl is the formula for table salt. If you think of symbols of the elements as being like letters of the alphabet, a formula is like a "word" that represents a compound.

Besides identifying the elements in a compound, a formula also shows the ratio of the different atoms that make up that substance. By glancing at the formula for propane, you can see which elements make up this compound. They are carbon and hydrogen. Notice that there are numbers in the formula that are written smaller and lower than the letter symbols. These numbers are subscripts. **Subscripts** show the ratio of the atoms of different elements in a compound. For propane, the ratio is 3 atoms of carbon to 8 atoms of hydrogen.

If a letter symbol in a formula doesn't have a subscript, the number 1 is understood. For example, in carbon dioxide, CO_2, there is one carbon atom to every two oxygen atoms. What is the ratio of atoms in iron oxide (rust) Fe_2O_3? The formula tells you there are two atoms of iron for every three atoms of oxygen.

Ratios and Subscripts

A ratio compares two numbers. In a chemical formula, subscripts show the ratio of one kind of atom to another. $CaBr_2$ for instance, shows that there are 2 bromide atoms for every 1 calcium atom. Write a formula for a compound that has atoms in the following ratios:

- twice as many silver atoms as carbon atoms
- three times as many oxygen atoms as carbon atoms

In this formula, show the elements in this order: silver (Ag), carbon (C), and oxygen (O).

Structure of an Equation A chemical equation summarizes a reaction. It tells you the substances you start with and the substances you get at the end. The materials you have at the beginning are called the **reactants.** When the reaction is complete, you have different materials, called the **products** of the reaction. **A chemical equation uses symbols and formulas to show the reactants and the products of a chemical reaction.**

Chemical equations have a definite structure. The formulas for the reactants are written on the left, followed by an arrow. You read the arrow as "yields." The products are written on the right. When there are two or more reactants—or two or more products—they are separated from each other by plus signs.

$$\text{Reactant} + \text{Reactant} \rightarrow \text{Product} + \text{Product}$$

The number of reactants and products can vary. Some reactions have only one reactant or product. Other reactions have two, three, or more reactants or products. Find the number of products that result when limestone ($CaCO_3$) is heated.

$$\underset{\text{Reactant}}{CaCO_3} \quad \rightarrow \quad \underset{\text{Product}}{CaO} \quad + \quad \underset{\text{Product}}{CO_2}$$

Conservation of Mass No matter how many reactants and products are involved, all the atoms present at the start of a reaction are present at the end. Think about what happens when classes change at your school. A class is made up of a group of students and a teacher together in a room. When the bell rings, people from each class move from room to room, ending up in new and different classes. The number of students and teachers in the school has not changed. But their arrangement is different and the new groups interact differently.

Figure 19 When iron filings and sulfur are mixed and heated, the product is the compound iron sulfide. *Interpreting Diagrams* How do you know that mass has been conserved in the reaction?

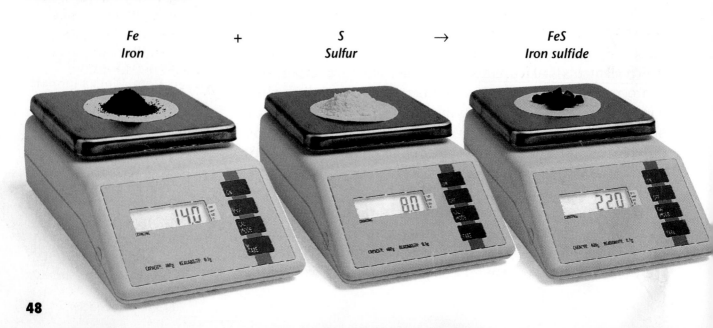

$$\underset{\textbf{Iron}}{Fe} \quad + \quad \underset{\textbf{Sulfur}}{S} \quad \rightarrow \quad \underset{\textbf{Iron sulfide}}{FeS}$$

Figure 20 Burnt wood and gray ash are all that remain from a roaring fire.
Problem Solving When wood burns, it reacts with oxygen in the air. What masses would you need to measure before and after the fire to show conservation of mass?

Now imagine that all the students and teachers are atoms, and each class is a molecule. At the end of a reaction (similar to a class change), the same atoms are present, but they are grouped together in different molecules. **The amount of matter involved in a chemical reaction does not change. The total mass of the reactants must equal the total mass of the products.** This principle, called the **conservation of mass,** means that during a chemical reaction, matter is not created or destroyed.

At first glance, some reactions seem to violate the principle of conservation of mass. If you measured the cooled ash left from a wood fire, for example, it wouldn't have the same mass as the wood that had been burned. What happened to the missing mass? It has escaped into the air as carbon dioxide gas and water vapor. If you could trap and measure these gases, you'd be able to prove that the mass didn't change.

☑ *Checkpoint* *How do the masses of the atoms in the reactants of a chemical reaction compare with the atoms in the products?*

Balancing Chemical Equations

How does the principle of conservation of mass relate to a chemical equation? It indicates that the same number of atoms exist in the products as were present in the reactants. So to describe a reaction accurately, a chemical equation must show the same number of each type of atom on both sides of the equation. When that happens, chemists say the equation is balanced. To balance an equation, begin by looking at the formulas.

$$H_2 + O_2 \rightarrow H_2O$$

How many atoms does the hydrogen molecule have? How about oxygen? How many of each kind of atom are present in one water molecule?

Still There

ACTIVITY

Use nuts and bolts to model the principle of conservation of mass.

1. Measure the mass of a collection of bolts, each with a nut attached to it.

2. Remove all the nuts from the bolts. Measure the total mass of the nuts. Then do the same with the bolts. Add these values.

3. Rearrange your collection, putting two or three nuts on one bolt, one nut on another bolt, and so on. You can even leave a few pieces unattached.

4. Measure the total mass again. Compare this figure with the totals from Steps 1 and 2.

Making Models How are the nuts and bolts similar to atoms and molecules in a chemical reaction? How do your observations model conservation of mass?

Calculating ACTIVITY

Each chemical formula below is written just as it might be in a balanced chemical equation. For each formula, calculate the number of each kind of atom.

$3 H_2O$

$2 H_2SO_4$

$4 Fe_2O_3$

$6 NaCl$

NO_2

When a coefficient is in front of a formula, how do you find the total number of atoms of one kind? What do you do if there is no coefficient?

Look at the chemical equation and models for the reaction:

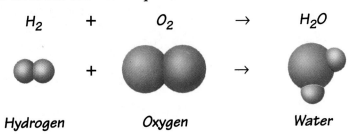

$$H_2 \quad + \quad O_2 \quad \rightarrow \quad H_2O$$

Hydrogen   Oxygen   Water

Count the number of atoms of each element on each side of the equation. You find 2 atoms of oxygen in the reactants but only 1 atom of oxygen in the products.

How can you get the number of oxygen molecules on both sides to be the same? You might be tempted to balance the oxygen by changing the formula for water to H_2O_2. Don't even think about it! You would be writing H_2O_2, which is the formula for hydrogen peroxide, a completely different compound.

To balance the equation, use a coefficient. A **coefficient** (koh uh FISH unt) is a number placed *in front of* a chemical formula in an equation. It tells you how many atoms or molecules of each reactant and product take part in the reaction. If the coefficient is 1, you don't need to write it. Balance the number of oxygen atoms by writing the coefficient 2 for water. That's like saying "2 × H_2O." Now there are 2 oxygen atoms in the product.

$$H_2 \quad + \quad O_2 \quad \rightarrow \quad 2 H_2O$$

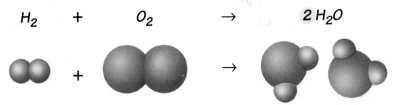

Okay, you've balanced the oxygen atoms. But now there are 2 hydrogen atoms in the reactants and 4 in the product. How can you balance the hydrogen? Try doubling the number of hydrogen atoms on the left side of the equation by changing the coefficient for hydrogen to 2. That's it!

$$2 H_2 \quad + \quad O_2 \quad \rightarrow \quad 2 H_2O$$

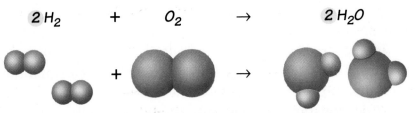

Now there are 4 hydrogen atoms and 2 oxygen atoms on each side. The equation is balanced. It tells you that 2 molecules of hydrogen react with 1 molecule of oxygen to yield 2 molecules of water. Count the atoms in the final diagram. Prove to yourself that the balanced equation is correct.

When magnesium metal, Mg, reacts with oxygen gas, O_2, the product of the reaction is magnesium oxide, MgO. Write a balanced equation for this reaction.

Write the word equation.	Magnesium + Oxygen → Magnesium oxide
Write the chemical equation.	Mg + O_2 → MgO
Count the number of atoms of each element on each side of the equation.	Mg — one O — two Mg — one O — one
Choose coefficients to balance the equation.	$2\,Mg$ + O_2 → $2\,MgO$
Think about it.	The answer shows 2 magnesium atoms and 2 oxygen atoms on each side, so the equation is balanced.

Practice Problems

1. Balance the equation: $C + Cl_2 \rightarrow CCl_4$
2. Balance the equation: $Al_2O_3 \rightarrow Al + O_2$

Classifying Chemical Reactions

Chemical reactions can be classified by what happens to the reactants and products. Substances may add together to make a more complex substance. They may break apart to make simpler substances. Or substances may even exchange parts. In each case, new materials form. **Many chemical reactions can be classified in one of three categories: synthesis, decomposition, or replacement.** As you read about each of these kinds of reactions, look at the examples. Compare the reactants and the products to see how they change.

Synthesis Have you ever listened to music from a synthesizer? You can hear many different notes and types of musical sounds. The synthesizer combines these sounds to make a complicated piece of music. When two or more substances (elements or compounds) combine to make a more complex substance, the process is called **synthesis** (SIN thuh sis). To synthesize is to put things together. Look back at the reaction of hydrogen and oxygen to make water. You should see now that this is a synthesis reaction—two elements come together, making a compound.

Figure 21 Iron combines with oxygen (top) to form iron oxide, or rust (bottom). This reaction is an example of synthesis.

 **INTEGRATING ENVIRONMENTAL SCIENCE** Acid rain is a product of synthesis reactions. In one case, sulfur dioxide, oxygen, and water combine to make sulfuric acid. Look at the equation for the reaction. Can you find the 8 oxygen atoms on each side of the equation?

$$2\,SO_2 + O_2 + 2\,H_2O \rightarrow 2\,H_2SO_4$$

Sulfur dioxide   Oxygen   Water   Sulfuric acid

Sulfur dioxide comes from car engines or from power plants that burn coal. Oxygen and water vapor are in the air. Together they produce sulfuric acid, which causes rainwater to become corrosive. This acid water then eats away at stone and metal, and can damage living organisms.

Decomposition While a synthesis reaction builds compounds from simpler reactants, a process called **decomposition** breaks down compounds into simpler products. Many people keep a bottle of hydrogen peroxide to clean cuts. If you keep such a bottle for a very long time, you'll have water instead. The hydrogen peroxide decomposes into water and oxygen gas.

$$2\,H_2O_2 \rightarrow 2\,H_2O + O_2$$

The oxygen that is produced escapes into the air.

☑ *Checkpoint* *How do synthesis and decomposition differ?*

Figure 22 Safety airbags in cars inflate as a result of a decomposition reaction. On impact, a detonator cap inside the air bag explodes. The explosion causes a compound made of sodium and nitrogen to decompose. One product is a large quantity of nitrogen gas.
Applying Concepts Why is quick inflation of airbags important?

Replacement When one element replaces another in a compound, or when two elements in different compounds trade places, the process is called **replacement.** Copper metal, for example, can be obtained by heating rock containing copper oxide in the presence of charcoal. The carbon of the charcoal takes the place of copper in the copper oxide.

$$2\ CuO + C \rightarrow 2\ Cu + CO_2$$

Medications for an upset stomach may contain calcium carbonate. Notice how this replacement reduces the amount of stomach acid (HCl).

$$CaCO_3 + 2\ HCl \rightarrow CaCl_2 + H_2CO_3$$

Although not all reactions can be classified as synthesis, decomposition, or replacement reactions, many everyday reactions can be grouped this way.

Figure 23 Copper metal can be chemically obtained from copper ore. Copper oxide (in the ore) reacts with carbon in a replacement reaction.

Section 4 Review

1. What information do you need in order to write a chemical equation?
2. What is the principle of conservation of mass?
3. List and define three types of chemical reactions.
4. **Thinking Critically** **Applying Concepts** Balance the following chemical equations by adding coefficients:
   a. $HCl + NaOH \rightarrow H_2O + NaCl$
   b. $Fe_2O_3 + C \rightarrow Fe + CO_2$
   c. $SO_2 + O_2 \rightarrow SO_3$
5. **Thinking Critically** **Classifying** Classify each of the following reactions as synthesis, decomposition, or replacement:
   a. $2\ NH_4NO_3 \rightarrow 2\ N_2 + O_2 + 4\ H_2O$
   b. $2\ Al + Fe_2O_3 \rightarrow Al_2O_3 + 2\ Fe$
   c. $P_4O_{10} + 6\ H_2O \rightarrow 4\ H_3PO_4$

> **Check Your Progress** ..... **CHAPTER PROJECT**
>
> Prepare a table to keep track of the chemical changes you observe. Have your teacher check your table to be sure it contains the proper headings. Record the different chemical changes you observe for a week. Make sure you can describe the evidence for each chemical change. If possible, classify each reaction as a synthesis, decomposition, or replacement reaction. Also classify it as occurring in a living or nonliving setting.

5 Controlling Chemical Reactions

Can You Speed Up or Slow Down a Reaction?

1. Put on your safety goggles and lab apron.

2. Obtain about 125 mL each of three solutions of vitamin C and water— one at room temperature, one at about 75°C, and one chilled to between 5° and 10°C.

3. Add three drops of iodine solution to each container and stir each with a clean spoon. Compare changes you observe in the solutions.

Iodine

4. Clean up your work area and wash your hands.

Think It Over

Inferring What conclusion can you make about the effect of temperature on the reaction of iodine and vitamin C?

GUIDE FOR READING

◆ How is activation energy related to the start of chemical reactions?

◆ How can you control the rate of a chemical reaction?

Reading Tip As you read, make a list of factors affecting reaction rate.

Key Terms activation energy
• concentration • catalyst
• enzyme • inhibitor

Figure 24 Building demolition requires a good understanding of chemical reactions.

You are working on an engineering team that tears down buildings. "3, 2, 1 . . . Let it go!" You push a button and suddenly a loud rumbling sound starts. The ground shakes, and clouds of dust pour into the street. In 15 seconds, a tall building is reduced to a pile of rubble. Careful control of energy in the explosion is critical to collapse only the structures meant to come down. If the demolition expert on your team doesn't understand the chemical reactions used, people could be injured or property damaged.

Although you may never demolish a building, you do use energy from controlled chemical reactions every day. Every time your body converts your lunch into the energy to play sports or to ride in a car, you are using controlled reactions.

Getting Reactions Started

If you have watched someone start a wood fire, you may have seen that it's not easy to do. Yet once wood begins to burn, it gives off a steady supply of heat and light. Why is it so hard to start some chemical reactions?

Activation Energy The rock at the top of the hill in Figure 25 contains stored energy because of its position. Yet it remains motionless until it's pushed over the small hump. After that, it falls down the hill rapidly, releasing its stored energy.

Every chemical reaction is like that rock. The reaction won't begin until the reactants get the energy needed to push them "over the hump." **Chemical reactions need a certain amount of energy to get started.** For example, energy is needed to break existing chemical bonds. Once that energy is available, the atoms begin to form the new chemical bonds that create the products. The minimum amount of energy needed to start a chemical reaction is called the **activation energy** of the reaction.

Consider the reaction in which hydrogen and oxygen form water. This chemical change gives off tremendous amounts of energy. But if you simply mix the two gases together, the mixture can remain unchanged for years. For the reaction to start, a tiny amount of activation energy—just a spark—is needed. Once a few molecules of hydrogen and oxygen react, the rest will follow because each reaction provides activation energy for new reactions. So every chemical reaction needs activation energy to begin. But do reactions also need energy to keep going? That depends on whether the reaction is exothermic or endothermic.

Figure 25 The rock at the top of this hill cannot roll down the hill until a small push gets it going. *Making Models How does this cartoon model the role of activation energy in a chemical reaction?*

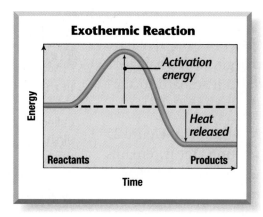
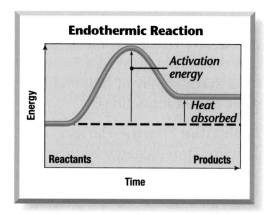

Figure 26 Every chemical reaction needs a certain amount of energy to get started.
Interpreting Diagrams Tell where increases and decreases in energy are shown in each diagram.

Designing Experiments

How can you tell whether a reaction between two solutions is endothermic or exothermic? Design an experiment that would make use of a stopwatch and two thermometers.

At the end of your experiment, how would you know whether the reaction was endothermic or exothermic? What would the result mean in terms of energy change?

Energy and Types of Reactions In Section 3, you learned that an exothermic reaction is one that gives off energy. Most chemical reactions are exothermic. They follow the pattern shown in Figure 26 in the graph on the left. Notice that a dotted line marks the energy level of the reactants before the reaction.

Like all reactions, exothermic reactions need activation energy to get started. But additional energy is not needed to complete the reaction. Instead, energy is given off as the reaction takes place. As a result, the energy level of the products is lower than the energy level of the starting materials. An example of an exothermic reaction is the burning of fuel to produce heat.

Now examine the graph of an endothermic reaction in Figure 26. Like all chemical reactions, endothermic reactions need activation energy to get started. But they also need a supply of energy to keep going. Because the materials absorb energy as the products are formed, the energy level of the final materials is higher than that of the starting materials.

That's what happens when baking soda and vinegar react in the Discover activity on page 38. Thermal energy already present in the solution is enough to start the reaction. As the reaction keeps going, it continues to draw the energy it needs from the solution. Another example of an endothermic reaction is baking bread. Bread dough won't bake unless it can absorb enough energy.

✓ *Checkpoint* *Why do exothermic reactions need activation energy?*

Rates of Chemical Reactions

Chemical reactions don't all occur at the same rate. Some, like explosions, are very fast. Others, like the rusting of metal, are much slower. Also, a particular reaction can occur at different rates depending on the conditions. A reaction's speed depends in part on how easily the particles of the reactants can get together.

If you want to make a chemical reaction happen faster, you need to get more reactant particles together more often. To slow down a reaction, you need to do the opposite—get fewer particles together less often. **Chemists can control the rates of reactions by changing factors such as concentration, temperature, and surface area, and by using substances called catalysts and inhibitors.**

Figure 27 Bubbles of hydrogen form when magnesium reacts with an acid. The test tube on the left has a lower concentration of acid than the test tube on the right. *Relating Cause and Effect How does the concentration of acid affect the rate of the reaction?*

Concentration One way to increase the rate of a reaction is to increase the concentration of the reactants. **Concentration** is the amount of one material in a given amount of another material. For example, adding a small spoon of sugar to a glass of lemonade will make it sweet. But adding a large spoon of sugar makes the lemonade a lot sweeter! The glass with more sugar has a greater concentration of sugar molecules.

Increasing the concentrations of the reactants makes more particles available to react. Compare the test tubes in Figure 27. In the test tube on the right, the greater concentration of acid means that more acid particles are present to react with the magnesium metal. You can see evidence for the increased rate of reaction in the greater number of bubbles that are produced.

Temperature Another way to increase the rate of a reaction is to increase its temperature. When you heat a substance, its particles move faster. Faster-moving particles increase the reaction rate in two ways. First, the particles come in contact more often, which

Figure 28 Unrefrigerated foods quickly spoil from the chemical reactions carried out by microorganisms. Keeping foods cold slows these changes.

Sharpen your Skills

Interpreting Data

1. Measure the length and width of a face of a gelatin cube. **ACTIVITY**
2. Calculate the area of that face of the cube.
   Area = length × width
   Repeat for each of the other five faces. Then add the six values together to get the total surface area.
3. Using a plastic knife, cut the cube in half and repeat Steps 1 and 2 for each piece of gelatin. Add the surface areas of the two pieces to get a new total.

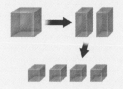

4. How did the total surface area of the cube before it was cut compare with the total after it was cut?
5. Predict what would happen to the total surface area if you cut each cube in two again. If you have time, test your prediction.

Figure 29 The concrete walls of this grain elevator in Kansas were blown apart by an explosion when grain particles and oxygen above the stored wheat exploded. Grain particles in the air have a greater surface area than the top surface of a pile of grain does.

means there are more chances for a reaction to happen. Second, faster-moving particles have more energy. This energy helps the reactants get over the activation energy "hump."

At home, you often use temperature to control reaction rates. Suppose that you forget to put milk back into the refrigerator before you leave for school. When you come home, the milk may smell sour. Milk contains bacteria, which carry out thousands of chemical reactions as they live and reproduce. At room temperature, those reactions happen more quickly. Some of the reactions cause food to spoil. Keeping foods cold slows down those reactions, so your food stays fresh longer.

Surface Area When a chunk of solid material reacts with a liquid or a gas, only the particles on the surface of the solid can come in contact with the other reactant. Now suppose you break the solid into smaller pieces. What happens? You've increased the surface area of the solid. More particles of the material are exposed, so the reaction happens faster. That's also what happens when you chew your food. Chewing breaks food into smaller pieces. Your digestive juices can then work more quickly to change the food into nutrients your body can use.

Catalysts Another way to control the rate of a reaction is to change the activation energy. If you decrease the activation energy, the reaction happens faster. A **catalyst** (KAT uh list) is a material that increases the rate of a reaction by lowering the activation energy. Although catalysts help change a reaction's rate, they are not permanently changed in the reaction. Thus they themselves are not considered reactants.

Many chemical reactions happen at temperatures that would be deadly to living things. Yet, some of these reactions are necessary for life. The cells in your body (as in all living things) contain biological catalysts called **enzymes** (EN zymz). Your body contains thousands of different enzymes. Each one is specific. That means it affects only one particular chemical reaction.

Enzymes provide a surface on which reactions take place. The surface helps reactions happen at lower temperatures because it lowers activation energy. In this way, enzymes safely increase the reaction rates of chemical reactions necessary for life. After the reaction, the enzyme breaks away unchanged.

Inhibitors Sometimes a reaction is more useful when it can be slowed down rather than speeded up. A material used to decrease the rate of a reaction is called an **inhibitor.** Inhibitors work in many different ways.

The discovery of one inhibitor had an important effect on the construction industry. Nitroglycerin is a powerful liquid explosive that decomposes quickly, releasing tremendous energy. An explosion can be caused just by shaking the bottle! In the 1860s, Alfred Nobel tried adding certain solid materials, such as wood pulp, to the nitroglycerin. The solids absorbed the liquid and kept it from reacting until it was ignited. This mixture could be handled more safely and still be used for blasting. Nobel's discovery is the more easily controlled material known as dynamite.

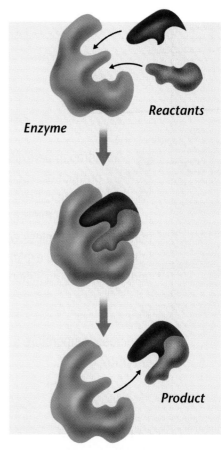

Reactants

Enzyme

Product

Figure 30 Enzyme molecules are shaped in ways that help reactant molecules come together.

Section 5 Review

1. What would happen if the activation energy for a particular chemical reaction was not available?
2. Describe three ways to increase the rate of a chemical reaction.
3. Which has greater surface area: a sugar cube or an equal mass of sugar crystals? Explain.
4. **Thinking Critically** **Relating Cause and Effect** Copy and complete the table below to show how some factors increase, decrease, or have no effect on the rate of a reaction.

Changes	Effect on Reaction Rate
Decreased concentration	
Increased surface area	
Heat added	
Catalyst	

Science at Home

Comparing Reaction Rates
Place an iron nail in a plastic cup. Add enough water to almost cover the nail. Place a small piece of fine steel wool in another cup and add the same amount of water. Ask family members to predict what will happen overnight. The next day, examine the nail and steel wool. Compare the amount of rust on each. Were your family's predictions correct? Explain how reaction rates are affected by surface areas.

Peroxide, Catalase, & You!

Hydrogen peroxide is a poisonous waste product of reactions in living cells. An enzyme called catalase, found in the blood, speeds up the breakdown of hydrogen peroxide into harmless water and oxygen gas. In this lab, you will explore the action of catalase under changing conditions.

Problem

How does temperature affect the action of an enzyme?

Skills Focus

measuring, controlling variables, drawing conclusions

Materials

forceps   stopwatch
test tube with a one-hole stopper
0.1% hydrogen peroxide solution
filter paper disks soaked in liver preparation (catalase enzyme) and kept at four different temperatures (room temperature, 0–4°C, 37°C, and 100°C)
container to hold water (beaker or bowl)

Procedure

1. Form a hypothesis that predicts how the action of the catalase enzyme will differ at the different temperatures to be tested.
2. Make a data table like the one below. Get the room temperature from your teacher.
3. Fill a container with water. Then fill a test tube with 0.1% hydrogen peroxide solution until the test tube is overflowing. Do this over a sink or the container of water.

DATA TABLE

Temperature (°C)	Time (sec)	Average Time for Class (sec)
0		
(room temperature)		
37		
100		

3. Make a data table similar to the one shown.

4. Moisten the small end of a one-hole stopper with water.

5. Using forceps, remove a filter paper disk soaked in liver preparation (catalase enzyme) that has been kept at room temperature. Stick it to the moistened end of the one-hole stopper.

6. Your partner should be ready with the stopwatch for the next step.

7. Place the stopper firmly into the test tube, hold your thumb over the hole, and quickly invert the test tube. Start the stopwatch. Put the inverted end of the test tube into the container of water, as shown in the photograph, and remove your thumb.

8. If the hydrogen peroxide breaks down, oxygen will be produced. Oxygen bubbles will cling to the disk and cause it to float. Record the time it takes for the disk to rise to the top. If the disk does not rise within 30 seconds, record "no reaction" and go on to Step 9.

9. Rinse the test tube and repeat the procedure with catalase enzyme disks kept at 0°C, 37°C, and 100°C. **CAUTION:** *When you remove the disk kept in the hot water bath, do not use your bare hands. Avoid spilling the hot water.*

Analyze and Conclude

1. Calculate the average time for each temperature based on the results of the entire class. Enter the results in your data table.

2. Make a line graph of the data you collected. Label the horizontal axis (*x*-axis) "Temperature" with a scale from 0°C to 100°C. Label the vertical axis (*y*-axis) "Time" with a scale from 0 to 30 seconds. Plot the class average time for each temperature.

3. What evidence do you have that your hypothesis from Step 1 is either supported or not supported?

4. How is the time it takes the disk to rise to the top of the tube related to the rate of the reaction?

5. What can you conclude about the activity of the enzyme at the various temperatures you tested? (*Hint:* Enzyme activity is greater when the rate of reaction is faster.)

6. Make a prediction about how active the enzyme would be at 10°C, 60°C, and 75°C. Give reasons to support your prediction.

7. **Apply** Oxygen kills many kinds of bacteria that can cause infection. Explain why hydrogen peroxide is often used as a treatment on cuts and scrapes.

Design an Experiment

The activity of an enzyme also depends upon the concentration of the enzyme. Design an experiment that explores the relationship between enzyme activity and enzyme concentration (your teacher can give you disks soaked with different enzyme concentrations).

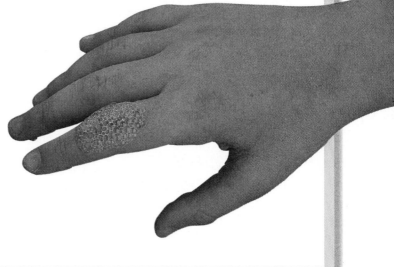

Transporting Hazardous Chemicals

Each year, millions of tons of hazardous substances criss-cross the country by truck and rail. These substances can be poisonous, flammable, and even explosive. But chemical reactions using these materials are also necessary to make the products that people use every day. They even make the trucks themselves run.

The chemical industry says that the transport of hazardous substances is safe and that problems are rare. But public health officials are worried. When accidents do happen, these compounds can damage the environment and threaten human lives. How can hazardous substances be transported safely?

The Issues

Why Do People Transport Hazardous Substances? Transporting hazardous substances can be dangerous. Useful products are made, however, from the hazardous materials that trucks and trains carry. Would people give up cars, computers, and CDs?

For example, CDs are made from plastics. To produce these plastics, manufacturers use compounds such as benzene and styrene. Benzene fumes are poisonous and flammable. Styrene can explode when exposed to air. Public health experts say it is important to find safe substitutes for dangerous substances. But finding alternatives will be difficult and expensive.

What Are the Risks? Serious accidents are rare. But recently in the United States, there were over 300 accidents involving hazardous chemical releases in one year. Public health experts say that some substances are too hazardous to transport on roads and railroads. An accidental release of these substances near a city could harm many people.

Some people say that vehicles carrying chemically reactive or hazardous substances should be restricted to isolated roads. However, many factories that use the chemical compounds are located in cities. Chemicals often must be transported from where they are made to where they are used. In the case of gasoline, cars are everywhere. Trucks and trains must transport the fuel to every neighborhood and region of the country.

How Should Transportation Be Regulated? Manufacturers that use hazardous chemicals say that there already are adequate laws. The Hazardous Materials Transportation Act (1975, revised 1994) requires carriers of hazardous substances to follow strict labeling and packaging rules. They must keep records of what they carry and where they travel. Local emergency officials in communities near transportation routes must also be trained to handle accidents involving these substances.

On the other hand, public health experts say there are not enough inspectors to check all trucks and trains and make sure rules are followed. But hiring more inspectors would cost additional tax money.

You Decide

1. Identify the Problem
In your own words, explain the problem of safely transporting hazardous substances.

2. Analyze the Options
Examine the pros and cons of greater regulation of the transport of hazardous substances. In each position, consider the effects on chemical industries and on the general public.

3. Find a Solution
Suppose there is a chemical factory in your city. You are the emergency planning director. Create regulations for transporting hazardous substances through your community.

SECTION 1 Inside an Atom

Key Ideas

◆ While electrons move around outside the nucleus of an atom, protons and neutrons stay inside the nucleus.

◆ The number of valence electrons determines the physical and chemical properties of an atom, and therefore, an element.

Key Terms

element	atomic number
atom	atomic mass unit (amu)
nucleus	valence electron
proton	chemical bond
neutron	electron dot diagram
electron	

SECTION 2 The Periodic Table

Key Ideas

◆ By arranging the elements according to atomic mass, Mendeleev identified patterns among their properties.

◆ An element's physical and chemical properties can be predicted from its location in the periodic table.

Key Terms

physical property	symbol	metal
chemical property	group	nonmetal
atomic mass	period	metalloid
periodic table		

SECTION 3 Observing Chemical Reactions

Key Idea

◆ A chemical reaction produces materials that have different properties than the starting materials had. Each reaction either absorbs or releases energy.

Key Terms

chemical reaction	exothermic reaction
precipitate	molecule
endothermic reaction	compound

SECTION 4 Writing Chemical Equations

Key Ideas

◆ A chemical equation uses symbols to show the reactants and products of a chemical reaction.

◆ Matter is neither created nor destroyed during a chemical reaction.

◆ Chemical reactions may be classified by the types of changes in reactants and products.

Key Terms

chemical equation	conservation of mass
formula	coefficient
subscript	synthesis
reactant	decomposition
product	replacement

SECTION 5 Controlling Chemical Reactions

Key Ideas

◆ Every chemical reaction needs activation energy to get started. Endothermic reactions need energy to continue.

◆ The rate of a chemical reaction can be controlled by such factors as concentration, surface area, temperature, and use of a catalyst or inhibitor.

Key Terms

activation energy	catalyst	inhibitor
concentration	enzyme	

Organizing Information

Concept Map Use key terms and ideas you learned in this chapter to construct a concept map about chemical reactions. (For more on concept maps, see the Skills Handbook.)

Reviewing Content

 Review key concepts online using iText at www.phschool.com

Multiple Choice

Choose the letter of the best answer.

1. The atomic number of an element is determined by
   a. the number of electrons.
   b. the number of protons.
   c. the number of neutrons.
   d. the valence electrons only

2. Elements that usually gain or share valence electrons are the
   a. metals.   b. metalloids.
   c. nonmetals.   d. precipitates.

3. A compost pile releases heat due to chemical reactions involving nitrogen. These chemical reactions are
   a. endothermic.   b. exothermic.
   c. organic.   d. decomposition.

4. The reaction between sulfur trioxide and water ($SO_3 + H_2O \rightarrow H_2SO_4$) is called
   a. replacement.
   b. synthesis.
   c. decomposition.
   d. combustion.

5. The rate of a chemical reaction can be increased by all the following, except:
   a. increasing temperature.
   b. decreasing activation energy.
   c. decreasing concentration.
   d. increasing surface area.

True or False

If the statement is true, write true. If it is false, change the underlined word or words to make the statement true.

6. Protons and neutrons are found in the <u>nucleus</u> of an atom.

7. <u>Valence electrons</u> hold atoms together.

8. A solid that falls out of solution during a chemical reaction is called a <u>precipitate</u>.

9. In a chemical formula, <u>symbols</u> identify which elements are present.

10. Chemical reactions will speed up if the concentration of the reactants <u>decreases</u>.

Checking Concepts

11. How is a molecule different from a compound?

12. You find the mass of a piece of iron metal, let it rust, and measure the mass again. The mass has increased. Does this violate the law of conservation of mass? Explain.

13. Why can't you balance a chemical equation by changing the subscripts?

14. **Writing to Learn** Suppose that you are a detective and you have a mystery to solve. You know that the suspect has the following characteristics: soft solid, tarnishes in air, one valence electron, and an atomic weight of 85.47. Use the periodic table and your knowledge about chemical reactions to identify the suspect. Explain your conclusion. What other characteristics would you expect the suspect to have?

Thinking Critically

15. **Applying Concepts** Balance the following equations and tell whether they are synthesis, decomposition, or replacement reactions.
    a. $Fe + HCl \rightarrow FeCl_2 + H_2$
    b. $N_2 + O_2 \rightarrow N_2O_5$
    c. $H_2CO_3 \rightarrow H_2O + CO_2$
    d. $CuO + H_2SO_4 \rightarrow CuSO_4 + H_2O$

16. **Problem Solving** Steel that is exposed to water and salt rusts quickly. If you were a shipbuilder, how would you protect a new ship? Explain why your idea works.

17. **Making Judgments** Many people think that the amount of sulfur dioxide in car emissions needs to be decreased. Why would this idea be a healthy change for the environment?

18. **Inferring** Some statues are made of materials that can react in acid rain and begin to dissolve. It has been found that statues with smooth surfaces are dissolved by acid rain much slower than statues with very detailed carvings. Explain why the rate of this reaction would be slower for the statues with smooth surfaces than the statues with carved surfaces.

Applying Skills

Use the energy diagram to answer Questions 19–21.

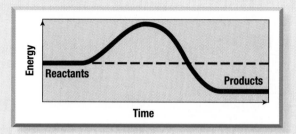

19. **Interpreting Data** How does the energy of the products compare with the energy of the reactants?
20. **Classifying** Tell whether this reaction is exothermic or endothermic.
21. **Predicting** What would happen to the graph if a catalyst were added to the reaction? Would adding heat to the reaction change the height of the curve? Explain.

Performance CHAPTER PROJECT **Assessment**

Present Your Project Compare the reactions in your chemical change log with those of your classmates. How many of the same processes did you observe? Defend your opinions as to whether or not your observations were chemical changes. Together make a list of the types of evidence you observed, and classify the reactions as endothermic or exothermic.

Reflect and Record In your journal, answer these questions. What evidence of chemical change is easiest to detect? What types of chemical reactions did you observe most frequently? Give an example of a chemical reaction you suspect was taking place, but for which you could not find direct evidence.

Test Preparation

Use these questions to prepare for standardized tests.

Read the information below. Then answer Questions 22–26.

A laboratory assistant was experimenting with chemical reactions when she combined a small amount of zinc (Zn) with hydrochloric acid (HCl). She discovered that zinc chloride ($ZnCl_2$) and hydrogen (H_2) were produced.

22. Which of the following substances are the reactants?
    A $Zn + HCl$
    B $ZnCl_2 + H_2$
    C $Zn + H_2$
    D $ZnCl_2 + HCl$

23. Which of the following substances are the products?
    F $Zn + HCl$
    G $ZnCl_2 + H_2$
    H $Zn + H_2$
    J $ZnCl_2 + HCl$

24. Which equation correctly describes this reaction?
    A $Zn + HCl \rightarrow ZnCl_2 + H_2$
    B $ZnCl_2 + H_2 \rightarrow Zn + 2 HCl$
    C $Zn + 2HCl \rightarrow ZnCl_2 + H_2$
    D $2 Zn + 2 HCl \rightarrow 2 (ZnCl_2 + H_2)$

25. How should the assistant classify this reaction?
    F synthesis   G decomposition
    H replacement   J combustion

26. Which of the following actions would probably speed up the reaction between zinc and hydrochloric acid?
    A making sure the masses of the reactants and the products are the same
    B cooling down the reactants before combining them
    C adding an inhibitor
    D breaking up the zinc into smaller pieces

Exploring Properties of Materials

This spider's web and the mountain thistle stems that support it are made of natural polymers.

WEB ACTIVITY

www.phschool.com

Polymer Profiles

A spider's delicate web glistens in the early morning sunshine. It was spun overnight from silken fibers produced by the spider's body. These fibers, much of the spider itself, and the flower stems that support the web are made from polymers— one of the types of materials you will study in this chapter. In your project, you will survey different polymers found around you. You will learn about the properties of these materials and see how their uses depend on their properties.

Your Goal To collect and investigate different polymers.

To complete your project you must

◆ collect at least eight polymer samples from at least three different locations
◆ identify the chemical and physical properties of the polymers by performing at least three tests
◆ create an informative display about these polymers
◆ follow the safety guidelines in Appendix A

Get Started Brainstorm with your classmates what you already know about polymers. Make a list of items you think are made of polymers. Look in Section 1 to get some hints about materials to investigate. Begin to think about how different polymers are used in everyday life, and why.

Check Your Progress You will be working on this project as you study this chapter. To keep your project on track, look for Check Your Progress boxes at the following points.

Section 1 Review, page 75: Collect samples of polymers and record data about their sources and uses.

Section 3 Review, page 88: Devise procedures to test properties of the polymers.

Section 4 Review, page 95: Carry out your tests and organize your results in your data table.

Present Your Project At the end of the chapter (page 99), you will present a showcase of polymers to the class.

TEKS

In addition to process TEKS, this chapter addresses these concept TEKS as they relate to the chapter's topics.

(8.8) The student knows that matter is composed of atoms. The student is expected to:
(A) describe the structure and parts of an atom.
(B) identify the properties of an atom including mass and electrical charge.

(8.9) The student knows that substances have chemical and physical properties. The student is expected to:
(A) demonstrate that substances may react chemically to form new substances.
(D) identify that physical and chemical properties influence the development and application of everyday materials such as cooking surfaces, insulation, adhesives, and plastics.

1 Polymers and Composites

DISCOVER • ACTIVITY

What Did You Make?

1. Look at a sample of borax solution and write down properties you observe. Do the same with white glue.

2. Measure about 2 large spoonfuls of borax solution into a paper cup.

3. Stir the solution as you add about one spoonful of white glue to the cup.

4. After 2 minutes, record the properties of the material in the cup. Wash your hands when you are finished.

Think It Over

Observing What evidence of a chemical reaction did you observe? How did the materials change? What do you think you made?

GUIDE FOR READING

◆ How does a polymer form?

◆ Why are composite materials often more useful than single polymers?

Reading Tip As you read, make a list of properties of polymers. Write one sentence describing each property.

Key Terms organic compound
• polymer • monomer
• plastic • composite

Figure 1 The clothing, boots, goggles, and helmet worn by this climber are all made of polymers. So is the rope that protects her from falling off this frozen waterfall in Colorado.

Did you ever step into tar on a hot summer day? Tar is a thick, smelly, black goo that sticks to your shoes. Tar, from crude oil or coal, can be made into rope, insulating fabric for clothes, and safety gear. Manufacturers use tar to make countless products ranging from sports equipment and automobile parts to plastic housewares and toys.

Plastic products are found everywhere today. Look around the room. How many things can you see that are made of plastic? What materials do you think people made these items from before plastic was invented? Many things that were once made of other materials are now made of plastic.

Carbon's Strings, Rings, and Other Things

Plastics and the cells in your body have something in common. They are made of organic compounds. An **organic compound** contains atoms of carbon bonded to one another and to other kinds of atoms. Carbon is present in more than two million known compounds, and more are being discovered or invented every day.

Carbon's unique ability to form so many compounds comes from two properties. Carbon atoms can form four chemical bonds. They can also bond to one another in chains and ring-shaped groups. These structures form the "backbones" to which other atoms attach.

Hydrogen is the most common element found with carbon in its compounds. Other elements include oxygen, nitrogen, phosphorus, sulfur, and the halogens, especially chlorine.

Carbon Compounds Form Polymers

Molecules of some organic compounds can hook together, forming larger molecules. A **polymer** (PAHL uh mur) is a large, complex molecule built from smaller molecules joined together. The smaller molecules from which polymers are built are called **monomers** (MAHN uh murz). **Polymers form when chemical reactions link monomers in a repeating pattern.** A polymer is a different substance with different properties from the hundreds or even thousands of monomers that compose it.

Many polymers consist of a single kind of monomer that repeats over and over again. You could think of these monomers as linked like the identical cars of a long passenger train. In other cases, two or three monomers may join in an alternating pattern. Sometimes links between monomer chains occur, forming large webs or netlike molecules. The physical and chemical properties of a polymer depend on the monomers from which it is made.

☑ *Checkpoint* *In what patterns may monomers become linked?*

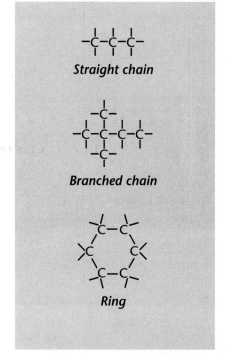

Figure 2 Carbon atoms can form straight chains, branched chains, and rings. In these drawings, lines represent chemical bonds that can form between atoms.
Interpreting Diagrams How many bonds are shown for each carbon atom?

Building a Polymer

One kind of monomer

Two kinds of monomers

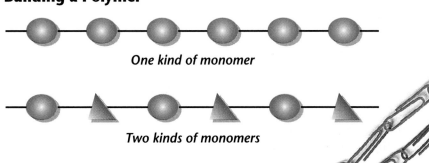

Figure 3 Like chains made of similar or different paper clips, polymers can be built from similar or different kinds of monomers.

Figure 4 Both animals and plants make polymers. **(A)** The leaves and stems of these desert plants are made of cellulose and other polymers. **(B)** A cotton plant is a source of polymers that people make into thread and cloth. **(C)** Silk fabric is made from the threads of silkworm cocoons. *Comparing and Contrasting What do the polymers shown in these photos have in common?*

Natural Polymers

INTEGRATING LIFE SCIENCE Polymers have been around as long as life on Earth. Plants, animals, and other living things produce the polymers they need from nutrients and other materials in the environment.

Plant Polymers Look closely at a piece of coarse paper, such as a paper towel. You can see that it is made of long strings, or fibers. These fibers are bundles of cellulose. Cellulose is a flexible but strong natural polymer that gives shape to plant cells. Cellulose is made in plants when sugar molecules (made earlier from carbon dioxide and water) are joined into long strands. The cellulose then is made into cell structures.

Animal Polymers Gently touch a spider web and feel how it stretches without breaking. It is made from chemicals in the spider's body. These chemicals mix and react to form a silken polymer that is one of the strongest materials known. Spiders spin webs, egg cases, and traps for prey from these fibers. You can wear polymers made by animals. Silk is made from the fibers of silkworm cocoons. Wool is made from sheep's fur. These polymers can be woven into thread and cloth.

Your own body makes polymers. Tap your fingernail on a tabletop. Your fingernails and the muscles that just moved your finger are made of proteins. Proteins are polymers. Within your body, proteins are assembled from combinations of smaller molecules (monomers), called amino acids. The properties of a protein depend on which amino acids are used and in what order. One combination builds the protein that forms your fingernails. Another combination forms the protein that carries oxygen in your blood. Yet another forms the hair that grows on your head.

☑ *Checkpoint* What are two examples of natural polymers from plants and animals?

Synthetic Polymers

Many polymers you use every day are synthesized from simpler materials. Recall that a synthesis reaction occurs when elements or simple compounds combine to form complex compounds. The starting materials for most polymers come from coal or oil. **Plastics,** which are synthetic polymers that can be molded or shaped, are the most common products. But there are many others. Carpets, clothing, adhesives, insulation, and even chewing gum can be made of synthetic polymers.

Figure 5 lists just a few of the hundreds of polymers people use. Although the names seem like tongue-twisters, see how many you recognize. You may be able to identify some polymers by the initials often printed on the bottoms of plastic containers.

Compare the uses of polymers listed in Figure 5 with their chemical or physical properties. Notice that many products require materials that are flexible, yet strong. Others must be hard or lightweight or nonreactive. When chemical engineers develop a new product, they have to think about how it will be used. Then they synthesize a polymer with properties to match.

Synthetic polymers are often used in place of natural materials that are too expensive or wear out too quickly. Polyester and nylon fabrics, for example, are used instead of wool, silk, and cotton to make clothes. Laminated countertops and vinyl floors replace wood in many kitchens. Other synthetic polymers have uses for which there is no suitable natural material. Compact discs, computer parts, artificial heart valves, and even nonstick cooking surfaces couldn't exist without synthetic polymers.

Language Arts CONNECTION

Many words in the English language use prefixes from Greek or Latin. In Greek, *mono-* means "one" and *poly-* means "many." These prefixes tell you that the molecules are made of either one or many parts.

In Your Journal

Make a list of words with other prefixes that tell you "how many," for example, the *tri-* in triangle. Tell what number the prefix indicates. Extend your list to include units of measurement, such as the millimeter. In each case, tell what information the prefix gives.

Figure 5 The properties of synthetic polymers make these everyday materials useful.

Some Synthetic Polymers You Use		
Name	Properties	Uses
Low-density polyethylene (LDPE)	Flexible, soft, melts easily	Plastic bags, squeeze bottles, electric wire insulation
High-density polyethylene (HDPE)	Stronger than LDPE; higher melting temperatures	Detergent bottles, gas cans, toys, milk jugs
Polypropylene (PP)	Hard, keeps its shape	Toys, car parts, bottle caps
Polyvinyl chloride (PVC)	Tough, flexible	Garden hoses, imitation leather, piping
Polystyrene (PS)	Lightweight, can be made into foam	Foam drinking cups, insulation, furniture, "peanut" packing material
Nylon	Strong, can be drawn into flexible thread	Stockings, parachutes, fishing line, fabric
Teflon (polytetrafluoroethylene)	Nonreactive, low friction	Nonstick coating for cooking pans

Composites

Every substance has its advantages and disadvantages. What would happen if you could take the best properties of two substances and put them together? **Composites** combine two or more substances as a new material with different properties. **By combining the useful properties of two or more substances in a composite, chemists can make a new material that works better than either one alone.** Many composite materials include one or more polymers.

The Development of Polymers

The first synthetic polymers were made by changing natural polymers in some way. Later, crude oil and coal became the starting materials. Now new polymers are designed in laboratories every year.

1869 Celluloid

Made using cellulose, celluloid became a substitute for ivory in billiard balls and combs and brushes. It was later used to make movie film. Because celluloid is very flammable, other materials have replaced it for almost all purposes, except table-tennis balls.

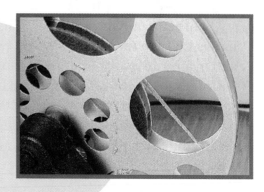

1825   **1875**

1839 Synthetic Rubber

Charles Goodyear invented a process that turned natural rubber into a hard, stretchable polymer. It did not get sticky and soft when heated or become brittle when cold, as natural rubber does. Bicycle tires were an early use.

1909 Bakelite

Bakelite was the first commercial polymer made from compounds in coal tar. Bakelite doesn't get soft when heated, and it doesn't conduct electricity. These properties made it useful for handles for pots and pans, telephones, and for parts in electrical outlets.

A Natural Composite The idea of putting two different materials together to get the advantages of both comes from the natural world. Many synthetic composites are designed to imitate a common natural composite—wood. Wood is made of long fibers of cellulose, held together by another plant polymer called lignin. Cellulose fibers are flexible and can't support much weight. At the same time, lignin is brittle and would crack under the weight of the tree branches. But the combination of the two polymers makes a strong tree trunk.

In Your Journal

Find out more about the invention of one of these polymers. Write a headline for a newspaper, announcing the invention. Then write the first paragraph of the news article telling how the invention will change people's lives.

1989 LEP

A light-emitting polymer (LEP) is a plastic that gives off light when exposed to low-voltage electricity. Research on LEPs points toward their use as flexible and more easy-to-read viewing screens in computers, digital camera monitors, watch-size phones, and televisions.

1934 Nylon

A giant breakthrough came with a synthetic fiber that imitates silk. Nylon replaced expensive silk in women's stockings and fabric for parachutes and clothing. It can also be molded to make objects like buttons, gears, and zippers.

1925   **1975**   **2025**

1952 Fiberglass Composite

Fiberglass is mixed with polymers to form a material with the strength of glass fibers and the moldability of plastic. Fiberglass composite is useful for boat and airplane parts because it is much lighter than metal, and it doesn't rust.

1971 Kevlar

Kevlar is five times as strong as the same weight of steel. This polymer is tough enough to substitute for steel ropes and cables in offshore oil-drilling rigs, but light enough to use in spacecraft parts. Kevlar is also used in protective clothing for firefighters and police officers.

Figure 6 Fiberglass makes a snowboard (left) both lightweight and strong. The composites in a fishing rod (right) make it flexible so that it does not break when pulling in a large fish.

Classifying ACTIVITY

Sit or stand where you have a clear view of the room you are in. Slowly sweep the room with your eyes, making a list of the objects you see. Do the same sweep of the clothes you are wearing. Check off those items on your list made (completely or partly) of natural or synthetic polymers. What percent of the items were *not* made with polymers?

Synthetic Composites The idea of combining the properties of two substances to make a more useful one has led to many new products. Fiberglass composites are one example. Strands of glass fiber are woven together and strengthened with a liquid plastic that sets like glue. The combination makes a strong, hard solid that may be molded around a form to give it shape. These composites are lightweight, but strong enough to be used as a boat hull or car body. Fiberglass also resists corrosion. It will not rust as metal does.

Other composites made from strong polymers combined with lightweight ones have many uses. Bicycles, automobiles, and airplanes built from such composites are much lighter than the same vehicles built from steel or aluminum. Some composites are used to make fishing rods, tennis racquets, and other sports equipment that need to be flexible but strong.

Too Many Polymers?

 **INTEGRATING ENVIRONMENTAL SCIENCE** It is difficult to look around without seeing something made of synthetic polymers. They have replaced many natural materials for several reasons. First, polymers are inexpensive to make. Second, they are strong. Finally, they last a long time.

But synthetic polymers have caused some problems, too. Many of the disadvantages of using plastics come from the same properties that make them so useful. It is often cheaper to throw away plastic materials and make new ones than it is to reuse them. As a result, they increase the volume of trash. Most plastics don't

react very easily with other chemical compounds. This means they don't break down into simpler materials in the environment. In contrast, natural polymers do. Some plastics are expected to last thousands of years. How do you get rid of something that lasts that long?

Is there a way to solve these problems? One solution is to use waste plastics as raw material for making new plastic products. You know this idea as recycling. Recycling has led to industries that create new products from discarded plastics. Bottles, fabrics for clothing, and parts for new cars are just some of the many items that can come from waste plastics. A pile of empty soda bottles can even be turned into synthetic wood. Look around your neighborhood. You may see park benches or "wooden" fences made from recycled plastics. Through recycling, the disposal problem is eased and new, useful items are created.

Figure 7 These rulers are just one product made from recycled plastic bottles.
Drawing Conclusions What would have happened to these bottles if they weren't recycled?

Section 1 Review

1. How are monomers related to polymers?
2. What advantage does a composite have over the individual materials from which it is made?
3. Why is it possible for carbon atoms to form chains and rings with other carbon atoms?
4. Make a list of polymers you can find in your home. Classify them as natural or synthetic.
5. **Thinking Critically Making Judgments** Think of something plastic that you have used today. Is there some other material that would be better than plastic for this use?

CHAPTER PROJECT

Check Your Progress
Collect a variety of different polymers. You might look in tool chests, kitchen cabinets, closets or drawers, art classrooms, hardware stores, or outdoors. Be sure to record where you found the polymer and what its function is. Record any information on labels or packaging. Try to identify each polymer as natural or synthetic. Organize this information into a list.

Packaging With Polymers

Y ou need to mail some breakable items to a friend. There are many different polymer materials that you could use to package these items. In this lab, you will design an experiment to find out more about these materials. Then you will decide which one you would use.

Problem

Which polymer material should you choose for packaging?

Skills Focus

designing experiments, controlling variables, drawing conclusions

Suggested Materials

water   hand lens   weights (or books)
scissors   tape   thermometers
balance   clock or timer
containers (beakers, trays, plastic cups)
iodine solution, 1% solution
hard-boiled eggs (optional)
polymers used in packaging (paper, Tyvek,
    plastic foam, ecofoam, cardboard, fabric,
    popcorn, sawdust, wood shavings, or plastic)
computer (optional)

Procedure

1. Write a hypothesis about the ideal properties a polymer should have if it is to be used for packaging.
2. Make a list of all the ways you can think of to test the properties of polymers. Think about properties including, but not limited to, the following:
   - ability to protect a fragile object
   - reaction to water   • appearance
   - heat insulation   • strength
   - reaction to iodine   • mass

   (*Note:* Iodine turns a dark blue-black color when starch is present. Starch may attract insects or other pests.)

DATA CHART

	Brief Description of Test 1	Brief Description of Test 2	Brief Description of Test 3	Brief Description of Test 4
Polymer A				
Polymer B				
Polymer C				

3. Select a property you wish to test. Choose a method that you think would be the best way to test that property.

4. Design a step-by-step procedure for the test. Do the same for each of the other properties you decide to investigate. Be sure that you change only one variable at a time. Include any safety directions in your procedure.

5. Predict which polymers you think will perform best in each test you plan.

6. After your teacher has approved your procedure, perform the tests on a sample of each polymer.

7.  In your notebook or on the computer, construct a chart that is similar to the one on the left to organize, examine, and evaluate your data.

Analyze and Conclude

1. Describe the similarities and differences that you discovered among your samples.

2. Review the different tests that you used. Which worked well? Are there any tests you would do differently if you were to do them another time?

3. Which polymer, or polymers, would you use to package your items for mailing? Explain your reasons for this choice.

4. Which polymer, or polymers, would you not want to use? Why?

5. **Apply** Tyvek costs more than paper. Ecofoam costs more than plastic foam. How would this information influence your decision on which material to use?

Design an Experiment

A cookie package must drop 1.5 m in a vending machine without allowing the cookie inside to break. Design an experiment to determine how you could make a package that is strong, cheap, and environmentally friendly. With your teacher's approval, perform the experiment.

SCIENCE AND SOCIETY

Grocery Bags: Paper or Plastic?

Americans use more than 32 billion grocery bags each year. About 80 percent of the bags are plastic. The other 20 percent are paper. Plastic bags are made from crude oil, a resource that cannot be replaced. Paper bags, on the other hand, are made from trees. Trees are a renewable resource, but it takes time to grow them.

Both paper and plastic grocery bags end up in the trash. Although some bags are incinerated, or burned, most end up buried in landfills. You need a way to carry groceries home. Which bag should you choose at the grocery store—paper or plastic?

The Issues

Should People Choose Paper Bags?

Paper bags can hold more items than plastic. A typical paper bag can hold about 12 items. A plastic bag might hold half as many.

A mature tree can yield about 700 bags. But just one large supermarket can use 700 bags in less than an hour! Most trees that are used to make paper come from forests. Only about 20 percent come from tree farms.

Hazardous chemicals are used in making paper bags. Wood and certain poisonous chemical compounds are heated. The mixture is cooked into a mush of wood fibers, which is pressed into paper.

Usually, paper bags are biodegradable, which means that decay organisms break them down. But in tightly packed landfills, even paper bags don't break down easily.

Should People Choose Plastic Bags?

Plastic bags are lightweight, compact, and waterproof. They take up 80 percent less space in landfills than an equal number of paper bags. But most plastic bags are not biodegradable. They cannot be broken down by natural processes. They can last a long time in landfills.

Some plastic bags end up in the ocean. There they are a danger to seabirds and animals who may eat or get caught in them.

Plastic bags are made from a compound that's left over when crude oil is made into fuel. This waste product used to be discarded or burned.

Most plastic can be recycled. Unfortunately, only about 10 percent of all plastic products are recycled today. Most people are just not recycling.

Which Is the Right Choice?

Some people want laws that would require manufacturers to make all bags—paper and plastic—out of recycled materials. Paper manufacturers say, however, that the fibers in recycled paper are too short to make bags that are strong enough.

The right choice of bags may depend on how your community handles trash. Does it collect paper or plastic or both to be recycled?

Both paper and plastic bags can be reused in many ways, such as for storage or trash containers liners. But the best choice may be neither paper nor plastic. One reusable cloth bag could replace hundreds of paper and plastic bags.

You Decide

1. Identify the Problem
In your own words, explain the problems in choosing paper or plastic bags.

2. Analyze the Options
List the pros and cons of using plastic and paper bags. In each case, who will benefit? Who might be harmed?

3. Find a Solution
Your community wants to pass a law to regulate the kind of grocery bags that stores should offer. Take a stand. Defend your position.

SECTION 2 Metals and Alloys

DISCOVER ·····························ACTIVITY

Are They Steel the Same?

1. Wrap a cut nail (low-carbon steel), a wire nail (high-carbon steel) and a stainless steel bolt together in a paper towel.

2. Place the towel in a plastic bag. Add about 250 mL of salt water and seal the bag.

3. After one or two days, remove the nails and bolt. Note any changes in the metals.

Think It Over

Developing Hypotheses What happened to the three types of steel? Which one changed the most, and which changed the least? What do you think accounts for the difference?

Over 6,000 years ago, people learned to make copper knives and tools that were sharper than stone tools. Later, they discovered that they could also use tin for tools. But these metals are soft, so they bend easily and are hard to keep sharp. About 5,000 years ago, metal makers discovered a way to make better tools. Copper and tin mixed together in the right amounts make a stronger, harder metal that keeps its sharp edge after long use. This discovery was the beginning of the Bronze Age. It also was the invention of the first alloy. An **alloy** is a mixture made of two or more elements that has the properties of metal. In every alloy, at least one of the elements is a metal.

Properties of Metals

You know a piece of metal when you see it. It's hard and usually shiny. At room temperature all metallic elements (except mercury) are solids. Metals share other properties, too. They can conduct electricity. They are ductile, that is, they can be drawn out into thin wire. Copper, for example, made into wire, is used to carry electric current to the outlets in your home. Metals are also malleable, that is, they can be hammered into a sheet. Aluminum, rolled flat, makes aluminum foil. You wouldn't be able to do that with a piece of glass!

GUIDE FOR READING

◆ What properties make alloys useful?

Reading Tip Before you read, rewrite the headings in the section as *how, why,* or *what* questions. As you read, look for answers to these questions.

Key Term alloy

Gold leaf dome of City Hall in Savannah, Georgia ▶

Figure 8 Stainless steel is the iron alloy used to make the spaghetti server and pot (left). The coins and chain of this necklace (right) are made from alloys of gold.
Applying Concepts Why are alloys used to make these objects rather than the pure metals?

Properties of Alloys

The properties of an alloy can differ greatly from those of its individual elements. Bronze, for example, is an alloy of copper and tin. It was a much better material for early toolmaking because it was harder than either element alone.

Pure gold is soft and easily bent. Gold jewelry and coins are made of an alloy of gold with another metal, such as copper or silver. These gold alloys are much harder than pure gold but still let its beauty show. Even after thousands of years, objects made of gold alloys still look exactly the same as when they were first made.

Alloys are used much more than pure metals because they are generally stronger and less likely to react with air or water. You have seen iron objects rust when they are exposed to air and water. But forks and spoons made of stainless steel can be washed over and over again without rusting. Stainless steel is an alloy of iron, carbon, nickel, and chromium. It does not react as easily with air and water as iron does. *Exploring Alloys and Metals in Aircraft* shows how other properties of alloys may be put to use.

☑ *Checkpoint Why is bronze more useful for tools than copper or tin?*

Making Alloys

Many alloys are made by melting metals and mixing them together in carefully measured amounts. Since the beginning of the Bronze Age, this technique has been used to make copper alloys. Some modern alloys are made by mixing the elements as powders and then heating them under high pressure. This process uses less energy because the metals blend at lower temperatures. The material then can be molded into the desired shape immediately. Another recent technique, called ion implantation, involves firing a beam of ions at a metal. A thin layer of alloy then forms on the metal's surface. Titanium, for example, may be bombarded with nitrogen ions to make a strong alloy for artificial bone and joint replacements.

EXPLORING Alloys and Metals in Aircraft

Much of the structure of an aircraft is made of metals. Engineers often design alloys with specific characteristics to fit the needs of the different parts of the aircraft.

Gold

A thin layer of pure gold coats the polymer (plastic) windshield. An electric current through the gold provides enough heat to keep the windshield frost-free. Gold works well for this purpose because it does not react with air and water.

Iron alloys

The structural supports that hold the airplane together must be extremely strong. Steel made of iron with carbon and other metals is the best choice for these parts.

Aluminum alloys

The outside of the plane has to be strong, light, and resistant to corrosion. The airplane's "skin" is aluminum, which is alloyed with magnesium, copper, and traces of other metals to increase strength.

Titanium alloys

Landing gear must be strong enough to hold the wheels of the airplane and support its great mass. Alloys of titanium with vanadium, iron, and aluminum are strong as steel but much lighter in weight.

Nickel alloys

The turbine blades in the jet engines have to spin around thousands of times per minute without changing shape. They also must withstand temperatures up to 1,100°C. Nickel alloyed with iron, carbon, and cobalt does the job.

Common Alloys

Alloy	Elements	Properties	Uses
Brass	Copper, zinc	Strong, resists corrosion, polishes well	Musical instruments, faucets, decorative hardware, jewelry
Bronze	Copper, tin	Hard, resists corrosion	Marine hardware, screws, grillwork
Stainless steel	Iron, carbon, nickel, chromium	Strong, resists corrosion	Tableware, cookware, surgical instruments
Carbon steel	Iron, carbon	Inexpensive, strong	Tools, auto bodies, machinery, steel girders, rails
Plumber's solder	Lead, tin	Low melting point	Sealing joints and leaks in metal plumbing
Sterling silver	Silver, copper	Shiny, harder than pure silver	Jewelry, tableware
Dental amalgam	Mercury, silver, tin, copper, zinc	Low melting point, easily shaped	Dental fillings
Pewter	Tin, antimony, copper*	Bright or satin finish, resists tarnish	Tableware, decorative objects
Wood's metal	Bismuth, lead, tin, cadmium	Low melting point	Fire sprinklers, electric fuses

*Pewter containing lead cannot be used with food.

Figure 9 Alloys have a wide variety of uses.
Making Generalizations How do the properties of each alloy make it well suited for its uses?

Using Alloys

When you want to describe something very hard or tough, you may use the expression "hard as steel." Steel is an alloy of iron with other elements. It is used for its strength, hardness, and resistance to corrosion. Without steel, suspension bridges, sky-scrapers, and surgical knives would not exist. Neither would artificial joints that replace damaged knees and hips.

Steels Not all steel is alike. Its properties depend on which elements are added to iron. High-carbon steel, for example, consists of about 0.5 percent manganese and up to 0.8 percent carbon. Carbon steel is stronger and harder than wrought iron, which is almost pure iron. Tools, knives, machinery, and appliances are just some of the uses for carbon steel. Steels with less than 0.8 percent carbon are more ductile and malleable. They may be used for nails, cables, and chains.

There are hundreds of different types of steel. Usually carbon is added to the iron plus one or more of the following metals: chromium, manganese, molybdenum, nickel, tungsten, and vanadium. Steel made with these metals is generally stronger and harder than carbon steel, and usually more corrosion-resistant. Depending on their properties, these steels may become bicycle frames, train rails, steel tubing, and construction equipment.

Figure 10 A plumber (left) takes advantage of the low melting point of the alloy solder to seal a leaking pipe. The brass in this doorknocker (below) is an alloy of copper and zinc.

Other Alloys Bronze, brass, and solder (SAHD ur) are just a few examples of other kinds of alloys. These materials are used to make items ranging from plumbing materials and sprinkler systems to tableware and doorknobs. Even your dentist uses alloys. Have you ever had a cavity in a tooth? A mixture of mercury with silver or gold (called an amalgam) makes a pasty solid. It rapidly hardens, filling the hole in your tooth. Look at Figure 9 and see how many of the examples listed in the table are alloys you have seen or used.

Section 2 Review

1. Name two properties of alloys that make them more useful than pure metals.
2. Describe one way in which alloys are made.
3. What advantage does stainless steel cookware have over cookware made of iron?
4. **Thinking Critically** **Applying Concepts** What properties would you look for to find out if an object was made of metal?
5. **Thinking Critically** **Problem Solving** The purity of gold is expressed in units called karats. A piece of 24-karat gold is pure gold metal. A piece of 12-karat gold is one half gold and one half another metal, often silver or copper. What fraction of the metal in a piece of 18-karat gold jewelry is actually gold?

Science at Home

Metal Inventory Identify items in your home that are made from metals or alloys. Look for cooking utensils, tools, toys, sports equipment, appliances, and other household items that are made with these materials. Discuss with members of your family how properties of the metals or alloys relate to the uses of the objects.

SECTION 3 Ceramics and Glass

DISCOVER

ACTIVITY

Does It Get Wet?

1. Find the masses of a glazed pottery flowerpot and an unglazed one of similar size. Record both values.
2. Place both pots in a basin of water for ten minutes.
3. Remove the pots from the water and blot dry gently with paper towels.
4. Find and record the masses of both flowerpots again.
5. Calculate the percent of change in mass for each pot.

Think It Over

Inferring Which pot gained the most mass? What can you infer about the effect that glazing has on the pot?

GUIDE FOR READING

◆ What physical properties of ceramics make them useful?

◆ How can glass be changed to make it useful?

Reading Tip Before you read, make a list of ceramic or glass items you use. As you read, look for reasons why these materials are well suited for their uses.

Key Terms ceramics • glass • optical fiber

Picture yourself on a warm day, walking through a slow-flowing stream. The mud at the bottom is soft. It squishes up between your toes. When you pick it up and shape it with your hands, it holds its form. If you let it dry in the sun, it becomes hard. This material is clay. You could also shape the clay into blocks, add some straw to make a composite material, and let the blocks dry. If you live where there is not much rain, you could use the blocks to build a house. In fact, people have used this type of brick to build sturdy homes. The Pueblo homes of the Southwest, for example, were built this way over a thousand years ago. Some of them are still standing today.

Making Ceramics

A discovery made thousands of years ago increased the usefulness of dried clay objects. Heating clay to about 1,000°C makes it harder and stronger. **Ceramics** are hard, crystalline solids made by heating clay and other mineral materials to high temperatures. Clay is made of very small mineral particles containing silicon, aluminum, and oxygen. Other elements, such as magnesium and iron may be present in clay, too. Clay forms when the minerals in

◄ **Pueblo homes in Taos, New Mexico**

rock are broken down. Unheated clay also contains water. When a clay object is heated, much of the water present on its surface evaporates, and the particles of clay stick together.

This process forms the hard ceramic pottery used for bricks and flowerpots. Once cooled, these materials have tiny spaces in their structure that absorb and hold water. If you grow a plant in this kind of pot, you can feel the moisture in the outer surface of the clay after you water the plant. When pottery is brushed with a layer of silicon dioxide and heated again, a glassy coating, called a glaze, forms. This glaze is shiny and waterproof. You might see glazed pottery used to serve or store food. Potters often use colorful glazes to create artistic designs on their work.

☑ *Checkpoint* *How does a glaze change the properties of a ceramic?*

Figure 11 Wet clay takes shape in the hands of a potter. *Predicting What will happen to the water in the clay when the potter heats it in a kiln, or hot oven?*

Properties and Uses of Ceramics

Have you ever heard the phrase "a bull in a china shop"? Imagine the damage. A bull in a bronze shop just wouldn't be as dramatic! The phrase comes from the fact that ceramics are brittle and can shatter when struck. Despite their tendency to break, ceramics have several physical properties that make them useful. **Ceramics resist moisture, do not conduct electricity, and can withstand temperatures higher than molten metals.**

Ceramic pottery has been used for thousands of years to store food, protecting it from moisture and animals. Roofing tiles, bricks, and sewer pipes are all long-standing uses of ceramics. Ceramics are also used as insulators in electric equipment and light fixtures.

Figure 12 Some ceramics, such as these roof tiles (left), have practical uses. Other ceramics (right) are valued for their delicate beauty.

Figure 13 Before the space shuttle *Columbia* can be launched again, tiles damaged during its last reentry must be replaced. *Predicting* What would happen to the spacecraft if many of the tiles were missing?

New uses for ceramics continue to be developed. The walls of ovens for making steel and other metal products are made of a type of brick that does not melt at the temperature of red-hot iron. And ceramic tiles are the only materials that can withstand the temperatures of over 1,600°C that build up on the bottom of the space shuttle during its reentry into the atmosphere. These tiles insulate the shuttle and protect the astronauts.

Making Glass

Have you ever looked closely at a handful of sand, or watched the varied grains as they slipped through your fingers? Thousands of years ago people learned that sand mixed with limestone can be melted into a thick, hot liquid. Most sand consists of tiny, hard pieces of quartz, a mineral made of silicon dioxide. When sand is heated to about 1,600°C, it flows like thick molasses. If this liquid cools quickly, it forms a clear, solid material with no crystal structure called **glass.**

The first glass objects were formed in clay molds that were chipped away after the glass hardened. Then about 2,000 years ago, glassmakers in ancient Persia invented glassblowing. The glassmaker put a blob of melted glass on the end of an iron pipe. By blowing air through the pipe, the glassmaker could produce a hollow glass vessel. If the glass was blown inside a wooden mold, jars and vases in beautiful patterns and shapes could be created.

Figure 14 Glass objects made in ancient Rome are on display at the Corning Museum in Corning, New York.

86

Figure 15 This cooktop surface is glass-ceramic—a hard, crystalline material made partially of glass. Although the cooktop looks glassy, it is composed only of 5% glass. Electric coils built into the cooktop supply the heat needed for cooking.

Different materials may be added to glass to make it useful for particular purposes. Early glassmakers added calcium (as limestone) and sodium (as sodium carbonate) to the melting sand. This mixture melts at a lower temperature than sand alone, so it is easier to work with. Window glass and the bottles and jars you use every day are still made with this type of glass.

Substituting lead oxide for the limestone makes a glass that bends light in useful ways. This kind of glass is used to make lenses for eyeglasses, telescopes, and microscopes. Adding boron oxide creates a glass that resists heat better than ordinary glass. It is used for cooking surfaces and laboratory glassware that must be heated. Colored glass is made by adding minerals containing various metals to the molten glass. Selenium and gold produce red glass. Cobalt makes beautiful, deep blue glass.

Scientists have used glass to develop a product that is heat-resistant to temperatures of about 700°C. Glass-ceramics are made by causing glass to react with other substances, including lithium and aluminum. Glass-ceramics are used in consumer products such as cooktop surfaces, cookware, and woodstove windows.

☑ *Checkpoint* *What are five materials that may be added to glass to make it useful for a particular purpose?*

Communication Through Glass

 There's a good chance that the next time you make a phone call, your message will travel through glass. An **optical fiber** is a threadlike piece of glass (or plastic) that can be used for transmitting light. Light shining into one end of the fiber travels through the glass to the other end. The effect is similar to electrons that carry a signal in copper wire. When you speak into a telephone, the signal created by your voice is converted to light signals that travel through the glass fiber. At the other end, the light may be converted into electronic signals that can then be converted to sound.

A Bright Idea

Can you communicate using an optical fiber?

1. Construct a barrier between you and a partner so that you cannot see each other.
2. Run a plastic optical fiber past the barrier.
3. Bring the bulb of a penlight flashlight close to your end of the fiber.
4. Using a single flash for "yes" and two flashes for "no," send your partner a message by responding to a series of yes and no questions he or she asks.
5. Change roles so that your partner has a chance to send signals in response to your questions.

Observing What happened when you and your partner sent signals to each other?

Figure 16 Even if optical fibers are twisted into a loop, light can move through the fibers.
Making Generalizations How can this property of optical fibers be useful?

You know that light can pass through glass from one side to the other. That's one reason you can see through a window. But when light moves through an optical fiber, it is reflected within the fiber. It doesn't pass through the outside surface. For this reason, there is little loss of light from one end to the other—an important condition for transmitting messages!

A pair of optical fibers, each the thickness of a human hair, can carry 625,000 phone calls at one time. One quarter pound of glass fiber can replace over two tons of copper wire. This difference is a big advantage when installing long lines like those that carry messages under the ocean. Because optical fibers are so efficient, they are being used to replace most copper telephone and cable television lines. Another benefit of glass fiber is its stability. Since the glass does not corrode as metals do, the lines are easier to maintain.

Section 3 Review

1. What physical property of ceramics makes them useful as the walls for ovens or as insulating materials?
2. In what ways can the physical properties of glass be changed?
3. How is a message transmitted through a glass fiber?
4. **Thinking Critically Applying Concepts** Before ceramics were invented, people stored food in containers such as baskets, leather bags, and wooden bowls. What properties of ceramics made them better containers for food?

CHAPTER PROJECT

Check Your Progress
Devise a plan to test some chemical and physical properties of the polymers you have collected. Tests might include hardness, fiber strength, flexibility, color, density, solubility in water, or reaction to corrosive chemicals. Construct a data table on which you can record results of your tests.

SECTION 4 Radioactive Elements

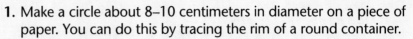

DISCOVER

How Much Goes Away?

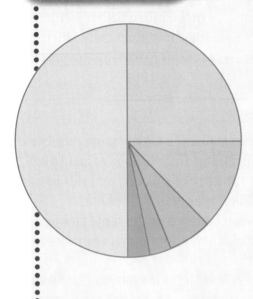

1. Make a circle about 8–10 centimeters in diameter on a piece of paper. You can do this by tracing the rim of a round container.

2. Use a straightedge to draw a line dividing the circle in half. Then divide one half into quarters, then into eighths, and so on, as shown in the diagram.

3. With scissors, cut out your circle. Now cut away the undivided half circle. Next, cut away the undivided quarter circle. Continue until you are left with one segment.

4. Place the segments on your desktop in the order you cut them.

Think It Over

Making Models How is the piece of paper changing each time? Suppose the original circle was a model for a sample of radioactive material, and the paper you cut away is material that became nonradioactive. What would eventually happen?

M ore than a thousand years ago, some people came up with what they thought was a great idea. Take some dull, cheap lead metal and turn it into valuable gold! They heated the lead, cooled it, added acid to it. They ground it into a powder and mixed it with everything they could think of. Of course, nothing worked. There is no chemical reaction that converts one element into another.

Even so, elements do sometimes change into other elements. A uranium atom can become a thorium atom. Atoms of carbon can become atoms of nitrogen. (But lead never changes into gold, unfortunately!) How is it possible for these changes to happen?

GUIDE FOR READING

◆ What is produced during radioactive decay?

◆ How is half-life a useful property of radioactive isotopes?

◆ In what ways are radioactive isotopes useful?

Reading Tip As you read, use the headings to make an outline about the properties and uses of radioactive isotopes.

Key Terms nuclear reaction • isotope • mass number • radioactive decay • nuclear radiation • alpha particle • beta particle • gamma radiation •half-life • radioactive dating • tracer • radiation therapy

Figure 17 This painting from 1570 shows people trying to change lead into gold. No such chemical reaction was ever accomplished.

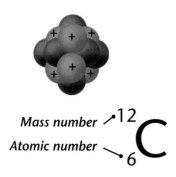

Carbon-12

Mass number ⟋^{12}C
Atomic number ⟍$_6$

Carbon-14

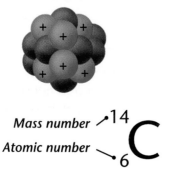

Mass number ⟋^{14}C
Atomic number ⟍$_6$

Figure 18 All carbon atoms have 6 protons in each nucleus, but the isotope carbon-12 has 6 neutrons and the isotope carbon-14 has 8 neutrons.

Figure 19 Radioactive elements give off mass and energy during radioactive decay.
Interpreting Diagrams Which type of decay does not result in a different element?

Nuclear Reactions

You have already learned that an atom consists of a nucleus of protons and neutrons, surrounded by a cloud of electrons. A chemical change always involves the electrons but doesn't affect the nucleus. Since the number of protons determines the identity of the atom, one element can't be made into another element by a chemical reaction. Such a change happens only during **nuclear reactions** (NOO klee ur)—reactions involving the particles in the nucleus of an atom.

Isotopes

Remember that all the atoms of an element have the same number of protons (same atomic number), but the number of neutrons can vary. Atoms with the same number of protons and different numbers of neutrons are called **isotopes** (EYE suh tohps).

To show the difference between isotopes of the same element, you write both the name of the element and the mass number of the isotope. **Mass number** is the sum of the protons and neutrons in the nucleus of an atom. Consider, for example, isotopes of carbon. Most carbon atoms are carbon-12, having six protons and six neutrons (and six electrons). About one out of every trillion carbon atoms, however, has eight neutrons. That isotope is carbon-14. Figure 18 shows you how to write the symbols for the two isotopes. Note that the atomic number is included, too.

☑ *Checkpoint* *Why do mass numbers for isotopes differ?*

Radioactive Decay

Some isotopes are unstable. The nucleus of an unstable atom does not hold together well. Unstable isotopes undergo nuclear reactions, often forming atoms with different atomic numbers or atomic masses. In a process called **radioactive decay,** the atomic nuclei of unstable isotopes release fast-moving particles and energy. There are three types of radioactive decay, each determined by the type of radiation released by the unstable

Alpha Decay	Beta Decay	Gamma Decay

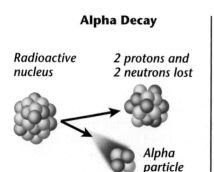

Radioactive nucleus → *2 protons and 2 neutrons lost*

Alpha particle

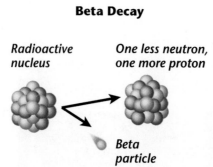

Radioactive nucleus → *One less neutron, one more proton*

Beta particle

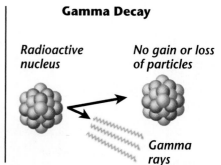

Radioactive nucleus → *No gain or loss of particles*

Gamma rays

nucleus. **Radioactive decay can produce alpha particles, beta particles, and gamma rays.** (Alpha, beta, and gamma are the first three letters of the Greek alphabet.) The particles and energy produced during radioactive decay are forms of **nuclear radiation.**

Alpha Decay An **alpha particle** consists of two protons and two neutrons. It is the same as a helium nucleus. Release of an alpha particle by an atom decreases the atomic number by 2 and the mass number by 4. Although alpha particles move very fast, they are stopped by collisions with atoms. Alpha radiation can cause an injury much like a bad burn. But a sheet of paper or thin piece of metal foil will act as a shield.

Beta Decay When a neutron inside the nucleus of an unstable atom breaks apart, it forms a beta particle and a proton. A **beta particle** is an electron given off by a nucleus during radioactive decay. The new proton remains in the nucleus. Therefore, the nucleus now has one less neutron and one more proton. Its mass number remains the same, but its atomic number increases by 1. Beta particles travel faster than alpha particles. They can pass through an aluminum sheet 3 millimeters thick. They can also travel into the human body and damage its cells.

Gamma Decay Alpha and beta decay are almost always accompanied by gamma radiation. **Gamma radiation** is high-energy waves, similar to X-rays. You will learn more about waves in Chapter 4. Gamma radiation (also called gamma rays) does not cause a change in either the atomic mass or the atomic number of the atom formed. But the energy released is the most penetrating type of radiation. You would need a piece of lead several centimeters thick or a concrete wall about a meter thick to stop gamma rays. They can pass right through a human body, causing severe damage to cells.

Sharpen your Skills

Predicting **ACTIVITY**

Look at the table of radioactive isotopes below.

Isotope	Type of Decay
$^{238}_{92}U$	Alpha
$^{63}_{28}Ni$	Beta
$^{131}_{53}I$	Beta
$^{226}_{88}Ra$	Alpha

1. With the help of a periodic table (see Appendix D), predict the element that forms in each case.

2. Label the symbol for each new element. Include the atomic number and mass number.

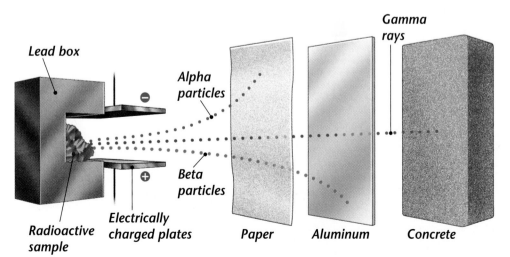

Lead box

Alpha particles

Beta particles

Gamma rays

Radioactive sample

Electrically charged plates

Paper

Aluminum

Concrete

Figure 20 The three types of nuclear radiation can be separated according to charge and penetrating power. *Inferring Which type of radiation is the most penetrating?*

Half-Lives of Some Radioactive Elements	
Element	**Half-Life**
Carbon-14	5,730 years
Chlorine-36	400,000 years
Cobalt-60	5.26 years
Iodine-131	8.07 days
Phosphorus-32	14.3 days
Polonium-216	0.16 second
Radium-226	1,600 years
Sodium-24	15 hours
Uranium-235	710 million years
Uranium-238	4.5 billion years

Figure 21 The half-lives of radioactive elements vary greatly. *Interpreting Data Which isotope in this table decays most rapidly?*

Half-Life

Not all the atoms of a sample of a radioactive isotope decay at once. They decay randomly, one at a time. If you watched a sample of iodine-131, for example, you couldn't predict when any particular nucleus would decay. But the time it takes for half the atoms to change can be measured. The **half-life** of an isotope is the time needed for half the atoms of a sample to decay. The half-life of each isotope differs. As shown in Figure 21, half-lives can range from less than a second to billions of years!

 **INTEGRATING EARTH SCIENCE** Fossils are the traces or remains of living things that have been preserved. **The half-lives of certain radioactive isotopes are useful in determining the ages of rocks and the fossils found in them.** As plants grow they use carbon dioxide (CO_2) from the air during photosynthesis. Some carbon dioxide contains carbon-14. This becomes part of the plant's structures the same way carbon-12 does. After the plant dies, it stops taking in carbon dioxide. If the plant's remains are preserved as a fossil, the ratio of carbon-14 to carbon-12 decreases. From the data, scientists can calculate how many half-lives have passed since the plant was alive. Thus, they can estimate the age of the plant and its surrounding rock. This process is called **radioactive dating.**

The half-life of carbon-14 is short compared to some other radioactive isotopes. It cannot be used to find the ages of objects older than about 60,000 years. Other isotopes, such as potassium-40 and uranium-238, are used to study older fossils, rocks, and objects used by early humans.

☑ *Checkpoint* *How does a sample of a radioactive isotope change after one half-life?*

Figure 22 Using the known half-lives of certain radioactive elements, such as potassium-40 and uranium-238, scientists can determine the age of ancient objects. This saber-toothed cat lived about 25 million years ago.

Phosphorus-32

**Phosphorus-32
in leaves**

Figure 23 Phosphorus-32 added to soil is absorbed through the plant's roots. The tracer can be detected in any plant structure in which the phosphorus is used.

Using Radioactive Isotopes

In addition to studying objects from the past, people use radioactive isotopes for work in the present. **Radioactive isotopes are useful both as sources of radiation and as tracers.** The radiation released by radioactive isotopes is itself useful. Nuclear power plants and some medical treatments, for example, depend on nuclear reactions as sources of radiation.

Another important use depends on the fact that the radiation given off by isotopes can be detected. Like a lighthouse flashing in the night, a radioactive isotope "signals" where it is. **Tracers** are radioactive isotopes that can be followed through the steps of a chemical reaction or industrial process. In chemical reactions, tracers behave the same way as nonradioactive forms of an element.

Tracers in Chemical Reactions Scientists can make use of tracers in chemical reactions. Equipment that detects radiation can track the tracer wherever it goes. This technique is helpful for studying reactions in living organisms. For example, phosphorus is used by plants in small amounts for healthy growth. A plant will absorb radioactive phosphorus-32 added to the soil just as it does the nonradioactive form. Radiation will be present in any part of the plant that contains the isotope. In this way, biologists can learn where and how plants use phosphorus.

Uses in Industry Radioactive isotopes are valuable in industry as tracers and for the radiation they produce. For example, tracers are used in finding weak spots in metal pipes, especially oil pipelines. When added to a liquid, tracers can easily be detected if they leak out of the lines.

Engineers use gamma radiation from radioactive isotopes to look for flaws in metal. Gamma rays can pass through metal and be detected on a photographic film. This is similar to using X-rays to take a picture inside your body. By looking at the

Sharpen your Skills

Calculating ACTIVITY
Carbon-14 has a half-life of 5,730 years. Data from several newly discovered fossils shows that carbon-14 has undergone decay in the fossils for five half-lives. Calculate the age of the fossils.

Figure 24 The radioactive isotope technetium-99 is used in medical studies of the heart, lungs, liver, and bones. **A.** In these healthy lungs, the red areas show greater absorption of the isotope than the yellow or green areas. **B.** In the hand, the bones are colored orange.

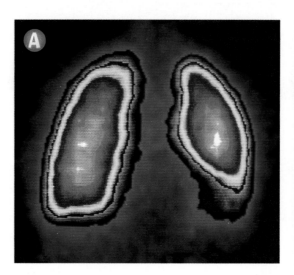
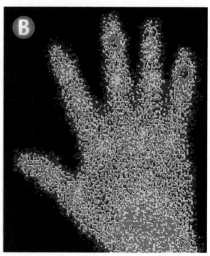

Social Studies
CONNECTION

Using radioactive materials can provide benefits such as electricity or advanced medical care. But what happens to the unavoidable radioactive waste? People aren't so comfortable having that around!

NIMBY is short for the phrase "not in my backyard." It stands for the idea that people don't want unpleasant or possible hazardous conditions near where they live. They would prefer to see radioactive wastes go elsewhere.

In Your Journal

Your local government has invited citizens to a meeting to discuss possible options for storing radioactive wastes from nearby medical or industrial uses. Write a one- or two-paragraph speech to the public meeting, expressing your opinion.

gamma-ray images, structural engineers can detect small cracks in the metal of bridges and building frames. Without these images, a problem might not be discovered until a disaster occurs.

Uses in Medicine Doctors use radioactive isotopes to detect medical problems and to treat some diseases. Tracers injected into the body travel to organs and other structures where that chemical is normally used. Using equipment that detects radiation, technicians make images of the bone, blood vessel, or organ affected. For example, tracers made with technetium-99 are frequently used to diagnose problems in the bones, liver, kidneys, and digestive system. Other isotopes, such as thallium-201 in the heart and xenon-133 in the lungs, help doctors diagnose disease in these organs.

INTEGRATING HEALTH

In a process called **radiation therapy,** radioactive elements are used to destroy unhealthy cells. Iodine-131, for example, is given to patients with tumors of the thyroid gland, a gland in the neck that controls the rate at which nutrients are used. Because the thyroid gland uses iodine, the radioactive iodine-131 collects in the gland. Radiation from this isotope destroys unwanted cells in the gland without serious effects on other parts of the body.

Cancer tumors of different kinds often are treated from outside the body with high-energy gamma rays. Many hospitals use cobalt-60 for this purpose. When gamma radiation is focused on a cancer tumor, it causes changes that kill the cancer cells.

Nuclear Power Nuclear reactions release enormous quantities of energy compared to chemical reactions. For this reason, some power plants use radioactive isotopes as fuel. Carefully controlled reactions, most often using uranium-235, provide electric power in many parts of the world.

✓ *Checkpoint* *What is a tracer?*

Safe Use of Radioactive Materials

Despite the positive uses of radioactive materials, they also are dangerous. Radiation penetrates living tissue, knocking electrons from atoms. This process produces ions that then can interfere with chemical reactions in living cells. Illness, disease, and even death may result from overexposure to radiation.

The dangers of radioactive materials mean that their use must be carefully managed. People who work with these materials must wear protective clothing and use insulating shields. Radioactive wastes can't just be thrown away. After radiation therapy, for example, contaminated equipment and clothing can still be hazardous. These items must be disposed of properly. Materials with low levels of radiation may be buried in landfills. Such landfills are carefully monitored to prevent contamination of the environment. Isotopes with long half-lives, however, will remain hazardous for hundreds or even thousand of years. Plans are under way to dispose of these kinds of materials in specially designed containers that will be buried in very dry underground tunnels. In that way the radioactive wastes can be isolated for many generations.

Figure 25 Waste Isolation Pilot Plant (WIPP) is a site in New Mexico where the United States government is developing safe storage for radioactive wastes. Large underground rooms (left), will house the wastes in secure barrels (right).

Section 4 Review

1. Describe the three types of radiation given off during radioactive decay.
2. How are radioactive isotopes helpful for studying rocks and fossils?
3. Give two examples of how tracers are used. Tell why radioactive isotopes work as tracers.
4. **Thinking Critically Making Judgments** If there were a proposal in your state to ban the use of radioactive materials because of the hazards of radioactive waste, would you support the idea? Why or why not?

Check Your Progress

CHAPTER PROJECT

After your teacher approves your plan, perform your tests. Record all results in your data table. If there is time, perform your tests more than once to obtain multiple sets of data. Try to organize your samples into groups based on the results of your tests. Identify similarities and differences among the groups.

THAT'S HALF-LIFE!

In this lab, you will use pennies to model how half-life is related to the decay of radioactive isotopes.

Problem

How does a sample of radioactive waste decay to a nonhazardous level?

Materials

100 pennies   graph paper
container such as a jar or a box
colored pencils (optional)

Procedure

1. Copy the data table into your notebook. Then place 100 pennies in a container.
2. Shake the pennies out onto the desktop. Separate the ones showing heads from those showing tails.
3. Count the number of pennies showing tails and calculate the number of pennies showing heads. Record both these values.
4. Put back only the pennies showing tails.
5. Repeat the process until there are two or fewer pennies left in the container.
6. Keep a tally of the total number of pennies removed from the container. Record this number after each trial.

Analyze and Conclude

1. Make a graph of your data. Label the horizontal axis with the trial number. Label the vertical axis with the number of pennies left in the container after each trial. Connect the data points with a smooth, curved line.
2. What does the graph tell you?
3. On the same set of axes, plot the total number of pennies removed from the container after each trial. Use a dotted line or different colored pencil to make this graph.
4. What does your second graph tell you?
5. Suppose the pennies represent nuclei of a radioactive element. What do you think the heads and tails represent?
6. What do you think is represented by each trial or shake of the pennies?
7. How many half-lives does it take for the substance modeled in this lab to decay to two or fewer "nuclei"?
8. **Think About It** Suppose 1,600 grams of low-level radioactive waste is buried at a waste disposal site. Assuming that 10 grams of radioactive material is an acceptable level of radiation exposure, about how many half-lives must pass before there is no longer a health risk at the site?

More to Explore

How could you use this model to show the decay of a sample that was twice as massive as the sample used in this lab? What would you do differently? Predict how you think the results would differ.

DATA TABLE

Trial	Tails Remaining	Heads Removed (each trial)	Total Pennies Removed
1			
2			
3			

1 Polymers and Composites

Key Ideas

◆ Polymers are large carbon compounds. They form when chemical bonds link many monomers in a repeating pattern.

◆ Polymers occur naturally as products of living cells. Polymers also are synthesized in factories and laboratories for a variety of uses.

◆ Composite materials combine the useful properties of two different substances.

Key Terms

organic compound   monomer   composite
polymer   plastic

2 Metals and Alloys

INTEGRATING TECHNOLOGY

Key Ideas

◆ An alloy is a mixture of two or more elements, one of which is a metal. Alloys have the properties of metals, but also are generally stronger and less likely to react with water or air than metals.

◆ Steel is one of the most frequently used alloys. Its properties make it useful for building materials, tools, and machinery.

Key Term
alloy

3 Ceramics and Glass

Key Ideas

◆ Ceramics are made by heating clay mixed with other materials to temperatures that produce a brittle, crystalline solid. Ceramics resist moisture, do not conduct electricity, and withstand high temperatures.

◆ Glass results when sand is melted to make a thick liquid that can be shaped when hot. Adding other materials gives glass properties such as heat resistance and color.

Key Terms

ceramics   glass   optical fiber

4 Radioactive Elements

Key Ideas

◆ Radioactive decay is a change in the nucleus of an atom that releases particles and energy. The products of radioactive decay are alpha and beta particles and gamma rays.

◆ The half-life is the amount of time it takes for half of the radioactive atoms of an isotope to decay. The half-lives of some radioactive isotopes are used to determine the ages of rocks and fossils.

◆ Radioactive isotopes are used as sources of radiation in industry, medicine, and research.

Key Terms

nuclear reaction   beta particle
isotope   gamma radiation
mass number   half-life
radioactive decay   radioactive dating
nuclear radiation   tracer
alpha particle   radiation therapy

Organizing Information

Compare/Contrast Table Copy the table about polymers, alloys, ceramics, and glass onto a separate sheet of paper. Then complete it and add a title. (For more on compare/contrast tables see the Skills Handbook.)

Material	Made From	How Made	How Used
Polymers	Monomers (carbon compounds)	a. ?	b. ?
Alloys	c. ?	Metals heated and mixed	d. ?
Ceramics	Clay; other minerals	e. ?	f. ?
Glass	g. ?	Melted, then cooled into desired shapes	h. ?

Reviewing Content

 Review key concepts online using iText at www.phschool.com

Multiple Choice

Choose the letter of the best answer.

1. A large molecule made of many monomers is called a
   a. plastic.
   b. polymer.
   c. protein.
   d. chain.
2. Fiberglass is a type of
   a. polymer.
   b. alloy.
   c. ceramic.
   d. composite.
3. The properties of alloys most resemble
   a. ceramics.
   b. glass.
   c. metals.
   d. polymers.
4. Clean sand is heated to its melting point to make
   a. ceramics.
   b. glass.
   c. alloys.
   d. composites.
5. Atoms that have the same atomic number but different mass numbers are
   a. radioactive.   b. alloys.
   c. isotopes.   d. alpha particles.

True or False

If the statement is true, write true. If it is false, change the underlined word or words to make the statement true.

6. <u>Oxygen</u> is the element that forms the backbone of most polymers.
7. Cellulose molecules are examples of <u>synthetic</u> polymers.
8. A useful alloy of copper and tin is <u>steel</u>.
9. The furnaces used to melt metals are insulated with <u>ceramic</u> materials.
10. Alpha, beta, and gamma radiation form as the result of <u>chemical reactions</u>.

Checking Concepts

11. Name some polymers that are products of nature. Tell where they come from.
12. Explain why some advantages of using polymers can become disadvantages.
13. List three properties of metals. Then for each property, give an example of how a specific metal is put to use.
14. Why is gold always mixed with other metals to make jewelry?
15. What is the purpose of the glaze on the surface of a pottery vase?
16. What properties of radioactive isotopes make them useful?
17. **Writing to Learn** Pretend you are a reporter for a consumer affairs magazine. Write a letter to a manufacturer of products such as glassware, plastic food containers, metal tools, or others discussed in this chapter. Ask about the physical and chemical properties of the products and how these properties influenced product development.

Thinking Critically

18. **Making Judgments** The plastic rings that hold beverage cans together are sometimes hazardous to living things in the ocean. Should companies that make soft drinks be allowed to continue using plastic rings? Consider what could replace them and the effects of the change.
19. **Applying Concepts** The earliest building bricks were dried by being left out in the sun. Why can this kind of brick be used only in areas with a dry climate?
20. **Comparing and Contrasting** Explain which material—steel, glass or polystyrene foam—would be the best choice for each of the following uses: cup for hot chocolate; hammer; wall of a salt-water aquarium; egg carton.
21. **Calculating** A wooden tool found in a cave has one-fourth as much carbon-14 as a living tree. How old is the tool? (*Hint:* The half-life of carbon-14 is 5,730 years.)

Applying Skills

The diagram below shows the first few steps of the radioactive decay of uranium-238. Use the diagram to answer Questions 22–24.

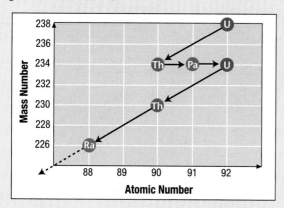

22. **Interpreting Data** How many elements are in the diagram? How many different isotopes of each element are there?
23. **Classifying** What type of radioactive decay resulted in uranium-238 becoming thorium-234? How do you know?

24. **Inferring** How do you know from the diagram that thorium-230 is radioactive?

CHAPTER PROJECT

Performance ▼ Assessment

Present Your Project Prepare a chart or poster to display the polymers you examined. Provide a sample of each polymer and include information such as its name, where it was found, what monomers it is made of (if known), and significant physical and chemical properties as shown by your tests. Be prepared to compare the polymers with other types of materials such as glass, ceramics, and metals.

Reflect and Record In your journal, explain how you might improve your collection and testing process. Describe one of the more interesting polymers that you found. Why do you think it is interesting?

Test Preparation
Use these questions to prepare for standardized tests.

Use the diagram to answer Questions 25–28.

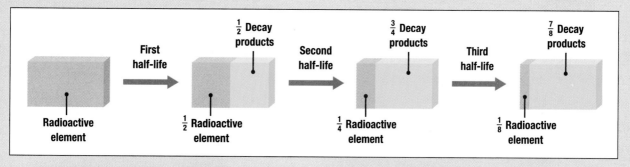

25. What is shown in this diagram?
    A the fraction of a radioactive element remaining after each half-life
    B the decay series for uranium
    C a three-step chemical reaction
    D the difference between long and short half-lives
26. How much of a radioactive-element sample will be left after the fourth half-life?
    F 1/8   G 7/8
    H 1/16   J 7/16

27. The half-life of sodium-24 is 15 hours. How much of a 100-gram sample will be left after 45 hours?
    A 50 grams   B 25 grams
    C 15 grams   D 12.5 grams
28. What is the decay product?
    F the element undergoing decay
    G the element that causes radioactive decay
    H the energy released during decay
    J one or more elements that form when the radioactive element changes

CHAPTER

3 Motion and Energy

Bright colors in this
thermogram show
areas that radiate
the most heat.

WEB ACTIVITY

www.phschool.com

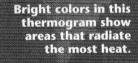

In Hot Water

This unusual image is not from a cartoon or horror movie. It's a thermogram of a house. A thermogram is an image formed by heat given off by an object. You might be very interested in a thermogram of your own house, because it can help you find expensive heat losses.

In this chapter, you will find out what heat is and how it relates to thermal energy and temperature. As you read the chapter, you will use what you learn to design and construct a device that will insulate a container of hot water.

Your Goal To build a container for a 355-mL (12-oz) aluminum can that keeps water hot.

Your project must

- ◆ reduce the loss of thermal energy from the container
- ◆ be constructed from available raw materials rather than be a ready-made insulating container
- ◆ have insulation no thicker than 3 cm
- ◆ not use electricity or heating chemicals
- ◆ follow the safety guidelines in Appendix A

Get Started With a group of classmates, brainstorm different materials that prevent heat loss. Consider such questions as the following: What properties do the materials seem to have in common? Which materials are easy to get? How can you find out which materials best prevent heat loss?

Check Your Progress You'll be working on this project as you study this chapter. To keep your project on track, look for Check Your Project boxes at the following points.

Section 3 Review, page 121: Perform experiments to determine the best insulating materials and keep a log of your results.

Section 4 Review, page 130: Build and test the device.

Present Your Project At the end of the chapter (page 133), you will evaluate your insulating device and recommend improvements.

TEKS

In addition to process TEKS, this chapter addresses these concept TEKS as they relate to the chapter's topics.

(8.7) The student knows that there is a relationship between force and motion. The student is expected to:

(A) demonstrate how unbalanced forces cause changes in the speed or direction of an object's motion.

(8.10) The student knows that complex interactions occur between matter and energy. The student is expected to:

(A) illustrate interactions between matter and energy including specific heat.

SECTION
1 Motion

DISCOVER

Where Are the Forces?

1. Hold a ball by pressing your fingertips into opposite spots on the ball. Press just hard enough to keep the ball from falling.

2. Have a partner press his or her fingertips into the ball as well. Your fingers should be arranged as shown in the photograph. Note what happens to the ball.

3. Now have your partner push in only one spot. Note what happens.

Think It Over

Inferring In which step did the ball stay up? In which step did it fall? Explain why.

GUIDE FOR READING

◆ When is an object in motion?

◆ How do unbalanced forces affect an object's motion?

◆ How are work and energy related?

Reading Tip Before you read, preview the section and make a list of the boldfaced terms. As you read, write a definition for each term in your own words.

Key Terms motion
• reference point • speed
• velocity • acceleration
• force • unbalanced force
• balanced force • work
• energy • potential energy
• kinetic energy

I t's a grey winter day as you travel across the bay on a ferryboat. You are cold and tired, so you stay in the car and close your eyes. As you rest, you feel as if you are moving, but when you open your eyes, the cars around you are in the same places. Are you moving or aren't you? The answer is yes—and no.

Motion

An object is in **motion** when its distance from another object is changing. When you looked at the other cars on board the ferryboat, you were not in motion. But, if you had looked at the shoreline, you would have been in motion. The cars on the ferryboat and the shoreline are both examples of a **reference point**—a place or object that can be used to determine if an object is in motion. **An object is in motion if the object changes position relative to a reference point.**

Figure 1 As you approach your reference point, the shoreline, you and the ferryboat are in motion.

Whether or not an object is in motion depends on the reference point you use. You always assume that the reference point is not moving. For instance, if you use the sun as your reference point, you are in motion even if you are sitting still in a chair. You, your chair, and everything around you are in motion because Earth is always traveling around the sun. Is the sun the ultimate reference point? No, because the sun moves in relation to other stars in the galaxy. An ultimate reference point does not exist. Therefore, to describe motion, you must always identify the reference point for the motion.

Speed How fast do you move between classes? To answer this question you must know two things about your motion. First, you must know the distance you move. Second, you must know how much time you took to move that distance. For example, if two classrooms are 60 meters apart and it takes you one minute to move between them, your speed is 60 meters per minute, or 1 meter per second. The **speed** of an object is the distance it travels divided by the time it takes to travel that distance.

$$Speed = Distance/Time$$

Figure 2 lists typical speeds for various objects in motion. Notice that the units differ, but every speed unit includes a unit of distance divided by a unit of time.

Velocity Knowing an object's speed is important. But you need more information to describe the object's motion completely. For example, if the airplane shown in Figure 3 leaves the Denver airport and flies in a straight line at a speed of 750 km/hr, where will it be in 2 hours? Although you know the airplane's speed, you can't answer that question without also knowing the direction in which the airplane is moving.

The speed of an object moving in a particular direction is called its **velocity.** Objects in motion can have the same speeds but different velocities. For example, an airplane traveling west from Denver to San Francisco at 750 km/hr has a different velocity than an airplane flying southeast from Denver to Houston at 750 km/hr.

Figure 3 The velocity of the airplane is defined by both its speed and direction.

Object	Speed
Jet	12.5 km/min
Automobile	100 km/h
Person walking	5 km/h
Snail	5 m/h
Glacier	1 m/day
Typical Speeds of Objects	

Figure 2 All of these objects are moving relative to the ground. *Comparing and Contrasting Which object is moving at the fastest speed? The slowest speed?*

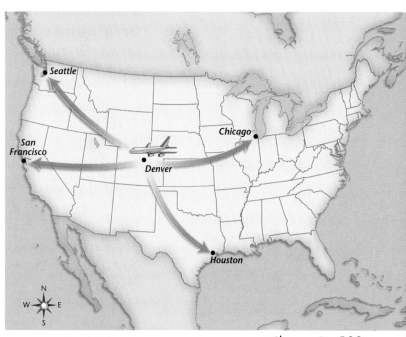

Figure 4 (A) The sprinter accelerates at the start of a race. (B) The passengers on the ride are accelerating as they change direction. (C) The race car's parachute helps it to slow down.

Falling Down

When the force of gravity pulls downward on an object, the object accelerates. Do this activity to find out if the height from which an object falls is related to its acceleration.

1. Divide modeling clay into four equal pieces. Roll each piece into a ball so that you have four identical balls of clay.

2. Using a meter stick, hold a clay ball one meter above the floor and let it go. Carefully lift the ball off the floor without disturbing its shape.

3. Repeat Step 2 for the other clay balls, but drop each one from a different height.

Drawing Conclusions How was the final shape of the clay ball related to the height from which it was dropped? Which ball was traveling at the greatest velocity when it hit the ground? Explain.

Acceleration Most objects do not move at the same velocity throughout their entire motion. For example, suppose you board a train in the station. The train is not moving when compared with the station platform. As the train pulls out of the station, it picks up speed. The velocity of the train changes during its trip to the next station. It slows down at crossings and it speeds up on flat land. It travels north, then northeast, and then north again. At the next station, it slows to a stop. The rate at which the velocity of an object changes is called **acceleration.**

Although you may think of acceleration as going faster, scientists use the term for any type of velocity change. That means that an object is accelerating whenever it speeds up, slows down, or changes direction. Figure 4 shows examples of objects that are all accelerating.

☑ *Checkpoint* **What is velocity?**

Force

What causes an object to accelerate? Look again at the examples in Figure 4. Each situation shows acceleration as a result of a push or a pull. A **force** is a push or a pull exerted on an object. You exert a force whenever you kick a ball, lift a book, or pedal your bicycle. When you exert a force on an object, you can change the object's motion. In other words, you cause the object to accelerate. An object's acceleration is always the result of a force. Whenever you see that an object is speeding up, slowing down, or changing direction, you know that a force is acting on the object.

Unbalanced Forces Although acceleration is always caused by a force, not every force causes acceleration. This is because several forces can act on an object at the same time. All the forces add together and may affect the object's motion.

For example, suppose that only two forces act on the balloon shown in Figure 5A. In the figure, the arrows represent the forces. In this textbook, the width of the arrow indicates the strength of the force. The balloon contains helium gas, which is lighter than air. Therefore, one force that acts on the balloon is the upward force of the air surrounding the balloon.

Gravity is the second force acting on the balloon. It is a downward force. Notice that the upward force is greater than the downward force on the balloon. When two forces act on the same object in opposite directions, the smaller force is subtracted from the greater force. The resulting force is called the net force. The net force on the balloon is in the upward direction. Therefore, the balloon rises.

After a while, some helium leaks out of the balloon. With less helium inside, the upward force on the balloon is less. Gravity still exerts a downward force on the balloon. Now, as shown in Figure 5B, the net force is in the downward direction. Therefore, the balloon falls to the ground.

In both cases, a net force caused the balloon to move. When a net force acts on an object, the forces are said to be unbalanced. **Unbalanced forces** acting on an object will change the object's motion. **Unbalanced forces can cause an object to start moving, stop moving, or change direction.**

Figure 5 (A) Forces can combine to produce a net force greater than the separate forces. (B) Forces can also combine to produce a smaller net force than the separate forces. *Applying Concepts What happens to the net force on the balloon if you refill it with helium?*

Figure 6 Forces can combine so that they cancel out.

Balanced Forces You can change the forces on the balloon by pulling down on the balloon's string while the balloon is rising. As shown in Figure 6, your pull is a downward force like the force of gravity. Therefore, the two forces add together. If the combined downward force equals the upward force, the opposing forces cancel out, and the net force is zero. Because no net force acts on the balloon, it neither rises nor falls. Equal forces that act on an object in opposite directions are called **balanced forces. Balanced forces do not change an object's motion.**

Newton's Laws of Motion

In the late 1600s, an English mathematician, Sir Isaac Newton, proposed three laws of motion. The laws explain the relationship among forces, matter, and motion.

First Law of Motion Newton's first law of motion states that an object at rest will remain at rest. Also, an object that is moving at a constant velocity will continue moving at a constant velocity unless it is acted upon by an unbalanced force.

The first part of this law is easy to observe. For example, if you place a book on your desk, the book won't move unless you push it. The second part of this law is less obvious than the first part. If you roll a marble across the floor, it will eventually stop. The marble stops because two unbalanced forces, friction and air resistance, slow it down. Friction is the force that two surfaces exert on each other when they rub against each other. In this case, the surface of the marble rubs against the floor's surface. Air resistance is the friction experienced by an object moving through the air.

Figure 7 These crash test dummies continue in motion until another unbalanced force, such as the one exerted by the air bags, acts on them.

Second Law of Motion Newton's second law of motion states that the net force on an object is equal to the mass of the object multiplied by its acceleration.

$$Force = Mass \times Acceleration$$

For example, suppose you have to push a box full of textbooks across the floor to the other side of the room. If you and a friend push together, the box will have a greater acceleration to begin with than if you push alone. You and your friend exert a greater force on the box than you do by yourself.

Third Law of Motion The third law of motion states that if one object exerts a force on a second object, the second object exerts a force of equal strength in the opposite direction on the first object. For example, think about what happens when you hit a ball with a bat. The bat pushes on the ball, but at the same time the ball pushes against the bat. You feel the force of the ball's collision with the bat in your hands. So, why don't you and the bat go flying backwards?

Newton's second law of motion explains why. The same force acting on two different masses results in less acceleration of the larger mass than of the smaller mass. The total mass of you and the bat is larger than the mass of the ball. Therefore, the acceleration of you and the bat is much less than the acceleration of the ball. In fact, the acceleration on the bat is so small you don't notice it.

☑ *Checkpoint* *What is Newton's second law of motion?*

You can make an object move if you apply enough force on it. In science, when you exert a force on an object that causes the object to move, you have done **work**. When you lift a pencil, push a lawnmower, or pull a sled, you are doing work. The amount of work done on an object can be calculated by multiplying the force's size by the distance it moves the object.

$$Work = Force \times Distance$$

Math TOOLBOX

Relationships

An equation shows the relationships among the variables. For example, the equation on the left shows how force, mass, and acceleration are related. Here is another way to show these relationships.

Acceleration = Force/Mass

When two numbers change together, they have a direct relationship. Force and acceleration have a direct relationship. If force increases, acceleration increases as long as the mass stays the same.

When two numbers change in opposite directions, they have an inverse relationship. Acceleration and mass have an inverse relationship. If mass increases, acceleration decreases as long as the total force stays the same.

Figure 8 A bat exerts a force on a ball, and a ball exerts an equal and opposite force in response.
Forming Operational Definitions
Which law of motion explains this?

Energy

The ability to do work is called **energy.** The more energy an object or organism has, the more work it can do. When you do work on an object, you transfer some of your energy to the object. For example, when you throw a ball, you transfer some of your energy to the ball. **You can think of work, then, as the transfer of energy.** Both work and energy are measured in a unit called the joule. Although many types of energy can do work, energy exists in two basic forms—kinetic energy and potential energy. Each form of energy can be changed, or converted, into the other.

Potential Energy   Sometimes when you do work on an object, you change its position or shape. For example, when you lift a box from the floor to a table, you do work on the box. The energy you transfer to the object is stored in the object. This stored energy can be released later to do work. Energy that is stored is called **potential energy** because it has the potential to do work.

Two examples of potential energy are elastic potential energy and gravitational potential energy. Objects that can be stretched or compressed have elastic potential energy. For example, some children's wind-up toys have springs. When you wind up the toy, you compress its spring and give it elastic potential energy.

Gravitational potential energy depends on the height of an object. When you lift an object, you do work in a direction opposite the force of gravity. As a result, the object gains gravitational potential energy. The higher you lift the object, the more gravitational potential energy it gains. That energy might be used later if the object falls to the ground.

Figure 9 (A) The arrow has elastic potential energy when it is drawn back in the bow. (B) The roller coaster has maximum gravitational potential energy at the top of the track.

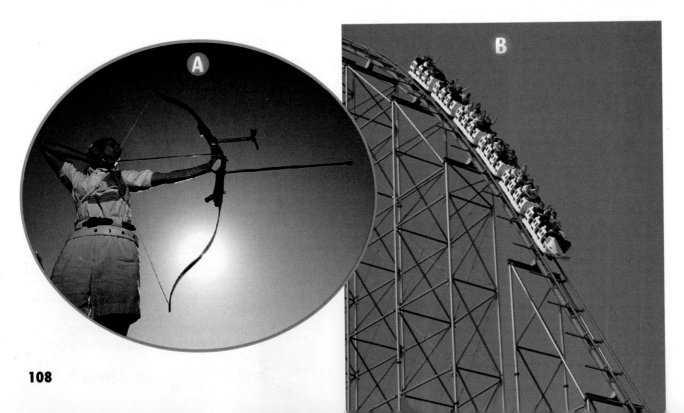

Kinetic Energy An object in motion can do work by exerting a force on another object. The force of a hurricane's wind can break apart buildings. The force of a moving hammer pushes a nail into a piece of wood. The force of a rolling bowling ball knocks down the pins. The energy of moving objects is called **kinetic energy.**

The amount of kinetic energy a moving object has depends on its mass and velocity. You can calculate an object's kinetic energy by using the following formula:

$$\text{Kinetic Energy} = \frac{\text{Mass} \times \text{Velocity}^2}{2}$$

Notice that the kinetic energy increases as mass increases. For example, a truck has more kinetic energy than a car traveling at the same velocity because the truck has more mass. Kinetic energy also increases as velocity increases. An ice skater has more kinetic energy when skating quickly than when skating slowly.

Large objects are not the only kinds of matter to have kinetic energy. Even the small particles that make up substances have kinetic energy. You will learn more about their kinetic energy in the following sections.

Figure 10 Falling water has kinetic energy. *Comparing and Contrasting How would you describe the energy of the water trapped by the dam?*

Section 1 Review

1. How do you know when an object is in motion?
2. How do balanced forces affect an object's motion? How do unbalanced forces affect an object's motion?
3. What is the relationship between work and energy?
4. **Thinking Critically: Comparing and Contrasting** How are speed, velocity, and acceleration similar? How do they differ?

Science at Home

Forces in Action As some family members watch, place a pencil on a table or counter so that a small part hangs over the edge. Ask them to predict what will happen as you move the pencil out little-by-little over the edge. Then move the pencil slowly until it falls to the floor. Ask your family members to identify the unbalanced forces on the pencil both before and after it fell. Draw a diagram to explain the forces and how they changed.

Sticky Sneakers

The appropriate sneaker for an activity should have a specific type of tread to grip the floor or the ground. In this lab you will test different sneakers by measuring the amount of friction between the sneakers and a table.

Problem

How does the amount of friction between a sneaker and a surface compare for different types of sneakers?

Skills Focus

forming operational definitions, measuring, controlling variables

Materials

three or more different types of sneakers
spring scale, 20 N or 5 N, or force sensor
mass set(s)   tape
large paper clip   balance

Procedure

1. Sneakers are designed to deal with various friction forces, including these:
   ◆ starting friction, which is involved when you start from a stopped position
   ◆ forward-stopping friction, which is involved when you come to a forward stop
   ◆ sideways-stopping friction, which is in-volved when you come to a sideways stop

2. Prepare a data table in which you can record each type of friction for each sneaker.
3. Place each sneaker on a balance. Then put masses in each sneaker so that the total mass of the sneaker plus the masses is 1,000 g. Distribute the masses evenly inside the sneaker.
4. You will need to tape the paper clip to each sneaker and then attach a spring clip to the paper clip. To measure
   ◆ starting friction, attach the paper clip to the back of the sneaker
   ◆ forward-stopping friction, attach the paper clip to the front of the sneaker
   ◆ sideways-stopping friction, attach the paper clip to the side of the sneaker

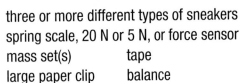

DATA TABLE

Sneaker	Starting friction (N)	Sideways-stopping friction (N)	Forward-stopping friction (N)
A			
B			

5. To measure starting friction, pull the sneaker backward until it starts to move. Use the 20-N spring scale first. If the reading is less than 5 N, use a 5-N scale. If using a force sensor, see your teacher for instructions. The force necessary to make the sneaker start moving is equal to the friction force. Record the starting friction force in your data table.

6. To measure either type of stopping friction, use the spring scale to pull each sneaker at a slow, constant speed. Record the stopping friction force in your data table.

7. Repeat Steps 4 through 6 for the remaining sneakers.

Analyze and Conclude

1. What are the manipulated and responding variables in this experiment? Explain. (See the Skills Handbook for a discussion of experimental variables.)

2. Why is the reading on the spring scale equal to the friction force in each case?

3. Do you think that using a sneaker with a small amount of mass in it is a fair test of the friction of the sneakers? (Consider the fact that sneakers are used with people's feet inside them.) Explain your answer.

4. Draw a diagram that shows the forces acting on the sneaker for each type of motion.

5. Why did you pull the sneaker at a slow speed to test for stopping friction? For starting friction, why did you pull a sneaker that wasn't moving?

6. Which sneaker had the most starting friction? Which had the most forward stopping friction? Which had the most sideways stopping friction?

7. Can you identify a relationship between the type of sneaker and the type of friction you observed? What do you observe about the sneakers that would cause one to have better traction than another?

8. **Apply** Wear a pair of your own sneakers. Start running and notice how you press against the floor with your sneaker. How do you think this affects the friction between the sneaker and the floor? How can you test for this variable?

Getting Involved

Go to a store that sells sneakers. If possible take a spring scale and, with the clerk's permission, do a quick friction test on sneakers designed for different activities. Also, note the materials they are made of, the support they provide for your feet, and other features. Then decide whether it is necessary to buy specific sneakers for different activities.

SECTION 2 Temperature and Thermal Energy

DISCOVER ·················· ACTIVITY

How Cold Is the Water?

1. Fill a plastic bowl with cold water, another with warm water, and a third with water at room temperature. Label each bowl.

2. Line up the three bowls. Place your right hand in the cold water and your left hand in the warm water.

3. After about a minute, place both your hands in the third bowl at the same time.

Think It Over

Observing How did the water in the third bowl feel when you touched it? Did it feel the same on each hand? If not, can you explain why?

GUIDE FOR READING

◆ What are the three common temperature scales?

◆ How does temperature differ from thermal energy?

Reading Tip As you read, write a sentence that states the main idea of each paragraph.

KeyTerms Fahrenheit scale
• Celsius scale • Kelvin scale
• absolute zero

The radio weather report says that today's high temperature will be 25 degrees. What should you wear? Do you need a coat and a scarf to keep warm, or only shorts and a T-shirt? What you decide depends on the temperature scale. On one scale, 25 degrees is below freezing, while on another scale 25 degrees is quite comfortable.

Temperature

You don't need a science book to tell you that the word *hot* means higher temperatures or the word *cold* means lower temperatures. You wear different clothes on a hot day than on a cold day. When scientists think about temperature, however, they are considering the particles that make up matter.

Recall that matter is made up of tiny particles called atoms and molecules. These particles are always in motion even if the object they make up isn't moving at all. You just learned that the energy of motion is called kinetic energy. All particles of matter have kinetic energy. The faster particles move, the more kinetic energy they have. Temperature is a measure of the average kinetic energy of the individual particles in an object.

Figure 11 The particles of hot cocoa move faster than those of cold chocolate milk.
Applying Concepts Which drink has particles with greater average kinetic energy?

Look at the mug of hot cocoa and the glass of cold chocolate milk in Figure 11. The hot cocoa has a higher temperature than the cold chocolate. Its particles are moving faster, so they have greater average kinetic energy. If the chocolate milk is heated, its particles will move faster, so their kinetic energy will increase. This means that the temperature of the milk will rise.

Temperature Scales

If you did the Discover activity, you know that whether something feels hot or cold depends on what you compare it to. Walking into an air-conditioned building on a hot day can give you a chill. You need a few minutes to get comfortable with the indoor temperature. Since you can't rely on your sense of touch, you need a scale to measure temperature accurately. **The three common scales for measuring temperature are the Fahrenheit, Celsius, and Kelvin scales.**

Fahrenheit Scale In the United States, the most common temperature scale is called the **Fahrenheit scale.** On this scale, the number 32 is assigned to the temperature at which water freezes. The number 212 is assigned to the temperature at which water boils. The interval between these two temperatures is divided into 180 equal intervals called degrees Fahrenheit (°F).

Celsius Scale The temperature scale used in most of the world is the **Celsius scale.** On this scale, the number 0 is assigned to the temperature at which water freezes. The number 100 is assigned to the temperature at which water boils. The interval between freezing and boiling is divided into 100 equal parts, called degrees Celsius (°C).

Kelvin Scale The temperature scale commonly used in physical science is the **Kelvin scale.** Units on the Kelvin scale are the same size as the units on the Celsius scale, and are called kelvins (K).

Figure 12 This illustration compares the three common temperature scales.
Comparing and Contrasting What are the differences among the scales?

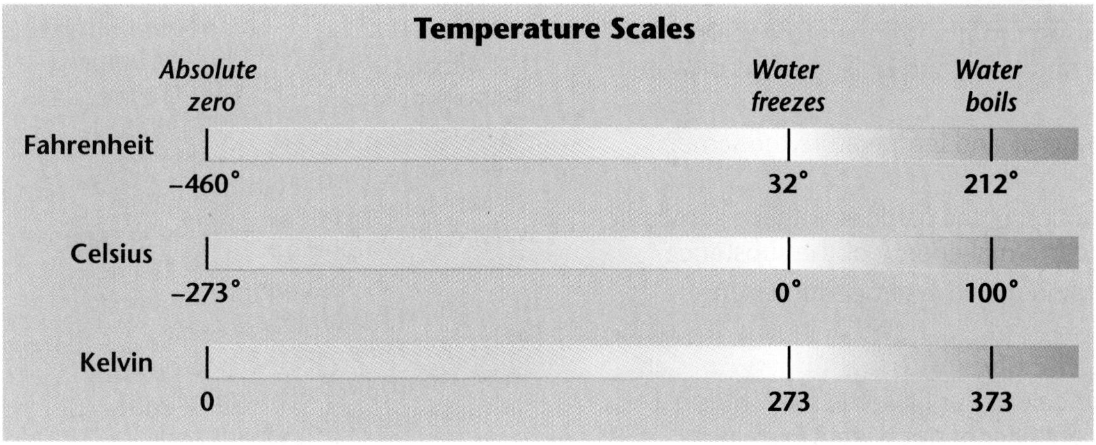

Temperature Scales

	Absolute zero	Water freezes	Water boils
Fahrenheit	−460°	32°	212°
Celsius	−273°	0°	100°
Kelvin	0	273	373

Figure 13 A large pot of hot cocoa can have the same temperature as a small cup of cocoa.
Comparing and Contrasting Do both containers and the cocoa in them have the same thermal energy?

Any temperature on the Kelvin scale can be changed to Celsius degrees by subtracting 273 from it. So the freezing point of water on the Kelvin scale is 273 K and the boiling point is 373 K.

Why is the number 273 special? Experiments have led scientists to conclude that the lowest temperature possible is about −273°C. This is called **absolute zero.** No more energy can be removed from matter at about −273°C. The Kelvin scale is defined so that zero on the Kelvin scale is absolute zero.

☑ *Checkpoint* What three points define the common temperature scales?

Thermal Energy

The total energy of all of the particles in a sample of matter is called thermal energy, or sometimes internal energy. Even if two samples of matter are at the same temperature, they do not necessarily have the same total energy.

The more particles a substance has at a given temperature, the more thermal energy it has. For example, 2 liters of hot cocoa at 75°C has more thermal energy than 0.15 liter at 75°C. **So temperature is a measure of the average kinetic energy of the individual particles of matter. Thermal energy is the total energy of all of the particles.**

Thermal energy does not depend on just temperature and the number of particles in a substance. It also depends on how the particles are arranged. In Section 4 you will learn about how thermal energies differ for solids, liquids, and gases.

Section 2 Review

1. Name the three common temperature scales. Give the freezing point and boiling point of water for each.
2. Are thermal energy and temperature the same? Explain.
3. How is the motion of the particles within a substance related to the thermal energy of the substance?
4. Why are there no negative temperatures on the Kelvin scale?
5. **Thinking Critically** **Applying Concepts** Can a container of cold water have the same thermal energy as a container of hot water? Explain.

Science at Home

Room Temperature Ask your family members to look around your home for situations in which temperature is important. Perhaps the temperature in the oven is important when you bake a cake. Or the temperature at which you set your air conditioning on a hot day is important. Make a table describing each situation. Your family members will probably use the Fahrenheit scale. Ask them to describe any situations they are familiar with that make use of the Celsius scale.

114

③ The Nature of Heat

What Does It Mean to Heat Up?

1. Obtain several utensils made of different materials, such as silver, stainless steel, plastic, and wood.

2. Press a small gob of frozen butter on the handle of each utensil. Make sure that when the utensils stand on end, the butter is at the same height on each.

3. Stand the utensils in a beaker so that they do not touch each other.

4. Pour hot water into the beaker until it is about 6 cm below the butter. Watch the utensils for the next several minutes. What do you see happening?

5. The utensils will be greasy. Wipe them off and wash them in soapy water.

Think It Over
Observing What happened to the butter? Did the same thing happen on every utensil? How can you account for your observations?

Blacksmithing is hot work. A piece of iron held in the forge becomes warmer and begins to glow as thermal energy from the fire travels along it. At the same time, the blacksmith feels hot air rising from the forge. He also feels the glow of the fire directly on his face and arms. Each of these movements of energy is a form of heat. **Heat** is the transfer of thermal energy from a substance at one temperature to a substance at a different temperature.

GUIDE FOR READING

◆ How is heat related to thermal energy?

◆ What are the three forms of heat transfer?

◆ What is specific heat?

Reading Tip Before you read, define heat in your own words. Make any necessary corrections to your definition as you read the section.

Key Terms heat • conduction • convection • radiation • insulator • specific heat

Figure 14 This blacksmith uses heat to soften a piece of iron before he hammers it into shape.

Notice that the scientific definition of heat is different from its everyday use. In a conversation, you might hear someone say that an object contains heat. Matter, however, contains not heat but thermal energy. Only when thermal energy is transferred is it called heat. **Heat is thermal energy moving from an object at one temperature to an object at a different temperature.** Recall from Section 1 that work also involves the transfer of energy. So work and heat are both examples of energy transfers. They are both measured with the same unit—joules.

How Is Heat Transferred?

There are three ways that heat can move. **Heat is transferred by conduction, convection, and radiation.** The blacksmith experienced all three.

Conduction In the process of **conduction,** heat is transferred from one particle of matter to another in an object without the movement of the object itself. Think of a metal spoon in a pot of water being heated on an electric stove. The fast-moving particles of the hot electric coil collide with the slow-moving particles of the cool pot. Because of these collisions, the slower particles move faster, and heat is transferred. Then the particles of the pot collide with the particles of the water, which in turn collide with the particles at one end of the spoon. As the particles move faster, the metal spoon becomes hotter. This process of conduction is repeated all along the metal until the entire spoon becomes hot.

In Figure 15, the horseshoes in a blacksmith's forge glow red as heat is transferred to the metal from the fire. This transfer of heat throughout the horseshoes is due to conduction.

Figure 15 The entire horseshoe becomes hot even though only its underside touches the hot coals. *Inferring By what method is heat transferred through the metal?*

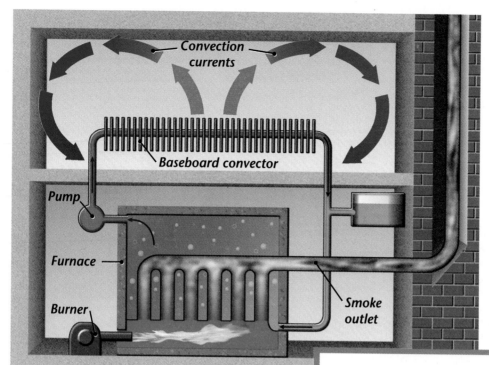

Convection currents

Baseboard convector

Pump

Furnace

Burner

Smoke outlet

Figure 16 Just as convection currents move heat throughout the liquid in a pot, convection currents move heat from the baseboard throughout the room.

Convection If you watch a pot of hot water on a stove, you will see the water moving. **Convection** is the movement that transfers heat within the water. In convection, heat is transferred by the movement of currents within a fluid (a liquid or gas).

When the water at the bottom of the pot is heated, its particles move faster, and they also move farther apart. As a result, the heated water becomes less dense. A less dense fluid will float on top of a more dense one. Therefore, the heated water rises in the pot. The surrounding cooler water flows into its place. This flow creates the circular motion you see in Figure 16, which is known as a convection current.

Convection currents are used to transfer heated air throughout a building. As the air near the baseboard heater in Figure 16 is heated, it becomes less dense and rises. When the warm air rises, the surrounding cool air flows into its place.

INTEGRATING EARTH SCIENCE Convection currents occur in the environment as well. A soaring bird, such as a hawk, takes advantage of this fact and rides updrafts where warm air rises. In fact, convection currents transfer air heated by the sun throughout Earth's atmosphere. They produce the global winds that form Earth's weather.

✓ *Checkpoint* How does convection transfer heat?

Figure 17 Radiation from the heat lamps above keeps food warm in a cafeteria. *Applying Concepts How does the heat transfer used in cooling food differ from that used to keep the food warm?*

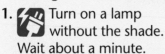

Feel the Warmth

How is heat transferred from a light bulb?

1.  Turn on a lamp without the shade. Wait about a minute.

2. Hold the palm of your hand about 10 cm from the side of the bulb for about 15 seconds. Remove it sooner if it gets too warm.

3. Now hold the palm of your hand about 10 centimeters above the top of the bulb for about 15 seconds.

Drawing Conclusions In which location did your hand feel warmer? Explain your observations in terms of heat transfer.

Radiation **Radiation** is the transfer of energy by electromagnetic waves. You can feel radiation from a bonfire or a heat lamp across a distance of several meters. And of course a blacksmith feels the glow of radiation from his forge. There is an important difference between radiation and the processes of conduction and convection. Radiation does not require matter to transfer thermal energy. All of the sun's energy that reaches Earth travels through millions of kilometers of empty space.

Heat Moves One Way

If two substances have different temperatures, heat will flow from the warmer object to the colder one. When heat flows into a substance, the thermal energy of the substance increases. As the thermal energy increases, its temperature increases. At the same time, the temperature of the substance giving off heat decreases. Heat will flow from one substance to the other until the two substances have the same temperature. A bowl of hot oatmeal cools to room temperature if you don't eat it quickly.

How is something cold, like ice cream, made? The ingredients used, such as milk and sugar, are not nearly as cold as the finished ice cream. In an ice cream maker, the ingredients are put into a metal can that is packed in ice and salt. You might think that the ice transfers cold to the ingredients in the can. But this is not the case. There is no such thing as "coldness" for scientists. Instead, the ingredients grow colder as thermal energy flows from them to the ice. Heat transfer occurs in only one direction.

✓ *Checkpoint* *In what direction does heat move?*

Conductors and Insulators

Have you ever stepped from a rug to a tile floor on a cold morning? The tile floor feels colder than the rug. Yet if you measured their temperatures, they would be the same—room temperature. The difference between them has to do with how materials conduct heat.

A material that conducts heat well is called a conductor. Metals such as silver and stainless steel are good conductors. A metal spoon conducts heat faster than a wooden or plastic spoon. A material that does not conduct heat well is called an **insulator.** Wood, wool, straw, paper, and cork are good insulators. Gases, such as air, are also good insulators.

A good conductor, such as a tile floor, will feel cool to the touch because it transfers heat away from your skin easily. An insulator such as a rug, on the other hand, slows the transfer of heat from your skin, so it feels warmer.

Clothes and blankets are insulators that slow the transfer of heat out of your body. Mammals and birds have natural insulation. Birds have feathers that trap air under them, and mammals such as walruses have a layer of fat called blubber.

A well-insulated building is comfortable inside when the weather is either hot or cold outdoors. Insulation prevents heat from entering the building in hot weather and prevents heat from escaping in cold weather. Fiberglass is a common insulating material in buildings. It is made of a tangle of thin glass fibers that trap air. Air is a poor conductor of heat, and trapped air cannot transfer heat by convection easily. So fiberglass slows the transfer of heat through the walls or roof.

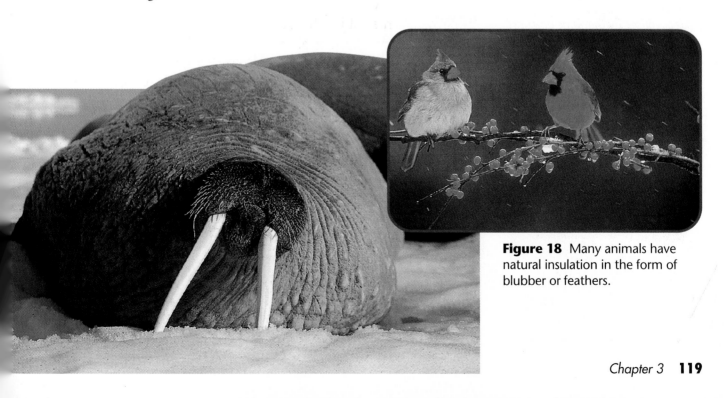

Figure 18 Many animals have natural insulation in the form of blubber or feathers.

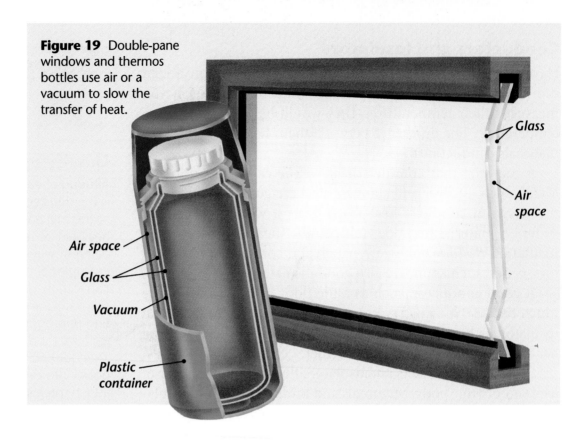

Figure 19 Double-pane windows and thermos bottles use air or a vacuum to slow the transfer of heat.

Glass

Air space

Air space

Glass

Vacuum

Plastic container

Much of the heat transfer in a house occurs through the windows. For this reason, insulating windows are made up of two panes of glass with a thin space of air between them. The air trapped between the glass panes does not transfer heat well. Thermos bottles use the same principle. They contain a vacuum, which is a better insulator than air.

Specific Heat

Imagine running across hot sand toward the ocean. You run to the water's edge, and stop short—the water is too cold. How can the sand be so hot and the water so cold? The answer is that complex interactions occur between matter and energy. Water requires more heat to raise its temperature than sand does.

When an object is heated its temperature rises. But the temperature does not rise at the same rate for all objects. The amount of energy required to raise an object's temperature depends on the chemical makeup of the object. Different materials need more or less energy to change their temperature by the same amount.

The specific heat of a substance tells how much energy is needed to raise the substance's temperature by a given amount. The amount of energy required to raise the temperature of 1 kilogram of a substance by 1 kelvin is the **specific heat** of the substance. Joules per kilogram-kelvin (J/(kg·K)) is the unit of measure for specific heat. Look at the specific heats of the substances listed in Figure 20. Notice that the specific heat

Figure 20 This table lists the specific heats of several substances. *Problem Solving How much more energy is required to raise the temperature of 1 kg of iron than is needed to raise the temperature of 1 kg of copper by the same amount?*

Specific Heat of Common Substances	
Substance	Specific Heat (J/(kg·K))
Aluminum	903
Brass	376
Copper	385
Glass	664
Ice	2,060
Iron	450
Sand	670
Silver	235
Water	4,180

120

of water is quite high. It takes 4,180 joules of energy to raise the temperature of 1 kilogram of water 1 kelvin. Materials with a high specific heat can absorb a great deal of thermal energy without a great change in temperature.

The energy gained or lost by an object is related to the mass, change in temperature, and specific heat of the material. You can calculate thermal energy changes with the following formula.

Change in energy =
      Mass × Specific heat × Change in temperature

How much heat is needed to raise the temperature of 5 kilograms of water 10 kelvins?

Heat absorbed = (5 kg)(4,180 J/(kg·K))(10 K) = 209,000 J

You need to transfer 209,000 joules to the water to increase its temperature by 10 kelvins.

Section 3 Review

1. How does heat differ from thermal energy?
2. Describe the three kinds of heat transfer.
3. What is specific heat?
4. **Thinking Critically** **Problem Solving** How much energy is gained by 10 kg of silver if it is heated from 21°C to 35°C?
5. **Thinking Critically** **Applying Concepts** Before homes were heated, people often placed hot water bottles in their beds at bedtime. Why is water a good choice?

Check Your Progress

CHAPTER PROJECT

Prepare a short summary of your experimental plan. How will you test insulating ability? (*Hint:* What variables do you want to keep constant? How can you make sure you control these?) Think about how you can design a fair test to compare the relative insulating abilities of each material. How often will you record the temperature? Then carry out your tests.

Just Add Water

If you add hot water to cold water, what will happen? In this lab, you'll make a device that measures changes in thermal energy. You will use the skill of interpreting data to calculate the thermal energy transferred.

Problem

When hot and cold water are mixed, how much thermal energy is transferred from the hot water to the cold water?

Materials

4 plastic foam cups   scissors
hot tap water   balance
pencil
beaker of water kept in an ice bath
2 thermometers or temperature probes

Procedure

1. Predict how the amount of thermal energy lost by hot water will be related to the amount of thermal energy gained by cold water.
2. Copy the data table into your notebook.
3. Follow the instructions in the box to make two calorimeters. Find the mass of each empty calorimeter (including the cover) on a balance and record each mass in your data table.

MAKING A CALORIMETER

A. Label a plastic foam cup with the letter C ("C" stands for cold water).
B. Cut 2 to 3 cm from the top of a second plastic foam cup. Invert the second cup inside the first. Label the cover with a C also. The cup and cover are your cold-water calorimeter.
C. Using a pencil, poke a hole in the cover large enough for a thermometer to fit snugly.
D. Repeat Steps A, B, and C with two other plastic foam cups. This time, label both cup and cover with an H. This is your hot-water calorimeter.

4. From a beaker of water that has been sitting in an ice bath, add water (no ice cubes) to the cold-water calorimeter. Fill it about one-third full. Put the cover on, find the total mass, and record the mass in your data table.
5. Add some hot tap water to the hot-water calorimeter. Fill it about one-third full. **CAUTION:** *Hot tap water can cause burns.* Put the cover on, find the total mass, and record the mass in your data table.

DATA TABLE

	Mass of Empty Cup (g)	Mass of Cup and Water (g)	Mass of Water (g)	Starting Temp. (°C)	Final Temp. (°C)	Change in Temp. (°C)
Cold-water calorimeter						
Hot-water calorimeter						

6. Calculate the mass of the water in each calorimeter. Record the results in your data table.

7. Put thermometers through the holes in the covers of both calorimeters. Wait a minute or two and then record the temperatures. If using temperature probes, see your teacher for instructions.

8. Remove both thermometers and covers. Pour the water from the cold-water calorimeter into the hot-water calorimeter. Put the cover back on the hot-water calorimeter, and insert a thermometer. Record the final temperature as the final temperature for both calorimeters.

Analyze and Conclude

1. What is the temperature change of the cold water? Record your answer in the data table.

2. What is the temperature change of the hot water? Record your answer in the data table.

3. Calculate the amount of thermal energy that enters the cold water. Specific heat of water is 4.18 J/(g·K). Use the following formula.

Thermal energy transferred =
    4.18 J/(g·K) × Mass of cold water × Temperature change of cold water
Remember that a change of 1°C is equal to a change of 1 K.

4. Now use the formula to calculate the thermal energy leaving the hot water.

5. What unit should you use for your results for Questions 3 and 4?

6. Was your prediction from Step 1 confirmed? How do you know?

7. **Think About It** What sources of error might have affected your results? How could the lab be redesigned in order to reduce the errors?

Design an Experiment

How would your results be affected if you started with much more hot water than cold? If you used more cold water than hot? Make a prediction. Then design a procedure to test your prediction. Get your teacher's approval, and try your new procedure.

Insulation—And a Breath of Clean Air

People want to save money. They also want to conserve the fossil fuels—oil, coal, and natural gas—used to heat and cool buildings. So, since the 1970s, new homes, offices, and schools have been built to be energy-efficient. Builders have constructed large, square buildings with thick insulation, less outside wall space, and smaller, airtight windows. These features slow the transfer of thermal energy into and out of buildings.

Limiting the transfer of thermal energy, however, often means limiting the transfer of air. As a result, viruses, bacteria, and pollutants are not carried away by fresh outdoor air. People who live and work in these buildings sometimes develop illnesses. These illnesses cost billions of dollars a year in medical expenses and lost work.

The Issues

How Can Indoor Air Be Made Cleaner?

Limiting indoor pollutants—or getting rid of them altogether—is a major way of reducing building-related illness. Toward this end, builders can construct buildings with materials and insulation that do not pollute the air. They can use natural wood, for instance, instead of plastics and particle board, which give off irritating chemicals. Indoor air can be filtered. Walls, floors, and carpets can be cleaned frequently. Machines that give off irritating chemicals, such as copiers, can be placed in specially ventilated rooms. In this way, pollution can be kept out of the air that most people in the building breathe.

How Can Ventilation Be Improved?

Good ventilation requires at least 10 liters per second of fresh air for each person. If less fresh air comes in, some people may get illnesses or eye, nose, and throat irritations. There are several ways to increase ventilation. In some buildings, machines such as fans and blowers are used to move air in and out. People in those buildings must be careful not to block air vents with furniture or equipment. Special attention must be paid to ventilation during times of increased pollution, such as when a room is being painted.

Increasing air flow into buildings means using more energy for heating and air conditioning. So the energy savings from efficient buildings are reduced. To make up for this loss, people can wear heavier clothing in winter. They can set their thermostats lower and use less energy for heating. They can also wear lighter clothes in summer, and use less energy for air conditioning.

Another way to obtain clean air while conserving energy is called energy recovery ventilation. Heat is transferred from warm air leaving a building to cold air entering a building. The air goes out, but the energy stays inside.

You Decide

1. Identify the Problem
In your own words, describe the problem caused by thick layers of insulation.

2. Analyze the Options
List five different options for reducing building-related illnesses. How would each option affect the amount of fuel needed for heating?

3. Find a Solution
You're building a new school. Make a checklist of steps to take to prevent illness but still keep heating costs down.

SECTION 4 Thermal Energy and States of Matter

DISCOVER •••••••••••••••••••••••••••••••••••• ACTIVITY ••••

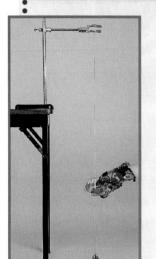

What Happens to Heated Metal?

1. Wrap one end of a one-meter-long metal wire around a clamp on a ring stand.

2. Tie the other end through several washers. Adjust the clamp so that the washers swing freely, but nearly touch the floor.

3. ⬛ Light a candle. Hold the candle with an oven mitt, and heat the wire. **CAUTION:** *Be careful near the flame, and avoid dripping hot wax on yourself.* Predict how heat from the candle will affect the wire.

4. With your hand in the oven mitt, swing the wire. Observe any changes in the motion of the washers.

5. Blow out the candle and allow the wire to cool. After several minutes, swing the wire again and observe its motion.

Think It Over

Inferring Based on your observations, what can you conclude about the effect of heating a solid?

Throughout the day, temperatures at an orange grove drop steadily. The anxious farmer awaits the updated weather forecast. The news is not good. The temperature is expected to fall even further during the night. Low temperatures could wipe out the entire crop. He considers picking the crop early, but the oranges are not yet ripe.

Instead, the farmer tells his workers to haul in long water hoses. He has them spray the orange trees with water. As the temperature drops, the water turns to ice. The ice keeps the oranges warm!

How can ice possibly keep anything warm? The answer has to do with how thermal energy is transferred as water becomes ice.

GUIDE FOR READING

◆ How do matter and energy interact in changes of state?

◆ Why does matter expand when it is heated?

Reading Tip As you read, take notes on how each illustration helps to explain the text.

Key Terms state
• thermal expansion
• thermostat • bimetallic strip

Figure 22 Imagine using ice to keep something warm! These oranges were sprayed with water because freezing temperatures threatened them.

125

Gas

Solid

Liquid

Three States of Matter

What happens when you hold an ice cube in your hand? It melts. The solid and the liquid are both the same matter. All matter can exist in three **states**—solid, liquid, and gas. Although the chemical composition of a substance remains the same, the arrangement of the particles that make up the matter differ from one state to another.

Solids An ice cube, a coin, a book, and the crystal of fluorite shown above are all solids. The particles that make up a solid are packed together in relatively fixed positions. Particles of a solid cannot move out of their positions. They can only vibrate back and forth. This is why solids retain a fixed shape and volume.

Liquids Water, orange juice, and the molten steel shown at the left are all liquids. The particles that make up a liquid are close together, but they are not held together as tightly as those of a solid. Because liquid particles can move around, liquids don't have a definite shape. But liquids do have a definite volume.

Gases Air, helium, and the neon in the colored sign shown above are all gases. In a gas, the particles are moving so fast that they don't even stay close together. Gases expand to fill all the space available. They do not have a fixed shape or volume.

Changes of State

The physical change from one state of matter to another is called a change of state. A change of state most often occurs between the solid and liquid states, and between the liquid and gas states.

The state of a substance depends on how much thermal energy it possesses. The more thermal energy the substance has, the faster its particles move. A gas has more thermal energy than a liquid.

Because of this, the particles of a gas move faster than the particles of the same substance in the liquid or solid state. Particles in a liquid move faster than particles in the solid state.

Matter will change from one state to another if thermal energy is absorbed or released. Figure 24 is a graph of changes of state. Thermal energy is shown on the horizontal axis and temperature is shown on the vertical axis. You can see that as thermal energy increases, a substance changes from a solid to a liquid and then to a gas. A substance changes from a gas to a liquid and then to a solid as thermal energy is removed from it.

The flat regions of the graph show conditions under which thermal energy is changing but temperature remains the same. Under these conditions matter is changing from one state to another. During a change of state, the addition or loss of thermal energy changes the distances among the particles. However, the average kinetic energy of those particles does not change. Since temperature is a measure of average kinetic energy, the temperature does not change as a substance changes state.

Solid–Liquid Changes of State

On the lower left portion of the graph in Figure 24, matter goes through changes between the solid and liquid states of matter. These changes are known as melting and freezing.

Melting The change of state from a solid to a liquid is called melting. Melting occurs when a solid absorbs thermal energy. As the thermal energy of the solid increases, the rigid structure of its particles begins to break down. The particles become freer to move around. The temperature at which a solid changes to a liquid is called the melting point.

☑ *Checkpoint* *What is a change of state?*

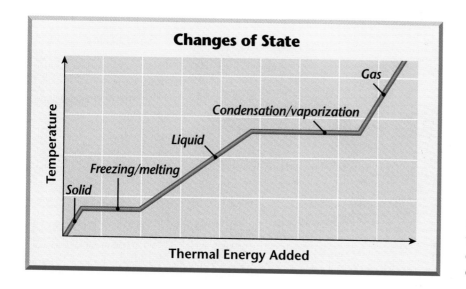

Figure 24 This graph shows how thermal energy and temperature change as a pure substance changes from one state to another.

Observing ACTIVITY

Put a teakettle on a stove or a hot plate, and bring the water to a boil. Look carefully at the steam coming out of the spout. CAUTION: *Steam and boiling water can cause serious burns.* What state of matter is the steam that you see? What is present, but not visible, in the small space between the steam and the spout?

Freezing The change of state from a liquid to a solid is called freezing. Freezing occurs when a liquid loses thermal energy. The temperature at which a substance changes from a liquid to a solid is called its freezing point. For a given substance, the freezing point and the melting point are the same. The only difference between the two is whether the substance is gaining or releasing thermal energy.

The fact that freezing involves a release of energy explains why the farmer had his workers spray the orange trees with water. The liquid water released thermal energy as it froze. Some of this thermal energy was transferred to the oranges, and kept them from freezing.

Liquid–Gas Changes of State

The upper right portion of Figure 24 on the previous page shows changes between the liquid and gas states of matter. These changes are known as vaporization and condensation.

Vaporization The process by which matter changes from the liquid to the gas state is called vaporization. During this process, particles in a liquid absorb thermal energy. This causes the particles to move faster. Eventually they move fast enough to escape the liquid, as gas particles.

If vaporization takes place at the surface of a liquid, it is called evaporation. At higher temperatures, vaporization can occur below the surface of a liquid as well. This process is called boiling. When a liquid boils, gas bubbles formed within the liquid rise to the surface. The temperature at which a liquid boils is called its boiling point.

Condensation You have probably noticed that beads of water appear on the outside of a cold drinking glass or on the bathroom mirror after you take a shower. Why do you think this occurs?

Figure 25 Water vapor in the air begins to condense soon after sunset. *Applying Concepts As it condenses, does water absorb or release thermal energy?*

Figure 26 Joints on bridges and spaces in sidewalks allow for the expansion and contraction of the matter that composes them. *Applying Concepts* What happens to the spaces in the expansion joint as the bridge gets warmer?

The water vapor in the air loses thermal energy when it comes in contact with the cold glass. When a gas loses a sufficient amount of thermal energy, it will change into a liquid. A change from the gas state to the liquid state is called condensation.

☑ *Checkpoint* What is the difference between boiling and evaporation of a liquid?

Thermal Expansion

Have you ever loosened a tight jar lid by holding it under a stream of hot water? This works because the metal lid expands a little. Most substances expand when heated. **As the thermal energy of a substance increases, its particles move faster and the substance expands.** This is true even when the substance is not changing state. The expanding of matter when it is heated is known as **thermal expansion.**

When a substance is cooled, thermal energy is released. This means that the motion of the particles slows down and the particles move closer together. So as a substance is cooled, it usually contracts, or decreases in size.

Thermometers You are already familiar with one application of thermal expansion—a thermometer. In a common thermometer, a liquid such as mercury or alcohol is sealed within a glass tube. As the liquid is heated, it expands and climbs up the tube. As the liquid is cooled, it contracts and flows down in the tube.

Expanding Teeth Your teeth also expand and contract with INTEGRATING HEALTH changes in temperature. If you have a filling, the material used for the filling must expand and contract with your tooth. If it didn't, the filling could cause the tooth to crack, or the filling could loosen. So dentists use fillings that have the same expansion properties as teeth.

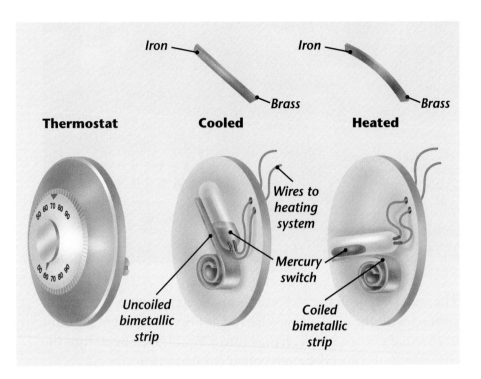

Figure 27 A bimetallic strip is an important part of many thermostats. When the temperature drops, the strip uncoils and closes a switch that starts a heating system. *Relating Cause and Effect What causes the bimetallic strip to coil and uncoil?*

Iron — Brass

Iron — Brass

Thermostat   **Cooled**   **Heated**

Wires to heating system

Mercury switch

Uncoiled bimetallic strip

Coiled bimetallic strip

Thermostats The principle of thermal expansion is used in the design of **thermostats,** or heat-regulating devices. Many thermostats contain **bimetallic strips,** which are strips of two different metals joined together. Different metals expand at different rates. When the bimetallic strip is heated, one side expands more than the other. This causes the strip to curve.

The movement of the strip operates a switch. If the switch is connected to a furnace or other heating system, the thermostat will turn the heating system on and off. In addition to home heating systems, thermostats are used on such devices as air conditioners, ovens, toasters, and electric blankets.

Section 4 Review

1. How does thermal energy produce a change from one state of matter to another?
2. What is thermal expansion?
3. What happens to the temperature of a substance during a change of state? What happens to thermal energy during a change of state?
4. How does a thermostat make use of thermal expansion?
5. **Thinking Critically Applying Concepts** Why do cookbooks recommend that you poke holes in a potato before baking it?

Check Your Progress

CHAPTER PROJECT

Build and test your container. Remember that you need to be able to get to the aluminum can at the beginning of the test so that hot water can be poured into it. You must also be able to measure the temperature of the water at the end of the test.

SECTION 1 Motion

Key Ideas

◆ An object is in motion when its distance changes relative to a reference point.
◆ A net force results from unbalanced forces. Unbalanced forces cause an object to accelerate.
◆ Balanced forces are equal forces exerted in opposite directions. Balanced forces do not change an object's motion.
◆ Energy is the ability to do work. When work is done, energy is transferred.
◆ Kinetic energy is energy of motion. Potential energy is energy of position or shape.

Key Terms

motion	unbalanced force
reference point	balanced force
speed	work
velocity	energy
acceleration	potential energy
force	kinetic energy

SECTION 2 Temperature and Thermal Energy

Key Ideas

◆ Three temperature scales are Fahrenheit, Celsius, and Kelvin.
◆ Temperature is a measure of the average kinetic energy of each particle within an object.
◆ Thermal energy is the total energy of the particles that make up an object.

Key Terms

Fahrenheit scale	Kelvin scale
Celsius scale	absolute zero

SECTION 3 The Nature of Heat

Key Ideas

◆ Heat is a transfer of thermal energy.
◆ Heat is transferred by conduction, convection, and radiation.
◆ The amount of energy needed to raise the temperature of 1 kilogram of a substance by 1 kelvin is the specific heat.

Key Terms

heat	convection	insulator
conduction	radiation	specific heat

SECTION 4 Thermal Energy and States of Matter

INTEGRATING CHEMISTRY

Key Ideas

◆ Matter can undergo a change of state when thermal energy is added or removed.
◆ As matter is heated, its particles move faster.

Key Terms

state	thermostat
thermal expansion	bimetallic strip

Organizing Information

Concept Map Copy the concept map onto a separate sheet of paper. Complete it and add a title. (For more on concept maps, see the Skills Handbook.)

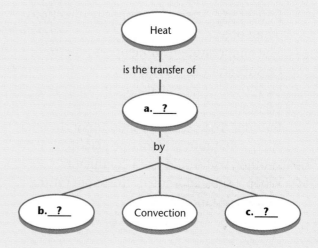

Reviewing Content

 Review key concepts online using iText at www.phschool.com

Multiple Choice

Choose the letter of the answer that best completes each statement.

1. Speed is equal to distance divided by
   a. time.
   b. acceleration.
   c. velocity.
   d. direction.
2. The average kinetic energy of the particles of an object is measured by the object's
   a. heat content.
   b. temperature.
   c. specific heat.
   d. thermal energy.
3. The process by which heat moves from one end of a solid to the other is called
   a. convection.
   b. conduction.
   c. radiation.
   d. insulation.
4. If you want to know the amount of heat needed to raise the temperature of 2 kg of steel by 10°C, you need to know steel's
   a. temperature.
   b. thermal energy.
   c. heat content.
   d. specific heat.
5. The change of state that occurs when a gas becomes a liquid is called
   a. evaporation.
   b. boiling.
   c. freezing.
   d. condensation.

True or False

If the statement is true, write true. If it is false, change the underlined word or words to make the statement true.

6. Equal forces exerted in opposite directions on an object are <u>unbalanced</u>.
7. The temperature reading of zero on the <u>Celsius</u> scale is absolute zero.
8. Heat transfer by <u>radiation</u> can occur in a vacuum.
9. In order to decrease the amount of thermal energy that moves from one place to another, you would use a <u>conductor</u>.
10. When a substance melts, the temperature of the substance <u>increases</u>.

Checking Concepts

11. One person says that an object is in motion. Another person says that the same object is not in motion. How can both people be correct? Give an example.
12. What happens to the particles of a solid as the thermal energy of the solid increases?
13. When night falls on a summer day, the air temperature drops by 10°C. Will the temperature of the water in a nearby lake change by the same amount? Explain why or why not.
14. How can you add thermal energy to matter without increasing its temperature?
15. When molten steel becomes solid, is energy absorbed or released by the steel?
16. Describe how a thermostat controls the temperature in a building.
17. **Writing to Learn** Haiku is a form of poetry that began in Japan. A haiku has three lines. The first and third lines have five syllables each. The second line has seven syllables. Write a haiku describing how you might feel on a frosty winter morning or a sweltering summer afternoon.

Thinking Critically

18. **Relating Cause and Effect** What are two ways of increasing an object's acceleration?
19. **Comparing and Contrasting** How are kinetic energy and potential energy similar? How are they different?
20. **Problem Solving** Suppose a mercury thermometer contains 2 g of mercury. How much thermal energy would be needed to change the thermometer's reading from 25°C to 40°C? The specific heat of mercury is 140 J/(kg·K).
21. **Relating Cause and Effect** Why is the air pressure in a car's tires different before and after the car has been driven for an hour?
22. **Applying Concepts** Telephone lines are allowed to sag when they are hung. Can you think of a reason why?

Applying Skills

Use the drawing of three containers of water to answer Questions 23–25.

30°C   30°C   60°C

100 g   200 g   200 g

23. **Interpreting Data** Compare the average motion of the molecules in the three containers. Explain your answer.

24. **Drawing Conclusions** Compare the total amount of thermal energy in the three containers. Explain your answer.

25. **Calculating** Determine how much heat you would need to raise the temperature of each container by 1°C. (See Figure 20 on page 120.) Show your work.

Performance   CHAPTER PROJECT   Assessment

Present Your Project Talk with your classmates about their designs. When you've had a chance to look them over, predict the final water temperature for each device. Record the starting temperature for each one, including your own. Record the final temperatures at the end of the demonstrations.

Reflect and Record In your journal, answer the following questions: Which insulating materials seemed to work the best? Which design worked best? How could you improve your model?

Test Preparation

Use these questions to prepare on the TAAS tests.

Read the passage. Then answer Questions 26–28.

Water has quite a high specific heat. This property of water affects the climate in many places. Because of the high specific heat of water, the temperature of water in the open ocean does not vary much from summer to winter. In winter, the water is warmer than the air, and so the water warms the air that moves over it. In summer, the water is cooler than the air, so the water cools the air that moves over it.

During the winter on the west coast, warm air over the Pacific Ocean blows onto land. In the summer, cooler air over the ocean blows onto land. As a result, the city of Portland, Oregon, is warmer in winter and cooler in the summer than the city of Minneapolis, Minnesota, which is at about the same latitude as Portland. Because Minneapolis is farther from the ocean than Portland, it is less affected by the temperature of the water.

26. What is this passage mostly about?
    A how latitude affects temperature
    B why the southern states are warmer than the northern states
    C how the ocean affects coastal climates
    D how the specific heat of water compares to that of other materials

27. Since the specific heat of water is higher than that of land,
    F the temperature of land rises less than that of water given the same amount of energy.
    G the temperature of water rises less than that of land given the same amount of energy.
    H land needs more energy than water to produce the same temperature change.
    J water is always warmer than land.

28. Why is Portland, Oregon, cooler than Minneapolis, Minnesota, in the summer?
    A Winds carry warm air to Minneapolis.
    B Winds carry cool air to Portland.
    C Minneapolis has a lower latitude.
    D Portland has a lower latitude.

WEB ACTIVITY

www.phschool.com

Over and Over and Over Again

Passersby watch as the Chinese dragon moves to the music.

It's time to celebrate the Chinese New Year! The parade passes through the streets to the delight of the people watching. The dragon dancers use poles to move the dragon up and down. The dragon moves just like a wave.

In this chapter, you will discover how waves travel through different materials. Some waves involve repeating patterns, or cycles. Any motion that repeats itself at regular intervals is called periodic motion. The hands on a clock, a child on a swing, a ride on a Ferris wheel, and the beating of your heart are just a few examples of periodic motion. As you work through the project, you will investigate the properties of periodic motion.

Your Goal To find and describe examples of periodic motion.

To complete this project you will

◆ identify several examples of periodic motion or other events that have periodic characteristics

◆ collect and organize data on the frequency and duration of each event

◆ present your findings as a poster, display, or demonstration

Get Started Brainstorm examples of repeating patterns you have observed. Think about objects or events that go back and forth or alternate from high to low, dark to light, loud to quiet, or crowded to uncrowded.

Check Your Progress You'll be working on this project as you study this chapter. To keep your project on track, look for Check Your Progress boxes at the following points.

Section 1 Review, page 139: List examples of periodic motion you'd like to study.

Section 2 Review, page 145: Record your observations of the frequency, length, and amplitude of the periodic events.

Present Your Project At the end of the project (page 159), you will present your findings to your class.

TEKS

In addition to process TEKS, this chapter addresses these concept TEKS as they relate to the chapter's topics.

(8.7) The student knows that there is a relationship between force and motion. The student is expected to:
(B) recognize that waves are generated and can travel through different media.

(8.10) The student knows that complex interactions occur between matter and energy. The student is expected to:
(A) illustrate interactions between matter and energy including specific heat.

What Are Waves?

How Do Waves Travel Through Water?

1. Fill a shallow pan with about 3 centimeters of water.

2. With a pencil, touch the surface of the water at one end of the pan twice each second for about a minute.

3. Describe the pattern the waves make. Sketch a rough diagram of what you see.

4. Float a cork on the water. How do you think the cork will move if there are waves? Repeat Step 2 to find out.

Think It Over

Observing What happened to the cork in Step 4? How is the cork's movement similar to the wave's movement? How is it different? Draw a diagram of what you see. Use arrows to show the movement of the cork.

GUIDE FOR READING

◆ **How do matter and energy interact when waves are generated?**

◆ **What are the three main types of waves?**

Reading Tip Before you read, think of what comes to mind when you hear the word *wave.* As you read, write a definition of *wave.*

Key Terms wave • medium • mechanical wave • vibration • transverse wave • crest • trough • longitudinal wave • compression • rarefaction • surface wave

---

Far out to sea, the wind disturbs the calm surface of the water. A ripple forms. As the wind continues to blow, the ripple grows into a powerful wave that can travel a great distance. Near the beach, surfers wait eagerly. They quickly paddle into deeper water to catch the monstrous wave. Surfers enjoy the power of nature as they ride the wave to the shore.

What are waves? How can they travel so far? Why are some waves more powerful than others? In this section, you will explore how waves begin and how they move.

Waves—Matter and Energy Interacting

Waves crashing on a beach show the tremendous energy waves can carry. A **wave** is a disturbance that transfers energy from place to place. In science, energy is defined as the ability to do work. To understand waves, think of a boat out on the ocean. If a wave disturbs the surface of the water, it will cause anything floating on the water to be disturbed, too. The energy carried by a wave can lift even a large ship as it passes.

The disturbance caused by a wave is temporary. After the wave has passed, the water is calm again.

◀ **A surfer riding a wave**

What Carries Waves? Many waves require something to travel through. For example, water waves travel along the surface of water, and sound waves travel through air. A wave can even travel along a rope. The material through which a wave travels is called a **medium** (plural *media*). Gases such as air, liquids such as water, and solids such as a rope all act as media. Waves that require a medium through which to travel are called **mechanical waves**.

Although waves travel through a medium, they do not carry the medium itself with them. Look at the duck in Figure 1. When a wave moves under the duck, the duck moves up and down. It does not move along the surface of the water. After the wave passes, the water and the duck are where they started.

Breaking waves at a beach behave a little differently. When waves hit a beach, the water does actually move along with the wave. This happens because the water near the beach is shallow. As the wave hits the shore, the bottom of the wave drags along the ocean floor. The top of the wave continues to move forward. Eventually the wave topples over, or breaks.

Not all waves require a medium to carry them along. Light from the sun, for example, can travel through empty space. Light is an example of an electromagnetic wave.

What Causes Waves? You can create waves by dipping your finger in water. **Waves are generated when a source of energy forces the matter in a medium to vibrate.** A **vibration** is a repeated back-and-forth or up-and-down motion. This motion is the source of the wave.

A moving object has energy. The moving object can transfer energy to a nearby medium, creating a wave. For example, as the propellers of a motorboat turn, they disturb the calm water surface. The boat's propeller transfers energy to the water. The propeller produces a wave that travels through the water. As the boat moves through the water, it also causes waves.

✓ *Checkpoint* What are mechanical waves?

Figure 1 Waves travel through water, but they do not carry the water with them. The duck moves up and down as a wave passes under it. The duck does not travel along with the wave.
Interpreting Diagrams If you add a sixth sketch to the diagram, which stage should it most resemble?

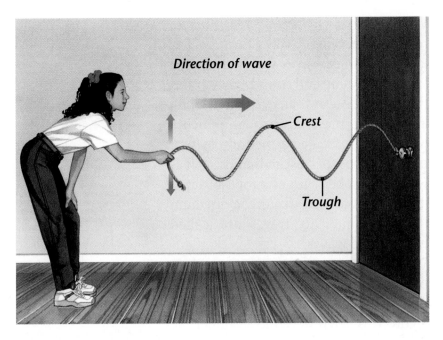

Figure 2 As she moves the free end of a rope up and down, the girl transfers energy to the rope. The energy travels along the rope, creating a transverse wave.

Direction of wave

Crest

Trough

Generating Different Types of Waves

Different types of waves travel through mediums in different ways. Waves are classified according to how they travel through a medium. **The three types of waves are transverse waves, longitudinal waves, and surface waves.**

Transverse Waves When you exert a force to move the end of a rope, you generate a wave that moves from one end of the rope to the other. The rope itself, however, moves up and down or from side to side. Waves that move the medium at right angles to the direction in which the waves are traveling are called **transverse waves.** Transverse means "across." As a transverse wave moves in one direction, the particles of the medium move across the direction of the wave. Figure 2 shows that some parts of the rope are high while some are low. The highest parts of the wave are called **crests,** and the lowest parts are called **troughs** (trawfs).

Figure 3 The coils in the spring toy move back and forth in the same direction as the motion of the wave. This is a longitudinal wave. *Comparing and Contrasting How does this wave compare with waves on a rope?*

Longitudinal Waves Figure 3 shows a different kind of wave. If you stretch out a spring toy and push and pull one end, you can produce a longitudinal wave. **Longitudinal waves** (lawn juh TOO duh nul) move the particles of the medium parallel to the direction that the waves are traveling. The coils in the spring move back and forth in the same direction as the wave travels.

As you can see in Figure 3, in some parts of the spring, the coils are close together.

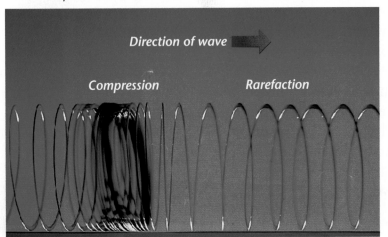

Direction of wave

Compression   Rarefaction

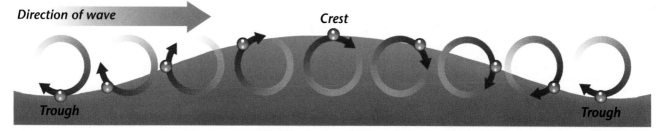

Figure 4 In a surface wave, up-and-down motion combines with back-and-forth motion. The combination produces circular motion.

In other parts, the coils are more spread out. The parts where the coils are close together are called **compressions** (kum PRESH uns). The parts where the coils are spread out, or rarefied, are called **rarefactions** (rair uh FAK shunz).

As compressions and rarefactions travel along the spring toy, each coil moves slightly forward and then back. The energy travels from one end of the spring to the other, creating a wave. After the wave passes, each part of the spring returns to the position where it started.

Combinations of Waves **Surface waves** are combinations of transverse and longitudinal waves. These waves occur at the surface between two media, such as water and air. When a wave passes through water, the water (and anything on it) moves up and down, like a transverse wave on a rope. The water also moves back and forth slightly in the direction that the wave is traveling, like the coils of the spring. But unlike the coils of a spring, water does not compress. The up-and-down and back-and-forth movements combine to make each particle of water move in a circle. Figure 4 shows the circular motion of surface waves.

Section 1 Review

1. How are waves generated?
2. Name the three types of waves. Give an example of each type.
3. When a wave passes a ship at sea, how does the wave affect the ship? What is the wave's medium?
4. **Thinking Critically** **Applying Concepts** The vibrations produced by a jackhammer are used to break up pavement. What type of waves do you think the jackhammer produces in the ground? Explain.

Check Your Progress CHAPTER PROJECT

Find and list as many examples of periodic motion as you can. Look for cycles and patterns that repeat in only a few seconds and others that take hours or days to repeat. Try to find examples that continue day after day, such as the rising and setting of the sun. Don't limit your search to your home or school. Look at the world around you and at the solar system for ideas. Describe and sketch each example you find.

SECTION
② Properties of Waves

DISCOVER •••••••••••••••••••••••••••••••• ACTIVITY

How Can You Change a Wave?

1. Lay a rope about 3 meters long on a smooth floor. Securely hold one end. Have a partner hold the other end.

2. Flick the end of the rope left and right about once per second to make a series of waves travel down the rope. Observe the waves as they travel toward your partner.

3. Now flick the end of the rope more often—about two times per second. Again, observe the waves.

4. Switch roles with your partner and repeat Steps 2 and 3.

Think It Over

Predicting What happened to the waves when you flicked the rope more often? How will the wave change if you flick the rope less often than once per second? Try it.

GUIDE FOR READING

◆ **What are the basic properties of waves?**

◆ **How is a wave's speed related to its wavelength and frequency?**

Reading Tip As you read, make a list of the properties of waves. Write a sentence that describes each property.

Key Terms amplitude
• wavelength
• frequency
• hertz (Hz)

Rhythmic gymnastics ▶

One of the most elegant and graceful Olympic sports is rhythmic gymnastics. In one routine, a ribbon dancer flicks a stick attached to a ribbon, making waves travel down the ribbon. Some of the waves are long, while others are shorter. The rate at which the gymnast flicks her hands affects the length and shape of the waves in the ribbon.

There are many different kinds of waves. Waves can carry a little energy or a lot. They can be short or long. They can be rare or frequent. They can travel fast or slow. All waves, however, share certain properties. **The basic properties of waves are amplitude, wavelength, frequency, and speed.**

Wave Diagrams

To understand the properties of waves, it helps to represent a wave on a diagram. Transverse waves like those on a rope are easy to draw. You can draw a transverse wave as shown in Figure 5. Think of the horizontal line as the position of the rope before it is disturbed. This is its rest position. As the wave passes, the rope goes above or below the rest position. Remember that the crests and the troughs are the highest and lowest points on the wave.

To draw longitudinal waves, think of the compressions in the spring toy as being similar to the crests of a transverse wave. The rarefactions in the spring toy are like the troughs of a transverse wave. By treating compressions as crests and rarefactions as troughs, you can draw longitudinal waves in the same way as transverse waves.

☑ *Checkpoint* Which part of a longitudinal wave is similar to the crest of a transverse wave?

Amplitude

Some waves are very high, while others are barely noticeable. The distance the water rises depends on the amplitude of the wave that passes through it. **Amplitude** is the maximum distance the particles of the medium carrying the wave move away from their rest positions. The amplitude is a measure of how much a particle in the medium moves when disturbed by the wave. The amplitude of a water wave is the maximum distance a water particle moves above or below the surface level of calm water.

You know that waves are produced by something vibrating. The farther the medium moves as it vibrates, the larger the amplitude of the resulting waves. You can increase the amplitude of the waves on a rope by moving your hand up and down a greater distance. To do this, you have to use more energy. This greater amount of energy is then transferred to the rope. Thus, the amplitude of a wave is a direct measure of its energy.

Amplitude of Transverse Waves Compare the two transverse waves in Figure 6. You can see that wave A goes up and down a greater distance than wave B. The amplitude of a transverse wave is the maximum distance the medium moves up or down from its rest position. You can find the amplitude of a transverse wave by measuring the distance from the rest position to a crest or to a trough.

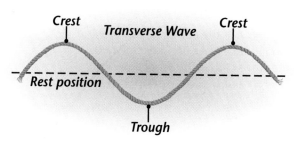

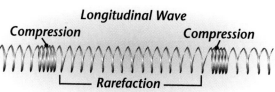

Figure 5 The crests and troughs of a transverse wave are the points at which the medium is farthest from the rest position. The compressions of a longitudinal wave correspond to the crests of a transverse wave.

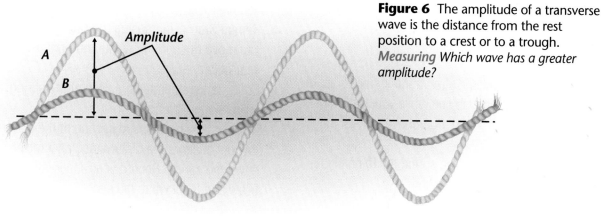

Figure 6 The amplitude of a transverse wave is the distance from the rest position to a crest or to a trough. *Measuring Which wave has a greater amplitude?*

Figure 7 If the compressions of a longitudinal wave are very crowded, the wave has a large amplitude. *Interpreting Diagrams Which longitudinal wave shown has the larger amplitude?*

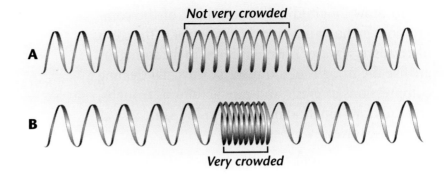

Not very crowded

A

B

Very crowded

Amplitude of Longitudinal Waves The amplitude of a longitudinal wave is a measure of how compressed or rarefied the medium becomes. High-energy vibrations cause the compressions to be very crowded. This makes the rarefactions quite loose. Crowded compressions and uncrowded rarefactions are like high crests and low troughs. They mean that the longitudinal wave has a large amplitude.

Skills Lab

Observing

Wavy Motions

*N*ow it's your turn to make some waves on a spring toy. In this lab, you will observe some properties of waves.

Problem

How do waves travel in a spring toy?

Materials (per group)

spring toy   meter stick

Procedure

1. On a smooth floor, stretch the spring to about 3 meters. Hold one end while your partner holds the other end. Do not overstretch the spring toy.
2. Pull a few coils of the spring toy to one side near one end of the spring.
3. Release the coils and observe the motion of the spring. What happens when the disturbance reaches your partner? Draw what you observe.
4. Have your partner move one end of the spring toy to the left and then to the right on the floor. Be certain to hold both ends of the spring securely. Draw a diagram of the wave you observe.
5. Repeat Step 4, increasing the rate at which you move the spring toy left and right. Record your observations.
6. Squeeze together several coils of the spring toy, making a compression.
7. Release the compressed section of the spring toy and observe the disturbance as it moves down the spring. Record your observations. Draw and label what you see.

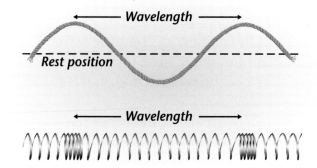

Wavelength

Rest position

Wavelength

Figure 8 The wavelength of a transverse wave is the distance from crest to crest. The wavelength of a longitudinal wave is the distance from compression to compression.

Wavelength

A wave travels a certain distance before it starts to repeat. The distance between two corresponding parts of a wave is its **wavelength.** You can find the wavelength of a transverse wave by measuring the distance from crest to crest or from trough to trough. You can find the wavelength of a longitudinal wave by measuring the distance from one compression to the next.

Analyze and Conclude

1. Compare the waves generated in Steps 1–5 with the waves generated in Steps 6–7.
2. Were the waves generated in Steps 1–5 transverse or longitudinal? Explain your answer.
3. In Step 3 of the procedure, compare the original wave to the wave that came back.
4. Were the waves generated in Steps 6 and 7 transverse or longitudinal? Explain your answer.
5. What happened to the wavelength and frequency when you increased the rate at which the spring toy moved left and right?
6. How did you change the amplitude of the waves you made?
7. **Think About It** Based on your observations, describe two ways that waves move through a spring toy. Use drawings and written explanations.

More to Explore

Obtain a wide variety of spring toys. Look for different sizes and materials, such as metal and plastic. Explore the differences among the waves you can produce on each spring. What accounts for these differences?

Frequency

The **frequency** of a wave is the number of complete waves that pass a given point in a certain amount of time. If you make waves on a rope so that one wave passes by every second, the frequency is 1 wave per second.

Since waves are produced by vibrations, frequency can also be described as the number of vibrations per second. To increase the frequency of the waves on a rope, you can move your hand up and down more often, perhaps two or three times per second. To decrease the frequency, you move your hand less often, perhaps once every two or three seconds.

Frequency is measured in units called **hertz (Hz).** A wave or vibration that occurs every second has a frequency of 1 Hz. If two waves pass you every second, then the frequency of the wave is 2 per second, or 2 hertz. The hertz was named after the German scientist Heinrich Hertz, who first produced radio waves.

☑ *Checkpoint* *How can you increase the frequency of waves on a rope?*

Speed

Imagine watching a distant thunderstorm on a hot summer day. First you see the flash of lightning. A few seconds later you hear the roll of thunder. Even though the lightning and thunder occurred at the same instant, they reach you seconds apart. This happens because sound and light travel at very different speeds. Light travels much faster than sound. Different waves travel at different speeds. The speed of a wave is how far the wave travels in one unit of time, or distance divided by time.

The speed, wavelength, and frequency of a wave are related to each other by a mathematical formula.

$$Speed = Wavelength \times Frequency$$

If you know any two of the quantities in the speed formula—speed, wavelength, and frequency—you can calculate the third quantity. For example, if you know the speed and the wavelength of a wave, you can calculate the frequency. If you know the speed and the frequency, you can calculate the wavelength.

$$Frequency = \frac{Speed}{Wavelength} \qquad Wavelength = \frac{Speed}{Frequency}$$

Waves in different media travel at different speeds. In a given medium under the same conditions, a wave's speed is constant. For example, all sound waves traveling through air at the same pressure and at the same temperature travel at the same speed.

If the temperature or pressure changes, the sound waves will travel at a different speed.

If the same type of wave travels at the same speed in the same medium, what do you think will happen if the frequency changes? When you multiply the wavelength and frequency after the change, you should get the same speed as before the change. Therefore, if you increase the frequency of a wave, the wavelength must decrease.

Sample Problem

The speed of a wave on a rope is 50 cm/s and its wavelength is 10 cm. What is the frequency?

Analyze. You know speed and wavelength. You want to find frequency.

Write the formula.
$$\text{Frequency} = \frac{Speed}{Wavelength}$$

Substitute and solve.
$$\text{Frequency} = \frac{50 \; cm/s}{10 \; cm}$$

$$\text{Frequency} = \frac{50 \; /s}{10}$$

$$\text{Frequency} = 5 \; /s \; (5 \text{ per second}) \text{ or } 5 \text{ Hz.}$$

Think about it. If you move your hand as often as 5 times a second, then fairly short waves, only 10 cm long, will move down the rope.

Practice Problems

1. A wave has a wavelength of 5 mm and a frequency of 2 Hz. At what speed does the wave travel?

2. The speed of a wave on a guitar string is 100 m/s, and the frequency is 1,000 Hz. What is the wavelength of the wave?

Section 2 Review

1. List the four basic properties of waves. Describe each property.
2. How are the speed, wavelength, and frequency of a wave related?
3. Can two waves have the same wavelength but different amplitudes? Explain.
4. **Thinking Critically** Inferring When you increase the tension on a piece of wire, the speed of waves on it increases, but the wavelength stays constant. What happens to the frequency of the waves as the tension on the wire is increased?

Check Your Progress CHAPTER PROJECT

Observe the amplitude, wavelength, frequency, and speed of one of the periodic motions on your list. How many complete repetitions of each periodic motion occur in a given amount of time? How long it does it take for a periodic event to finish and start again? Compare the highest and lowest position or the nearest and farthest position of the object showing periodic motion. Record your observations in your notebook.

SECTION 3 Interactions of Waves

DISCOVER ·ACTIVITY· · ·

How Does a Ball Bounce?

1. Choose a spot at the base of a wall. From a distance of 1 m, roll a wet ball along the floor at an angle to the spot you chose. Watch the angle at which the ball bounces back by looking at the path of moisture on the floor.

2. Wet the ball again. From a different position, roll the ball toward the same spot, but at an angle to the wall. Again, observe the angle at which the ball bounces back.

Think It Over

Developing Hypotheses How do you think the angle at which the ball hits the wall is related to the angle at which the ball bounces back? To test your hypothesis, roll the ball from several different positions toward the same spot on the wall. Use a protractor to measure the angles. Record your findings in a data table in your notebook or on the computer.

GUIDE FOR READING

◆ Why do waves bend?
◆ What happens to a wave at a barrier?

Reading Tip Before you read, preview *Exploring Interactions of Waves* on pages 150–151. Write down your questions. As you read, answer your questions.

Key Terms reflection
• angle of incidence
• angle of reflection
• refraction • diffraction
• interference
• constructive interference
• destructive interference
• standing wave • node
• antinode • resonance

It is a hot, sunny day. The water in the swimming pool is calm. To test the temperature of the water, you dip one foot in first. Your foot causes a series of ripples to travel across the water to the far wall of the pool. As each ripple hits the wall, it bounces off the wall and travels back toward you.

Reflection

When water waves hit the side of a swimming pool, they bounce back. When an object or wave hits a surface through which it cannot pass, it bounces back. This is called **reflection.**

To show reflection of a wave, draw a line in the direction of the motion of the wave. Now imagine a line perpendicular to the wall or surface. As shown in Figure 9, the **angle of incidence** is the angle between the incoming wave and the imaginary perpendicular line. The **angle of reflection** is the angle between the reflected wave and the imaginary line. The law of reflection states that the angle of reflection equals the angle of incidence. All waves obey the law of reflection.

There are many examples of reflection in your everyday life. A ball that hits a wall bounces back, or is reflected. When you look in a mirror, you use reflected light to see yourself. An echo is an example of reflected sound.

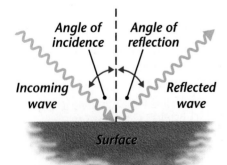

Figure 9 The angle of reflection is equal to the angle of incidence.

Refraction

Have you ever pushed a shopping cart that had a stiff wheel? If so, you know how difficult it is to control the direction of the cart. This is because the stiff wheel doesn't turn as fast as the other wheels. As you push the cart, it tends to veer to the side of the sticky wheel and so changes direction. Waves sometimes change direction when they enter a new medium. If a wave enters the new medium at an angle, one side changes speed before the other side. **When a wave moves from one medium into another medium at an angle, it changes speed as it enters the second medium, which causes it to bend.** The bending of waves due to a change in speed is called **refraction.**

Though all waves change speed when they enter a new medium, they don't always bend. Bending occurs when one side of the wave enters the new medium before the other side of the wave. The side of the wave that enters the new medium first changes speed first. The other side is still traveling at its original speed. The bending occurs because the two sides of the wave are traveling at different speeds.

☑ *Checkpoint* What is refraction?

Diffraction

Sometimes waves can bend around an obstacle in their path. For example, waves can pass through a narrow entrance to a harbor and then spread out inside the harbor. In Figure 10, notice how the water waves bend and spread out as they enter the harbor. **Whenever a wave passes around the edge of a barrier or moves through a hole in the barrier, the wave bends and spreads out.**

Figure 10 Waves from the ocean enter the harbor and spread out. This is an example of diffraction. *Predicting How do you think the waves in the harbor would change if the opening were wider?*

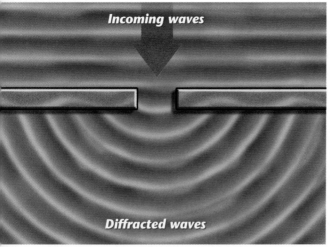
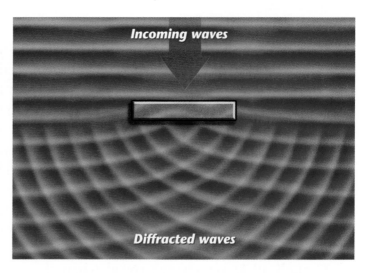

Incoming waves

Diffracted waves

Incoming waves

Diffracted waves

Figure 11 The diagram shows how waves diffract. A wave can go through a hole in a barrier and spread out (left). Or it can bend around a barrier (right).
Interpreting Diagrams What happens to the incoming waves as they bend around a barrier (right)?

The bending of waves around the edge of a barrier is known as **diffraction.** Figure 11 shows a water wave passing through a hole in a barrier and another bending around a barrier. In each case, you see the wave diffracting on the other side of the barrier.

☑ *Checkpoint* **What is diffraction?**

Interference

Suppose that you and a friend are each holding one end of a rope. If you both flick the ends at the same time, you send two waves toward each other. What happens when the waves meet?

When two or more waves meet, they have an effect on each other. This interaction is called **interference.** There are two types of interference: constructive and destructive.

Constructive Interference **Constructive interference** occurs whenever two waves combine to make a wave with a larger amplitude. You can think of constructive interference as waves "helping each other" to give a stronger result, or adding energy.

Figure 12A shows two identical waves (same amplitude, same wavelength) traveling in the same direction at the same time. If the two waves travel along the same path at the same time, they will behave as one. What will the combined wave look like? The crests of the first wave will occur at the same place as the crests of the second wave. The energy from the two waves will combine. Thus the amplitude of the new wave will be twice the amplitude of either of the original waves.

If the waves have the same wavelength but different amplitudes, the crests will still occur at the same place and add together. The resulting amplitude will be the sum of the two original amplitudes. Similarly, the troughs will occur together, making a deeper trough than either wave alone.

Figure 12 The diagrams show how identical waves can combine.

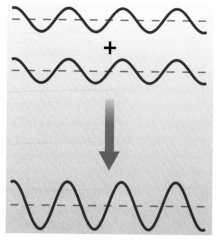

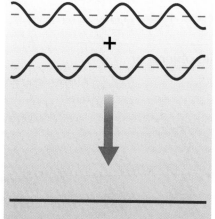

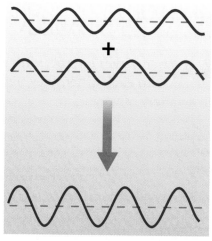

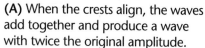

(A) When the crests align, the waves add together and produce a wave with twice the original amplitude.

(B) When the crests of one wave align with the troughs of another, they cancel each other out.

(C) If one wave travels a little behind the other, they combine both constructively and destructively at different places.

Destructive Interference When the amplitudes of two waves combine with each other producing a smaller amplitude, the result is called **destructive interference.** What happens if the crests don't meet at the same place? In this case, one wave comes after the other. Figure 12B shows what happens when the crests of the first wave occur at the same place as the troughs of the second wave. The amplitude of the first wave cancels out the amplitude of the second wave. This type of interference produces a wave with an amplitude of zero. The original waves seem to be destroyed. If the two waves have different amplitudes, they will not cancel each other out but will combine to produce a wave with a smaller amplitude.

In Figure 12C, two identical waves travel along the same path, one a little behind the other. When this happens, the waves combine constructively in some places and destructively in others.

Standing Waves

If you tie a rope to a doorknob and continuously shake the free end, waves will travel down the rope, reflect at the end, and come back. The reflected waves will collide with the incoming waves. When the waves meet, interference occurs. After they pass each other, they carry on as if the interference had never occurred.

If the incoming wave and the reflected wave combine at the right places, the combined wave appears to be standing still. A **standing wave** is a wave that appears to stand in one place, even though it is really two waves interfering as they pass through each other. If you make a standing wave on a rope, the wave looks as though it is standing still. But in fact, waves are traveling along the rope in both directions.

Standing Waves

 Here's how to generate a standing wave.

1. Tie a piece of elastic cord about 3 m long to a fixed, solid object. Hold the cord securely and pull it tight.

2. Slowly move the end of the cord up and down until you produce a standing wave.

3. Now move the cord up and down twice as fast to double the frequency. What happens?

Predicting What do you think will happen if you triple the original frequency? Try it. Be sure to keep a good grip on the cord.

EXPLORING Interactions of Waves

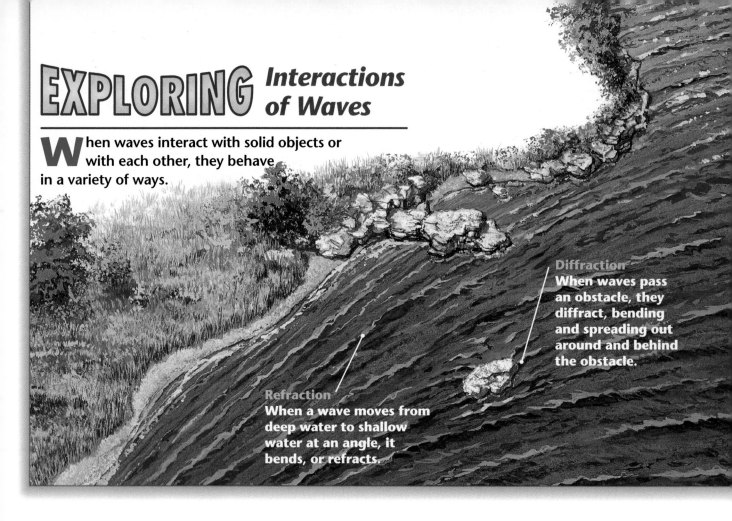

When waves interact with solid objects or with each other, they behave in a variety of ways.

Refraction
When a wave moves from deep water to shallow water at an angle, it bends, or refracts.

Diffraction
When waves pass an obstacle, they diffract, bending and spreading out around and behind the obstacle.

Nodes and Antinodes At certain points, destructive interference causes the two waves to combine to produce an amplitude of zero, as in Figure 13. These points are called **nodes.** The nodes always occur at the same place on the rope. The diagram also shows how the amplitudes of the two waves combine to produce amplitudes greater than zero. The crests and troughs of the standing wave are called **antinodes.** These are the points of maximum energy.

Resonance Have you ever pushed a child on a swing? At first, it is difficult to push the swing. But once you get it going, you need only push gently to keep it going. When an object is vibrating at a certain frequency, it takes very little energy to maintain or increase the amplitude of the wave.

Most objects have a natural frequency of vibration. Their particles vibrate naturally at a certain frequency. **Resonance** occurs when vibrations traveling through an object match the object's natural frequency. When vibrations of the same frequency are added, the amplitude of the object's vibrations increases.

Figure 13 A standing wave is set up when the reflected wave interacts with the incoming wave. The nodes are the points of zero amplitude. The antinodes are the points of maximum amplitude.

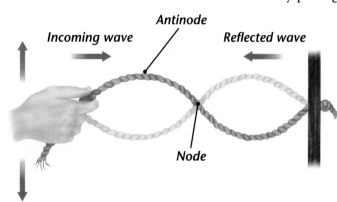

Incoming wave   *Antinode*   *Reflected wave*

Node

Constructive Interference
When two waves combine to make a wave with a larger amplitude, the result is constructive interference.

Destructive Interference
When two waves combine to make a wave with a smaller amplitude, the result is destructive interference.

Reflection
When a wave hits a barrier, it reflects at the same angle at which it hit the barrier.

An object that is vibrating at its natural frequency absorbs energy from objects that vibrate at the same frequency. Resonance occurs in music and adds a distinct quality to the sound.

If an object is not very flexible, resonance can cause it to shatter. For this reason, marching troops are told to break step as they cross a bridge. If they all march across the bridge in perfect step, it is possible that the pounding could match the natural frequency of the bridge. The increased vibration could cause the bridge to collapse.

 Section 3 Review

1. What causes refraction?
2. When does diffraction occur?
3. How do constructive and destructive interference differ?
4. What is the law of reflection?
5. **Thinking Critically** **Predicting** Two water waves have the same wavelength. The crests of one occur at the same place as the crests of the second. If one wave has twice the amplitude of the other, will the waves interfere constructively or destructively? Explain.

Science at Home

Waves in a Sink With your parent's permission, fill the kitchen sink with water to a depth of about 10 cm. Dip your finger in the water repeatedly to generate waves. Demonstrate reflection and interference to your family members. Try to think of ways to demonstrate refraction and diffraction as well.

Making Waves

Making Waves

In this lab, you will use a model to investigate wave behavior.

Problem

How do water waves interact with each other and with solid objects in their paths?

Materials

water · plastic dropper
metric ruler · paper towels
modeling clay
cork or other small floating object
ripple tank (aluminum foil lasagna pan with mirror at the bottom)

Procedure

1. Fill the pan with water to a depth of 1.5 cm. Let the water come to rest. Make a data table like the one shown below.
2. Fill a plastic dropper with water. Then release a drop of water from a height of about 10 cm above the center of the ripple tank. Observe the reflection of the waves that form and record your observations.

3. Predict how placing a paper towel across one end of the ripple tank will affect the reflection of the waves. Record your prediction in your notebook.
4. Drape a paper towel across one end of the ripple tank so it hangs in the water. Repeat Step 2, and record your observations of the waves.
5. Remove the paper towel and place a stick of modeling clay in the water near the center of the ripple tank.
6. From a height of about 10 cm, release a drop of water into the ripple tank halfway between the clay and one of the short walls. Record your observations.
7. Place the clay in a different position so that the waves strike it at an angle. Then repeat Step 6.

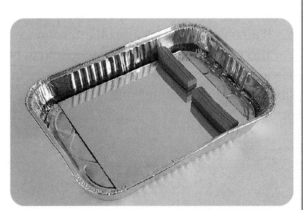

DATA TABLE		
Type of Barrier	Observations Without Cork	Observations With Cork

8. Place two sticks of clay end-to-end across the width of the tank. Adjust the clay so that there is a gap of about 2 cm between the ends of the two pieces. Repeat Step 6. Now change the angle of the modeling clay barrier in the ripple tank. Again repeat Step 6, and watch to see if the waves interact with the barrier any differently. Record your observations in the table.

9. Cut each of the two pieces of modeling clay in half. Rearrange the pieces of clay in the tank to make a barrier with three 2-cm gaps. Wait for the motion of the water to settle down. Then repeat Step 6.

10. Remove all the modeling clay and add a small floating object, such as a cork, to the water. Then repeat Steps 2–9 with the floating object. Observe what happens to the cork in each step. Record your observations in the data table.

11. Once you have finished all of the trials, clean and dry your work area.

Analyze and Conclude

1. How are waves affected by the paper towel hanging in the water?
2. What happens when waves strike a barrier head on? What happens when waves strike a barrier at an angle?
3. What happens when waves strike a barrier with a gap in it? What happens when they strike a barrier with three gaps in it?
4. **Think About It** How does the behavior of waves in your model compare to the behavior of waves in a harbor?

Design an Experiment

Predict what would happen if you could send a steady train of uniform waves the length of the ripple tank for an extended time. Use a plastic bottle with a pinhole in the bottom to make a model that will help to test your prediction. Get permission from your teacher to try out your dropper device.

SECTION 4 Seismic Waves

DISCOVER ·········· ACTIVITY···

Can You Find the Sand?

1. Fill a plastic film canister with sand and replace the lid tightly.

2. Place the canister on a table with four other identical but empty canisters. Mix them around so that a classmate does not know which can is which.

3. With your fist, pound on the table a few times. Have your classmate try to figure out which canister contains the sand.

4. Stick each canister to the table with some modeling clay. Pound on the table again. Now can your classmate figure out which canister contains the sand?

Think It Over

Inferring Pounding on a table generates waves. Why might the canister containing the sand respond differently from the empty ones?

GUIDE FOR READING

◆ What happens when the rock medium beneath Earth's surface moves?

◆ What are the different types of seismic waves?

◆ How does a seismograph work?

Reading Tip As you read, make a table comparing primary, secondary, and surface waves.

Key Terms seismic wave
• primary wave
• secondary wave
• tsunami
• seismograph

Some of the most dramatic waves originate deep inside Earth. On August 27, 1883, the eruption of Krakatau volcano in Indonesia caused a series of earthquakes. Vibrations from the earthquakes formed waves that traveled from the island through the surrounding water. On the open ocean, the waves were only about 1 meter high. As they entered shallower water, near land, the waves traveled more slowly. This caused the waves at the back to catch up to the waves at the front and to pile on top. The first wave grew into a wall of water over 35 meters high. People on ships far out at sea could not even tell when the waves went by. But on the islands of Java and Sumatra thousands of people were killed as the enormous waves crashed onto the land.

Figure 14 This illustration shows a giant wave reaching the coast of Java. The wave was caused by earthquakes related to the eruption of Krakatau volcano 40 kilometers away.

Types of Seismic Waves

An earthquake occurs when rock beneath Earth's surface moves. The movement of Earth's plates creates stress in the rock. **When the stress in the rock medium builds up enough, the rock breaks or changes shape, releasing energy in the form of waves or vibrations.** The waves generated by earthquakes are known as **seismic waves.** The word *seismic* comes from the Greek word *seismos,* meaning "earthquake."

Seismic waves ripple out in all directions from the point where the earthquake occurred. The medium for a seismic wave is Earth itself. The waves can travel from one side of Earth to the other. **Seismic waves include primary waves, secondary waves, and surface waves.**

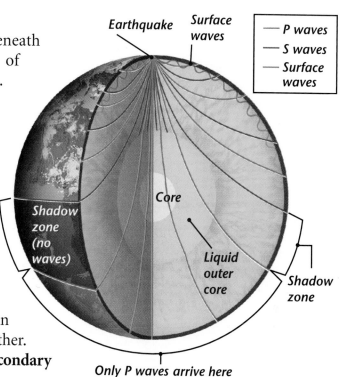

Figure 15 P waves travel through all parts of Earth. S waves do not travel through Earth's core. Surface waves travel only along Earth's surface. The shadow zone is where there are no seismic waves. *Applying Concepts Why don't S waves travel through Earth's core?*

Primary Waves Some seismic waves are longitudinal waves. Longitudinal seismic waves are also known as **primary waves,** or P waves. They are called primary waves because they move faster than other seismic waves and so arrive at distant points before other seismic waves. Primary waves are made up of compressions and rarefactions of rock inside Earth.

Secondary Waves Other seismic waves are transverse waves with crests and troughs. Transverse seismic waves are known as **secondary waves,** or S waves. Secondary waves cannot travel through liquids. Since part of Earth's core is liquid, S waves do not travel directly through Earth and cannot be detected on the side of Earth opposite an earthquake. Because of this, scientists on the side of Earth opposite the earthquake detect mainly P waves.

Surface Waves When P waves and S waves reach Earth's surface, some of them are transformed into surface waves similar to waves on the surface of water. Recall that surface waves are a combination of longitudinal and transverse waves. Even though surface waves travel more slowly than either P or S waves, they produce the most severe ground movements.

Earthquakes that occur underwater can generate huge surface waves on the ocean called **tsunamis** (tsoo NAH meez). Tsunamis can cause great damage when they reach land.

✓ *Checkpoint* How are P waves different from S waves?

Detecting Seismic Waves

If you did the Discover activity, you saw how waves can affect different masses by different amounts. To detect and measure earthquake waves, scientists use instruments called **seismographs** (SYZ muh grafs). **A seismograph records the ground movements caused by seismic waves as they move through Earth.**

The frame of the seismograph is attached to the ground, so the frame shakes when seismic waves arrive at the seismograph's location. Seismographs used to have pens attached to the frame that made wiggly lines on a roll of paper as the ground shook. Now scientists use electronic seismographs that use computers to record data about Earth's motion.

Since P waves travel through Earth faster than S waves, P waves arrive at seismographs before S waves. By measuring the time between the arrival of the P waves and the S waves, scientists can tell how far away the earthquake was. By comparing readings from at least three seismographs at different places on Earth, scientists can tell where the earthquake occurred.

Oil, water, minerals, and other valuable substances are hidden under Earth's surface. To find out what is under the ground, geologists may set off explosives to produce a small earthquake. The seismic waves resulting from the explosion reflect off different materials deep underground to seismographs located around the site of the explosion. The readings help geologists to locate mineral resources underground.

Figure 16 A scientist studies the printout from a seismograph.

Section 4 Review

1. What causes seismic waves?
2. Describe the different types of seismic waves.
3. How do seismographs help scientists determine where an earthquake occurred?
4. **Thinking Critically Inferring** S waves can travel from one side of the moon, through the core, to the other side. What does this tell you about the center of the moon? Explain.

Science at Home

Sounds Solid Find out how disturbances travel through different solids. Have a family member or friend tap one end of the table with a spoon. Now put your ear down on the other side of the table and listen to the tapping again. What difference do you notice? Repeat the tapping on various surfaces around your home. What observations have you made?

SECTION 1 What Are Waves?

Key Ideas

◆ Waves are generated when a source of energy forces the matter in a medium to vibrate.
◆ The three main types of waves are transverse waves, longitudinal waves, and surface waves.

Key Terms

wave	transverse wave	compression
medium	crest	rarefaction
mechanical wave	trough	surface wave
vibration	longitudinal wave	

SECTION 2 Properties of Waves

Key Ideas

◆ The basic properties of waves are amplitude, wavelength, frequency, and speed.
◆ The speed, frequency, and wavelength of a wave are related to each other by a mathematical formula.

$$Speed = Wavelength \times Frequency$$

Key Terms

amplitude	frequency
wavelength	hertz (Hz)

SECTION 3 Interactions of Waves

Key Ideas

◆ When a wave moves from one medium into another medium at an angle, it changes speed as it enters the second medium and bends.
◆ When a wave passes a barrier or moves through a hole in a barrier, it bends and spreads out.
◆ Two waves moving through the same medium can combine to produce a new wave.

Key Terms

reflection	constructive interference
angle of incidence	destructive interference
angle of reflection	standing wave
refraction	node
diffraction	antinode
interference	resonance

SECTION 4 Seismic Waves

INTEGRATING TECHNOLOGY

Key Ideas

◆ When stress in the rock medium beneath Earth's surface builds up enough, the rock breaks or changes shape, releasing energy in the form of seismic waves.
◆ Seismic waves include primary waves, secondary waves, and surface waves.
◆ A seismograph records the ground movements caused by seismic waves as they move through Earth.

Key Terms

seismic wave
primary wave
secondary wave
tsunami
seismograph

Organizing Information

Concept Map Copy the concept map about waves onto a separate sheet of paper. Then complete it and add a title. (For more on concept maps, see the Skills Handbook.)

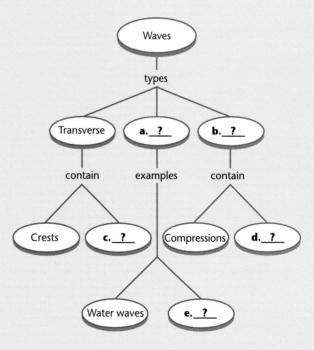

Reviewing Content

Review key concepts online using iText at www.phschool.com

Multiple Choice

Choose the letter of the best answer.

1. A wave carries
   a. energy.　　b. matter.
   c. water.　　d. air.
2. The distance between one crest and the next crest is the wave's
   a. amplitude.　　b. wavelength.
   c. frequency.　　d. speed.
3. In a given medium, if the frequency of a wave increases, its
   a. wavelength increases.
   b. speed increases.
   c. amplitude decreases.
   d. wavelength decreases.
4. The bending of a wave due to a change in its speed is
   a. interference.
   b. diffraction.
   c. reflection.
   d. refraction.
5. Seismic waves that do *not* travel through liquids are
   a. P waves.
   b. S waves.
   c. surface waves.
   d. tsunamis.

True or False

If the statement is true, write true. If it is false, change the underlined word or words to make the statement true.

6. <u>Transverse</u> waves have compressions and rarefactions.
7. When the particles of a medium move a great distance as the wave passes, the wave has a large <u>amplitude</u>.
8. When a wave changes speed as it enters a new medium at an angle, it undergoes <u>diffraction</u>.
9. Nodes and antinodes occur in <u>longitudinal</u> waves.
10. <u>Secondary</u> waves arrive at distant points before other seismic waves.

Checking Concepts

11. Explain the difference between transverse and longitudinal waves. Use diagrams to illustrate your explanation.
12. How can you find the amplitude of a longitudinal wave?
13. How are a wave's speed, wavelength, and frequency related?
14. Describe the difference between constructive and destructive interference.
15. Explain how seismographs work.
16. **Writing to Learn** Suppose you are a sportswriter with a background in science. While at a baseball game, you notice that at various times, entire sections of people stand up and sit down again. This "wave" travels around the stadium. Write a short newspaper article that describes what the crowd is doing. Be sure to use terms such as amplitude, frequency, wavelength, and speed in your description. Give your article a title.

Thinking Critically

17. **Calculating** A wave travels at 10 m/s and has a wavelength of 2 m. What is the frequency of the wave? If the speed of the wave doubles but the wavelength remains the same, what is the new frequency? Show your work.
18. **Comparing and Contrasting** One wave has half the amplitude of a second wave. The two waves interfere constructively. Draw a diagram and describe the resulting wave. Describe the resulting wave if two waves of equal amplitude interfere destructively.
19. **Making Models** Describe a way to model refraction of a wave as it enters a new medium.
20. **Applying Concepts** Suppose a wave moves from one side of a lake to the other. Does the water move across the lake? Explain.

Applying Skills

The wave in the illustration is a giant ocean wave produced by an underwater earthquake. Use the illustration to answer Questions 21–24.

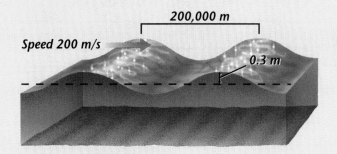

200,000 m

Speed 200 m/s

0.3 m

21. **Classifying** What kind of wave is shown in the above diagram?
22. **Interpreting Diagrams** What is the amplitude of the wave shown? What is its speed? Find the frequency of the wave. Show your work.

23. **Predicting** What could happen if this wave hits a coastal city? What property of a wave determines how much damage it could do?
24. **Calculating** How long would it take this wave to travel 5,000 km?

Performance CHAPTER PROJECT **Assessment**

Present Your Project Share your examples of periodic events and patterns with your classmates. On your display, highlight the repeating patterns and the frequency of each example. Which periodic events involve the transmission of waves through the vibrations of a medium?

Reflect and Record In your journal, describe the common or unusual events in your life that repeat periodically. Did you and your classmates observe the same things, or did your classmates surprise you with the examples they found?

Test Preparation   Use these questions to practice for standardized tests.

Read the passage. Then answer Questions 25–29.

During a visit to a nearby lake, you throw a stone into the water. As you sit back, you watch the ripple of waves created by the rock. Not far from where you threw the stone, you see a leaf bobbing up and down on the water.

25. What type of waves did you generate by throwing the stone?
    A transverse
    B longitudinal
    C surface
    D seismic
26. What is the medium for the waves?
    F stone
    G water
    H leaf
    J air

27. What was transferred by the waves?
    A water
    B energy
    C objects floating on the water
    D air
28. When the leaf was raised to its highest position by the wave, it was at the wave's
    F trough.
    G compression.
    H crest.
    J rarefaction.
29. What two factors do you need to know to determine the wave's speed?
    A amplitude and frequency
    B amplitude and wavelength
    C angle of incidence and angle of reflection
    D wavelength and frequency

CHAPTER 5 Sound Waves

WEB ACTIVITY
www.phschool.com

Music to Your Ears

Music, one of the oldest arts, forms an important part of many occasions. Early Chinese, Egyptian, and Babylonian people made stringed instruments from animal hair, whistles from bones, and trumpets from animal horns. Today, musical instruments are made of wood, brass, silver, and nylon.

In this chapter you will investigate the properties of sound. You will learn how sound is produced by different objects, including musical instruments. As you work through the chapter, you will gather enough knowledge to help you to complete the project.

Your Goal To design, build, and play a simple musical instrument.

To complete this project you must
◆ design a simple musical instrument
◆ construct and modify your instrument
◆ play a simple tune on your instrument

Get Started Begin now by discussing different kinds of instruments with your classmates. What kind of music do you enjoy? What instruments are common in your favorite type of music? Do you or any of your classmates already play an instrument? Which type of instrument would you like to build?

Check Your Progress You'll be working on this project as you study this chapter. To keep your project on track, look for Check Your Progress boxes at the following points.
Section 2 Review, page 173: Make a list of materials you could use to build your instrument.
Section 3 Review, page 181: Design and construct your instrument.
Section 5 Review, page 192: Test your instrument. Modify and test it again.

Present Your Project At the end of the chapter (page 195), you will demonstrate how you can vary the loudness and pitch of the sound of your instrument and play a simple tune.

These musical instruments play a part in African ceremonial life.

TEKS

In addition to process TEKS, this chapter addresses these concept TEKS as they relate to the chapter's topic

(8.6) The student knows that interdependence occurs among living systems. The student is expected to:
(A) describe interactions among systems in the human organism.
(8.7) The student knows that there is a relationship between force and motion. The student is expected to:
(B) recognize that waves are generated and can travel through different media.

(8.10) The student knows that complex interactions occur between matt and energy. The student is expected to:
(A) illustrate interactions between matter and energy including specific heat.

SECTION 1 The Nature of Sound Waves

What Is Sound?

1. Fill a bowl with water.

2. Tap a tuning fork against the sole of your shoe. Place the tip of one of the prongs in the water. What do you see?

3. Tap the tuning fork again. Predict what will happen when you hold it near your ear. What do you hear?

Think It Over

Observing How do you think your observations are related to the sound you hear? What might change if you use a tuning fork of a different size? What would change in the sound you hear?

GUIDE FOR READING

◆ What is sound?

◆ What physical properties of a medium affect the speed at which sound travels through it?

Reading Tip Before you read, preview the headings in the section. Record the headings in outline form, leaving room to add notes.

Key Terms sound • larynx • elasticity

Here is an old riddle: If a tree falls in a forest and no one is there to hear it, does the falling tree make a sound? To answer the question, you must decide how to define the word "sound." If sound is something a person must hear with his or her ears, then you might say the falling tree makes no sound.

When a tree crashes down, the energy with which it strikes the forest floor is transmitted through two kinds of media: the ground and the surrounding air. This energy causes the ground and the air to vibrate. If sound is a disturbance that travels through the ground or the air, then sound is created even if no one is around. So the falling tree does make a sound.

Sound and Longitudinal Waves

Just like the waves you studied in Chapter 4, sound begins with a vibration. When a tree crashes to the ground, the surrounding air particles are disturbed. This disturbance causes other vibrations in nearby particles.

How Sound Travels Like all waves, **sound** waves carry energy through a medium without the particles of the medium traveling along. A common medium for sound is air. Each molecule in the air moves back and forth as the disturbance goes by. **Sound is a disturbance that travels through a medium as a longitudinal wave.** When the disturbance reaches the air near your ears, you hear the sound.

How Sounds Are Made A drum also makes sounds by generating vibrations. When you beat a drum, the surface of the drum begins to vibrate so quickly that you cannot see any movement.

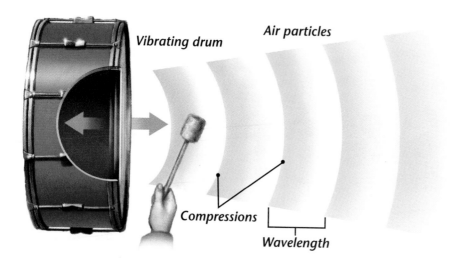

Vibrating drum

Air particles

Compressions

Wavelength

Figure 1 As the drum vibrates back and forth, it creates compressions and rarefactions in the air. *Classifying What type of wave does a drum make?*

Air is mostly made up of tiny particles, or molecules, of gases. Figure 1 shows how the vibration of a drum generates a disturbance in the molecules in the air near it. When the drumhead moves to the right, the force pushes the molecules together, generating a compression. When the drumhead moves to the left, the molecules move farther apart, generating a rarefaction.

When you pluck a guitar string, it vibrates back and forth, generating compressions and rarefactions. These compressions and rarefactions travel through the air as longitudinal waves similar to the longitudinal waves that you saw travel along a spring.

 INTEGRATING LIFE SCIENCE Your vocal cords act like vibrating guitar strings. Whenever you speak or sing, you force air from your lungs up through your voice box, or **larynx.** Your larynx consists of two folds of tissue called vocal cords, shown in Figure 2. The forced air rushes by your vocal cords, making them vibrate. As your vocal cords move toward each other, the air between them is compressed. As they move apart, the air spreads out, or is rarefied. Like vibrating guitar strings, your vocal cords generate compressions and rarefactions in the air. The air carries these longitudinal waves to other people's ears as well as to your own.

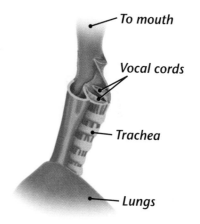

To mouth

Vocal cords

Trachea

Lungs

Figure 2 When a person speaks or sings, the vocal cords vibrate. The vibrations produce longitudinal sound waves in the air.

Sound in Solid and Liquid Media

Sound can also travel through solids and liquids. When you knock on a door, the particles of the door vibrate. The vibration generates sound waves that travel through the door. When the sound waves reach the other side of the door, they generate sound waves in the air on the far side. In old western movies, you may have seen someone put an ear to a railway track.

Figure 3 When sound waves enter a room through an open door, they spread out. This is called diffraction.

Figure 4 The speed of sound depends upon the medium through which it is traveling. *Making Generalizations In general, does sound travel faster in solids, liquids, or gases?*

Speed of Sound	
Medium	**Speed (m/s)**
Gases	
Air (0°C)	330
Air (20°C)	342
Liquids	
Fresh water	1,490
Salt water	1,530
Solids (25°C)	
Lead	1,210
Plastic	1,800
Silver	2,680
Copper	3,100
Gold	3,240
Brick	3,650
Hard wood	4,000
Glass	4,540
Iron	5,000
Steel	5,200

If a train is on the way, its sound will travel more quickly through the steel tracks than through the air. If you put your ear to a street, you might hear distant traffic. Sound waves from the traffic are traveling through the ground as well as through the air.

Sound can travel only if there is a medium to transmit the compressions and rarefactions. In outer space, there are no molecules to compress or rarefy. The energy of the original vibrations has no matter through which to travel. So sound does not travel through outer space.

How Sound Bends When sound waves hit a barrier with a small hole in it, some of the waves pass through the hole. Just as diffraction causes water waves to spread out in a harbor, the sound waves spread out, or diffract, as they go through the hole. When sound waves go through a doorway, they spread out. Even if you are off to the side of the room, you may still hear sound from outside. If you are outside the room and not too far from the doorway, you can hear sound coming from inside the room.

Because of diffraction, you can also hear sounds from around corners. Waves passing a corner spread out as they pass.

The Speed of Sound in Different Media

If you have ever seen a live band perform, you've noticed that the sounds produced by the different instruments and singers all reach your ears at the same time. If they did not travel at the same speed, the sounds that were played together would reach you at different times and would not sound very pleasant.

The speed of sound depends on the physical properties of the medium it travels through. At room temperature, about 20°C, sound travels at about 342 m/s. This is much faster than most jet airplanes travel through the air. Figure 4 shows the speed of sound through some common materials.

As the physical properties of a medium change, so does the speed of the sound that travels through it. **The speed at which sound travels through a medium depends on the elasticity, density, and temperature of the medium.**

Elasticity Since sound is a transfer of energy, its speed depends on how well the particles in the medium bounce back after being disturbed. If you stretch a rubber band and then let it go, it returns to its original shape. However, when you stretch modeling clay and then let it go, it stays stretched. Rubber bands are more elastic than modeling clay. **Elasticity** is the ability of a material to bounce back after being disturbed. If a medium is very elastic, its particles easily go back to their original positions. Sound travels more quickly in mediums that have a high degree of elasticity because when the particles are compressed, they quickly spread out again.

Solid materials are usually more elastic than liquids or gases, so compressions and rarefactions travel very well in solids. The particles of a solid do not move very far, so they bounce back and forth quickly as the compressions and rarefactions of the sound waves go by. Most liquids are not very elastic. Sound is not transmitted as well in liquids as it is in solids. Gases are generally very inelastic and are the poorest transmitters of sound.

Density The speed of sound also depends on how close together the particles of the substance are. The density of a medium is how much matter, or mass, there is in a given amount of space, or volume.

In materials in the same state of matter—solid, liquid, or gas—sound travels more slowly in denser mediums. The denser the medium, the more mass it has in a given volume. The particles of a dense material do not move as quickly as those of a less-dense material. Sound travels more slowly in dense metals, such as lead or silver, than in iron or steel.

Temperature In a given medium, sound travels more slowly at lower temperatures than at higher temperatures. As you learned in Chapter 3, at a low temperature, the particles of a medium are sluggish. They move and return to their original positions more slowly than they would at a high temperature.

At 20°C, the speed of sound in air is about 340 m/s. At 0°C, the speed is about 330 m/s. At higher altitudes the air is colder, so sound travels more slowly at higher altitudes.

☑ *Checkpoint* *How does elasticity affect the speed of sound?*

Figure 5 Some substances are more elastic than others. Sponges and rubber bands are more elastic than modeling clay. *Predicting Is sound likely to travel faster through a sponge, a rubber band, or a piece of modeling clay?*

Sharpen your **Skills**

Graphing ACTIVITY

🖥 Use a pencil or the computer to graph the following data that shows how the speed of sound in air changes with temperature changes. Show temperatures from –20°C to 30°C on the horizontal axis. Plot speed from 300 m/s to 400 m/s on the vertical axis.

Air Temperature (°C)	Speed (m/s)
–20	318
–10	324
0	330
10	336
20	342
30	348

How does air temperature affect the speed of sound?

Moving Faster Than Sound

On October 14, 1947, the supersonic age began with a bang. Far above the California desert, Captain Chuck Yeager of the United States Air Force had just "broken the sound barrier." Captain Yeager was at an altitude of 12,000 meters and just about out of fuel. He had used much of his fuel to get higher rather than faster because the speed of sound is less higher up. Wide open throttles accelerated his plane to over 293 meters per second, the speed of sound at that altitude. Thus, when he hit 294 meters per second, he exceeded the speed of sound at that altitude. At a lower altitude, the speed of sound is much higher and he would not have had the power or speed to exceed it. Yeager's team chose to go high in part because the temperature there is lower and the speed of sound is less. Each pilot today who "goes supersonic" owes Chuck Yeager a debt of gratitude.

Fifty years later, Andy Green stood poised on Nevada's Black Rock desert. He had traveled all the way from Great Britain to go supersonic—on the ground! He chose the desert because it is flat, wide open, and cold in the morning. All of these factors were important to the attempt. On October 15, 1997, at the coolest time of the day, Green blasted off in his jet-powered car, *Thrust*. A short time later he traveled a measured distance at an average speed of 339 meters per second—7 meters per second faster than the speed of sound at that altitude. Andy Green was the first person to break the sound barrier on the ground.

Figure 6 On October 14, 1947, Captain Chuck Yeager became the first person to fly a plane faster than the speed of sound (top). On October 15, 1997, Andy Green officially became the first person to drive a land vehicle faster than the speed of sound (bottom).

Section 1 Review

1. How does sound travel through a medium?
2. How do elasticity, density, and temperature affect the speed at which sound travels through a medium?
3. Why can't sound travel through outer space?
4. **Thinking Critically Applying Concepts** Sound travels faster through glass than through gold. Based on this information, which material would you say is more dense? Explain.

Science at Home

Ear to the Sound Find a long metal railing or water pipe. **CAUTION:** *Beware of sharp edges and rust.* Put one ear to the pipe while a family member taps on the pipe some distance away. Do you hear the sound first with the ear touching the pipe or with your other ear? Compare the sound you hear through the metal medium with the sound coming through the air. What accounts for the difference?

The Speed of Sound

Sound travels at different speeds through different media. In this lab, you will measure the speed of sound in air.

Problem

How fast does sound travel in air?

Materials (per group of 3)

metric tape measure
drum and drumstick
   (or empty coffee can
   and metal spoon)

weather thermometer
digital stopwatch

Procedure

1. With the approval of your teacher, select an outdoor area such as a football field.
2. Record the outdoor air temperature in °C.
3. Measure a distance of 100 meters in a straight line. How long do you think it should take for a sound to travel the 100 m?
4. Stand at one end of this measured distance with the drum. Have two teammates go to the other end with a stopwatch. One teammate, the "watcher," should watch you and the drum. The other, the "listener," should face away from the drum and listen for the sound.
5. Strike the drum to create a short but loud noise.
6. As you strike the drum, the watcher should start the stopwatch. When the listener hears the sound, he or she should immediately say "stop." Then the watcher stops the watch. Record the time to one tenth of a second.
7. Repeat Steps 1–6 five times. How consistent are your times? What accounts for any differences?
8. Now switch roles. Repeat Steps 1–6 with different students beating the drum, watching, and listening.

Analyze and Conclude

1. How far did the sound travel? How long did it take? (Calculate the average of the five measured times.)
2. To calculate the speed of sound in air, use this formula:

$$Speed = \frac{Distance}{Time}$$

3. How well does your result compare with the prediction you made in Step 3? Make a list of reasons for any differences. What could you do to improve the accuracy of your measurements?
4. **Think About It** Another way to measure the speed of sound would be to stand near a tall building, shout, and wait to hear the echo. To use the echo method, what adjustments would you have to make to the procedure in this lab?

Design an Experiment

How could you find out the effect of changing air temperature on the speed of sound? Write a set of procedures you could use to conduct such an experiment.

SECTION 2 Properties of Sound Waves

How Does Amplitude Affect Loudness?

1. Your teacher will give you a wooden board with two nails in it. Fasten a guitar string to the board by wrapping each end tightly around a nail.

2. Hold the string near the middle. Pull it about 1 cm to one side. This distance is the amplitude of vibration. Let it go. How far does the string move to the other side? Describe the sound you hear.

3. Repeat Step 2 four more times. Each time, pull the string back a greater distance. Describe how the sound changes each time.

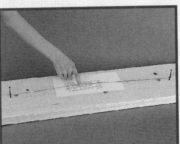

Think It Over

Forming Operational Definitions How would you define the amplitude of the vibration? How did you change the amplitude each time? What effect did changing the amplitude have on the sound?

◆ How are sound intensity and loudness related?

◆ How are frequency and pitch related?

◆ What causes the Doppler effect?

Reading Tip As you read, use your own words to write a phrase or sentence describing each boldfaced word.

Key Terms intensity • loudness • decibels (dB) • ultrasound • infrasound • pitch • Doppler effect

---

Suppose you and a friend are standing next to each other. You are talking in your normal speaking voice. After you say good-bye and your friend has walked away, you realize you have forgotten to tell your friend something important. How do you get your friend's attention? You will need to shout to be heard. When you shout, you take a deep breath and exhale very fast, and your voice sounds louder.

Intensity and Loudness

Compare the sound of a whisper to that of a hearty shout. The sounds are different because the amount of energy carried by the sound waves is different. The sound waves caused by a shout carry much more energy than those of a whisper.

Intensity You have seen how you can change the amplitude of a wave along a rope. If you move the rope a greater distance, you give it more energy as you shake it. When a sound wave carries a large amount of energy, the molecules of the medium move a greater distance as the waves pass by, and the sound wave has a greater amplitude. The **intensity** of a sound wave is the amount of energy the wave carries per second through a unit area. Intensity is measured in watts per square meter (W/m^2).

Loudness If you did the Discover activity with the guitar string, you should have noticed how pulling the string back different distances affected the loudness of the sound you heard.

The amplitude of the string's vibration changed. Sound waves of higher amplitude have a greater intensity because they carry more energy per second through a given area. Though intensity and loudness are not the same, the greater the intensity of a sound wave, the louder it is. **Loudness** describes what you actually hear. **A sound wave of greater intensity generally sounds louder.**

To increase the loudness of the music coming from a CD player, you adjust the volume control. Loudspeakers or headphones give off sound by vibrating a cone of material. Figure 7 shows how the vibrations make compressions and rarefactions in the air, just like a vibrating drumhead. As you turn up the volume, the cone vibrates with a greater amplitude and the sound you hear is louder.

Loudness, or sound level, is measured in **decibels (dB)**. Figure 8 shows the loudness of some familiar sounds. The loudness of a sound you can barely hear is about 0 dB. Each 10 dB increase in sound level represents a tenfold increase in intensity. For example, a sound at 30 dB is ten times more intense than a sound at 20 dB. Sounds louder than 100 dB can cause damage to your ears, especially if you listen to those sounds for long periods of time. Sounds louder than 120 dB can cause pain and sometimes permanent hearing loss.

Figure 7 A loudspeaker gives out sound by vibrating cones of material. The greater the amplitude of vibration, the greater the volume, or loudness, of the sound.

✓ *Checkpoint* *How does amplitude affect the loudness of a sound?*

Loudness of Sounds

Sound	Loudness (dB)	Hearing Damage
Threshold of human hearing	0	None
Rustling leaves	10	
Whisper	20	
Very soft music	30	
Classroom	35	
Average home	40–50	
Loud conversation	60–70	
Heavy street traffic	70	
Loud music	90–100	After long exposure
Subway train	100	
Rock concert	115–120	Progressive
Jackhammer	120	Threshold of pain
Jet engine	120–170	
Space shuttle engine	200	Immediate and irreversible

Figure 8 Some sounds are so soft, you can barely hear them. Others are so loud that they can damage your ears. *Applying Concepts How is the sound of a space shuttle engine different from that of a whisper?*

The Short Straw

Try this activity **ACTIVITY** to see how the length of a straw affects the sound it makes when you blow through it.

1. Flatten one end of a drinking straw and cut the end to form a point.

2. Blow through the straw. Describe what you hear.

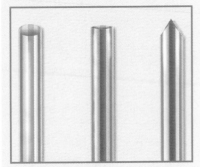

Predicting What changes would you hear if you shortened the straw by cutting off some of the straight end? Test your prediction.

Frequency and Pitch

A barbershop quartet consists of four singers with very different voices. When all four people sing together, the different voices combine to make a pleasing sound.

Frequency When a person sings, muscles in the throat stretch and relax the vocal cords. This changes the frequency of the sounds. When the vocal cords are stretched, they vibrate more often as the air rushes past them. This creates higher-frequency sound waves. When the vocal cords are relaxed, they vibrate less often and produce lower-frequency sound waves. The frequency of a sound wave is the number of vibrations that occur per second. A frequency of 50 Hz means fifty vibrations per second. A bass singer can produce a range of frequencies from about 80 Hz to about 260 Hz. A trained soprano voice can produce frequencies over 1,000 Hz.

Most people can hear sounds with frequencies between 20 Hz and 20,000 Hz. Sound waves with frequencies above the normal human range of hearing are called **ultrasound.** The prefix *ultra-* means "above." Sounds with frequencies below the normal human range of hearing are called **infrasound.** The prefix *infra-* means "below."

Pitch Before a barbershop quartet begins to sing, one member plays a note on a pitch pipe. This gives the lead singer the correct starting note. The **pitch** of a sound is a description of how high or low the sound seems to a person. **The pitch of a sound that you hear depends on the frequency of the sound wave.** Sound waves of high frequency have a high pitch, while sound waves of low frequency have a low pitch.

Figure 9 A barbershop quartet consists of four singers, whose voices sound good together. *Comparing and Contrasting In what way are the four voices different?*

Figure 10 The key farthest to the left on a piano is attached to the longest string. This key plays the note with the lowest pitch. *Developing Hypotheses Why do longer strings generally produce lower notes than shorter ones?*

When a string vibrates, the pitch of the sound depends on the material used, the length and thickness of the string, and on how tightly it is stretched. You can change the pitch of a sound by changing the physical properties of the string that produces it. For example, violinists and guitarists tune their instruments by turning knobs that stretch the strings. A tighter string produces a higher frequency. You hear the higher frequency as a sound with higher pitch.

Different lengths of string produce different frequencies, too. In general, a short string produces a higher pitch than a long string under the same tension. Consider the range of notes you can play on a piano. The key farthest to the left on a piano keyboard produces the note with the lowest pitch. It is attached to the longest string, which vibrates at a frequency of about 27 Hz. The key farthest to the right on a piano keyboard produces the note with the highest pitch. It is attached to the shortest string, which vibrates at a frequency of 4,186 Hz.

☑ *Checkpoint* *How are frequency and pitch related?*

Resonance Have you ever heard of an opera singer who could shatter a glass with a sustained high note? How can that happen? All objects vibrate naturally. The vibrations are so frequent that you usually cannot see them. The frequency of the vibrations depends on the type and shape of the object. If the frequency of sound waves exactly matches the natural frequency of an object, the sound waves can add to the object's vibrations. Resonance occurs when the frequency of the sound waves and the natural frequency of the object are the same.

Suppose a note has the same frequency as the natural vibration of a crystal glass. If the note is played steadily, the sound waves can add to the amplitude of vibration of the glass. If the note is played loudly enough and for long enough, the amplitude of vibration can increase so much that the glass shatters.

Figure 11 Some musical instruments can produce notes with vibrations that match the natural frequency of a crystal glass. If the note is sustained, the amplitude of vibration can cause the glass to shatter.

The Doppler Effect

Even though a sound may have a constant frequency, it does not always sound that way to a listener. Have you ever heard a police car speed by with its siren on? If you listen carefully you will notice something surprising. As the car moves toward you, the pitch of the siren is higher. As the car goes by and moves away, the pitch drops. But the frequency of the siren is not really changing. If you were riding in the police car, you would hear the same pitch all the time. The apparent change in frequency as a wave source moves in relation to the listener is called the **Doppler effect.** If the waves are sound waves, the change in frequency is heard as a change in pitch.

The Doppler Demonstration The Doppler effect was named after Christian Doppler, an Austrian scientist who described it about 150 years ago. To demonstrate the effect, Doppler put a musical band on an open flatcar of a train. He stood on the ground nearby. As the train approached him, the notes the musicians played seemed to be a higher pitch. As the train passed, the notes seemed to drop in pitch. Doppler repeated the experiment, but this time he stood on the train and had the musicians play while they were seated on the ground. Doppler heard the same changes in pitch as the train he rode approached and passed the band. The effect was the same regardless of who was moving, the band or Doppler.

Changing Pitch To understand what causes this apparent change in pitch, suppose you are standing still and throwing tennis balls at a wall. If you could throw one ball each second, the balls would hit the wall at a rate of one per second. The frequency would be 1 per second, or 1 Hz. Now, suppose you walk toward the wall, while still throwing one ball per second.

Figure 12 As the police car speeds by, the pitch of the siren seems to change. Ahead of the car, the sound waves are piling up, so the pitch is higher. Behind the car the waves spread out, so the pitch is lower. *Applying Concepts How would the siren's pitch sound to the two people if the police car stopped?*

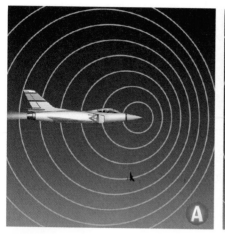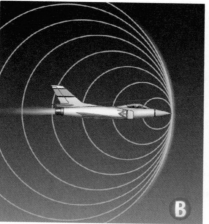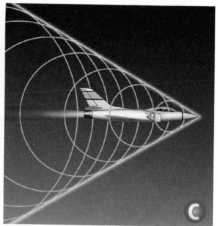

Figure 13 When a plane flies faster than the speed of sound, waves pile up to form the shock wave known as the sound barrier.

Because each ball has a shorter distance to travel than the one before, it takes less time to get there. The balls hit the wall more often than one per second, or with a higher frequency than before. Similarly, if you throw balls at the wall as you back away, the balls will hit the wall with lower frequency. Each ball has farther to travel before it hits the wall, so it takes longer to get there.

Figure 12 shows how sound waves from a moving source behave. **As a sound source moves toward the listener, the waves reach the listener with a higher frequency. The pitch appears to increase because of the Doppler effect.**

This piling up of sound waves has a spectacular effect in the air. Figures 13A and B show how as a plane travels almost as fast as the speed of sound, the sound waves pile up in front of the plane. This pile-up is the "sound barrier." When the plane flies faster than the speed of sound, it breaks through the barrier. When the sound barrier is broken, as in Figure 13C, a huge amount of energy is released in the form of a shock wave. People on the ground nearby hear a loud noise called a sonic boom.

Section 2 Review

1. What makes some sounds louder than others?
2. What happens to a sound's frequency if its pitch is increased?
3. How can you change the pitch of a vibrating string?
4. Explain how resonance can cause a crystal glass to shatter.
5. What is the Doppler effect?
6. **Thinking Critically Relating Cause and Effect** If you are riding in a fire truck with the siren blaring, you do not hear the Doppler effect. Explain.

DISCOVER ··· ACTIVITY ····

How Can You Produce Patterns of Sound?

1. Obtain an empty coffee can.

2. Stretch the palm area of a latex glove over the open end. Glue a small mirror tile in the center of the glove.

3. Shine a flashlight so that the light reflects off the mirror and onto a wall.

4. Ask a classmate to continuously tap a spoon on the closed end of the can. Make sure you keep the light shining on the mirror. Observe the light patterns that are reflected on the wall. What do the patterns look like? Draw and label what you observe.

5. Have your classmate change the frequency of the tapping. Draw what you observe.

Think It Over

Inferring What causes the moving patterns on the wall? What happens when you change the frequency of the tapping? Explain.

GUIDE FOR READING

◆ What is sound quality?

◆ How are music and noise different?

◆ What happens when two or more sound waves interact?

Reading Tip Before you read, list as many musical instruments as you can. Write a short description of how you think each one works. Revise your list as you read.

Key Terms timbre • music • noise • dissonance • acoustics • beats

Imagine you are waiting for a train at a busy station. In the middle of all the hustle and bustle, you notice lots of different sounds. A baby wails while a teenager listens to a favorite radio station. Then the train rolls in. Why are some sounds pleasing to hear while others make you want to cover your ears? The answer is in the way sound waves combine.

Busy train station ▶

Sound Quality

Think of all the different sounds you hear on a given day. Some sounds are pleasant, such as your favorite kind of music, a babbling brook, or a baby cooing. Other sounds are unpleasant, such as loud power tools, fingernails scratching on a chalkboard, or a constant drip of water from a tap. Your ears hear all kinds of sounds—some that you like and some that you don't.

To understand the quality of sound, consider the example of a violin string. As the string vibrates, waves travel along the string and then reflect back, setting up a standing wave. Figure 14 shows how a string vibrates with different frequencies. The frequency at which a standing wave occurs is the string's resonant frequency. Every object, including musical instruments, has its own resonant frequency.

The resonant frequency produces a pitch called the fundamental tone. However, most of the sounds you hear are not pure tones. Although a tuning fork or pitch pipe produces a single tone, more complex instruments produce several tones at once. For example, a string can vibrate at several frequencies at the same time. The higher frequencies produce sounds heard as having higher pitch. The higher pitches, or overtones, have frequencies of two, three, or four times the frequency of the fundamental tone.

Timbre (TAM bur) describes the quality of the sound you hear. Overtones can be weak, strong, or missing. The timbre of a sound depends on which overtones are present. **The blending of the fundamental tone and the overtones makes up the characteristic sound quality, or timbre, of a particular sound.**

Sounds produced by different instruments have different timbres. The sound of a note played on a trumpet has a different timbre from the same note played on a violin or flute. The trumpet, the violin, and the flute produce different overtones. The size, shape, and materials used also affect the timbre of an instrument.

☑ *Checkpoint* What factors affect the quality of a sound?

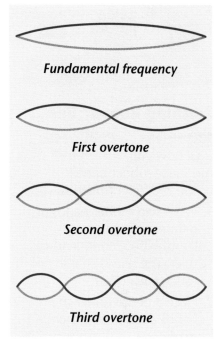

Fundamental frequency

First overtone

Second overtone

Third overtone

Figure 14 When half a wave takes up the whole string, a fundamental tone is produced (top). When some sections of the string vibrate faster than other parts, overtones are produced. *Inferring How does the pitch of each overtone compare with the pitch of the fundamental tone?*

Plucking Rubber Bands

Making Music

If the combination of the fundamental tone and the overtones results in a sound with a pleasing timbre and a clear pitch, the sound is considered **music.** Most music contains only a few fundamental tones and their overtones. **Music is a set of tones combined in ways that are pleasing to the ear.** The design of a musical instrument affects the overtones it produces when a note is played. All musical instruments produce vibrations when played. The material that vibrates varies. The major groups of instruments are strings, brass, woodwinds, and percussion.

Strings Stringed instruments have strings that vibrate when plucked, struck, or rubbed with a bow. A short string vibrates at a higher frequency and so produces a higher-pitched sound than a long string. As they play, musicians place their fingers on different places along the string to vary the pitch. The material, thickness, and tightness of a string also affects the pitch it produces. Instruments such as guitars, violins, and cellos also have a box, or sounding board. The box improves the quality of the sound produced by the strings. Larger stringed instruments, such as the cello and the double bass, produce lower pitches.

Brass and Woodwinds Brass instruments, such as trumpets and trombones, produce sound when the player's lips vibrate against the mouthpiece. This vibration causes the air column inside the instrument to vibrate. The musician adjusts the length of the air column by pressing valves or moving slides.

Figure 15 Violins are stringed instruments, flutes and clarinets are woodwinds, and trumpets are brass instruments. *Making Generalizations What do all these musical instruments have in common?*

176

Many woodwind instruments, such as clarinets and oboes, have a thin, flexible strip of material called a reed. When the player blows into the mouthpiece, the reed vibrates along with the column of air. The longer the column of air, the lower the pitch. Larger woodwind and brass instruments, such as the bassoon and the tuba, produce lower pitches.

Percussion Percussion instruments, such as drums, bells, cymbals, and xylophones, vibrate when struck. The sound they produce depends on the material from which they are made. It also depends on the size of the instrument, and the part of the instrument that is played. For example, larger drums usually produce lower pitches.

Figure 16 Percussion instruments vibrate when struck. *Predicting Describe the sound produced by a large drum compared with that of a small drum of the same material.*

☑ *Checkpoint* *What are the main groups of musical instruments?*

Noise

You are sitting comfortably in your classroom chair, watching a classmate write on the board. Suddenly, you hear the accidental scratch of fingernails as the chalk flies from your friend's grasp. The sound makes you wince.

Why is the squeak of fingernails on a chalkboard so unpleasant? One answer is that the squeak is noise. **Noise** is a mixture of sound waves that do not sound pleasing together. **Noise has no pleasing timbre and no identifiable pitch.** Consider the noise of chalk squeaking on a chalkboard or the noise of a jackhammer working in the street. The vibrations that produce these sounds are random. Even if an engine produces a hum that has a fundamental tone and overtones, the lack of rhythm in the sound makes us call it noise instead of music.

Sounds that are music to some people are noise to others. Some rock bands and orchestras play compositions with tones that seem to have no musical relationship. The sound produced when these notes are played together is called **dissonance.** Dissonance is music to the ears of people who enjoy the sound.

Music
CONNECTION

One of the most widely known compositions of Sergei Prokofiev, a Russian composer who lived from 1891 to 1953, is *Peter and the Wolf*. In this work, each instrument, or group of instruments, represents a character in the story.

In Your Journal

Listen to a recording of *Peter and the Wolf*. Write a review of this work. Do you agree with how Prokofiev matched instruments with characters? Which instrument would you have chosen to represent each character?

EXPLORING *Making Music*

The sound produced by a musical instrument depends on the instrument's size and shape. The material from which the instrument is made and the way it is played also affect the timbre of the sound.

Violin
The violin is a carefully crafted wooden box with strings. The strings are attached to tuning pegs, which can be turned to adjust the tension. When the strings are rubbed with a bow, they vibrate. The violinist controls the pitch by placing the fingers at different positions along the string.

Harp
The harp consists of a row of strings, each one a different length. The harpist gracefully plucks the strings with the fingers to produce music. The short strings produce higher pitches than the long strings do.

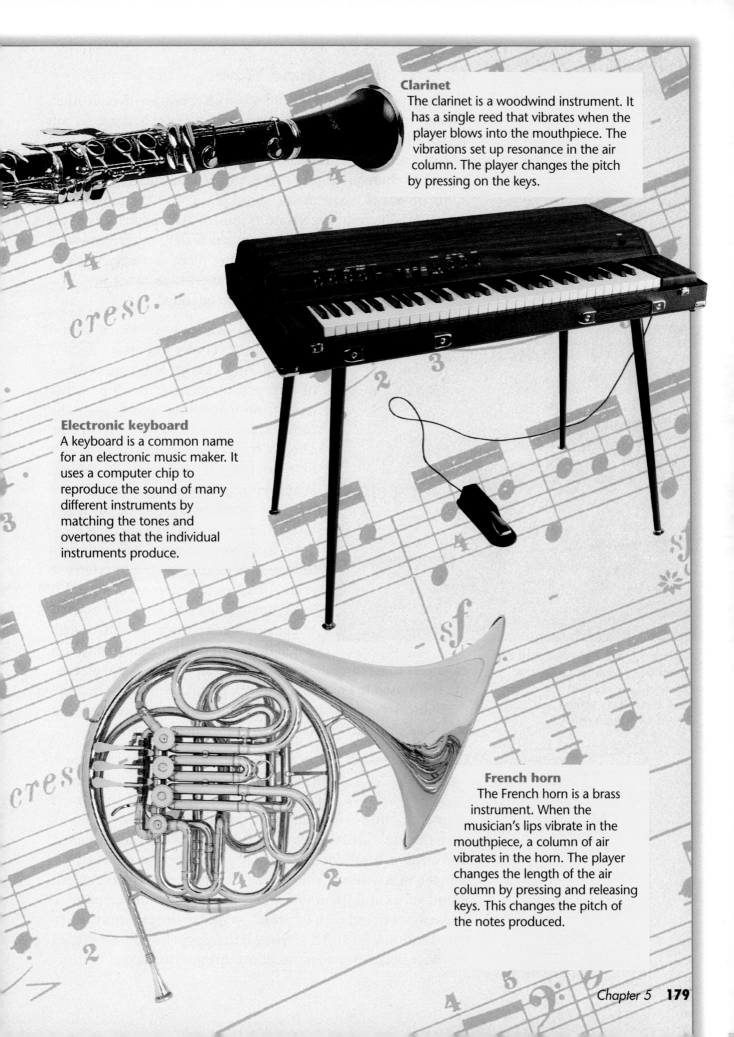

Clarinet
The clarinet is a woodwind instrument. It has a single reed that vibrates when the player blows into the mouthpiece. The vibrations set up resonance in the air column. The player changes the pitch by pressing on the keys.

Electronic keyboard
A keyboard is a common name for an electronic music maker. It uses a computer chip to reproduce the sound of many different instruments by matching the tones and overtones that the individual instruments produce.

French horn
The French horn is a brass instrument. When the musician's lips vibrate in the mouthpiece, a column of air vibrates in the horn. The player changes the length of the air column by pressing and releasing keys. This changes the pitch of the notes produced.

Interference of Sound Waves

You have probably heard sound waves interfering with each other, though you may not have known what you were hearing. As you recall, interference occurs when waves interact. **The amplitudes of two sound waves can combine, causing the loudness of the sound to change.** When interference is constructive, compressions of waves occur at the same place, and the amplitudes combine. The resulting sound is louder than either of the two original sounds. When the interference is destructive, compressions of one wave occur at the same place as rarefactions of another wave and the amplitudes cancel each other out. The resulting wave is softer or completely concealed.

Figure 17 A concert hall must be designed to provide the highest sound quality possible. The design should eliminate echoes and destructive interference.

Acoustics The way in which sound waves interact is very important in concert halls. In a concert hall, sound waves of different frequencies reach each listener from many directions at the same time. These sound waves may come directly from the orchestra or they may first bounce off the walls or ceiling. People sitting in various seats may hear different sounds because of the particular interactions of sound waves at their locations. In a poorly designed hall, seats may be located where destructive interference occurs. The sound will seem distorted.

Acoustics describe how well sounds can be heard in a particular room or hall. When designing auditoriums, acoustical engineers must carefully consider the shape of the room and the materials used to cover walls, floors, ceilings, and seats. Because they absorb sound instead of reflecting it, some materials can eliminate the reflected waves that cause interference.

Canceling Sounds Sometimes destructive interference is welcome. *INTEGRATING TECHNOLOGY* Airplane passengers use earphones to listen to music, but the throbbing of the plane's engines can drown out much of the sound. Some airline earphones use destructive interference to cancel out the steady engine noise. The earphones produce sound waves that interfere destructively with the engine sound. The passenger's ears receive both the engine sound waves and the sound waves produced by the earphones. These waves cancel each other out, so the passenger hears neither. Only the music is left. This type of technology also allows factories to reduce noise levels to protect the hearing of workers.

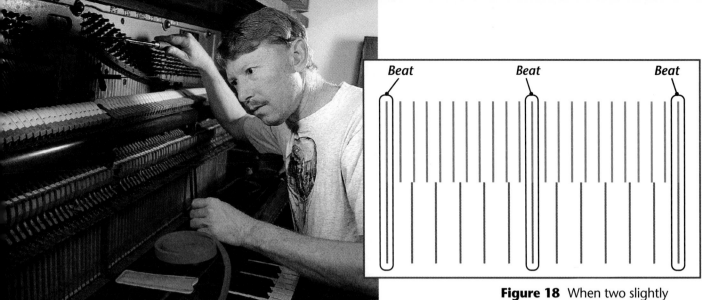

Figure 18 When two slightly different frequencies are combined, they interfere constructively at regular intervals (above right). A piano tuner listens to the sound of a note and a tuning fork together (above left). *Inferring How does the piano tuner know when a key is perfectly tuned?*

Beats If two sound waves are close in frequency, they can combine so that they interfere both constructively and destructively at regular intervals. Figure 18 shows how two frequencies can combine at certain times. The resulting sound gets louder and softer at regular intervals. The intervals depend on the difference between the two frequencies. The repeated changes in loudness are called **beats.**

Piano tuners use beats to tune pianos. A piano tuner strikes a tuning fork of a particular frequency and hits the corresponding key on a piano at the same time. If the tuner hears beats, that means that the frequency of vibration of the piano string does not exactly match that of the tuning fork. The tuner then adjusts the piano string until no beat can be heard. Then the piano key is perfectly tuned.

Section 3 Review

1. What factors determine the quality of a sound?
2. What is the difference between music and noise?
3. How can sounds cancel each other out?
4. How can the interference of two sound waves produce a louder sound?
5. What are beats?
6. **Thinking Critically Applying Concepts** Explain why a sound in an empty room will sound different from the same sound in a room with a carpet, curtains, and furniture.

Check Your Progress

CHAPTER PROJECT

Begin building the instrument you have designed. As you build your instrument, experiment with different materials to find the most appealing sound. How do different kinds of materials affect the sounds? Explore and experiment with the sounds your instrument makes. How does adding or removing certain parts or materials affect the loudness of the sound? How can you vary the pitch of your instrument?

Musical Notes

Musical instruments produce sound by setting up standing waves. Those waves can be on a string or in a column of air. In this lab, you will see how you can use bottles to produce different musical notes, maybe enough to play a simple tune.

Problem

How can you produce different musical notes with bottles of water?

Skills Focus

predicting, observing, inferring

Materials

3 identical glass bottles
water
masking tape
marking pen
pencil

Procedure

1. Label the bottles A, B, and C.
2. Put water in each bottle so that bottle A is one-fourth full, bottle B is half full, and bottle C is three-fourths full.
3. Make a chart in your lab notebook to organize your data. Measure the distance from the top of each bottle to the surface of the water. Then measure the height of the water in each bottle. Record your measurements.
4. Predict the difference in pitch you will hear if you blow across the top of each bottle in turn. Give reasons for your prediction.
5. Test your prediction by blowing over the top of each bottle. Listen to the sound you produce. Describe each sound in terms of its pitch— low, medium, or high. Record the pitch of each sound in your chart.

DATA CHART

Bottle	Length of Column of Air (cm)	Height of Water (cm)	Pitch Produced by Blowing Across Top of Bottle	Pitch Produced by Tapping Pencil on Side of Bottle
A				
B				
C				

6. When you gently tap the side of a bottle with a pencil, you produce another sound. Do you think the sound will be similar to or different from the sound produced by blowing across the top of the bottle? Explain.

7. Test your prediction by tapping on the side of each bottle with a pencil. Record the pitch of each sound.

Analyze and Conclude

1. Describe how the sound is produced in Step 5. Which bottle produced the highest pitch? Which bottle produced the lowest pitch?

2. What caused the change in pitch from bottle to bottle?

3. Describe how the sound is produced in Step 7. Which bottle produced the highest pitch? Which bottle produced the lowest pitch?

4. What caused the change in pitch from bottle to bottle? What change in pitch can you produce by tapping on a different part of the bottle?

5. Compare the sounds you produced by blowing across the bottles with those produced by tapping on the bottles. What was the difference in pitch for each bottle? Explain your observations.

6. Look at your chart to examine and evaluate your data. How does the length of the column of air affect the pitch? How does the height of the water affect the pitch?

7. **Think About It** Based on your observations in this lab, what statements can you make about the relationship between the sounds produced and the medium through which the sound travels?

More to Explore

To play simple tunes, you will need eight notes. Set up a row of eight bottles, each with a different amount of water. Adjust the water level in each bottle until you can play a simple scale. Practice playing a simple tune on your bottles.

SECTION 4 How You Hear Sound Waves

DISCOVER ···ACTIVITY····

Where Is the Sound Coming From?

1. Ask your partner to sit on a chair, with eyes closed.

2. Clap your hands near your partner's left ear. Ask your partner to tell you the direction the sound came from.

3. Now clap near your partner's right ear. Again, ask your partner to tell you the direction the sound came from. Continue clapping above your partner's head, in front of the face, and below the chin in random order. How well can your partner detect the direction the sound is coming from?

4. Switch places with your partner and repeat Steps 1–3.

Think It Over
Observing As you clap, record the answers given by your partner. Which locations are easily identified? Which locations were impossible to identify? Is there a pattern? If so, can you think of a possible explanation for this pattern?

GUIDE FOR READING

◆ What body systems interact to send sound messages to your brain?

◆ How do you hear sound?

Reading Tip As you read, draw a flowchart to show how you hear sound.

Key Terms ear canal • eardrum • middle ear • cochlea

The house is quiet. You are sound asleep. All of a sudden, your alarm clock goes off. Startled, you jump up out of bed. Your ears detected the sound waves produced by the alarm clock. **Your skeletal, circulatory, and nervous systems all play an important role in getting information to your brain.**

How You Hear Sound

How do your skeletal, circulatory, and nervous systems work together to get a sound message to your brain? Your ear has three main sections: the outer ear, the middle ear, and the inner ear. Each section has its own function. **The outer ear funnels sound waves, the middle ear transmits the waves inward, and the inner ear converts the sound waves into a form that your brain can understand.** The circulatory system carries food to and wastes away from all parts of the ear.

Outer Ear As the alarm clock rings, the sound waves reach your ears. The curved surface of the outermost part

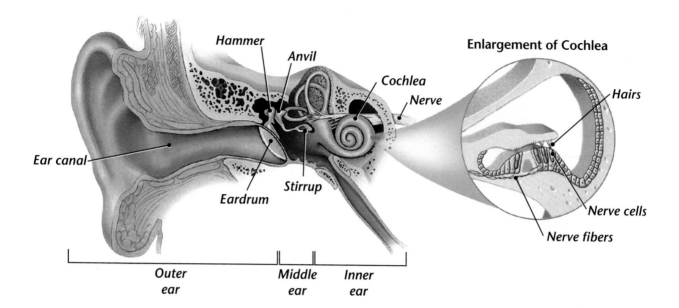

Hammer
Anvil
Cochlea
Nerve
Ear canal
Eardrum
Stirrup

Enlargement of Cochlea
Hairs
Nerve cells
Nerve fibers

Outer ear   Middle ear   Inner ear

Figure 19 The illustrations show the structure of the human ear and the inside of the cochlea. *Interpreting Diagrams How is sound transmitted through the middle ear?*

of your ear looks and acts like a funnel. It collects sound waves and directs them into a narrower region known as the **ear canal.** Your ear canal is a few centimeters long and ends at the eardrum. As shown in Figure 19, the **eardrum** is a small, tightly stretched, drumlike membrane. The sound waves make your eardrum vibrate, just as a drum vibrates when you beat it.

Middle Ear Behind the eardrum is an area called the middle ear. The **middle ear** contains the three smallest bones in the skeletal system—the hammer, the anvil, and the stirrup. The hammer is attached to the eardrum, so when the eardrum vibrates, the hammer does too. The hammer then hits the anvil, which then shakes the stirrup.

Inner Ear Another membrane separates the inner ear and middle ear. Behind this membrane is a cavity filled with liquid. This cavity, the **cochlea** (KAHK lee uh), is shaped like a snail shell. Inside, it is lined with over 10,000 nerve cells, called hair cells. These nerve cells have hairlike structures that float in the liquid in the cochlea. When the stirrup vibrates against the membrane, the vibrations pass into the cochlea and through the liquid. As the liquid moves, the hair-like structures sway, sending messages to the brain. The brain processes these messages and tells you that you've heard sound.

☑ *Checkpoint* **What are the three main areas of the ear?**

Listen to Sounds

How does sound travel to your ears?

ACTIVITY

1. Tie two strings to the handle of a metal spoon. Each string should be about 40 cm long.

2. Hold one end of each string in each hand. Bump the bowl of the spoon against a desk or other hard solid object. Listen to the sound.

3. Now wrap the ends of the string around your fingers.

4. Put your index fingers up against your ears and bump the spoon against the object again.

Inferring How does the first sound compare with the sound you heard with your fingers up against your ears? What can you conclude about how sound travels to your ears?

Figure 20 Hearing aids can make sounds louder as the sounds enter the ear.

Hearing Loss

INTEGRATING HEALTH The human ear can normally detect sounds as soft as breathing (about 2–10 dB). The normal range of frequencies a person can hear is 20–20,000 Hz. However, when hearing loss occurs, a person may have difficulty hearing soft sounds or high-pitched sounds. Many people suffer hearing loss as a result of injury, infection, or aging.

Hearing Loss Due to Injury or Infection A head injury can cause the tiny hammer, anvil, and stirrup to disconnect from each other. When this happens, sound cannot be transmitted through the middle ear. Surgery can usually correct this type of hearing loss.

If your eardrum becomes damaged or punctured, you may experience hearing loss. (Imagine trying to play a torn drum!) For this reason, it is dangerous to put objects into your ear, even to clean it. Viral or bacterial infections can also damage the delicate inner ear, causing permanent hearing loss.

Hearing Loss Due to Aging The most common type of hearing loss occurs gradually as people age. As a person gets older, the tiny hair cells in the cochlea become less effective at detecting the signals. Many older people have difficulty hearing higher-frequency sounds.

Extended exposure to loud sounds can damage the hair cells. If these cells are damaged by loud sounds, they can no longer transmit signals to the brain. You can prevent this type of hearing loss by wearing ear plugs or other hearing protection when you know you are going to be exposed to loud noises.

Some types of hearing loss can be helped using hearing aids. Hearing aids are amplifiers. Some are so tiny that they can fit invisibly in the ear. Others are made specifically for a person's hearing loss and amplify mainly the frequencies that the person has lost the ability to hear.

Section 4 Review

1. How do the skeletal, circulatory, and nervous systems interact to help you hear sound?
2. How do your ears detect sound waves?
3. How can sound damage your hearing?
4. **Thinking Critically Classifying** Make a chart that lists some common sounds you might hear in a day. Estimate the loudness of each sound and state whether each one could produce hearing loss. (*Hint:* Refer to Figure 8 on page 169.)

Science at Home

Sound Survey Invite family members to make a survey of the kinds of sounds they hear throughout one day. Have each member rate the sounds as quiet, normal, loud, or painful. Then rate each sound as pleasant, neutral, or annoying. State the source of each sound, the location, the time of day, and the approximate length of time that they are exposed to the sound. How are the ratings alike and different?

Keeping It Quiet...

A construction worker operates a jackhammer; a woman waits in a noisy subway station; a factory worker uses loud machinery. All three are victims of noise pollution. In the United States, 80 million people say they are "continually" bothered by noise, and 40 million face danger to their health.

One burst of sound from a passing truck can be enough to raise blood pressure. People start to feel pain at about 120 decibels. Exposure to even 85 decibels (the noise level of a kitchen blender or a loudly crying baby) can eventually damage the hair cells of the cochlea. Noise that "doesn't hurt" can still damage your hearing. As many as 16 million Americans may have permanent hearing loss caused by noise. What can we do to keep it quiet?

The Issues

What Can Individual People Do? Some work conditions are noisier than others. Construction workers, factory employees, and people who drive large vehicles are often at risk. All workers in noisy environments can benefit from ear protectors, such as plugs or headphone-like mufflers. Ear protectors can reduce noise levels by 35 decibels.

A listener at a rock concert, a hunter firing a rifle, or someone using an electric drill can also prevent damage with ear protectors. In addition, people should, if possible, avoid extreme noise. They can buy quieter machines and respect neighbors by not using noisy machines, such as lawn mowers and snow blowers, at quiet times of day or night. Simply turning down the volume on headphones, radios, CD players, and tape players can prevent one of the most frequent causes of permanent hearing loss in young people.

What Can Communities Do?
Transportation—planes, trains, trucks, and cars— is the largest source of noise pollution. Fifteen million Americans live near airports or under airport flight paths. Careful planning to locate highways and airports away from homes and buildings can reduce noise. Cities and towns can also prohibit flights late at night.

Many communities have laws against noise of more than a fixed decibel level, but these laws are not always enforced. In some cities "noise police" can fine the owners of noisy equipment.

What Can Government Do? A national Office of Noise Abatement and Control was set up in the 1970s. It required labels on power tools and lawnmowers telling how much noise they make. In 1982, this office was closed down. Some lawmakers want to bring the office back and have nationwide limits to many types of noise. However, critics say that national laws have little effect in controlling noise. The federal government could also encourage—and pay for—research into making quieter vehicles and machines.

You Decide

1. **Identify the Problem**
   In your own words, describe the problem of noise pollution.

2. **Analyze the Options**
   List as many methods as you can for dealing with noise. How would each method work to reduce noise or to protect people from noise? Who would be affected by each method?

3. **Find a Solution**
   Propose one method for reducing noise in your community. Make a poster that encourages people to carry out your proposal.

Applications of Sound Waves

DISCOVER

How Can You Use Time to Measure Distance?

1. Measure a distance 3 meters from a wall and mark the spot with a piece of masking tape.

2. Roll a soft ball in a straight line from that spot toward the wall. What happens to the ball?

3. Roll the ball again. Try to roll the ball at the same speed each time. Have a classmate use a stopwatch to record the time it takes for the ball to leave your hand, reflect off the wall, and then return to you.

4. Now move 6 meters away from the wall. Mark the spot with tape. Repeat Steps 2 and 3.

5. Compare the time for both distances.

Think It Over

Inferring What does the difference in time tell you about the distance the ball has traveled?

GUIDE FOR READING

◆ How is sonar used to measure distances?

◆ Why do some animals use echolocation?

◆ How is ultrasound used in medicine?

Reading Tip As you read, write a sentence or two that describes each application of sound waves.

Key Terms sonar
• echolocation • sonogram

You and your friend are in a long, dark cave. Every sound you make seems to come right back to you. For fun, both of you shout and scream and then listen as the echoes bounce around the cave.

Reflection of Sound Waves

When a sound wave hits a surface through which it cannot pass, it bounces back, or reflects. A reflected sound wave is called an echo.

Sometimes an echo is much fainter than the original sound. This is usually because some of the energy of the wave is absorbed along the way. Some materials reflect sound very well, while others absorb most of the sound that strikes them. Most of the practical applications of sound are based on the fact that sound reflects off some surfaces. The physical properties of everyday materials determine their sound applications.

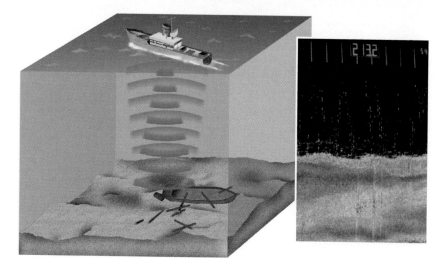

Figure 21 Sonar is used to determine distances and to locate objects under water.
Applying Concepts What two quantities must be known to calculate how far a sound wave has traveled?

Sonar

Reflected sound waves have many uses. They can be used to determine the depth of water, to locate a sunken shipwreck or cargo, to find schools of fish, or to locate boats out on the ocean.

Sonar is a system of detecting reflected sound waves. The word *sonar* comes from the initial letters of **so**und **n**avigation **a**nd **r**anging. "Navigation" means finding your way around on the ocean (or in the air), and "ranging" means finding the distance between objects. Submarines and ships use sonar to detect other submarines and ships by sending sound waves through the water close to the surface. When the waves hit another boat near the surface of the water, they reflect back and are picked up by the sonar device.

How Sonar Works A sonar machine, or depth finder, produces a burst of high-frequency ultrasonic sound waves that travels through the water. When the waves hit an object or the ocean floor, they reflect. The reflected waves are detected by the sonar machine. **The sonar device measures the time it takes to detect the reflected sound waves.** It uses the data to calculate the distance that the sound has traveled. The intensity of the reflected waves tells the size and shape of the object that reflected the waves.

Calculating Distances The farther a sound wave travels before bouncing off a barrier, the longer it takes to come back. To calculate the depth of water, the sonar machine must calculate the distance traveled by the sound waves. It measures the time taken for the waves to come back. The sonar device then multiplies the speed of sound in water by the time taken. The total distance traveled by the sound is twice the depth of the water. Because the waves traveled to the bottom and then back, the sonar machine divides the total distance by two to find the actual depth.

☑ *Checkpoint* What are three uses for sonar?

Figure 22 Elephants communicate using low-frequency, or infrasonic, sound waves.
Applying Concepts How do elephants benefit from an ability to hear and produce infrasonic sound waves?

Uses of Ultrasound and Infrasound

The dog trainer stands quietly, watching the dog a short distance away. To get the dog's attention, the trainer blows into a small whistle. You don't hear a thing. But the dog stops, cocks an ear, and then comes running toward the trainer. What did the dog hear that you didn't? Dogs can hear ultrasonic frequencies of over 20,000 Hz, which is the upper limit for humans.

Some animals communicate using sounds with frequencies that humans cannot hear. When elephants get upset, they stomp on the ground. The stomping produces low-frequency, or infrasonic, sound waves—too low for humans to hear. The waves travel through the ground for distances of up to 50 kilometers and can be detected by other elephants.

Ultrasound in the Ocean Dolphins and whales emit pings of sound at frequencies that are high, but not too high for you to hear. **Echolocation** (ek oh loh KAY shun) is the use of sound waves to determine distances or to locate objects. Dolphins and whales use echolocation to find their way in the ocean, and to find their prey.

INTEGRATING
LIFE SCIENCE

It was once thought that fish couldn't hear the high frequencies that dolphins and whales emit. But scientists have discovered that shad, herring, and some other fish can hear sounds as high as 180,000 Hz, nine times as high as the highest frequency you can hear. The fish may use this ability to avoid being eaten by dolphins and whales.

Because sound waves travel so well in water, ultrasound has many uses in the sea. Some fisherman attach ultrasonic beepers to their nets. The ultrasound annoys the dolphins, who then swim away from the nets and do not get caught. Other devices can protect divers from sharks by surrounding the divers with ultrasonic waves that keep sharks away.

Figure 23 Dolphins emit high-frequency sounds to communicate with each other, to navigate, and to find food.

Echolocation in Bats Imagine walking around in a totally dark room. You would bump into the walls and furniture quite often. Bats, however, can fly around dark areas and not bump into anything. **Bats use echolocation to navigate and to find food.**

As bats fly, they send out pulses of sound at frequencies of about 100,000 Hz. Then they listen to how long the sound takes to return. By picking up the reflections, or echoes, a bat can tell if it is about to bump into something. Though bats are not blind, they rely more on their hearing than on their vision to "see" where they are going. Bats also can use echolocation to hunt. Most bats hunt insects, but some hunt small animals such as mice and frogs.

Figure 24 Bats use echolocation to locate food and to avoid bumping into objects. Their large ears are used for collecting sound waves.

☑ *Checkpoint* *How does echolocation benefit animals that use it?*

Ultrasound in Medicine Ultrasound allows doctors to get a picture, called a **sonogram,** of the inside of the human body. **Doctors use ultrasound to look inside the human body and to diagnose and treat medical conditions.**

INTEGRATING HEALTH

To examine a pregnant woman, the doctor holds a small probe on the woman's abdomen. The probe generates very high-frequency sound waves (about 4 million Hz). The ultrasound device detects and measures the ultrasonic waves that bounce back. By analysing the intensity and frequency of the reflected waves, the device builds up a picture. The sonogram can show the position of the developing baby. Sonograms can also show if more than one baby is to be born.

Because of their high frequency, carefully focused ultrasound waves can also painlessly destroy unwanted tissues. In many cases ultrasound can eliminate the need for surgery.

Figure 25 A doctor examines a pregnant woman with an ultrasound machine. A picture of the developing baby is displayed on a screen.

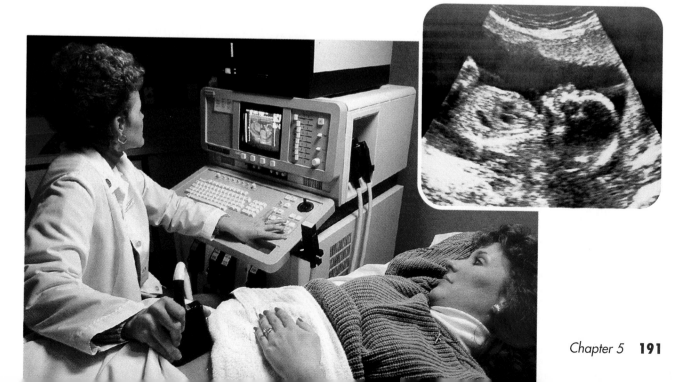

Figure 26 Some examples of common household objects that use ultrasound include an automatic focus camera, an ultrasonic toothbrush, and an ultrasonic jewelry cleaner.

Ultrasound at Home As technology progresses, more and more everyday objects use ultrasonic waves. Imagine cleaning your teeth with sound! If you have used one of the newer electric toothbrushes, you have done just that. The toothbrush sends out high-frequency sound waves that can reach into places that the bristles of the brush cannot.

Ultrasonic jewelry cleaners can clean delicate pieces of jewelry that might be damaged by brushes or harsh detergents. The tub is filled with water and a mild detergent. When the cleaner is switched on, the sound waves move through the water. When they reach the jewelry, the vibrations shake the dirt away, without causing scratches or other damage.

Some cameras use ultrasound to focus automatically. You look through the viewfinder at the object to be photographed. As you push the button to take a picture, the camera sends out ultrasonic waves that reflect off the object and travel back to the camera. The camera measures the time taken for the waves to come back, just like a sonar machine. The camera then calculates the distance to the object and adjusts the lens accordingly.

Section 5 Review

1. What is sonar?
2. How do animals use ultrasound and infrasound?
3. How is ultrasound used in medicine?
4. What household devices use sound waves? What is the function of sound in each device?
5. **Thinking Critically** **Calculating** The speed of sound in ocean water is about 1,530 m/s. If it takes 3 seconds for a sound wave to travel from the bottom of the ocean back to a ship, what is the depth of the water?

Check Your Progress
```
CHAPTER PROJECT
```
Test your musical instrument. Is it pleasing to the ear? Can you play a wide range of notes? Can you vary the loudness? Make further adjustments to your instrument. From what you have learned about pitch and frequency, what changes can you make to produce different notes? You may want to try tuning your instrument with a piano or pitch pipe. Try to play a musical scale or a simple song. Or make up your own song.

SECTION 1 — The Nature of Sound Waves

Key Ideas

◆ Sound is a disturbance that travels through a medium as a longitudinal wave.

◆ The speed at which sound travels through a medium depends on the elasticity, density, and temperature of the medium.

Key Terms

sound   larynx   elasticity

SECTION 2 — Properties of Sound Waves

Key Ideas

◆ A sound wave of greater intensity sounds louder. Loudness is measured in decibels.

◆ The pitch of a sound that you hear depends on the frequency of the sound wave.

◆ As a sound source moves toward the listener, the waves reach the listener with a higher frequency. The pitch appears to increase because of the Doppler effect.

Key Terms

intensity   infrasound
loudness   pitch
decibels (dB)   Doppler effect
ultrasound

SECTION 3 — Combining Sound Waves

Key Ideas

◆ The blending of the fundamental tone and the overtones makes up the characteristic sound quality, or timbre, of a particular sound.

◆ Music is a set of tones that combine in ways that are pleasing to the ear.

◆ Noise has no pleasing timbre or identifiable pitch.

◆ Interference occurs when two or more sound waves interact.

Key Terms

timbre   noise   acoustics
music   dissonance   beats

SECTION 4 — How You Hear Sound Waves

INTEGRATING LIFE SCIENCE

Key Ideas

◆ The skeletal, circulatory, and nervous systems interact and help you hear sound.

◆ The outer ear funnels sound waves, the middle ear transmits the sound inward, and the inner ear converts the sound for your brain.

Key Terms

ear canal   eardrum   middle ear   cochlea

SECTION 5 — Applications of Sound Waves

Key Ideas

◆ A sonar system detects reflected sound waves.

◆ Animals use sound waves to communicate, to navigate, and to find food.

◆ Ultrasound is used to diagnose and treat medical conditions.

Key Terms

sonar   echolocation   sonogram

Organizing Information

Concept Map Copy the concept map about sound onto a separate sheet of paper. Then complete it and add a title. (For more on concept maps, see the Skills Handbook.)

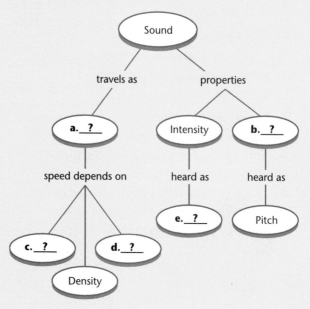

Reviewing Content

 Review key concepts online using iText at www.phschool.com

Multiple Choice
Choose the letter of the best answer.

1. Sound does *not* travel through
   a. water.
   b. steel rails.
   c. wooden doors.
   d. outer space.

2. The Doppler effect causes an apparent change in
   a. loudness.
   b. intensity.
   c. pitch.
   d. resonance.

3. Beats result from
   a. reflection.
   b. refraction.
   c. diffraction.
   d. interference.

4. The hammer, anvil, and stirrup are in the
   a. outer ear.
   b. middle ear.
   c. inner ear.
   d. cochlea.

5. Sonar is used to find
   a. time.
   b. speed.
   c. angle of reflection.
   d. distance.

True or False
If the statement is true, write true. If it is false, change the underlined word or words to make the statement true.

6. Sound travels <u>faster</u> in air than in water.
7. Loudness is how the ear perceives <u>pitch</u>.
8. <u>Timbre</u> is what you hear as the quality of sound.
9. The <u>inner</u> ear contains the cochlea.
10. The system of using sound to measure distance is called <u>acoustics</u>.

Checking Concepts

11. When a drum vibrates, the air molecules that begin vibrating next to it do not reach your ear, yet you hear the sound of the drum. Explain.

12. What are the factors that affect the sound of a vibrating guitar string?

13. As a car drives past you, the driver keeps a hand on the horn. Describe what you hear as the car approaches you, then passes by.

14. How can loud noises damage your hearing?

15. Why is ultrasound useful in medicine?

16. **Writing to Learn** You have been hired to produce an informational brochure about sound. This brochure will be presented to soon-to-arrive visitors from outer space. They have no concept of sound, and everything they learn will come from your brochure. Write a brief description of sound for the visitors.

Thinking Critically

17. **Comparing and Contrasting** How do sound waves behave like the waves in spring toys? How are they different?

18. **Controlling Variables** If you are measuring the speed of sound, what variable(s) should you try to keep constant?

19. **Calculating** At 0°C, sound travels through air at a speed of 330 m/s. At this speed, how long would it take sound to travel a distance of 1000 m? *(Hint: Speed = Distance/Time)*

20. **Applying Concepts** If one musician plays a note on an instrument and another plays a slightly higher note on a similar instrument, what will you hear?

21. **Inferring** Thunder and lightning happen at the same time. Why do you think you usually see the lightning before you hear the thunder?

Applying Skills

The table below shows the range of frequencies produced and heard by various animals and birds. Use the data to answer Questions 22–23.

Animal	Highest Frequency Heard (Hz)	Highest Frequency Produced (Hz)
Human	20,000	1,100
Dog	50,000	1,800
Cat	65,000	1,500
Bat	120,000	120,000
Porpoise	150,000	120,000
Frog	10,000	8,000
Robin	21,000	13,000

22. **Graphing** Draw a bar graph to compare the highest frequencies heard by each animal and the highest frequencies produced by each animal.

23. **Calculating** If the speed of sound in air is 330 m/s, calculate the wavelength of the highest-frequency sound heard by humans. Use the following formula:

$$Wavelength = \frac{Speed}{Frequency}$$

CHAPTER PROJECT

Performance Assessment

Present the Project Describe your instrument and explain how it was built. Discuss how you solved any design problems. Using your instrument, demonstrate how you can play different sounds. Show how you change the pitch or loudness of your instrument.

Reflect and Record In your journal write an evaluation of your project. How would you improve on the design of the instrument? How is your instrument like or different from the instruments your classmates built?

Test Preparation
Use these questions to practice for standardized tests.

Study the chart. Then answer Questions 24–26.

Medium	Speed of Sound (m/s)
Rubber	60
Air at 0°C	330
Air at 25°C	346
Lead	1,210
Water at 25°C	1,498
Silver	2,680
Wood (Oak)	3,850
Glass	4,540
Aluminum	5,000
Iron	5,100
Steel	5,200

24. What information does this table provide?
    A the speed of sound in different states of the same matter
    B the speed of sound over different distances
    C the speed of sound at several different temperatures
    D the speed of sound in different media

25. In which medium does sound travel most slowly?
    F water   G air
    H steel   J rubber

26. Sound travels faster through air at 25°C than it does at 0°C. This shows that sound travels
    A faster at lower temperatures.
    B more slowly at lower temperatures.
    C more slowly at higher temperatures.
    D only at temperatures above 0°C.

Turning Down the Volume on
SONIC BOOMS

Dr. Christine Mann Darden (center) grew up in Monroe, North Carolina. She received her Ph.D. in Mechanical Engineering at George Washington University in Washington, D.C. A national expert on sonic booms, she now works at NASA's Langley Research Center in Hampton, Virginia. She manages a group of scientists who are developing supersonic airplanes. Dr. Darden is shown here with other members of the Sonic Boom Group, Kathy Needleman (left) and Robert Mack (right).

*I*t happens every time a space shuttle returns to Earth. The spacecraft drops down from orbit and streaks toward its landing site in Florida or California. A few seconds after it passes overhead—BOOM! A window-rattling sound like a giant cannon shot is heard. Most scientists at the space center are monitoring the shuttle itself when it comes down from a mission. But Dr. Christine Darden is more interested in that big boom.

Dr. Darden is a research engineer at the National Aeronautics and Space Administration (NASA). She is in charge of the space agency's Sonic Boom Group. Her team of scientists is investigating the distinctive "sound print" made by aircraft that travel faster than the speed of sound. Dr. Darden and her co-workers are looking for ways to soften sonic booms. They hope to make supersonic travel—travel at speeds faster than the speed of sound—more common in the future.

Talking with Dr. Christine Darden

Breaking the Sound Barrier

The sound barrier was first broken in 1947. Since then, people have complained about sonic booms so much that the government has passed regulations. It's now against the law to fly most aircraft at supersonic speeds over the United States.

"If it is loud enough, a sonic boom can actually break windows and do damage to buildings," says Dr. Darden. "People find it very disturbing. Right now, the boom is one of the biggest obstacles to commercial supersonic air service."

Today supersonic aircraft such as the Concorde fly mainly over the ocean. But what if scientists can find ways to lower the volume of sonic booms? Then someday supersonic commercial jets may be allowed to fly across the country.

What Is a Sonic Boom?

You have probably heard the sound that is made when an airplane breaks the sound barrier. A sonic boom sounds like a clap of thunder or a sharp explosion high in the sky. Just what are you hearing?

"A sonic boom is a compression or pressure wave," Dr. Darden explains. "An airplane pushes a wave of air molecules ahead of it as it travels forward, just as a ship's bow pushes out a wave as it moves through the water. Those compressions travel outward from the plane as a shock wave of high pressure. When that shock wave reaches our ears, we hear it as a boom."

Both the SR-71 Blackbird (above) and F-16 (opposite page) are military supersonic planes.

"Think of blowing up a balloon," Dr. Darden says. "With the balloon inflated, the air on the inside is much more compressed than the air on the outside. When the balloon pops, the compression immediately flies outward in the form of a shock wave."

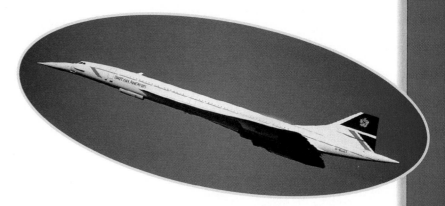

Scheduled flights (to the United States) of the Concorde, a supersonic commercial plane, are made only between New York and London or Paris.

How Do You Research What You Can't See?

"Part of our work is coming up with new ways to observe and measure the phenomenon we're studying," says Dr. Darden. "For example, we know that all waves have similar properties. So we look at how waves behave in water to tell us something about how they behave in the air."

Choosing Engineering

Dr. Darden's study of waves in water and air is a long way from her first career as a math teacher. In the late 1960s, she was teaching in a school in Hampton, Virginia. At that time, the NASA labs nearby were working on a program to send astronauts to the moon. Dr. Darden went to work for NASA as a mathematician.

She quickly became fascinated with the work of the NASA research engineers. "They were the ones who were working with the really tough challenges of the program," she says. "They were doing the interesting, hands-on work." As a result of her experience, she decided to get a graduate degree in engineering.

How Do You Test Supersonic Aircraft?

Working hands-on is one way that Dr. Darden and her team study how airplanes create sonic booms. They

1 A sonic boom results when an airplane moves at supersonic speed. Air is compressed at the front of the plane, creating shock waves.

2 The shock waves move out behind the plane in a cone shape.

3 When the shock waves reach the ground, people hear them as a sonic boom.

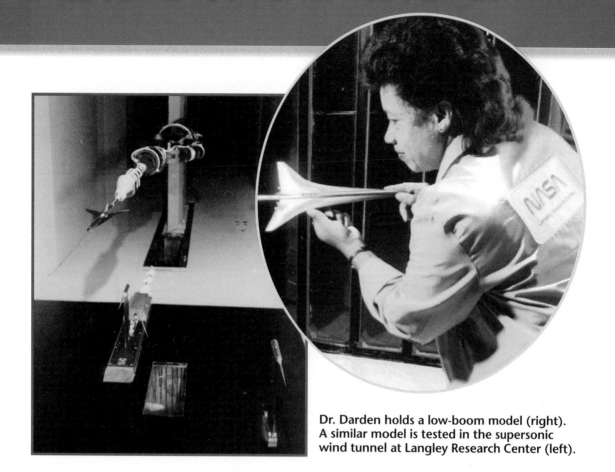

Dr. Darden holds a low-boom model (right). A similar model is tested in the supersonic wind tunnel at Langley Research Center (left).

"fly" model aircraft in a high-speed wind tunnel. The scientists place the steel models in the tunnel and watch how they behave in winds moving at up to three times the speed of sound. (The speed of sound varies with altitude and air pressure. At sea level on a 16°C day, the speed of sound is about 1,207 kilometers per hour.)

Instruments on the sides of the tunnel allow Dr. Darden to "hear" the sonic boom created by the model. By adding very fine smoke, she can even watch how the air moves over the plane. "We can actually see the shock wave," she says.

Can the Sonic Boom Effect Be Reduced?

Dr. Darden and her group at NASA have found that the shape of an aircraft determines the size of the boom it creates. They have performed tests with computer programs, on actual supersonic

jets, and in wind tunnels. Their experiments have shown that angling the wings back sharply reduces the size of the shock wave and the loudness of the sonic boom. But the same features that make planes quieter also make them harder to fly.

"You could put a needle up there supersonically and you wouldn't get a sonic boom," explains Dr. Darden. "But you wouldn't have much of an airplane, either."

In Your Journal

In her research, Dr. Darden made predictions about how the angle of an airplane wing might affect a sonic boom. Then her team set up a series of experiments to test these predictions.

Now think of different-shaped boats moving through water: a kayak, a tugboat, and a rowboat. Predict the type of wave that each boat will make. How could you use models to test your predictions?

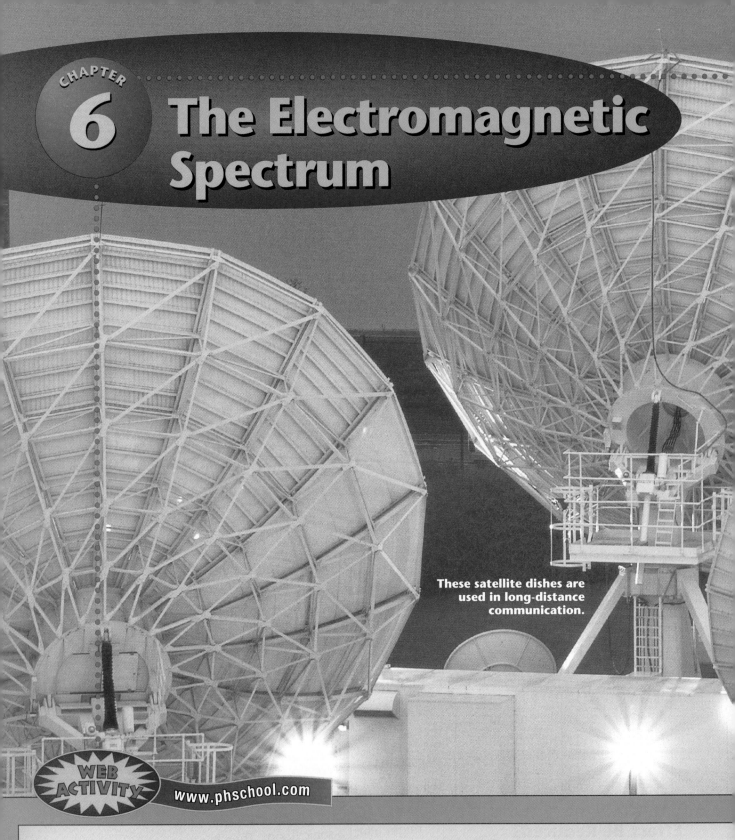

CHAPTER

6 The Electromagnetic Spectrum

These satellite dishes are used in long-distance communication.

WEB ACTIVITY
www.phschool.com

You're on the Air

Communication technology is developing at a rapid rate. Technology now makes it possible to store and process huge amounts of information. Communication technology will continue to improve as scientific advances are made. Look around you! How do people communicate? Radios, televisions, cellular phones, and electronic pagers are part of everyday life. Wireless communication has made it convenient for people to communicate anytime and anywhere.

In this chapter you will study and research the use of several wireless communication devices.

Your Goal To collect data about when, where, and why people use radios, televisions, cellular telephones, and other kinds of communication devices.

To complete this project you must
- design a survey sheet about the use of communication devices
- distribute your survey sheet to students in your school and to adults in your community
- compile and analyze your data
- create graphs to show your results

Get Started To get started, brainstorm what kinds of questions you will ask. Think about the format and content of your survey sheet. How might you involve students in other classes so you can gather more data?

Check Your Progress You will be working on this project as you study this chapter. To keep your project on track, look for Check Your Progress boxes at the following points.
Section 2 Review, page 214: Design and distribute your survey.
Section 4 Review, page 229: Compile, analyze, and graph your results.

Present Your Project At the end of the chapter (page 235), you will present the results of your survey to the class.

TEKS

In addition to process TEKS, this chapter addresses these concept TEKS as they relate to the chapter's topics.

(8.7) The student knows that there is a relationship between force and motion. The student is expected to:
(B) recognize that waves are generated and can travel through different media.

(8.10) The student knows that complex interactions occur between matter and energy. The student is expected to:
(A) illustrate interactions between matter and energy including specific heat.

1 The Nature of Electromagnetic Waves

How Does a Beam of Light Travel?

1. Punch a small hole (about 0.5 cm in diameter) in each of four large index cards.

2. Stand each card upright so that the long side of the index card is on the tabletop. Use binder clips or modeling clay to hold the cards upright.

3. Space the cards about 10 cm apart. To make sure the holes in the cards are in a straight line, run a piece of string through the four holes and pull it tight.

4. Place the flashlight in front of the card nearest you. Shut off all the lights, so that the only light you see comes from the flashlight. What do you see on the wall?

5. Move one of the cards sideways about 3 cm and repeat Step 4. Now what do you see on the wall?

Think It Over

Inferring Explain what happened in Step 5. What does this activity tell you about the path of light?

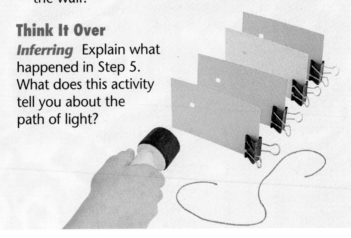

GUIDE FOR READING

◆ What is an electromagnetic wave?

◆ What are the properties of light?

Reading Tip As you read, keep a list of the words that are used to describe the nature of electromagnetic waves.

Key Terms
• electromagnetic wave
• electromagnetic radiation
• polarized light
• photoelectric effect
• photon

Close your eyes for a moment and imagine you are in a shower of rain. Are you getting wet? Do you feel anything? Believe it or not, you are being "showered." Not by rain but by waves, most of which you cannot feel or hear. As you read this, you are surrounded by radio waves, infrared waves, visible light, ultraviolet waves, and maybe even tiny amounts of X-rays and gamma rays. If you have ever tuned a radio, spoken on a cordless or cellular phone, felt warmth on your skin, turned on a light, or had an X-ray taken, you have experienced electromagnetic waves.

Figure 1 Even though you may not feel them, you are being showered by electromagnetic waves.

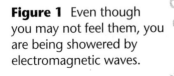

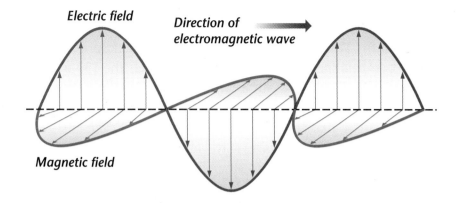

Figure 2 An electromagnetic wave consists of electric and magnetic fields, which vibrate at right angles to each other.

Electromagnetic Waves

You have seen waves travel through water and move along ropes and springs. You have also heard sound waves travel through air, metal, and water. All these waves have two things in common—they transfer energy from one place to another, and they require a medium through which to travel. Recall that a medium is the matter through which a wave travels.

However, waves called electromagnetic waves can transfer energy with or without a medium. **Electromagnetic waves** are transverse waves that have some electrical properties and some magnetic properties. **An electromagnetic wave consists of changing electric and magnetic fields.**

Electric and Magnetic Fields Electromagnetic waves travel as vibrations in electric and magnetic fields. An electric field is a region in which charged particles can be pushed or pulled. Wherever there is an electric charge, there is an electric field associated with it. A moving electric charge is part of an electric current.

An electric current is surrounded by a magnetic field. A magnetic field is a region in which magnetic forces are present. If you place a paper clip near a magnet, the paper clip moves toward the magnet because of the magnetic field surrounding the magnet.

When the electric field changes, so does the magnetic field. The changing magnetic field causes the electric field to change. When one field vibrates, so does the other. In this way, the two fields constantly cause each other to change. The result is an electromagnetic wave, as shown in Figure 2.

Electromagnetic Radiation The energy that is transferred by electromagnetic waves is called **electromagnetic radiation.** Because electromagnetic radiation does not need a medium, it can travel through the vacuum of outer space. If it could not, light from the sun and stars could not travel through space to Earth. NASA officials could not make contact with space shuttles in orbit.

How Do Light Beams Behave?

1. Fill two plastic cups with water. Slowly pour the water from the two cups into a sink. Aim the stream of water from one cup across the path of the water from the other cup.

2. How do the two streams interfere with each other?

3. Now darken a room and project a slide from a slide projector onto the wall. Shine a flashlight beam across the projector beam.

4. How do the two beams of light interfere with each other? What effect does the interference have on the projected picture?

Drawing Conclusions How is the interference between light beams different from that between water streams? Does this activity support a wave model or a particle model of light? Explain.

Speed of Electromagnetic Waves All electromagnetic waves travel at the same speed—about 300,000,000 meters per second in a vacuum. You can also express this as 300,000 kilometers per second. At this speed, light from the sun travels the 150 million kilometers to Earth in about 8 minutes. That's really fast! When electromagnetic waves travel through a medium such as the atmosphere or glass, they travel more slowly. But even at slower speeds, electromagnetic waves travel about a million times faster than sound can travel in air.

☑ *Checkpoint* *What is the speed of electromagnetic waves when they travel in a vacuum?*

Waves or Particles?

In general, the wave model can explain many of the properties of electromagnetic radiation. However, some properties of electromagnetic radiation do not fit the wave model. **Light has many of the properties of waves. But light can also act as though it is a stream of particles.**

When light passes through a polarizing filter, it has the properties of a wave. An ordinary beam of light has waves that vibrate in all directions. A polarizing filter acts as though it has tiny slits that are either horizontal or vertical. When light enters a polarizing filter, only some waves can pass through. The light that passes through is called **polarized light.**

To help you understand polarization, think of waves of light as being like transverse waves on a rope. They vibrate up and down, left and right, or at any other angle. If you shake a rope through a fence with vertical slats, as shown in Figure 3, only waves that vibrate up and down will pass through. The other waves are blocked. A polarizing filter acts like the slats in a fence. It allows only waves that vibrate in one direction to pass through.

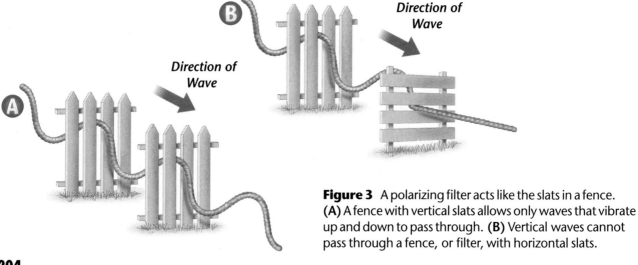

Figure 3 A polarizing filter acts like the slats in a fence. **(A)** A fence with vertical slats allows only waves that vibrate up and down to pass through. **(B)** Vertical waves cannot pass through a fence, or filter, with horizontal slats.

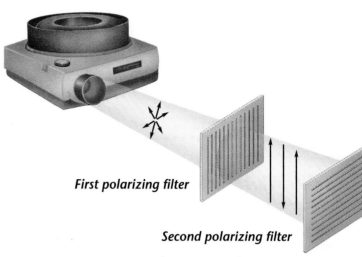

First polarizing filter

Second polarizing filter

Figure 4 The first polarizing filter allows only waves that vibrate up and down to pass through. When a second polarizing filter is placed in front of the first, and at right angles to it, no light passes through. *Applying Concepts Does the way that light passes through a polarizing filter support the wave model or the particle model of light?*

If you place one polarizing filter on top of another and rotate one of them, you will see how the amount of light coming through changes. If the two polarizing filters are placed so that one is rotated 90° from the other, no light can come through. All the light is blocked.

Here is an example of how light can act like a stream of particles. When a beam of light shines on some substances, it causes the electrons of their atoms to move. This movement causes an electric current to flow. Sometimes light can even knock electrons out of the substance. This is called the **photoelectric effect.** The photoelectric effect can only be explained by thinking of light as a stream of tiny packets, or particles, of energy. Each packet is called a **photon.** Albert Einstein explained the photoelectric effect in 1905.

It may be difficult for you to picture light as being particles and waves at the same time. Many scientists find it difficult, too. However, both models are necessary to explain the properties of light and other forms of electromagnetic radiation.

 Section 1 Review

Science at Home

1. What do electromagnetic waves consist of?
2. Describe one behavior that shows that light is a stream of particles.
3. Describe one behavior that shows that light is a wave.
4. **Thinking Critically Comparing and Contrasting** How are light and sound alike? How are they different?

Sunglasses On the next sunny day, have family members go outside wearing their sunglasses. Compare the sunglasses. Which sunglasses have polarizing lenses? How can you tell? Through the sunglasses, look at surfaces that create glare, such as water or glass. Compare the effects of different pairs of sunglasses. Which kind of sunglasses are best designed to reduce glare on a sunny day? **CAUTION:** Do not look directly at the sun.

Waves of the Electromagnetic Spectrum

What Is White Light?

1. Line the inside of a cardboard box with white paper. Hold a small triangular prism up to direct sunlight. **CAUTION:** *Do not look directly at the sun.*

2. Rotate the prism until the light coming out of the prism appears on the inside of the box. What colors do you see? What is the order of the colors? Describe how the colors progress from one to the next.

3. Using colored pencils, draw a picture of what you see inside the box.

Think It Over

Forming Operational Definitions The term *spectrum* describes a range. How do you think this term is related to what you just observed?

GUIDE FOR READING

◆ How do electromagnetic waves differ from each other?

◆ How does the energy in electromagnetic waves interact with matter?

Reading Tip Before you read, use the headings to make an outline about the different electromagnetic waves. As you read, make notes about each type of wave.

Key Terms
• electromagnetic spectrum
• radio wave
• microwave • radar
• magnetic resonance imaging
• infrared ray • thermogram
• visible light • ultraviolet ray
• X-ray • gamma ray

C an you imagine trying to keep food warm with a flashlight? How about trying to tune in a radio station on your television? Light and radio waves are both electromagnetic. But each has properties that make it useful for some purposes and useless for others. What makes radio waves different from light or ultraviolet rays?

Characteristics of Electromagnetic Waves

All electromagnetic waves travel at the same speed, but they have different wavelengths and different frequencies. Radiation in the wavelengths that your eyes can see is called visible light. Only a small portion of electromagnetic radiation is visible light. The rest of the wavelengths are invisible. Your radio detects wavelengths that are much longer and have a lower frequency than visible light.

Recall how speed, wavelength, and frequency are related:

$$Speed = Wavelength \times Frequency$$

Since the speed of all electromagnetic waves is the same, as wavelength decreases, frequency increases. Waves with the longest wavelengths have the lowest frequencies. Waves with the shortest wavelengths have the highest frequencies. The amount of energy carried by an electromagnetic wave increases with frequency. The higher the frequency of a wave, the higher its energy.

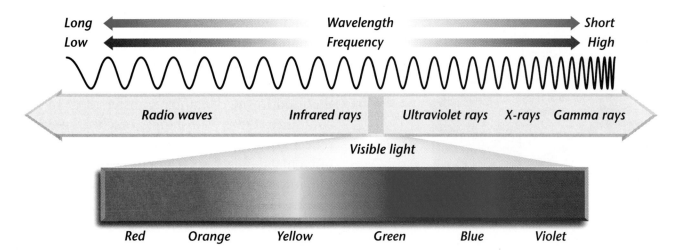

| Long | | Wavelength | | Short |
| Low | | Frequency | | High |

| Radio waves | Infrared rays | Ultraviolet rays | X-rays | Gamma rays |

Visible light

| Red | Orange | Yellow | Green | Blue | Violet |

The **electromagnetic spectrum** is the name for the range of electromagnetic waves when they are placed in order of increasing frequency. Figure 5 shows the electromagnetic spectrum. **The electromagnetic waves in the electromagnetic spectrum possess energy. Complex interactions occur between the energy in electromagnetic waves and matter.**

✓ *Checkpoint* *How are the frequency and wavelength of electromagnetic waves related?*

Radio Waves

Radio waves are the electromagnetic waves with the longest wavelengths and lowest frequencies. Like all electromagnetic waves, radio waves can travel through a vacuum. Most of the radio waves we receive, though, have traveled through air. Antennas pick up radio waves from the air and send them through wires to your radio. The radio converts the electromagnetic waves into the sound that comes out of the radio speakers.

Each radio station in an area broadcasts at a different frequency. To change the station on your radio, you adjust the tuning dial or press a button. This makes the tuner pick up waves of a different frequency. The numbers on your radio tell you the frequency of the station you are listening to.

Microwaves The radio waves with the shortest wavelengths and the highest frequencies are **microwaves.** One of their most common uses is in microwave ovens. When you switch on a microwave oven, it gives off electromagnetic waves that bounce around inside the oven, penetrating the food. Matter and energy interact when water molecules in the food absorb the energy from the microwaves, causing the food to get hot.

Figure 5 The electromagnetic spectrum shows the different electromagnetic waves in order of increasing frequency and decreasing wavelength. *Interpreting Diagrams Which electromagnetic waves have the highest frequencies?*

Social Studies CONNECTION

In 1920, only about 20,000 people using homemade radio sets were receiving radio signals. As an experiment, Frank Conrad of the Westing-house Company began to broadcast recorded music and sports results. Because public response was so enthusiastic, the company began broadcasting programs on a regular basis. By 1922, there were more than 500 radio stations in the United States.

In Your Journal

Imagine you are the advertising director for an early radio station. Write a letter to a business of your choice telling the owners why they should buy advertising time from your radio station.

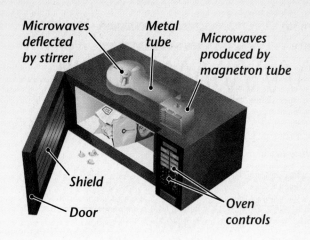

Microwaves deflected by stirrer

Metal tube

Microwaves produced by magnetron tube

Shield

Door

Oven controls

Figure 6 Microwaves produced in a microwave oven are absorbed by water molecules in foods. The energy raises the temperature of the food faster than an ordinary oven, so the food takes less time to cook. *Applying Concepts Why are metal containers not suitable for use in a microwave oven?*

Microwaves can pass right through some substances, such as glass and plastic. For this reason, microwaves do not heat glass and plastic containers. If the container gets hot, it is because the food in the container transfers heat to the container. Other substances, such as metals, reflect microwaves. If you have ever accidentally put a metal object, such as a piece of aluminum foil, into a microwave oven, you may have seen sparks. The sparks are the result of a buildup of electrical energy in the metal caused by the microwaves. Metal containers and utensils should never be used in microwave ovens.

Microwaves are not easily blocked by structures such as trees, buildings, and mountains. For this reason, microwaves are used to transmit cellular telephone calls. You will read more about cellular phones in Section 4.

Radar Short-wavelength microwaves are used in radar. **Radar,** which stands for **ra**dio **d**etection **a**nd **r**anging, can be used to locate objects. A radar device sends out short pulses of radio waves. These waves are reflected by objects that they strike. A receiver detects the stronger reflected waves and measures the time it takes for them to come back. From the time and the known speed of the waves, the receiver calculates the distance to the object. Radar is used to monitor airplanes landing and taking off at airports, as Figure 7 shows. Radar is also used to locate ships at sea and to track weather systems.

In Chapter 5, you learned how the frequency of a sound wave seems to change when the source of the sound moves toward you or away from you. The Doppler effect occurs with electromagnetic waves too, and has some very useful applications. Police use radio waves and the Doppler effect to find the speeds of vehicles.

Figure 7 Radar is used to monitor airplanes taking off and landing at airports.

Figure 8 Radio waves and the Doppler effect are used to find the speeds of moving vehicles (left) and of moving balls at sporting events such as tennis matches (right).

A radar gun sends blips of radio waves toward a moving car. The waves are then reflected. Because the car is moving, the frequency at which the reflected blips arrive is different from the frequency at which the waves were sent out. The radar device uses the difference in frequency to calculate the speed of the car. If the car is going faster than the speed limit, the police often give a speeding ticket.

Radar is also used at some sports events to measure the speed of a moving ball. The radio waves bounce off a moving ball. The speed at which the ball is hit or thrown can then be displayed on a board like the one in Figure 8.

Magnetic Resonance Imaging (MRI) Radio waves are also

INTEGRATING HEALTH used in medicine to produce pictures of tissues in the human body. This process is called **magnetic resonance imaging,** or MRI. In MRI, a person is placed in a machine that gives out short bursts of radio waves. The radio waves, combined with strong magnetic fields, cause atoms within the body to line up in one direction. The atoms return to their original directions at different rates. By analyzing the rates, the MRI machine can create pictures of internal body organs. The pictures show clear images of muscles and other soft tissues not shown on X-rays. MRI is used to detect brain disorders and soft tissue disorders near the spine.

☑ *Checkpoint* *What are three uses of radio waves?*

Infrared Rays

If you switch on an electric stove, you can feel infrared rays even before the element turns red. As the element warms up, it gives off energy as light and heat. This energy is infrared radiation, or infrared rays. **Infrared rays** have shorter wavelengths and higher frequencies than radio waves.

Figure 9 Magnetic resonance imaging (MRI) uses radio waves to create pictures of human tissue. It is used to examine the brain, spinal cord, and other organs.

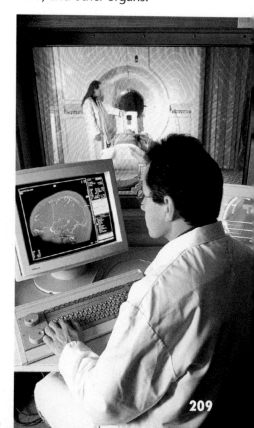

Infra- is a Latin prefix that means "below." Put *infra-* and *red* together, and you get *infrared*, which means "below red." The next waves in the spectrum are red light.

Infrared rays range in wavelength from a little shorter than radio waves to just longer than visible red light. Because you can feel the longest infrared rays as warmth, these rays are often called heat rays. Heat lamps have bulbs that give off more infrared rays and fewer visible light waves than regular bulbs. Some people have heat lamps in their bathrooms. You may also have seen heat lamps keeping food warm at cafeteria counters.

Most objects give off some infrared rays. Warmer matter gives off infrared rays with higher energy than cooler matter. An infrared camera takes pictures using infrared rays instead of light.

EXPLORING *the Electromagnetic Spectrum*

Electromagnetic waves are all around you—in your home, around your neighborhood and town, at the beach or pool, and in hospitals.

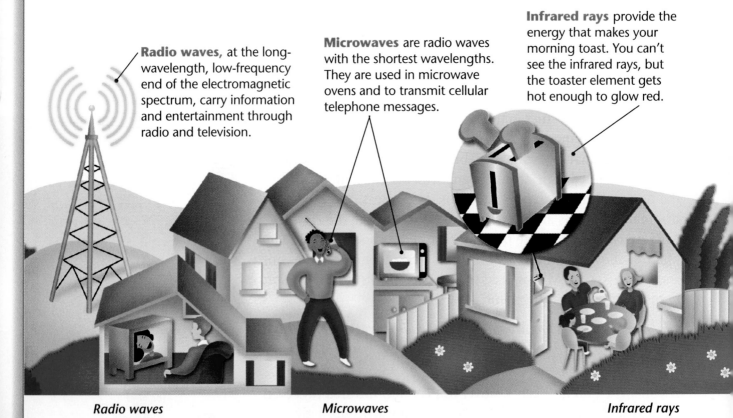

Infrared rays provide the energy that makes your morning toast. You can't see the infrared rays, but the toaster element gets hot enough to glow red.

Microwaves are radio waves with the shortest wavelengths. They are used in microwave ovens and to transmit cellular telephone messages.

Radio waves, at the long-wavelength, low-frequency end of the electromagnetic spectrum, carry information and entertainment through radio and television.

Radio waves	Microwaves	Infrared rays
10^3 Hz	10^{10} Hz	10^{13} Hz

These pictures are called thermograms. Figure 10 shows a thermogram of a person. A **thermogram** shows regions of different temperatures in different colors. Thermograms identify the warm and cool parts of an object by analyzing the infrared rays it gives off. Thermograms are especially useful for checking structures, such as houses, for energy leaks.

Even though your eyes cannot see the wavelengths of infrared rays, you can use an infrared camera or binoculars to detect people or animals in the dark. Satellites in space use infrared cameras to study the growth of plants and to observe the motions of clouds to help determine weather patterns.

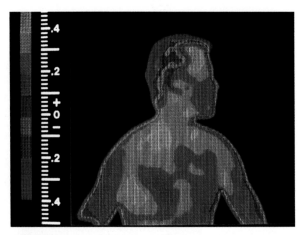

Figure 10 Infrared rays can be used to produce a thermogram. *Inferring What color do you think represents cooler body temperatures?*

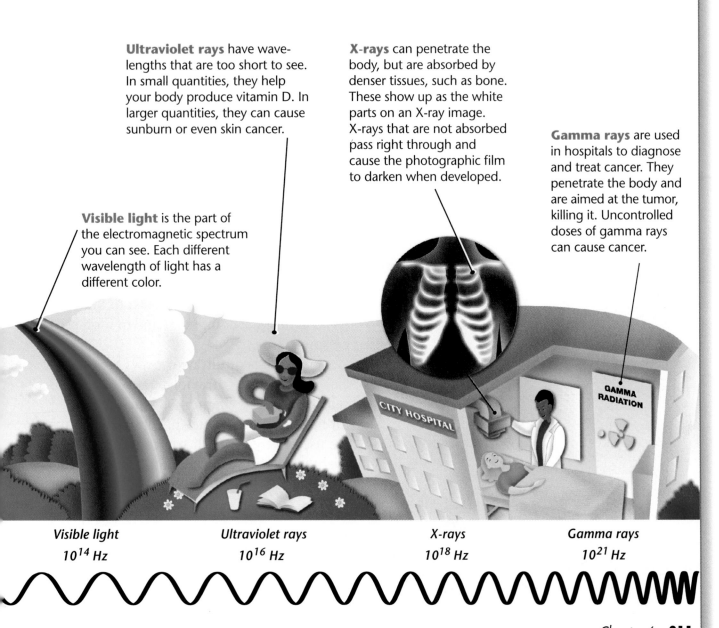

Ultraviolet rays have wavelengths that are too short to see. In small quantities, they help your body produce vitamin D. In larger quantities, they can cause sunburn or even skin cancer.

X-rays can penetrate the body, but are absorbed by denser tissues, such as bone. These show up as the white parts on an X-ray image. X-rays that are not absorbed pass right through and cause the photographic film to darken when developed.

Gamma rays are used in hospitals to diagnose and treat cancer. They penetrate the body and are aimed at the tumor, killing it. Uncontrolled doses of gamma rays can cause cancer.

Visible light is the part of the electromagnetic spectrum you can see. Each different wavelength of light has a different color.

Visible light	Ultraviolet rays	X-rays	Gamma rays
10^{14} Hz	10^{16} Hz	10^{18} Hz	10^{21} Hz

Visible Light

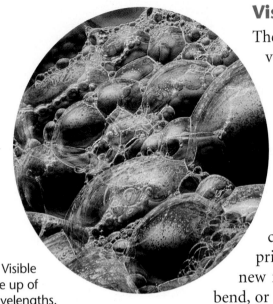

The electromagnetic waves that you can see are visible light. They make up only a small part of the electromagnetic spectrum. **Visible light** has shorter wavelengths and higher frequencies than infrared waves. The longest wavelengths of visible light are red. As the wavelengths decrease and the frequencies increase, you can see other colors of light. The shortest wavelengths are purple, or violet.

Have you ever seen a rainbow in the sky, colors on a bubble, or light passing through a prism? Recall what happens when waves enter a new medium, such as water or glass. The waves bend, or refract. Different wavelengths of light refract by different amounts, so the waves separate into the various colors of the visible spectrum. The colors are red, orange, yellow, green, blue, and violet, in order of increasing frequencies. Most visible light is made up of a mixture of these colors.

Figure 11 Visible light is made up of different wavelengths. Each wavelength has its own color. When light bounces off a bubble, interference removes some of the colors of the visible spectrum and leaves others for us to see.

☑ *Checkpoint* *What are the colors of the visible spectrum?*

Ultraviolet Rays

Electromagnetic waves with wavelengths just shorter than those of visible light are called **ultraviolet rays,** or UV. *Ultra-* is a Latin prefix that means "beyond." So *ultraviolet* means "beyond violet." UV waves have higher frequencies than visible light, so they carry more energy. Because the energy of ultraviolet rays interacts with matter, they can damage or kill living cells. Ultraviolet lamps are often used to kill bacteria on hospital equipment and in food processing plants.

Small doses of ultraviolet rays are beneficial to humans. Ultraviolet rays cause skin cells to produce vitamin D, which is needed for healthy bones and teeth. Ultraviolet lamps are used to treat jaundice, a condition of the liver that causes yellowing of the skin, in newborn babies.

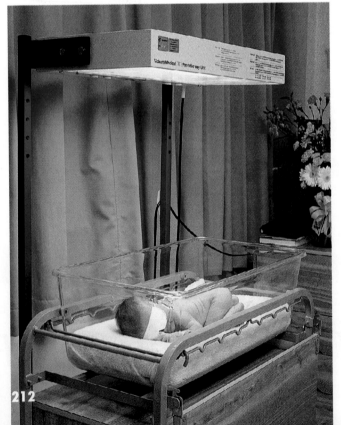

Figure 12 Ultraviolet light is used to treat jaundice in newborn babies. The baby's eyes are protected because too much ultraviolet light could damage them.

The ultraviolet rays present in sunlight can burn your skin. Too much exposure can cause skin cancer and damage your eyes. If you apply sunblock lotion and wear sunglasses, you can limit the damage to your body caused by UV rays.

INTEGRATING LIFE SCIENCE Although ultraviolet light is invisible to humans, many insects can see it. For example, bees have good color vision, but they do not see the same range of wavelengths that humans do. Bees see less of the lower frequency red waves and more of the higher frequency ultraviolet waves. Flowers that appear to be one color to a human appear very different to a honeybee. To the bee, the part of a flower that contains nectar looks different from the rest of the flower. The bee can head straight for the nectar!

X-Rays

X-rays are electromagnetic waves with very short wavelengths. Their frequencies are just a little higher than ultraviolet rays. Because of their high frequencies, X-rays carry more energy than ultraviolet rays and can interact with most matter. Dense matter, such as bone or lead, absorbs X-rays and does not allow them to pass through. For this reason, X-rays are used to make images of bones inside the body. X-rays pass right through both skin and soft tissues and change the photographic film in the X-ray machine so that it darkens when it is developed. The bones, which absorb X-rays, appear as the lighter areas on the film, as shown in Figure 13.

Too much exposure to X-rays can cause cancer. If you've ever had a dental X-ray, you'll remember how the dentist gave you a lead apron to wear during the procedure. The lead absorbs X-rays and prevents them from reaching your body.

X-rays are sometimes used in industry and engineering. For example, to find out if a steel or concrete structure has tiny cracks, engineers can take an X-ray image of the structure. X-rays will pass through tiny cracks that are invisible to the human eye. Dark areas on the X-ray film show the cracks. This technology is often used to check the quality of joints in oil and gas pipelines.

What Does a Bee See?

Load a roll of UV-sensitive film into a camera. Take photos of a variety of flowers. Include white flowers and flowers that you see bees near. Have the film developed and look at the prints.

Observing What can bees see that you cannot? How is this useful to the bees?

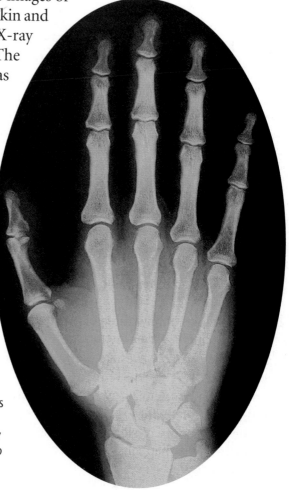

Figure 13 X-rays pass through softer human tissues and cause the photographic plate to darken behind them when developed. Bones absorb X-rays, so they show up as lighter areas. *Applying Concepts Why do you think that dental X-rays are useful to dentists?*

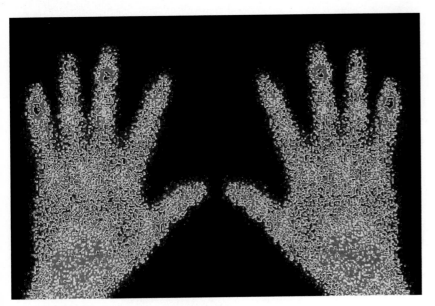

Figure 14 Doctors can inject radioactive liquids into the body and use gamma ray detectors to trace them. The detectors build images that doctors can use to examine the inside of the body.

Gamma Rays

Gamma rays have the shortest wavelengths and highest frequencies of the electromagnetic spectrum. Because they have the greatest amount of energy, they are the most penetrating of all the electromagnetic waves.

Some radioactive substances and certain nuclear reactions produce gamma rays. Because of their great ability to penetrate matter, gamma rays can cause serious illness. However, when used in controlled conditions, gamma rays have some medical uses. For example, gamma rays can be used to kill cancer cells in radiation therapy. Gamma rays can also be used to examine the body's internal structures. A patient can be injected with a fluid that emits gamma rays. Then a gamma ray detector can form an image of the inside of the body.

 INTEGRATING SPACE SCIENCE Some objects far out in space give off bursts of gamma rays. The gamma rays travel for billions of years before they reach Earth. Earth's atmosphere blocks these gamma rays, so gamma-ray telescopes that detect them must orbit above Earth's atmosphere. Astronomers think that collisions of dying stars in distant galaxies are one way of producing these gamma rays. Some gamma-ray telescopes detected the stronger gamma rays given off in the atmosphere as a result of nuclear weapons tests on Earth.

Section 2 Review

1. How are all electromagnetic waves alike? How are they different?
2. Give examples of how three different types of electromagnetic waves interact with matter.
3. Explain how radio waves are used to find the speed of a moving object.
4. How are X-rays useful? How are they dangerous?
5. **Thinking Critically Applying Concepts** As the wavelength of electromagnetic waves decreases, what happens to the frequency? To the energy?

CHAPTER PROJECT

Check Your Progress

Write the questions for your survey. Some categories you might want to include are types of communication devices, how often they are used, when and where they are used, and the purposes for which they are used. Do people use these devices for personal reasons or for business? (*Hint:* To make your survey easy to complete, ask questions that require short answers.) Give the survey sheet to your classmates and other students in the school for their families and neighbors to complete.

Food Irradiation

Food sometimes travels a long way to reach your plate. Potatoes from Maine and strawberries from Florida or Mexico must stay fresh until you eat them. But every so often, food makes people ill. Millions of Americans get sick every year from contaminated or spoiled food.

One way to prevent such illness is food irradiation. In the most common method, gamma rays are sent through fresh or frozen food. The radiation slows decay and kills organisms that could make people sick. It makes food safer to eat and also helps the food stay fresh longer. Five minutes of irradiation will allow strawberries to stay fresh for an extra nine or ten days.

Some people worry about the possible dangers of eating irradiated food. More than 40 countries, including the United States, permit food irradiation. Others forbid it. Is food irradiation safe?

TREATED BY
IRRADIATION

The Issues

Does Irradiation Destroy Nutrients in Food? Radiation kills living cells. But it can also make chemical changes in the food itself. It may destroy useful nutrients, such as vitamins A, B-1, E, and K. Up to ten percent of these vitamins can be lost when food is irradiated. Of course, other methods of protecting and preserving food—such as refrigeration or canning fruits and vegetables—also lead to small losses in nutrition. Even cooking food makes it lose some vitamins.

Does Irradiation Change the Food Itself? Irradiating food doesn't make the food radioactive. But irradiation may change the molecular structure of some foods, creating chemicals such as benzene and formaldehyde. In small doses, these substances have little effect. But large amounts can be harmful to people. Supporters say that these same substances are found naturally in food. Some critics say irradiation should not be used until

there is further research. Researchers want to determine whether people who eat irradiated food for a long time are more likely to develop cancer or other diseases. Other experts say that the short-term research already done shows that irradiation is safe. Some alternatives to irradiation, such as spraying with pesticides, are clearly more harmful.

Will Irradiating Food Make People Less Careful About Handling Food? In the United States, all irradiated food must be labeled. But if people are not careful about washing their hands before preparing food, irradiated food can still become contaminated. Also, the amounts of radiation allowed won't kill all harmful organisms. It's still necessary to cook food properly before eating it, especially meat and eggs. Some food experts worry that irradiation will make people feel falsely safe and become careless about preparing food.

You Decide

1. Identify the Problem

In your own words, explain the problem of food irradiation.

2. Analyze the Options

List reasons for and against: (a) requiring all food to be irradiated; (b) permitting, but not requiring, food irradiation; and (c) banning food irradiation.

3. Find a Solution

You see two containers of a food at the supermarket. One is irradiated; one is not. The price is the same. Which would you buy? Explain why.

SECTION 3 Generating Visible Light Waves

DISCOVER

How Do Light Bulbs Differ?

1. Your teacher will give you one incandescent and one fluorescent light bulb.

2. Examine each bulb closely. What is the shape and size of each? Describe the differences between the bulbs. Draw each type of bulb and record your observations.

3. How do you think each bulb produces light?

Think It Over

Posing Questions Make a list of five questions you could ask to help you understand how each bulb works.

GUIDE FOR READING

◆ **What happens when matter and energy interact in a light bulb?**

◆ **What colors of light does an incandescent bulb generate?**

Reading Tip As you read, compare and contrast the different ways in which light can be generated.

Key Terms illuminated
• luminous • spectroscope
• incandescent light
• fluorescent light • neon light
• sodium vapor light
• tungsten-halogen light
• bioluminescence

Figure 15 An incandescent light bulb glows when electricity passes through the tungsten filament.

Look around the room. Most of the matter you see is visible because it reflects light. If no light source were present, you could not see matter. An object that can be seen because it reflects light is an **illuminated** object. Light illuminates the page you are reading and your desk. An object that gives off its own light is a **luminous** object. A light bulb, a burning match, and the sun are examples of luminous objects.

There are many different types of light bulbs. Common types of light bulbs include incandescent, fluorescent, neon, sodium vapor, and tungsten-halogen. **Complex interactions between matter and energy occur in light bulbs to generate a continuous spectrum of wavelengths.** An instrument called a **spectroscope** can be used to view the different colors of light produced by each type of bulb.

Incandescent Lights

Have you heard the phrase "red hot"? When some objects get hot enough, they glow, giving off a faint red light. If they get even hotter, the glow turns into white light. The objects are said to be "white hot." **Incandescent lights** (in kun DES unt) glow when a filament inside them gets hot.

Look closely at a clear, unlit incandescent bulb. Notice inside the thin wire coil called a filament. It is made of a metal called tungsten. When an electric current passes through the filament, it heats up. When the filament gets hot enough, it gives off red light, which has low frequencies. As it gets hotter, the filament gives off light with higher frequencies. Once the filament gets hot enough to give off

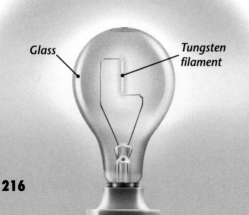

Glass

Tungsten filament

enough violet light, all the frequencies of light combine to produce white light. **Incandescent lights give off all the colors of visible light: red, orange, yellow, green, blue, and violet.**

The American inventor Thomas Edison is credited with developing a long-lasting incandescent light bulb in 1879. Edison knew that if he passed an electric current through a wire, it would get hot and glow. By experimenting with different types of filaments, Edison developed a light bulb that would glow for a long time.

Incandescent bulbs are not very efficient in giving off light. Less than ten percent of the energy is actually given out as light. Most of the energy produced by an incandescent bulb is given off as infrared rays. Incandescent bulbs can get quite hot when they have been left on for a while.

Fluorescent Lights

Have you ever noticed the long, narrow light bulbs in stores and offices? They are **fluorescent lights** (floo RES uhnt). Maybe you have some in your school. Each glass tube contains a gas and is coated on the inside with a powder.

When an electric current passes through a fluorescent bulb, it causes the gas to emit ultraviolet waves. When the ultraviolet waves hit the powder coating inside the tube, the coating emits visible light. This process is called fluorescing.

Unlike incandescent lights, fluorescent lights give off most of their energy as light. They usually last longer than incandescent bulbs and use less electricity for the same brightness, which makes them less expensive to run.

☑ *Checkpoint* *Why are fluorescent bulbs more economical than incandescent bulbs?*

Figure 16 Fluorescent lights are commonly used in offices, stores, and schools.
Applying Concepts Why might fluorescent light bulbs be used in an office rather than incandescent light bulbs?

Figure 17 Neon lights are used in advertising signs and decoration.
Applying Concepts Why are neon lights so colorful?

Neon Lights

Some gases can be made to produce light by passing an electric current through them. For example, a **neon light** consists of a sealed glass tube filled with neon. When an electric current passes through the neon gas, matter interacts with energy as the gas absorbs the energy. However, the gas cannot hold the energy for very long. The energy is released by the gas in the form of light. This process is called electric discharge through gases.

Pure neon gives out red light. Often, what is called a neon light has a different gas, or a mixture of gases, in the tube. Different gases produce different colors of light. For example, both argon gas and mercury vapor produce greenish blue light. Helium gives a golden yellow light. Krypton gives a pale violet light. Sometimes the gases are put into colored glass tubes to produce other colors. Neon lights are commonly used for bright, flashy signs.

Sodium Vapor Lights

Sodium vapor lights contain a small amount of solid sodium as well as some neon and argon gas. When the neon and argon gas are heated, they begin to glow. This glow heats up the sodium, causing it to change from a solid into a gas. The particles of sodium vapor give off energy in the form of yellow light.

Sodium vapor lights are commonly used for street lighting. They require very little electricity to give off a great deal of light, so they are quite economical.

Figure 18 Sodium vapor light bulbs give off a yellow light. They are commonly used to illuminate streets and parking lots.

Tungsten-Halogen Lights

Tungsten-halogen lights work partly like incandescent bulbs. They have tungsten filaments and contain a gas. The gas is one of a group of gases called the halogens. When electricity passes through the filament, the filament gets hot and glows. The halogen makes the filament give off a bright white light.

Tungsten-halogen lights have become very popular. These small bulbs use relatively little electricity for the bright light they provide. They are used in overhead projectors and in floor lamps. Because some halogen bulbs become very hot, they must be kept away from flammable materials, such as paper and curtains.

Figure 19 Tungsten-halogen light bulbs contain a tungsten filament and a halogen gas. Even small bulbs can produce very bright light.

Bioluminescence

INTEGRATING LIFE SCIENCE Have you ever seen a firefly? On a warm summer evening, they flash their lights in patterns to attract mates. Fireflies are examples of organisms that produce their own light in a process called bioluminescence. **Bioluminescence** (by oh loo muh NES uns) occurs as a result of a chemical reaction among proteins and oxygen in an organism. The reaction produces energy that is given off in the form of light. Recall from Chapter 1 that an energy-producing chemical reaction is called an exothermic reaction. Unlike a light bulb, which gives off most of its energy as infrared rays, the reaction that produces bioluminescence gives off almost all of its energy as light.

There are also bioluminescent organisms in the oceans. Some types of jellyfish give off light when they are disturbed. Deep in the ocean, where sunlight cannot reach, bioluminescence is the only source of light. Some deep-sea fish use bioluminescence to search for food or to attract mates.

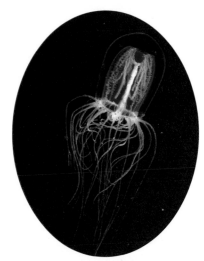

Figure 20 This jellyfish produces its own light by bioluminescence.

Section 3 Review

1. How do light bulbs generate light?
2. How does an incandescent light bulb generate white light?
3. Compare luminous objects with illuminated objects. Give two examples of each.
4. Why are fluorescent lights commonly used in businesses and schools?
5. **Thinking Critically Making Judgments** Which type of light is best for each room in your home? Give reasons for your choices.

Science at Home

Buying Bulbs Invite family members to visit a hardware store that sells light bulbs. Ask the salesperson to describe the different kinds of bulbs available. Read the information about each bulb on the side panel of each package. Ask the salesperson to explain any terms you don't understand. Look for the cost and expected life of the bulbs, too. How does this information help you and your family purchase the most economical bulbs?

Comparing Light Bulbs

In this lab, you will design an experiment to compare the illumination provided by different brands and powers of light bulbs.

Problem

Which light bulb provides the best illumination?

Skills Focus

designing experiments, controlling variables, measuring, drawing conclusions

Materials (per group)

computer (optional)
a variety of incandescent light bulbs that
   can fit in the same lamp or socket
medium-sized cardboard box
light socket or lamp (without shade)
meter stick   wax paper
scissors   plain paper

Procedure

1. Following the instructions below, construct your own light box. The box allows you to test the illumination that is provided by each light bulb.
2. With a partner, examine the different bulbs. What is the power (watts), light output (lumens), and life (hours) for each bulb? Predict which light bulb will be the brightest. Explain your choice.
3. How will you test your prediction?
   - What kinds of incandescent light bulbs will you use?
   - What variables will you keep constant? What variables will you change?
4. On a sheet of paper or on the computer, make a data table like the one shown at the right to record your data.
5. Review your plan. Will your procedure help you find an answer to the problem?

How to Build and Use a Light Box

A. Use a medium-sized cardboard box, such as the kind of box copy paper comes in. If the box has flaps, cut them off.

B. Carefully cut a viewing hole (about 2 cm × 4 cm) in the bottom of the box. This will be on top when the box is used. This is hole A.

C. Punch another hole (about 1 cm × 1 cm) on one side of the box. This is hole B. It will allow light from the bulb to enter the box.

D. To decrease the amount of light entering, cover hole B with two layers of wax paper.

E. Put a light bulb in the lamp and place it to the side of the box, 1 m from hole B.

F. Have your partner write a secret letter on a piece of plain paper. Put the paper on the table. Place the light box over the paper with the viewing hole facing up.

G. Now look through hole A.

H. Turn the lamp on and move the light toward the box until you can read the secret letter. Measure the distance between the light bulb and hole B.

DATA TABLE

Bulb #	Brand Name	Power (watts)	Light Output (lumens)	Life (hrs)	Cost ($)	Distance from Bulb to Light Box (cm)

6. Ask your teacher to check your procedure.
7. Before you repeat the steps for a second light bulb, look back at your procedure. How could you improve the accuracy of your results?
8. Test the illumination of the rest of your light bulbs.

Analyze and Conclude

1. How does the distance between the bulb and hole B affect how easily you can read the secret letter?
2. Based on your observations, what can you infer about the illumination provided by each bulb? Which bulb gave the most illumination?
3. Which bulb gave the most illumination over its lifetime?
4. Which bulb gave the most illumination for its cost?
5. How did your results compare with your prediction? What did you learn that you did not know when you made your prediction?
6. What factors affect the illumination given by a light bulb?
7. Apply Based on your results, do you think that the most expensive bulb is the best?

More to Explore

Modify your light box and repeat the activity. What different materials would you use? Would you make the light box smaller or larger than the original? How do different light boxes compare in testing illumination by light bulbs?

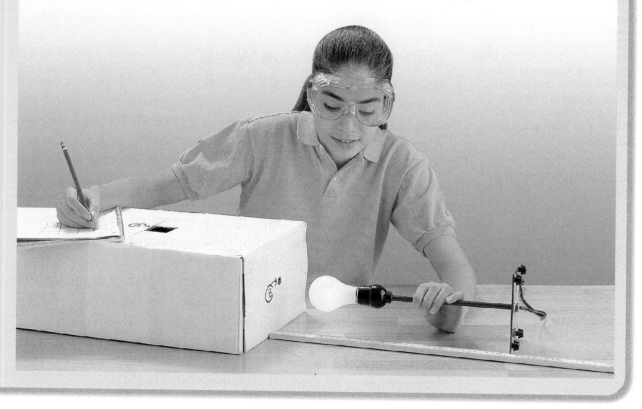

SECTION 4 Wireless Communication

DISCOVER ··· ACTIVITY····

How Can Radio Waves Change?

1. Trace the wave diagram onto a piece of tracing paper. Then transfer the wave diagram onto a flat piece of latex from a balloon or latex glove.

2. Stretch the latex horizontally. How is the stretched wave different from the wave on the tracing paper?

3. Now stretch the latex vertically. How is this wave different from the wave on the tracing paper? How is it different from the wave in Step 2?

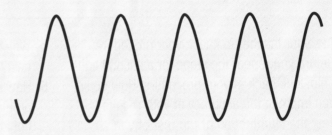

Think It Over

Making Models Which stretch changes the amplitude of the wave? Which stretch changes the frequency of the wave?

GUIDE FOR READING

◆ How do AM and FM radio waves transmit information?

◆ How do cellular phones and pagers use electromagnetic waves?

◆ How are satellites used to relay information?

Reading Tip Before you read, preview the diagrams and captions in the section. List any terms you are not familiar with. As you read, write the definition of each term on your list.

Key Terms
• amplitude modulation (AM)
• frequency modulation (FM)

Recent advances in technology have turned our world into a global village. Today you can communicate with people on the other side of the world in just seconds. You can watch a television broadcast of a soccer game from Europe or a news report from the Middle East. Once scientists discovered that messages could be carried on electromagnetic waves, they realized that communication signals could travel at the speed of light.

Radio and Television Waves

How does your favorite radio station or television program travel to you? Both radio and television programs are carried, or transmitted, by radio waves. Radio waves are generated when charged particles move back and forth in transmission antennas. These transmissions are broadcast, or sent out in all directions. Radio waves carry information from the antenna of a broadcasting station to the receiving antenna of your radio or television. Don't confuse the sound that comes from your radio with radio waves. Your radio converts the radio transmission into sound waves. Sound waves travel through matter to your ear.

There are many different radio and television stations, all sending out signals. How can each station's signal come through so clearly? As you move your radio tuner up and down the dial, you hear different radio stations. Look at the radio dial in Figure 21. Each number on the dial represents a different frequency measured either in kilohertz (kHz) or megahertz (MHz).

Figure 21 The radio dial shows the FM and AM frequency bands. Each radio station is assigned a different carrier frequency.

Recall that a hertz is one cycle per second. If something vibrates 1,000 times a second, it has a frequency of 1,000 Hz, or 1 kilohertz (kHz). (The prefix *kilo-* means "one thousand.") If something vibrates 1,000,000 times a second, it has a frequency of 1,000,000 Hz, or 1 megahertz (MHz). (The prefix *mega-* means "one million" and is represented by a capital M.)

In the United States, the Federal Communications Commission, or FCC, assigns different frequencies of radio waves for different uses. Radio stations are allowed to use one part of the spectrum, and television stations are assigned different parts of the spectrum. Taxi and police radios are also each assigned their own set of frequencies. In this way, the entire spectrum of radio waves is divided into bands. These bands are used for different purposes.

Each radio or television station in the United States is assigned a basic broadcast frequency, known as a carrier frequency. Each station is identified by the frequency at which it broadcasts. Radio stations broadcast in one of two main frequency bands—AM and FM.

AM Radio AM stands for **amplitude modulation.** On AM broadcasts, the frequency of the wave remains constant. The information that will become sound, such as speech and music, is coded in changes, or modulations, in the amplitude of the wave. **At the broadcasting station, music and speech are converted from sound into electronic signals. The electronic signals for AM broadcasts are then converted into a pattern of changes in the amplitude of a radio wave.**

Figure 22 Sound signals are carried by varying either the amplitude (AM) or the frequency (FM) of radio waves.
Interpreting Diagrams What remains constant in the AM wave? In the FM wave?

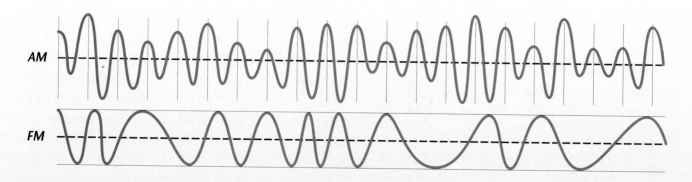

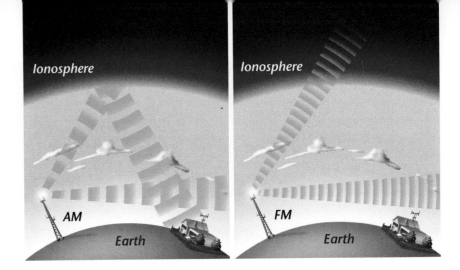

Figure 23 AM radio waves are reflected by the ionosphere. FM radio waves pass through the ionosphere. *Applying Concepts Which type of broadcast has a longer range on Earth?*

Your radio picks up the wave and converts the coded information back into an electronic signal. This signal travels to your radio's speaker and comes out as sound waves.

The AM frequencies used for radio broadcasts range from 535 kHz to 1,605 kHz. These radio waves vibrate at frequencies ranging from 535 to 1,605 thousand times per second.

AM waves have relatively long wavelengths and are easily reflected by Earth's ionosphere. The ionosphere is an electrically charged layer high in the atmosphere. Figure 23 shows how this reflection allows the AM waves to bounce back to Earth's surface. This is why AM radio stations can broadcast over long distances, especially at night when the absorption of radio waves by the ionosphere is reduced. However, the reception of AM waves is sometimes not very clear. For this reason, AM radio stations usually broadcast more talk shows than music.

FM Radio FM stands for **frequency modulation.** On FM broadcasts, the amplitude of the wave remains constant. **FM signals travel as changes, or modulations, in the frequency of the wave.**

If you look at an FM dial on a radio, you will see that the stations broadcast at frequencies from 88 MHz to 108 MHz. FM radio waves vibrate from 88 million to 108 million times each second. The frequencies of FM stations are much higher than the frequencies of AM radio stations, which vibrate only thousands of times per second.

Because FM waves have higher frequencies and more energy than AM waves, they penetrate the atmosphere instead of being reflected back to Earth. For this reason, FM waves do not travel as far as AM waves. Have you ever gone on a long car trip and tried to listen to radio stations along the way? Then you have probably lost reception of radio stations and had to tune in new ones as you traveled. FM waves are usually received clearly and produce a better sound quality than AM waves. They are generally used to broadcast music.

Produce Electro-magnetic Interference

ACTIVITY

Find out which appliances produce radio waves.

1. Turn on a non-cabled television set. Keep the volume low. Observe the image on the screen.

2. Plug an electric mixer or a hair dryer into a nearby outlet and switch it on. What happens to the image on the television?

3. Change the speed of the mixer or hair dryer. What happens to the image on the television?

Drawing Conclusions What can you conclude about the electric mixer or the hair dryer? Explain.

Television Television broadcasts are similar to radio broadcasts, except that the electromagnetic waves carry picture signals as well as sound. There are two main bands of television wave frequencies: Very High Frequency (VHF) and Ultra High Frequency (UHF). VHF television channels range from frequencies of 54 MHz to 216 MHz, and correspond to Channels 2 through 13 on your television set. This band of frequencies includes some FM radio frequencies, so television stations are restricted from using the frequencies that are reserved for radio stations. UHF channels range from frequencies of 470 MHz to 806 MHz, and correspond to Channels 14 through 69.

Weather can affect the reception of television signals. For better reception, cable companies now pick up the signals, improve them, and send them through cables into homes. Cable television reception is usually clearer than reception with an antenna. Many American homes that have television now have cable reception.

✓ *Checkpoint* What do the terms VHF and UHF mean?

Cellular Telephones

Cellular phones have become very common. **Cellular telephones transmit and receive signals using high-frequency radio waves, or microwaves.** The cellular system works over regions divided up into many small cells. Each cell has its own transmitter and receiver. Cells that are next to each other are assigned different frequencies, but cells that are not next to each other can be assigned the same frequency. Cellular telephone signals are strong enough to reach only a few nearby cells. They cannot travel great distances. This allows many phones in different areas to use the same frequency at the same time, without interfering with each other.

As cellular phone users travel from one cell to another, the signals are transferred from one cell to another with very little interruption. If you travel outside one cellular phone company's area, another company becomes responsible for transmitting the signals.

Many cellular phones are more expensive to use than wired phones. But they are becoming more affordable and more popular. Cellular phones allow users to make and receive calls without having to use someone else's phone or to look for a pay phone.

Figure 24 Cellular telephones transmit and receive radio waves that travel short distances.

Cordless Telephones

Cellular telephones should not be confused with cordless telephones. The bases of cordless telephones are connected to the telephone system just like ordinary phones. The only difference is that there is no cord between the handset and the base. The information is transmitted from the handset to the base by radio waves, so you can walk away from the base as you talk on the phone.

Pagers

Pagers are small electronic devices that people can carry in their pockets or attached to their clothes. Have you ever paged someone?

SCIENCE & History

Wireless Communication

Since the late 1800s, many developments in communication have turned our world into a global village.

1895
First Wireless Transmission

Italian engineer and inventor Guglielmo Marconi successfully used radio waves to send a coded wireless signal a distance of more than 2 km.

1923
Ship-to-Ship Communication

For the first time, people on one ship could talk to people on another. The signals were sent as electromagnetic waves, received by an antenna, and converted into sound.

1900   **1920**

1888
Electromagnetic Waves

German scientist Heinrich Hertz proved James Clerk Maxwell's prediction that radio waves exist. Hertz demonstrated that the waves could be reflected, refracted, diffracted, and polarized just like light waves.

1901
First Transatlantic Signals

On December 12, the first transatlantic radio signal was sent from Poldhu Cove, Cornwall, England, to Signal Hill, Newfoundland. The coded electromagnetic waves traveled more than 3,000 km through the air.

Cornwall, England

Signal Hill, Newfoundland

You dial the telephone number of the pager from a telephone or another pager. Depending on the pager, you can then enter your telephone number or leave a voice message, which will appear as a text message on the pager's screen.

When you leave a message for a pager, the information is first sent to a receiving station. There it is coded and sent as electromagnetic waves to the correct pager. The pager then beeps or vibrates, letting the owner know that there is a message. Some pagers are two-way pagers. This means that the pager can return electromagnetic signals to the receiving station, which sends them to the person who sent the original message.

In Your Journal

At your local or school library, find out more about Guglielmo Marconi. Imagine you were hired as his assistant. Write a letter to a friend that describes your new job.

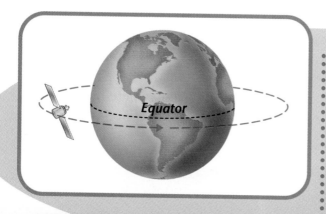

1963
Geosynchronous Orbit

Communications satellites are launched into orbits at altitudes of about 35,000 km. At this altitude, a satellite orbits Earth at the same rate as Earth rotates. A satellite orbiting above the equator remains above the same location as Earth turns.

1940   **1960**   **1980**

1957
Sputnik I

On October 4, the Soviet Union became the first country to successfully launch an artificial satellite into orbit. This development led to a new era in communications. Since then, more than 5,000 artificial satellites have been placed in orbit.

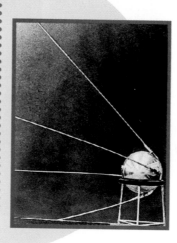

1979
Cellular Phone Network

The world's first cellular phone network was set up in Japan. It allowed people to make and receive telephone calls without wired phones.

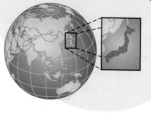

Communications Satellites

Since the development of satellite technology, long-distance communications have become faster and cheaper. Communications satellites work like the receivers and transmitters of a cellular phone system. Satellites orbiting Earth receive radio, television, and telephone signals, and transmit them around the world. **The radio waves are sent from Earth up to the satellite, which then relays the waves to other receivers on Earth.** Most satellites strengthen the signals before sending them back to Earth. Communications satellites can relay several signals at the same time.

Because a satellite can only "see" part of Earth at any given time, it is necessary to have more than one satellite in orbit for any given purpose. In this way, signals can be sent all around the world at any time.

Satellite Telephone Systems In recent years, the use of telephones has increased so much that telephone companies have had to develop new ways of transmitting electromagnetic waves. Several companies have developed or are developing satellite telephone systems. The radio waves from one phone are sent up through the atmosphere, received by one of the communications satellites, and transmitted back to Earth to the receiving phone. This system makes calling available anywhere in the world, but may be more expensive than a cellular telephone system.

Figure 25 Communications satellites are remote-controlled spacecraft that orbit Earth. Because electromagnetic waves travel in straight lines, they cannot curve around Earth. Satellites receive signals from Earth and transmit them to parts of the world they could not otherwise reach.

Television Satellites Television networks use communications satellites to send their signals to local stations across the country. The television signals are changed into radio waves using frequency modulation.

Some people have their own antennas to receive signals directly from satellites. Because the antennas are dish-shaped, they are known as satellite dishes. Older satellite dishes were very large. As the signals broadcast from satellites have become more powerful and the data in the signals has been compressed, the dishes required to receive them have become a lot smaller.

The Global Positioning System The Global Positioning System (GPS) was originally designed for use by the United States military. Now, many thousands of civilians use the system for navigation. The Global Positioning System uses a group of two dozen communications satellites that work together. The GPS satellites broadcast radio signals to Earth. These signals carry information that can tell you your exact location on Earth's surface, or even in the air. Anybody on Earth with a GPS receiver can receive these signals.

Today, GPS receivers are becoming increasingly common in airplanes, boats, and even in cars. In some cars you can type your destination into a computer and have the GPS system map out your route. A computerized voice might even tell you when to turn right or left.

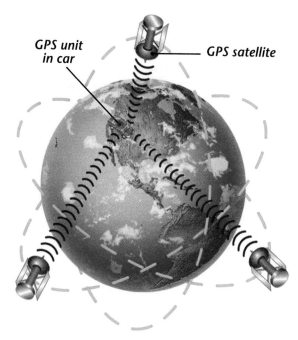

GPS unit in car

GPS satellite

Figure 26 The Global Positioning System (GPS) uses a group of 24 satellites, each traveling in its own orbit. Receivers in cars, boats, and airplanes use signals from at least three satellites at a time to determine their exact location on Earth.

Section 4 Review

1. Describe how the sounds from a radio station, such as speech or music, are converted into radio waves.
2. What is the difference between AM and FM radio broadcasts?
3. How does the cellular phone system work?
4. How does a satellite relay radio and television signals?
5. **Thinking Critically Predicting** What do you think might happen if the Federal Communications Commission did not control the use of different frequencies of radio waves?

Check Your Progress
Collect your surveys and tally your results. As you analyze your data, look for patterns. You can use bar graphs or circle graphs to display your findings. Include information about cost, time, and any other questions you asked in your survey. Write one or two paragraphs explaining your conclusions.

CHAPTER PROJECT

Build a Crystal Radio

The first radio, called a crystal set, was invented in the early 1900s. At first, people built their own crystal sets to receive broadcast transmissions from local radio stations. In this lab, you will build your own crystal radio and learn how science and technology are related.

Problem

How can you collect and convert radio signals?

Skill Focus

measuring, observing, problem solving, making models, drawing conclusions

Materials (per group)

cardboard tube (paper towel roll)
3 pieces of enameled or insulated wire, 1 about 30 m long, and 2 about 30 cm long
wirestrippers or sandpaper
2 alligator clips
scissors
aluminum foil
2 pieces of cardboard (sizes can range from 12.5 cm × 20 cm to 30 cm × 48 cm)
masking tape
crystal diode
earphone
2 pieces of insulated antenna wire, 1 about 30 m long, and 1 about 0.5 m long

Procedure

Part 1 Wind the Radio Coil

(*Hint:* All ends of the insulated wires need to be stripped to bare metal. If the wire is enameled, you need to sandpaper the ends.)

1. Carefully punch two holes approximately 2.5 cm apart in each end of a cardboard tube. The holes should be just large enough to thread the insulated wire through.
2. Feed one end of the 30-m piece of insulated wire through one set of holes. Leave a 50-cm lead at that end. Attach alligator clip #1 to this lead. See Figure 1.
3. Wind the wire tightly around the cardboard tube. Make sure the coils are close together but do not overlap one another.
4. Wrap the wire until you come to the end of the tube. Feed the end of the wire through the other set of holes, leaving a 50-cm lead as before. Attach alligator clip #2 to this lead. See Figure 2.

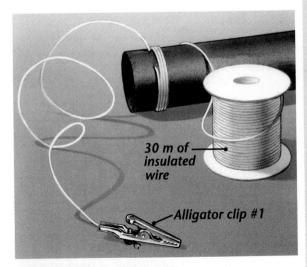

30 m of insulated wire

Alligator clip #1

Figure 1 Winding the Coil

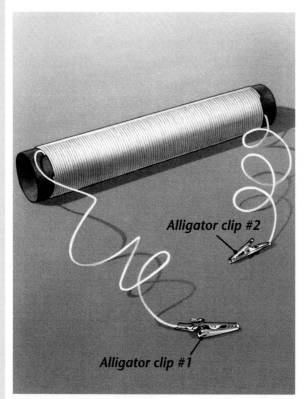

Figure 2 The Finished Coil

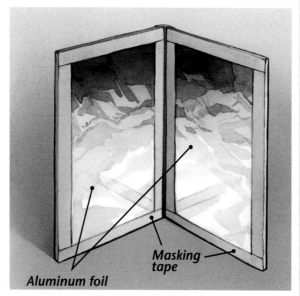

Figure 3 The Tuning Plates

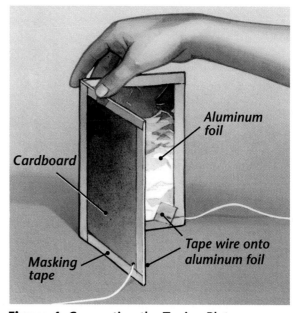

Figure 4 Connecting the Tuning Plates

Part 2 Make the Tuning Plates

5. Without wrinkling the aluminum foil, cover one side of each piece of cardboard with the foil. Trim off any excess foil and tape the foil in place.

6. Hold the pieces of cardboard together with the foil facing inward. Tape along one edge to make a hinge. It is important for the foil pieces to be close together but not touching. See Figure 3.

7. Make a small hole through the cardboard and foil near a corner of one side. Feed one of the short pieces of insulated wire through the hole and tape it onto the foil as shown. Tape the other short piece of insulated wire to the corner of the other side. See Figure 4.

8. Connect one end of the wire from the foil to alligator clip #1. Connect the other wire from the foil to alligator clip #2.

Part 3 Prepare the Earphone

9. Handle the diode carefully. Connect one wire from the diode to alligator clip #1. The arrow on the diode should point to the earphone. Tape the other end of the diode wire to one of the earphone wires.

10. Connect the other wire from the earphone to alligator clip #2. See Figure 5.

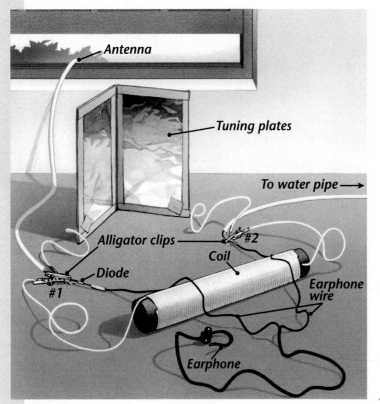

Antenna

Tuning plates

To water pipe →

Alligator clips

#2

Coil

Diode

#1

Earphone wire

Earphone

Figure 5 The Completed Radio

Part 4 Hook Up the Antenna

11. String the long piece of antenna wire along the floor to an outside window. Connect the other end of the wire to alligator clip #1.

12. Connect one end of the shorter piece of antenna wire to a cold-water pipe or faucet. Connect the other end to alligator clip #2. See Figure 5.

13. Put on the earphone and try to locate a station by squeezing the tuning plates slowly until you hear a signal. Some stations will come in when the plates are close together. Other stations will come in when the plates are opened far apart.

Analyze and Conclude

1. Evaluate your model. How many stations can you pick up? Where are the stations located geographically? Which station has the strongest signal? Keep a log of the different stations you receive.

2. How can you improve your model? How does adjusting the tuning plates affect the radio signals?

3. A crystal radio is not a powerful receiver. You can improve reception by having a good antenna. How can you improve your antenna?

4. **Apply** What are the similarities and differences between a modern radio and a crystal radio? How is one more efficient?

Design an Experiment

Use your crystal radio or any radio to test signal reception at various times of the day. Do you receive more stations at night or in the morning? Explain your results.

SECTION 1 The Nature of Electromagnetic Waves

Key Ideas

◆ An electromagnetic wave is a transverse wave with electrical and magnetic properties. It does not have to travel through a medium.
◆ Light has both wave and particle properties.

Key Terms

electromagnetic wave   photoelectric effect
electromagnetic radiation   photon
polarized light

SECTION 2 Waves of the Electromagnetic Spectrum

Key Ideas

◆ Electromagnetic waves travel at the same speed but have different wavelengths and frequencies.
◆ Electromagnetic wave energy interacts in complex ways with matter.

Key Terms

electromagnetic spectrum   thermogram
radio wave   visible light
microwave   ultraviolet ray
radar   X-ray
magnetic resonance imaging   gamma ray
infrared ray

SECTION 3 Generating Visible Light Waves

Key Ideas

◆ Interactions between matter and energy in light bulbs generate a continuous spectrum of wavelengths.
◆ An incandescent light bulb generates and combines all of the colors of visible light to create white light.

Key Terms

illuminated   neon light
luminous   sodium vapor light
spectroscope   tungsten-halogen light
incandescent light   bioluminescence
fluorescent light

SECTION 4 Wireless Communication

INTEGRATING TECHNOLOGY

Key Ideas

◆ At broadcasting stations, music and speech are converted from sound into an electrical signal and then into a pattern of changes in a radio wave.
◆ AM broadcasts transmit information by modifying the amplitude of the signal. FM broadcasts change the frequency of the signal.
◆ Cellular telephones transmit and receive signals using high-frequency radio waves.
◆ When you leave a message for a pager, the information is first sent to a receiving station. There it is coded and directed to the correct pager.
◆ Radio, television, and telephone signals are sent from Earth up to communications satellites, which then relay the signals to receivers around the world.

Key Terms

amplitude modulation (AM)
frequency modulation (FM)

Organizing Information

Concept Map Copy the concept map about electromagnetic waves onto a sheet of paper. Then complete it and add a title. (For more on concept maps, see the Skills Handbook.)

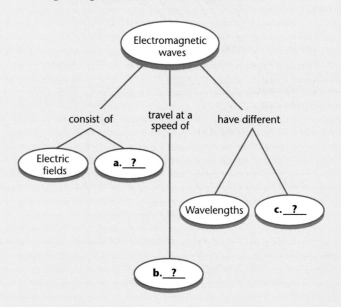

Reviewing Content

 Review key concepts online using iText at www.phschool.com

Multiple Choice

Choose the letter of the best answer.

1. All electromagnetic waves have the same
   a. frequency.
   b. speed.
   c. wavelength.
   d. energy.

2. The electromagnetic waves with the longest wavelengths are
   a. radio waves.
   b. infrared rays.
   c. X-rays.
   d. gamma rays.

3. Which of the following does *not* belong in the electromagnetic spectrum?
   a. X-ray
   b. sound
   c. infrared ray
   d. radio wave

4. Light bulbs that glow when a filament inside them gets hot are called
   a. bioluminescent lights.
   b. fluorescent lights.
   c. incandescent lights.
   d. neon lights.

5. Television signals are transmitted by
   a. gamma rays.   b. infrared rays.
   c. X-rays.   d. radio waves.

True or False

If the statement is true, write true. If it is false, change the underlined word or words to make the statement true.

6. The photoelectric effect is evidence that light can act as a <u>particle</u>.

7. <u>Ultraviolet</u> rays can be felt as heat.

8. Fluorescent lights give off most of their energy as <u>infrared rays</u>.

9. A radio station is identified by the <u>amplitude</u> at which it broadcasts.

10. Radio and television transmitters can be placed on <u>satellites</u> and sent into orbit.

Checking Concepts

11. How do you know that electromagnetic waves can travel through a vacuum?

12. How does polarization show that light can act as a wave?

13. How is the Doppler effect used to find the speeds of moving objects?

14. Explain the difference between cellular telephones and cordless telephones.

15. A person lost in the woods at night may signal for help by turning a flashlight on and off according to a code known as Morse code. This is actually a modulated signal. Is it AM or FM? Explain your answer.

16. **Writing to Learn** Develop an advertising campaign to sell fluorescent lights. Your ad should describe two advantages of fluorescent lights over incandescent lights. Be sure to include a catchy slogan.

Thinking Critically

17. **Applying Concepts** What important information can be gathered from a thermogram of a house? How could this information be used to help save energy?

18. **Relating Cause and Effect** The waves of the electromagnetic spectrum that have the greatest frequency are also the most penetrating and can cause the most harm. Explain.

19. **Classifying** List five examples of luminous objects and five examples of illuminated objects.

20. **Problem Solving** Suppose you are building an incubator for young chicks and need a source of heat. What type of light bulbs would you use? Explain.

21. **Comparing and Contrasting** Make a table to compare the different types of wireless communication. Include headings such as: type of information transmitted; distance over which signal can be transmitted; one-way or two-way communication.

Applying Skills

The table below gives information about four radio stations. Use the table to answer Questions 22–24.

Call letters	Frequency
KSIS	91.9 MHz
KMOM	1400 kHz
WDAD	103.5 MHz
WJFO	580 kHz

22. **Interpreting Data** Which radio station broadcasts at the longest wavelength? The shortest wavelength?
23. **Classifying** Which radio stations are AM? Which are FM?
24. **Predicting** You are going on a car trip across the United States. Which station would you expect to receive for the greater distance: KSIS or KMOM?

Performance CHAPTER PROJECT **Assessment**

Present Your Project Now you are ready to present your findings to your classmates. You could mount your graphs on posterboard. Alternatively, you could put your graphs on transparencies and use an overhead projector to show the results of your survey. You could also use a computer to create a slide show.

Reflect and Record What in your results was most surprising? How could you have done a better job of collecting your data? Has this project given you a better understanding of the usage of the various devices? Think about the world 25 years from now. Use the information you collected to predict the types of devices that will be used in the future.

Test Preparation

Use these questions to practice for standardized tests.

Use the diagram to answer Questions 25–28.

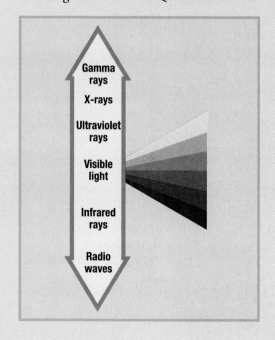

25. What would be the best title for this diagram?
    A Colors of the Spectrum
    B The Electromagnetic Spectrum
    C Visible Light
    D The Speed of Electromagnetic Waves
26. Which waves have the lowest frequency?
    F radio waves   G infrared rays
    H visible light   J gamma rays
27. Which waves have the shortest wavelength?
    A radio waves   B infrared rays
    C visible light   D gamma rays
28. What color would be at the "top" of the visible light spectrum?
    F violet   G green
    H yellow   J red

CHAPTER 7

Light Waves

This kaleidoscope image is formed by two mirrors at right angles. Colored objects between the mirrors are reflected to form a repeated pattern.

WEB ACTIVITY
www.phschool.com

What a Sight!

Look inside a kaleidoscope. Small beads or pieces of colored glass are reflected by mirrors, forming colorful, ever-changing patterns. Kaleidoscopes are optical instruments, devices that use arrangements of mirrors or lenses to produce images.

In this chapter, you will study how mirrors and lenses reflect and refract light. You will learn what causes the different colors of the objects all around you. You will use these ideas to create your own optical instrument.

Your Goal To construct an optical instrument that serves a specific purpose. It can be a kaleidoscope, a telescope, a periscope, a microscope, or something of your own creation.

To complete this project successfully you must
- design and build an optical instrument that includes at least one mirror or one lens
- demonstrate how your instrument works
- prepare a manual that explains the purpose of each part of your instrument

Get Started Begin to think about what you would like your optical instrument to do. Which would you like to see better—tiny objects or distant objects? Would you like to see around corners? Maybe you would prefer your instrument to produce striking images!

Check Your Progress You'll be working on this project as you study this chapter. To keep your project on track, look for Check Your Progress boxes at the following points.

Section 1 Review, page 242: Draw your optical instrument.
Section 3 Review, page 253: Build your optical instrument.
Section 5 Review, page 268: Test and modify your instrument. Prepare a manual explaining how your instrument works.

Present Your Project At the end of the chapter (page 271), you will demonstrate how your instrument works. You will also present your manual, showing the design and use of the instrument.

TEKS

In addition to process TEKS, this chapter addresses these concept TEKS as they relate to the chapter's topics.

(8.6) The student knows that interdependence occurs among living systems. The student is expected to:
(A) describe interactions among systems in the human organism.
(8.7) The student knows that there is a relationship between force and motion. The student is expected to:
(B) recognize that waves are generated and can travel through different media.

SECTION 1 Wave Reflection and Mirrors

DISCOVER · ACTIVITY · · · ·

How Does Your Reflection Wink?

1. Look at your face in a mirror. Wink your right eye. Which eye does your reflection wink?

2. Tape two mirrors together so that they open and close like a book. Open them so they form a 90° angle with each other. **CAUTION:** *Be careful of any sharp edges.*

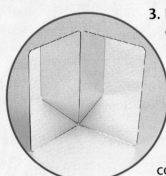

3. Looking into both mirrors at once, wink at your reflection again. Which eye does your reflection wink now?

Think It Over
Observing How does your reflection wink at you? How does the second reflection compare with the first reflection?

GUIDE FOR READING

◆ What happens when light strikes an object?

◆ What are the two kinds of reflection?

◆ What types of images are produced by plane, concave, and convex mirrors?

Reading Tip Before you read, preview the section and write down any unfamiliar terms. As you read, find the meaning of each term.

Key Terms opaque
• transparent • translucent
• ray • regular reflection
• diffuse reflection • image
• plane mirror • virtual image
• concave mirror • focal point
• real image • convex mirror

Have you ever looked at a store window on a bright, sunny day? In order to see inside, you may have used your hands to block the glare. The glare is actually reflected light. The glare from the store window shows that glass can reflect light. But if you look at a clear glass window with no glare, you can see right through it.

When Light Waves Strike an Object

When light waves strike an object, they can be reflected, absorbed, or transmitted, depending on the properties of the object. Most objects reflect or absorb light. A material that reflects or absorbs all of the light that strikes it is **opaque** (oh PAYK). Most objects are opaque. You cannot see through opaque objects because light cannot pass through them. Examples of opaque materials include wood, metal, cardboard, and cotton and wool fabrics.

A **transparent** material transmits light. When light strikes a transparent object, it passes through its medium, allowing you to see what is on the other side. Clear glass, water, and air are examples of transparent materials.

Other materials allow some light to pass through. This type of material is translucent. **Translucent** (trans LOO sunt) materials scatter light as the light passes through. You can usually tell that there is something behind a translucent material, but you cannot see the details of the objects behind the material clearly. Frosted glass and wax paper are translucent. Figure 1 shows opaque, transparent, and translucent objects.

Figure 1 The spools of thread are opaque. They reflect light of various colors. The pitcher and glass are transparent. They transmit light, allowing you to see the milk inside. The leaf is translucent. The frog can be seen through the leaf but lacks detail.

Kinds of Wave Reflection

When you look at some objects, such as a shiny metal fixture or a mirror, you can see yourself. But when you look at other objects, such as a book, a wooden table, or your pencil, you see only the object itself. You can see most objects because light reflects, or bounces, off them. What you see when you look at an object depends on how its surface reflects light. **The two kinds of reflection are regular and diffuse reflection.**

Regular Reflection To show how light travels and reflects, you can represent light waves as straight lines called **rays.** Light rays reflect from a surface according to the law of reflection: the angle of reflection equals the angle of incidence.

Regular reflection occurs when parallel rays of light hit a smooth surface. All the rays are reflected at the same angle. For example, if you look at a sheet of shiny metal, you can see your own reflection. The light rays coming from you strike the smooth surface and are reflected regularly.

Diffuse Reflection When parallel rays of light hit a bumpy, or uneven, surface, **diffuse reflection** occurs. Each ray obeys the law of reflection. But since each ray hits the surface at a different angle, the rays are reflected at different angles. Because the reflected rays travel in all directions, diffuse reflection allows you to see an object from any position.

The physical properties of most objects cause them to reflect light diffusely. This is because most objects do not have smooth surfaces. Even surfaces that appear to be smooth, such as a freshly painted wall, have small bumps that scatter light. If you look at a wall through a magnifying glass, you will see that the surface is not really smooth.

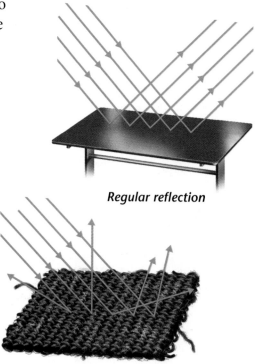

Regular reflection

Diffuse reflection

Figure 2 When light strikes a surface at an angle, it is reflected at the same angle. If the surface is smooth, the reflection is regular (top). If the surface is uneven, the reflection is diffuse (bottom).

Look at the back of a shiny spoon. What kind of image do you see? How does changing the distance between your eyes and the spoon affect what you see? What kind of mirror does the back of the spoon represent? Now look at the front of the spoon. What kind of mirror is the front of the spoon? What kind of image do you see ?

Mirrors

Did you look in a mirror this morning? Maybe you combed your hair or brushed your teeth in front of a mirror. A mirror is a sheet of glass that has a smooth, silver-colored coating on one side. When light passes through the glass, the properties of the coating on the back cause the light to reflect regularly, allowing you to see an image. An **image** is a copy of an object formed by reflected or refracted rays of light.

Mirrors can be flat or curved. The shape of the surface determines how the image will look. Depending on the shape of the mirror, the image can be the same size as the object, or it can be larger or smaller.

Plane Mirrors Look into a flat mirror, or **plane mirror.** You will see an image that is the same size as you are. Your image will seem to be the same distance behind the mirror as you are in front of it. **A plane mirror produces an image that is right-side up and the same size as the object being reflected.**

The image you see when you look in a plane mirror is a virtual image. **Virtual images** are right-side up, or upright. "Virtual" describes something that you can see, but does not really exist. You can't reach behind a mirror and touch your image.

Why do you see a virtual image? Figure 3 shows how the image of the dancer is formed by a plane mirror. Light rays reflected from the dancer travel out in all directions. The rays strike the mirror and are reflected toward the eye. The human brain assumes that light travels in a straight line. Even though the rays are reflected, the brain treats the rays as if they had come from behind the mirror. It is easiest to consider just the rays from the top and the bottom of the dancer. The dashed lines show the points from which the light rays appear to come. Since the dashed lines appear to come from behind the mirror, this is where the dancer's image appears to be located.

☑ *Checkpoint* *What is a virtual image?*

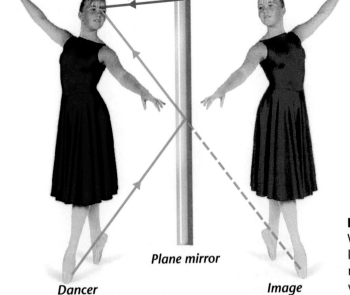

Plane mirror

Dancer

Image

Figure 3 A plane mirror forms a virtual image. When the dancer looks in the mirror, the rays of light from her body are reflected toward her. The rays appear to come from behind the mirror, where the image is formed.

Concave Mirrors A mirror with a surface that curves inward like the inside of a bowl is a **concave mirror.** Figure 4 shows how a concave mirror can reflect parallel rays of light so that they meet at a point. The point at which the rays meet is called the **focal point.**

Concave mirrors can form virtual images, real images, or no images. The type of image formed by a concave mirror depends on the position of the object in relation to the focal point. Figure 5 shows how concave mirrors form images. If the object is farther away from the mirror than the focal point, the reflected rays form a real image. A **real image** is formed when rays actually meet at a point. Real images are upside down, or inverted. A real image may be larger or smaller than the object. A virtual image is formed if the object is between the focal point and the mirror. The image appears to be behind the mirror and right-side up.

Some concave mirrors are used to project rays of light. For example, the bulb of a car's headlight is at the focal point of a concave mirror. When the light from the bulb hits the mirror, no image forms because the rays are reflected parallel to each other. This projects the light on the road ahead. Concave mirrors are also used to produce magnified images, as in makeup mirrors.

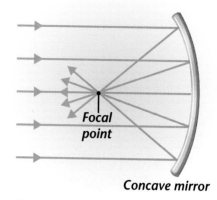

Concave mirror

Figure 4 This concave mirror reflects parallel rays of light back through the focal point.

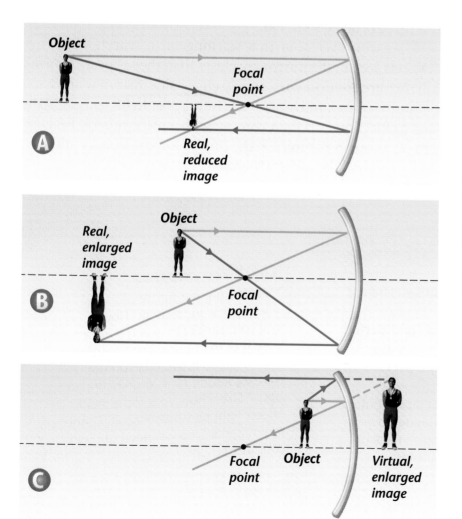

Figure 5 The type of image formed by a concave mirror depends on the position of the object in relation to the focal point. **(A), (B)** If the object is farther from the mirror than the focal point, the image is real and inverted. **(C)** If the object is between the mirror and the focal point, the image is virtual and upright. *Interpreting Diagrams How can you tell that the images in **A** and **B** are real?*

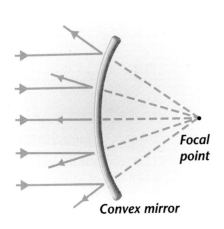

Focal
point

Convex mirror

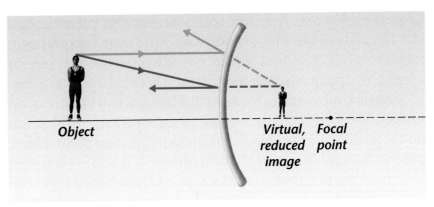

Object

Virtual,
reduced
image

Focal
point

Figure 6 A convex mirror reflects parallel rays of light as though they came from the focal point behind the mirror. The image formed by a convex mirror is always virtual. *Applying Concepts What is a convex mirror?*

Convex Mirrors A mirror with a surface that curves outward is called a **convex mirror.** Figure 6 shows how some convex mirrors reflect parallel rays of light. The rays spread out but appear to come from a focal point behind the mirror. The focal point of a convex mirror is the point from which the rays appear to come. **Since the rays do not actually meet, images formed by convex mirrors are always virtual.**

Have you ever seen this warning on a rearview mirror? "Objects seen in the mirror are closer than they appear." Convex mirrors are used in cars as passenger-side rearview mirrors. Because a convex mirror spreads out rays of light, you can see a larger reflection area than you can with a plane mirror. Because you see more in the mirror, the images appear smaller and farther away than the objects themselves.

Section 1 Review

1. Explain what happens when light strikes different types of objects.
2. Describe two ways in which light can be reflected.
3. What types of images are produced by a plane mirror? A concave mirror? A convex mirror?
4. **Thinking Critically Applying Concepts**
   A slide projector projects an upright image onto a screen. The slides must be placed upside down in the projector. Is the image on the screen real or virtual? Give two reasons for your answer.

Check Your Progress
CHAPTER PROJECT

Decide on the purpose of your optical instrument. How will you use it? Draw and label a sketch of the optical instrument you would like to build. Will you use mirrors, lenses, or a combination of both? Show how your instrument affects light rays that enter it. Gather the materials you will need to build your instrument.

② Wave Refraction and Lenses

DISCOVER •••••••••••••••••••••••••••••••••••• ACTIVITY ••••

How Can You Make an Image Appear on a Sheet of Paper?

1. Hold a hand lens about 2 meters from a window. Look through the lens. What do you see? **CAUTION:** *Do not look at the sun.*

2. Move the lens farther away from your eye. What changes do you notice?

3. Now hold the lens between the window and a sheet of paper, but closer to the paper. Slowly move the lens away from the paper and toward the window. Keep watching the paper. What do you see? What happens as you move the lens?

Think It Over

Observing How do you think an image is formed on a sheet of paper? Describe the image. Is it real or virtual? How do you know?

A fish tank can play tricks on your eyes. If you look through the side, the fish seems closer than if you look over the top. If you look through the corner, you may see the same fish twice. You see one image of the fish through the front of the tank and another image through the side of the tank. The two images appear in different places!

Refraction of Light Waves

As you look into a fish tank, you are seeing the light bend as it passes through three different media. The media are the water, the glass of the tank, and the air. As the light passes from one medium to the next, it refracts. **When light waves enter a new medium at an angle, their speed changes. The change in speed causes them to bend, or change direction.**

Refraction can cause you to see something that may not actually be there. For example, refraction can form a mirage. It can also help cause a beautiful sight, a rainbow. In a rainbow, raindrops refract and reflect sunlight, producing colors.

GUIDE FOR READING

◆ What happens when light waves enter a new medium at an angle?

◆ What kinds of images do convex and concave lenses form?

Reading Tip As you read, draw diagrams to show how each type of lens refracts light.

Key Terms index of refraction • mirage • lens • concave lens • convex lens

Figure 7 There is only one fish in this tank, but the refraction of light makes it look as though there are two.

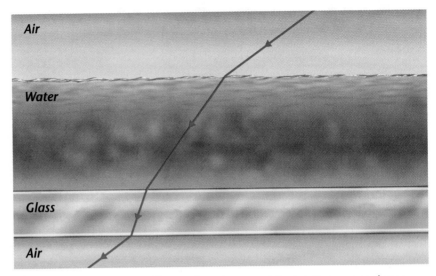

Disappearing Glass

Try this activity to see how light waves are refracted in different liquid media.

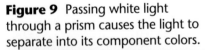

1. Place a small drinking glass inside a larger drinking glass. Can you see the small glass inside the larger one?

2. Fill both glasses with water. Look at the glasses from the side. Can you still see the smaller glass?

3. Empty and dry the glasses and refill them with vegetable oil. Describe what you see.

Inferring Why does the vegetable oil create a different effect from the water's effect?

Figure 8 As light passes from a less dense medium into a more dense medium, it slows down and is refracted. *Inferring Why does the light leaving the glass and entering air travel in its original direction?*

Index of Refraction Some media cause light to bend more than others. Figure 8 shows how light passes from air into water, from water into glass, and from glass into air again. When light passes from air into water, the light slows down. Light slows down even more when it passes from water into glass. Light travels fastest in air, a little slower in water, and slower still in glass. When light passes from glass back into air, the light speeds up. Notice that the ray that leaves the glass is traveling in the same direction as it was before it entered the water.

Glass causes light to bend more than either air or water because glass refracts light more. Another way to say this is that glass has a higher index of refraction than either air or water. A material's **index of refraction** is a measure of how much a ray of light bends when it enters that material. The higher the index of refraction of a medium, the more it bends light. The index of refraction of a vacuum is 1. The index of refraction of diamond is 2.42.

Figure 9 Passing white light through a prism causes the light to separate into its component colors.

Prisms Figure 9 shows that a beam of white light can be separated to show all the colors of the visible spectrum. Remember that white light is actually a mixture of many wavelengths of light, each with its own color. When white light enters a prism, each wavelength is refracted by a different amount. The longer the wavelength, the less the wave will be bent by a prism.

244

Rainbows When white light from the sun shines through tiny drops of water, a rainbow may appear. Raindrops act like tiny prisms, refracting and reflecting the light and separating the colors. The colors of the rainbow always appear in the same order because raindrops refract the shorter wavelengths the most. Red, with the longest wavelength, is refracted the least. Violet, with the shortest wavelength, is refracted the most. The result is that white light is separated into the colors of the visible spectrum: red, orange, yellow, green, blue, and violet.

INTEGRATING EARTH SCIENCE

Mirages Imagine that you are in a car moving down a road on a hot, sunny day. The road ahead looks wet. Yet when you get there, the road is perfectly dry. Did the puddles disappear just before you got there? No, they were never there at all! What you saw was a mirage. A **mirage** (mih RAHJ) is an image of a distant object caused by refraction of light.

Figure 11 shows how a mirage forms. The air higher up is cooler than the air near the road. Light travels faster when it reaches the warmer air. As a result, the rays bend as they travel downward. Near the ground, the rays are traveling almost parallel to the ground but continue to bend until they begin to travel upward. As they travel upward they bend in the other direction. Your brain assumes that the rays have traveled in a straight line. They look just like rays reflected off a smooth surface, such as water. The observer sees a mirage.

☑ *Checkpoint* *What causes a mirage?*

Figure 10 A rainbow forms when sunlight is refracted and reflected by tiny water droplets.

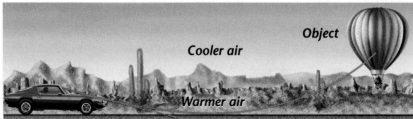
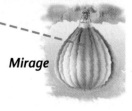

Figure 11 Light travels faster through hot air than through cool air. This causes light from the sky to bend as it approaches the ground. You see a mirage when refracted light appears to come from the ground.

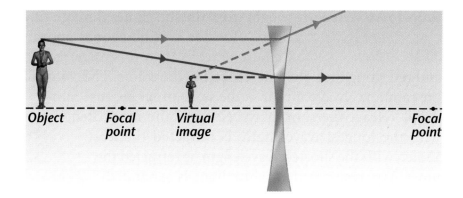

Figure 12 The ray that travels horizontally from the top of the object is refracted as though it is coming from the focal point on the same side of the lens as the object. The ray that travels toward the other focal point is refracted so it travels horizontally.
Interpreting Diagrams Why do the rays from a concave lens never meet?

Object   Focal point   Virtual image   Focal point

Light Waves and Lenses

Have you ever looked through binoculars, used a microscope or a camera, or worn eyeglasses? If so, you have used a lens to bend light. A **lens** is a curved piece of glass or other transparent material that is used to refract light. A lens forms an image by refracting light rays that pass through it. Like mirrors, lenses can have different shapes. The type of image formed by a lens depends on the shape of the lens.

Concave lens

Convex lens

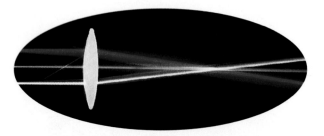

Figure 13 **(A)** A concave lens refracts parallel rays of light so that they appear to come from one of the focal points. **(B)** A convex lens refracts parallel rays of light so that they meet at the focal point.

Concave Lenses A **concave lens** is thinner in the center than at the edges. As parallel rays of light pass through a concave lens, they are bent away from the center of the lens. Figure 12 shows how the rays spread out, but appear to come from the focal point on the opposite side of the lens. **Because the light rays never meet, a concave lens can produce only a virtual image.**

Convex Lenses A **convex lens** is thicker in the center than at the edges. As parallel light rays pass through a convex lens, they are bent toward the center of the lens as shown in Figure 13B. The rays meet at the focal point of the lens and then continue on. The more curved the lens, the more it refracts light.

A convex lens acts somewhat like a concave mirror, because it focuses rays of light. **The type of image formed by a convex lens depends on the position of the object in relation to the focal point.** Figure 14 shows three examples. If the object is farther away than the focal point, the refracted rays form a real image on the other side of the lens. If the object is between the lens and the focal point, a virtual image forms on the same side of the lens as the object.

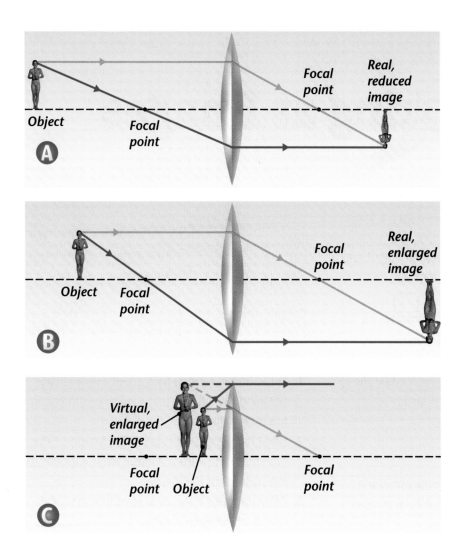

Figure 14 The type and size of image formed by a convex lens depend on the position of the object. **(A)**, **(B)** If the object is farther from the focal point than the lens, the image is real and inverted. **(C)** If the object is between the focal point and the lens, the image is virtual.

Section 2 Review

1. What happens to light waves as they pass from one medium into another medium?
2. What determines the type of image that is formed by a convex lens?
3. Why is it impossible for a concave lens to form a real image?
4. Explain why you sometimes see a rainbow during a rain shower or shortly afterward.
5. **Thinking Critically Problem Solving** Suppose you wanted to closely examine the leaf of a plant. Which type of lens would you use? Explain.

Science at Home

Pencil Bending Here's how you can bend a pencil without touching it. Put a pencil in a glass of water, as shown in the photograph. Have your family members look at the pencil from the side. Using the idea of refraction, explain to your family why the pencil appears as it does.

Looking at Images

In this lab, you will explore how images are formed by a convex lens.

Problem

How does the distance between an object and a convex lens affect the image formed?

Materials (per group)

tape
cardboard stand
light bulb and socket
battery and wires
computer (optional)

convex lens
blank sheet of paper
clay, for holding the lens
meter stick

Procedure

1. Tape the paper onto the cardboard stand.
2. Place a lit bulb more than 2 m from the paper. Use the lens to focus light from the bulb onto the paper. Measure the distance from the lens to the paper. This is the approximate focal length of the lens you are using. Also measure the height of the bulb.
3. Use a pencil and paper or the computer to make a data table like the one below. Add the data table to your notebook.
4. Now place the bulb more than twice the focal length away from the lens. Record the position and size of the focused image on the paper.
5. Repeat Step 4, except move the bulb so that it is just over one focal length away from the lens.

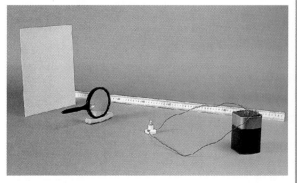

Analyze and Conclude

1. Is the image formed by a convex lens always upside down? If not, under what conditions is the image upright?
2. What happens to the size of the image as the bulb moves toward the lens? What happens to the position of the image?
3. What happens if the bulb is within one focal length of the lens? Explain.
4. **Think About It** Make a list of the variables in this experiment. Which variables did you keep constant? Which was the manipulated variable? Which was the responding variable?

Design an Experiment

With your teacher's approval and supervision, design an experiment to study images formed by convex lenses of various focal lengths. How does the focal length of the lens affect the position and size of the images produced?

DATA TABLE

Focal Length of Lens: _____ cm   Height of Bulb: _____ cm

Distance from Bulb to Lens (cm)	Image Position (upright or upside down)	Image Size (height in cm)

SECTION 3 Color

DISCOVER · ACTIVITY · · ·

How Do Colors Mix?

1. ✂ Carefully cut a disk with a diameter of about 10 cm out of a piece of sturdy white cardboard. Divide the disk into three equal-sized segments. Use colored pencils to color one segment red, the next green, and the third blue.

2. Carefully punch two holes, about 2 cm apart, on opposite sides of the center of the disk.

3. Thread a string about 1 m long through the holes. Tie the ends of the string together so that the string forms a loop that passes through both holes.

4. With equal lengths of string on each side of the disk, turn the disk so that you are winding up the string. Predict what color(s) you will see if the disk spins fast.

5. Spin the disk by pulling and relaxing the string.

Think It Over

Observing What color do you see as the wheel spins fast? Was your prediction correct?

As the morning sun slowly rises over the flower garden, the sunlight begins to reveal bright pink and orange poppies, purple pansies, and a striking display of many other colors. Each flower is beautiful, yet different. The light from the sun allows you to see each color clearly. But sunlight is white light. What makes each flower appear to be a different color?

The Color of Objects

Color is a physical property of many objects, including flowers. The colors of flowers and other objects depend on how they reflect light. Each flower absorbs some wavelengths of light and reflects other wavelengths. **The color of an object is determined by the color of the light it reflects.**

GUIDE FOR READING

◆ What determines the color of an object?

◆ What are the primary colors of light?

◆ How is mixing pigments different from mixing light?

Reading Tip Before you read, use the section headings to make an outline about color. Leave space to take notes.

Key Terms primary color
• secondary color
• complementary color
• pigment

249

Objects in White Light Flowers and other objects reflect different colors of light. For example, when white light strikes the orange petals of a lily, the petals reflect mostly orange wavelengths. The petals absorb the other wavelengths. You see the petals as orange because orange wavelengths of light bounce off them and enter your eyes. On the other hand, the stem and leaves appear green. They reflect mostly green wavelengths and absorb the other colors.

What happens with black and white objects? A skunk looks black and white because some parts of it reflect all wavelengths of light while other parts do not reflect any light. When white light strikes the skunk's stripe, all the colors are reflected. The colors combine, so you see white light. When white light strikes the black parts of the skunk, all the light is absorbed and none is reflected back to you. Your eyes see black.

Even colored and white objects can appear black if there is no light to reflect off them. Imagine being in a dark room. If there is no light present, then no light can reflect off the things in the room. No light enters your eyes, so you see nothing. If there is a small amount of light in the room, you may be able to make out the shapes of objects. However, you will not be able to tell their colors.

Objects in Colored Light Objects can look a different color depending on the color of the light in which they are seen. Figure 17 shows two photographs of a desktop, each taken under different light. The picture on the left was taken under ordinary white light. In it, the keyboard is blue and the folder is red. The picture on the right was taken under green light. When green light shines

Figure 15 The petals of this lily appear orange because they reflect orange light. The stems and leaves appear green because they reflect green light.

Figure 16 This skunk's white fur reflects all colors of light. *Applying Concepts Why do the skunk's legs look black?*

Figure 17 In white light, objects appear in many different colors (left). If viewed under green light, the same objects appear in shades of green or black (right).
Predicting How would these objects look under blue light?

on an object, the object either reflects or absorbs the green light. Since red and blue objects reflect only red and blue light, they absorb all of the green light. The binder looks black.

Objects Seen Through Filters Some transparent materials allow only certain colors of light to pass through them. They reflect or absorb the other colors. Such materials are called color filters. For example, a red filter is a piece of glass or plastic that allows only red light to pass through. Spotlights on theater stages often use color filters to produce different color effects. Photographic slides are color filters, too. A slide projector shines white light through a combination of color filters. The image you see on the screen shows the colors that each part of the slide allows through.

☑ *Checkpoint* What is a color filter?

Combining Colors

An understanding of color is very useful in photography, art, theater lighting, and printing. People who work with color must know how to produce a wide range of colors from just a few basic colors. It is possible to produce any color by mixing colors of the spectrum in varying amounts. Three colors that can be used to make any other color are called **primary colors.** Any two primary colors combined in equal amounts produce a **secondary color.**

Mixing Colors of Light **The primary colors of light are red, green, and blue. When combined in equal amounts, the primary colors produce white light.** But if they are combined in varying amounts, they can produce any other color. For example, red and green combine to form yellow light. Yellow is a secondary color of light because it is produced from two primary colors.

Developing Hypotheses

1. Carefully make a **ACTIVITY** color wheel with eight segments. Use colored pencils to color alternate blue and yellow segments.

2. Predict what color you will see if you spin the wheel. Write a hypothesis of what you think the outcome will be.

3. Spin the wheel. What do you see? Does it confirm your hypothesis?

4. Repeat the activity with color wheels that have different pairs of colors.

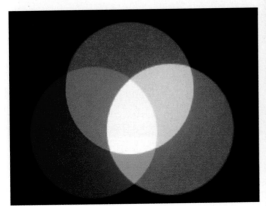

Primary colors of light

Figure 18 The primary colors of light are red, green, and blue. When combined in equal amounts, the primary colors of light form white light. A color television produces all colors of light by combining red, green, and blue light in varying amounts. *Interpreting Photographs How does a television show black?*

Visual Arts
CONNECTION

Ever since the first cave artists painted about 20,000 years ago, pigments made from natural materials have been used to create pictures. In the 1400s, Renaissance painters such as Leonardo da Vinci and Raphael used many more colorful pigments to create their vivid paintings. Pigments were derived from minerals, plants, and animals.

In Your Journal

Look at the color names for markers, paints, or crayons. Do you see vermilion (red), azure (blue) or ochre (brown)? These colors were all originally made from minerals. Now these colors are made from chemicals. Can you find the names of other colors that may have originally come from minerals?

The secondary colors of light are yellow (red + green), cyan (green + blue), and magenta (red + blue). Figure 18 shows the primary colors of light.

A primary color and a secondary color can combine to make white. Any two colors that combine to form white light are called **complementary colors.** Yellow and blue are complementary colors, as are cyan and red, and magenta and green.

INTEGRATING TECHNOLOGY A color television screen produces only three colors of light. Figure 18 shows a magnified portion of a color television screen. Notice that the picture on the screen is made up of little groups of red, green, and blue lights. By varying the brightness of each colored light, the television produces pictures of many different colors.

Mixing Pigments How do artists produce the many shades of colors you see in paintings? Paints and dyes have different colors because of the pigments they contain. **Pigments** are substances that are used to color other materials. Color pigments are opaque substances that reflect particular colors. The color you see is the color that particular pigment reflects.

Mixing colors of pigments is different from mixing colors of light. **As pigments are added together, fewer colors of light are reflected and more are absorbed.** The more pigments that are combined, the darker the mixture looks.

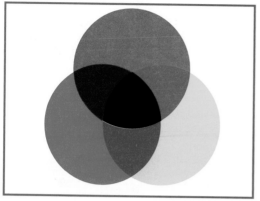

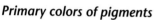
Primary colors of pigments

Figure 19 The primary colors of pigments are cyan, yellow, and magenta (left). The photograph shows a printed image and the round inset shows an enlargement of it. Four-color printing uses the three primary colors of pigment, plus black.

The primary colors of pigments are cyan, yellow, and magenta. If you combine all three primary colors of pigments in equal amounts, you get black. If you combine two primary colors of pigments in equal amounts, you get a secondary color. The secondary colors of pigments are red (magenta + yellow), green (cyan + yellow), and blue (magenta + cyan). By combining pigments in varying amounts, you can produce any other color. Figure 19 shows the primary colors of pigments.

If you use a magnifying glass to look at color pictures in this book, you will see that the pictures are made up of tiny dots of different colors of ink. The colors used are cyan, yellow, and magenta. Black ink is also used to make pictures darker. Because of the four colors of ink used, the process that produced this book is called four-color printing.

Section 3 Review

1. Why do objects have different colors?
2. What are the primary colors of light? What happens when the primary colors of light are mixed in equal amounts?
3. What happens when the primary colors of pigments are mixed in equal amounts?
4. What colors are used in the four-color printing process?
5. **Thinking Critically Comparing and Contrasting** Make a table that compares and contrasts the primary and secondary colors of light and those of pigments.

Check Your Progress CHAPTER PROJECT
Build your optical instrument according to the sketch you prepared. How does your instrument use reflection or refraction to produce and clarify images? Do you need to be able to change the focus of the image? Does your instrument have moving parts? How will you combine the different parts of the instrument?

Changing Colors

Stage lighting in theaters uses color filters to control the colors of light on stage. In this lab you will study the effect of color filters on white light.

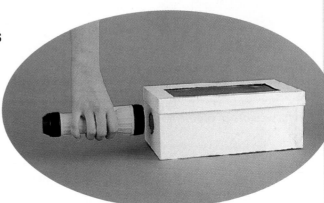

Skills Focus

observing, predicting, inferring

Materials (per group)

shoe box
flashlight
scissors
removable tape
red object (such as a ripe tomato)
yellow object (such as a ripe lemon)
blue object (such as blue construction paper)
red, green, and blue cellophane, enough to cover the top of the shoe box

Procedure

1. Carefully cut a large rectangular hole in the lid of the shoe box. The hole should be just a little smaller than the lid of the box.
2. Carefully cut a small, round hole in the center of one of the ends of the shoe box.
3. Tape the red cellophane under the lid of the shoe box, covering the hole in the lid.
4. Place the objects in the box and put the lid on.
5. In a darkened room, shine the flashlight into the shoe box through the side hole. Note the apparent color of each object in the box.
6. Repeat Steps 3–5 using the other colors of cellophane.

Analyze and Conclude

1. What did you see when you looked through the red cellophane? Explain why each object appeared as it did.
2. What did you see when you looked through the blue cellophane? Explain.
3. What color of light does each piece of cellophane allow through?
4. Predict what you would see under each piece of cellophane if you put a white object in the box. Test your prediction.
5. Use diagrams to show how each color of cellophane affects the white light from the flashlight.
6. **Think About It** Do color filters work more like pigments or like colors of light? What would happen if you shined a flashlight through both a red and a green filter? Explain.

Getting Involved

Visit a local theater or talk to a lighting designer to find out how color filters are used to produce different stage effects.

SECTION 4 Seeing Light Waves

DISCOVER ···················· ACTIVITY····

Can You See Everything With One Eye?

1. Write an X and an O on a sheet of paper. They should be about 5 cm apart.
2. Hold the sheet of paper at arm's length.
3. Close or cover your left eye. Stare at the X with your right eye.
4. Slowly move the paper toward your face while staring at the X. What do you notice?

5. Repeat the activity, keeping both eyes open. What difference do you notice?

Think It Over
Posing Questions Write two questions about vision that you could investigate using the X and the O.

The excitement mounts as the pitcher goes into his windup. As he goes through his motion, he keeps his eye on the strike zone. The batter watches the pitcher release the ball, then swings. Crack! The batter strikes the ball, drops the bat, and sprints toward first base. From your seat behind home plate, you watch the ball travel toward the outfield. Will it be a base hit? The left fielder watches the ball leave the bat and travel toward him. It goes over his head—a two-base hit!

Everyone involved has been following the first rule of baseball: Keep your eye on the ball. As the ball moves, the eyes must adjust continuously to keep it in focus. Fortunately, this change in focus happens seemingly automatically thanks to the interaction of your nervous, muscular, and circulatory systems. These same systems work together to help the batter run to second base and to help you jump up and cheer.

GUIDE FOR READING

◆ How do your eyes allow you to see?

◆ What kind of lenses are used to correct vision problems?

Reading Tip As you read, make a flowchart that shows how light travels through the eye and how the brain interprets the image.

Key Terms cornea • iris • pupil • retina • rod • cone • optic nerve • nearsighted • farsighted

Figure 20 As the ball moves through the air, your eyes must continuously adjust their focus to see the ball.

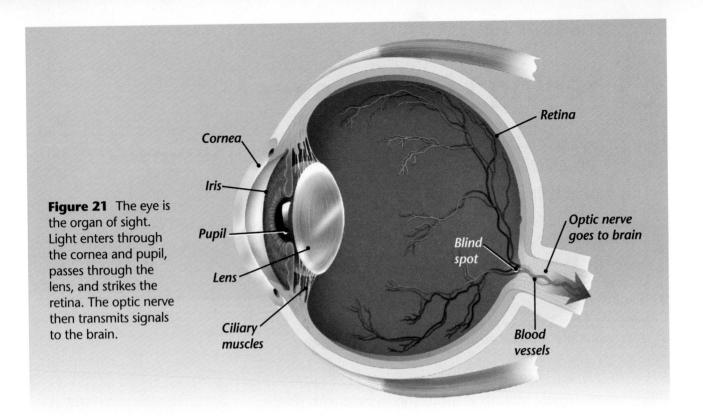

Cornea

Iris

Pupil

Lens

Ciliary muscles

Retina

Blind spot

Optic nerve goes to brain

Blood vessels

Figure 21 The eye is the organ of sight. Light enters through the cornea and pupil, passes through the lens, and strikes the retina. The optic nerve then transmits signals to the brain.

The Eye—An Organ System

Your eyes are complicated organs, with each part playing its own role in helping you see. **Seeing objects begins in the eye. Interactions among the nervous, muscular, and circulatory systems occur in the eye as light waves from an object enter the organ.** Look at the parts of the eye in Figure 21.

The Cornea Light enters the eye through the transparent surface structure called the **cornea.** The cornea protects the eye. It also acts as a lens, bending light waves as they enter the eye. Each time you blink, your eyelids act like little windshield wipers, cleansing and moistening the cornea.

The Iris The **iris** is a ring of muscle that contracts and expands to change the amount of light that enters the eye. The iris gives the eye color. The iris can be blue, brown, gray, green, or shades of these colors.

Figure 22 In dim light, the iris contracts. The pupil gets bigger and allows more light into the eye. *Relating Cause and Effect What happens in bright light?*

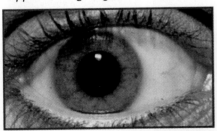

The Pupil The **pupil** is the part of the eye that looks black. It is actually an opening into the dark inside of the eye and is covered by the cornea. The size of the pupil depends on whether the iris is contracted or expanded. As light dims, the pupil enlarges, allowing in more light. As light brightens, the pupil becomes smaller, allowing in less light.

The Lens Just behind the pupil is the lens. The lens of your eye is a convex lens. The lens refracts light, forming an image on the lining of your eyeball. Figure 23 shows how the lens changes its focus. When you focus on a distant object, the ciliary muscles holding the lens relax, making the lens longer and thinner. When you focus on a nearby object, the muscles contract and the lens becomes shorter and fatter.

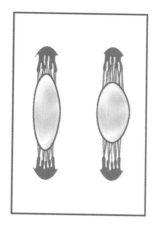

Figure 23 The ciliary muscles holding the lens in place contract and relax to change the shape of the lens.

The Retina The layer of cells lining the inside of the eye is the **retina.** As the cornea and the lens refract light, an upside-down image is formed on the retina. The retina is made up of millions of tiny, light-sensitive cells called rods and cones. The rods and cones generate nerve signals in response to light. The body's circulatory system brings food and removes wastes from the rods and cones.

The **rods** contain a pigment that reacts to small amounts of light. The rods distinguish among black, white, and shades of gray. They allow you to see in dim light, so they are important for night vision. In contrast, the **cones** respond to colors. There are three types of cones: those that detect red light, those that detect green light, and those that detect blue light. The cone cells function only in bright light. This is why it is difficult to distinguish colors in dim light.

The Optic Nerve and the Brain The signals generated by the rods and cones travel to your brain along a short, thick nerve called the **optic nerve.** When the signals reach your brain, the brain turns the image right-side up. It also combines the two images, one from each eye, into a single three-dimensional image.

There is one spot on the retina that does not have any rods or cones. This blind spot is the part of the retina where the optic nerve begins. You cannot see light that falls on the blind spot. However, an object whose light falls on the blind spot of one eye can usually be seen with the other eye. If you keep both eyes open, you do not notice the effect of the blind spots.

☑ *Checkpoint* *Where in the eye is the image formed?*

Correcting Vision

In some people, the shape of the eyeball causes the image on the retina to be slightly out of focus. Fortunately, wearing glasses or contact lenses can usually correct this type of vision problem. **Some lenses in eyeglasses are convex and some are concave. The type of lens used depends on whether the eye is too long or too short.**

True Colors ACTIVITY

When you stare too long at a color, the cones in your eyes get tired.

1. Stare at the bottom right star of the flag for at least 60 seconds. Do not move your eyes or blink during that time.

2. Now stare at a sheet of blank white paper.

Observing What do you see when you look at the white paper? How are the colors you see related to the colors in the original art?

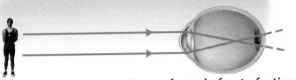

Nearsightedness (eyeball too long)

Image forms in front of retina

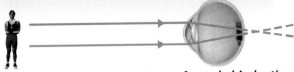

Farsightedness (eyeball too short)

Image forms behind retina

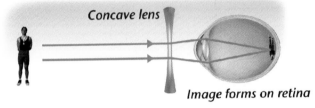

Correction

Concave lens

Image forms on retina

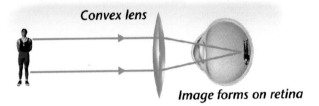

Correction

Convex lens

Image forms on retina

Figure 24 Nearsightedness and farsightedness are caused when the eyeball is a little too long or too short. Both can be corrected by wearing lenses.

Nearsightedness A **nearsighted** person can see nearby things clearly, but objects at a distance appear blurry. This happens because the eyeball is a little too long. The lens focuses the image in front of the retina. A nearsighted person can wear eyeglasses with concave lenses to see more clearly. A concave lens spreads out the rays a little before they enter the lens of the eye. This causes the image to form a little farther back, on the retina.

Farsightedness A **farsighted** person can see distant objects clearly, but nearby objects appear blurry. This happens when the eyeball is a little too short. The lens focuses the rays of light so that they would meet behind the retina. The image that falls on the retina is out of focus. A farsighted person can wear glasses with convex lenses. A convex lens makes the rays bend toward each other a little before they enter the eye. A clear image is then formed on the retina.

Section 4 Review

1. What happens in the eye to allow you to see?
2. What causes nearsightedness? Farsightedness? How can each be corrected?
3. Describe briefly the function of each of these structures in allowing a person to see: the cornea, pupil, lens, retina, optic nerve, brain.
4. **Thinking Critically Comparing and Contrasting** Compare and contrast the functions of the rods and the cones.

Science at Home

Optical Illusion Roll a sheet of paper into a tube and hold one end up to your right eye. Hold your left hand against the left side of the far end of the tube with your palm facing toward you. Keeping both eyes open, look at a distant object. Draw and label a diagram of what you see. What do you think causes this optical illusion?

DISCOVER •• ACTIVITY •••

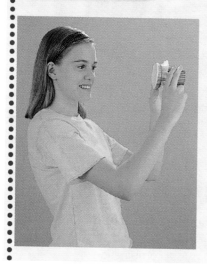

How Does a Pinhole Viewer Work?

1. ✂ Carefully use a pin to make a tiny hole in the center of the bottom of a paper cup.

2. Place a piece of wax paper over the open end of the cup. Hold the paper in place with a rubber band.

3. Turn off the room lights. Point the end of the cup with the hole in it at a bright window. **CAUTION:** *Do not look directly at the sun.*

4. Look at the image formed on the wax paper.

Think It Over

Classifying Describe the image you see. Is it upside down or right-side up? Is it smaller or larger than the actual object? What type of image is it?

Have you ever seen photos of the moons of Jupiter? Have you ever thought it would be exciting to fly close to the rings of Saturn? Of course you know that traveling in space has been done for only a few decades. But you might be surprised to know that the moons of Jupiter and the rings of Saturn had not been seen by anyone before the year 1600. It was only about 1609 that a new invention, the telescope, made those objects visible to people on Earth.

Since the 1600s, astronomers have built ever more powerful telescopes, allowing them to see greater detail of objects in space. The Trifid Nebula, for example, is visible as a cloud of gas and dust 28,000 trillion kilometers from Earth. It took about 3,000 years for light from this nebula to travel to Earth.

In this section you will learn how simple a device the telescope is. You may wonder why no one invented it sooner!

GUIDE FOR READING

◆ How do telescopes and microscopes work?

◆ How does a camera work?

◆ How is laser light different from ordinary light?

Reading Tip Before you read, preview the section to identify devices that use light. As you read, make notes about how each device is commonly used.

Key Terms telescope
• refracting telescope
• objective lens • eyepiece lens
• reflecting telescope
• microscope • camera • laser
• hologram • optical fiber
• total internal reflection

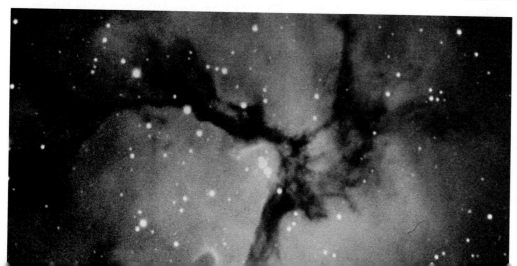

◀ The Trifid Nebula

259

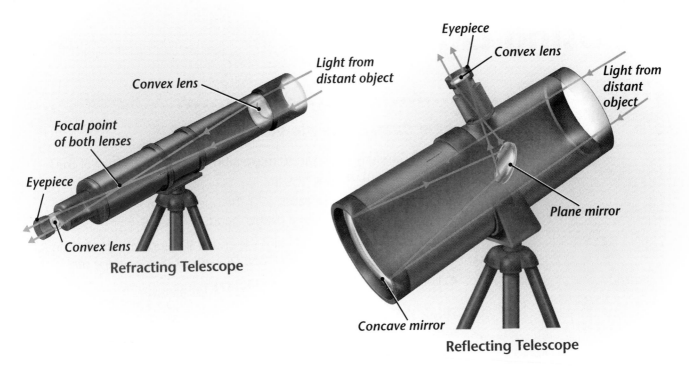

Refracting Telescope

Convex lens
Light from distant object
Focal point of both lenses
Eyepiece
Convex lens

Reflecting Telescope

Eyepiece
Convex lens
Light from distant object
Plane mirror
Concave mirror

Figure 25 A refracting telescope (left) uses a combination of lenses to form an image. A reflecting telescope (right) uses a combination of lenses and mirrors to form an image.

Telescopes

Distant objects are difficult to see because light from them has spread out by the time it reaches your eyes. Your eyes are too small to gather much light. A **telescope** forms enlarged images of distant objects. **Telescopes use lenses or mirrors to collect and focus light from distant objects.** The most common use of telescopes is to collect light from space. This allows astronomers to see objects they could not see with their eyes alone.

There are two main types of telescopes: refracting telescopes and reflecting telescopes. Both types are shown in Figure 25. A **refracting telescope** consists of two convex lenses, one at each end of a long tube. The larger lens is the objective lens. The **objective lens** gathers the light coming from an object and focuses the rays to form a real image. The lens close to your eye is the eyepiece lens. The **eyepiece lens** magnifies the image so you can see it clearly. The image you see through a refracting telescope is upside down.

A **reflecting telescope** uses a large concave mirror to gather light. The mirror collects light from distant objects and focuses the rays to form a real image. A small mirror inside the telescope reflects the image to the eyepiece lens. The eyepiece can be replaced by a camera to record the image. The image you see through a reflecting telescope is upside down also.

✓ *Checkpoint* What are the two main types of telescopes?

What a View!

ACTIVITY

You can use two hand lenses of different strengths to form an image.

1. Hold the stronger lens close to your eye.
2. Hold the other lens at arm's length.
3. Use your lens combination to view a distant object. **CAUTION:** *Do not look at the sun.* Adjust the distance of the farther lens until the image is clear.

Classifying What type of image do you see? What type of telescope is similar to this lens combination?

260

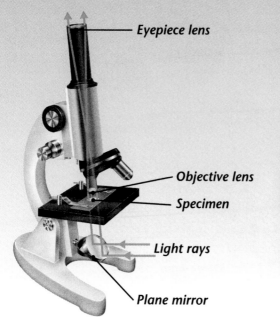

Eyepiece lens

Objective lens

Specimen

Light rays

Plane mirror

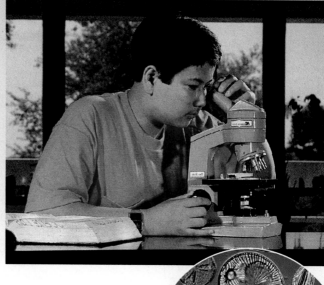

Figure 26 A microscope uses a combination of lenses to form enlarged images of tiny objects. You can use a microscope to look at microorganisms such as these single-celled algae. *Interpreting Photographs How does light move through a microscope to your eye?*

Microscopes

What would happen if you used a telescope to look at small objects close up? The principle of a refracting telescope can also be used to enlarge very small objects. A **microscope** forms enlarged images of tiny objects. **A microscope uses a combination of lenses to produce and magnify an image.**

Figure 26 shows how a microscope works. The specimen to be viewed is placed on a glass or plastic slide and covered with a coverslip. The slide is then placed on the platform of the microscope. A light source or a mirror illuminates the slide from below. The objective lens, placed very close to the slide, forms a real, but enlarged, image of the tiny object. The eyepiece lens enlarges the image even more. The image can be hundreds of times larger than the object itself. Most microscopes have two or three objective lenses so you can change the magnifying power.

Cameras

A **camera** uses lenses to focus light and record an image of an object. Cameras range from simple pinhole cameras to high-tech models used by professional photographers. They all work in basically the same way.

In a pinhole camera, an object's light rays enter a small box through a tiny pinhole. This light forms a real upside down image on the back of the box. However, most cameras are more complex.

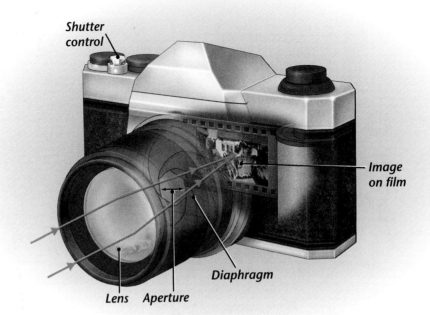

Figure 27 A camera uses a lens to project an image onto film. *Comparing and Contrasting Compare the lens, diaphragm, aperture, and film of the camera to the corresponding parts of the eye.*

Figure 27 shows the structure of a camera. The shutter is a little door behind an aperture, or hole. **When you press the button of a camera to take a photograph, you briefly open the shutter. This allows light to hit the film.** The shutter speed is the amount of time the shutter is open, or the exposure time. The diaphragm controls the amount of light that enters the camera by changing the size of the aperture. This is similar to the way that the iris of your eye controls the amount of light that enters your eye through the pupil.

Inside the camera, light passes through a convex lens or a combination of lenses. The lens focuses the light to form a real image on the film. To get a clear, properly focused image, the lens must move closer to or away from the film, depending on whether the object is close or far away. Most cameras allow you to move the lens by turning a ring on the front of the camera. An automatic camera moves the lens itself until the image is focused.

Photographic film is a material that undergoes a chemical change when exposed to light. The film is developed into negatives by treating it with chemicals. The negative is used to print the image on paper. The result is a photograph.

☑ *Checkpoint* *What part of a camera controls the amount of light that enters the camera?*

Lasers

In a laser show, thin beams of light flash across the walls and ceiling. These are not ordinary beams of light. The light can be focused into a narrow beam with very little spread. It can produce a clear, sharp image on a flat surface. The properties of these beams of light allow them to have many different uses.

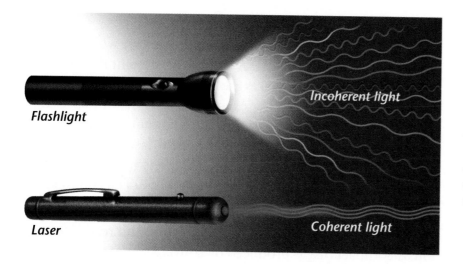

Flashlight

Incoherent light

Laser

Coherent light

Figure 28 White light is made up of many different wavelengths, or colors. Laser light consists of light of only one wavelength. All the crests of laser light are in step with each other.

When you turn on an ordinary light bulb, the light spreads out and is visible around the room. Ordinary white light is made up of light of many different colors and wavelengths. **A laser beam consists of waves that all have the same wavelength, or color. The waves are coherent, or in step.** All the crests of the waves align with each other, as do all the troughs.

The word **laser** comes from the first letters of the words that describe how it works: **l**ight **a**mplification by **s**timulated **e**mission of **r**adiation. *Light amplification* means that the light is strengthened, or given more energy. *Stimulated emission* means that the atoms emit light when exposed to radiation.

A laser consists of a tube that contains a material such as ruby or a helium-neon mixture. The material used determines the wavelength of the light waves that are generated.

Electricity, a light flash, or a chemical reaction causes the material in the tube to emit light. Recall that light consists of photons, which act like waves and particles. These photons travel up and down the tube. One end of the tube is covered with a mirror which reflects the photons that hit it. The photons then travel to a partially reflecting mirror at the other end of the tube. As the photons travel through the tube, they bump into other atoms, which emit more photons with the same amount of energy as the one that caused the collision. This process continues until there is a stream of in-step photons traveling up and down the tube. Finally, some of the light "leaks" through the partially reflecting mirror. The light that comes out of the tube is the laser beam.

Figure 29 This diagram of a ruby laser shows photons moving up and down the tube. The light that comes out of the tube is the laser beam.

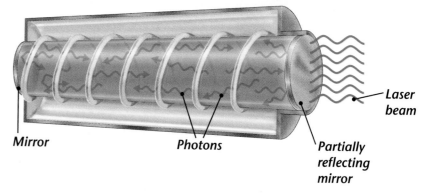

Mirror

Photons

Laser beam

Partially reflecting mirror

Uses of Lasers

Lasers have many practical applications. Lasers are widely used by surveyors and engineers. A laser beam is so straight that it can be used to make sure that surfaces are level and that bridges and tunnels are properly aligned. For example, a laser beam was used to guide the tunnel diggers who dug the Channel Tunnel between England and France. Some very powerful lasers can even cut through steel. Many stores and supermarkets use lasers. A laser scans the universal product code, or bar code. The store's computer then displays the price of the object.

Compact Discs Lasers can be used to store and read information. A compact disc is produced by converting data into electrical signals. The electrical signals are converted to a laser beam, which cuts a pattern of pits on a blank disc. When you play a compact disc or read one with a computer, a laser beam shines on the disc's surface. The beam is reflected onto a light detector.

SCIENCE & History

Optical Instruments

The development of optical instruments has changed the way we look at the world and beyond. It has allowed major scientific discoveries.

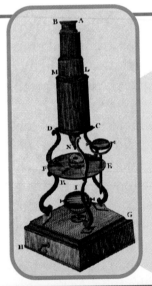

1595 THE NETHERLANDS
Microscopes

The first useful microscope is thought to have been constructed by Zacharias Jansen or his father, Hans. The Jansen microscope could magnify images up to nine times the size of the object. By the mid-1600s, microscopes looked like the one shown.

1300   **1400**   **1500**   **1600**

1350 ITALY
Spectacles

Craftsmen made small disks of glass that could be framed and worn in front of the eyes. Early spectacles consisted of convex lenses. They were used as reading glasses.

1607 THE NETHERLANDS
Telescopes

The first telescope was made of two convex lenses. It was from this simple invention that the Italian scientist Galileo developed his more powerful telescopes shown here.

The reflection patterns vary due to the pits on the disc's surface. The compact disc player or disc drive changes these patterns into electrical signals. You sense the signals as sound or visual images.

Surgery  Doctors can use lasers instead of scalpels to make incisions. The beam of light can be powerful enough to cut through flesh. As the laser makes the incision, it seals the cut blood vessels. This reduces the amount of blood a patient loses. Laser incisions usually heal faster than scalpel cuts, so the patient's recovery time is reduced.

Eye doctors use lasers to repair detached retinas. If the retina falls away from the inside of the eye, the rods and cones can no longer send signals to the brain. This can lead to total or partial blindness. The doctor can use a laser to attach the retina back onto the eyeball. Lasers can also be used to destroy or remove skin blemishes and cancerous growths.

In Your Journal

Find out more about early photography and people's reactions to it. Then imagine you are an early photographer explaining photography to someone who has never seen a photo. Create a two-page dialog in which you answer that person's questions on the process and possible uses of photography.

1990 UNITED STATES

Hubble Space Telescope

This large reflecting telescope was launched by the crew of the space shuttle *Discovery*. It can detect infrared, visible, and ultraviolet rays in space and send pictures back to Earth.

1700　　**1800**　　**1900**　　**2000**

1826 FRANCE

Cameras

The earliest camera, the pinhole camera, was adapted to form and record permanent images by Joseph Nicéphore Niépce and Louis-Jacques-Mandé Daguerre of France. This is one of Nicéphore Niépce's earliest photographic images.

1960 UNITED STATES

Lasers

The first laser, built by American Theodore Maiman, used a rod of ruby to produce light. Since then, lasers have been used in numerous ways, including engineering, medicine, and communications.

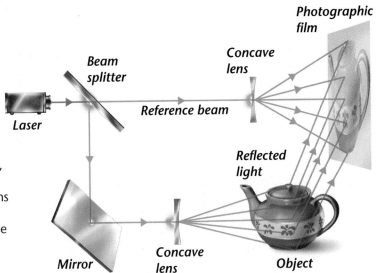

Photographic film

Beam splitter

Concave lens

Reference beam

Laser

Reflected light

Mirror

Concave lens

Object

Figure 30 To form a hologram, the light from a laser is split into two beams. When the two beams strike the photographic film, an interference pattern produces the image, or hologram.

Holography Check out your local video store or newsstand. Some videos and magazines have pictures that appear to move as you walk by. A **hologram** is a three-dimensional photograph created by using the light from a laser. The process is called holography.

Figure 30 shows how a hologram is produced. A laser beam is split into two beams. One beam passes through a concave lens. Behind the lens is a piece of photographic film. The concave lens bends the rays of light before they hit the film. The second beam is sent to a mirror and reflected toward another concave lens. The object being photographed is behind this lens. Again, the rays are bent by the lens before they hit the object. The object then reflects these rays toward the film, where they interfere with rays from the first beam. The interference pattern between the two beams of light creates a three-dimensional image that is recorded on the film.

☑ *Checkpoint* *What are four uses of lasers?*

Figure 31 Optical fibers are thin strands of glass or plastic that carry light.

Optical Fibers

Lasers are also used in communications. A laser beam is electromagnetic radiation of a single wavelength. It is similar to radio waves and so can carry signals by modulation. Unlike radio waves, laser beams are not usually sent through the air. Instead, they are sent through optical fibers. **Optical fibers** are long, thin strands of glass or plastic that can carry light for long distances without allowing the light to fade out. The physical properties of glass and plastic make them ideal everyday materials to use in optical fibers. They can carry many more signals than metal wiring.

EXPLORING Uses of Lasers

The invention of the laser has led to many developments in technology and communication.

A laser beam reads information from tiny pits on a compact disc. ▲

▲ Civil engineers use laser beams to ensure that buildings are straight.

▼ Optical fibers carry beams of laser light great distances. One tiny fiber can carry thousands more phone conversations than the traditional copper wire cable.

▲ A supermarket scanner reflects a laser off a set of lines known as a universal product code, or UPC. Each product has a unique code. This code represents a number that is programmed into the store's computer. The computer then displays the name of the object and the price on a screen near the cash register.

Small, hand-held lasers are commonly used as pointers in lectures and presentations.

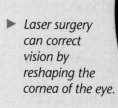

◀ Banks now commonly put small holograms on credit cards for security reasons. The hologram makes credit cards difficult to copy.

▶ Laser surgery can correct vision by reshaping the cornea of the eye.

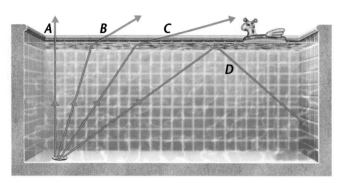

Figure 32 The angle of the light beam determines whether or not the light can leave the medium. If the angle is great enough, the light is reflected back into the water.

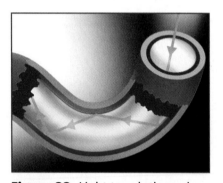

Figure 33 Light travels through an optical fiber by total internal reflection.

Figure 32 shows how the light can stay inside a medium and not pass through the surface to the outside. When a light beam hits a surface at a 0° angle of incidence, it goes through the surface without being bent. As the angle of incidence gets larger, the light is bent more and more. When it travels nearly parallel to the surface, all of the light is reflected. This complete reflection of light by the inside surface of a medium is called **total internal reflection.** Figure 33 shows how a laser beam reflects off the inside of an optical fiber and keeps going, even if the optical fiber is bent.

Communications To send signals through optical fibers, the electrical signals that start out over copper wires are changed into pulses of light by tiny lasers. Then the signals can travel over long ranges in the optical fiber. Optical fibers have led to great improvements in telephone service, computer networks, and cable television systems. Signals sent over optical fibers are usually faster and clearer than those sent over copper wire. One tiny optical fiber can carry thousands of phone conversations at the same time. Optical fibers are much thinner than copper wire. Therefore, many more optical fibers than copper wire can be placed in a given amount of space.

Medicine Optical fibers are commonly used in medical instruments. Doctors can insert a thin optical fiber inside various parts of the body, such as the heart or the stomach. The optical fiber can be attached to a microscope or a camera. In this way, doctors can examine internal organs without having to perform surgery.

 Section 5 Review

1. Compare and contrast refracting telescopes and reflecting telescopes.
2. How does a microscope work?
3. Why does a camera produce an upside-down image?
4. How does a laser generate light waves that are different from those generated by ordinary light bulbs?
5. **Thinking Critically Making Judgments** Do you think it would be dangerous to look into a laser beam? Explain your answer.

Check Your Progress
CHAPTER PROJECT

Now it is time to test your optical instrument. Does it work as you designed it to? Can you adjust the mirror or lenses to change the focus of the image? Do moving parts move smoothly and easily? Modify any parts of your instrument to help it work better. Prepare a manual that describes and explains each part of the instrument.

SECTION 1 Wave Reflection and Mirrors

Key Ideas
◆ Light that strikes an object can be reflected, absorbed, or transmitted.
◆ Regular reflection occurs with smooth surfaces. Diffuse reflection occurs with uneven surfaces.
◆ Concave mirrors can form virtual images, real images, or no images. Images formed by convex mirrors are always virtual.

Key Terms
opaque	plane mirror
transparent	virtual image
translucent	concave mirror
ray	focal point
regular reflection	real image
diffuse reflection	convex mirror
image	

SECTION 2 Wave Refraction and Lenses

Key Ideas
◆ When light waves hit the surface of a medium at an angle, they bend, or change direction.
◆ The type of image formed by a convex lens depends on the position of the object in relation to the focal point.
◆ Concave lenses produce only virtual images.

Key Terms
index of refraction	concave lens
mirage	convex lens
lens	

SECTION 3 Color

Key Ideas
◆ Light reflected by an object is the object's color.
◆ The primary colors of light are red, green, and blue.
◆ As pigments are added together, fewer colors of light are reflected and more are absorbed.

Key Terms
primary color	complementary color
secondary color	pigment

SECTION 4 Seeing Light Waves

INTEGRATING LIFE SCIENCE

Key Ideas
◆ You see objects because of interactions among the nervous, muscular, and circulatory systems.
◆ Lenses can correct some vision problems.

Key Terms
cornea	retina	optic nerve
iris	rod	nearsighted
pupil	cone	farsighted

SECTION 5 Using Light

Key Ideas
◆ Cameras, microscopes, and telescopes use lenses or mirrors to gather light.
◆ Laser light waves have the same wavelength.

Key Terms
telescope	camera
refracting telescope	laser
objective lens	hologram
eyepiece lens	optical fiber
reflecting telescope	total internal reflection
microscope	

Organizing Information

Compare/Contrast Table Copy the tables about mirrors and lenses onto a sheet of paper. Then fill in the empty spaces and add a title to each table. (For more on compare/contrast tables, see the Skills Handbook.)

Type of Mirror	How It Affects Light	Type of Image Formed
Plane	Reflects	a. _?_
b. _?_	c. _?_	Real or virtual
Convex	Reflects	d. _?_

Type of Lens	How It Affects Light	Type of Image Formed
Convex	e. _?_	f. _?_
g. _?_	h. _?_	Virtual

Reviewing Content

 Review key concepts online using iText at www.phschool.com

Multiple Choice

Choose the letter of the best answer.

1. A substance that does not transmit light is
   a. translucent.
   b. opaque.
   c. transparent.
   d. polarized.

2. The scattering of light off an uneven surface is called
   a. regular reflection.
   b. refraction.
   c. diffuse reflection.
   d. total internal reflection.

3. A convex lens can form
   a. either a real image or a virtual image.
   b. a virtual image.
   c. a real image.
   d. a reflection.

4. The colored part of the eye is the
   a. retina.
   b. cornea.
   c. iris.
   d. pupil.

5. A laser produces light that
   a. has many colors.
   b. spreads out in many directions.
   c. is incoherent.
   d. is coherent.

True or False

If the statement is true, write true. If it is false, change the underlined word or words to make the statement true.

6. An image that only seems to be where it is seen is a <u>real</u> image.

7. A lens that is thinner in the middle than at the edges is a <u>concave</u> lens.

8. Under green light a red object appears <u>blue</u>.

9. <u>Farsightedness</u> can be corrected by a convex lens.

10. <u>Holograms</u> are long, thin strands of glass or plastic that can carry light for long distances.

Checking Concepts

11. Explain the differences among transparent, translucent, and opaque materials. Give an example of each type of material.

12. Describe the differences and similarities between real and virtual images. How can each type of image be formed?

13. How is the index of refraction of a substance related to the speed of light in the substance?

14. Explain how mirages form.

15. Why do you see the petals of a rose as red and the leaves as green?

16. Explain how the lenses in your eyes adjust to focus on near and distant objects.

17. Explain how a camera works.

18. **Writing to Learn** You have been asked to nominate an optical instrument for an award. Choose the instrument that you think has played the most significant role in society. Write a nomination speech that describes several reasons for your choice.

Thinking Critically

19. **Applying Concepts** Can a plane mirror ever produce a real image? Explain.

20. **Comparing and Contrasting** How is mixing colors of light different from mixing pigments?

21. **Relating Cause and Effect** Explain why you can only see shades of gray in dim light.

22. **Comparing and Contrasting** How is a microscope similar to a refracting telescope? How is it different?

23. **Problem Solving** A telescope produces a real, upside-down image. If you want to see a boat that is far out to sea, how could you modify your telescope so the boat appears right-side up?

24. **Making Generalizations** Explain why laser light can never be white.

Applying Skills

Use the diagram to answer Questions 25–27.

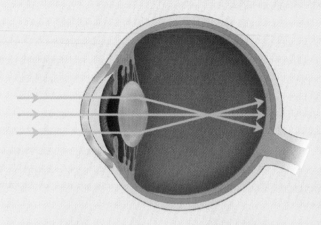

25. Classifying Which type of vision problem does this eye have?

26. Problem Solving What type of lens can correct this vision problem?

27. Communicating Copy the diagram into your notebook. Add a correcting lens to your diagram and show how the lens makes the image focus on the retina.

Performance ▼CHAPTER PROJECT Assessment

Present Your Project Demonstrate your optical instrument to your class. Explain how your instrument works and how it can be used. Present diagrams that show how the mirrors or lenses in your instrument reflect or refract light.

Reflect and Record Consider the design and performance of your instrument. What parts of the instrument worked as expected? What improvements could you make? What are the similarities and differences between your instrument and other students' instruments?

Test Preparation

Use these questions to prepare for standardized tests.

Read the passage. Then answer Questions 28–31.

As the sun sets, it is still visible for several minutes after it has really sunk below the horizon. This is because light is refracted by Earth's atmosphere. The density of the atmosphere decreases as its altitude above Earth's surface increases. For this reason, the refracted rays bend gradually to produce a curved path.

Refraction can also cause the shape of the sun to appear different just before it sets. When the sun is near the horizon, the rays from the lower edge are bent more than the rays from the upper edge. This makes the sun look oval rather than round.

28. What would be a good title for this passage?
   A The Sun Sets Earlier Each Day
   B Why Light Lingers After the Sunset
   C How the Atmosphere Lights Earth
   D How Sunlight Travels Through the Atmosphere

29. According to this passage, what happens to sunlight as it passes through the atmosphere?
   F It is separated into colors.
   G It is bent because of reflection.
   H It is bent because of refraction.
   J It is absorbed and does not reach Earth's surface.

30. How does the fact that the atmosphere is thicker in some places than in others affect sunlight?
   A It causes the light to curve.
   B It causes the light to be reflected.
   C It causes the light to stay in the atmosphere.
   D It causes rainbows to form.

31. What is the result of refraction of sunlight?
   F Daylight is several minutes longer.
   G Daylight is several minutes shorter.
   H The shape of the sun can be seen even after it has set.
   J The sun appears round when it is really oval in shape.

CHAPTER 8
Characteristics of the Universe

These telescopes on top of Mauna Kea, a mountain in Hawaii, are used to study distant stars and galaxies.

WEB ACTIVITY www.phschool.com

Star Stories

In the spring of 1997, you could easily see comet Hale-Bopp, shown here, without any special equipment. But many of the objects astronomers study just look like tiny pinpoints of light—if you can see them at all. However, astronomers have found many ways to learn about these "pinpoints."

In this chapter, you will discover how astronomers study characteristics of the universe and its stars and galaxies. In your project, you will find out how people in the past created stories to explain the patterns of stars they saw in the sky. You'll learn how the names of constellations you see in the Texas night sky reflect the cultures of the people who named them.

Your Goal To recognize major constellations, learn the stories behind their names, and create your own star story.

To complete the project you will
◆ learn the star patterns of at least three major constellations
◆ research the stories that gave one constellation its name
◆ write a Texas star story

Get Started Begin your project by previewing page 274 to learn what a constellation is. With a group of your classmates, make a list of constellations you have heard about. Then look at the star charts in Appendix G. From the chart for the current season, choose three or four constellations to explore further.

Check Your Progress You'll be working on this project as you study this chapter. To keep your project on track, look for Check Your Progress boxes at the following points.

Section 1 Review, page 280: Locate constellations and research one.
Section 3 Review, page 296: Draw a new picture for the star pattern in your constellation and give it a name.
Section 5 Review, page 304: Write your Texas star story.

Present Your Project At the end of the chapter (page 307), you will present your constellation along with your story that explains its name.

TEKS

In addition to process TEKS, this chapter addresses these concept TEKS as they relate to the chapter's topics.

(8.13) The student knows characteristics of the universe. The student is expected to:
(A) describe characteristics of the universe such as stars and galaxies;
(B) explain the use of light years to describe distances in the universe; and
(C) research and describe historical scientific theories of the origin of the universe.

SECTION 1 Tools of Modern Astronomy

DISCOVER · ACTIVITY · · ·

Are Those Stars Really a Group?

1. Cut ten pieces of thread to different lengths between 5 cm and 25 cm. Tape a 1-cm plastic foam ball to the end of each piece of thread.

2. Obtain a piece of cardboard about 50 cm by 50 cm. Tape the free ends of the thread pieces to various points on the cardboard.

3. Turn the cardboard over so the balls hang down. While your partner holds the cardboard horizontally, look at the balls from the side.

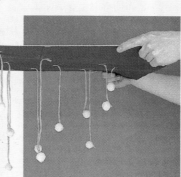

4. Imagine that the balls are stars in a constellation. With one eye closed, sketch the pattern the balls make.

Think It Over

Observing Can you tell which balls are farther away and which are closer? Do you think you can tell how close to one another the stars in a constellation are?

GUIDE FOR READING

◆ What do telescopes do?

◆ Why do astronomers use spectrographs?

Reading Tip Before you read, rewrite the main headings of the section as *how, why,* or *what* questions.

Key Terms constellation
• radio telescope
• observatory
• spectrograph

Before the Civil War, thousands of enslaved African Americans fled north to freedom. Traveling in secret by night, they looked to the stars for direction. They told one another to "follow the drinking gourd"—the star pattern that points to the North Star. Most Americans today call this pattern the Big Dipper.

Patterns of stars in the sky are called **constellations.** Stars in a constellation can look as if they are close together, even though they are at very different distances from Earth. For example, the star at the end of the handle in the Big Dipper is about twice as far from Earth as most of the other stars in the Big Dipper. So the stars in a constellation are not, in fact, all close together. Constellations are just patterns formed by stars that happen to be in the same direction in the sky.

Big Dipper ▶

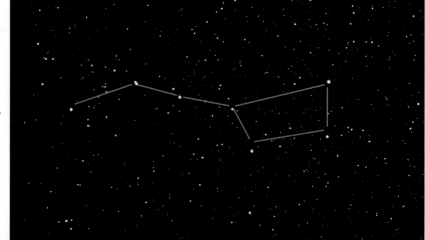

Looking at Stars

The stars in constellations appear as points of light. In fact, stars are huge spheres of hot, glowing gas, like the sun. Visible light is only one type of electromagnetic radiation given off by stars. Stars also give off radiation that you can't see. For example, some stars give off radiation in the form of radio waves. These waves are like the ones that carry signals to radios and televisions.

Astronomers use telescopes to observe stars and learn more about them. Many telescopes produce images using visible light. However, much of modern astronomy is based on detection of other types of electromagnetic radiation. **Most telescopes collect and focus different types of electromagnetic radiation from stars, including visible light.**

Visible Light Telescopes

In 1609, Galileo used a simple refracting telescope to look at objects in the sky. Among the objects he saw were the moons of the planet Jupiter, sun spots, and the terrain of the moon. Recall that a refracting telescope uses convex lenses to gather a large amount of light and focus it onto a small area.

Galileo's telescope, like the refracting telescope shown in Figure 1, used two lenses—an objective lens and an eyepiece lens. When light passes through the objective lens, the lens focuses the light at the focal point of the lens. The distance from the focal point to the objective lens is the focal length of the objective lens. The larger the objective lens, the more light the lens can collect. This makes it easier for astronomers to see faint objects. The eyepiece lens is also a convex lens. It has a focal point that coincides with that of the objective lens.

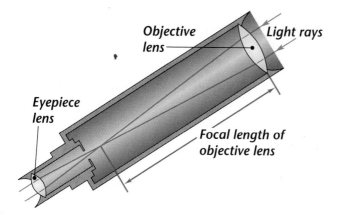

Figure 1 A refracting telescope uses an objective lens to focus the light rays from an image, which can be seen with the eyepiece lens. Both lenses are convex lenses. *Interpreting Photographs* Which of the two lenses is closest to the astronomer in the photograph to the right?

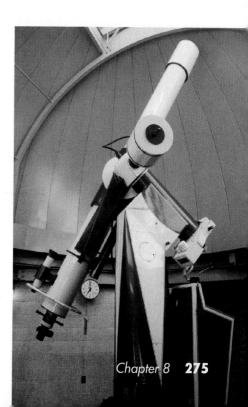

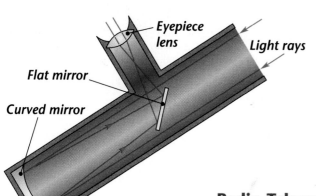

Eyepiece lens

Light rays

Flat mirror

Curved mirror

Figure 2 In a reflecting telescope, a mirror focuses a large amount of light onto a small area.

Isaac Newton built the first reflecting telescope in 1668. As you can see in Figure 2, a reflecting telescope uses a mirror instead of an objective lens. Like the lenses in a refracting telescope, the mirror in a reflecting telescope focuses a large amount of light onto a small area. The larger the mirror, the more light the telescope can collect. The largest visible light telescopes are now all reflecting telescopes.

Radio Telescopes Devices used to detect radio waves from objects in space are called **radio telescopes.** Most radio telescopes have curved, reflecting surfaces. These surfaces can be several hundred meters in diameter. They focus radio waves the way the mirror in a reflecting telescope focuses light waves. Radio telescopes concentrate the faint radio waves from outer space onto an antenna like that on a radio. As with visible light telescopes, the larger a radio telescope is, the more radio waves it can collect.

Checkpoint *In what way are radio telescopes similar to reflecting telescopes?*

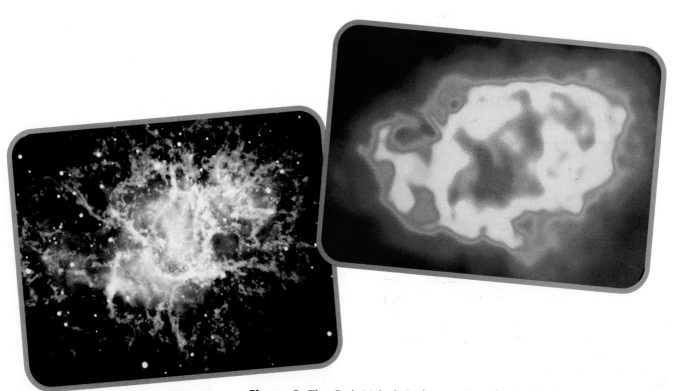

Figure 3 The Crab Nebula is the remains of a star that exploded about 1,000 years ago. The left image was photographed using visible light. The right image was made using radio waves. *Interpreting Photographs What colors in the image made using radio waves correspond to the brightest part of the photograph made using visible light?*

Figure 4 The Otto Struve Telescope is one of four telescopes at the McDonald Observatory in Texas. It sits about 2 kilometers above sea level.

Other Telescopes Some telescopes detect infrared radiation, which has longer wavelengths than visible light. There are also telescopes that detect the shortest wavelengths—ultraviolet radiation, X-rays, and gamma rays.

Observatories

A building that contains one or more telescopes is called an **observatory**. Most large observatories are located on mountaintops. Why have astronomers built the largest visible light telescopes on the tops of mountains? Earth's atmosphere makes objects in space look blurry. The sky on some mountaintops is clearer and is not brightened by city lights.

The best observatory site on Earth is probably the top of Mauna Kea, an ancient volcano on the Island of Hawaii in the Pacific Ocean. Mauna Kea is so tall—4,200 meters above sea level—that it is above 40 percent of Earth's atmosphere. The sky there is very dark at night, and many nights are free of clouds.

The McDonald Observatory in the Davis Mountains of southwest Texas has four operating telescopes. The largest is the Hobby-Eberly reflecting telescope. It sits on Mount Fowlkes, about 2 kilometers above sea level. It collects light on a mirror that is over 9 meters in diameter!

To collect data from visible light telescopes on Earth, astronomers must sometimes stay awake all night. Radio telescopes, however, can be used 24 hours a day and do not have to be on mountaintops.

Locating Radio Waves

You can use an umbrella to focus radio waves.

1. Line the inside of an umbrella with aluminum foil.

2. Turn on a small radio and tune it to a station.

3. Move the radio up and down along the umbrella handle. Find the position where the station is clearest. Radio waves reflecting off the foil focus at this point. Tape the radio to the handle.

4. Hold the umbrella at different angles. At which angle is the station the clearest?

Inferring In which direction do you think the radio station is located? Explain.

Satellites

 INTEGRATING TECHNOLOGY Most ultraviolet radiation, X-rays, and gamma rays are blocked by Earth's atmosphere. To detect these wavelengths, astronomers have placed telescopes on satellites.

The Hubble Space Telescope is a reflecting telescope with a mirror 2.4 meters in diameter. Because it is above the atmosphere, its images of stars in visible light are about seven times more detailed than the best images from telescopes on Earth. The Hubble Space Telescope can also collect ultraviolet and infrared radiation. The Chandra X-ray Observatory, similar in size to Hubble, makes images in the X-ray portion of the spectrum.

Development of Modern Telescopes

During the last century, astronomers have built larger telescopes, which can collect more light and other types of radiation. Today's astronomers use tools that could not have been imagined 100 years ago.

1897

Yerkes Telescope

The 1-meter-diameter telescope at Yerkes Observatory in Wisconsin is the largest refracting telescope ever built. Because its main lens is so large, the Yerkes telescope can collect more light than any other refracting telescope.

 **1900** **1920** **1940**

1931

Beginning of Radio Astronomy

Karl Jansky, an American engineer, was trying to find the source of static that was interfering with radio communications. Using a large antenna, he discovered that the static was coming from objects in space giving off radio waves. Jansky's accidental discovery led to the beginning of radio astronomy.

Spectrographs

Most large telescopes today have spectrographs. A **spectrograph** (SPEK truh graf) breaks the light from an object into colors and photographs the resulting spectrum. **Astronomers use spectrographs to get information about stars, including their chemical compositions and temperatures.**

Chemical Compositions Chemical elements in a star's atmosphere absorb light from the star. Each element absorbs light at different wavelengths, and each absorbed wavelength appears as a dark line on a spectrum. Just as each person has a unique set of fingerprints, each chemical element has a unique set of such lines.

In Your Journal

Research a telescope that is located in Texas. Create a publicity brochure that describes the telescope, when and where it was built, and what types of research it is used for.

1963
Arecibo Radio Telescope

This radio telescope in Puerto Rico was built in a natural bowl in the ground. It is 305 meters in diameter, more than three times the size of the next-largest radio telescope.

1990
Hubble Space Telescope

The Hubble Space Telescope can see objects in space more clearly than any other telescope. Astronauts have visited the telescope several times to repair or replace equipment.

1960   1980   2000

1980
Very Large Array

The Very Large Array is a set of 27 radio telescopes in New Mexico. The telescopes can be moved close together or far apart. The telescopes are linked, so they can be used as if they were one giant telescope 25 kilometers in diameter.

1999
Chandra X-ray Observatory

The hottest objects in space give off X-rays. NASA launched the Chandra X-ray Observatory into orbit to make detailed images in that part of the spectrum. Chandra X-ray images match Hubble visible-light images in detail.

Figure 5 Astronomers can use line spectrums to find the temperatures of stars.

Sharpen your Skills

Inferring  ACTIVITY

The lines on the spectrums below are from three different stars. Each of these star spectrums is made up of an overlap of spectrums from the individual elements shown in Figure 5. In Star A, which elements have the strongest lines? Which are the strongest in Star B? In Star C?

By comparing a star's spectrum with the known spectrums of different elements, such as those shown in Figure 5, astronomers can infer which elements are found in a star.

Temperatures Most stars have a chemical composition similar to the sun, about 73% hydrogen, 25% helium, and 2% other elements. The amount of energy each of these elements absorbs depends on the temperature of the star. Because of this, stars at different temperatures produce different line spectrums. By comparing a star's spectrum with the known spectrums of elements at different temperatures, astronomers can infer how hot the star is. Hydrogen, for example, produces very strong spectral lines when it is at about 10,000 degrees Celsius. If astronomers do not see a strong hydrogen line on a spectrum, this does not mean there is no hydrogen in the star. It just means that the star is either cooler or hotter than 10,000 degrees Celsius.

Section 1 Review

1. For what purpose are most telescopes designed?
2. What can astronomers tell from looking at a star's spectrum?
3. What does a spectrum without strong hydrogen lines tell you about a star's temperature?
4. **Thinking Critically** **Applying Concepts** Why are images from the Hubble Space Telescope clearer than images from telescopes on Earth?

Check Your Progress

CHAPTER PROJECT

Using the star charts in Appendix G, try to locate constellations in the night sky. (*Hint:* Remember that you may be looking at a constellation upside down. Also, light conditions may affect how many stars you can see.) Sketch the constellations you can locate and compare them with the ones your classmates saw. Now choose one constellation and research the myths or legends that gave it its name. Find as many stories as you can about your constellation and make notes about them.

Make Your Own Telescope

In this lab you will learn how to construct and use a simple refracting telescope. You can then try out your telescope.

Problem

How can you build a telescope?

Skill Focus

making models, observing, drawing conclusions

Materials

2 paper towel tubes of slightly different diameters
plastic objective lens
plastic eyepiece lens
foam holder for eyepiece (optional)
transparent tape
meter stick

Procedure

1. Fit one of the paper towel tubes inside the other. Make sure you can move the tubes but that they will not slide on their own.
2. Place the large objective lens flat against the end of the outer tube. Tape the lens in place.

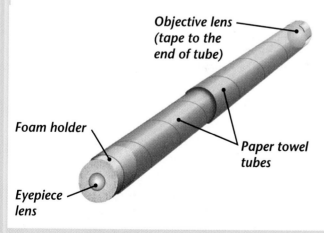

Objective lens (tape to the end of tube)

Foam holder

Paper towel tubes

Eyepiece lens

3. Insert the small eyepiece lens into the opening in the foam holder.
4. Place the foam eyepiece lens holder into the inner tube at the end of the telescope opposite to the objective lens.
5. Tape a meter stick to the wall. Look through the eyepiece at the meter stick from 5 m away. Slide the tubes in and out to focus your telescope until you can read the numbers on the meter stick. Draw your telescope. On the drawing, mark the tube position that allows you to read the numbers most clearly.
6. Use your telescope to look at other objects at different distances, both in your classroom and through the window. For each object you view, draw your telescope, marking the position at which you see the objects most clearly. **CAUTION:** *Do not look at the sun. You will damage your eyes.*

Analyze and Conclude

1. Why do you need two tubes?
2. If you focus on a nearby object and then focus on something farther away, do you have to move the tubes together or apart?
3. How does this telescope compare to the telescopes astronomers use?
4. **Apply** How could you improve on the design of your telescope? What effects would different lenses or tubes have?

More to Explore

With an adult, go outside in the evening on several days when the moon is clearly visible. Point the telescope at the moon. Draw the moon with all the features you see.

Light Pollution

Suppose you are in a dark theater watching a movie when the lights come on. You can still see the movie, but it seems dull and faded. For the same reason, you may not see very many stars if you live in or near a city. Light from street lights and advertising signs masks much of the starlight. Artificial light that makes it difficult to see the night sky clearly is known as light pollution.

Astronomers build modern observatories far from cities and outdoor lights. But light pollution is still a problem for older observatories and for amateur astronomers like the one in this photo. If light pollution increases, how will you see glittering stars in the night sky, the broad Milky Way, meteor showers, or an occasional passing comet?

The Issues

How Important Are Outdoor Lights?
Artificial lighting is one of the great advantages of the modern age. Street lights make it easier to drive safely, reducing accidents. Night lighting allows businesses to stay open later. In addition, lighting helps people feel safer in their homes and on the streets.

What Can Be Done? Street lights are the biggest cause of light pollution. However, some types of street lights cause more light pollution than others. Three types of street light bulbs are mercury-vapor bulbs, high-pressure sodium bulbs, and low-pressure sodium bulbs. Low-pressure sodium lights cause the least problem for astronomers, because they shine in only a very narrow range of wavelengths. A simple filter on a telescope can eliminate this light from the telescope's view. In addition, street lights of all types can be shielded so they don't shine upward. They can also be pointed only where the light is needed.

Would Reducing Light Pollution Save Money? Mercury-vapor lights are the most common type of street light. High-pressure sodium and low-pressure sodium lights use less electricity, however.

Initially, modifying street lights to reduce light pollution would cost a lot of money. However, reducing unneeded light and using light bulbs that require less electricity would also reduce energy usage, which could save money.

You Decide

1. Identify the Problem
In your own words, explain the problem of light pollution.

2. Analyze the Options
List possible solutions. What procedures are involved in each solution? List the advantages and disadvantages of each solution.

3. Find a Solution
Find out what types of street lights your town or city has. Write a letter to your city council about light pollution in your city or town.

DISCOVER • ACTIVITY • • • •

How Does Your Thumb Move?

1. Stand facing a wall, at least an arm's length away. Stretch your arm out with your thumb up and your fingers curled.

2. Close your right eye and look at your thumb with your left eye. Line your thumb up with something on the wall.

3. Now close your left eye and open your right eye. How does your thumb appear to move along the wall?

4. Bring your thumb closer to your eye, about half the distance as before. Repeat Steps 2 and 3.

Think It Over

Observing How does your thumb appear to move in Step 4 compared to Step 3? How are these observations related to how far away your thumb is at each step? How could you use this method to estimate distances?

What if you could travel to the stars at the speed of light? To travel from Earth to the sun would take about 8 minutes, not very long for such a long trip! Yet the next nearest star, Proxima Centauri, is much farther away—a trip to Proxima Centauri would take 4.2 years!

Most stars are much farther away than Proxima Centauri. Our sun and Proxima Centauri are only two of the stars that make up the Milky Way. The Milky Way is a cluster of stars, called a **galaxy.** It contains hundreds of billions of stars. At the speed of light, it would take you 25,000 years to travel the 250 million billion kilometers to the center of our galaxy. If you left our galaxy and traveled at the speed of light for about 2 million years, you would eventually reach another galaxy, the Andromeda Galaxy.

There are billions of galaxies in the **universe,** which astronomers define as all of space and everything in it. Since galaxies are so far apart, most of the universe is empty space. If our galaxy were the size of a dime, the Andromeda Galaxy would be about half a meter away. The rest of the universe, as far as astronomers can see, would extend for about 2 kilometers in all directions.

GUIDE FOR READING

◆ What units do astronomers use to measure distances to stars?

◆ How are stars classified?

Reading Tip As you read, make a list of the characteristics of stars. Write a sentence describing each characteristic.

Key Terms galaxy • universe
• light-year • parallax • giant star
• apparent magnitude
• absolute magnitude
• Hertzsprung-Russell diagram
• main sequence

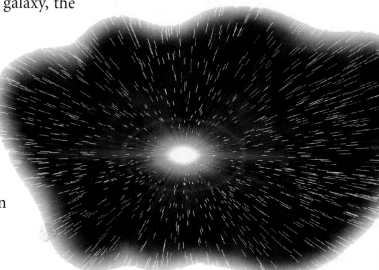

Distances to Stars

Distances on Earth are often measured in kilometers. However, as you have seen, distances to stars are so large that the kilometer is not a very practical unit. **Instead of kilometers, astronomers use a unit called the light-year.** In space, light travels at a speed of 300,000 kilometers per second. A **light-year** is the distance that light travels in one year, or about 9.5 million million kilometers. Note that the light-year is a unit of distance, not time.

To help you understand what a light-year is, consider an everyday example. If you bicycle at 10 kilometers per hour, it would take you 1 hour to go to a mall 10 kilometers away. You could say that the mall is "1 bicycle-hour" away.

It takes light about 4.2 years to reach Earth from Proxima Centauri, so Proxima Centauri is 4.2 light-years, or 40 million million kilometers, away.

✓ *Checkpoint* How many kilometers are in three light-years?

Measuring Distances to Stars

Standing on Earth looking up at the sky, it seems as if there is no way to tell how far away the stars are. However, astronomers have found a way to measure those distances. Astronomers often use parallax to measure distances to nearby stars.

Parallax is the apparent change in position of an object when you look at it from different places. For example, imagine that you and a friend have gone to a movie. After you sit down, a woman with a large hat sits down in front of you. Because you and your friend are sitting in different positions, the woman's hat blocks different parts of the screen. If you are sitting on her left, the woman's hat appears to be in front of the dinosaur. But to your friend, who is sitting on her right, she appears to be in front of the bird.

Have the woman and her hat moved? No. But because of your relative positions, she appears to have moved. This apparent movement is parallax.

Astronomers use parallax to measure the distances to nearby stars. First, they observe a star when Earth is on one side of the sun.

Figure 6 You and your friend are sitting in a theater behind a woman with a large hat. *Applying Concepts Why is your view of the screen different from your friend's view?*

Your view

Your friend's view

284

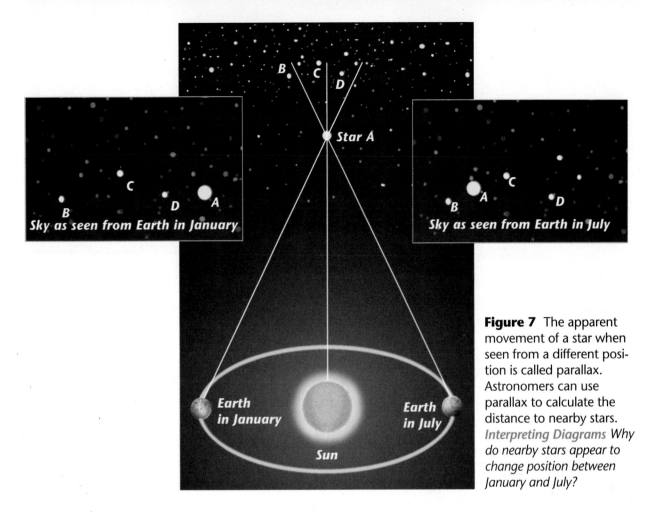

B C D

Star A

Sky as seen from Earth in January
C
B D A

Sky as seen from Earth in July
C
B A D

Earth
in January

Earth
in July

Sun

Figure 7 The apparent movement of a star when seen from a different position is called parallax. Astronomers can use parallax to calculate the distance to nearby stars. *Interpreting Diagrams Why do nearby stars appear to change position between January and July?*

Then, they observe the same star again six months later, when Earth is on the other side of the sun. Astronomers measure how much the star appears to move against a background of stars that are much farther away. They can then use this measurement, called the parallax shift, to calculate how far away the star is. The less the star appears to move, the farther away it is.

Parallax cannot be used to measure distances any greater than 1,000 light-years. The distance that a star that far away would appear to move when seen from opposite sides of Earth's orbit is too small to measure accurately.

Classifying Stars

Like the sun, all stars are huge spheres of glowing gas. They are made up mostly of hydrogen, and they make energy by nuclear fusion. This energy makes stars shine brightly. The sun is only an average-brightness star. However, the sun is much closer to Earth than any other star. Because it is so close, the sun appears much brighter and much larger than any other star. But the sun is neither the brightest nor the largest star in the galaxy.

Astronomers classify stars according to their physical characteristics. **The main characteristics used to classify stars are size, temperature, and brightness.**

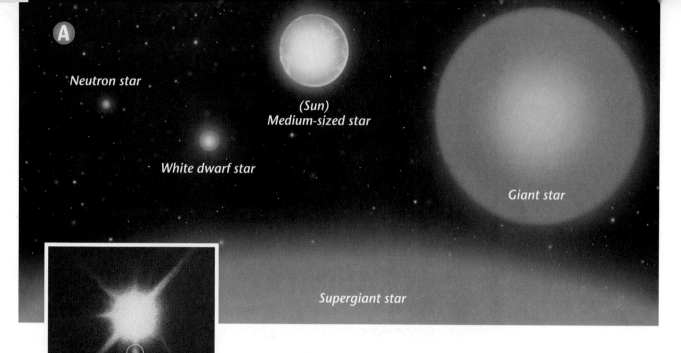

Figure 8 (A) Stars range in size from tiny neutron stars to enormous supergiants. (B) The brighter star is Sirius A. The fainter star, circled in yellow, is Sirius B, a white dwarf. *Observing* What size star is the sun?

Sizes of Stars

When you look at stars in the sky, they all appear to be the same size. Many stars are actually about the size of the sun, which is a medium-sized star. However, some stars are much larger than the sun. Very large stars are called **giant stars** or supergiant stars. If the supergiant star Betelgeuse (BAY tul jooz) were located where our sun is, it would be large enough to fill the solar system as far out as Jupiter.

Some stars are much smaller than the sun. White dwarf stars are about the size of Earth. Neutron stars are even smaller, only about 20 kilometers in diameter.

☑ *Checkpoint* *Name five sizes of stars, in order from largest to smallest.*

Color and Temperature of Stars

If you look around the sky at night, you can see slight differences in the colors of the stars. Figure 9 shows the constellation known as Orion the Hunter. The red star in Orion's shoulder is Betelgeuse. The blue-white star in Orion's heel is called Rigel.

A star's color reveals its temperature. Hot objects on Earth display the same range of colors as stars. If you watch a toaster heat up, you can see the wires glow red-hot. The wires inside a light bulb are even hotter and glow white. Similarly, the coolest stars—about 3,200 degrees Celsius—appear reddish in the sky. Reddish Betelgeuse is a cool star. With a surface temperature of about 5,500 degrees Celsius, the sun glows white. The hottest stars in the sky—over 10,000 degrees Celsius—appear slightly bluer than the sun. Blue-white Rigel is a very hot star, more than 15,000 degrees Celsius.

Brightness of Stars

Stars also differ in brightness, the amount of light they give off. The brightness of a star depends upon its size and temperature. For example, Betelgeuse is fairly cool. It is also very large, so it shines brightly. Rigel, on the other hand, is very hot, so it gives off a lot of light. Even though it is much smaller than Betelgeuse, Rigel also shines brightly.

How bright a star looks from Earth depends on both how far the star is from Earth and how bright the star actually is. Because of these factors, a star's brightness is described in two different ways: by its apparent magnitude and by its absolute magnitude.

Apparent Magnitude A star's **apparent magnitude** is its brightness as seen from Earth. Astronomers can measure apparent magnitude fairly easily.

Astronomers cannot tell how much light a star gives off just from the star's apparent magnitude. Just as a flashlight looks brighter the closer it is to you, a star looks brighter the closer it is to Earth. For example, the sun looks very bright. This does not mean that the sun gives off more light than all other stars. The sun looks bright simply because it is close to Earth.

Social Studies
CONNECTION

During the Middle Ages Arab astronomers in Southwest Asia and North Africa named many stars. Some Arabic star names are Vega ("falling vulture") and Rigel ("the left leg of the giant").

In Your Journal

Many other words used in astronomy and mathematics come from Arabic. Find *zenith, nadir, algorithm,* and *algebra* in a dictionary. Write their definitions in your own words.

Figure 9 The constellation Orion includes the red supergiant star Betelgeuse and the blue supergiant star Rigel.

Figure 10 The stars in a globular cluster are all about the same distance from Earth.

Star Bright ACTIVITY

Here's how you can compare absolute and apparent magnitudes.

1. Dim the lights. Put two equally bright flashlights next to each other on a table. Turn them on.

2. Look at the flashlights from the other side of the room. Think of the flashlights as two stars. Then compare them in terms of absolute and apparent magnitudes.

3. Move one of the flashlights closer to you and repeat Step 2.

4. Replace one of the flashlights with a brighter one. Repeat Step 1 with the unequally bright flashlights. Then repeat Step 2.

Making Models How could you place the flashlights in Step 4 so that they have the same apparent magnitude? Try it.

Absolute Magnitude A star's **absolute magnitude** is the brightness the star would have if it were at a standard distance from Earth. Finding a star's absolute magnitude is more complicated than finding its apparent magnitude. An astronomer must determine the star's apparent magnitude and its distance from Earth. The astronomer can then calculate the star's brightness if it were at a standard distance from Earth.

Figure 10 shows a globular cluster, a group of stars that are close together. The stars in a globular cluster are all at about the same distance from Earth. Because of this, astronomers study globular clusters to compare the brightnesses of stars. If one star in a globular cluster appears brighter than another star, it really is brighter than that other star.

The Hertzsprung-Russell Diagram

Two of the most important characteristics of stars are temperature and absolute magnitude. About 100 years ago, Ejnar Hertzsprung (EYE nahr HURT sprung) in Denmark and Henry Norris Russell in the United States each made graphs to find out if temperature and brightness are related. They plotted the temperatures of stars and their brightness on a graph. The points formed a pattern.

The graph they made is still used by astronomers. It is called the **Hertzsprung-Russell diagram,** or H-R diagram. As you can see in Figure 11, most of the points representing stars in the H-R diagram form a diagonal band called the **main sequence.** More than 90% of all stars are main sequence stars, including the sun. In the main sequence, surface temperature increases as brightness increases. In contrast, white dwarf stars are hot but not very bright, so they appear at the bottom center of the diagram.

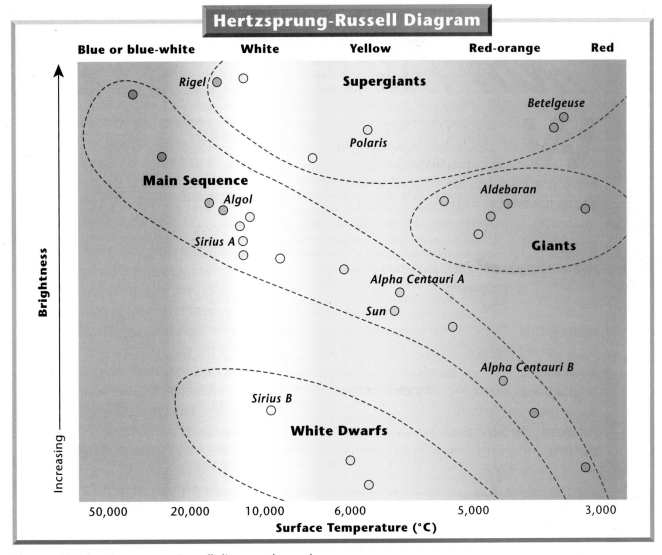

Hertzsprung-Russell Diagram

Blue or blue-white   White   Yellow   Red-orange   Red

Rigel

Supergiants

Betelgeuse

Polaris

Main Sequence

Aldebaran

Algol

Sirius A

Giants

Alpha Centauri A

Sun

Alpha Centauri B

Sirius B

White Dwarfs

Brightness

Increasing

Surface Temperature (°C)

50,000   20,000   10,000   6,000   5,000   3,000

Figure 11 The Hertzsprung-Russell diagram shows the relationship between surface temperature and brightness. *Interpreting Diagrams Which star is hotter: Rigel or Aldebaran?*

Section 2 Review

1. Why do astronomers use light-years instead of kilometers to measure distances to stars?
2. List three characteristics used to classify stars.
3. Which is hotter—a red star or a blue star? Why?
4. **Thinking Critically** **Applying Concepts** Stars A and B have about the same apparent magnitude, but Star A is about twice as far from Earth as Star B. Which star has the greater absolute magnitude? Explain your answer.

Science at Home

View Orion With adult family members, go outside on a clear, dark night. Determine which way is north, south, east, and west. Using the star chart for the correct season in Appendix G, look for the constellation Orion. Find the stars Betelgeuse and Rigel in Orion, and explain to your family why they are different colors.

HOW FAR IS THAT STAR?

When astronomers measure parallax, they record the positions of stars on film in cameras attached to telescopes. In this lab, you will set up a model of a telescope and use it to estimate distances.

Problem

How can parallax be used to determine distances?

Materials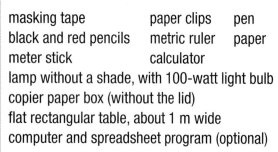

masking tape   paper clips   pen
black and red pencils   metric ruler   paper
meter stick   calculator
lamp without a shade, with 100-watt light bulb
copier paper box (without the lid)
flat rectangular table, about 1 m wide
computer and spreadsheet program (optional)

Procedure

Part 1 Telescope Model

1. Place the lamp on a table in the middle of the classroom.
2. Carefully use the tip of the pen to make a small hole in the middle of one end of the box. The box represents a telescope.
3. At the front of the classroom, place the box on a flat table so the hole points toward the lamp. Line the left side of the box up with the left edge of the table.

4. Put a small piece of tape on the table below the hole. Use the pen to make a mark on the tape directly below the hole. The mark represents the position of the telescope when Earth is on one side of its orbit.

Part 2 Star 1

5. Label a sheet of paper Star 1 and place it inside the box as shown in the drawing. Hold the paper in place with two paper clips. The paper represents the film in a telescope.
6. Darken the room. Turn on the light to represent the star.
7. With the red pencil, mark the paper where you see a dot of light. Label this dot A. Dot A represents the image of the star on the film.
8. Move the box so the right edge of the box lines up with the right edge of the table. Repeat Step 4. The mark on the tape represents the position of the telescope six months later, when Earth is on the other side of its orbit.
9. Repeat Step 7, and use a black pencil to mark the second dot B. Dot B represents the image of the star as seen 6 months later from the other side of Earth's orbit.
10. Remove the paper. Before you continue, copy the data table into your notebook or your spreadsheet.
11. Measure and record the distance in milli-meters between dots A and B. This distance represents the parallax shift for Star 1.

DATA TABLE						
Star	Parallax Shift (mm)	Focal Length (mm)	Diameter of Orbit (mm)	Calculated Distance to Star (mm)	Calculated Distance to Star (m)	Actual Distance to Star (m)

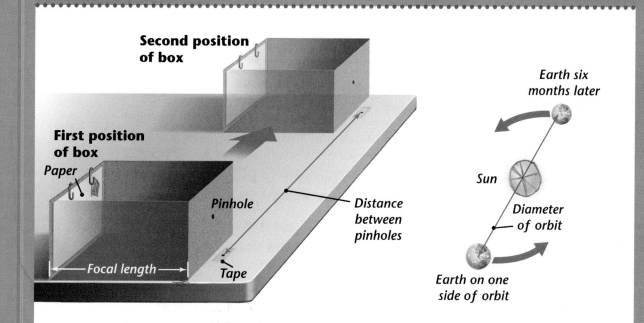

Second position of box

First position of box

Paper

Pinhole

Distance between pinholes

Focal length

Tape

Earth six months later

Sun

Diameter of orbit

Earth on one side of orbit

12. Measure and record the distance from the hole in the box to the lamp. This distance represents the actual distance to the star.

13. Measure and record the distance from the hole (lens) to the paper (film) at the back of the box in millimeters. This distance represents the focal length of your telescope.

14. Measure and record the distance in millimeters between the marks on the two pieces of masking tape. This distance represents the diameter of Earth's orbit.

Part 3 Stars 2 and 3

15. Move the lamp away from the table—about half the distance to the back of the room. The bulb now represents Star 2. Predict what you think will happen to the light images on your paper.

16. Repeat Steps 6–12 with a new sheet of paper to find the parallax shift for Star 2.

17. Move the lamp to the back of the classroom. The bulb now represents Star 3. Repeat Steps 6–12 with a new sheet of paper to find the parallax shift for Star 3.

Analyze and Conclude

1. What caused the apparent change in position of the dots of light for each star? Explain.

2. Use the following formula to calculate the distance from the telescope to Star 1.

$$\text{Distance} = \frac{\text{Diameter} \times \text{Focal length}}{\text{Parallax shift}}$$

3. Divide your result from Question 2 by 1,000 to get the distance to the light bulb in meters.

4. Repeat Questions 2 and 3 for Stars 2 and 3.

5. Was your prediction in Step 15 correct? Why or why not?

6. Is the parallax shift greater or smaller the farther away the star is? Relate each star's parallax shift to its distance from Earth.

7. **Think About It** How did your calculation for Star 3 compare with the actual distance? What could you do to improve your results?

Design an Experiment

What would happen if you kept moving the lamp away from the box? Is there a distance at which you can no longer find the distance to the star? Design an experiment to find out.

SECTION 3 Lives of Stars

DISCOVER ·· ACTIVITY

What Determines How Long Stars Live?

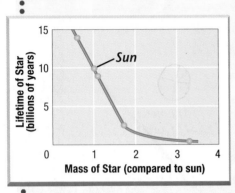

1. This graph shows how the mass of a star is related to its lifetime—how long the star lives before it runs out of fuel.

2. How long does a star with 0.8 times the mass of the sun live? How long does a star with 1.7 times the mass of the sun live?

Think It Over
Drawing Conclusions Describe the general relationship between a star's mass and its lifetime.

GUIDE FOR READING

- How does the life of a star begin?
- What determines how long a star will live?
- What happens to a star when it runs out of fuel?

Reading Tip As you read, make a flowchart showing the stages in the life of a medium-sized star.

Key Terms pulsar • nebula
• protostar • white dwarf
• supernova • neutron star
• black hole • quasar

In 1967, Jocelyn Bell Burnell, an astronomy student, detected an object in space that appeared to give off regular pulses of radio waves. Some astronomers hypothesized that the pulses might be a signal from an extraterrestrial civilization. At first, astronomers even named the source LGM, for "Little Green Men" in science-fiction stories. Eventually, astronomers concluded that the source of the radio waves was a neutron star. A neutron star is a tiny star left over when a giant star explodes. Neutron stars like the one Burnell discovered are called **pulsars**—pulsating radio sources.

Studying the Lives of Stars

Stars do not last forever. Each star is born, goes through its life cycle, and eventually dies. (Of course, stars are not really alive. The words *born, live,* and *die* are just helpful comparisons.) How did astronomers figure out that the neutron star Burnell discovered had been a larger star earlier in its life?

Imagine that you want to study how people age. You wish you could watch a few people for 50 years, but your assignment is due next week! You have to study a lot of people for a short time, and classify the people into different age groups. You may come up with groups like *babies, children, teenagers, young adults, middle-aged people,* and *elderly people.* You don't have time to see a single person go through all these stages, but you know the stages exist.

Astronomers have a similar problem with stars. They can't watch a single star for billions of years, so they study many stars and see how they differ from one another.

◀ Jocelyn Bell Burnell today

A Star Is Born

A star is made up of a large amount of gas in a relatively small volume. A **nebula,** on the other hand, is a large amount of gas and dust spread out in an immense volume. All stars begin their lives as parts of nebulas.

Gravity can pull some of the gas and dust in a nebula together. The contracting cloud is then called a protostar. *Proto* means "earliest" in Greek, so a **protostar** is the earliest stage of a star's life. **A star is born when the contracting gas and dust become so hot that nuclear fusion starts.** Nuclear fusion is the process by which atoms of hydrogen combine to form helium. During fusion, enormous amounts of energy are released.

Lifetimes of Stars

Before they can tell how old a star is, astronomers must determine its mass. **How long a star lives depends on how much mass it has.**

You might think that stars with more mass would last longer than stars with less mass. However, the reverse is true. You can think of stars as being like cars. A small car has a small gas tank, but it also has a small engine that burns gas slowly. A large car, on the other hand, has a larger gas tank, but it also has a larger engine that burns gas rapidly. So the small car might be able to travel farther on one small tank of gas than the larger car can on one large tank of gas. Small stars use up their fuel more slowly than large stars, so they have much longer lives.

Generally, stars that have less mass than the sun use their fuel slowly, and can live for up to 200 billion years. Medium-mass stars like the sun live for about 10 billion years. Astronomers think the sun is about 4.6 billion years old, so it is almost halfway through its lifetime.

Stars that have more mass than the sun have shorter lifetimes. A star that is 15 times as massive as the sun may live only about ten million years. That may seem like a long time, but it is only one tenth of one percent of the lifetime of the sun.

Checkpoint *If a star is twice as massive as the sun, will it have a longer or shorter life than the sun?*

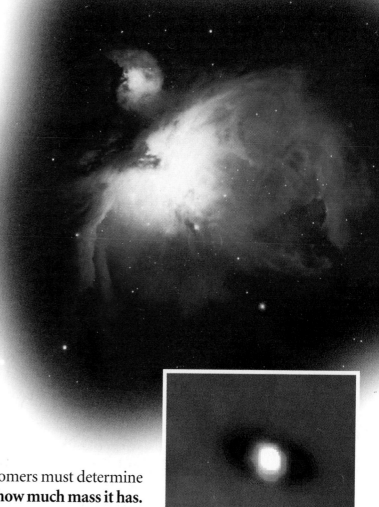

Figure 12 The Orion Nebula (top) is a giant cloud of gas and dust. The Hubble Space Telescope took this photo of a protostar (bottom) in the Orion Nebula. A protostar is a star in the earliest stage of its life. *Applying Concepts How do some of the gas and dust in a nebula become a protostar?*

Figure 13 Supernova 1987A was the brightest supernova seen in hundreds of years. The arrow in the photo at the left points to the original star, before it exploded. *Making Generalizations* Why were ancient astronomers able to see supernovas?

Sharpen your Skills

Predicting ACTIVITY

Find Algol, Polaris, and Sirius B in the H-R diagram on page 289. For each star, write a sentence predicting what the next stages in its life will be.

Deaths of Stars

When a star begins to runs out of fuel, the center of the star shrinks and the outer part of the star expands. The star becomes a red giant or supergiant.

All main sequence stars eventually become red giants or supergiants. However, what happens next depends on the mass of the star, as *Exploring the Lives of Stars* shows. **When a star runs out of fuel, it becomes a white dwarf, a neutron star, or a black hole.**

White Dwarfs Small and medium stars take 10 billion or more years to use up their nuclear fuel. Then their outer layers expand, and they become red giants. Eventually, the outer parts grow bigger still and drift out into space. The blue-white hot core of the star that is left behind is a **white dwarf.**

White dwarfs are only about the size of Earth, but they have about as much mass as the sun. Since a white dwarf has the same mass as the sun but only one millionth the volume, it is one million times as dense as the sun. A spoonful of material from a white dwarf has as much mass as a large truck. White dwarfs have no fuel, but they glow faintly from leftover energy. When a white dwarf stops glowing, it is dead. Then it is called a black dwarf.

Neutron Stars A dying giant or supergiant star can suddenly explode. Within hours, the star blazes millions of times brighter. The explosion is called a **supernova.** You can see a supernova in Figure 13. After a supernova, some of the material from the star expands into space. This material may become part of a nebula. The nebula can then contract to form a new, "recycled" star. Astronomers think the sun began as a nebula that contained material from a supernova explosion.

After the star explodes, some of the material from the star is left behind. This material may form a neutron star. **Neutron stars** are even smaller and denser than white dwarfs. A neutron star may contain as much as three times the mass of the sun but be only about 20 kilometers in diameter, the size of a large asteroid or a town on Earth.

Black Holes The most massive stars—those having more than 40 times the mass of the sun—become **black holes** when they die. After this kind of star becomes a supernova, more than five times the mass of the sun may be left. The gravity of this mass is so strong that the gas is pulled inward, packing the gas into a smaller and smaller space. Eventually five times as much mass as the sun becomes packed within a sphere 30 kilometers in diameter. At that point, the gravity is so strong that nothing can escape, not even light. The remains of the star become a black hole.

EXPLORING the Lives of Stars

A star's life history depends on its mass. The sun is a medium-mass star that will become a white dwarf, then a black dwarf.

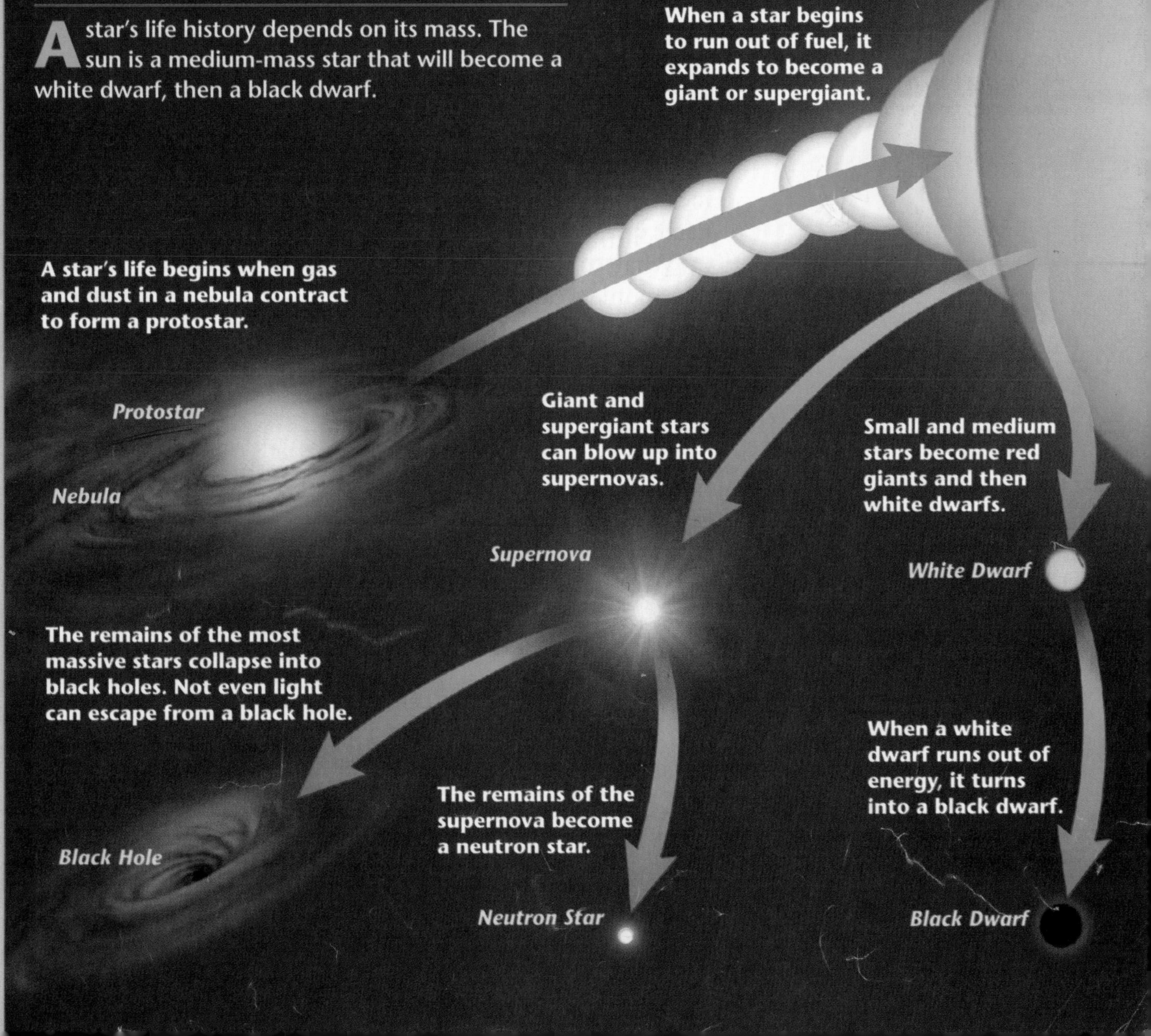

Red Giant or Supergiant

When a star begins to run out of fuel, it expands to become a giant or supergiant.

A star's life begins when gas and dust in a nebula contract to form a protostar.

Protostar

Nebula

Giant and supergiant stars can blow up into supernovas.

Small and medium stars become red giants and then white dwarfs.

Supernova

White Dwarf

The remains of the most massive stars collapse into black holes. Not even light can escape from a black hole.

When a white dwarf runs out of energy, it turns into a black dwarf.

The remains of the supernova become a neutron star.

Black Hole

Neutron Star

Black Dwarf

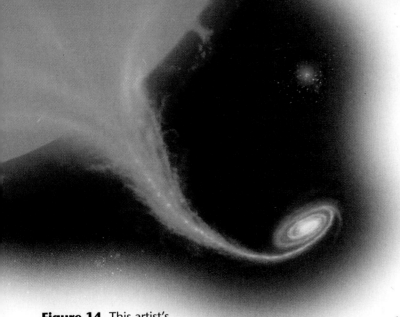

No light, radio waves, or any other form of radiation can ever get out of a black hole, so it is not possible to detect a black hole directly. But astronomers can detect black holes indirectly.

For example, gas near a black hole is pulled so strongly that it rotates faster and faster around the black hole. Friction heats the gas up. Astronomers can detect X-rays coming from the hot gas and infer that a black hole is present. Similarly, if another star is near a black hole, astronomers can calculate the mass of the black hole from the effect of its gravity on the star. Scientists at the Chandra X-ray Observatory, which you read about on page 279, are looking for black holes by studying sources of X-rays.

Figure 14 This artist's impression shows a black hole pulling matter from a companion star. The material glows as it is pulled into the black hole. *Applying Concepts If it is impossible to detect a black hole directly, how do astronomers find them?*

Quasars In the 1960s, astronomers discovered objects that are unusual because they are very bright and also very far away. Many of these objects are about 12 billion light-years away, making them among the most distant objects in the universe. These distant bright objects looked almost like stars. Since *quasi* means "something like" in Latin, these objects were given the name **quas**i-stell**ar** objects, or **quasars.**

What could be so bright even though it is so far away? Astronomers have concluded that quasars are actually distant galaxies with giant black holes at their centers. Each black hole has a mass a billion times or more as great as that of the sun. As enormous amounts of gas revolve around such a black hole, the gas heats up and shines brightly.

Section 3 Review

1. What is the earliest stage in the life of a star?
2. Why do small stars have longer lifetimes than large stars?
3. What is the difference between stars that become white dwarfs and stars that become neutron stars?
4. What evidence do astronomers use to detect black holes?
5. **Thinking Critically Inferring** What will happen to the sun when it dies? Explain your answer.

Check Your Progress

CHAPTER PROJECT

Draw and label the stars in your constellation *without* the connecting lines that form the usual image. What different patterns can you see? (*Hint:* Use a pencil to "doodle" different connections among the stars.) What does each pattern look like? Choose one pattern, and use it to name your constellation. Then write an outline of a brief story that explains why this constellation is in the sky.

SECTION
4 Star Systems and Galaxies

Why Does the Milky Way Look Hazy?

1. Using a pencil, carefully poke at least 20 holes close together in a sheet of white paper.

2. Tape the paper to a chalkboard or dark-colored wall.

3. Go to the other side of the room and look at the paper. From the far side of the room, what do the dots look like? Can you see individual dots?

Think It Over

Making Models How is looking at the paper from the far side of the room like trying to see many very distant stars that are close together? How does your model compare to the photograph of the Milky Way below?

O n a clear, dark summer night in the country, you can see a hazy band of light stretched across the sky. This band of stars is called the Milky Way. It looks as if the Milky Way is very far away from Earth. Actually, though, Earth is inside the Milky Way! How is this possible? Before you can understand the answer to this question, you need to know more about how stars are grouped together.

Star Systems and Planets

Our solar system has only one star, the sun. **But more than half of all stars are members of groups of two or more stars, called star systems.** If you were on a planet in one of these star systems, you might see two or more suns in the sky.

Double and Triple Stars A star system with two stars is called a **binary star.** (The prefix *bi* means "two.") Those with three stars are called triple stars. Proxima Centauri is probably part of a triple-star system close to our sun. The other two stars in the system, Alpha Centauri A and Alpha Centauri B, form a double star. Scientists are not sure whether Proxima Centauri is really part of the same star system or whether it is just passing close to the other two stars temporarily.

Astronomers can sometimes detect a binary star even if only one of the stars in the pair can be seen from Earth. For example, the darker star in the pair may pass in front of the other star and eclipse the other star.

GUIDE FOR READING

◆ What is a star system?

◆ What are the three types of galaxies?

Reading Tip Before you read, preview the boldfaced terms. As you read, look for a photograph or diagram that illustrates each term.

Key Terms binary star
• eclipsing binary • spiral galaxy
• elliptical galaxy
• irregular galaxy

The Milky Way ▶

Figure 15 Algol is an eclipsing binary star system, consisting of a bright star and a dim companion star. Each time the dimmer star passes in front of the brighter one, Algol becomes less bright. *Interpreting Diagrams When does Algol become brighter?*

Bright star

Dim companion star

Figure 16 If you saw someone dancing but couldn't see a partner, you could infer that the partner was there by watching the dancer you could see. Astronomers use a similar method to detect faint stars in star systems.

A system in which one star blocks the light from another is called an **eclipsing binary.** As Figure 15 shows, the star Algol is actually part of an eclipsing binary.

Often astronomers can tell that there is a second star in a system only by observing the effects of its gravity. As the second star revolves around the first star, the second star's gravity makes the first star move back and forth. Imagine you are watching a pair of dancers twirling each other around. Even if one dancer were invisible, you could tell that the invisible dancer was there from watching the motion of the visible dancer.

Planets Around Other Stars In 1995, astronomers discovered a planet revolving around a star using a method similar to the one they use to detect binary stars. The star they were observing, 51 Pegasi, moved back and forth only very slightly. Therefore, they knew the invisible object could not have enough mass to be a star. They deduced that it must be a planet.

Before this discovery, there was no way to know whether stars other than the sun had planets revolving around them. Now astronomers think that our solar system is not the only one. All of the planets found beyond our solar system so far are very large, at least half Jupiter's mass. A small planet would be difficult to detect, because it would have little gravitational effect on the star it revolved around.

Astronomers are trying to find new ways to use telescopes to see planets directly. Seeing a planet around another star is like trying to see a firefly near a street light. The glare of the light makes it hard to see anything near the light. To see a planet directly, astronomers will have to shield their view from the glare of the star that the planet revolves around. This may not be possible for many years.

Some scientists hypothesize that life may exist on planets revolving around other stars. A few astronomers are using radio telescopes to search for signals that could not have come from natural sources. Such a signal might be evidence that an extraterrestrial civilization existed and was sending out radio waves.

✓ *Checkpoint* *What evidence have astronomers used to conclude that there are planets around other stars?*

Galaxies

Now you are ready to learn about the Milky Way. The Milky Way is the galaxy in which our solar system is located. Like other galaxies, it contains single stars, double stars, star systems, and lots of gas and dust between the stars. The Milky Way Galaxy, often just called "our galaxy," looks milky or hazy because the stars are too close together for your eyes to see them individually. The dark blotches in the Milky Way are clouds of dust that block light coming from stars behind them.

There are billions of galaxies in the universe. **Astronomers have classified most galaxies into three main categories: spiral galaxies, elliptical galaxies, and irregular galaxies.**

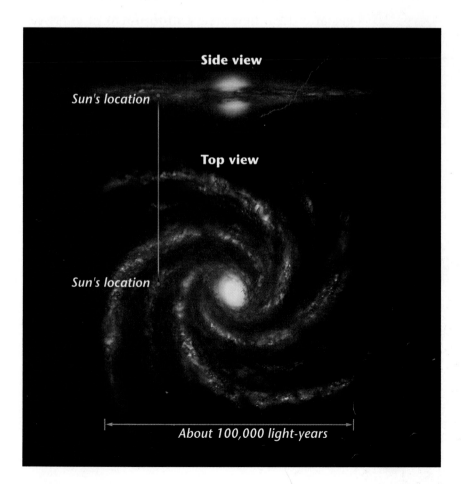

Side view

Sun's location

Top view

Sun's location

About 100,000 light-years

A Spiral Galaxy

You can make a model of our galaxy.

1. Using pipe cleaners, make a pinwheel with two spirals.

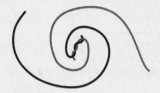

2. View the spirals along the surface of the table. Sketch what you see. Can you see the spiral shape?

3. Next, view the spirals from above the table and sketch them.

Observing The sun is inside a flat spiral galaxy. From Earth's position on the flat surface, is it possible to get a good view of stars in the spiral arms? Why or why not?

Figure 17 From the side, the Milky Way Galaxy appears to be a narrow disk. The spiral structure would be visible only from above the galaxy.

Figure 18 (A) This spiral galaxy is similar to our galaxy. (B) An elliptical galaxy looks like a flattened ball. (C) The Large Magellanic Cloud is an irregular galaxy.

Spiral Galaxies Figure 18A shows a galaxy that has the shape of twin spirals, called a **spiral galaxy.** Astronomers can see other spiral galaxies from different angles. These views show that spiral galaxies have arms that spiral outward, like pinwheels.

Our galaxy has the same spiral, pinwheel shape. It is hard for us to see the spiral shape of our galaxy because our solar system is inside the galaxy, about two thirds of the way out in one of the spiral arms. The Milky Way you see in the sky is the view people on Earth get when they look toward the main part of the rest of our galaxy. The center of our galaxy is about 25,000 light-years from the sun. However, we cannot see the center of our galaxy. The center is hidden from our view by the dust associated with massive clouds of dust between the sun and the center.

Elliptical Galaxies Not all galaxies have spiral arms. **Elliptical galaxies** look like flattened balls. Look at the elliptical galaxy in Figure 18B. These galaxies contain billions of stars but have little gas and dust between the stars. Because of the lack of gas and dust, new stars cannot form in elliptical galaxies. Elliptical galaxies contain mostly old stars.

Irregular Galaxies Some galaxies do not have regular shapes. Because of this, they are known as **irregular galaxies.** The Large Magellanic Cloud in Figure 18C is an irregular galaxy about 160,000 light-years away from our galaxy. It is one of our closest neighboring galaxies in the universe.

Section 4 Review

1. What is a star system?
2. Describe the three main types of galaxies.
3. Where is the sun in our galaxy?
4. **Thinking Critically Applying Concepts** Some binary stars are called eclipsing binaries. Explain why this term is appropriate. (*Hint:* Think about Algol as you come up with an answer.)

Science at Home

Stargazing Plan an evening of stargazing with adult family members. Choose a dark, clear night. Use binoculars if available and the star charts in Appendix G to locate the Milky Way and some interesting stars you have learned about. Explain to your family what you know about the Milky Way and each star you observe.

DISCOVER

How Does the Universe Expand?

1. Use a marker to put 10 dots on an empty balloon. The dots represent galaxies.

2. Blow up the balloon. What happens to the distances between galaxies that are close together? Galaxies that are far apart?

Think It Over

Inferring If the universe is expanding, do galaxies that are close together move apart faster or slower than galaxies that are far apart?

The Andromeda Galaxy is the most distant object you can see with your unaided eyes. Light from this galaxy has traveled for 2 million years before reaching your eyes. When that light finally reaches your eye, you are seeing what the galaxy looked like 2 million years ago. It is as though you are looking back in time.

Astronomers have photographed galaxies that are billions of light-years away. As you recall, this means that light from these galaxies traveled for billions of years before it reached Earth. From these observations, astronomers have inferred that the universe is incredibly old—billions of years old.

Moving Galaxies

Astronomers use information about how galaxies are moving as one way to develop ideas about how the universe formed. Astronomers can measure how far away different galaxies are. By examining the visible light spectrum of a galaxy, astronomers can tell how fast the galaxy is moving and whether it is moving toward our galaxy or away from it. Only a few nearby galaxies are moving toward our galaxy. All of the other galaxies are moving away from our galaxy.

In the 1920s, Edwin Hubble, an American astronomer, discovered that the farther away a galaxy is from us, the faster it is moving away from us. The Hubble Space Telescope was named after Hubble in honor of this and other important discoveries.

GUIDE FOR READING

◆ According to the big bang theory, how did the universe form?

◆ What is one theory about how the solar system formed?

Reading Tip Before you read, write down what you have already heard about the big bang theory. Then read how the theory explains the history of the universe.

Key Term big bang

▼ Galaxies photographed by the Hubble Space Telescope

Figure 19 The galaxies in the expanding universe are like the raisins in rising bread dough.
Making Models How does rising raisin bread dough model the expanding universe?

To understand how the galaxies are moving, think of raisin bread dough that is rising. If you could shrink yourself to sit on a raisin, you would see all the other raisins moving away from you as the bread dough rose. The farther away a raisin was from you, the faster it would move away, because there would be more bread dough to expand between you and the raisin. No matter which raisin you sat on, all the other raisins would seem to be moving away from you. You could tell that the bread dough was expanding by watching the other raisins.

The universe is something like the raisin bread dough. The galaxies in the universe, like the raisins in the dough, are moving away from each other. In the universe, it is space that is expanding, like the dough between the raisins.

Origin of the Universe

To understand one theory of the origin of the universe, suppose you could run time backward. All of the galaxies would then be moving together instead of apart. All of the matter in the universe would eventually come together at a single point. At that time, billions of years ago, the universe was small, hot, and dense. The universe then exploded in what astronomers call the **big bang.**

According to the big bang theory, the universe began with an enormous explosion about 10 to 15 billion years ago. Since this explosion, the universe has been expanding. Because of this expansion, the universe is billions of times larger than it was billions of years ago.

Figure 20 All of the distant galaxies astronomers have observed are moving away from our galaxy.

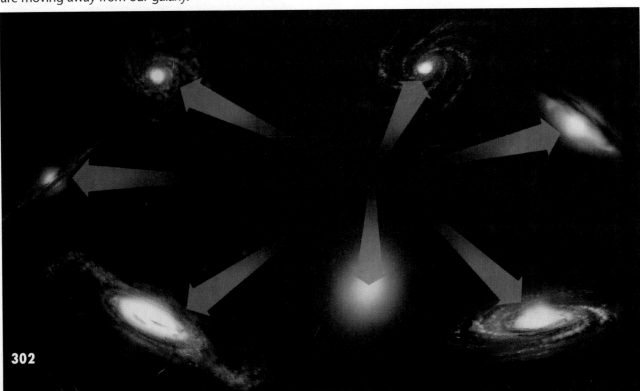

A cloud of gas and dust formed a spinning disk.

Gas in the center of the disk collapsed to form the sun.

The remaining gas and dust formed the planets.

The solar system includes the sun, planets, and belts of rock, ice, and dust.

Figure 21 The solar system formed from a collapsing cloud of gas and dust.

Astronomers know approximately how fast the universe is expanding now. They can use this information to infer how long it has been expanding. Astronomers estimate that the universe has been expanding for 10 billion to 15 billion years.

☑ *Checkpoint* How do galaxies move relative to each other?

Origin of the Solar System

According to the big bang theory, matter in the universe formed galaxies. Where this matter was dense enough, giant stars formed. Eventually, these stars died in supernova explosions. These explosions added new elements to the matter in the universe.

Then about five billion years ago, a nebula collapsed to form the solar system. Slowly the nebula shrank to form a spinning disk. As gravity pulled the matter into the disk's center, the matter became hot and dense. Nuclear fusion began, and the sun was born.

Elsewhere in this disk, gas and dust formed solid spheres smaller than the sun. The spheres closest to the sun lost most of their gases and became the inner planets Mercury, Venus, Earth, and Mars. The spheres farthest from the sun became the gas giants Jupiter, Saturn, Uranus, and Neptune. Between the inner planets and the gas giants, the asteroids formed. Pluto was formed just beyond Neptune. Far beyond Pluto is a huge cloud of ice and other substances. This cloud is probably the main source of comets.

Unanswered Questions About the Universe

The big bang theory does not explain all the observations made about the universe. For example, the measurement of the distance between two objects in the universe may vary depending on how the measurement was made. Some of the measurements indicate that the universe may be younger than the big bang theory predicts. The estimated ages of stars in some globular clusters also suggest some uncertainty about the age of the universe. Measurements of the energy left over from the big bang have been made by the Cosmic Background Explorer Spacecraft, but they don't pinpoint when the big bang occurred.

Figure 22 This engineer is checking data from the Hubble Space Telescope. The telescope can be controlled from this room.

In addition, the big bang theory does not answer all the questions that scientists have about the universe. What caused the big bang? What came before the big bang? Scientists also want to know what will happen to the universe in the future. One possible answer is that the universe will continue to expand. Indeed, some current observations of scientists suggest that the rate of expansion is speeding up. Another possible answer is that the universe will someday start to contract. According to this idea, all of the galaxies will be pulled back together, resulting in a "big crunch."

Astronomy is one of the oldest sciences. However, there are still many discoveries to be made and puzzles to be solved about the universe. New telescopes and electronic detectors will give astronomers much more information in the first decades of the twenty-first century. These new instruments will allow the next generation of astronomers to see farther and more clearly into the universe.

Section 5 Review

1. What is the big bang theory?
2. Describe a theory of how the solar system formed.
3. What observations show that the universe is expanding?
4. **Thinking Critically Inferring** What can astronomers infer from the fact that other galaxies are moving away from ours?

Check Your Progress

CHAPTER PROJECT

Now you are ready to write the first draft of your Texas star story. After you have written a first draft, read it over carefully and look for ways to improve it. Here are things to look for as you edit your first draft. Does the beginning grab the reader's interest? Does your story make sense? Should you add more details? Should you rethink your choice of words? Rewrite and revise as much as necessary.

SECTION 1 Tools of Modern Astronomy

INTEGRATING **PHYSICS**

Key Ideas

◆ Telescopes collect and focus different types of electromagnetic radiation from stars and galaxies.
◆ Astronomers use spectrographs to get information about stars.

Key Terms

constellation   observatory
radio telescope   spectrograph

 SECTION 2 Characteristics of Stars

Key Ideas

◆ Astronomers measure distances to stars and galaxies in light-years.
◆ The main characteristics used to classify stars are size, temperature, and brightness.

Key Terms

galaxy   apparent magnitude
universe   absolute magnitude
light-year   Hertzsprung-Russell diagram
parallax   main sequence
giant star

 SECTION 3 Lives of Stars

Key Ideas

◆ A star is born when nuclear fusion starts.
◆ The length of a star's life depends on its mass.
◆ When a star runs out of fuel, it becomes a white dwarf, a neutron star, or a black hole.

Key Terms

pulsar   white dwarf   black hole
nebula   supernova   quasar
protostar   neutron star

SECTION 4 Star Systems and Galaxies

Key Ideas

◆ More than half of all stars are members of groups of two or more stars, called star systems.
◆ There are three types of galaxies: spiral galaxies, elliptical galaxies, and irregular galaxies.

Key Terms

binary star   elliptical galaxy
eclipsing binary   irregular galaxy
spiral galaxy

 SECTION 5 History of the Universe

Key Ideas

◆ According to the big bang theory, the universe formed in an enormous explosion about 10 to 15 billion years ago.
◆ About five billion years ago, a cloud of gas and dust collapsed to form the solar system.

Key Term

big bang

Organizing Information

Concept Map Copy the concept map about telescopes onto a separate sheet of paper. Then complete it and add a title. (For more on concept maps, see the Skills Handbook.)

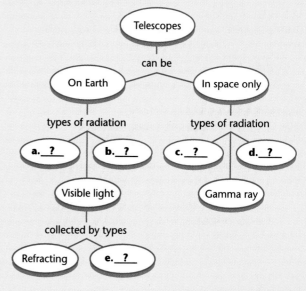

Reviewing Content

Review key concepts online using iText at www.phschool.com

Multiple Choice

Choose the letter of the answer that best completes each statement.

1. The Hubble Space Telescope is a
   a. gamma ray telescope.
   b. reflecting telescope.
   c. refracting telescope.
   d. radio telescope.

2. The most common chemical element in a star is
   a. hydrogen.
   b. helium.
   c. carbon.
   d. sodium.

3. To measure the distance to a nearby star, an astronomer would use
   a. visible light.
   b. quasars.
   c. parallax.
   d. a spectrograph.

4. Stars more massive than the sun
   a. live longer than the sun.
   b. are redder than the sun.
   c. have shorter lives than the sun.
   d. live as long as the sun.

5. The sun formed out of a
   a. pulsar.   b. supergiant star.
   c. black hole.   d. nebula.

True or False

If the statement is true, write true. If it is false, change the underlined word or words to make the statement true.

6. Telescopes that detect radio waves from stars are called <u>refracting</u> telescopes.

7. The sun is a <u>main-sequence</u> star.

8. Pulsars are a kind of <u>neutron star</u>.

9. More than half of all stars are <u>single</u> stars.

10. Acccording to the <u>big bang</u> theory, the universe has been expanding for 10–15 billion years.

Checking Concepts

11. Explain how a visible light reflecting telescope and a radio telescope are alike.

12. What kinds of information can astronomers obtain by studying the spectrum of a star?

13. Describe what will happen to the sun when it runs out of fuel.

14. Why can astronomers see the spiral arms of the Andromeda Galaxy more clearly than the spiral arms of the Milky Way Galaxy?

15. Describe the process by which the sun was formed.

16. **Writing to Learn** Imagine you have a spaceship that can travel much faster than the speed of light. Write a letter describing your three-part trip from Earth: to the nearest star other than the sun, to the center of our galaxy, and to the next-nearest spiral galaxy.

Thinking Critically

17. **Applying Concepts** Is a light-year a unit of distance or a unit of time? Explain.

18. **Applying Concepts** Describe a real-world situation involving absolute and apparent magnitudes. (*Hint:* Think about riding in a car at night.)

19. **Comparing and Contrasting** Compare the life histories of a medium-sized star and a giant star. How are they similar? How are they different?

20. **Relating Cause and Effect** Once every three days a small, bright star becomes much dimmer, only to return to its original brightness within six hours. Based on this information, what is causing the small star to become dimmer?

21. **Making Generalizations** What information does knowing the rate at which the universe is expanding give astronomers about the big bang?

Applying Skills

Use the data about moving galaxies in the table below to answer Questions 22–24.

Cluster of Galaxies	Distance (millions of light-years)	Speed (kilometers per second)
Virgo	80	1,200
Ursa Major	980	15,000
Bootes	2,540	39,000
Hydra	3,980	61,000

22. Graphing Make a line graph showing how each cluster's distance from our galaxy is related to its speed. Put distance on the *x*-axis and speed on the *y*-axis.

23. Interpreting Data How are the distance and speed of a galaxy related?

24. Drawing Conclusions Does your graph indicate that the universe is expanding, contracting, or staying the same size? Explain.

Test Preparation   *Use these questions to prepare for standardized tests.*

Study the diagram. Then answer Questions 25–29.

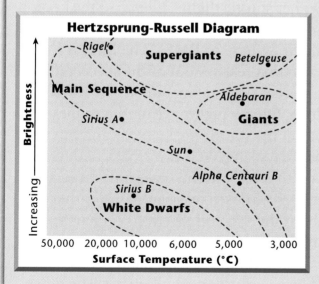

Hertzsprung-Russell Diagram

25. To which group do most stars belong ?
   A supergiants   **B** giants
   C main sequence   **D** white dwarfs

26. Which star is hotter than the sun?
   F Betelgeuse
   G Aldebaran
   H Alpha Centauri B
   J Sirius B

27. Which star is most likely to be red?
   A Rigel
   B Sirius A
   C Sirius B
   D Betelgeuse

28. Compared to Rigel, Alpha Centauri B is
   F cooler and brighter.
   G cooler and dimmer.
   H hotter and brighter.
   J hotter and dimmer.

29. Which star has a greater absolute magnitude?
   A Rigel
   B Betelgeuse
   C Sirius B
   D Aldebaran

AN ELECTRICAL ENGINEER IN
OUTER SPACE

Ellen Ochoa was born and raised in California. She earned a doctorate in electrical engineering from Stanford University and became an astronaut in 1991. She has flown on two space-shuttle missions. Currently she is a Spacecraft Communicator, an astronaut at Mission Control who talks with other astronauts while they are in space. She is a talented flute player who has taken her flute with her on the shuttle. She hopes to be aboard more missions in space soon.

When she was studying electricity in school science classes, Ellen Ochoa didn't know that some day her studies would help take her into space. "I just always liked math and science," the California-born Dr. Ochoa says. Today she is an astronaut and has flown on two space-shuttle missions. Trained as an electrical engineer, she is an expert in the uses of electricity. This is the important skill she brings to the astronaut team.

Astronaut Ochoa has worked in the testing and training process for robotics — humanlike machines that can carry out complicated tasks in space. On her shuttle flights, Ellen had the key job of controlling one of these machines, the Remote Manipulator System, or RMS. "The RMS is a robotic arm that reaches out of the spacecraft," she explains. "We use electricity to operate it. The RMS is about 50 feet long. On my flights, we used it to pick up a satellite that was in the shuttle payload bay and put it in orbit. Then a few days later, we'd come back and retrieve the satellite and put it back in the spacecraft cargo area." One of the satellites was used by scientists to gather information about the sun and its effects on Earth. Another was used to study Earth's atmosphere.

"We have a work station with two hand controllers. One is sort of like a joystick on a kid's game. The other is like a square knob that you hold. You push and pull, or move up and down or left and right, to move the electrical RMS arm to the correct position."

Talking with Dr. Ellen Ochoa

◄ Ellen Ochoa training on Earth with the RMS

◄ A satellite in the grasp of the RMS arm of the space shuttle *Atlantis*

This diagram of the RMS arm shows its three joints and mechanical hand (at the right). The arm is about 15 meters long.

Q *How did you become interested in science?*

A I got into science because I liked math. I always enjoyed math and did well at it. I was interested in finding out about all the ways that people could use math. So I studied physics at college. I didn't know until then that I would have a career in science.

Q *Did you follow the space program when you were young?*

A Oh sure. It was a very big thing in the 1960s when I was in elementary school. At the time, the Apollo program was sending astronauts to the moon. But it wasn't until I was in graduate school in electrical engineering that I learned how to apply for the space program and what they were looking for in selecting astronauts.

Q *What happened when you applied to the space program?*

A The first time I applied in 1985 I was not selected. So I tried again in 1990 and was chosen. That's been the case with many astronauts. Persistence is one of our qualities.

Q *How do astronauts use electricity in the space shuttle?*

A We use electrical power for many of the systems on board the shuttle. It's used for the computers and for the sensors and detectors to make sure that the life-support systems are working correctly. Many of our instruments for research use other forms of energy related to electricity, like light or radio waves. We can use these instruments, for instance, to measure the chemicals in the atmosphere that affect climate and weather. And, of course, we use radio for communicating with the ground crew.

Q *Where does the electricity you use come from?*

A We have fuel cells on board. We bring up cryogenic (very cold) oxygen and hydrogen. Then we allow the two chemicals to mix together in the fuel cells. Fuel cells use chemical reactions, like batteries. The chemical reactions in fuel cells produce both electricity and water, which we use on board. We would like to carry up more oxygen and hydrogen fuel cells, to make more electric power. But more fuel cells would mean we could carry less of other things, such as the equipment for the scientific experiments we do.

Q *Are you studying other ways to make electricity?*

A We've had two shuttle flights that experimented with tethered satellites. Basically, the idea was to drag a satellite through space on a tether—a long conducting cable. As the conductor passes through Earth's magnetic field, electric current is generated. Tethered satellites are just at the research stage now.

Ellen Ochoa at the controls of the RMS arm with astronaut Donald R. McMonagle

Ellen Ochoa entertains other crew ▶ members during a flight.

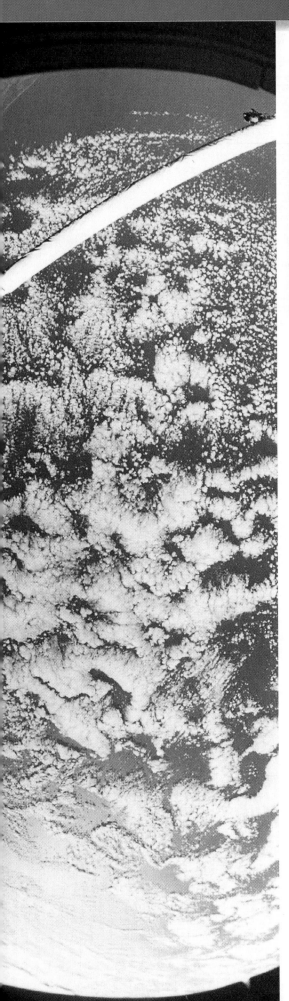

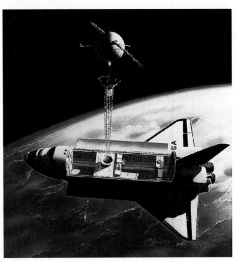

But eventually, we'd like to use power from tethers to move satellites up and down in orbit without using up precious fuel.

Q *What parts of working as an astronaut do you enjoy?*

A I think the whole flight is fun— the launch, viewing Earth from space, and living in weightlessness, although that can be frustrating, too. Doing the activities we've been trained for is hard work, but it's really enjoyable as well. There are a lot of interesting, exciting careers for people with backgrounds in science and math. Being an astronaut is just one of them.

In Your Journal

Ellen talks about persistence, a quality that helped her become an astronaut. Think of a time when you succeeded in doing something after many attempts. Describe what happened. How did persistence and determination help you? Why would these qualities be important for scientists to have?

CHAPTER

9 Plate Tectonics

This is a satellite image of the San Francisco Bay area. The row of lakes below marks the line of the San Andreas fault, a crack in Earth's crust.

WEB ACTIVITY

www.phschool.com

Moving Plates

Along the San Andreas fault in California, two vast pieces of Earth's lithosphere called plates slowly slide past each other. In this chapter you will learn how movements deep within Earth cause plate movements on the surface. You will build a model that shows plate movements and how they result in mountain building and other changes in the planet's surface.

Your Goal To build a three-dimensional model that shows how plate movement changes Earth's surface features.

To complete this project, you must

◆ choose one of the plates that forms Earth's surface and become an expert in its movements
◆ build a scale model showing how one edge of your plate interacts with another plate
◆ show how the two plates push together, pull apart, or slide past each other, and indicate the direction and rate of their movement
◆ construct a map showing your prediction of future plate movement
◆ label all physical features clearly
◆ follow the safety guidelines in Appendix A

Get Started Begin now by previewing the chapter to learn about Earth's structure and how plates move and interact. Brainstorm a list of the kinds of materials that could be used to make a three-dimensional model. Start a project folder in which you will keep your sketches, ideas, and any information needed to design and build your model.

Check Your Progress You will be designing and building your model as you study this chapter. To keep your project on track, look for Check Your Progress boxes at the following points.

Section 1 Review, page 322: Choose a plate and begin gathering information about its movements.
Section 4 Review, page 337: Sketch and design your model.
Section 5 Review, page 345: Revise your design and start building your model.
Section 6 Review, page 353: Complete the construction of your model.

Present Your Project At the end of the chapter (page 357), you will present your completed model to the class and discuss the movements of your tectonic plate.

TEKS

In addition to process TEKS, this chapter addresses these concept TEKS as they relate to the chapter's topics.

(8.7) The student knows that there is a relationship between force and motion. The student is expected to:
(A) demonstrate how unbalanced forces cause changes in the speed or direction of an object's motion; and
(B) recognize that waves are generated and can travel through different media.

(8.10) The student knows that complex interactions occur between matter and energy. The student is expected to:
(A) illustrate interactions between matter and energy including specific heat.

(8.14) The student knows that natural events and human activity can alter Earth systems. The student is expected to:
(A) predict land features resulting from gradual changes such as mountain building, beach erosion, land subsidence, and continental drift.

How Do Scientists Determine What's Inside Earth?

1. Your teacher will provide you with three closed film canisters. Each canister contains a different material. Your goal is to determine what is inside each canister—even though you can't directly observe what it contains.

2. Stick a label made from a piece of tape on each canister.

3. To gather evidence about the contents of the canisters, you may tap, roll, shake, or weigh them. Record your observations.

4. What differences do you notice between the canisters? Apart from their appearance on the outside, are the canisters similar in any way? How did you obtain this evidence?

Think It Over

Inferring Based on your observations, what can you infer about the contents of the canisters? How do you think scientists gather evidence about Earth's interior?

I n November 1963, the people of Iceland got to see how new land can be added to Earth's surface. With no warning, the waters south of Iceland began to hiss and bubble. Soon there was a fiery volcanic eruption from beneath the ocean. Steam and ash belched into the sky. Molten rock from inside Earth spurted above the ocean's surface and hardened into a small island. Within the next several years, the new volcano added 2.5 square kilometers of new, raw land to Earth's surface. The Icelanders named the island "Surtsey." In Icelandic mythology, Surtsey is the god of fire.

Figure 1 The island of Surtsey formed in the Atlantic Ocean.

The Science of Geology

Newspapers reported the story of Surtsey's fiery birth. But much of what is known about volcanoes like Surtsey comes from the work of geologists. **Geologists** are scientists who study the forces that make and shape planet Earth. Geologists study the chemical and physical characteristics of **rock,** the material that forms Earth's hard surface. They map where different types of rock are found on and beneath the surface. Geologists describe landforms, the features formed in rock and soil by water, wind, and waves. Geologists study the processes that create Earth's features and search for clues about Earth's history.

The modern science of **geology,** the study of planet Earth, began in the late 1700s. Geologists of that time studied the rocks on the surface. These geologists concluded that Earth's landforms are the work of natural forces that slowly build up and wear down the land.

Studying Surface Changes   Forces beneath the surface are constantly changing Earth's appearance. Throughout our planet's long history, its surface has been lifted up, pushed down, bent, and broken. Thus Earth looks different today from the way it did millions of years ago.

Today, geologists divide the forces that change Earth's surface features into two groups: constructive forces and destructive forces. **Constructive forces shape the surface by building up mountains and landmasses. Destructive forces are those that slowly wear away mountains and, eventually, every other feature on the surface.** The formation of the island of Surtsey is an example of constructive forces at work. The ocean waves that will wear away Surtsey's shoreline are an example of Earth's destructive forces.

Two hundred years ago, the science of geology was young. Then, geologists knew only a few facts about Earth's surface. They knew that Earth is a sphere with a radius at the equator of more than 6,000 kilometers. They knew that there are seven great landmasses, called continents, surrounded by oceans. They knew that the continents are made up of many layers of rock.

Figure 2 The work of geologists often takes them outdoors—from caves beneath the surface to mountainsides. *Observing What are the geologists in each picture doing?*

These layers can sometimes be seen on the walls of canyons and the sides of valleys. However, many riddles remained: How old is Earth? How has Earth's surface changed over time? Why are there oceans, and how did they form? For more than 200 years, geologists have tried to answer these and other questions about the planet.

Indirect Evidence—Seismic Waves One of the most difficult questions that geologists have tried to answer is, What's inside Earth? Much as geologists might like to, they cannot dig a hole to the center of Earth. The extreme conditions in Earth's interior prevent exploration far below the surface. The deepest mine in the world, a gold mine in South Africa, reaches a depth of 3.8 kilometers. But it only scratches the surface. You would have to travel more than 1,600 times that distance—over 6,000 kilometers—to reach Earth's center.

Geologists cannot observe Earth's interior directly. Instead, they must rely on indirect methods of observation. Have you ever hung a heavy picture on a wall? If you have, you know that you can knock on the wall to locate the wooden beam underneath the plaster that will support the picture. When you knock on the wall, you listen carefully for a change in the sound.

When geologists want to study Earth's interior, they also use an indirect method. But instead of knocking on walls, they use seismic waves. Recall from Chapter 4 that when earthquakes occur, they produce seismic waves. Geologists record the seismic waves and study how they travel through the medium of Earth. The speed of these seismic waves and the paths they take reveal how the planet is put together. Using data from seismic waves, geologists have learned that Earth's interior is made up of several layers. Each layer surrounds the layers beneath it, much like the layers of an onion.

Figure 3 This cave in Georgia may seem deep. But even a deep cave is only a small nick in Earth's surface.

✓ *Checkpoint* *What kind of indirect evidence do geologists use to study the structure of Earth?*

A Journey to the Center of the Earth

If you really could travel through these layers to the center of Earth, what would your trip be like? To begin, you will need a vehicle that can travel through solid rock. The vehicle will carry scientific instruments to record changes in temperature and pressure as you descend.

Temperature As you start to tunnel beneath the surface, you might expect the rock around you to be cool. At first, the surrounding rock is cool. Then at about 20 meters down your instruments report that the surrounding rock is getting warmer. For every 40 meters that you descend from that point, the temperature rises 1 Celsius degree. This rapid rise in temperature continues for several kilometers. After that, the temperature increases more slowly, but steadily.

Pressure During your journey to the center of Earth, your instruments also record an increase in pressure in the surrounding rock. The deeper you go, the greater the pressure. **Pressure** is the force pushing on a surface or area. Because of the weight of the rock above, pressure inside Earth increases as you go deeper.

As you go toward the center of Earth, you travel through several different layers. **Three main layers make up Earth's interior: the crust, the mantle, and the core. Each layer has its own conditions and materials.** You can see these layers in *Exploring Earth's Interior* on pages 320–321.

Figure 4 The deeper this swimmer goes, the greater the pressure from the surrounding water. *Comparing and Contrasting* How is the water in the swimming pool similar to Earth's interior? How is it different?

Pressure Increases

Depth
0
.5m
1m
1.5m
2m

The Crust

Your journey to the center of Earth begins in the crust. The **crust** is a layer of rock that forms Earth's outer skin. On the crust you find rocks and mountains. But the crust also includes the soil and water that cover large parts of Earth's surface.

This outer rind of rock is much thinner than what lies beneath it. In fact, you can think of Earth's crust as being similar to the paper-thin skin of an onion. The crust includes both the dry land and the ocean floor. It is thinnest beneath the ocean and thickest under high mountains. The crust ranges from 5 to 40 kilometers thick.

The crust beneath the ocean is called oceanic crust. Oceanic crust consists mostly of dense rocks such as basalt. **Basalt** (buh SAWLT) is dark, dense rock with a fine texture. Continental crust, the crust that forms the continents, consists mainly of less dense rocks such as granite. **Granite** is a rock that has larger crystals than basalt and is not as dense. It usually is a light color.

Figure 5 Two of the most common rocks in the crust are basalt and granite. **A.** The dark rock is basalt, which makes up much of the oceanic crust. **B.** The light rock is granite, which makes up much of the continental crust.

The Mantle

Your journey downward continues. At a depth of between 5 and 40 kilometers beneath the surface, you cross a boundary. Above this boundary are the basalt and granite rocks of the crust. Below the boundary is the solid material of the **mantle,** a layer of hot rock.

The crust and the uppermost part of the mantle are very similar. The uppermost part of the mantle and the crust together form a rigid layer called the **lithosphere** (LITH uh sfeer). In Greek, *lithos* means "stone." The average thickness of the lithosphere is about 100 kilometers.

Figure 6 At the surface, Earth's crust forms peaks like these in the Rocky Mountains of Colorado. Soil and plants cover much of the crust. *Comparing and Contrasting How does the thickness of Earth's crust compare to the thickness of the mantle?*

Next you travel farther into the mantle below the lithosphere. Here your vehicle encounters material that is hotter and under increasing pressure. In general, temperature and pressure in the mantle increase with depth. The heat and pressure make the part of the mantle just beneath the lithosphere less rigid than the rock above. Like road tar softened by the heat of the sun, the material that forms this part of the mantle is somewhat soft—it can bend like plastic. This soft layer is called the **asthenosphere** (as THEHN uh sfeer). In Greek, *asthenes* means "weak." Just because *asthenes* means "weak," you can't assume this layer is actually weak. But the asthenosphere is soft. The material in this layer can flow slowly.

The lithosphere floats on top of the asthenosphere. Beneath the asthenosphere, which extends to a depth of 350 kilometers, solid mantle material extends all the way to Earth's core. The mantle is nearly 3,000 kilometers thick.

✓ *Checkpoint How does the material of the asthenosphere differ from the material of the lithosphere?*

The Core

After traveling through the mantle, you reach the core. Earth's core consists of two parts—a liquid outer core and a solid inner core. The metals iron and nickel make up both parts of the core. The **outer core** is a layer of molten metal that surrounds the inner core. In spite of enormous pressure, the outer core behaves like a thick liquid. The **inner core** is a dense ball of solid metal. In the inner core, extreme pressure squeezes the atoms of iron and nickel so much that they cannot spread out and become liquid.

The outer and inner cores make up about one third of Earth's mass, but only 15 percent of its volume. The inner and outer cores together are just slightly smaller than the moon.

Sharpen your Skills

Creating Data Tables

ACTIVITY

Imagine that you have invented a super-strong vehicle that can resist extremely high pressure as it bores a tunnel deep into Earth's interior. You stop several times on your trip to collect data using devices located on your vehicle's outer hull. To see what conditions you would find at various depths on your journey, refer to *Exploring Earth's Interior* on pages 320–321. Copy the table in your notebook or make one on the computer. Then complete the table.

Depth	Name of Layer	What Layer Is Made Of
20 km		
150 km		
2,000 km		
4,000 km		
6,000 km		

EXPLORING Earth's Interior

Earth's interior is divided into layers: the crust, mantle, outer core, and inner core. Although Earth's crust seems stable, the extreme heat of Earth's interior causes changes that slowly reshape the surface.

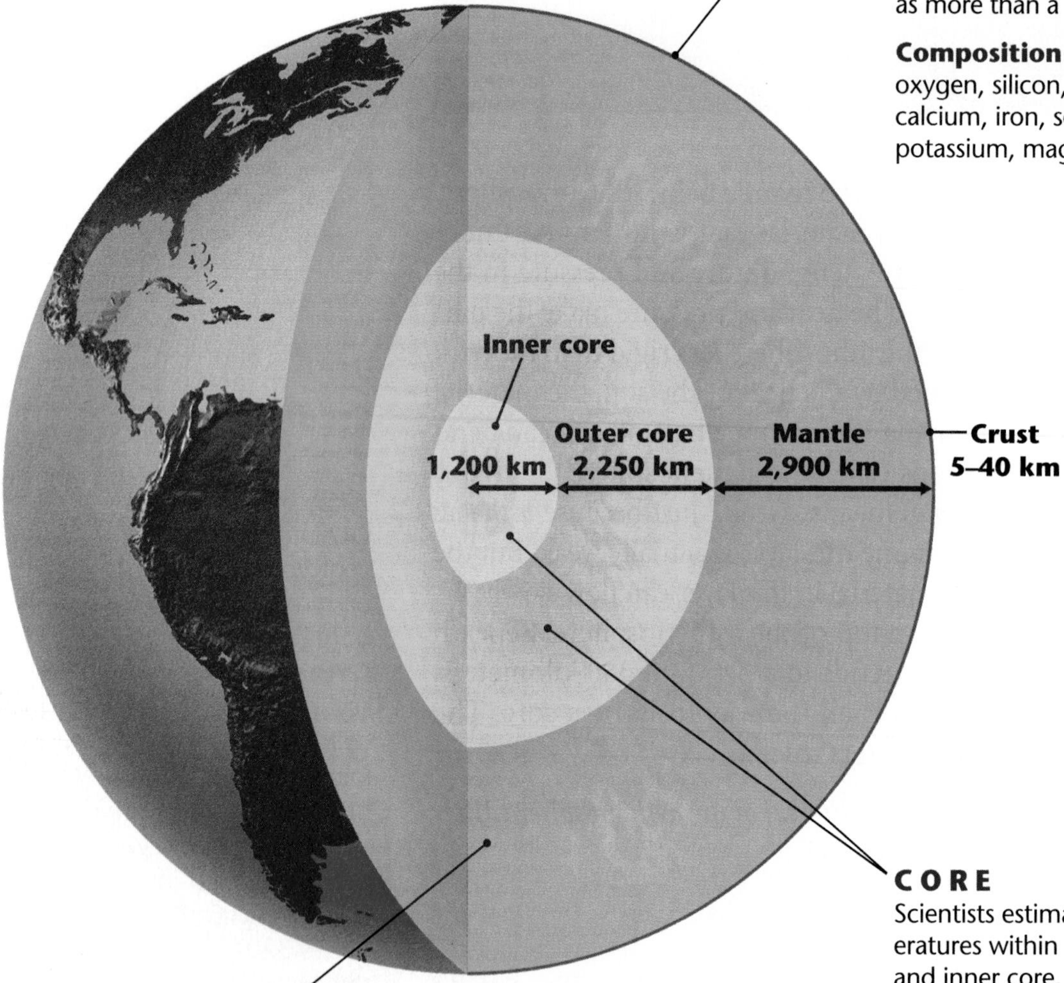

CRUST

The crust is Earth's solid and rocky outer layer, including both the land surface and the ocean floor. The crust averages 32 km thick. At the scale of this drawing, the crust is too thin to show up as more than a thin line.

Composition of crust:
oxygen, silicon, aluminum, calcium, iron, sodium, potassium, magnesium

Inner core
1,200 km

Outer core
2,250 km

Mantle
2,900 km

Crust
5–40 km

MANTLE

A trip through Earth's mantle goes almost halfway to the center of Earth. The chemical composition of the mantle does not change much from one part of the mantle to another. However, physical conditions in the mantle change because pressure and temperature increase with depth.

Composition of mantle:
silicon, oxygen, iron, magnesium

CORE

Scientists estimate that temperatures within Earth's outer core and inner core, both made of iron and nickel, range from about 2,000°C to 5,000°C. If these estimates are correct, then Earth's center may be as hot as the sun's surface.

Composition of core:
iron, nickel

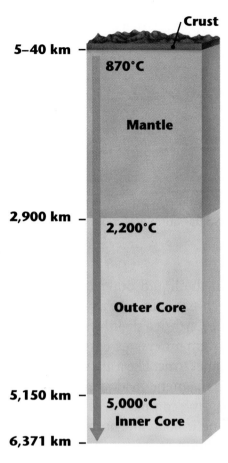

5–40 km —

Crust

870°C

Mantle

2,900 km —

2,200°C

Outer Core

5,150 km —

5,000°C
Inner Core

6,371 km —

◀ **CROSS SECTION FROM SURFACE TO CENTER**

From Earth's surface to its center, the layers of Earth's interior differ in their composition, temperature, and pressure. Notice how temperature increases toward the inner core.

CRUST-TO-MANTLE

The rigid crust and lithosphere float on the hot, soft material of the asthenosphere. Notice that continental crust, made mostly of granite, is several times thicker than oceanic crust, made mostly of basalt. ▼

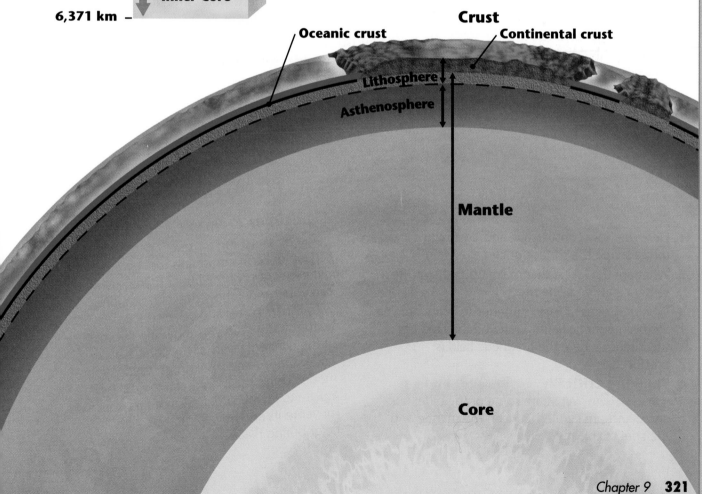

Oceanic crust

Crust

Continental crust

Lithosphere

Asthenosphere

Mantle

Core

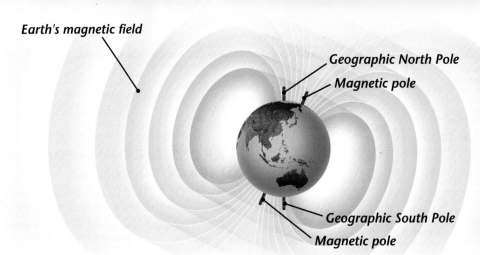

Earth's magnetic field

Geographic North Pole
Magnetic pole

Geographic South Pole
Magnetic pole

Figure 7 Like a magnet, Earth's magnetic field has north and south poles.

Earth's Magnetic Field

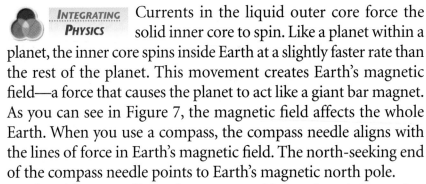

INTEGRATING PHYSICS Currents in the liquid outer core force the solid inner core to spin. Like a planet within a planet, the inner core spins inside Earth at a slightly faster rate than the rest of the planet. This movement creates Earth's magnetic field—a force that causes the planet to act like a giant bar magnet. As you can see in Figure 7, the magnetic field affects the whole Earth. When you use a compass, the compass needle aligns with the lines of force in Earth's magnetic field. The north-seeking end of the compass needle points to Earth's magnetic north pole.

Consider an ordinary bar magnet. If you place it beneath a piece of paper and sprinkle iron filings on the paper, the iron filings line up with the bar's magnetic field. If you could cover the entire planet with iron filings, they would form a similar pattern.

Section 1 Review

1. Describe how constructive and destructive forces shape the surface of Earth.
2. What are the layers that make up Earth? Write a sentence about each one.
3. What happens in Earth's interior to produce Earth's magnetic field? Describe the layers of the interior where the magnetic field is produced.
4. **Thinking Critically Comparing and Contrasting** What are some of the differences and similarities between the mantle and the core? Explain.

CHAPTER PROJECT

Check Your Progress

Begin by sketching a cross section of Earth's crust and the different layers of the upper mantle. How can your model show these layers along with Earth's plates and other surface features? How can you show the thickness of the different layers at the correct scale? Think about materials you can use for your model. Using the map on page 341, pick a plate to investigate. Research this plate's movements and how it interacts with neighboring plates.

SECTION 2 Convection Currents and the Mantle

DISCOVER ••• ACTIVITY

How Can Heat Cause Motion in a Liquid?

1. ⚠️ Carefully pour some hot water into a small, shallow pan. Fill a clear, plastic cup about half-full with cold water. Place the cup in the pan.

2. Allow the water to stand for two minutes until all motion stops.

3. Fill a plastic dropper with some food coloring. Then, holding the dropper under the water surface and slightly away from the edge of the cup, gently squeeze a small droplet of the food coloring into the water.

4. Observe the water for one minute.

5. Add another droplet at the water surface in the middle of the cup and observe again.

Think It Over

Inferring How do you explain what happened to the droplets of food coloring? Why do you think the second droplet moved in a way that was different from the way the first droplet moved?

E arth's molten outer core is nearly as hot as the surface of the sun. To explain how heat from the core affects the mantle, you need to recall how heat is transferred in solids and liquids. If you have ever touched a hot pot accidentally, you have discovered for yourself (in a painful way) that heat moves. In this case, it moved from the hot pot to your hand. The movement of energy from a warmer object to a cooler object is called heat transfer.

Heat is always transferred from a warmer substance to a cooler substance. For example, holding an ice cube will make your hand begin to feel cold in a few seconds. But is the coldness in the ice cube moving to your hand? Since cold is the absence of heat, it's the heat in your hand that moves to the ice cube! **Heat is transferred through radiation, conduction, and convection.**

Radiation

Recall from Chapter 3 that radiation is the transfer of energy by electromagnetic waves. Radiation does not require matter to transfer heat, or thermal energy. Sunlight is radiation that warms Earth's surface. The process takes place with no direct contact between the sun and Earth's surface. Other familiar forms of radiation include the heat you feel around a flame or open fire.

GUIDE FOR READING

◆ How is heat transferred?

◆ What causes convection currents in Earth's mantle?

Reading Tip As you read, draw a concept map of the three types of heat transfer. Include supporting ideas about convection.

Key Term density

Figure 8 In conduction, the heated particles of a substance transfer heat to other particles through direct contact. That's how the spoon and the pot itself heat up.

Conduction

Remember that heat transfer by direct contact of particles of matter is called conduction. What happens as a spoon heats up in a pot of soup? Heat is transferred from the hot soup and the pot to the particles that make up the spoon. The particles near the bottom of the spoon vibrate faster as they are heated, so they bump into other particles and heat them, too. Gradually the entire spoon heats up. When your hand touches the spoon, conduction transfers heat from the spoon directly to your skin. Then you feel the heat. Look at Figure 8 to see how heat flows in this system.

Convection

Conduction heats the spoon, but how does the soup inside the pot heat up? Recall from Chapter 5 that heat transfer involving the movement of fluids—liquids and gases—is called convection. Convection is heat transfer by the movement of a heated fluid. During convection, heated particles of fluid begin to flow, transferring heat energy from one part of the fluid to another.

Heat transfer by convection is caused by differences of temperature and density within a fluid. **Density** is a measure of how much mass there is in a volume of a substance. For example, rock is more dense than water because a given volume of rock has more mass than the same volume of water.

When a liquid or gas is heated, the particles move faster. As the particles move faster, they spread apart. Because the particles of the heated fluid are farther apart, they occupy more space. The density decreases. But when a fluid cools, its particles move more slowly and settle together more closely. As the fluid becomes cooler, its density increases.

Convection occurs when you heat soup on a stove. As the soup at the bottom of the pot gets hot, it expands and therefore becomes less dense. The warm, less dense soup moves upward and floats over the cooler, denser soup. At the surface, the warm soup spreads out and cools, becoming denser. Then, gravity pulls this cooler, denser soup back down to the bottom of the pot, where it is heated again. Figure 9 shows this pattern of movement.

Figure 9 In this pot, the soup close to the heat source is hotter and less dense than the soup near the surface. These differences in temperature and density cause convection currents.

A constant flow begins as the cooler soup continually sinks to the bottom of the pot and the warmer soup rises. A convection current is the flow that transfers heat within a fluid.

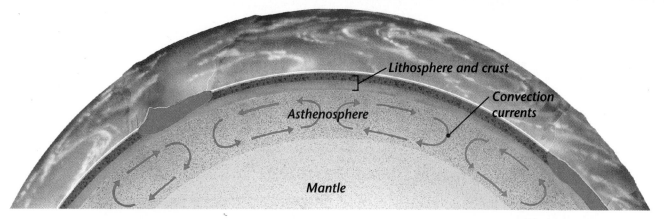

Lithosphere and crust

Asthenosphere

Convection currents

Mantle

The heating and cooling of a fluid, changes in the fluid's density, and the force of gravity combine to set convection currents in motion. Convection currents continue as long as heat is added. What happens after the heat source is removed? Without heat, the convection currents will eventually stop when all of the material has reached the same temperature.

 Checkpoint What is convection?

Figure 10 Heat from Earth's mantle and core causes convection currents to form in the asthenosphere. Some geologists think convection currents extend throughout the mantle. *Applying Concepts What part of Earth's interior is like the soup in the pot? What part is like the burner on the stove?*

Convection in Earth's Mantle

Like soup simmering in a pot, Earth's mantle responds to heat. Notice in Figure 10 how convection currents flow in the asthenosphere. **Heat from Earth's core and from the mantle itself causes the convection currents in the mantle.** Hot columns of mantle material rise slowly through the asthenosphere. At the top of the asthenosphere, the hot material spreads out and pushes the cooler material out of the way. This cooler material sinks back into the asthenosphere. Over and over, the cycle of rising and sinking takes place. Convection currents like these have been moving inside Earth for more than four billion years!

Section 2 Review

1. What are the three types of heat transfer?
2. Describe how convection currents form.
3. In general, what happens to the density of a fluid when it becomes hotter?
4. What happens to convection currents when a fluid reaches a constant temperature?
5. **Thinking Critically** **Predicting** What will happen to the flow of hot rock in Earth's mantle if the planet's core eventually cools down? Explain your answer.

Science at Home

Convection and Home Heating
Convection currents may keep the air inside your home at a comfortable temperature. Air is made up of gases, so it is a fluid. Regardless of the type of home heating system, heated air circulates through a room by convection. You may have tried to adjust the flow of air in a stuffy room by opening a window. When you did so, you were making use of convection currents. With an adult family member, study how your home is heated. Look for evidence of convection currents.

DISCOVER •••••••••••••••••••••••••••••••• ACTIVITY ••••

How Are Earth's Continents Linked Together?

1. Find the oceans and the seven continents on a globe showing Earth's physical features.

2. How much of the globe is occupied by the Pacific Ocean? Does most of Earth's "dry" land lie in the Northern or Southern hemisphere?

3. Find the points or areas where most of the continents are connected. Find the points at which several of the continents almost touch, but are not connected.

4. Examine the globe more closely. Find the great belt of mountains running from north to south along the western side of North and South America. Look for another great belt of mountains on the globe.

Think It Over

Posing Questions What questions can you pose about how oceans, continents, and mountains are distributed on Earth's surface?

GUIDE FOR READING

◆ What was Wegener's hypothesis of continental drift?

◆ Why was Alfred Wegener's hypothesis rejected by most scientists of his day?

Reading Tip As you read, look for evidence that supports the hypothesis of continental drift.

Key Terms Pangaea • continental drift • fossil

Five hundred years ago, the sea voyages of Columbus and other explorers changed the map of the world. The continents of Europe, Asia, and Africa were already known to mapmakers. Soon mapmakers were also showing the outlines of the continents of North and South America. Looking at these world maps, many people wondered why the coasts of several continents matched so neatly.

Look at the modern world map in Figure 11. Notice how the coasts of Africa and South America look as if they could fit together like jigsaw-puzzle pieces. Could the continents have once been a single landmass? In the 1700s, the first geologists thought that the continents had remained fixed in their positions throughout Earth's history. Early in the 1900s, however, one scientist began to think in a new way about this riddle of the continents. His idea changed the way people look at the map of the world.

World map drawn by Juan Vespucci in 1526 ▶

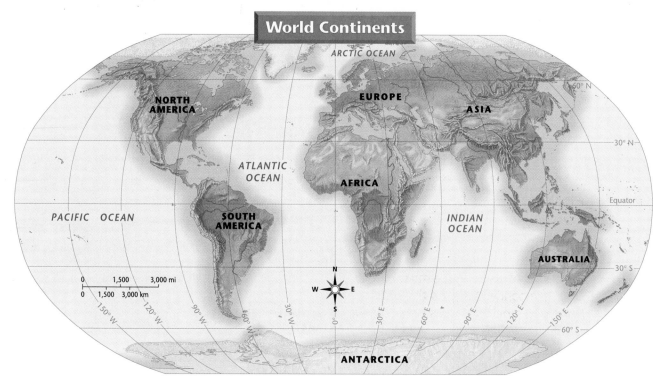

World Continents

Continental Drift

In 1910, a young German scientist named Alfred Wegener (VAY guh nur) became curious about the relationship of the continents. He formed a hypothesis that Earth's continents had moved! **Wegener's hypothesis was that all the continents had once been joined together in a single landmass and have since drifted apart.**

Wegener named this supercontinent **Pangaea** (pan JEE uh), meaning "all lands." According to Wegener, Pangaea existed about 300 million years ago. This was the time when the fossil record contains the first evidence that reptiles and winged insects lived on Earth. Also, tropical forests, which later formed coal deposits, covered much of Earth.

Wegener hypothesized that over tens of millions of years, Pangaea began to break apart. The pieces of Pangaea slowly moved toward their present-day locations, becoming the continents as they are today. Wegener's idea that the continents slowly moved over Earth's surface became known as **continental drift.**

Have you ever tried to persuade a friend to accept a new idea? You probably had to provide some convincing evidence. Wegener gathered evidence from different scientific fields to support his ideas about continental drift. In particular, he studied landforms, fossils, and evidence that showed how Earth's climate had changed over many millions of years. Wegener published all his evidence for continental drift in a book called *The Origin of Continents and Oceans*, first published in 1915.

Figure 11 Today's continents provide clues about Earth's history. *Observing Which coastlines of continents seem to match up like jigsaw-puzzle pieces?*

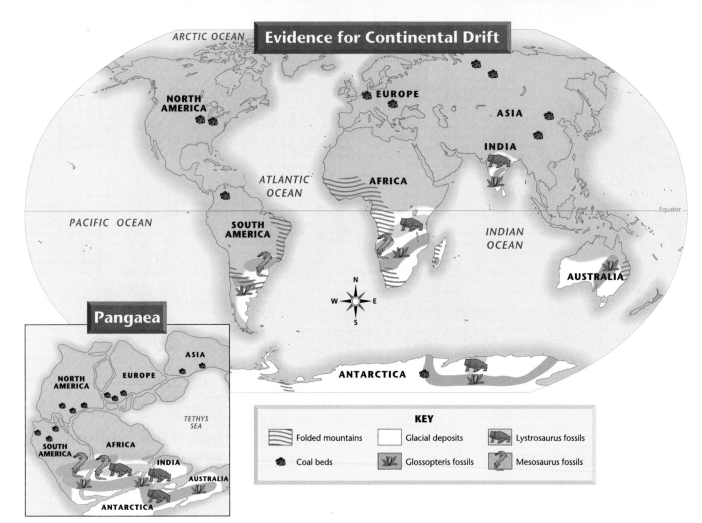

Evidence for Continental Drift

ARCTIC OCEAN

NORTH AMERICA

EUROPE

ASIA

INDIA

ATLANTIC OCEAN

AFRICA

PACIFIC OCEAN

SOUTH AMERICA

INDIAN OCEAN

AUSTRALIA

Equator

ANTARCTICA

Pangaea

ASIA

NORTH AMERICA

EUROPE

TETHYS SEA

SOUTH AMERICA

AFRICA

INDIA

AUSTRALIA

ANTARCTICA

KEY

Folded mountains		Glacial deposits		Lystrosaurus fossils	
Coal beds		Glossopteris fossils		Mesosaurus fossils	

Figure 12 Wegener used several types of evidence to support his idea that the continents were once joined in a single landmass called Pangaea. *Inferring According to Wegener's hypothesis, what does the presence of similar mountain ranges in Africa and South America indicate?*

Figure 13 Fossils of the freshwater reptile *Mesosaurus* found in Africa and South America provide evidence of continental drift.

Evidence From Landforms Wegener thought that mountain ranges and other features on the continents provided evidence for continental drift. When he pieced together maps of Africa and South America, he saw a mountain range running from east to west in South Africa that lined up with a mountain range in Argentina. European coal fields matched up with similar coal fields in North America. Wegener compared matching these features to reassembling a torn-up newspaper. If the pieces could be put back together, the "words" would match.

Evidence From Fossils Wegener also used fossil evidence as support for continental drift. A **fossil** is a trace of an organism that has been preserved in rock. For example, fossils of the reptiles *Mesosaurus* and *Lystrosaurus* had been found in places now separated by oceans. Neither reptile could have swum long distances across salt water. Therefore, Wegener concluded that these reptiles once lived on a single landmass. Another example was *Glossopteris* (glaw SAHP tuh ris), a fernlike plant that lived 250 million years ago. *Glossopteris* fossils had been found in rocks in Africa, South America, Australia, India, and Antarctica. The occurrence of *Glossopteris* on these widely separated landmasses convinced Wegener that the continents had once been united.

Figure 14 Fossils of *Glossopteris* are found on continents in the Southern Hemisphere and in India.

INTEGRATING LIFE SCIENCE The seedlike structures of *Glossopteris* could not have traveled across the distances that separate the continents today. The "seeds" were too large for the wind to carry and too fragile to have survived an ocean trip. How did *Glossopteris* come to live on such widely separated continents? Wegener inferred that the continents at that time were joined as the supercontinent Pangaea.

Evidence From Climate Wegener also used evidence of climate change to support his hypothesis of continental drift. Spitsbergen is an island in the Arctic Ocean north of Norway. This island is ice-covered and has a harsh polar climate. But fossils of tropical plants had been found on Spitsbergen. When these plants lived about 300 million years ago, the island must have had a warm and mild climate. Wegener concluded that Spitsbergen must have been located closer to the equator at that time.

Thousands of kilometers to the south, geologists had found evidence that at the same time it was warm in Spitsbergen, the climate was much colder in South Africa. This evidence included deep scratches in rocks that showed that continental glaciers once covered South Africa. Continental glaciers are thick layers of ice that cover hundreds of thousands of square kilometers. But the climate of South Africa is too mild today for continental glaciers to form. Wegener concluded that, when Pangaea existed, South Africa was much closer to the South Pole.

According to Wegener, these clues provide evidence that continental drift happened. The climates of Spitsbergen and South Africa changed because the positions of these places on Earth's surface changed. As a continent moves toward the equator, its climate becomes warmer. As a continent moves toward the poles, its climate becomes colder. But the continent carries with it the fossils and rocks that formed at its previous location.

☑ *Checkpoint* *What were the three types of evidence Wegener used to support his hypothesis of continental drift?*

Figure 15 Although scientists rejected his hypothesis, Wegener continued to collect evidence for continental drift and to update his book. He died in 1930 on an expedition to explore Greenland's continental glacier.

Scientists Reject Wegener's Hypothesis

Wegener did more than provide a hypothesis about continental drift. He attempted to explain how drift took place. He even offered a new explanation for how mountains form. Wegener thought that when drifting continents collide, their edges crumple and fold. The folding continents slowly push up huge chunks of rock to form great mountains.

However, Wegener could not provide a satisfactory explanation for the force that pushes or pulls the continents. Because Wegener could not identify the cause of continental drift, most geologists rejected his idea. In addition, for geologists to accept Wegener's idea, they would need to change their own explanations of what caused continents and mountains to form.

Many geologists in the early 1900s thought that Earth was slowly cooling and shrinking. According to this idea, mountains formed when the crust wrinkled like the skin of a dried-up apple. Wegener said that if the apple hypothesis were correct, then mountains should be found all over Earth's surface. But mountains usually occur in narrow bands along the edges of continents. Wegener thought that his own hypothesis better explained where mountains occur and how they form.

For nearly half a century, from the 1920s to the 1960s, most scientists paid little attention to the idea of continental drift. Then new evidence about Earth's structure led scientists to reconsider Wegener's bold hypothesis.

Section 3 Review

1. What was Wegener's hypothesis of continental drift?
2. How did Wegener use evidence based on fossils to support his hypothesis that the continents had moved?
3. What was the main reason scientists rejected Wegener's hypothesis of continental drift?
4. **Thinking Critically** **Inferring** Coal deposits have also been found beneath the ice of Antarctica. But coal only forms in warm swamps. Use Wegener's hypothesis to explain how coal could be found so near the poles.

Science at Home

Moving the Continents You can demonstrate Wegener's idea of continental drift. Use the world map in Figure 11. On a sheet of tracing paper, trace the outlines of the continents bordering the Atlantic Ocean. Label the continents. Then use scissors to carefully cut the map along the eastern edge of South America, North America, and Greenland. Next, cut along the western edge of Africa and Europe (including the British Isles). Throw away the Atlantic Ocean. Place the two cut-out pieces on a dark surface and ask family members to try to fit the two halves together. Explain to them about the supercontinent Pangaea and its history.

SECTION 4 Sea-Floor Spreading

DISCOVER · ACTIVITY

What Is the Effect of a Change in Density?

1. Partially fill a sink or dishpan with water.

2. Open up a dry washcloth in your hand. Does the washcloth feel light or heavy?

3. Moisten one edge of the washcloth in the water. Then gently place the washcloth so that it floats on the water's surface. Observe the washcloth carefully (especially at its edges) as it starts to sink.

4. Remove the washcloth from the water and open it up in your hand. Is the mass of the washcloth the same as, less than, or greater than when it was dry?

Think It Over

Observing How did the washcloth's density change? What effect did this change in density have on the washcloth?

Deep in the ocean, the temperature is near freezing. There is no light, and living things are generally scarce. Yet some areas of the deep-ocean floor are teeming with life. One of these areas is the East Pacific Rise, a region of the Pacific Ocean floor off the coasts of Mexico and South America. Here, ocean water sinks through cracks, or vents, in the crust. The water is heated by contact with hot material from the mantle and then spurts back into the ocean.

Around these hot-water vents live some of the most bizarre creatures ever discovered. Giant, red-tipped tube worms sway in the water. Nearby sit giant clams nearly a meter across. Strange spiderlike crabs scuttle by. Surprisingly, the geological features of this strange environment provided scientists with evidence that strongly supports Wegener's hypothesis of continental drift.

GUIDE FOR READING

◆ What is the process of sea-floor spreading?

◆ What happens to the ocean floor at deep ocean trenches?

Reading Tip Before you read, preview the art and captions looking for new terms. As you read, find the meanings of these terms.

Key Terms mid-ocean ridge
• sea-floor spreading
• deep-ocean trench
• subduction

Figure 16 Tube worms cluster near hot water vents in the ocean floor.

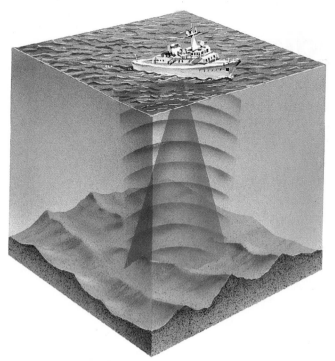

Figure 17 Scientists use sonar to map the ocean floor.

Mapping the Mid-Ocean Ridge

The East Pacific Rise is just one part of the **mid-ocean ridge,** the longest chain of mountains in the world. In the mid-1900s, scientists mapped the mid-ocean ridge using sonar. Recall from Chapter 5 that a sonar device bounces sound waves off underwater objects and then records the echoes of these sound waves. The time it takes for the echo to arrive indicates the distance to the object.

The mid-ocean ridge curves like the seam of a baseball along the sea floor, extending into all of Earth's oceans. Most of the mountains in the mid-ocean ridge lie hidden under hundreds of meters of water. However, there are places where the ridge pokes above the surface. For example, the island of Iceland is a part of the mid-ocean ridge that rises above the surface in the North Atlantic Ocean. A steep-sided valley splits the top of the mid-ocean ridge for most of its length. The valley is almost twice as deep as the Grand Canyon. The mapping of the mid-ocean ridge made scientists curious to know what the ridge was and how it got there.

☑ *Checkpoint* *What device is used to map the ocean floor?*

Figure 18 The mid-ocean ridge is more than 50,000 kilometers long.

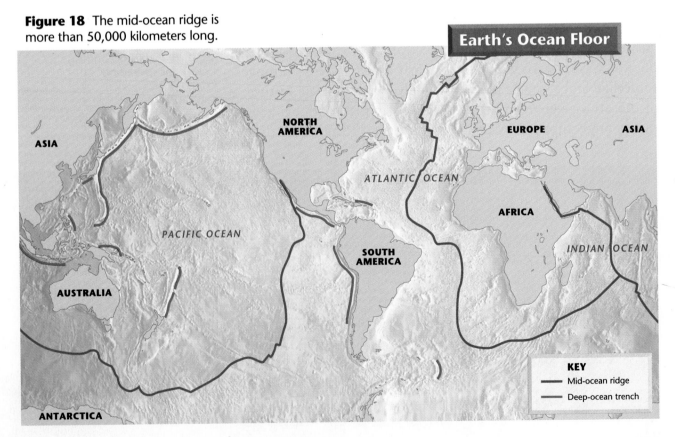

Earth's Ocean Floor

ASIA

NORTH AMERICA

EUROPE

ASIA

ATLANTIC OCEAN

PACIFIC OCEAN

AFRICA

INDIAN OCEAN

SOUTH AMERICA

AUSTRALIA

ANTARCTICA

KEY
— Mid-ocean ridge
— Deep-ocean trench

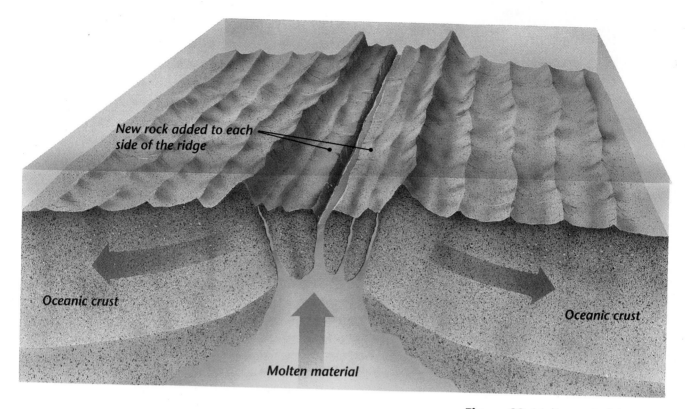

New rock added to each side of the ridge

Oceanic crust

Oceanic crust

Molten material

Figure 19 Molten material erupts though the valley that runs along the center of the mid-ocean ridge. This material hardens to form the rock of the ocean floor.
Applying Concepts What happens to the rock along the ridge when new molten material erupts?

Evidence for Sea-Floor Spreading

Harry Hess, an American geologist, was one of the scientists who studied the mid-ocean ridge. Hess carefully examined maps of the mid-ocean ridge. Then he began to think about the ocean floor in relation to the problem of continental drift. Finally, he reconsidered an idea that he previously had thought impossible: Maybe Wegener was right! Perhaps the continents do move.

In 1960, Hess proposed a radical idea. He suggested that the ocean floors move like conveyor belts, carrying the continents along with them. This movement begins at the mid-ocean ridge. The mid-ocean ridge forms along a crack in the oceanic crust. **At the mid-ocean ridge, molten material rises from the mantle and erupts. The molten material then spreads out, pushing older rock to both sides of the ridge.** As the molten material cools, it forms a strip of solid rock in the center of the ridge. Then more molten material flows into the crack. This material splits apart the strip of solid rock that formed before, pushing it aside.

Hess called the process that continually adds new material to the ocean floor **sea-floor spreading.** He realized that the sea floor spreads apart along both sides of the mid-ocean ridge as new crust is added. Look at Figure 19 to see the process of sea-floor spreading.

Several types of evidence from the oceans supported Hess's idea of sea-floor spreading—evidence from molten material, magnetic stripes, and drilling samples. This evidence also led scientists to look again at Wegener's hypothesis of continental drift.

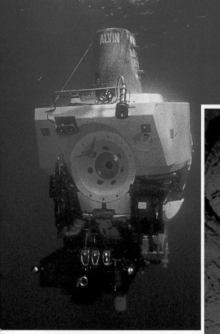

Evidence From Molten Material In the 1960s, scientists found evidence that new material is indeed erupting along the mid-ocean ridge. The scientists were carried to the ocean floor in *Alvin*, a small submersible built to withstand the crushing pressures four kilometers below the ocean's surface. In the central valley of the mid-ocean ridge, *Alvin*'s crew found strange rocks shaped like pillows or like toothpaste squeezed from a tube. Such rocks can form only when molten material hardens quickly after erupting under water. The presence of these rocks showed that molten material has erupted again and again from cracks along the central valley of the mid-ocean ridge.

Figure 20 The submersible *Alvin* photographed pillow lava along the mid-ocean ridge. These "pillows" form under water when cold ocean water causes a crust to form on erupting molten material. Each pillow expands until it bursts, allowing molten material to flow out and form the next pillow.

Evidence From Magnetic Stripes When scientists studied

INTEGRATING PHYSICS

patterns in the rocks of the ocean floor, they found more support for sea-floor spreading. In Section 1 you read that Earth behaves like a giant magnet, with a north pole and a south pole. Evidence shows that Earth's magnetic poles have reversed themselves. This last happened 780,000 years ago. If the magnetic poles suddenly reversed themselves today, you would find that your compass needle pointed south. Scientists discovered that the rock that makes up the

Figure 21 Magnetic stripes in the rock of the ocean floor show the direction of Earth's magnetic field at the time the rock hardened.
Interpreting Diagrams How does the pattern of matching stripes show evidence of sea-floor spreading?

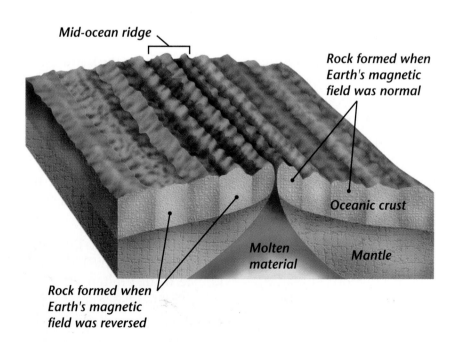

Mid-ocean ridge

Rock formed when Earth's magnetic field was normal

Oceanic crust

Molten material

Mantle

Rock formed when Earth's magnetic field was reversed

334

ocean floor lies in a pattern of magnetized "stripes." These stripes hold a record of reversals in Earth's magnetic field.

The rock of the ocean floor, which contains iron, began as molten material. As the molten material cooled, the iron bits inside lined up in the direction of Earth's magnetic poles. When the rock hardened completely, it locked the iron bits in place, giving the rocks a permanent "magnetic memory." You can think of it as setting thousands of tiny compass needles in cement.

Using sensitive instruments, scientists recorded the magnetic memory of rocks on both sides of the mid-ocean ridge. They found that a stripe of rock that shows when Earth's magnetic field pointed north is followed by a parallel stripe of rock that shows when the magnetic field pointed south. As you can see in Figure 21, the pattern is the same on both sides of the ridge. Rock that hardens at the same time has the same magnetic memory.

Evidence From Drilling Samples Additional proof of sea-floor spreading came from rock samples obtained by drilling into the ocean floor. The *Glomar Challenger*, a drilling ship built in 1968, gathered the samples. The *Glomar Challenger* sent drilling pipes through water 6 kilometers deep to drill holes in the ocean floor. This feat has been compared to using a sharp-ended wire to dig a hole into a sidewalk from the top of the Empire State Building.

Samples from the sea floor were brought up through the pipes. Then the scientists determined the ages of the rocks in the samples. They found that the farther away from the ridge, the older the rocks were. The youngest rocks were always in the center of the ridges. The combined evidence is strong support for the idea that sea-floor spreading has taken place.

Checkpoint *What evidence did scientists find for sea-floor spreading?*

Reversing Poles

1. Cut six short pieces, each about 2.5 cm long, from a length of audiotape.
2. Tape one end of each piece of audiotape to a flat surface. The pieces should be spaced 1 cm apart and line up lengthwise in a single line.
3. Touch a bar magnet's north pole to the first piece of audiotape. Then reverse the magnet and touch its south pole to the next piece.
4. Repeat Step 3 until you have applied the magnet to each piece of audiotape.
5. Sweep one end of the magnet about 1 cm above the line of audiotape pieces. Observe what happens.

Making Models What characteristic of the ocean floor did you observe as you swept the magnet along the line of audiotape pieces?

Figure 22 The *Glomar Challenger* was the first research ship designed to drill samples of rock from the deep-ocean floor.

Subduction at Deep-Ocean Trenches

How can the ocean floor keep getting wider and wider? The answer is that the ocean floor generally does not just keep spreading. Instead, the ocean floor plunges into deep underwater canyons called **deep-ocean trenches.** A deep-ocean trench forms where the oceanic crust bends downward.

Where there are deep-ocean trenches, subduction takes place. **Subduction** (sub DUK shun) is the process by which the ocean floor sinks beneath a deep-ocean trench and back into the mantle. Convection currents under the lithosphere push new crust that forms at the mid-ocean ridge away from the ridge and toward a deep-ocean trench.

New oceanic crust is hot. But as it moves away from the mid-ocean ridge, it cools and becomes more dense. Eventually, as shown in Figure 23, gravity pulls this older, denser oceanic crust down beneath the trench. The sinking crust is like the washcloth in the Discover activity at the beginning of this section. As the dry washcloth floating on the water gets wet, its density increases and it begins to sink.

At deep-ocean trenches, subduction allows part of the ocean floor to sink back into the mantle in a process that takes tens of millions of years. You can think of sea-floor spreading and subduction together as if the ocean floor were moving out from the mid-ocean ridge on a giant conveyor belt.

Figure 23 Oceanic crust formed along the mid-ocean ridge is recycled at a deep-ocean trench. In the process of subduction, oceanic crust sinks down beneath the trench into the mantle. *Drawing Conclusions Where would denser oceanic crust be found?*

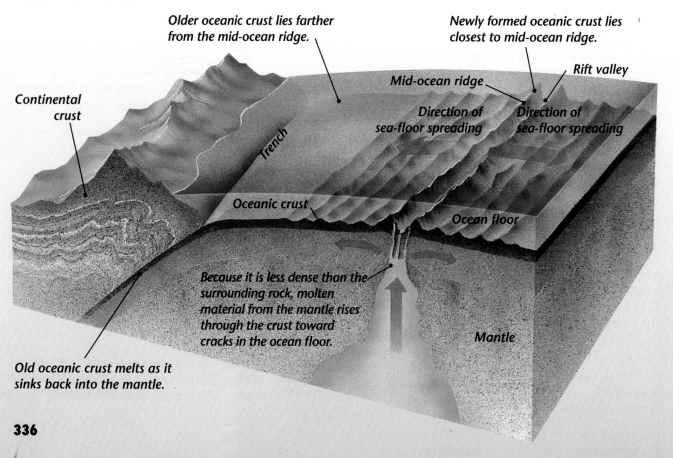

Older oceanic crust lies farther from the mid-ocean ridge.

Newly formed oceanic crust lies closest to mid-ocean ridge.

Rift valley

Mid-ocean ridge

Continental crust

Direction of sea-floor spreading

Direction of sea-floor spreading

Trench

Oceanic crust

Ocean floor

Because it is less dense than the surrounding rock, molten material from the mantle rises through the crust toward cracks in the ocean floor.

Mantle

Old oceanic crust melts as it sinks back into the mantle.

Subduction and Earth's Oceans

The processes of subduction and sea-floor spreading can change the size and shape of the oceans. Because of these processes, the ocean floor is renewed about every 200 million years. That is the time it takes for new rock to form at the mid-ocean ridge, move across the ocean, and sink into a trench.

Subduction in the Pacific Ocean The vast Pacific Ocean covers almost one third of the planet. And yet it is shrinking. How could that be? Sometimes a deep ocean trench swallows more oceanic crust than the mid-ocean ridge can produce. Then, if the ridge does not add new crust fast enough, the width of the ocean will shrink. This is happening to the Pacific Ocean, which is ringed by many trenches.

Subduction in the Atlantic Ocean The Atlantic Ocean, on the other hand, is expanding. Unlike the Pacific Ocean, the Atlantic Ocean has only a few short trenches. As a result, the spreading ocean floor has virtually nowhere to go. In most places, the oceanic crust of the Atlantic Ocean floor is attached to the continental crust of the continents around the ocean. So as the Atlantic's ocean floor spreads, the continents along its edges also move. Over time, the whole ocean gets wider. The spreading floor of the North Atlantic Ocean and the continent of North America move together like two giant barges pushed by the same tugboat.

Figure 24 It is cold and dark in the deep ocean trenches where subduction occurs. But even here, scientists have found living things, such as this fish.

Section 4 Review

1. What is the role of the mid-ocean ridge in sea-floor spreading?
2. Describe the process of subduction at a deep-ocean trench.
3. What is the evidence for sea-floor spreading?
4. **Thinking Critically** **Relating Cause and Effect** Where would you expect to find the oldest rock on the ocean floor? Explain your answer.
5. **Thinking Critically** **Predicting** As you can see in Figure 18, the mid-ocean ridge extends into the Red Sea between Africa and Asia. What do you think will happen to the Red Sea in the future? Explain your answer.

Check Your Progress CHAPTER PROJECT
Now that you have learned about sea-floor spreading, begin to sketch your model. Does the plate that you chose include oceanic crust, part of the mid-ocean ridge, or a trench? How will you show these features in your model? Improve your original ideas for your model and add new ideas. Revise your list of materials if necessary.

Skills Lab

MODELING SEA-FLOOR SPREADING

Along the entire length of Earth's mid-ocean ridge, the sea floor is spreading. Although this process takes place constantly, it is difficult to observe directly. You can build a model to help understand this process.

Problem

How does sea-floor spreading add material to the ocean floor?

Materials

scissors
metric ruler
2 sheets of unlined paper
colored marker

Procedure

1. Draw stripes across one sheet of paper, parallel to the short sides of the paper. The stripes should vary in spacing and thickness.
2. Fold the paper in half lengthwise and write the word "Start" at the top of both halves of the paper. Using the scissors, carefully cut the paper in half along the fold line to form two strips.
3. Lightly fold the second sheet of paper into eighths. Then unfold it, leaving creases in the paper. Fold this sheet in half lengthwise.

4. Starting at the fold, draw lines 5.5 cm long on the middle crease and the two creases closest to the ends of the paper.

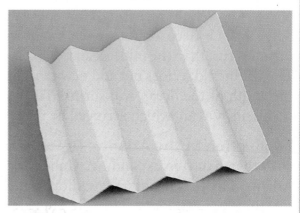

5. Now carefully cut along the lines you drew. Unfold the paper. There should be three slits in the center of the paper.

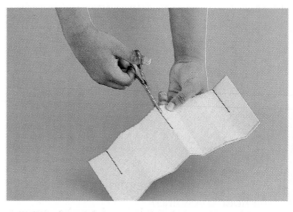

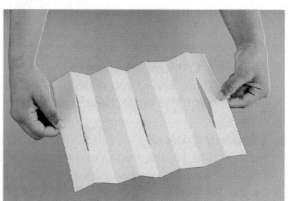

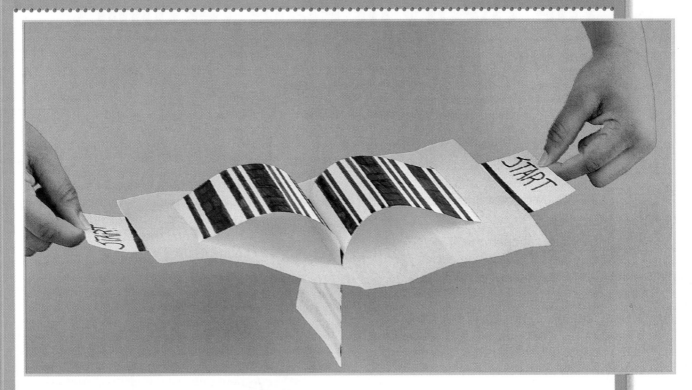

6. Put the two striped strips of paper together so their Start labels touch one another. Insert the Start ends of the strips up through the center slit and then pull them toward the side slits.

7. Insert the ends of the strips into the side slits. Pull the ends of the strips and watch what happens at the center slit.

8. Practice pulling the strips through the slits until you can make the two strips come up and go down at the same time.

Analyze and Conclude

1. What feature of the ocean floor does the center slit stand for? What prominent feature of the ocean floor is missing from the model at this point?

2. What do the side slits stand for? What does the space under the paper stand for?

3. How does the ocean floor as shown by the part of a strip close to the center slit differ from the ocean floor as shown by the part near a side slit? How does this difference affect the depth of the ocean?

4. What do the stripes on the strips stand for? Why is it important that your model have an identical pattern of stripes on both sides of the center slit?

5. Explain how differences in density and temperature provide some of the force needed to cause sea-floor spreading and subduction.

6. **Think About It** Use your own words to describe the process of ocean-floor spreading. What parts of the process were not shown by your model?

More to Explore

Imagine that so much molten rock erupted from the mid-ocean ridge that an island formed there. How could you modify your model to show this island? How could you show what would happen to it over a long period of time?

The Theory of Plate Tectonics

DISCOVER · ACTIVITY · · ·

How Well Do the Continents Fit Together?

1. Using a world map in an atlas, trace the shapes of the continents North America, South America, Africa, and Europe, including Great Britain and Ireland.

2. ✂ Carefully cut apart the landmasses. When you cut out Europe, leave Britain and Ireland attached to Europe.

3. Piece together these landmasses as they may have looked before Pangaea split apart, creating the Atlantic Ocean.

4. Attach your partial reconstruction of Pangea to a piece of paper.

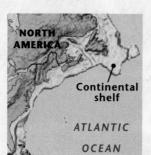
NORTH AMERICA
Continental shelf
ATLANTIC OCEAN

5. Obtain a map that shows the continental shelf. The continental shelf is the apron of continental crust that extends under water around the edges of the continents. Trace around the continental shelves of the same continents used in Step 1.

6. Repeat Steps 2 through 4.

Think It Over

Drawing Conclusions Do your observations support the idea that the continents were once joined together? When did they fit together better: when you cut them out along their coastlines or along their continental shelves? Explain.

GUIDE FOR READING

◆ What is the theory of plate tectonics?

◆ What are the three types of plate boundaries?

Reading Tip Before you read, preview *Exploring Plate Tectonics* on pages 342–343. Write a list of any questions you have about plate tectonics. Look for answers as you read.

Key Terms plate
• plate tectonics
• fault • transform boundary
• divergent boundary
• rift valley
• convergent boundary

Have you ever dropped a hard-boiled egg? If so, you may have noticed that the eggshell cracked in an irregular pattern of broken pieces. Earth's lithosphere, its solid outer shell, is not one unbroken layer. It is more like that cracked eggshell. It's broken into pieces separated by jagged cracks.

A Canadian scientist, J. Tuzo Wilson, observed that there are cracks in the continents similar to those on the ocean floor. In 1965, Wilson proposed a new way of thinking about these cracks. According to Wilson, the lithosphere is broken into separate sections called **plates.** The plates fit closely together along cracks in the lithosphere. As shown in Figure 25, the plates carry the continents or parts of the ocean floor, or both.

A Theory of Plate Motion

Wilson combined what geologists knew about sea-floor spreading, Earth's plates, and continental drift into a single theory—the theory of plate tectonics (tek TAHN iks). **Plate tectonics** is the geological theory that states that pieces of Earth's lithosphere are in constant, slow motion, driven by convection currents in the mantle. **The theory of plate tectonics explains the formation, movement, and subduction of Earth's plates.**

As the plates move, they collide, pull apart, and grind past each other. No plate can budge without affecting the other plates surrounding it. What force causes Earth's plates to move? Many geologists think that convection currents in the mantle cause the movement of Earth's plates. The plates of the lithosphere float on top of the asthenosphere. Convection currents rise in the asthenosphere and spread out beneath the lithosphere. The force of the convection current drags the overlying plate along. Slowly, the convection current cools and sinks deeper into the mantle. Scientists think that this downward movement may provide the force that causes the subduction of plates carrying oceanic crust.

Some geologists think that there are other causes of plate movement. According to the "slab push" hypothesis, magma rising along the mid-ocean ridge exerts a force that pushes an oceanic plate away from the ridge. In the "slab pull" hypothesis, the force of gravity causes plate movement by pulling cooler, denser oceanic plates down toward the mantle. Slab push and slab pull may work together with convection currents to move Earth's plates.

Sharpen your Skills

Predicting ACTIVITY

Study the map of Earth's plates in Figure 25. Draw South America on a new piece of paper. Include compass markings on the paper. Now draw the South American plate and the Nazca plate. Show the plate boundaries and their directions of movement. In which directions are these plates moving? What do you think will happen as these plates continue to move?

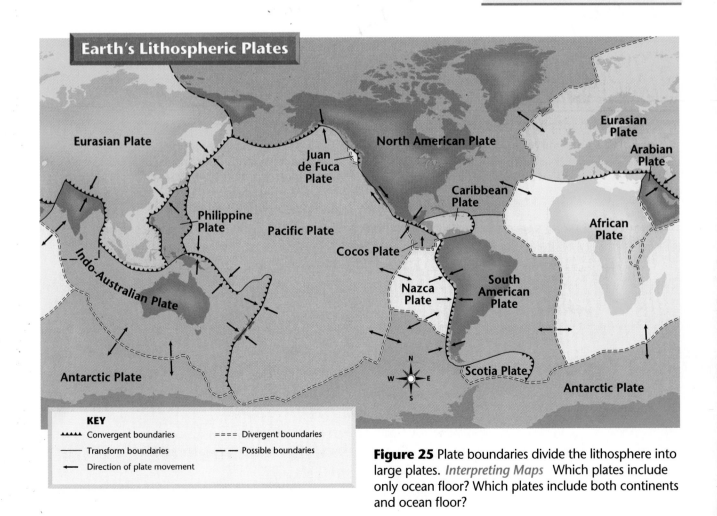

Earth's Lithospheric Plates

Eurasian Plate

Juan de Fuca Plate

North American Plate

Eurasian Plate

Arabian Plate

Philippine Plate

Pacific Plate

Caribbean Plate

African Plate

Cocos Plate

Indo-Australian Plate

Nazca Plate

South American Plate

Antarctic Plate

Scotia Plate

Antarctic Plate

N W E S

KEY

ᴧᴧᴧᴧ Convergent boundaries
==== Divergent boundaries
—— Transform boundaries
— — Possible boundaries
←— Direction of plate movement

Figure 25 Plate boundaries divide the lithosphere into large plates. *Interpreting Maps* Which plates include only ocean floor? Which plates include both continents and ocean floor?

Plate Boundaries

The edges of different pieces of the lithosphere—Earth's rigid shell—meet at lines called plate boundaries. Plate boundaries extend deep into the lithosphere. **Faults**—breaks in Earth's crust where rocks have slipped past each other—form along these boundaries. **There are three kinds of plate boundaries: transform boundaries, divergent boundaries, and convergent boundaries.** For each type of boundary, there is a different type of plate movement, as you can see in *Exploring Plate Tectonics*.

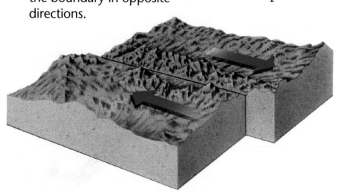

Figure 26 At a transform boundary, two plates move along the boundary in opposite directions.

Transform Boundaries Along transform boundaries, crust is neither created nor destroyed. A **transform boundary** is a place where two plates slip past each other, moving in opposite directions. Earthquakes occur frequently along these boundaries. Look at Figure 26 to see the type of plate movement that occurs along a transform boundary.

EXPLORING *Plate Tectonics*

Plate movements have built many of the features of Earth's land surfaces and ocean floors.

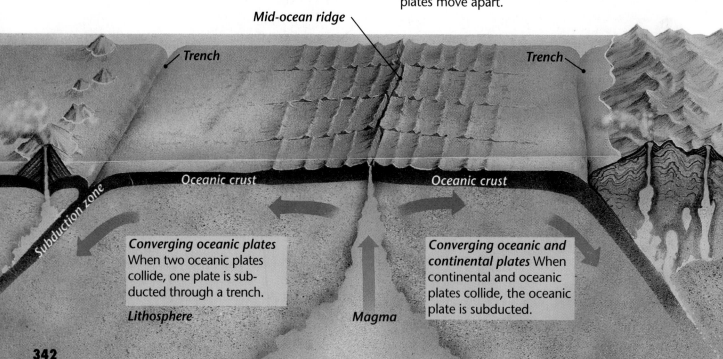

Diverging oceanic plates
The mid-ocean ridge marks a divergent boundary where plates move apart.

Mid-ocean ridge

Trench

Trench

Oceanic crust

Oceanic crust

Subduction zone

Converging oceanic plates
When two oceanic plates collide, one plate is subducted through a trench.

Lithosphere

Magma

Converging oceanic and continental plates When continental and oceanic plates collide, the oceanic plate is subducted.

Divergent Boundaries The place where two plates move apart, or diverge, is called a **divergent boundary** (dy VUR junt). Notice in *Exploring Plate Tectonics* that divergent boundaries are found both in the oceans and on land. Most divergent boundaries occur at the mid-ocean ridge. In Section 4, you learned how oceanic crust forms along the mid-ocean ridge as sea-floor spreading occurs.

Other divergent boundaries occur on land. When a divergent boundary develops on land, two of Earth's plates slide apart. A deep valley called a **rift valley** forms along the divergent boundary. For example, the Great Rift Valley in east Africa marks a deep crack in the African continent that runs for about 3,000 kilometers. Along this crack, a divergent plate boundary is slowly spreading apart. The rift may someday split the eastern part of Africa away from the rest of the continent. As a rift valley widens, its floor drops. Eventually, the floor may drop enough for the sea to fill the widening gap.

☑ *Checkpoint* *What is a rift valley? How are rift valleys formed?*

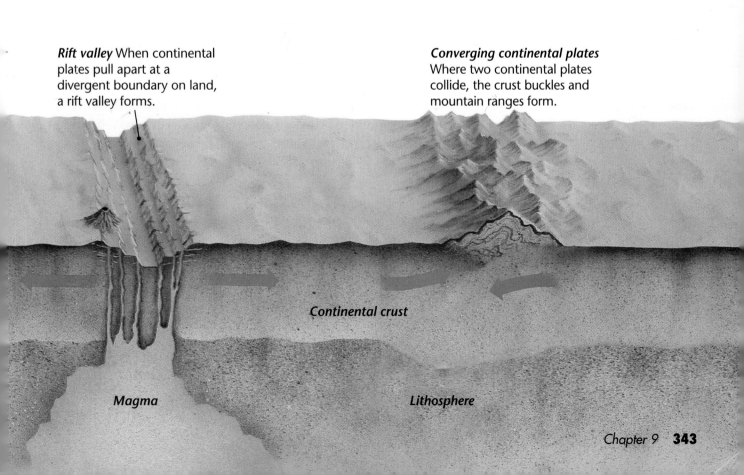

Rift valley When continental plates pull apart at a divergent boundary on land, a rift valley forms.

Converging continental plates Where two continental plates collide, the crust buckles and mountain ranges form.

Continental crust

Magma

Lithosphere

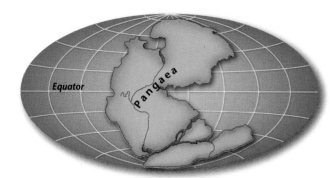

225 million years ago
All Earth's major landmasses were joined in the super-continent Pangaea before plate movements began to split it apart.

180–200 million years ago
Pangaea continued to split apart, opening narrow seas that later became oceans.

Figure 27 A collision between two continental plates produced the majestic Himalayas. The collision began 50 million years ago, when the plate that carries India slammed into Asia.

Convergent Boundaries The place where two plates come together, or converge, is called a **convergent boundary** (kun VUR junt). When two plates converge, the result is called a collision. Collisions may bring together oceanic crust and oceanic crust, oceanic crust and continental crust, or continental crust and continental crust.

When two plates collide, the density of the plates determines which one comes out on top. Oceanic crust, which is made mostly of basalt, is more dense than continental crust, which is made mostly of granite. And oceanic crust becomes cooler and denser as it spreads away from the mid-ocean ridge.

Where two plates carrying oceanic crust meet at a trench, the plate that is more dense dives under the other plate and returns to the mantle. This is the process of subduction that you learned about in Section 4.

Sometimes a plate carrying oceanic crust collides with a plate carrying continental crust. The less dense continental crust can't sink under the more dense oceanic crust. Instead, the oceanic plate begins to sink and plunges beneath the continental plate.

When two plates carrying continental crust collide, subduction does not take place. Both continental plates are mostly low-density granite rock. Therefore, neither plate is dense enough to sink into the mantle. Instead, the plates crash head-on. The collision squeezes the crust into mighty mountain ranges.

☑ *Checkpoint* **What types of plate movement occur at plate boundaries?**

135 million years ago Gradually, the landmasses that became today's continents began to drift apart.

Earth today
Note how far to the north India has drifted—farther than any other major landmass.

65 million years ago
India was still a separate continent, charging toward Asia, while Australia remained attached to Antarctica.

Figure 28 It has taken about 225 million years for the continents to move to their present locations. *Posing Questions* What questions would you need to answer in order to predict where the continents will be in 50 million years?

The Continents' Slow Dance

The plates move at amazingly slow rates: from about one to ten centimeters per year. The North American and Eurasian plates are floating apart at a rate of 2.5 centimeters per year—that's about as fast as your fingernails grow. This may not seem like much, but these plates have been moving for tens of millions of years.

About 260 million years ago, the continents were joined together in the supercontinent that Wegener called Pangaea. Then, about 225 million years ago, Pangaea began to break apart. Figure 28 shows how Earth's continents and other landmasses have moved since the break-up of Pangaea.

Section 5 Review

1. What is the theory of plate tectonics?
2. What are the different types of boundaries found along the edges of Earth's plates?
3. What major event in Earth's history began about 225 million years ago? Explain.
4. **Thinking Critically** **Predicting** Look at Figure 25 on page 341 and find the divergent boundary that runs through the African plate. Predict what could eventually happen along this boundary.

Check Your Progress   CHAPTER PROJECT
Complete your research on your chosen plate. You should be able to describe the makeup of the plate as well as the direction and rate of its movement. Now that you have learned about plate tectonics, add to your sketch any transform boundary, convergent boundary on land, or divergent boundary on land. How will you show what happens *where* your plate interacts with another plate? Begin building your model.

SECTION 6 Changing Earth's Surface

DISCOVER •••ACTIVITY••••

Where Are Volcanoes Found on Earth's Surface?

1. Look at the map of Earth's active volcanoes on page 351. What symbols are used to represent volcanoes? What other symbols are shown on the map?

2. Do the locations of the volcanoes form a pattern? Do the volcanoes seem related to any other features on Earth's surface?

Think About It

Developing Hypotheses Develop a hypothesis to explain where Earth's volcanoes are located. Are there any volcanoes on the map whose location cannot be explained by your hypothesis?

GUIDE FOR READING

◆ How does plate movement change Earth's surface?

◆ How do mountains form?

◆ What is land subsidence?

Reading Tip Before you read, write the headings in this section. As you read, write down the main point of each heading.

Key Terms stress
• deformation • earthquake
• fault • strike-slip fault
• normal fault
• hanging wall • footwall
• reverse fault
• fault-block mountain
• land subsidence • volcano
• hot spot

In 1983, a fault near Borah Peak in Idaho slipped, causing a powerful earthquake. The earthquake pushed the land along one side of the fault up by nearly 3 meters. The result was a long, clifflike ridge marking where the fault movement occurred. In only a few seconds, the Borah Peak earthquake produced a dramatic change in Earth's surface. More often, changes in the surface take place gradually. But over time, even gradual change can produce new features.

Forces in the Lithosphere

The Borah Peak earthquake is an example of how the forces of plate movement affect the lithosphere. **Plate movement can alter Earth systems and produce changes in Earth's surface. These changes include deformation of the crust, faults, mountain building, land subsidence, and volcanoes.** Scientists try to predict

Figure 29 An earthquake pushed up the land along this fault, forming a long ridge.

the Earth features, or landforms, that will develop in an area by studying the plates around the area and how they move.

Plate movements produce powerful forces that push, pull, bend, and twist the lithosphere. They produce stress in rock. **Stress** is a force that adds potential energy to rock until the rock changes shape or breaks and moves. Stress leads to **deformation,** a change in the rock's shape or volume.

Deformation takes place so slowly that you cannot observe it directly. But over a very long time, deformation changes Earth's surface. Stress produces three types of deformation: shearing, tension, and compression. Shearing pushes a mass of rock in two opposite directions. Tension pulls on rock, making it thinner in the middle. Compression squeezes rock, making it thicker in the middle.

Deformation caused by plate movement can put so much stress on the lithosphere that it breaks. Where the lithosphere breaks, a fault forms. During plate movement, stress builds up along the fault, storing potential energy in the rock. Eventually, the rock along the fault suddenly breaks and slides, causing an **earthquake.** Each time an earthquake occurs, potential energy changes to kinetic energy as the rock along the fault moves. In this way, every earthquake changes Earth's surface.

Figure 30 Deformation pushes, pulls, or twists the rocks in Earth's crust. *Relating Cause and Effect* Which type of deformation tends to shorten part of the crust?

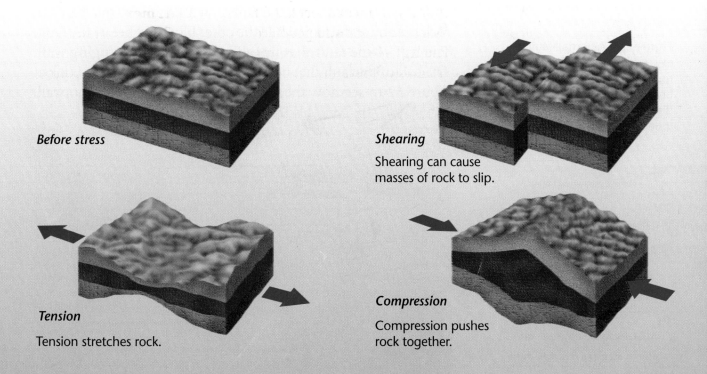

Before stress

Shearing
Shearing can cause masses of rock to slip.

Tension
Tension stretches rock.

Compression
Compression pushes rock together.

Figure 31 The San Andreas fault is a strike-slip fault that slices through California.

Strike-slip fault

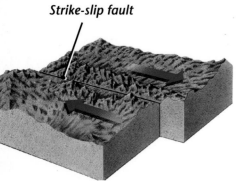

Faults and Fault Movements

If you try to break a caramel candy bar in two, it may only bend and stretch at first. Like a candy bar, many types of rock can bend or fold. But beyond a certain limit, even these rocks will break. Rocks that easily bend take more stress to break than brittle ones.

When enough stress builds up in rock, the rock breaks, creating a fault. A **fault** is a break in the crust where slabs of crust slip past each other. The rocks on both sides of a fault can move up or down or sideways. **Faults usually occur along plate boundaries, where the forces of plate motion compress, pull, or shear the crust so much that the crust breaks.** There are three main types of faults: strike-slip faults, normal faults, and reverse faults.

Strike-Slip Faults   Shearing creates strike-slip faults. In a **strike-slip fault,** the rocks on either side of the fault slip past each other sideways with little up or down motion. Figure 31 shows the type of movement that occurs along a strike-slip fault. As you learned in the previous section, this type of motion results in a transform boundary between plates. The San Andreas fault in California is an example of a transform boundary.

Normal Faults   Tension forces in Earth's crust cause normal faults. In a **normal fault,** the fault is at an angle, so one block of rock lies above the fault while the other block lies below the fault. The half of the fault that lies above is called the **hanging wall.** The half of the fault that lies below is called the **footwall.** Look at Figure 32 to see how the hanging wall lies above the footwall.

Figure 32 A normal fault is exposed in this road cut. The rock layers no longer line up because the hanging wall has dropped down relative to the footwall.

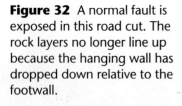

Footwall

Hanging Wall

Key
Force deforming the crust →
Movement along the fault →

348

When movement occurs along a normal fault, the hanging wall slips downward. Tension forces create normal faults where plates diverge, or pull apart. For example, normal faults occur along the Rio Grande rift valley in New Mexico, where two pieces of Earth's crust are diverging.

Reverse Faults Compression forces produce reverse faults. A **reverse fault** has the same structure as a normal fault, but the blocks move in the opposite direction. Look at Figure 33 to see how the rocks along a reverse fault move. As in a normal fault, one side of a reverse fault lies at an angle above the other side. The rock forming the hanging wall of a reverse fault slides up and over the footwall. Reverse faults produced mountains in the Canadian Rockies.

Mountain Building

Over millions of years, plate movement can cause folding and faulting. **Folding and faulting driven by plate movement result in mountain building.** A mountain is a landform that rises high above the surrounding land. A mountain range is a group of mountains that are closely related in shape, structure, and age.

Folding When continental plates collide, the collision squeezes the two plates together. Slowly, layers of rock in the plate fold, like a rug when its ends are pushed toward each other. For example, when Pangaea began to form, the North American plate collided with the Eurasian plate. As these huge plates collided, thick layers of rock near the edges of the plates were compressed and folded. This folding formed the Appalachian Mountains.

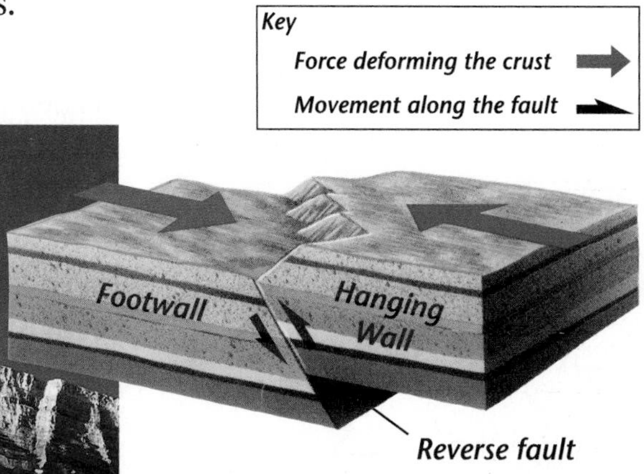

Key

Force deforming the crust ➡

Movement along the fault ➤

Footwall

Hanging Wall

Reverse fault

Figure 33 A reverse fault formed this mountain in Alberta, Canada, as compression forces pushed one mass of rock up and over another.

Figure 34 Two normal faults can form fault-block mountains, such as the Teton range in Wyoming.

Normal faults

Key
Movement along normal faults ➡

Faulting Sometimes, plate movements cause tension in the crust. If the tension is great enough the crust breaks, forming a normal fault. Faulting can cause mountains to form. For example, geologists think that plate movements have placed tension on Earth's crust in Nevada and Utah and parts of nearby states. The tension caused many normal faults to form in this region. Blocks of crust then slid along these normal faults, forming mountains called **fault-block mountains.** One example of a fault-block mountain range is shown in Figure 34.

Land Subsidence

When plate movement and deformation of the crust push up a wide area of crust, uplift occurs. These forces also can lead to land subsidence. **Land subsidence occurs when the land surface sinks, or subsides, as a result of geologic processes or human activities.** In Chapter 12, you will learn how certain human activities can cause a different kind of land subsidence.

Plate movements along diverging plate boundaries are one cause of land subsidence. This type of subsidence leads to the formation of rift valleys and ocean basins.

Sometimes, as uplift raises one part of the crust, land subsidence occurs in an adjoining area. In the area of subsidence, the force of plate movement warps the crust downward. The crust may sink until it is below sea level. About 65–70 million years ago, this process resulted in shallow seas covering the central part of North America. The seas extended all the way from Texas to northern Canada!

Volcanic Mountains

Some of Earth's most spectacular mountains are volcanoes. A **volcano** is a weak spot in the crust where molten, rock-forming material called magma comes to the surface. Magma that reaches the surface is called lava. Lava cools to form solid rock. **Volcanic activity builds mountains made of lava rock and other volcanic materials.** Plate movements determine where volcanoes develop on Earth's surface.

Location of Volcanoes

There are about 600 active volcanoes on land. Many more lie beneath the sea. Volcanoes occur in belts that extend across continents and oceans. One major volcanic belt is the Ring of Fire, formed by the many volcanoes that rim the Pacific Ocean.

Volcanic belts form along the boundaries of Earth's plates. Here, the lithosphere is weak and fractured, allowing magma to reach the surface. Most volcanoes occur along diverging plate boundaries, such as the mid-ocean ridge, or in subduction zones around the edges of oceans. But there are exceptions to this pattern. Some volcanoes form far from the boundaries of continental or oceanic plates.

Language Arts CONNECTION

The word *volcano* comes from the name of the Roman god of fire, Vulcan. According to Roman mythology, Vulcan lived beneath Mount Etna, a huge volcano on the island of Sicily in the Mediterranean Sea. Vulcan used the heat of Mount Etna to make metal armor and weapons for the ancient gods and heroes.

In Your Journal

Use the dictionary to find the definition of *plutonic* rock. Explain why the name of another Roman god was used for this term.

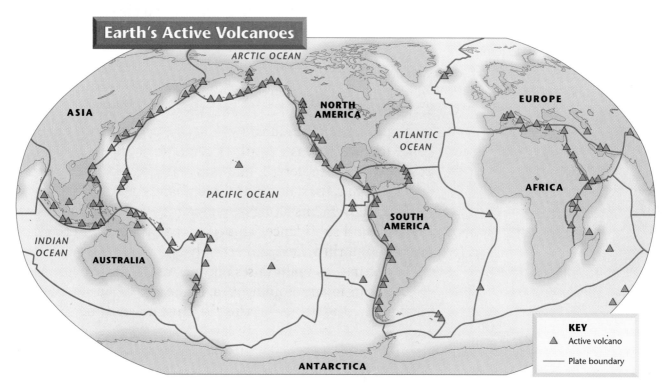

Earth's Active Volcanoes

ARCTIC OCEAN
ASIA
NORTH AMERICA
EUROPE
ATLANTIC OCEAN
AFRICA
PACIFIC OCEAN
SOUTH AMERICA
INDIAN OCEAN
AUSTRALIA
ANTARCTICA

KEY
▲ Active volcano
— Plate boundary

Figure 35 The Ring of Fire is a belt of volcanos that circles the Pacific Ocean. *Observing* What other patterns can you see in the locations of Earth's volcanoes?

Volcanoes at Diverging Plate Boundaries Volcanoes form along the mid-ocean ridge, which marks a diverging plate boundary. Along the ridge, lava pours out of cracks in the ocean floor. Volcanoes also form along rift valleys, such as the Great Rift Valley in Africa.

Volcanoes at Converging Boundaries Many volcanoes form near the plate boundaries where some oceanic crust returns to the mantle. There, the crust melts and forms magma, which then rises back toward the surface. When the magma from the melted crust erupts as lava, volcanoes are formed.

Many volcanoes occur on islands, near boundaries where two oceanic plates collide. Recall that at such places, the older, denser plate dives under the other plate, creating a deep-ocean trench. The lower plate sinks beneath the deep-ocean trench into the asthenosphere. There it begins to melt, forming magma. Because the magma is less dense than the surrounding rock, it seeps upward through cracks in the crust. Eventually, the magma breaks through the ocean floor, creating volcanoes. The resulting volcanoes create a string of islands called an island arc. Major island arcs include Japan, New Zealand, Indonesia, the Caribbean islands, the Philippines, and the Aleutians.

Subduction also occurs where the edge of a continental plate collides with an oceanic plate. Collisions between oceanic and continental plates produced both the volcanoes of the Andes mountains on the west coast of South America and the volcanoes of the Pacific Northwest in the United States.

Figure 36 Volcanoes form when two oceanic plates collide or when an oceanic plate collides with a continental plate. In both cases, oceanic crust sinks beneath a deep-ocean trench and melts to form magma that erupts to the surface as lava.

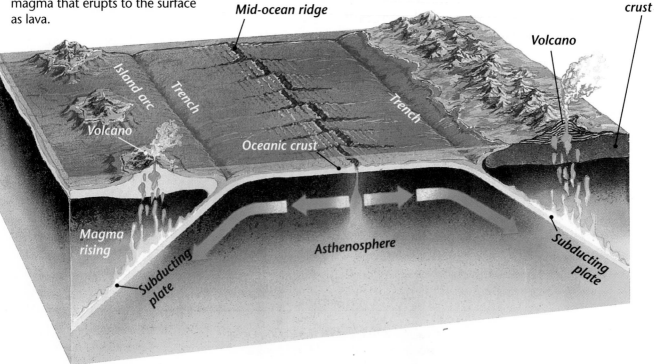

Mid-ocean ridge

Continental crust

Volcano

Island arc

Trench

Trench

Volcano

Oceanic crust

Magma rising

Asthenosphere

Subducting plate

Subducting plate

Figure 37 Hawaii sits on the moving Pacific plate. Beneath it is a powerful hot spot. Eventually, the plate's movement will carry the island of Hawaii away from the hot spot. *Inferring* *Which island on the map formed first?*

Hot Spot Volcanoes Some volcanoes result from "hot spots" in Earth's mantle. A **hot spot** is an area where magma from deep within the mantle melts through the crust like a blowtorch through steel. Hot spots often lie in the middle of continental or oceanic plates far from any plate boundaries.

A hot spot volcano in the ocean floor can gradually form a series of volcanic mountains. For example, the Hawaiian Islands formed one by one over millions of years as the Pacific plate drifted over a hot spot.

Hot spots can also form under the continents. Yellowstone National Park in Wyoming marks a major hot spot under the North American plate. The last volcanic eruption in Yellowstone occurred about 75,000 years ago.

Hot Spot in a Box

ACTIVITY

1. Fill a plastic box half-full of cold water. This represents the ocean.

2. Mix red food coloring with hot water in a small, narrow-necked bottle to represent magma.

3. Hold your finger over the mouth of the bottle as you place the bottle in the center of the box with the bottle's mouth under water.

4. Float a flat piece of plastic foam on the water to model a tectonic plate. Make sure the "plate" is floating above the bottle.

5. Take your finger off the bottle and observe what happens to the "magma."

Making Models Move the plastic foam slowly along. Where does the magma touch the "plate"? How does this model a hot spot volcano?

Section 6 Review

1. Explain how the three types of deformation affect Earth's crust.
2. Describe two ways that mountains form.
3. What is land subsidence and why does it occur?
4. Where do most volcanoes occur?
5. **Thinking Critically** **Predicting** If oceanic crust is subducted beneath continental crust, what Earth features will form on the continental crust?

Check Your Progress CHAPTER PROJECT
Complete the construction of your model by adding the surface features. Be sure to label the features on your model. Include arrows that indicate the direction of plate movement. Predict how Earth's surface features might change along the plate boundaries in your model. Construct a map showing what your plate might look like 20 million years in the future.

Mapping Earthquakes and Volcanoes

In this lab, you will interpret data on the locations of earthquakes and volcanoes to find patterns.

Problem

Is there a pattern in the locations of earthquakes and volcanoes?

Materials

outline world map showing longitude and latitude
4 pencils of different colors

Procedure

1. Use the information in the table to mark the location of each earthquake on the world map. Use one of the colored pencils to draw a letter E inside a circle at each earthquake location.
2. Use a pencil of a second color to mark the locations of the volcanoes on the world map. Indicate each volcano with the letter V inside a circle.
3. Use a third pencil to lightly shade the areas in which earthquakes are found.
4. Use a fourth colored pencil to lightly shade the areas in which volcanoes are found.

Analyze and Conclude

1. How are earthquakes distributed on the map? Are they scattered evenly over Earth's surface? Are they concentrated in zones?
2. How are volcanoes distributed? Are they scattered evenly or concentrated in zones?
3. From your data, what can you infer about the relationship between earthquakes and volcanoes?

4. **Apply** Based on the data, which area of the North American continent would have the greatest risk of earthquake damage? Of volcano damage? Why would knowing this information be important to urban planners, engineers, and builders in this area?

More to Explore

On a map of the United States, locate active volcanoes and areas of earthquake activity. Determine the distance from your home to the nearest active volcano.

Earthquakes		Volcanoes	
Longitude	Latitude	Longitude	Latitude
120° W	40° N	150° W	60° N
110° E	5° S	70° W	35° S
77° W	4° S	120° W	45° N
88° E	23° N	61° W	15° N
121° E	14° S	105° W	20° N
34° E	7° N	75° W	0°
74° W	44° N	122° W	40° N
70° W	30° S	30° E	40° N
10° E	45° N	60° E	30° N
85° W	13° N	160° E	55° N
125° E	23° N	37° E	3° S
30° E	35° N	145° E	40° N
140° E	35° N	120° E	10° S
12° E	46° N	14° E	41° N
75° E	28° N	105° E	5° S
150° W	61° N	35° E	15° N
68° W	47° S	70° W	30° S
175° E	41° S	175° E	39° S
121° E	17° N	123° E	13° N

SECTION 1 Earth's Interior

Key Ideas

◆ Constructive forces and destructive forces both change Earth's features.
◆ Earth's interior is divided into the crust, the mantle, the outer core, and the inner core.

Key Terms

geologist	crust	lithosphere
rock	basalt	asthenosphere
geology	granite	outer core
pressure	mantle	inner core

SECTION 2 Convection Currents and the Mantle

INTEGRATING PHYSICS

Key Idea

◆ Heat is transferred by radiation, conduction, and convection. Heat from Earth's core causes convection currents in the mantle.

Key Term

density

SECTION 3 Drifting Continents

Key Ideas

◆ Wegener thought that the continents were once joined, then drifted apart.
◆ Wegener could not identify a force that could move the continents.

Key Terms

Pangaea	continental drift	fossil

SECTION 4 Sea-Floor Spreading

Key Ideas

◆ In sea-floor spreading, molten material forms new rock along the mid-ocean ridge.
◆ In subduction, the ocean floor sinks back to the mantle beneath deep ocean trenches.

Key Terms

mid-ocean ridge	deep-ocean trench
sea-floor spreading	subduction

SECTION 5 The Theory of Plate Tectonics

Key Ideas

◆ The theory of plate tectonics explains plate movements and how they cause continental drift.
◆ Plates slip past each other at transform boundaries, move apart at divergent boundaries, and come together at convergent boundaries.

Key Terms

plate	divergent boundary
plate tectonics	rift valley
fault	convergent boundary
transform boundary	

SECTION 6 Changing Earth's Surface

Key Ideas

◆ Plate movement changes Earth's surface by altering Earth's systems and producing faults, mountains, land subsidence, and volcanoes.
◆ Mountains are formed as a result of folding and faulting of Earth's crust driven by plate movements.
◆ Land subsidence occurs when the land surface sinks, or subsides, as a result of geologic processes.

Key Terms

stress	footwall
deformation	reverse fault
earthquakes	fault-block mountain
fault	land subsidence
strike-slip fault	volcano
normal fault	hot spot
hanging wall	

Organizing Information

Compare/Contrast Table Make a table about deformation forces on a separate piece of paper. Include rows for the three forces of deformation: shearing, tension, and compression. For each type of deformation fill in the type of fault it produces and the type of movement that occurs along the fault. Give your table a title.

Reviewing Content

 Review key concepts online using *iText at www.phschool.com*

Multiple Choice

Choose the letter of the answer that best completes each statement.

1. The layer of the upper mantle that can flow is the
   a. asthenosphere.   b. lithosphere.
   c. inner core.   d. continental crust.

2. Most scientists rejected Wegener's theory of continental drift because the theory failed to explain
   a. coal deposits in Antarctica.
   b. formation of mountains.
   c. climate changes.
   d. how the continents move.

3. Subduction of the ocean floor takes place at
   a. the lower mantle.   b. mid-ocean ridges.
   c. rift valleys.   d. trenches.

4. Two plates collide with each other at
   a. a divergent boundary.
   b. a convergent boundary.
   c. the boundary between the mantle and the crust.
   d. a transform boundary.

5. A fault in which the hanging wall slides up and over the footwall is a
   a. reverse fault.   b. syncline.
   c. normal fault.   d. strike-slip fault.

True or False

If the statement is true, write true. If it is false, change the underlined word or words to make the statement true.

6. The Earth's <u>outer core</u> is made of basalt and granite.

7. The spinning of the <u>asthenosphere</u>, made of iron and nickel, explains why Earth has a magnetic field.

8. <u>Magnetic stripes</u> on the ocean floor are where oceanic crust sinks back to the mantle.

9. When two continental plates <u>converge</u>, a rift valley forms.

10. <u>Land subsidence</u> occurs when Earth's surface sinks as a result of geologic processes.

Checking Concepts

11. How is the inner core different from the outer core?

12. Explain why there are convection currents in the mantle.

13. How does a hot spot form a volcanic island?

14. What evidence of Earth's climate in the past supports the hypothesis of continental drift?

15. What was the importance of the discovery that molten rock was coming out of cracks along the mid-ocean ridge?

16. Describe the processes that create a fault-block mountain.

17. What happens when a plate of oceanic crust collides with a plate of continental crust? Why?

18. **Writing to Learn** Imagine that Alfred Wegener is alive today to defend his hypothesis of continental drift. Write a short interview that Wegener might have on a daytime talk show. You may use humor.

Thinking Critically

19. **Classifying** Classify these layers of Earth's interior as liquid, solid, or solid but able to flow slowly: crust, lithosphere, asthenosphere, outer core, inner core.

20. **Comparing and Contrasting** How are oceanic and continental crust alike? How do they differ?

21. **Relating Cause and Effect** What do geologists think is the driving force of plate tectonics? Explain.

22. **Relating Cause and Effect** What events can cause land subsidence and what is formed as a result?

23. **Making Generalizations** State in one sentence the most significant discovery that geologists found through their study of plate tectonics.

24. **Predicting** A community has just built a street across a strike-slip fault that has frequent earthquakes. How will movement along the fault affect the street?

Applying Skills

Geologists think that a new plate boundary is forming in the Indian Ocean. The part of the plate carrying Australia is twisting away from the part of the plate carrying India.

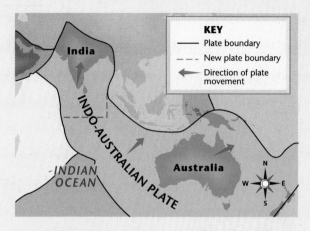

KEY
— Plate boundary
– – – New plate boundary
← Direction of plate movement

25. **Interpreting Maps** Look at the arrows showing the direction of plate motion. In what direction is the part of the plate carrying Australia moving? In what direction is the part carrying India moving?

26. **Predicting** As India and Australia move in different directions, what type of plate boundary will form between them?

27. **Inferring** On the map you can see that the northern part of the Indo-Australian plate is moving north and colliding with the Eurasian plate. What features would occur where these plates meet? Explain.

Performance ▼ Assessment
CHAPTER PROJECT

Presenting Your Project Present your model to the class. Point out the types of plate boundaries on the model. Discuss the plate motions and landforms that result in these areas. What similarities and differences exist between your model and those of your classmates?

Reflect and Record In your journal, write an evaluation of your project. What materials would you change? How could you improve your model?

Test Preparation
Use these questions to prepare for standardized tests.

Use the diagram to answer Questions 28–31.

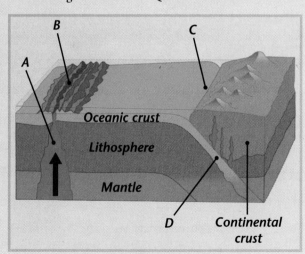

Oceanic crust
Lithosphere
Mantle
Continental crust

28. The arrow at A represents
   A a transform boundary.
   B continental crust.
   C a subduction zone.
   D molten magma rising from the mantle.

29. What is occurring at the feature labeled B?
   F New rock is being added to the oceanic plate.
   G The ocean floor is sinking.
   H Subduction is occurring.
   J Two plates are colliding.

30. As sea-floor spreading occurs, the oceanic plate
   A does not move.
   B moves from C toward B.
   C moves from B toward C.
   D floats higher on the mantle.

31. What is occurring at D?
   F New material is rising from the mantle.
   G The oceanic plate is melting as it sinks into the mantle.
   H Sedimentary rock is being added to the plate.
   J The oceanic plate is pushing the continental plate into the mantle.

These aurichalcite (oh rih KAL syt) crystals were found in a copper mine in Mexico. This mineral is formed from the metals zinc, copper, and other elements.

WEB ACTIVITY
www.phschool.com

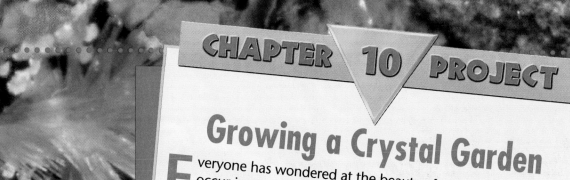

Growing a Crystal Garden

Everyone has wondered at the beauty of minerals. Minerals occur in an amazing variety of colors and crystal shapes—from clear, tiny cubes of halite (table salt) to precious rubies and sapphires. Some crystals look like dandelion puffs. In this project, you will grow crystals to see how different types of chemicals form different crystal shapes.

Your Goal To design and grow a crystal garden.

To complete this project successfully, you must
◆ create a three-dimensional garden scene as a base on which to grow crystals
◆ prepare at least two different crystal-growth solutions
◆ observe and record the shapes and growth rates of your crystals
◆ follow the safety guidelines in Appendix A.

Get Started Begin by deciding what materials you will use to create your garden scene. Your teacher will suggest a variety of materials and also describe the types of crystal-growth solutions that you can use.

Check Your Progress You'll be working on this project as you study this chapter. To keep your project on track, look for Check Your Progress boxes at the following points.

Section 1 Review, page 368: Design and build a setting for your crystal garden and add the solutions.
Section 2 Review, page 374: Observe and record the growth of the crystals.

Present Your Project At the end of the chapter (page 385), display your finished crystal garden to your class. Be prepared to describe your procedure, observations, and conclusions.

TEKS

In addition to process TEKS, this chapter addresses these concept TEKS as they relate to the chapter's topics.

(8.9) The student knows that substances have chemical and physical properties. The student is expected to:
(A) demonstrate that substances may react chemically to form new substances.

(8.12) The student knows that cycles exist in Earth systems. The student is expected to:
(A) analyze and predict the sequence of events in the lunar and rock cycles.

SECTION 1 Properties of Minerals

DISCOVER •••••••••••••••••••••••••••••••••• ACTIVITY

What Is the True Color of a Mineral?

1. Examine samples of magnetite and black hematite. Both minerals contain iron. Describe the color and appearance of the two minerals. Are they similar or different?

2. Rub the black hematite across a streak plate or the back of a porcelain or ceramic tile. Observe the color of the streak on the tile.

3. Wipe the tile clean before you test the next sample.

4. Rub the magnetite across the back of the tile. Observe the color of the streak on the tile.

Think It Over

Observing Does the color of each mineral's streak match its color? How could this streak test be helpful in identifying them as two different minerals?

GUIDE FOR READING

◆ What are the characteristics of a mineral?

◆ What physical and chemical properties can be used to identify minerals?

Reading Tip As you read, use the headings to make an outline showing what minerals are and how they can be identified.

Key Terms mineral • inorganic • crystal • element • compound • Mohs hardness scale • streak • luster • cleavage • fracture • fluorescence

If you visit a science museum, you might wander into a room named the "hall of minerals." There you would see substances you have never heard of. For example, you might see deep-red crystals labeled "sphalerite" (SFAL uh ryt). You might be surprised to learn that sphalerite is a source of zinc and gallium. These metals are used in products from "tin" cans to computer chips! Although you may have never seen sphalerite, you are probably familiar with other common minerals, such as turquoise, a blue-green mineral used in jewelry.

Figure 1 The Hall of Minerals at the American Museum of Natural History in New York City contains one of the world's largest collections of minerals.

Figure 2 **A.** Red crystals of the mineral sphalerite are called ruby zinc. **B.** Borax is a mineral that forms in dry lake beds. **C.** Coal is not a mineral because it is made of the remains of ancient plants.
Comparing and Contrasting How are sphalerite and borax similar? How are they different?

What Is a Mineral?

Sphalerite and turquoise are just two of more than 3,000 **minerals** that geologists have identified. Of all these minerals, only about 100 are common. Most of the others are harder to find than gold. About 20 minerals make up most of the rocks of Earth's crust. These minerals are known as rock-forming minerals. As the materials that make up Earth's rocks, rock-forming minerals, along with all other minerals, are involved in the rock cycle. You will learn about the rock cycle in Chapter 11.

A mineral is a naturally occurring, inorganic solid that has a crystal structure and a definite chemical composition. For a substance to be a mineral, it must have all of these characteristics. In Figure 2, you can compare sphalerite with another mineral, borax, and with coal, which is not a mineral.

Naturally Occurring To be classified as a mineral, a substance must occur naturally. Cement, brick, steel, and glass all come from substances found in Earth's crust. However, these building materials are manufactured by people. Because they are not naturally occurring, such materials are not considered to be minerals.

Inorganic A mineral must also be **inorganic.** This means that the mineral cannot arise from materials that were once part of a living thing. For example, coal forms naturally in the crust. But geologists do not classify coal as a mineral because it comes from the remains of plants and animals that lived millions of years ago.

Solid A mineral is always a solid, with a definite volume and shape. The particles that make up a solid are packed together very tightly, so they cannot move like the particles that make up a liquid. A solid keeps its shape because its particles can't flow freely.

Crystal Structure The particles of a mineral line up in a pattern that repeats over and over again. The repeating pattern of a mineral's particles forms a solid called a **crystal.** A crystal has flat sides, called faces, that meet at sharp edges and corners.

Sometimes, the crystal structure is obvious from the mineral's appearance. In other minerals, however, the crystal structure is visible only under a microscope. A few minerals, such as opal, are considered minerals even though their particles are not arranged in a crystal structure.

Definite Chemical Composition A mineral has a definite chemical composition. This means that a mineral always contains certain elements in definite proportions. An **element** is a substance composed of a single kind of atom. All the atoms of the same element have the same chemical and physical properties.

Almost all minerals are compounds. In a **compound,** two or more elements are combined so that the elements no longer have distinct properties. The elements that make up a compound are said to be chemically joined. For example, a crystal of the mineral quartz has one atom of silicon for every two atoms of oxygen. Each compound has its own properties, which usually differ greatly from the properties of the elements that form it. Figure 3 compares the mineral cinnabar to the elements that make it up.

Figure 3 Minerals are usually a compound of two or more elements. **A.** Mercury is a metal that is a silvery liquid at room temperature. **B.** The element sulfur is bright yellow. **C.** The mineral cinnabar is a compound of the elements mercury and sulfur. Cinnabar has red crystals.

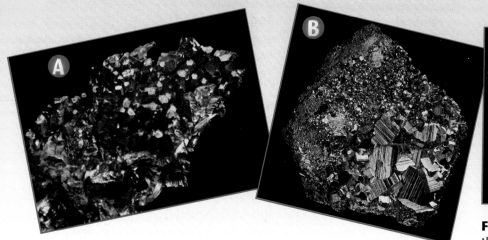

Figure 4 An old saying warns "All that glitters is not gold." **A.** Real gold can occur as a pure metal. **B.** Pyrite, or fool's gold, contains iron and sulfur. **C.** Chalcopyrite is a compound of copper, iron, and sulfur. *Observing These minerals are similar in color. But do you notice any differences in their appearance?*

Some elements occur in nature in a pure form, not as part of a compound with other elements. These elements, such as copper, silver, and gold, are considered to be minerals. Almost all pure elements are metals.

☑ *Checkpoint* *What does it mean to say that a mineral has a definite chemical composition?*

Identifying Minerals

During the California Gold Rush of 1849, thousands of people headed west to find gold in the California hills. Some found gold, but most found disappointment. Perhaps the most disappointed of all were the ones who found pyrite, or "fool's gold." All three minerals in Figure 4 look like gold, yet only one is the real thing.

Because there are so many different kinds of minerals, telling them apart can be a challenge. The color of a mineral alone often provides too little information to make an identification. **Each mineral has its own specific physical and chemical properties that can be used to identify it.** When you have learned to recognize the properties of minerals, you will be able to identify many common minerals around you.

You can see some of the properties of a mineral just by looking at a sample. To observe other properties, however, you need to conduct tests on that sample. As you read about the properties of minerals, think about how you could use them to identify a mineral.

Hardness When you identify a mineral, one of the best clues you can use is the mineral's hardness. In 1812, Friedrich Mohs, an Austrian mineral expert, invented a series of tests to describe and compare the hardness of minerals. Called the **Mohs hardness scale,** this scale ranks ten minerals from softest to hardest.

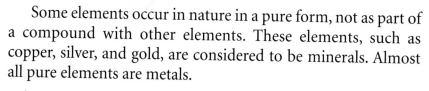

Classifying

1. Use your fingernail to try to scratch talc, calcite, and quartz. Record which minerals you were able to scratch.

2. Now try to scratch the minerals with a penny. Were your results different? Explain.

3. Were there any minerals you were unable to scratch with either your fingernail or the penny?

4. How would you classify the three minerals in order of increasing hardness?

Figure 5 The Mohs hardness scale rates the hardness of minerals on a scale of 1 to 10.

Drawing Conclusions You find a mineral that can be scratched by a steel knife, but not by a copper penny. What is this mineral's hardness on the Mohs scale?

Mohs Hardness Scale

Mineral	Rating	Testing Method
Talc	1	Softest known mineral. It flakes easily when scratched by a fingernail.
Gypsum	2	A fingernail can easily scratch it.
Calcite	3	A fingernail cannot scratch it, but a copper penny can.
Fluorite	4	A steel knife can easily scratch it.
Apatite	5	A steel knife can scratch it.
Feldspar	6	Cannot be scratched by a steel knife, but it can scratch window glass.
Quartz	7	Can scratch steel and hard glass easily.
Topaz	8	Can scratch quartz.
Corundum	9	Can scratch topaz.
Diamond	10	Hardest known mineral. Diamond can scratch all other substances.

Look at the table in Figure 5 to see which mineral is the softest and which is the hardest. A mineral can scratch any mineral softer than itself, but will be scratched by any mineral that is harder. How would you determine the hardness of a mineral not listed on the Mohs scale, such as sphalerite? You could try to scratch sphalerite with talc, gypsum, or calcite. But you would find that none of them scratch sphalerite. Apatite, the mineral rated 5 on the scale, does scratch sphalerite. Therefore, you would conclude that sphalerite's hardness is about 4 on Mohs hardness scale.

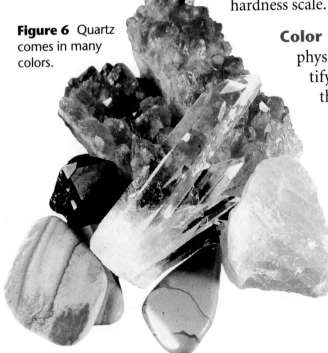

Figure 6 Quartz comes in many colors.

Color The color of a mineral is an easily observed physical property. But color can be used to identify only those few minerals that always have their own characteristic color. The mineral malachite is always green. The mineral azurite is always blue. No other minerals look quite the same as these. Many minerals, however, like the quartz in Figure 6, can occur in a variety of colors.

Streak A streak test can provide a clue to a mineral's identity. The **streak** of a mineral is the color of its powder. You can observe a streak by rubbing a mineral against a piece of unglazed tile called a streak plate. Even though the color of the mineral may vary, its

Figure 7 **A.** Galena, which contains lead, has a metallic luster. **B.** Malachite, which contains copper, has a silky luster.

streak does not. Surprisingly, the streak color and the mineral color are often different. For example, although pyrite has a gold color, it always produces a greenish black streak. Real gold, on the other hand, produces a golden yellow streak.

Luster Another simple test to identify a mineral is to check its luster. **Luster** is the term used to describe how a mineral reflects light from its surface. Minerals containing metals are often shiny. For example, galena is an ore of lead that has a bright, metallic luster. Look at Figure 7 to compare the luster of galena with the luster of malachite. Other minerals, such as quartz, have a glassy luster. Some of the other terms used to describe luster include earthy, waxy, and pearly.

Density Each mineral has a characteristic density. Recall from Chapter 1 that density is the mass in a given space, or mass per unit volume. No matter what the size of a mineral sample, the density of that mineral always remains the same.

You can compare the density of two mineral samples of about the same size. Just pick them up and heft them, or feel their weight, in your hands. You may be able to feel the difference between low-density quartz and high-density galena. If the two samples are the same size, the galena is almost three times as heavy as the quartz.

But heft provides only a rough measure of density. When geologists measure density, they use a balance to determine precisely the mass of a mineral sample. The mineral is also placed in water to determine how much water it displaces. The volume of the displaced water equals the volume of the sample. Dividing the sample's mass by its volume gives the density of the mineral.

☑ *Checkpoint* *How can you determine a mineral's density?*

Crystal Systems The crystals of each mineral grow atom by atom to form that mineral's particular crystal structure. Geologists classify these structures into six groups based on the number and angle of the crystal faces. These groups are called crystal systems. For example, all halite crystals are cubic. Halite crystals have six sides that meet at right angles, forming a perfect cube. Sometimes you can see that a crystal has the particular crystal structure of its mineral. Crystals that grow in an open space can be almost perfectly formed. But crystals that grow in a tight space are often incompletely formed. Figure 8 shows minerals that belong to each of the six crystal systems.

Figure 8 This chart lists some common minerals and their properties. *Interpreting Data Which mineral is lowest in density and hardness? Which mineral could you identify by using a compass?*

Properties and Uses of Minerals

Name	 Magnetite	 Quartz	 Rutile	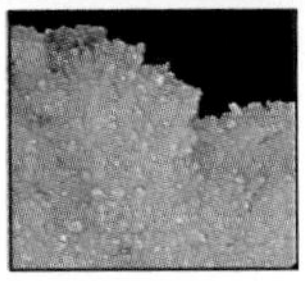 Sulfur	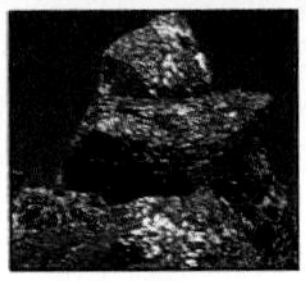 Azurite	 Microcline Feldspar
Hardness	6	7	$6 - 6\frac{1}{2}$	2	$3\frac{1}{2} - 4$	6
Color	Black	Transparent or in a range of colors	Black or reddish brown	Lemon yellow to yellowish brown	Blue	Green, red-brown, pink, or white
Streak	Black	Colorless	Light brown	White	Pale blue	Colorless
Crystal System	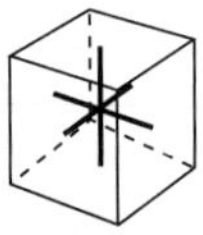 Cubic	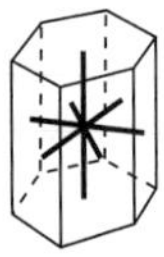 Hexagonal	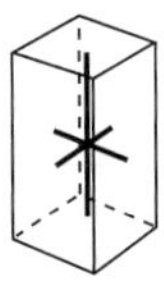 Tetragonal	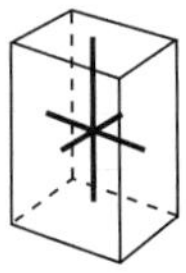 Orthorhombic	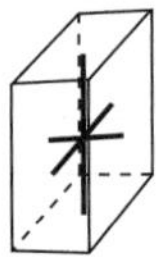 Monoclinic	 Triclinic
Luster	Metallic	Glassy	Metallic or gemlike	Greasy	Glassy to dull or earthy	Glassy
Special Properties	Magnetic	Fractures like broken glass	Not easily melted	Melts easily	Reacts to acid	Cleaves well in two directions
Density (g/cm³)	5.2	2.6	4.2–4.3	2.0–2.1	3.8	2.6
Uses	A source of iron used to make steel	Used in making glass and electronic equipment, or as a gem	Contains titanium, a hard, light-weight metal used in aircraft and cars	Used in fungicides, industrial chemicals, and rubber	A source of copper metal; also used as a gem	Used in pottery glaze, scouring powder, or as a gem

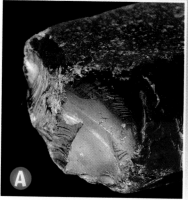

Figure 9 **A.** When quartz fractures, the break looks like the surface of a seashell. **B.** A piece of feldspar cleaves at right angles. **C.** Mica cleaves into thin, flat sheets that are almost transparent.
Applying Concepts *How would you test a mineral to determine its cleavage and fracture?*

Cleavage and Fracture The way a mineral breaks apart can help to identify it. A mineral that splits easily along flat surfaces has the property called **cleavage.** Whether a mineral has cleavage depends on how the atoms in its crystals are arranged. Depending on the arrangement of atoms in the mineral, it will break apart more easily in one direction than another. Look at the minerals in Figure 9. Mica separates easily in only one direction, forming flat sheets. Feldspar splits at right angles, producing square corners. These minerals have cleavage.

Most minerals do not split apart evenly. Instead, they have a characteristic type of fracture. **Fracture** describes how a mineral looks when it breaks apart in an irregular way. Geologists use a variety of terms to describe fracture. For example, quartz has a shell-shaped fracture. When quartz breaks, it produces curved, shell-like surfaces that look like chipped glass. Pure metals, like copper and iron, have a hackly fracture—they form jagged points. Some soft minerals that crumble easily like clay have an earthy fracture. Minerals that form rough, irregular surfaces when broken have an uneven fracture.

✓ *Checkpoint* *How are cleavage and fracture similar? How are they different?*

Crystal Hands

You can grow two different kinds of salt crystals. **ACTIVITY**

1. Put on your goggles.

2. ☠ Pour a solution of halite (table salt) into one shallow pan and a solution of Epsom salts into another shallow pan.

3. Put a large piece of black construction paper on a flat surface.

4. Dip one hand in the halite solution. Shake off the excess liquid and make a palm print on the paper. Repeat with your other hand and the Epsom salt solution, placing your new print next to the first one. **CAUTION:** *Do not do this activity if you have a cut on your hand.* Wash your hands after making your hand prints.

5. Let the prints dry overnight.

Observing Use a hand lens to compare the shape of the crystals. Which hand print has more crystals?

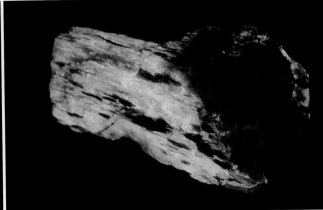

Figure 10 Scheelite looks quite ordinary in daylight, but glows with brilliant color under ultraviolet light.

Special Properties Some minerals can be identified by special physical properties. For example, minerals that glow under ultraviolet light have a property known as **fluorescence** (floo RES uns). The mineral scheelite is fluorescent. Magnetism occurs naturally in a few minerals. Lodestone, which is a form of magnetite, acts as a natural magnet. Early magnets—such as compass needles—were made by striking a piece of iron with lodestone. Uraninite and a few other minerals are radioactive. They set off a Geiger counter. Some minerals react chemically to acid. Calcite, a compound of calcium, carbon, and oxygen, fizzes and gives off carbon dioxide when a drop of vinegar is placed on it.

A few minerals, such as quartz, have electrical properties. Pressure applied to these crystals produces a small electric current. In addition, these crystals vibrate if they come in contact with an electric current. Because of these properties, quartz crystals are used in microphones, radio transmitters, and watches.

Section 1 Review

1. What characteristics must a substance have to be considered a mineral?
2. Describe how you can test a mineral to determine its hardness, density, and streak.
3. What is the major difference between an element and a compound?
4. **Thinking Critically** **Classifying** According to the definition of a mineral, can water be classified as a mineral? Explain your answer.
5. **Thinking Critically** **Making Generalizations** Explain why you can't rely on any single test or property when you are trying to identify a mineral.

Check Your Progress CHAPTER PROJECT
Select a container for your crystal garden such as a plastic shoe box or a large-mouth jar. Make a sketch showing the shapes and locations of the "plants" you plan to grow. When you have designed your garden, decide what materials to put in the box for the crystals to grow on. Decide what crystal-growth solutions you will use. Halite, Epsom salts, and alum are possibilities. Check with your teacher to make sure the chemicals you plan to use are safe. ☠

THE DENSITY OF MINERALS

In this lab, you will use water to help you measure the density of minerals.

Problem

How can you compare the density of different minerals?

Materials

graduated cylinder, 100 mL
3 mineral samples: pyrite, quartz, and galena
water
balance
computer and spreadsheet program (optional)

Procedure

1. Check to make sure the mineral samples are small enough to fit in the graduated cylinder.
2. Copy the data table into your notebook or create a spreadsheet on the computer. Place the pyrite on the balance and record its mass in the data table.
3. Fill the cylinder with water to the 50-mL mark.
4. Carefully place the pyrite into the cylinder of water. Try not to spill any of the water.
5. Read the level of the water on the scale of the graduated cylinder. Record the level of the water with the pyrite in it.
6. Calculate the volume of water displaced by the pyrite. To do this, subtract the volume of water without the pyrite from the volume of water with the pyrite. Record your answer.
7. Calculate the density of the pyrite by using this formula.

$$\text{Density} = \frac{\text{Mass of mineral}}{\text{Volume of water displaced by the mineral}}$$

(Note: Density is expressed as g/cm³. One mL of water has a volume of 1 cm³.)

8. Remove the water and mineral from the cylinder.
9. Repeat steps 2–8 for quartz and galena.

Analyze and Conclude

1. Which mineral had the highest density? The lowest density?
2. How does finding the volume of the water that was displaced help you find the volume of the mineral itself?
3. Why won't the procedure you used in this lab work for a substance that floats or one that dissolves in water?
4. **Apply** Pyrite is sometimes called "fool's gold" because its color and appearance are similar to real gold. How could a scientist determine if a sample was real gold?
5. **Think About It** Does the shape or size of a mineral sample affect its density? Explain.

More to Explore

Repeat the activity by finding the density of other minerals or materials. Then compare the densities of these materials with pyrite, quartz, and galena.

DATA CHART			
	Pyrite	Quartz	Galena
Mass of Mineral (g)			
Volume of Water Without Mineral (mL)	50 mL	50 mL	50 mL
Volume of Water With Mineral (mL)			
Volume of Water Displaced (mL)			
Density (g/cm³)			

2 How Minerals Form

DISCOVER •••••••••••••••••••••••••••••••••••••• ACTIVITY ••••

How Does the Rate of Cooling Affect Crystal Growth?

1. ☠ Put on your goggles. Use a plastic spoon to place a small amount of salol near one end of each of two microscope slides. You need just enough to form a spot 0.5 to 1.0 cm in diameter.

2. 🔥🔦 Carefully hold one slide with tongs. Warm it slowly over a lit candle until the salol is almost completely melted. **CAUTION:** *Move the slide in and out of the flame to avoid cracking the glass.*

3. Set the slide aside to cool slowly.

4. While the first slide is cooling, hold the second slide with tongs and heat it as in Step 2. Cool the slide quickly by placing it on an ice cube. Carefully blow out the candle.

5. Observe the slides under a hand lens. Compare the appearance of the crystals that form on the two slides.

6. Wash your hands when you are finished.

Think It Over
Relating Cause and Effect
Which sample had larger crystals? If a mineral forms by rapid cooling, would you expect the crystals to be large or small?

GUIDE FOR READING

◆ What are the processes by which minerals form?

Reading Tip Before you read, rewrite the headings of the section as how, why, or what questions. As you read, look for answers to these questions.

Key Terms solution • vein

Picture yourself digging for diamonds. At Crater of Diamonds State Park in Arkansas, that's exactly what people do. The park is one of the very few places in the United States where diamonds can be found. Visitors are permitted to prospect, or search, for diamonds. Since the area became a park in 1972, visitors have found more than 20,000 diamonds!

How did the diamonds get there? Millions of years ago, a volcanic pipe formed in the mantle at a depth of 120 kilometers or more. At that depth, great

Diamonds ▶

pressure and heat changed carbon atoms into the hardest known substance—diamond. Then the pipe erupted, carrying diamonds and other materials toward the surface. Today, geologists recognize this type of volcanic pipe as an area of unusual bluish-colored rock made up of a variety of minerals, including diamond. Volcanic pipes containing diamonds are found in only a few places on Earth. Most occur in South Africa and Australia, where many of the world's diamonds are mined today.

Processes That Form Minerals

You probably have handled many products made from minerals. But you may not have thought about how the minerals formed. The minerals that people use today have been forming deep in Earth's crust or on the surface for several billion years. **In general, minerals can form in two ways: through the crystallization of melted materials, and through the crystallization of materials dissolved in water.** Crystallization is the process by which atoms are arranged to form a material with a crystal structure.

Minerals From Magma

Minerals form as hot magma cools inside the crust, or as lava hardens on the surface. When these liquids cool to the solid state, they form crystals. The size of the crystals depends on several factors. The rate at which the magma cools, the amount of gas the magma contains, and the chemical composition of the magma all affect crystal size.

When magma remains deep below the surface, it cools slowly over many thousands of years. Slow cooling leads to the formation of large crystals. If the crystals remain undisturbed while cooling, they grow by adding atoms according to a regular pattern.

Magma closer to the surface cools much faster than magma that hardens deep below ground. With more rapid cooling, there is no time for magma to form large crystals. Instead, small crystals form. If magma erupts to the surface and becomes lava, the lava will also cool quickly and form minerals with small crystals.

Figure 11 The gray crystal of the mineral spodumene is 24 cm long. But it's not the largest crystal. Spodumene crystals the size of telephone poles have been found in South Dakota.
Inferring Under what conditions did such large crystals probably form?

Figure 12 A. Silver sometimes occurs as a pure metal, forming delicate, treelike shapes. B. Solutions containing dissolved metals form veins like the ones in this silver mine in Idaho.

Minerals From Hot Water Solutions

Sometimes, the elements that form a mineral dissolve in hot water. Magma has heated the water to a high temperature beneath Earth's surface. These dissolved minerals form solutions. A **solution** is a mixture in which one substance dissolves in another. When a hot water solution begins to cool, the elements and compounds leave the solution and crystallize as minerals. The silver shown in Figure 12A formed by this process.

Pure metals that crystallize underground from hot water solutions often form veins. A **vein** is a narrow channel or slab of a mineral that is much different from the surrounding rock. Deep underground, solutions of hot water and metals often follow cracks within the rock. Then the metals crystallize into veins. Figure 12B shows a vein of silver in a mine.

Many minerals form from solutions at places where tectonic plates spread apart along the mid-ocean ridge. First, ocean water seeps down through cracks in the crust. There, the water comes

Figure 13 Many minerals form at chimneys along the mid-ocean ridge. Chimneys occur in areas where sea-floor spreading causes cracks in the oceanic crust. *Interpreting Diagrams What is the energy source for this process?*

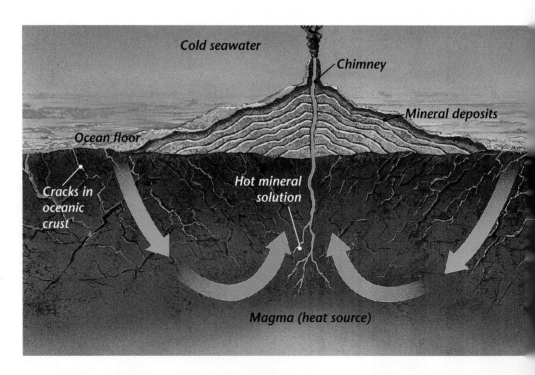

Cold seawater

Chimney

Mineral deposits

Ocean floor

Cracks in oceanic crust

Hot mineral solution

Magma (heat source)

Figure 14 In Death Valley, California, water carries dissolved minerals from the surrounding mountains into the valley. When the water evaporates under the blazing desert sun, the minerals form a crust on the valley floor.

in contact with magma that heats it to a very high temperature. The heated water dissolves minerals from the crust and rushes upward. This hot solution then billows out of vents, called "chimneys." When the hot solution hits the cold sea, minerals crystallize and settle to the ocean floor.

☑ *Checkpoint* *What is often found in veins? How do veins form?*

Minerals Formed by Evaporation

Minerals can also form when solutions evaporate. You know that if you stir salt crystals into a beaker of water, the salt dissolves, forming a solution. But if you allow the water in the solution to evaporate, it will leave salt crystals on the bottom of the beaker. In a similar way, thick deposits of the mineral halite formed over millions of years when ancient seas slowly evaporated. In the United States, such halite deposits occur in the Midwest, the Southwest, and along the Gulf Coast.

Several other useful minerals also form by the evaporation of seawater. These include gypsum, used in making building materials; calcite crystals, used in microscopes; and minerals containing potassium, used in making fertilizer.

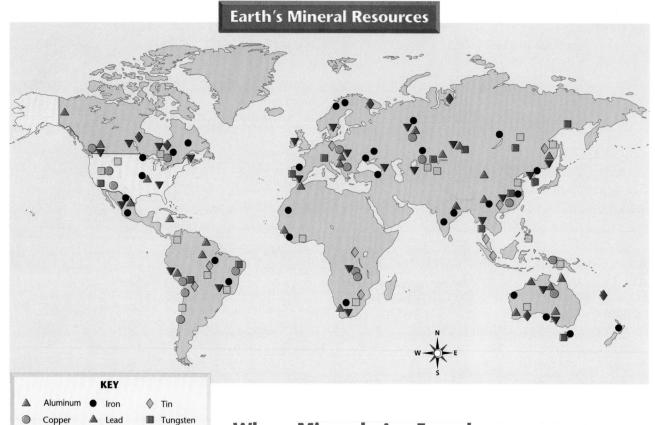

KEY

▲	Aluminum	●	Iron	◆	Tin
●	Copper	▲	Lead	■	Tungsten
▢	Gold	◆	Nickel	▼	Zinc

Figure 15 The map shows where important mineral resources are found throughout the world. *Interpreting Maps Which metals are found in the United States? Which ones must be imported from other countries?*

Where Minerals Are Found

Earth's crust is made up mostly of the common rock-forming minerals combined in various types of rock. Less common and rare minerals, however, are not distributed evenly throughout the crust. Instead, there are several processes that concentrate minerals, or bring them together, in deposits. Look at the map of the world's mineral resources in Figure 15. Do you see any patterns in the distribution of minerals such as gold and copper? Many valuable minerals are found in or near areas of volcanic activity and mountain building. For example, rich copper deposits are found along the Andes mountains in Chile.

Section 2 Review

1. What are the two main ways in which minerals form?
2. Describe how the cooling rate of magma affects the size of the mineral crystals formed.
3. What are the steps by which mineral deposits form along mid-ocean ridges?
4. **Thinking Critically Relating Cause and Effect** A miner finds a vein of silver. Describe a process that could have formed the vein.

CHAPTER PROJECT

Check Your Progress
Remember to record your daily observations of how your crystal garden grows. Sketch the shapes of the crystals and describe how the crystals grow. Compare the shapes and growth rates of the crystals grown from the various solutions. (*Hint:* If crystals do not begin growing, add more of the appropriate solution.)

Who Owns the Ocean's Minerals?

Rich mineral deposits lie on and just beneath the ocean floor. Many nations would like to mine these deposits. Coastal nations already have the right to mine deposits near their shores. Today, they are mining materials such as tin, titanium, diamonds, and sulfur from the continental shelf—the wide area of shallow water just off the shores of continents.

But the ocean floor beyond the continental shelves is open for all nations to explore. Mineral deposits in volcanic areas of the ocean floor include manganese, iron, cobalt, copper, nickel and platinum. Who owns these valuable underwater minerals?

▲ This sample from the floor of the Pacific Ocean near New Guinea may contain copper and gold.

The Issues

Who Can Afford to Mine? Although the ocean floor is open to all for exploration, mining the ocean floor will cost a huge amount of money. New technologies must be developed to obtain mineral deposits from the ocean floor.

Only wealthy industrial nations such as France, Germany, Japan, and the United States will be able to afford these costs. Industrial nations that have spent money and effort on mining think that they should be allowed to keep all the profits. However, developing nations that lack money and technology disagree. Landlocked nations that have no coastlines also object.

What Rights Do Other Nations Have?
As of 1996, 87 nations had signed the Law of the Sea treaty. Among other things, this treaty stated that ocean mineral deposits are the common property of all people. It also stated that mining profits must be shared among all nations.

Some people think that, because of the treaty, wealthy nations should share their technology and any profits they get from mining the ocean floor.

How Can the Wealth Be Shared?
What can nations do to prevent conflict over mining the ocean floor? They might arrange a compromise. Perhaps wealthy nations should contribute part of their profits to help developing or landlocked nations. Developing nations could pool their money for ocean-floor mining. Whatever nations decide, some regulations for ocean-floor mining are necessary. In the future, these resources will be important to everyone.

You Decide

1. **Identify the Problem**
   In your own words, state the controversy about ocean mineral rights.

2. **Analyze the Options**
   Compare the concerns of wealthy nations with those of developing nations. How could you reassure developing nations that they will not be left out?

3. **Find a Solution**
   Look at a map of the world. Who should share the mineral profits from the Pacific Ocean? From the Atlantic Ocean? Write one or two paragraphs stating your opinion. Support your ideas with facts.

3 Mineral Resources

DISCOVER ··· ACTIVITY ····

How Are Minerals Processed Before They Are Used?

1. Examine a piece of the mineral bauxite and use your knowledge of the properties of minerals to describe it.

2. Examine an aluminum can. (The metal aluminum comes from bauxite.) Compare the properties of the aluminum can with the properties of bauxite.

3. Examine a piece of the mineral graphite and describe its properties.

4. Examine the lead in a pencil. (Pencil "lead" is made from graphite.) Compare the properties of the pencil lead with the properties of graphite.

Think It Over

Posing Questions How is each mineral similar to or different from the object made from it? What questions would you need to answer to understand how bauxite and graphite are made into useful materials?

GUIDE FOR READING

◆ How are minerals used?

◆ What are the three types of mines?

◆ How are ores processed to obtain metals?

Reading Tip As you read, draw a concept map that explains how metal ores are located, mined, and smelted.

Key Terms gemstone • ore • smelting • alloy

Figure 16 The copper to make this Hopewell ornament may have come from an area in Michigan that is still a source of copper ore.

More than a thousand years ago, the Hopewell people lived in the Mississippi River valley. These ancient Native Americans are famous for the mysterious earthen mounds they built near the river. There these people left beautiful objects made from minerals: tools chipped from flint (a variety of quartz), the shape of a human hand cut out of a piece of translucent mica, or a flying bird made from a thin sheet of copper.

To obtain these minerals, the Hopewell people traded with peoples across North America. The copper, for example, came from near Lake Superior. There, copper could be found as a pure metal. Because copper is a soft metal, this copper was easy to shape into ornaments or weapons.

The Uses of Minerals

Like the Hopewell people, people today use minerals in many ways. You are surrounded by materials that come from minerals—for example, the metal body and window glass of a car. **Minerals are the source of metals, gemstones, and other materials used to make many products.** Are you familiar with any products that are made from minerals? You might be surprised at how important minerals are in everyday life.

Gemstones Beautiful gemstones such as rubies and sapphires have captured the imagination of people throughout the ages. Usually, a **gemstone** is a hard, colorful mineral that has a brilliant or glassy luster. People value gemstones for their color, luster, and durability—and for the fact that they are rare. Once a gemstone is cut and polished, it is called a gem. Gems are used mainly for jewelry and decoration. They are also used for mechanical parts and for grinding and polishing.

Metals Some minerals are the sources of metals such as aluminum, iron, copper, or silver. Metals are useful because they can be stretched into wire, flattened into sheets, and hammered or molded without breaking. Metal tools and machinery, the metal filament in a light bulb, even the steel girders used to frame office buildings—all began as minerals inside Earth's crust.

Figure 17 Gems like these red rubies and blue and yellow sapphires are among the most valuable minerals. These precious gems are varieties of the mineral corundum.

Other Useful Minerals There are many other useful minerals besides metals and gems. People use materials from these minerals in foods, medicines, fertilizers, and building materials. The very soft mineral talc is ground up to make talcum powder. Fluorite is important in making aluminum and steel. Clear crystals of the mineral calcite are used in optical instruments such as microscopes. Quartz, a mineral found in sand, is used in making glass as well as in electronic equipment and watches. Kaolin occurs as white clay, which is used for making high-quality china and pottery. Gypsum, a soft, white mineral, is used to make wallboard, cement, and stucco. Corundum, the second hardest mineral after diamond, is often used in polishing and cleaning products.

☑ *Checkpoint* *What is a gemstone? Why are gemstones valuable?*

Ores

A rock that contains a metal or economically useful mineral is called an **ore**. Unlike the copper used by the Hopewell people, most metals do not occur in a pure form. A metal usually occurs as a mineral that is a combination of that metal and other elements. Much of the world's copper, for example, comes from ores containing the mineral chalcopyrite (kal kuh PY ryt). Before metals, gemstones, and other useful minerals can be separated from their ores, however, geologists must find them.

Prospecting

A prospector is anyone who searches, or prospects, for an ore deposit. Geologists prospect for ores by looking for certain features on Earth's surface. These geologists observe what kind of rocks are on the land surface. They examine plants growing in an area and test stream water for the presence of certain chemicals.

Geologists also employ some of the tools used to study Earth's interior. In one technique, they set off explosions below ground to create shock waves. The echoes of these shock waves are used to map the location, size, and shape of an ore deposit.

Mining

The geologist's map of an ore deposit helps miners decide how to mine the ore from the ground. **There are three types of mines: strip mines, open pit mines, and shaft mines.** In strip mining,

Advances in Metal Technology

For thousands of years, people have been inventing and improving methods for smelting metals and making alloys.

4000 B.C. Cyprus

The island of Cyprus was one of the first places where copper was mined and smelted. In fact, the name of the island provided the name of the metal. In Latin, *aes cyprium* meant "metal of Cyprus." It was later shortened to *cuprum*, meaning "copper." The sculptured figure is carrying a large piece of smelted copper.

4000 B.C.	2500 B.C.	1000 B.C.

3500 B.C.
Mesopotamia

Metalworkers in Sumer, a city between the Tigris and Euphrates rivers, made an alloy of tin and copper to produce a harder metal—bronze. Bronze was poured into molds to form statues, weapons, or vessels for food and drink.

1500 B.C.
Turkey

The Hittites learned to mine and smelt iron ore. Because iron is stronger than copper or bronze, its use spread rapidly. Tools and weapons could be made of iron. This iron dagger was made in Austria several hundred years after the Hittites' discovery.

earthmoving equipment scrapes away soil to expose ore. In open pit mining, miners use giant earthmoving equipment to dig a tremendous pit. Miners dig an open pit mine to remove ore deposits that may start near the surface, but extend down for hundreds of meters. Some open pit mines are more than a kilometer wide and nearly as deep. For ore deposits that occur in veins, miners dig shaft mines. Shaft mines often have a network of tunnels that extend deep into the ground, following the veins of ore.

INTEGRATING ENVIRONMENTAL SCIENCE Mining for metals and other minerals can harm the environment. Strip mining and pit mining leave scars on the land. Waste materials from mining can pollute rivers and lakes. In the United States, laws now require that mine operators do as little damage to the environment as possible. To restore land damaged by strip mining, mine operators grade the surface and replace the soil.

In Your Journal

When people discover how to use metals in a new way, the discovery often produces big changes in the way those people live. Choose a development in the history of metals to research. Write a diary entry telling how the discovery happened and how it changed people's lives.

A.D. 1860s
England

Steel-making techniques invented by Henry Bessemer and William Siemens made it possible to produce steel cheaply on a large scale. Siemens' invention, the open-hearth furnace, is still widely used, although more modern methods account for most steel production today.

A.D. 500

A.D. 2000

A.D. 600s
Sri Lanka

Sri Lankans made steel in outdoor furnaces. Steady winds blowing over the top of the furnace's front wall created the high temperatures needed to make steel. Because their steel was so much harder than iron, the Sri Lankans were able to trade it throughout the Indian Ocean region.

A.D. 1960s TO THE PRESENT
United States

Scientists working on the space program have developed light and strong alloys for use in products ranging from bicycles to soda cans. For example, a new alloy of nickel and titanium can "remember" its shape. It is used for eyeglasses that return to their original shape after being bent.

Smelting

Ores must be processed before the metals they contain can be used. **After miners remove ore from a mine, smelting is necessary to remove the metal from the ore.** In the process of **smelting,** an ore is melted to separate the useful metal from other elements the ore contains. People around the world have used smelting to obtain metals from ores. The time line in *Science and History* on the previous two pages describes how this technology has developed over time.

How does smelting separate iron metal from hematite, a common form of iron ore? In general, smelting involves mixing an ore with other substances and then heating the mixture to a very high temperature. The heat melts the metal in the ore. The heat also causes the metal to separate from the oxygen with which it is combined. Metalworkers can then pour off the molten metal. Follow the steps in *Exploring Smelting Iron Ore.*

After smelting, additional processing is needed to remove impurities from the iron. The result is steel, which is harder and stronger than iron. Steel is an **alloy,** a solid mixture of two or more metals. Steelmakers mix iron with other elements to create alloys with special properties. For stronger steel, the metal manganese and a small amount of carbon are added. For rust-resistant steel, the metals chromium and nickel are added. You can compare plain steel with rust-resistant stainless steel in Figure 18.

Figure 18 Plain steel rusts easily. But stainless steel—an alloy of iron, chromium, and nickel—doesn't rust. The chromium and nickel slow down the process by which the oxygen in the air combines with iron in the steel to form iron oxide, or rust.

Section 3 Review

1. What are some of the ways that people use gems and metals?
2. Describe three different kinds of mines.
3. What process is used to separate useful metals from ores?
4. What are alloys, and why are they useful?
5. **Thinking Critically** In smelting, what causes a metal to separate from its ore?

Science at Home

Rust Protection You can demonstrate to your family how rust damages objects that contain iron. Obtain three iron nails. Coat one of the nails with petroleum jelly and coat the second nail with clear nail polish. Do not put anything on the third nail. Place all the nails in a glass of water with a little vinegar. (The vinegar speeds up the rusting process.) Allow the nails to stand in the glass overnight. Which nails show signs of rusting? Explain these results to your family.

EXPLORING *Smelting Iron Ore*

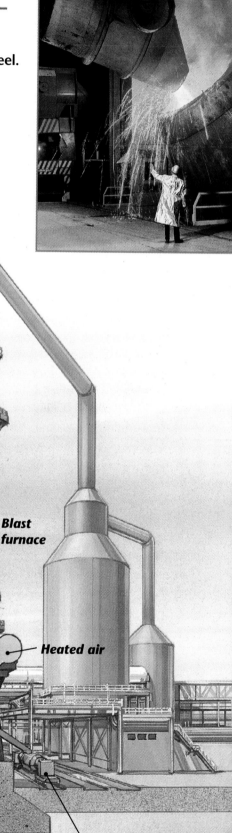

Iron usually occurs as the ores hematite or magnetite. Iron ores must be smelted to separate the iron from the oxygen and other substances in the ores. Then the iron is refined and processed into steel.

1. Iron ore is crushed and then mixed with crushed limestone and coke (baked coal), which is rich in carbon.

2. The coke and iron ore mixture is placed in a blast furnace, where extremely hot air is blown through, making the coke burn easily.

3. As the coke burns, chemical changes in the mixture produce carbon dioxide gas and molten iron.

4. The iron sinks to the bottom of the furnace. Impurities left in the ore combine with the limestone to create slag.

5. The slag and molten iron are poured off through taps in the blast furnace.

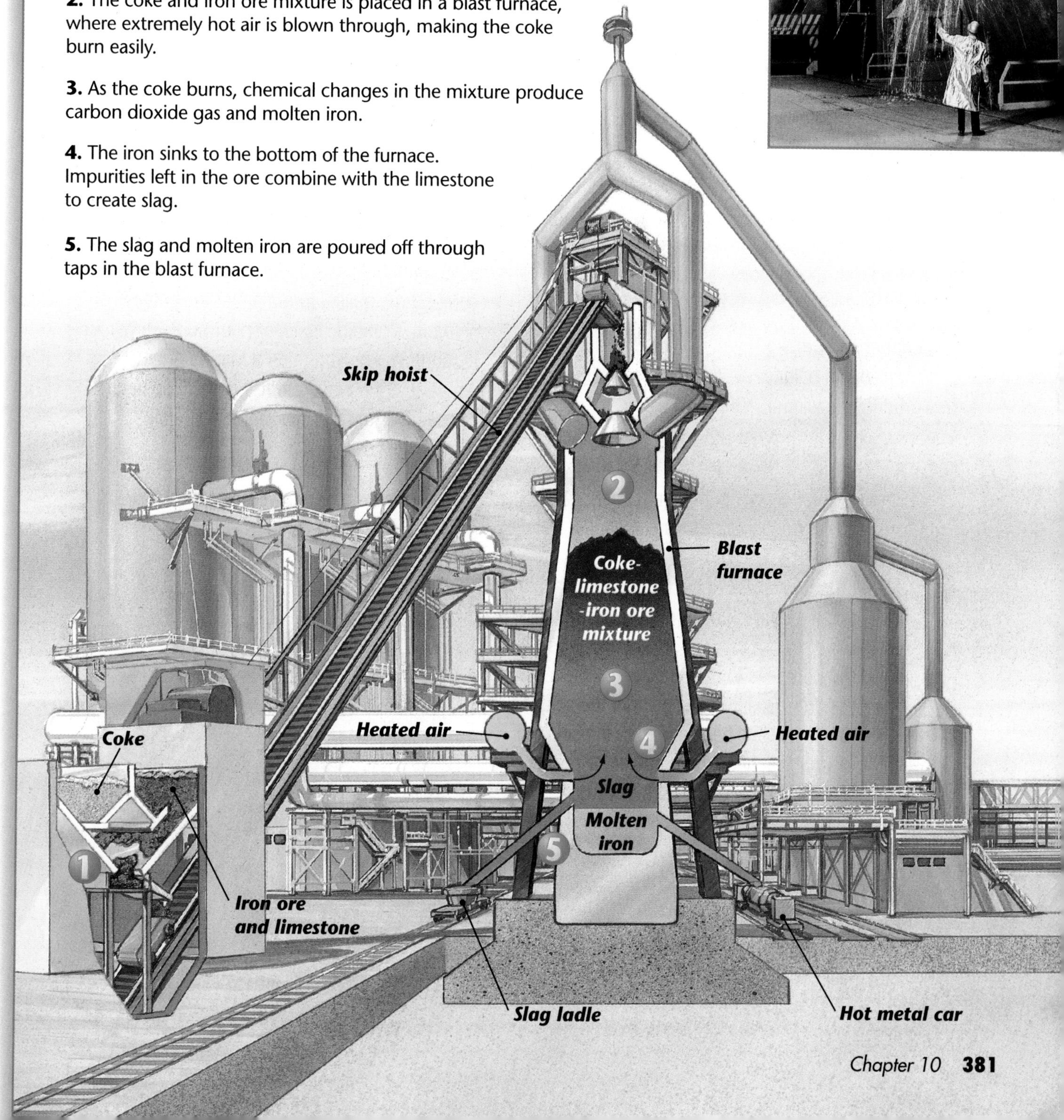

Skip hoist

2

Blast furnace

Coke-limestone-iron ore mixture

3

Heated air

4

Heated air

Coke

Slag

Molten iron

1

5

Iron ore and limestone

Slag ladle

Hot metal car

COPPER RECOVERY

If you were a mining engineer, one of your tasks would be to make mining and processing ores more efficient. When copper ore is processed at copper mines, wastewater containing copper sulfate is produced. Mining engineers have invented a way to recover copper metal from the wastewater. They make the wastewater flow over scrap iron.

Problem

How is copper recovered from a solution?

Skills Focus

observing, inferring, developing hypotheses

Materials

copper sulfate, 3 g
triple-beam balance
graduated cylinder, 100 mL
beaker, 400 mL
5 iron nails
water

Procedure

1. Place 3 g of copper sulfate in a beaker. **CAUTION:** *Copper sulfate is poisonous. Handle it with care.*
2. Add 50 mL of water to the beaker to dissolve the copper sulfate. Observe the color of the solution.
3. Add the iron nails to the beaker. The nails act as scrap iron. Describe the color of the solution after the nails have been added to the solution.
4. Follow your teacher's instructions for proper disposal. Wash your hands when you are finished.

Analyze and Conclude

1. What happened to the nails after you placed them in the solution? What is the material on the nails? Explain your answer.
2. How does the material on the nails compare with the copper sulfate?
3. Form a hypothesis that describes how a mine might recover copper from wastewater using the method that you have just tried.
4. What additional step would you have to perform to obtain copper useful for making copper wire or pennies?
5. **Apply** Why do you think the operator of a copper mine would want to collect copper from the wastewater?

Move to Explore

Repeat the experiment. This time test the solution with litmus paper both before and after you add the nails. Litmus paper indicates if a solution is acidic, basic, or neutral. Record your results. Why do you think a mining engineer would test the water from this process before releasing it into the environment?

SECTION 1 — Properties of Minerals

Key Ideas

◆ A mineral is a naturally occurring inorganic solid that has a crystal structure and a distinct chemical composition.

◆ Each mineral can be identified by its own physical and chemical properties.

◆ Some of the properties of minerals include hardness, color, streak, luster, density, cleavage and fracture, and crystal structure. Hardness is measured by the Mohs hardness scale.

◆ Minerals usually consist of two or more elements joined together in a compound.

Key Terms

mineral	Mohs hardness scale
inorganic	streak
crystal	luster
element	cleavage
compound	fracture
	fluorescence

SECTION 2 — How Minerals Form

Key Ideas

◆ Minerals form inside Earth through crystallization as magma or lava cools.

◆ Minerals form on Earth's surface when materials dissolved in water crystallize through evaporation.

◆ Mineral deposits form on the ocean floor from solutions heated by magma. The hot-water solutions containing minerals erupt through chimneys on the ocean floor, then crystallize when they come in contact with cold sea water.

Key Terms
solution
vein

SECTION 3 — Mineral Resources

INTEGRATING TECHNOLOGY

Key Ideas

◆ Minerals are useful as the source of all metals, gemstones, and of many other materials.

◆ Geologists locate ore deposits by prospecting—looking for certain features on and beneath Earth's surface.

◆ Ores can be removed from the ground through open pit mines, strip mines, or shaft mines.

◆ Smelting is the process of heating an ore to extract a metal.

Key Terms
gemstone
ore
smelting
alloy

Organizing Information

Venn Diagram Copy the Venn diagram comparing the mineral hematite and the human-made material brick onto a separate piece of paper. Then complete it and add a title. (For more on Venn diagrams, see the Skills Handbook.)

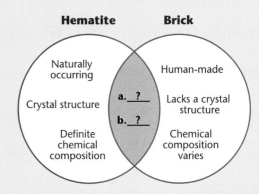

Hematite — Brick

- Naturally occurring
- Crystal structure
- Definite chemical composition
- a. __?__
- b. __?__
- Human-made
- Lacks a crystal structure
- Chemical composition varies

Reviewing Content

 Review key concepts online using iText at www.phschool.com

Multiple Choice

Choose the letter of the answer that best completes each statement.

1. In a mineral, the particles line up in a repeating pattern to form
   a. an element.   b. a crystal.
   c. a mixture.   d. a compound.
2. The softest mineral in the Mohs hardness scale is
   a. quartz.   b. talc.
   c. apatite.   d. gypsum.
3. Halite is a mineral formed by
   a. chimneys on the ocean floor.
   b. cooling of magma.
   c. evaporation.
   d. cooling of lava.
4. Metals are useful for tools because they
   a. are compounds.
   b. have a metallic luster.
   c. are hard yet can be easily shaped.
   d. are elements.
5. Minerals from which metals can be removed in usable amounts are called
   a. gemstones.
   b. crystals.
   c. alloys.
   d. ores.

True or False

If the statement is true, write true. If it is false, change the underlined word or words to make the statement true.

6. <u>Luster</u> is the term that describes how a mineral reflects light from its surface.
7. A piece of unglazed tile is used to test a mineral's <u>hardness</u>.
8. If magma cools very slowly, minerals with <u>small</u> crystals will form.
9. Minerals form from <u>hot-water solutions</u> at chimneys on the ocean floor.
10. The process of removing an ore deposit from the ground is known as <u>prospecting</u>.

Checking Concepts

11. What is the difference in composition between most minerals and a pure element?
12. How can the streak test be helpful in identifying minerals?
13. Compare cleavage and fracture.
14. Describe two different ways that minerals can form.
15. Describe the process used to extract metal from hematite ore. What metal would be obtained?
16. **Writing to Learn** You are a prospector searching for gold. In a letter home, describe where you plan to look, how you will know if you have found gold, and how you will feel about your discovery.

Thinking Critically

17. **Comparing and Contrasting** Color and luster are both properties of minerals. How are these properties similar? How are they different? How can each be used to help identify a mineral?
18. **Classifying** Obsidian forms when magma cools very quickly, creating a type of glass. In glass, the particles are not arranged in an orderly pattern as in a crystal. Obsidian is a solid, inorganic substance that occurs naturally in volcanic areas. Should it be classified as a mineral? Explain why or why not.
19. **Relating Cause and Effect** Describe how a vein of ore forms underground. What is the energy source for this process?
20. **Applying Concepts** Explain the roles of elements, solutions, and compounds in the process that forms minerals around chimneys on the ocean floor.
21. **Predicting** What would happen if steelmakers forgot to add enough chromium and nickel to a batch of stainless steel?

Applying Skills

Working as a geologist, you have found a sample of the mineral wulfenite. Testing the wulfenite reveals that it has a hardness of about 3 on the Mohs hardness scale and a density of 6.8 grams per cubic centimeter. You also determine that the mineral contains oxygen as well as the metals lead and molybdenum.

Wulfenite

22. Observing Describe wulfenite's color, luster, and crystal structure.

23. Inferring Did the wulfenite form slowly or quickly? Explain your answer.

24. Drawing Conclusions Is wulfenite hard enough for use as a gem? What would you use these crystals for? Explain.

Performance ▽ Assessment

CHAPTER PROJECT

Present Your Project Before you present your crystal garden to the class, share it with a classmate. Can your classmate identify which solution created which crystals? Do your data show differences in crystal growth rates? What conclusions can you draw from your data? Now you are ready to present your project to your class.

Reflect and Record In your journal, identify any changes that would improve your crystal garden. Which materials worked best for crystals to grow on? Which ones did not work well?

Test Preparation

Use these questions to prepare for standardized tests.

Study the table. Then answer Questions 25–29.

Properties of Six Minerals				
Mineral	Hardness	Density (g/cm³)	Luster	Streak
Corundum	9.0	4.0	glassy	white
Quartz	7.0	2.6	glassy	white
Magnetite	6.0	5.2	metallic	black
Copper	2.8	8.9	metallic	red
Galena	2.5	7.5	metallic	lead gray
Talc	1.0	2.8	pearly	white

25. Which mineral in the table could be scratched by all the others?
A quartz   **B** galena
C copper   **D** talc

26. The mineral in the table with the greatest density is
F copper.   **G** galena.
H magnetite.   **J** talc.

27. To be suitable as a gemstone, a mineral usually must be very hard and have a glassy luster. Which mineral on the list would probably make the best gemstone?
A copper   **B** corundum
C magnetite   **D** galena

28. Quartz and talc both produce a white streak and have similar density. What property or properties could you easily test to tell them apart?
F hardness and luster
G streak only
H density only
J none of the above

29. Suppose that you have found a dense, dark-colored mineral with a metallic luster. What property would you test quickly and easily to determine if the mineral were copper rather than galena?
A hardness   **B** luster
C streak   **D** density

 WEB ACTIVITY

www.phschool.com

Hikers cross a landscape
of rock in the Cascade
Range, a mountain range
in Washington state.

CHAPTER 11 PROJECT

Collecting Rocks

E ach rock, whether a small pebble or a giant boulder, tells a story. By observing a rock's characteristics, geologists learn about the forces that shaped the portion of Earth's crust where the rock formed. The rocks in your own community tell the story of Earth's crust in your area.

In this chapter, you will learn how three different types of rocks form. You can apply what you learn about rocks to create your own rock collection and explore the properties of these rocks.

Your Goal To make a collection of the rocks in your area.

To complete this project, you must

◆ collect samples of rocks, keeping a record of where you found each sample
◆ describe the characteristics of your rocks, including their color, texture, and density
◆ classify each rock as igneous, sedimentary, or metamorphic
◆ create a display for your rock collection
◆ follow the safety guidelines in Appendix A

Get Started With your classmates and teacher, brainstorm locations in your community where rocks are likely to be found. Are there road cuts, outcroppings of bedrock, riverbanks, or beaches where you could safely and legally collect your rocks?

Check Your Progress You will be working on this project as you study the chapter. To keep your project on track, look for Check Your Progress boxes at the following points.

Section 1 Review, page 391: Plan your rock-hunting expeditions.
Section 2 Review, page 395: Collect your rocks.
Section 3 Review, page 401: Begin to describe, test, and catalog your rock collection.
Section 5 Review, page 409: Classify your rocks and plan your presentation.

Present Your Project At the end of the chapter (page 413), prepare a display of your rock collection. Be prepared to discuss the properties of the rocks you collected, how the rocks formed, and how people can use them.

TEKS

In addition to process TEKS, this chapter addresses these concept TEKS as they relate to the chapter's topics.

(8.12) The student knows that cycles exist in Earth systems.
The student is expected to:
(A) analyze and predict the sequence of events in the lunar and rock cycles.

SECTION 1 Classifying Rocks

...

DISCOVER ········· ········· ACTIVITY

How Are Rocks Alike and Different?

1. Look at samples of marble and conglomerate with a hand lens.

2. Describe the two rocks. What is the color and texture of each?

3. Try scratching the surface of each rock with the edge of a penny. Which rock seems harder?

4. Hold each rock in your hand. Allowing for the fact that the samples aren't exactly the same size, which rock seems denser?

Think It Over

Observing Based on your observations, how would you compare the physical properties of marble and conglomerate?

GUIDE FOR READING

◆ What characteristics are used to identify rocks?

◆ What are the three major groups of rocks?

Reading Tip Before you read, use the headings to make an outline about rocks. Then fill in details as you read.

Key Terms texture
• grains • igneous rock
• sedimentary rock
• metamorphic rock

Figure 1 Geology students collect and study samples of rocks.

Between 1969 and 1972, the Apollo missions to the moon returned to Earth with pieces of the moon's surface. Space scientists eagerly tested these samples. They wanted to learn what the moon is made of. They found that the moon's surface is made of material very similar to the material that makes up Earth's surface—rock. Some moon samples are dark rock called basalt. Other samples are light-colored rock made mostly of the mineral feldspar.

How Geologists Classify Rocks

For both Earth and its moon, rocks are important building blocks. On Earth, rock forms mountains, hills, valleys, beaches, even the ocean floor. Earth's crust is made of rock. Rocks are made of mixtures of minerals and other materials, although some rocks may contain only a single mineral. Granite, which is shown in Figure 2, is made up of the minerals quartz, feldspar, mica, and hornblende, and sometimes other minerals.

Geologists collect and study samples of rock in order to classify them. Imagine that you are a geologist exploring a mountain range for the first time. How would you study a particular rock found in these mountains?

Figure 2 Granite is made up of quartz, mica, feldspar, and hornblende. It may also contain other minerals. *Observing* Which mineral seems most abundant in the sample of granite shown?

You might use a camera or notebook to record information about the setting where the rock was found. (In classifying a rock, it's important for a geologist to know what other types of rock occur nearby). Then, you would use a chisel or the sharp end of a rock hammer to remove samples of the rock. Finally, you would break open the samples with a hammer to examine their inside surfaces. You must look at the inside of a rock because the effects of water and weather can change the outer surface of a rock.

When studying a rock sample, geologists observe the rock's color and texture and determine its mineral composition. Using these characteristics, geologists can classify a rock according to its origin, or where and how it formed.

Texture

As with minerals, color alone does not provide enough information to identify a rock. A rock's texture, however, is very useful in identifying the rock. To a geologist, a rock's **texture** is the look and feel of the rock's surface. Some rocks are smooth and glassy. Others are rough or chalky. Most rocks are made up of particles of minerals or other rocks, which geologists call **grains.** A rock's grains give the rock its texture. To describe a rock's texture, geologists use a number of terms based on the size, shape, and pattern of the rock's grains.

Figure 3 Texture helps geologists classify rocks. *Forming Operational Definitions* Looking at the rocks below, describe the characteristics of a rock that help you to define what a rock's "grain" is.

Fine-grained
Slate

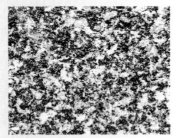

Coarse-grained
Diorite

No visible grain
Flint

Grain Size Often, the grains in a rock are large and easy to see. Such rocks are said to be coarse-grained. In other rocks, the grains are so small that they can only be seen with a microscope. These rocks are said to be fine-grained. Notice the difference in texture between the fine-grained slate and the coarse-grained diorite at left.

Grain Shape The grains in a rock vary widely in shape. Some grains look like tiny particles of fine sand. Others look like small seeds or exploding stars. In some rocks, such as granite, the grain results from the shapes of the crystals that form the rock. In other rocks, the grain shape results from fragments of other rock. These fragments can be smooth and rounded, like the fragments in conglomerate, or they can be jagged, like the fragments in breccia. You can compare examples of conglomerate and breccia below.

Grain Pattern The grains in a rock often form patterns. Some grains lie in flat layers that look like a stack of pancakes. Other grains form wavy, swirling patterns. Some rocks have grains that look like rows of multicolored beads, as in the sample of gneiss shown below. Other rocks, in contrast, have grains that occur randomly throughout the rock.

No Visible Grain Some rocks have no grain, even when they are examined under a microscope. Some of these rocks have no crystal grains because when they form, they cool very quickly. This quick cooling gives these rocks the smooth, shiny texture of a thick piece of glass. Other rocks with no visible grain are made up of extremely small particles of silica that settle out of water. One familiar rock that forms in this manner is flint.

✓ *Checkpoint* *What terms describe a rock's texture?*

Jagged grain
Breccia

Rounded grain
Conglomerate

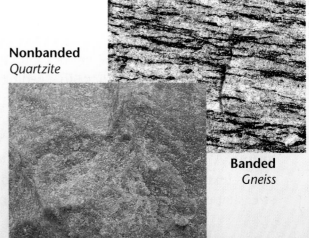

Nonbanded
Quartzite

Banded
Gneiss

Mineral Composition

Often, geologists must look more closely at a rock to determine its mineral composition. By looking at a small sliver of a rock under a microscope, a geologist can observe the shape and size of crystals in the rock and identify the minerals it contains. To prepare a rock for viewing under the microscope, geologists cut the rock very thin, so that light can shine through its crystals.

In identifying rocks, geologists also use some of the tests that are used to identify minerals. For example, testing the rock's surface with acid determines whether the rock includes minerals made of compounds called carbonates. Testing with a magnet detects the elements iron or nickel.

Origin

There are three major groups of rocks: igneous rock, sedimentary rock, and metamorphic rock. These terms refer to how the rocks in each group formed.

Rock belonging to each of these groups forms in a different way. **Igneous rock** forms from the cooling of molten rock—either magma below the surface or lava at the surface. Most **sedimentary rock** forms when particles of other rocks or the remains of plants and animals are pressed and cemented together. Sedimentary rock forms in layers below the surface. **Metamorphic rock** is formed when an existing rock is changed by heat, pressure, or chemical reactions. Most metamorphic rock forms deep underground.

Figure 4 A scientist is preparing to cut a thin slice from a piece of moon rock. He will then examine it under a microscope to determine its composition.

Section 1 Review

1. What three characteristics do geologists use to identify a rock sample?
2. What are the three groups into which geologists classify rocks?
3. What is meant by the *texture* of a rock?
4. What methods do geologists use to determine the mineral composition of a rock?
5. **Thinking Critically Comparing and Contrasting** What do the three major groups of rocks have in common? How are they different?

CHAPTER PROJECT

Check Your Progress
Your neighborhood might be a good place to begin your rock collection. Look for gravel and crushed rock in flower beds, driveways or parking lots, and beneath downspouts. **CAUTION:** *If the area you choose is not a public place, make sure that you have permission to be there.* Begin to collect samples of rocks with different colors and textures. Plan with your teacher or an adult family member to visit other parts of your community where you could collect rocks.

② Igneous Rocks

How Do Igneous Rocks Form?

1. Use a hand lens to examine samples of granite and obsidian.

2. Describe the texture of both rocks using the terms coarse, fine, or glassy.

3. Which rock has coarse-grained crystals? Which rock has no crystals or grains?

Think It Over

Inferring Granite and obsidian are igneous rocks. Given the physical properties of these rocks, what can you infer about how each type of rock formed?

GUIDE FOR READING

◆ What characteristics are used to classify igneous rocks?

Reading Tip As you read, make a list of the characteristics of igneous rocks. Write one sentence describing each characteristic.

Key Terms extrusive rock
• intrusive rock
• porphyritic texture

Figure 5 A lava flow soon cools and hardens to form igneous rock.

You are in a spacecraft orbiting Earth 4.6 billion years ago. Do you see the blue and green globe of Earth that astronauts today see from space? No—instead, Earth looks like a glowing piece of charcoal from a barbecue, or a charred and bubbling marshmallow heated over the coals.

Soon after Earth formed, the planet became so hot that its surface was a glowing mass of molten material. Hundreds of millions of years passed before Earth cooled enough for a crust to solidify. Then lava probably flowed from Earth's interior, spread over the surface, and hardened. The movement of magma and lava has continued ever since.

Characteristics of Igneous Rock

The first rocks to form on Earth probably looked much like the igneous rocks that harden from lava today. Igneous rock (IG nee us) is any rock that forms from magma or lava. The name "igneous" comes from the Latin word *ignis*, meaning "fire."

Most igneous rocks are made of mineral crystals. The only exceptions to this rule are the different types of volcanic glass—igneous rock that lacks minerals with a crystal structure. **Igneous rocks are classified according to their origin, texture, and mineral composition.**

Origin Geologists classify igneous rocks according to where they formed. **Extrusive rock** is igneous rock formed from lava that erupted onto Earth's surface. Basalt is the most common extrusive rock. Basalt forms much of the crust, including the oceanic crust, shield volcanoes, and lava plateaus.

Igneous rock that formed when magma hardened beneath Earth's surface is called **intrusive rock.** Granite is the most abundant intrusive rock in continental crust. Granite forms the core of many mountain ranges.

Texture The texture of an igneous rock depends on the size and shape of its mineral crystals. Igneous rocks may be similar in mineral composition and yet have very different textures. The texture of an igneous rock may be fine-grained, coarse-grained, glassy, or porphyritic. Rapid cooling lava forms fine-grained igneous rocks with small crystals. Slow cooling magma forms coarse-grained rock with large crystals.

Intrusive and extrusive rocks usually have different textures. Intrusive rocks have larger crystals than extrusive rocks. If you examine a coarse-grained rock such as granite, you can easily see that the crystals vary in size and color.

Some intrusive rocks have a texture that looks like a gelatin dessert with chopped-up fruit mixed in. A rock with large crystals scattered on a background of much smaller crystals has a **porphyritic texture** (pawr fuh RIT ik).

Figure 6 Igneous rocks can vary greatly in texture.
A. Rhyolite is a fine-grained igneous rock with a mineral composition similar to granite.
B. Pegmatite is a very coarse-grained variety of granite.
C. Porphyry has large crystals surrounded by fine-grained crystals.
Relating Cause and Effect What conditions caused rhyolite to have a fine-grained texture?

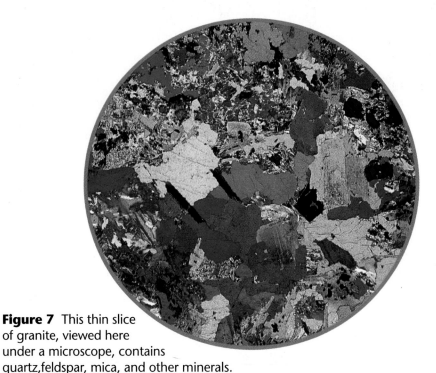
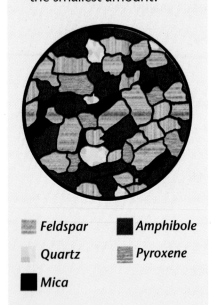
How can a rock have two textures? Porphyritic rocks form when intrusive rocks cool in two stages. As the magma begins to cool, large crystals form slowly. The remaining magma, however, cools more quickly, forming small crystals. The change in the rate of cooling may occur as magma moves nearer to the surface.

Extrusive rocks have a fine-grained or glassy texture. Basalt is an extrusive rock. It consists of crystals too small to be seen without a microscope.

Mineral Composition Recall from Chapter 3 that the silica content of magma and lava affects how easily the magma or lava will flow. Lava that is low in silica usually forms dark-colored rocks such as basalt. Basalt contains feldspar as well as certain dark-colored minerals, but does not contain quartz.

INTEGRATING CHEMISTRY Magma that is high in silica usually forms light-colored rocks, such as granite. However, granite comes in many shades and colors. Granite can be dark to light gray, red, and pink. Granite's color changes along with its mineral composition. Granite that is rich in reddish feldspar is a speckled pink. But granite rich in hornblende and dark mica is light gray with dark specks. Quartz crystals in granite add light gray or smoky specks. Geologists can make thin slices of granite and study each type of crystal in the rock to determine its mineral composition more exactly.

☑ *Checkpoint* *How do igneous rocks differ in origin, texture, and mineral composition?*

Uses of Igneous Rocks

Many igneous rocks are hard, dense, and durable. For this reason, people throughout history have used igneous rock for tools and building materials. For example, ancient Native Americans used obsidian for making very sharp tools for cutting and scraping.

Granite, one of the most abundant igneous rocks, has a long history as a building material. More than 3,500 years ago, the ancient Egyptians used granite for statues like the one shown in Figure 8. About 600 years ago, the Incas of Peru carefully fitted together great blocks of granite and other igneous rocks to build a fortress near Cuzco, their capital city. In the United States during the 1800s and early 1900s, granite was widely used to build bridges and public buildings and for paving streets with cobblestones. Thin, polished sheets of granite are still used in decorative stonework, curbstones, and floors.

Igneous rocks such as basalt, pumice, and obsidian also have important uses. Basalt is crushed to make gravel that is used in construction. The rough surface of pumice makes it a good abrasive for cleaning and polishing. Perlite, formed from the heating of obsidian, is often mixed with soil for starting vegetable seeds.

Figure 8 The ancient Egyptians valued granite for its durability. These statues at a temple in Luxor, Egypt, were carved in granite.

Section 2 Review

1. What are the three major characteristics that geologists use to identify igneous rocks?
2. What is the difference between extrusive and intrusive rocks? Give an example of each.
3. Explain what causes an igneous rock to have a fine-grained or coarse-grained texture.
4. Why are some igneous rocks dark and others light?
5. **Thinking Critically Comparing and Contrasting** How are basalt and granite different in their origin, texture, and mineral composition? How are they similar?

CHAPTER PROJECT

Check Your Progress

With an adult, visit an area where you can collect samples of rocks. As you collect your samples, observe whether the rock is loose on the ground, broken off a ledge, or in a stream. Begin to classify your rocks into groups. Do any of your rocks consist of a single mineral? Do you recognize any of the minerals in these rocks? Notice the texture of each rock. Did you find any rocks made of pieces of other rocks?

SECTION 3 Sedimentary Rocks

GUIDE FOR READING

◆ How do sedimentary rocks form?

◆ What are the three major types of sedimentary rocks?

Reading Tip Before you read, preview the headings in the section and predict how you think sedimentary rocks form.

Key Terms sediment
• erosion • deposition
• compaction • cementation
• clastic rock • organic rock
• chemical rock • coral reef
• atoll

isitors to Arches National Park in Utah see some of the strangest scenery on Earth. The park contains dozens of natural arches sculpted out of colorful rock and layered like a birthday cake. The layers of these "cakes" are red, orange, pink, or tan. One arch, named Landscape Arch, is nearly 90 meters across and about 30 meters high. Delicate Arch looks like the legs of a striding giant. The forces that wear away rock on Earth's surface have been carving these arches out of solid rock for 100 million years. The arches are made of sandstone, one of the most common sedimentary rocks.

From Sediment to Rock

Sedimentary rocks form from particles deposited by water and wind. If you have ever walked along a stream or beach, you may have noticed tiny sand grains, mud, and pebbles. These are some of the sediments that form sedimentary rock. **Sediment** is small, solid pieces of material that come from rocks or living things. Water, wind, and ice can carry sediment and deposit it in layers. But what turns these sediments into solid rock?

◀ Delicate Arch, Arches National Park, Utah

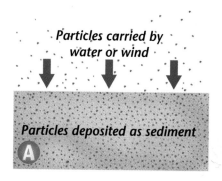

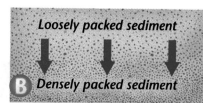

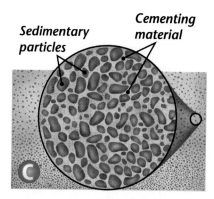

Figure 9 Sedimentary rocks form through the deposition, compaction, and cementation of sediments. **A.** Water or wind deposits sediment. **B.** The heavy sediments press down on the layers beneath. **C.** Dissolved minerals flow between the particles and cement them together.
Relating Cause and Effect What conditions are necessary for sedimentary rock to form?

Erosion Destructive forces are constantly breaking up and wearing away all the rocks on Earth's surface. These forces include heat and cold, rain, waves, and grinding ice. **Erosion** occurs when running water or wind loosen and carry away the fragments of rock.

Deposition Eventually, the moving water or wind slows and deposits the sediment. If water is carrying the sediment, rock fragments and other materials sink to the bottom of a lake or ocean. **Deposition** is the process by which sediment settles out of the water or wind carrying it. **After sediment has been deposited, the processes of compaction and cementation change the sediment into sedimentary rock.**

In addition to particles of rock, sediment may include shells, bones, leaves, stems, and other remains of living things. Over time, any remains of living things in the sediment may slowly harden and change into fossils trapped in the rock.

Compaction At first the sediments fit together loosely. But gradually, over millions of years, thick layers of sediment build up. These layers are heavy and press down on the layers beneath them. Then compaction occurs. **Compaction** is the process that presses sediments together. Year after year more sediment falls on top, creating new layers. The weight of the layers further compacts the sediments, squeezing them tightly together. The layers often remain visible in the sedimentary rock.

Cementation While compaction is taking place, the minerals in the rock slowly dissolve in the water. The dissolved minerals seep into the spaces between particles of sediment. **Cementation** is the process in which dissolved minerals crystallize and glue particles of sediment together. It often takes millions of years for compaction and cementation to transform loose sediments into solid sedimentary rock.

☑ *Checkpoint* *What are the processes that change sediment to sedimentary rock?*

Rock Absorber

Find out if water can soak into rock.

1. Using a hand lens, observe samples of sandstone and shale. How are they alike? How are they different?

2. Use a balance to measure the mass of each rock.

3. Place the rocks in a pan of water. Observe the samples. Which sample has bubbles escaping? Predict which sample will gain mass.

4. Leave the rocks submerged in the pan overnight.

5. The next day, remove the rocks from the pan and find the mass of each rock.

Drawing Conclusions How did the masses of the two rocks change after soaking? What can you conclude about each rock based on your observations?

Types of Sedimentary Rock

Geologists classify sedimentary rocks according to the type of sediments that make up the rock. **There are three major groups of sedimentary rocks: clastic rocks, organic rocks, and chemical rocks.** Different processes form each of these types of sedimentary rocks.

Clastic Rocks

Most sedimentary rocks are made up of the broken pieces of other rocks. A **clastic rock** is a sedimentary rock that forms when rock fragments are squeezed together. These fragments can range in size from clay particles too small to be seen without a microscope to large boulders too heavy for you to lift. Clastic rocks are grouped by the size of the rock fragments, or particles, of which they are made.

Shale One common clastic rock is shale. Shale forms from tiny particles of clay. For shale to form, water must deposit clay particles in very thin, flat layers, one on top of another. No cementation is needed to hold clay particles together. Even so, the spaces between the particles in the resulting shale are so small that water cannot pass through them. Shale feels smooth, and splits easily into flat pieces.

Sandstone Sandstone forms from the sand on beaches, on the ocean floor, in riverbeds, and in sand dunes. Sandstone is a clastic rock formed from the compaction and cementation of small particles of sand. Most sand particles consist of quartz. Because the cementation process does not fill all the spaces between sand grains, sandstone contains many small holes. Sandstone can easily absorb water through these holes.

Conglomerate and Breccia Some sedimentary rocks contain a mixture of rock fragments of different sizes. The fragments can range in size from sand and pebbles to boulders. If the fragments have rounded edges, they form a clastic rock called conglomerate. A rock made up of large fragments with sharp edges is called breccia (BRECH ee uh).

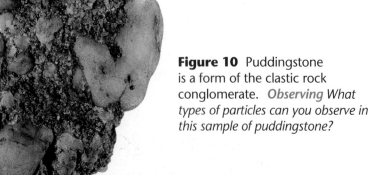

Figure 10 Puddingstone is a form of the clastic rock conglomerate. *Observing What types of particles can you observe in this sample of puddingstone?*

Organic Rocks

INTEGRATING LIFE SCIENCE Not all sedimentary rocks are made from particles of other rocks. **Organic rock** forms where the remains of plants and animals are deposited in thick layers. The term "organic" refers to substances that once were part of living things or were made by living things. Two important organic sedimentary rocks are coal and limestone.

Coal Coal forms from the remains of swamp plants buried in water. As layer upon layer of plant remains build up, the weight of the layers squeezes the decaying plants. Over millions of years, they slowly change into coal.

Limestone The hard shells of living things produce some kinds of limestone. How does limestone form? In the ocean, many living things, including coral, clams, oysters, and snails, have shells or skeletons made of calcite. When these animals die, their shells pile up as sediment on the ocean floor. Over millions of years, these layers of sediment can grow to a depth of hundreds of meters. Slowly, the pressure of overlying layers compacts the sediment. Some of the shells dissolve, forming a solution of calcite that seeps into the spaces between the shell fragments. Later, the dissolved material comes out of solution, forming calcite. The calcite cements the shell particles together, forming limestone.

Everyone knows one type of limestone: chalk. Chalk forms from sediments made of the skeletons of microscopic living things found in the oceans.

☑ *Checkpoint* *What are two important organic sedimentary rocks?*

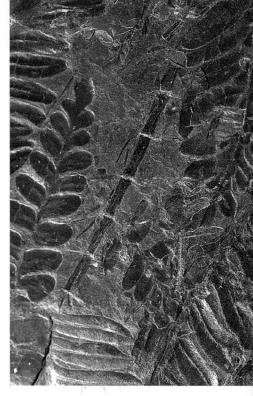

Figure 11 When broken apart, a piece of shale from a coal mine may reveal the impression of an ancient plant. Geologists estimate that it takes about 20 meters of decayed plants to form a layer of coal about one meter thick.

Figure 12 These limestone cliffs are along the Eleven Point River in Missouri.

Figure 13 These rock "towers" in Mono Lake, California, are made of tufa, a type of limestone. Tufa forms from solutions containing dissolved minerals. *Classifying What type of sedimentary rock is tufa?*

Chemical Rocks

Chemical rock forms when minerals that are dissolved in a solution crystallize. For example, limestone can form when calcite that is dissolved in lakes, seas, or underground water comes out of solution and forms crystals. This kind of limestone is considered a chemical rock.

Chemical rocks can also form from mineral deposits left when seas or lakes evaporate. Rock salt is a chemical rock made of the mineral halite, which forms by evaporation. Gypsum is another chemical rock formed by evaporation. Large deposits of rocks formed by evaporation form only in dry climates.

Limestone Deposits From Coral Reefs

Coral animals are tiny relatives of jellyfish that live together in vast numbers. They produce skeletons that grow together to form a structure called a **coral reef.** Coral reefs form only in the warm, shallow water of tropical oceans.

Coral animals absorb the element calcium from the ocean water. The calcium is then changed into calcite and forms their skeletons. When coral animals die, their skeletons remain, and more corals build on top of them. Over thousands of years, reefs may grow to be hundreds of kilometers long and hundreds of meters thick. Reefs usually grow outward toward the open ocean. If the sea level rises or if the sea floor sinks, the reef will grow upward, too.

There are three types of coral reefs: fringing reefs, barrier reefs and atolls. Fringing reefs lie close to shore, separated from land by

Figure 14 The island of Bora Bora in the south Pacific Ocean is ringed by a fringing reef. Someday, erosion will wear away the island, leaving an atoll.

shallow water. Barrier reefs lie farther out, at least 10 kilometers from the land. The Great Barrier Reef that stretches 2,000 kilometers along the coast of Australia is a barrier reef. An **atoll** is a ring-shaped coral island found far from land. An atoll develops when coral grows on top of a volcanic island that has sunk beneath the ocean's surface. How can a volcanic island sink? As the oceanic crust moves away from the mid-ocean ridge, it cools and becomes more dense. This causes the sea floor to sink.

A coral reef is really organic limestone. Like modern-day coral animals, ancient coral animals thrived in warm, tropical oceans. Their limestone fossils are among the most common fossils on Earth. Limestone that began as coral can be found on continents in places where uplift has raised ancient sea floors above sea level.

In parts of the United States, reefs that formed under water millions of years ago now make up part of the land. The movement of Earth's plates slowly uplifted the ocean floor where these reefs grew until the ocean floor became dry land. There are exposed reefs in Wisconsin, Illinois, and Indiana, as well as in Texas, New Mexico, and many other places.

Figure 15 A striking band of white rock tops El Capitan Peak in the Guadalupe Mountains of Texas. This massive layer of limestone formed from coral reefs that grew in a warm, shallow sea more than 250 million years ago.

Uses of Sedimentary Rocks

For thousands of years, people have used sandstone and limestone as building materials. Both types of stone are soft enough to be easily cut into blocks or slabs. You may be surprised to learn that the White House in Washington, D.C., is built of sandstone. Builders today use sandstone and limestone for decorating or for covering the outside walls of buildings.

Limestone also has many industrial uses. Recall from Chapter 10 that limestone is important in smelting iron ore. Limestone is also used in making cement.

Section 3 Review

1. Once sediment has been deposited, what processes change it into sedimentary rock?
2. What are the three major kinds of sedimentary rocks?
3. Describe two ways in which limestone can form.
4. Explain how coral reefs form.
5. **Thinking Critically Comparing and Contrasting** Compare and contrast shale and sandstone. Include what they are made of and how they form.

Check Your Progress

CHAPTER PROJECT

Begin to make an information card for each of your rocks, and decide how to store the rocks. Each rock's card should include the following information: where and when the rock was found; the type of geologic feature where you found the rock; a description of the rock's texture; a description of the minerals that make up the rock; and the results of any tests you performed on the rock. Are any of your rocks organic rocks? How could you tell?

DISCOVER ·································· ACTIVITY···

How Do the Grain Patterns of Gneiss and Granite Compare?

1. Using a hand lens, observe samples of gneiss and granite. Look carefully at the grains or crystals in both rocks.

2. Observe how the grains or crystals are arranged in both rocks. Draw a sketch of both rocks and describe their textures.

Think It Over
Inferring Within the crust, some granite becomes gneiss. What do you think must happen to cause this change?

GUIDE FOR READING

◆ Under what conditions do metamorphic rocks form?

◆ How do geologists classify metamorphic rocks?

Reading Tip Before you read, rewrite the headings in the section as questions. As you read, look for answers to those questions.

Key Term foliated

Every metamorphic rock is a rock that has changed its form. In fact, the word *metamorphic* comes from the Greek words *meta*, meaning "change," and *morphosis*, meaning "form." But what causes a rock to change into metamorphic rock? The answer lies inside Earth.

How Metamorphic Rocks Form

Heat and pressure deep beneath Earth's surface can change any rock into metamorphic rock. When rock changes into metamorphic rock, its appearance, texture, crystal structure, and mineral content change. Metamorphic rock can form out of igneous, sedimentary, or other metamorphic rock.

Collisions between Earth's plates can push the rock down toward the heat of the mantle. Pockets of magma rising through the crust also provide heat that can produce metamorphic rocks.

The deeper rock is buried in the crust, the greater the pressure on that rock. Under pressure hundreds or thousands of times greater than at Earth's surface, the minerals in a rock can change into other minerals. The rock has become a metamorphic rock.

Figure 16 Great heat and pressure can change one type of rock into another. Granite becomes gneiss, shale becomes slate, and sandstone changes to quartzite. *Observing* How does quartzite differ from sandstone?

Granite   *Gneiss*

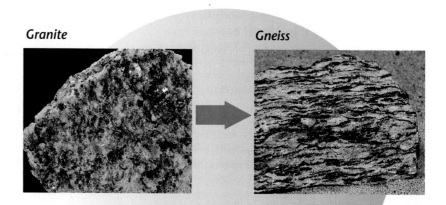

Classifying Metamorphic Rocks

While metamorphic rocks are forming, high temperatures change the size and shape of the grains, or mineral crystals, in the rock. In addition, tremendous pressure squeezes rock so tightly that the mineral grains may line up in flat, parallel layers. **Geologists classify metamorphic rocks by the arrangement of the grains that make up the rocks.**

Metamorphic rocks that have their grains arranged in parallel layers or bands are said to be **foliated.** The term *foliated* comes from the Latin word for "leaf." It describes the thin, flat layering found in most metamorphic rocks. Foliated rocks—including slate, schist, and gneiss—may split apart along these bands. In Figure 16, notice how the crystals in granite have been flattened to create the foliated texture of gneiss.

One common foliated rock is slate. Heat and pressure change the sedimentary rock shale into slate. Slate is basically a denser, more compact version of shale. During the change, new minerals such as mica and hornblende form in the slate.

Sometimes metamorphic rocks are nonfoliated. The mineral grains in these rocks are arranged randomly. Metamorphic rocks that are nonfoliated do not split into layers. Marble and quartzite both have a nonfoliated texture. Quartzite forms out of sandstone. The weakly cemented quartz particles in the sandstone recrystallize to form quartzite, which is extremely hard. Notice in Figure 16 how much smoother quartzite looks than sandstone.

☑ *Checkpoint* **What is a foliated rock?**

A Sequined Rock

1. Make three balls of clay about 3 cm in diameter. Gently mix about 25 sequins into one ball. **ACTIVITY**

2. Use a 30-cm piece of string to cut the ball in half. How are the sequins arranged?

3. Roll the clay with the sequins back into a ball. Stack the three balls with the sequin ball in the middle. Set these on a block of wood. With another block of wood, press slowly down until the stack is about 3 cm high.

4. Use the string to cut the stack in half. Observe the arrangement of the sequins.

Making Models What do the sequins in your model rock represent? Is this rock foliated or nonfoliated?

Shale

Slate

Sandstone

Quartzite

Figure 17 The pure white marble for the Taj Mahal came from a quarry 300 kilometers away. It took 20,000 workers more than 20 years to build the Taj Mahal.

Visual Arts
CONNECTION

The architect of the Taj Mahal used symmetry and repetition to design a beautiful building. Notice how the left side mirrors the right side, creating balance. Also notice how different parts of the building, such as domes, arches, and minarets (towers), are repeated. Repetition of these shapes creates rhythms as you look at the building.

In Your Journal

On your computer, write a letter to a friend describing what you feel walking toward the Taj Mahal. Explain how the building's symmetry and other features help to create this effect.

Uses of Metamorphic Rock

Marble and slate are two of the most useful metamorphic rocks. Marble usually forms when limestone is subjected to heat and pressure deep beneath the surface. Because marble has a fine, even grain, it is relatively easy to cut into thin slabs. And marble can be easily polished. These qualities have led architects and sculptors to use marble for many buildings and statues. For example, one of the most beautiful buildings in the world is the Taj Mahal in Agra, India. An emperor of India had the Taj Mahal built during the 1600s as a memorial to his wife, who had died in childbirth. The Taj Mahal, shown in Figure 17, is made of gleaming white marble.

Slate, because it is foliated, splits easily into flat pieces that can be used for flooring, roofing, outdoor walkways, or chalkboards. Like marble, slate comes in a variety of colors, including gray, black, red, and purple, so it has been used as trim for stone buildings.

Section 4 Review

1. Describe the process by which metamorphic rocks form.
2. What characteristics are used to classify metamorphic rocks?
3. Which properties of a rock may change as the rock becomes metamorphic?
4. How does pressure change rock?
5. **Thinking Critically** **Relating Cause and Effect** Why are you less likely to find fossils in metamorphic rocks than in sedimentary rocks?

Science at Home

How are rocks used in your neighborhood? Take a walk with your family to see how many uses you can observe. Identify statues, walls, and buildings made from rocks. Can you identify which type of rock is used? Look for limestone, sandstone, granite, and marble. Share a list of the rocks you found with your class. For each rock, include a description of its color and texture, where you observed the rock, and how it was used.

MYSTERY ROCKS

Problem

What properties can be used to classify rocks?

Materials

1 "mystery rock"   hand lens
2 unknown igneous rocks
2 unknown sedimentary rocks
2 unknown metamorphic rocks

Procedure

1. For this activity, you will be given six rocks and one sample that is not a rock. They are labeled A through G.
2. Make a data chart to organize your observations.
3. Using the hand lens, examine each rock for clues that show the rock formed from molten material. Record the rock's color and texture. Look for crystals or grains in the rock.
4. Use the hand lens to look for clues that show the rock formed from particles of other rocks. Observe the texture of the rock to see if it has any tiny, well-rounded grains.
5. Use the hand lens to look for clues that show the rock formed under heat and pressure. Observe if the rock has a flat layer of crystals or shows colored bands.
6. Record your observations in the data chart.

Analyze and Conclude

1. Use your completed data chart to examine and evaluate your observations. Infer from your observations which group each rock belongs in.
2. Decide which sample is not a rock. How did you determine that the sample you chose is not a rock? What do you think the "mystery rock" is? Explain.
3. Which of the samples could be classified as igneous rocks? What physical properties do these rock share with the other samples? How are they different?
4. Which of the samples could be classified as sedimentary rocks? How do you think these rocks formed? What are the physical properties of these rocks?
5. Which of the samples could be classified as metamorphic rocks? What are their physical properties?
6. **Think About It** What physical property was most useful in classifying rocks? Why?

More to Explore

Can you name each rock? Use a field guide to rocks and minerals to find the specific name of each rock sample.

DATA CHART				
Sample	Color (dark, medium, light, or mixed colors)	Texture (fine, medium, or coarse-grained)	Foliated or Banded	Rock Group (igneous, metamorphic, sedimentary)
A				
B				

The Rock Cycle

Which Rock Came First?

1. Referring to the photos below, make sketches of quartzite, granite, and sandstone on three index cards.

2. In your sketches, try to portray the color and texture of each rock. Look for similarities and differences.

3. To which major group does each rock belong?

Think It Over

Developing Hypotheses How are quartzite, granite, and sandstone related? Arrange your cards in the order in which these three rocks formed. Given enough time in Earth's crust, what might happen to the third rock in your series?

Quartzite

Granite

Sandstone

GUIDE FOR READING

◆ What is the rock cycle?

◆ What is the role of plate tectonics in the rock cycle?

Reading Tip Before you read, preview *Exploring the Rock Cycle* on page 408. Write a list of questions you have about the rock cycle. Then look for answers to the questions as you read.

Key Term rock cycle

The enormous granite dome that forms Stone Mountain in Georgia looks as if it will be there forever. The granite formed hundreds of millions of years ago as a batholith—a mass of igneous rock beneath Earth's surface. But this rock has stood exposed to the weather for millions of years. Bit by bit, the granite is flaking off. Washed away in streams, the bits of granite will eventually be ground down into sand. But that's not the end of the story. What will become of those sand particles from Stone Mountain? They are part of a series of changes that happen to all the rocks of Earth's crust.

A Cycle of Many Pathways

Earth's rocks are not as unchanging as they seem. **Forces inside Earth and at the surface produce a rock cycle that builds, destroys, and changes the rocks in the crust.** The **rock cycle** is a series of processes on Earth's surface and inside the planet that slowly change rocks from one kind to another. What drives the rock cycle? Earth's constructive and destructive forces—including plate tectonics—move rocks through the rock cycle.

The rock cycle can follow many different pathways. You can follow the rock of Stone Mountain along one of the pathways of the rock cycle.

Figure 18 Stone Mountain, near Atlanta, Georgia, rises 210 meters above the surrounding land.

One Pathway Through the Rock Cycle

In the case of Stone Mountain, the rock cycle began millions of years ago. First, a granite batholith formed beneath Earth's surface. Then the forces of mountain building slowly pushed the granite upward. Over millions of years, water and weather began to wear away the granite of Stone Mountain. Today, particles of granite still break off the mountain and become sand. Streams carry the sand to the ocean.

Over millions of years, layers of sediment will pile up on the ocean floor. Slowly, the sediments will be compacted by their own weight. Dissolved calcite in the ocean water will cement the particles together. Eventually, the quartz that once formed the granite of Stone Mountain will become sandstone, a sedimentary rock.

More and more sediment will pile up on the sandstone. As sandstone becomes deeply buried, pressure on the rocks will increase. The rock will become hot. Pressure will compact the particles in the sandstone until no spaces are left between them. Silica, the main ingredient in quartz, will replace the calcite as the cement holding the rock together. The rock's texture will change from gritty to smooth. After millions of years, the sandstone will have changed into the metamorphic rock quartzite.

What will happen next? You could wait tens of millions of years to find out how the quartzite completes the rock cycle. Or you can trace alternative pathways in *Exploring the Rock Cycle.*

Sharpen your Skills

Classifying

ACTIVITY

Some metamorphic rocks form out of igneous rocks, and other metamorphic rocks form out of sedimentary rocks.

1. If you find a fine-grained metamorphic rock with thin, flaky layers, from which group of rocks did it probably form? Explain.

2. If you find a metamorphic rock with distinct grains of different colors and sizes arranged in parallel bands, from which group of rocks did it probably form? Explain.

EXPLORING *the Rock Cycle*

Earth's constructive and destructive forces build up and wear down the crust. Igneous, sedimentary, and metamorphic rocks change continuously through the rock cycle. Rocks can follow many different pathways. The outer circle shows a complete cycle. The arrows within the circle show alternate pathways.

Sedimentary Rock

Igneous Rock

Erosion

Melting

Heat and pressure

Volcanic activity

Melting

Erosion

Heat and pressure

Magma

Metamorphic Rock

Melting

The Rock Cycle and Plate Tectonics

The changes of the rock cycle are closely related to plate tectonics. Recall that plate tectonics causes the movement of sections of Earth's lithosphere called plates. **Plate movements drive the rock cycle by pushing rocks back into the mantle, where they melt and become magma again. Plate movements also cause the folding, faulting, and uplift of the crust that move rocks through the rock cycle.** At least two types of plate movement advance the rock cycle. One type is a collision between subducting oceanic plates. The other type is a collision between continental plates.

Figure 19 This fossil trilobite lived on an ocean floor about 500 million years ago. As plate tectonics moved pieces of Earth's crust, the rock containing this fossil became part of a mountain.

Subducting Oceanic Plates Consider what could happen to the sand grains that once were part of Stone Mountain. The sand may become sandstone attached to oceanic crust. On this pathway through the rock cycle, the oceanic crust carrying the sandstone drifts toward a deep-ocean trench. At the trench, subduction returns some of the sandstone to the mantle. There, it melts and forms magma, which eventually becomes igneous rock.

Colliding Continental Plates Collisions between continental plates can also change a rock's path through the rock cycle. Such a collision can squeeze some sandstone from the ocean floor. As a result, the sandstone will change to quartzite. Eventually, the collision could form a mountain range or plateau. Then, as the mountains or plateaus containing quartzite are worn away, the rock cycle continues.

Section 5 Review

1. What process gradually changes rocks from one form to another?
2. How can plate movements move rocks through the rock cycle?
3. What rock comes before quartzite in the rock cycle? What rock or rocks could come just after quartzite in the rock cycle? Explain your answer.
4. **Thinking Critically Applying Concepts** Begin with a grain of sand on a beach. Describe what happens as you follow the grain through the rock cycle until it returns to a beach as a grain of sand again.
5. **Thinking Critically Making Judgments** In your opinion, at what point does the rock cycle really begin? Give reasons for your answer.

Check Your Progress CHAPTER PROJECT
Now that you have collected, described, tested, and recorded your rocks, classify them as igneous, sedimentary, or metamorphic. Are any of your rocks foliated? Try to identify specific types of rock. Compare your rock samples with pictures of rocks in a field guide or other library reference sources.

TESTING ROCK FLOORING

You are building your own house. For the kitchen floor, you want to use some rock such as granite, marble, or limestone. You need to know which material is easiest to maintain and keep clean.

Problem

What kind of rock makes the best flooring?

Skills Focus

designing experiments, forming operational definitions, drawing conclusions

Suggested Materials

steel nail   wire brush water
plastic dropper   hand lens
samples of igneous, sedimentary, and metamorphic rocks with flat surfaces
staining agents, such as ink and paints
greasy materials such as butter and crayons

Procedure

1. Brainstorm with your partner the qualities of good flooring. For example, good flooring should resist stains, scratches, and grease marks, and be safe to walk on when wet.
2. Predict what you think is the best building stone for a kitchen floor. Why?
3. Write the steps you plan to follow to answer the problem question. As you design your plan, consider the following factors:
   - What igneous, sedimentary, and metamorphic rocks will you test? (Pick at least one rock from each group.)
   - What materials or equipment will you need to acquire, and in what amounts?
   - What tests will you perform on the samples?
   - How will you control the variables in each test?
   - How will you measure each sample's resistance to staining, grease, and scratches?
   - How will you measure slipperiness?
4. Review your plan. Will it lead to an answer to the problem question?
5. Check your procedure and safety plan with your teacher.
6. Create a data table that includes a column in which you predict how each material will perform in each test.

Analyze and Conclude

1. Which material performed the best on each test? Which performed the worst on each test?
2. Which material is best for the kitchen flooring? Which material would you least want to use?
3. Do your answers support your initial prediction? Why or why not?
4. The person installing the floor might want rock that is easy to cut to the correct size or shape. What other qualities would matter to the flooring installer?
5. **Apply** Based on your results for flooring, what materials would you use for kitchen counters? How might the qualities needed for countertops differ from those for flooring?

More to Explore

Find out the cost per square meter of some materials used to build kitchen floors in your community. How does cost influence your decision on which material to use? What other factors can influence the choice of materials?

SECTION 1 Classifying Rocks

Key Ideas

◆ A rock is a hard piece of Earth's crust.
◆ Geologists classify rocks according to their color, texture, mineral composition, and origin.
◆ Rocks can be igneous, sedimentary, and metamorphic.

Key Terms

texture igneous rock metamorphic rock
grain sedimentary rock

SECTION 2 Igneous Rocks

Key Ideas

◆ Igneous rocks form from magma or lava.
◆ Igneous rocks are classified according to their origin, texture, and mineral composition.

Key Terms

extrusive rock intrusive rock porphyritic texture

SECTION 3 Sedimentary Rocks

Key Ideas

◆ Most sedimentary rocks form from sediments that are compacted and cemented together.
◆ The three types of sedimentary rocks are clastic rocks, organic rocks, and chemical rocks.

Key Terms

sediment cementation chemical rock
erosion clastic rock coral reef
deposition organic rock atoll
compaction

SECTION 4 Metamorphic Rocks

Key Ideas

◆ Heat and pressure deep beneath the surface can change any type of rock into metamorphic rock.
◆ Geologists classify metamorphic rock according to whether the rock is foliated or nonfoliated.

Key Term

foliated

SECTION 5 The Rock Cycle

Key Ideas

◆ The series of processes on and beneath Earth's surface that change rocks from one type of rock to another is called the rock cycle.
◆ Plate movements drive the rock cycle by pushing rocks back into the mantle, where they melt and become magma again. Plate movements also advance the rock cycle by causing folding, faulting, and uplifting of the crust.

Key Term

rock cycle

Organizing Information

Cycle Diagram Construct a cycle diagram that shows one pathway through the rock cycle. Include the following steps in your diagram in the correct order: sediments build up; igneous rock wears away; sedimentary rock forms; igneous rock forms from magma and lava; rock melts inside Earth to form magma. (For tips on making cycle diagrams, see the Skills Handbook.)

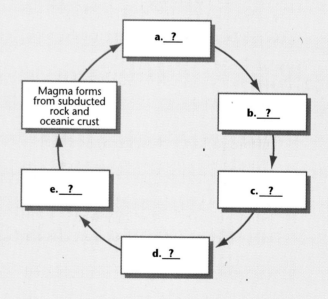

Reviewing Content

Review key concepts online using iText at www.phschool.com

Multiple Choice

Choose the letter of the best answer.

1. Which of the following sedimentary rocks is a chemical rock?
   a. shale
   b. sandstone
   c. rock salt
   d. breccia
2. Metamorphic rocks can be formed from
   a. igneous rocks.
   b. sedimentary rocks.
   c. metamorphic rocks.
   d. all rock groups.
3. The rock formed when granite changes to a metamorphic rock is
   a. marble.   b. basalt.
   c. gneiss.   d. pumice.
4. Which of the following helps create both metamorphic and sedimentary rocks?
   a. cementation   b. pressure
   c. evaporation   d. heat
5. Millions of years ago, a deposit of organic limestone was probably
   a. a swampy forest.   b. a lava flow.
   c. a coral reef.   d. an intrusive rock.

True or False

If the statement is true, write true. If it is false, change the underlined word or words to make the statement true.

6. Igneous rocks are classified by how they formed and by their color, texture, and <u>shape</u>.
7. Granite is a <u>fine-grained</u> igneous rock.
8. Sedimentary rocks that form when minerals come out of solution are classified as <u>porphyritic</u>.
9. A <u>barrier reef</u> is a ring-shaped coral island found in the open ocean.
10. The series of processes that slowly change rocks from one kind to another is called the <u>rock cycle</u>.

Checking Concepts

11. What is the relationship between an igneous rock's texture and where it was formed?
12. Why can water pass easily through sandstone but not through shale?
13. Describe how a rock can form by evaporation. What type of rock is it?
14. How do the properties of a rock change when the rock changes to metamorphic?
15. What are the sources of the heat that helps metamorphic rocks to form?
16. **Writing to Learn** You are a camp counselor taking your campers on a mountain hike. One of your campers cracks open a rock and finds a fossilized fish inside. The camper wants to know how a fish fossil from the sea floor ended up on the side of a mountain. What explanation would you give the camper?

Thinking Critically

17. **Applying Concepts** The sedimentary rocks limestone and sandstone are used as building materials. However, they wear away more rapidly than marble and quartzite, the metamorphic rocks that are formed from them. Why do you think this is so?
18. **Inferring** As a geologist exploring for rock and mineral deposits, you come across an area where the rocks are layers of coal and shale. What kind of environment probably existed in this area millions of years ago when these rocks formed?
19. **Comparing and Contrasting** How are clastic rocks and organic rocks similar? How are they different?
20. **Relating Cause and Effect** In the rock cycle, igneous, metamorphic, and sedimentary rocks can all become magma again. What step in the rock cycle causes this to happen? Explain your answer.

Applying Skills

Answer Questions 21–23 using the photos of three rocks.

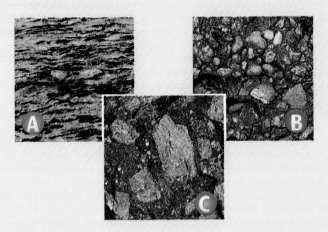

21. **Observing** How would you describe the texture of each rock?
22. **Classifying** Which of the three rocks would you classify as a metamorphic rock? Explain your answer.

23. **Inferring** A rock's texture gives clues about how the rock formed. What can you infer about the process by which rock B formed?

Performance ▼ Assessment
CHAPTER PROJECT

Present Your Project Construct a simple display for your rocks. Your display should clearly give your classification for each of your rock samples. In your presentation, describe where you went hunting for rocks and what kinds of rocks you found. Describe which of your discoveries surprised you the most.

Reflect and Record In your journal, write about how you developed your rock collection. Were there any rocks that were hard to classify? Did you find rocks from each of the three major groups? Can you think of any reason why certain types of rocks would not be found in your area?

Test Preparation
Use these questions to prepare for standardized tests.

Use the diagram to answer Questions 24–28.

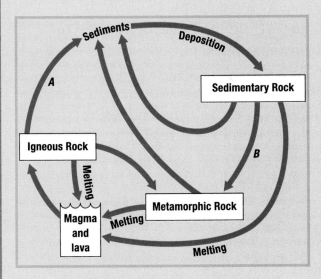

24. A good title for this diagram is
   A Different Kinds of Rock
   B Deposition of Sediment
   C How Metamorphic Rock Forms
   D Pathways of the Rock Cycle

25. The process shown by letter A is called
   F extrusion.   G crystallization.
   H erosion.   J intrusion.

26. The process shown by letter B involves
   A cementation only.
   B heat and pressure.
   C erosion and deposition.
   D compaction only.

27. According to the diagram, metamorphic rock forms from
   F igneous rock and sedimentary rock.
   G sedimentary rock only.
   H magma and lava.
   J melting rock.

28. According to the diagram, magma and lava may form through the melting of
   A any type of rock.
   B metamorphic rock only.
   C sediments.
   D igneous rock only.

FOCUS ON FAULTS

"When I was about fourteen, my family was living in Taiwan," Geologist Carol Prentice recalls. "One day I was playing pinball, and a little earthquake happened. It tilted my pinball machine."

Unlike most people experiencing their first quake, her reaction was not fright but fascination. "*What in the world is that?* I wondered. That was the first time I consciously remember thinking that earthquakes were something interesting." Later, she recalls, "When I was teaching earth science in high school, I realized that my favorite section to teach was on earthquakes and faults."

During an earthquake, forces from inside Earth fracture, or break, Earth's crust, producing a powerful jolt called an earthquake. As Earth's crust moves and breaks, it forms cracks called faults. Over the centuries, the faults may move again and again.

Geologist Carol Prentice climbs into these faults to study the soil and rocks. She hunts for clues about the history of a fault and estimates the risk of a serious earthquake in the future.

Carol Prentice studied geology at Humboldt State University and the California Institute of Technology. She is currently a Research Geologist for the United States Geological Survey in Menlo Park, California.

414

Finding Clues to Ancient Earthquakes

Today, Dr. Prentice is an expert in the field of paleoseismology. *Paleo* means "ancient" and *seismology* is "the study of earthquakes." So it's the study of ancient earthquakes. "Paleoseismologists search for evidence of earthquakes that happened hundreds or thousands of years ago," explains Dr. Prentice.

There are written records about earthquakes that happened years ago. But the real story of a quake is written in the rocks and soil. Years after an earthquake, wind, rain, and flowing water can wear the fault lines away from Earth's surface. Then the evidence of the quake is buried under layers of sediment. But the fault is still there.

The cracks of recent earthquakes, such as the Gobi-Altay fault shown here, are sometimes visible for hundreds of kilometers. Because this quake happened in the Mongolian desert, it is especially easy to see.

Choosing a Site

How do you pick a site to research? "First we study aerial photographs, geological maps, and satellite images of the fault line," Dr. Prentice explains. "We will have some sites in mind. Then, we go out and look at the sites and do some digging with a shovel to get samples."

"We look for places where sediments, such as sand and gravel, have been building up. If sediments have been depositing there for many thousands of years, you're likely to have a good record of prehistoric earthquakes at that site. When you dig, you're likely to see not only the most recent earthquake buried and preserved in the sediments, but also earlier earthquakes. That's a really good site." Once the site is established, the geological team begins digging a trench across the fault.

Earthquakes in Mongolia

RUSSIA

50° N

1905

1905

MONGOLIA

1957

CHINA

40° N

90° E

100° E

110° E

120° E

130° E

SEA OF JAPAN

NORTH KOREA

SOUTH KOREA

JAPAN

EAST CHINA SEA

PACIFIC OCEAN

0   250   500 mi
0   250   500 km

N W E S

KEY
Major earthquakes since 1900

415

Working in the Trenches

What's it like to work in a spot where Earth's surface ruptured? Does Carol Prentice ever think that an earthquake might occur when she is digging in the fault? "It's always in the back of your mind when you are working in the trench," she admits.

But, she says, "The trenches are dangerous, not so much because there might be an earthquake while you are working there but because the trench can cave in. If a trench is 4 to 5 meters deep, or just over your head, it needs shores—braces and supports—or it might cave in. When sediments are soft, and the trench is deep, it's more likely to cave in. That could happen in a place like Mongolia."

Carol (in back) and another geologist in a deep trench.

String grid lines are used to map out sections of the trench.

Shores support the trench walls.

In Mongolia, in northeast Asia, it's difficult for geologists to find the right materials to support a deep trench. It could cave in while someone is in it. "That would be very frightening," she says.

Looking at the Gobi-Altay Quake

Carol Prentice travels to earthquake sites around the world—Dominican Republic, Thailand, Mongolia—as well as to the San Andreas fault in California. One of Dr. Prentice's most recent research expeditions was to the site of the monster Gobi-Altay earthquake of 1957 in the Mongolian desert. In earthquakes like this one, the faults are easy to see. "We're taking a look at this Gobi Altay earthquake and seeing whether the next-to-last earthquake had the same pattern," Dr. Prentice says.

The faults of the Gobi-Altay earthquake are similar in some ways to the San Andreas fault and to the faults of other earthquakes in the United States. That's one of the reasons the Gobi-Altay is so interesting to geologists.

Interpreting the Data

When Dr. Prentice finds evidence of several earthquakes in one spot, she takes measurements that tell her when the layers of rocks, sand, and gravel were deposited and when they split. From that she knows when and how frequently earthquakes have occurred there.

She also determines how fast the opposite sides of the fault are slipping past each other. "Those two pieces of information— the dates of prehistoric earthquakes and the slip rate—are very, very important in trying to

An earthquake is caused by movement on a fault deep beneath Earth's surface. If this movement is large enough, it can cause cracks in the ground surface. Over the years, layers of sediment are deposited on top of the crack. The next earthquake causes a new crack in the surface, and new sediments are deposited. By studying evidence of the cracks in these layers of sediment, geologists learn about past earthquakes along the fault.

figure out how dangerous a particular fault is," Dr. Prentice explains.

Since faults don't move every year, but over thousands of years, you can figure out the average slip per year and make some predictions. The faster the fault is moving, the greater the danger. "We can look at the landforms around a fault.

> **"** ... the real story of a quake is written in the rocks and soil. **"**

We can look at what our instruments record, and say: This is an active fault. Someday it might produce a big earthquake, but what we really want to know is when. Is that earthquake likely to happen in the next fifty years, in the next hundred years, or is it going to be a thousand years before the next big earthquake?"

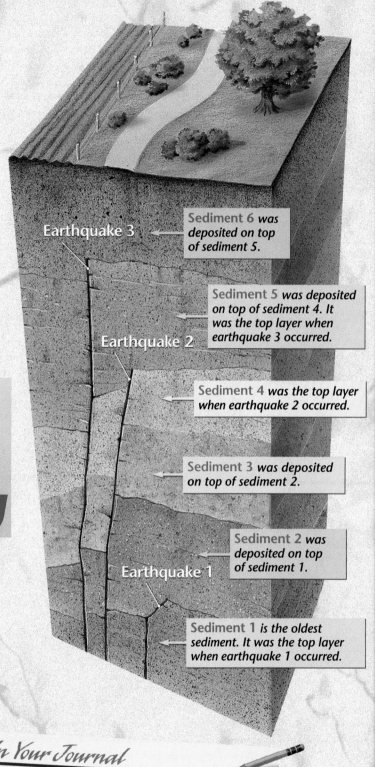

Earthquake 3

Earthquake 2

Earthquake 1

Sediment 6 *was deposited on top of sediment 5.*

Sediment 5 *was deposited on top of sediment 4. It was the top layer when earthquake 3 occurred.*

Sediment 4 *was the top layer when earthquake 2 occurred.*

Sediment 3 *was deposited on top of sediment 2.*

Sediment 2 *was deposited on top of sediment 1.*

Sediment 1 *is the oldest sediment. It was the top layer when earthquake 1 occurred.*

In Your Journal

Carol Prentice relies on close observation and making inferences in her study of earthquakes. Write a paragraph describing some of the other skills that Dr. Prentice needs to do her work as a paleoseismologist.

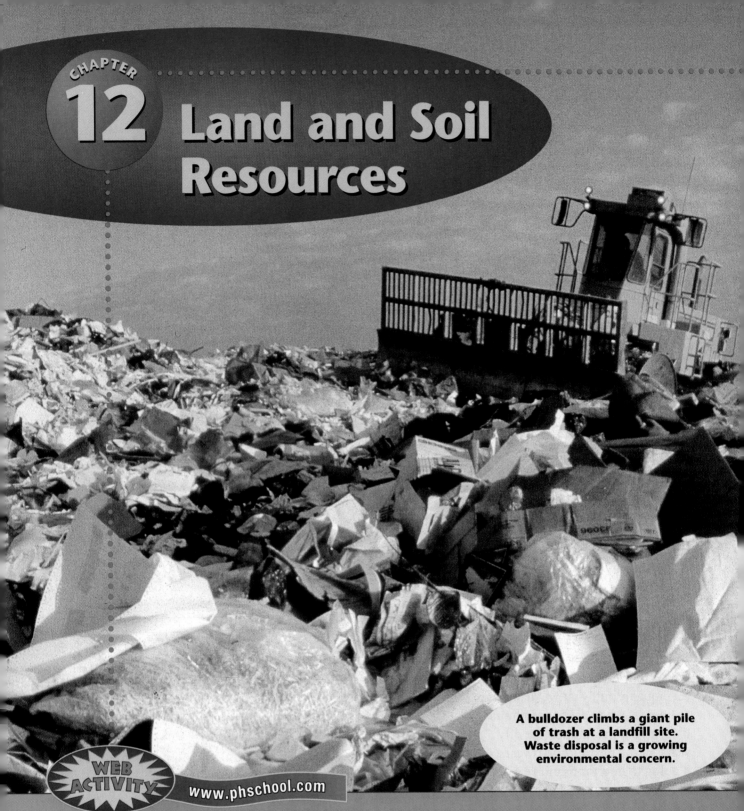

A bulldozer climbs a giant pile of trash at a landfill site. Waste disposal is a growing environmental concern.

WEB ACTIVITY

www.phschool.com

What's in a Package?

The next time you're in the supermarket, take a look at all the different kinds of packages. There are glass bottles, plastic bottles, metal cans, cardboard boxes, plastic bags, paper wrappers, and more! Different kinds of packages are used for different kinds of products.

Many of these packages are opened and then thrown away. But where is "away"? In this chapter, you will read about what happens to wastes after they are discarded. While you study the chapter, you will be analyzing the anatomy of a package.

Your Goal To analyze and display information about a product package.

Your display must

- Include a cutaway portion of the package with the different materials labeled.
- Identify the purpose of each part of the package.
- Describe what happens to each part of the package after it is thrown away in your community.

Get Started Obtain a product package to study. Empty the package and clean it out.

Check Your Progress You'll be working on this project as you study this chapter. To keep your project on track, look for Check Your Progress boxes at the following points.

Section 1 Review, page 427: Cut the package open and identify the materials from which it is made.

Section 3 Review, page 442: Investigate what happens to the materials that make up the package.

Wrap Up At the end of the chapter (page 445), you will assemble your product display and present it to your class.

TEKS

In addition to process TEKS, this chapter addresses these concept TEKS as they relate to the chapter's topics.

(8.12) The student knows that cycles exist in Earth systems. The student is expected to:
(C) predict the results of modifying Earth's nitrogen, water, and carbon cycles.

(8.14) The student knows that natural events and human activity can alter Earth systems. The student is expected to:
(C) describe how human activities have modified soil, water, and air quality.

① Conserving Land and Soil

How Does Mining Affect the Land?

1.  You will be given a pan filled with sand and soil representing a mining site. There are at least 10 deposits of "ore" (sunflower seeds) buried in your mining site.

2. Your goal is to locate and remove the ore from your site. You may use a pencil, a pair of tweezers, and a spoon as mining tools.

3. After you have extracted the chunks of ore, break them open to remove the "minerals" inside. **CAUTION:** Do not eat the sunflower seeds.

4. Observe your mining site and the surrounding area after your mining operations are finished.

Think It Over

Predicting How did mining change the land at your mining site? Predict whether it would be easy or difficult to restore the land to its original state. Explain.

◆ How do people use land?

◆ What kinds of problems occur when soil is not properly managed?

◆ What is the nitrogen cycle?

Reading Tip Before you read, use the section headings to make an outline about land and soil conservation. Leave space in the outline to take notes.

Key Terms development
• land reclamation • litter
• topsoil • subsoil • bedrock
• erosion • desertification
• nutrient depletion
• fallow • crop rotation
• nitrogen cycle

Less than a quarter of Earth's surface is dry land. Except for the land formed when volcanoes erupt or river deltas grow, new land generally is not added to the surface. All the people on Earth must share this limited amount of land to produce their food, build shelter, and obtain other resources. Land is a precious resource. As the American author Mark Twain once said about land, "They don't make it anymore."

Types of Land Use

People use land in many ways. **Three uses that change the land are agriculture, development, and mining.** Examples of these land uses are shown in Figure 2.

Agriculture Land is the source of most food. Crops such as wheat, rice, and potatoes require large areas of fertile land. But less than a third of Earth's land can be farmed. The rest is too dry, too wet, too salty, or too mountainous. To provide food for the growing population, new farmland must be created by clearing forests, draining wetlands, and irrigating deserts. When people make these changes, organisms that depended on the natural ecosystem must find new homes.

Many crops are grown to feed livestock such as hogs, chicken, and cattle. Other land serves as pasture or rangeland for grazing animals.

Development People settled the first villages in areas that had good soil and were near a source of fresh water. As populations grew, these settlements became towns and cities. People built more houses and paved roads. The construction of buildings, roads, bridges, dams, and other structures is called **development.**

In the United States, about a million hectares of farmland (an area half the size of New Jersey) are developed each year. Development not only reduces the amount of farmland, but can also destroy wildlife habitats.

Mining Mining is the removal of nonrenewable resources such as iron, copper, and coal from the land. Resources just below the surface are strip mined. Strip mining involves removing a strip of land to obtain the minerals and then replacing the strip. Strip mines expose the soil. It can then be blown or washed away more easily. Strip-mined areas may remain barren for years before the soil becomes rich enough to support the growth of plants again.

For resources located deep underground, it is necessary to dig a tunnel, or shaft. The minerals are carried up through the shafts. This process is called underground mining.

☑ *Checkpoint* *Why isn't all land suitable for farming?*

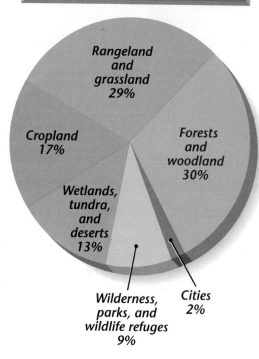

Land Use in the United States

Rangeland and grassland 29%

Forests and woodland 30%

Cropland 17%

Wetlands, tundra, and deserts 13%

Wilderness, parks, and wildlife refuges 9%

Cities 2%

Figure 1 Land in the United States is used in many ways. *Classifying Which of these land uses change the natural ecosystems of the land?*

Figure 2 Three major uses of land are agriculture, development, and mining.

Figure 3 It's hard to believe that cows now graze on the same hillside that used to be an open mine. Thanks to land reclamation practices, many mining areas are being restored for other uses.

Restoring the Land

Fortunately, it is often possible to restore land damaged by erosion or mining. The process of restoring an area of land to a more natural, productive state is called **land reclamation.** In addition to restoring lands for agriculture, land reclamation can restore habitats for wildlife. Many different types of land reclamation projects are currently underway all over the world. But it is generally more difficult and expensive to restore damaged land and soil than it is to protect them in the first place.

Figure 3 shows an example of land reclamation. When the mining in the first scene was completed, the mine operators smoothed out the sides of the mining cuts. Then they replaced the subsoil and topsoil that had been removed before mining. Finally, they planted grass. The former mine is now agricultural land.

Protecting the Soil

INTEGRATING EARTH SCIENCE Do you think of soil only as something that has to be washed off your hands or swept off the floor? Then you may not realize how much you depend on soil! Soil is a complex system made up of living and nonliving things. It contains the minerals and nutrients that plants need to grow. Soil also absorbs, stores, and filters water. Bacteria, fungi, and other organisms that live in soil break down the wastes and remains of living things. These decomposers recycle the chemical substances that are necessary for life.

Figure 4 Fertile soil is a valuable resource. The rich volcanic soil in Hawaii (right) is good for growing crops such as pineapple, sugar cane, and coffee.

Figure 5 shows the general structure of soil. Notice that it is composed of several layers. The very top layer of dead leaves and grass is called **litter.** The next layer, **topsoil,** is a mixture of rock fragments, nutrients, water, air, and decaying animal and plant matter. The water and nutrients are absorbed by the many plant roots located in this layer. Below the topsoil is the **subsoil.** The subsoil also contains rock fragments, water, and air, but has less animal and plant matter than the topsoil.

It can take hundreds of years to form just a few centimeters of new soil. All soil begins as the rock that makes up Earth's crust, called **bedrock.** Natural processes such as freezing and thawing gradually break apart the bedrock. Plant roots wedge between rocks and break them into smaller pieces. Chemicals released by lichens slowly break the rock into smaller particles. Animals such as earthworms and moles help grind rocks into even smaller particles. As dead organisms break down, their remains also contribute to the mixture.

Have you ever seen a flourishing vegetable garden with tall corn stalks, trailing squash vines, and string bean tendrils spiraling up bean poles? A successful garden requires fertile soil. Soil that is well suited for growing plants is said to be fertile. The most important quality of fertile soil is the amount of humus the soil contains. Humus is a dark-colored substance that forms as plant and animal remains decay. Humus provides plants with the nutrients that they need to grow. These nutrients include nitrogen, phosphorus, sulfur, and potassium. As soil develops, humus slowly builds up in the topsoil layer. Then, as plants grow, they remove from the topsoil the nutrients that the humus contains.

Because rich topsoil takes a long time to form, it is important to protect Earth's soil. **Poor soil management can result in three problems: erosion, nutrient depletion, and desertification.**

Figure 5 Soil consists of several layers. *Applying Concepts In which layer are most plant roots located? What do the roots absorb there?*

Erosion The process by which water, wind, or ice moves particles of rocks or soil is called **erosion.** Normally, plant roots hold soil in place. But when soil is exposed to wind and water, erosion occurs more rapidly. Many uses of land, including logging, mining, and farming, expose the soil and can cause erosion. Some farming methods that help reduce erosion are described in *Exploring Soil Conservation.*

EXPLORING *Soil Conservation*

These farming practices can help reduce soil erosion.

◄ **Strip cropping and contour plowing**
Farmers alternate strips of tall crops, such as corn, with short crops, such as squash. The short crops prevent soil from washing out of the tall crop rows, which are less protected. Crops are planted in curving rows that follow the slope, or contour, of the land. Contour plowing can reduce soil erosion as much as 50 percent on gently sloping land.

▲ **Windbreaks**
Rows of trees are planted along the edges of fields. These windbreaks block the wind and also trap eroding soil. Using fruit or nut trees as windbreaks provides an extra benefit for the farmer and wildlife.

Conservation plowing ▼
Rather than plowing fields and leaving them bare, farmers use machines that break up only the subsoil. This method leaves the dead stalks and weeds from the previous year's crop in the ground to hold the topsoil in place.

Terracing ▶
Steep hillsides are built up into a series of flat "terraces." The ridges of soil at the edges of the terraces slow down runoff and catch eroding soil.

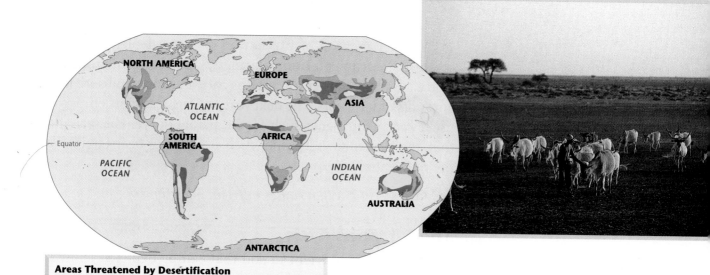

Areas Threatened by Desertification

☐ Existing desert   ▨ High risk   ▨ Moderate risk

Figure 6 Large areas of the world are at risk of desertification. One cause is overgrazing. Without grass to hold the soil in place, the Senegal plain in Africa is becoming a barren desert.
Interpreting Maps Which continent shows the largest area at high risk of desertification?

Desertification   Plants cannot grow without the moisture and nutrients in fertile soil. The advance of desertlike conditions into areas that previously were fertile is called **desertification.** In the past 50 years, desertification has occurred on about five billion hectares of land.

One cause of desertification is climate. During periods of drought, crops fail. Without plant cover, the exposed soil easily blows away. Overgrazing of grasslands by cattle and sheep also exposes the soil. Excessive cutting of trees for firewood can also contribute to desertification.

Desertification is a very serious problem. People cannot grow crops and graze livestock where desertification has occurred. People may face famine and starvation as a result. In central Africa, where desertification is severe, millions of rural people are moving to the cities because they can no longer support themselves on the land.

Nutrient Depletion   Plants make their own food through photosynthesis. But plants also require nitrogen, potassium, phosphorus, and other nutrients. Decomposers supply these nutrients to the soil as they break down the remains of dead organisms.

Sometimes, a farmer plants the same crops in a field year after year. As a result, the plants use more nutrients than the decomposers can replace. The soil becomes less fertile, a situation that is called **nutrient depletion.**

One way to prevent nutrient depletion is to periodically leave fields **fallow,** or unplanted with crops. A second way to prevent nutrient depletion is to leave the unused parts of crops, such as cornstalks and watermelon vines, in the fields rather than clearing them away. The stalks and vines decompose in the fields, adding nutrients to the soil.

Another method of preventing nutrient depletion is crop rotation. In **crop rotation,** a farmer plants different crops in a field each year. Some crops, such as corn and cotton, absorb large amounts of nutrients. The next year, the farmer plants crops that use fewer soil nutrients, such as oats, barley, or rye. The year after that, the farmer sows legumes such as alfalfa or beans to restore the nutrient supply.

☑ *Checkpoint* *What causes nutrient depletion?*

The Nitrogen Cycle

One important nutrient in soil that can be depleted is nitrogen. Nitrogen is a necessary building block in the matter that makes up living things. Since the air around you is about 78 percent nitrogen gas, you might think that it would be easy for living things to obtain nitrogen. However, most organisms cannot use the nitrogen gas in the air. Nitrogen gas is called "free" nitrogen, meaning it is not combined with other kinds of atoms. Most organisms can use nitrogen only once it has been "fixed," or combined with other elements to form nitrogen-containing compounds. You can follow this process, called the **nitrogen cycle,** in Figure 7 below. **The nitrogen cycle is the process by which nitrogen is removed from the atmosphere, fixed in the soil by bacteria, incorporated in other living things, and then released back into the atmosphere.**

Figure 7 In the nitrogen cycle, nitrogen moves from the air to the soil, into living things, and back into the air.
Interpreting Diagrams How does the rabbit in the diagram obtain nitrogen?

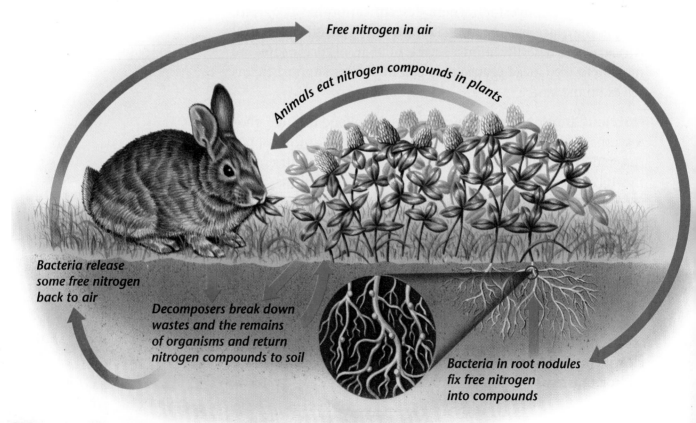

Free nitrogen in air

Animals eat nitrogen compounds in plants

Bacteria release some free nitrogen back to air

Decomposers break down wastes and the remains of organisms and return nitrogen compounds to soil

Bacteria in root nodules fix free nitrogen into compounds

Nitrogen Fixation The process of changing free nitrogen gas into a usable form of nitrogen is called nitrogen fixation. Most nitrogen fixation is performed by certain kinds of bacteria. Some of these bacteria live in bumps called nodules (NAHJ oolz) on the roots of certain plants. These plants, known as legumes, include clover, beans, peas, alfalfa, and peanuts.

The relationship between the bacteria and the legumes is an example of mutualism. A relationship in which both species benefit is called mutualism. Both the bacteria and the plant benefit from this relationship: The bacteria feed on the plant's sugars, and the plant is supplied with nitrogen in a usable form.

INTEGRATING TECHNOLOGY To enrich their fields, many farmers make use of the nitrogen-fixing bacteria in legumes. Every few years, a farmer may plant a legume such as alfalfa in a field. The bacteria in the alfalfa roots build up a new supply of nitrogen compounds in the soil. The following year, the new crops planted in the field benefit from the improved soil.

Return of Nitrogen to the Environment Once the nitrogen has been fixed into chemical compounds, it can be used by organisms to build proteins and other complex substances. Decomposers break down these complex compounds in animal wastes and in the bodies of dead organisms. This returns simple nitrogen compounds to the soil. Nitrogen can cycle from the soil to producers and consumers many times. At some point, however, bacteria break down the nitrogen compounds completely. These bacteria release free nitrogen back into the air. Then the nitrogen cycle starts again.

Figure 8 Lumpy nodules are clearly visible on the roots of this clover plant. Bacteria inside the nodules carry out nitrogen fixation.

Section 1 Review

1. List three ways that people use land.
2. What are three problems that can occur when topsoil is not properly managed?
3. Why is it important to protect topsoil?
4. Describe two methods for reducing soil erosion.
5. How is nitrogen fixation a necessary part of the nitrogen cycle?
6. **Thinking Critically** **Relating Cause and Effect** How may human activities be related to desertification?

Check Your Progress

CHAPTER PROJECT

Cut your package open so that you can observe its construction. Create a data table identifying each part of the package, the material it is made of, and its purpose. What properties of these materials make them desirable as packaging? (*Hint:* Packaging benefits include protecting a product from breakage, preventing spoilage, making it more attractive, or making it easier to use. Can you think of other benefits of the materials in your package?)

Save That Soil

In this lab, you'll decide how to control variables as you investigate the way rainfall causes soil erosion.

Problem

How are different types of land surfaces affected by rainfall?

Materials

newspaper	2 unbreakable pans
2 blocks	sod
loose soil	"rainmaker"
water	

Procedure

1. Cover a table with newspaper. Obtain two pans. Insert a block under one end of each pan to raise the two ends to the same height.
2. Read over the rest of the lab. Write a hypothesis that you will test. Pay careful attention to the variables you must control.
3. Place loose soil in the raised end of one pan. Place a small square of sod (soil with grass growing in it) in the raised end of the second pan. One variable is the amount of soil in each pan. Find a way to make the two amounts of soil the same. Record your procedures.
4. Create a "rainmaker" that controls the amount of water and the way it falls on the two soil samples. Then use your rainmaker to test the effect of the same amount of "rain" on the two kinds of soil. Record the results.
5. Review your experiment and your results. Do you see any procedure you wish to change? If so, get your teacher's permission to try the lab again with your revised procedures.

Analyze and Conclude

1. What effects did the "rainwater" produce on each type of soil you tested?
2. This experiment models soil erosion. What can you conclude about actual soil erosion caused by rain? How could a farmer use the information gained from this experiment to conserve topsoil?
3. **Think About It** Why was it essential for you to control the amounts of soil and "rainfall" in the two pans?

Design an Experiment

How does soil erosion caused by a gentle, steady rain compare with that caused by a heavy downpour? Design an experiment to find out. Be sure to control the way you imitate the two types of rain. Obtain your teacher's permission before conducting this experiment.

DISCOVER •••ACTIVITY••••

What's in the Trash?

Your teacher will give you a trash bag. The items in the bag represent the most common categories of household waste in the United States.

1. Before you open the bag, predict what the two most common categories are.

2. Put on some plastic gloves. Open the bag and sort the trash items into categories based on what they are made of.

3. 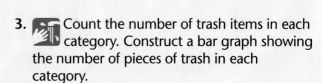 Count the number of trash items in each category. Construct a bar graph showing the number of pieces of trash in each category.

Think It Over

Interpreting Data Based on your graph, what are the two most common types of household waste? Was your prediction correct?

How much trash does your family throw away in a year? If it's your job to take the trash out, you might say that it's a large amount. But the amount of trash produced in the United States may be even greater than you think. Consider these facts:

◆ The average person produces about 2 kilograms of trash daily.

◆ Every hour, people throw away 2.5 million plastic bottles.

◆ Every two weeks, people throw away enough glass bottles and jars to fill the World Trade Center towers in New York City.

◆ Every year, people throw away enough white paper to build a wall 4 meters high that stretches from coast to coast.

◆ Every year, people throw away 1.6 billion pens, 2.9 million tons of paper towels, and 220 million automobile tires.

You can see why people call the United States a "throw-away society"! Disposable products can be cheap and convenient. But they have created a big problem—what to do with all the trash.

GUIDE FOR READING

◆ **What can be done with solid waste?**

◆ **What are the four major types of waste that can be recycled?**

◆ **What are the "three R's"?**

Reading Tip Before you read, preview *Exploring a Landfill* on page 430. Make a list of any unfamiliar words in the diagram. Look for the meanings of these words as you read.

Key Terms municipal solid waste • leachate • sanitary landfill • incineration • recycling • biodegradable • resins • composting

The Problem of Waste Disposal

In their daily activities, people generate many types of waste, including used paper, empty packages, and food scraps. The waste materials produced in homes, businesses, schools, and other places in a community are called **municipal solid waste.** Other sources of solid waste include construction debris and certain agricultural and industrial wastes. **Three methods of handling solid waste are to bury it, to burn it, or to recycle it.** Each method has advantages and disadvantages.

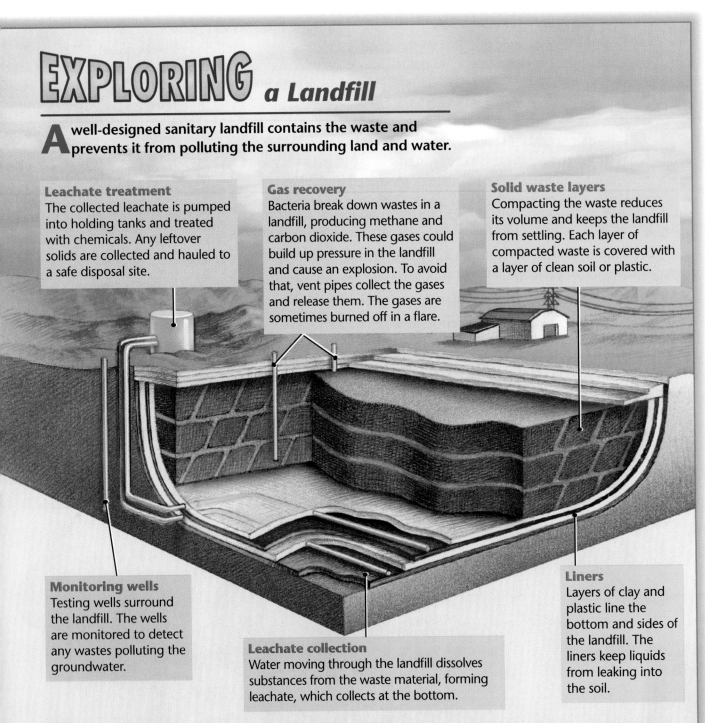

EXPLORING a Landfill

A well-designed sanitary landfill contains the waste and prevents it from polluting the surrounding land and water.

Leachate treatment
The collected leachate is pumped into holding tanks and treated with chemicals. Any leftover solids are collected and hauled to a safe disposal site.

Gas recovery
Bacteria break down wastes in a landfill, producing methane and carbon dioxide. These gases could build up pressure in the landfill and cause an explosion. To avoid that, vent pipes collect the gases and release them. The gases are sometimes burned off in a flare.

Solid waste layers
Compacting the waste reduces its volume and keeps the landfill from settling. Each layer of compacted waste is covered with a layer of clean soil or plastic.

Monitoring wells
Testing wells surround the landfill. The wells are monitored to detect any wastes polluting the groundwater.

Leachate collection
Water moving through the landfill dissolves substances from the waste material, forming leachate, which collects at the bottom.

Liners
Layers of clay and plastic line the bottom and sides of the landfill. The liners keep liquids from leaking into the soil.

Landfills Until fairly recently, people usually disposed of waste in open holes in the ground. But these open dumps were dangerous and unsightly. Rainwater falling on the wastes dissolved chemicals from the waste, forming a polluted liquid called **leachate.** Leachate could run off into streams and lakes, or trickle down into the groundwater below the dump.

In 1976, the government banned open dumps. Now much solid waste is buried in landfills that are constructed to hold the wastes more safely. A **sanitary landfill** holds municipal solid waste, construction debris, and some types of agricultural and industrial waste. *Exploring a Landfill* shows the parts of a well-designed sanitary landfill. Once a landfill is full, it is covered with a clay cap to keep rainwater from entering the waste.

However, even well-designed landfills still pose a risk of polluting groundwater. And while capped landfills can be reused in certain ways, including as parks and sites for sports arenas, they cannot be used for other needs, such as housing or agriculture.

Incineration The burning of solid waste is called **incineration** (in sin ur AY shun). Incineration has some advantages over the use of landfills. The burning facilities, or incinerators, do not take up as much space. They do not pose a risk of polluting groundwater. The heat produced by burning solid waste can be used to generate electricity. These "waste-to-energy" plants supply electricity to many homes in the United States.

Unfortunately, incinerators do have drawbacks. Even the best incinerators release some pollution into the air. And although incinerators reduce the volume of waste by as much as 90 percent, some waste still remains. This waste needs to be disposed of somewhere. Finally, incinerators are much more expensive to build than sanitary landfills. Many communities cannot afford to replace an existing landfill with an incinerator.

☑ *Checkpoint* *What is a waste-to-energy plant?*

Figure 9 This waste-to-energy plant generates electricity while disposing of municipal solid waste.

Figure 10 Metal and glass are two frequently recycled materials.
A. Crumpled aluminum cans ride up a conveyor belt in a recycling center. **B.** A giant mound of crushed glass awaits recycling.
Predicting Without recycling, what might eventually happen to the landfills that hold municipal solid waste?

Recycling

INTEGRATING TECHNOLOGY The process of reclaiming raw materials and reusing them is called **recycling.** Recycling reduces the volume of solid waste. Recycling enables people to use the materials in wastes again, rather than discarding those materials. As you know, matter in ecosystems is naturally recycled through the water cycle, carbon cycle, and other processes. A substance that can be broken down and recycled by bacteria and other decomposers is **biodegradable** (by oh dih GRAY duh bul).

Unfortunately, many of the products people use today are not biodegradable. Plastic containers, metal cans, rubber tires, and glass jars are examples of products that do not naturally decompose. Instead, people have developed techniques to recycle the raw materials in these products.

A wide range of materials, including motor oil, tires, and batteries, can be recycled. **Most recycling focuses on four major categories of products: metal, glass, paper, and plastic.**

Metal In your classroom, you are surrounded by metal objects that can be recycled. Your desk, scissors, staples, and paper clips are probably made of steel. Another very common metal, aluminum, is used to make soda cans, house siding, window screens, and many other products.

Metals such as iron and aluminum can be melted and reused. Recycling metal saves money and causes less pollution than making new metal. With recycling, no ore needs to be mined, transported to factories, or processed. In addition, recycling metals helps conserve these nonrenewable resources.

Glass Glass is made from sand, soda ash, and limestone mixed together and heated. Glass is one of the easiest products to recycle because glass pieces can be melted down over and over to make new glass containers. Recycled glass is also used to make fiberglass, bricks, tiles, and the reflective paints on road signs.

Recycling glass is less expensive than making glass from raw materials. Because the recycled pieces melt at a lower temperature than the raw materials, less energy is required. Recycling glass also reduces the environmental damage caused by mining for sand, soda, and limestone.

☑ *Checkpoint* *Why is it easy to recycle glass?*

Paper It takes about 17 trees to make one metric ton of paper. Paper mills turn wood into a thick liquid called pulp. Pulp is spread out and dried to produce paper. Pulp can also be made from used paper such as old newspapers. The newspapers must be washed to remove the inks and dyes. The paper is then mixed with more water and other chemicals to form pulp.

Most paper products can only be recycled a few times. Recycled paper is not as smooth or strong as paper made from wood pulp. Each time paper is recycled to make pulp, the new paper is rougher, weaker, and darker.

Plastic When oil is refined to make gasoline and other petroleum products, solid materials called **resins** are left over. Resins can be heated, stretched, and molded into plastic products. Have you ever noticed a symbol like the ones in Figure 11 on a plastic container? This number indicates what type of plastic a container is made of. For example, plastics labeled with a *1* or a *2* are made from plastics that are often recycled. Common products made from these types of plastic include milk jugs, detergent containers, and soda bottles.

Figure 11 These plastic bottles have numbers indicating the type of plastic they are made of. Plastics must be sorted by type before they are recycled.

Energy Savings in Manufacturing	
Material	**Using Recycled Rather Than Raw Materials**
Aluminum	90–97%
Glass	4–32%
Paper	23–74%

Figure 12 As this table shows, some kinds of recycling save more energy than others.
Interpreting Data Which type of recycling saves the most energy?

When they are recycled, they take on very different forms: as fiber filling for sleeping bags and jackets, carpeting, park benches, shower stalls, floor tiles, trash cans, or dock pilings!

Is Recycling Worthwhile? In addition to conserving resources, recycling saves energy. Figure 12 shows how much energy can be saved by using recycled materials instead of raw materials.

Recycling is not a complete answer to the solid waste problem. Many materials can be recycled. But scientists have not found good ways to recycle other materials, such as plastic-coated paper and plastic foam. There are not enough uses for some recycled products, such as low-quality recycled newspaper. Finally, all recycling processes require energy and create some pollution.

☑ *Checkpoint* **What are some advantages and disadvantages of recycling?**

Solid Waste Management

In the past few decades, people have become more aware of the solid waste problem. Many communities now collect recyclable items along with other household trash. Many supermarkets recycle paper and plastic grocery bags. Many states charge deposit fees on certain glass, metal, and plastic containers. When people return the containers to be recycled, they get their deposit back. This return system encourages people to recycle the containers instead of throwing them away. You might have seen recycling bins for metal and glass drink containers in movie theaters, parks, and other public areas. Consumers can also choose to buy products made with recyclable materials.

Figure 13 These students are sorting materials for a school recycling project.

434

As a result of these efforts, the amount of municipal solid waste that is recycled has increased. But most municipal solid waste in the United States still goes to landfills. Yet as usable land becomes more scarce, it will be even more critical to reduce the need for landfills.

What Can You Do?

The good news is that there are lots of ways individuals can help control the solid waste problem. **These are sometimes called the "three R's"—reduce, reuse, and recycle.** *Reduce* refers to creating less waste in the first place. For example, you can use a cloth shopping bag rather than a disposable paper or plastic bag. *Reuse* refers to finding another use for an object rather than discarding it. For example, you could refill plastic drink bottles with drinking water or juice you mix instead of buying drinks in new bottles. And *recycle* refers to reclaiming raw materials to create new products. You can make sure you recycle at home, and you can also encourage others to recycle. How about starting a used paper collection and recycling program at your school?

One way to significantly reduce the amount of solid waste your family produces is to start a compost pile. **Composting** is the process of helping the natural decomposition processes break down many forms of waste. Compost piles can be used to recycle yard trash such as grass clippings and raked leaves, and food waste such as fruit and vegetable scraps, eggshells, and coffee grounds. Some farms use compost piles to naturally recycle animal manure. Compost is an excellent natural fertilizer for plants.

Figure 14 Many communities have neighborhood compost bins like this one in Brooklyn, in New York City. *Applying Concepts How does composting help solve the solid waste problem?*

Section 2 Review

1. What happens to most solid waste in the United States?
2. List the four major categories of solid waste that are most often recycled.
3. Name and define the "three R's" of solid waste management.
4. Give an example of a way in which communities can reduce their solid waste.
5. What is composting?
6. **Thinking Critically Comparing and Contrasting** Compare the recycling of metal and paper. How are they similar? How are they different?

Science at Home

Trash Weigh-In For one week, have your family collect their household trash in large bags. Do not isnclude food waste. At the end of the week, hold a trash weigh-in. Multiply the total amount by 52 to show how much trash your family produces in a year. Together, can you suggest any ways to reduce your family's trash load?

Waste, Away!

About two thirds of municipal solid waste ends up in a landfill. In this lab, you'll investigate how landfills are constructed to be most effective and safe.

Problem

How do different kinds of landfills work?

Skills Focus

making models, drawing conclusions

Materials

measuring cup	metric ruler	soil
small pebbles	cheesecloth	scissors
plastic wrap	water	newspaper
5 rubber bands	red food coloring	tweezers

heavy-duty plastic bag
12 small sponge cubes
3 transparent, wide-mouthed jars

Procedure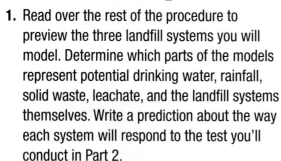

1. Read over the rest of the procedure to preview the three landfill systems you will model. Determine which parts of the models represent potential drinking water, rainfall, solid waste, leachate, and the landfill systems themselves. Write a prediction about the way each system will respond to the test you'll conduct in Part 2.

Part 1 Modeling Three Landfill Systems

2. Obtain 3 identical jars. Label them *System 1, System 2,* and *System 3.* Pour clean, clear water into each jar to a depth of 5 cm.

3. Add equal amounts of small pebbles to each jar. The pebbles should be just below the surface of the water.

4. For System 1, cover the pebble and water mixture with 2.5 cm of soil.

5. For System 2, suspend a piece of cheesecloth in the jar about 5 cm above the water line, as shown in the photograph. Hold the cheesecloth in place with a rubber band around the outside mouth of the jar. Gently pour a handful of small pebbles into the cheesecloth.

6. For System 3, suspend a plastic bag in the jar about 5 cm above the water line. Hold the bag in place with a rubber band around the outside mouth of the jar. Gently pour a handful of small pebbles into the plastic bag.

7. Observe the water and pebbles at the bottom of each system. Record your observations.

Part 2 Testing the Systems

8. Soak 12 identical sponge cubes in water tinted with red food coloring. Use tweezers to place four soaked sponge cubes onto the top surface in each jar.

9. Cover the sponge cubes in Systems 2 and 3 with a thin layer of soil. Leave the sponge cubes in System 1 uncovered.

10. Make a labeled drawing of each system. Explain what each part of the model represents.

11. Pour 150 mL of water over each system. Then cover each jar with plastic wrap, and hold the wrap in place with a rubber band. Let the systems stand overnight.

12. Observe each landfill system. Note especially any changes in the color or clarity of the "groundwater." Record your observations.

Analyze and Conclude

1. Explain how your models represent three common types of landfills: a well-designed, or sanitary, landfill; a landfill with a poor design; and an open dump. Compare the way the three systems work.

2. Which part of the model represented the leachate? How well did each landfill system protect the groundwater from the leachate?

3. Do you think a community's water supply is protected when waste is placed in landfills that are not immediately above groundwater sources? Explain.

4. **Apply** Based on your results, which landfill system is safest for the environment? Explain your answer.

Design an Experiment

Solid waste can be compacted (crushed into smaller pieces) and have liquid removed before it is placed in a landfill. Does preparing the waste in this way make it safer for the environment? Write a hypothesis, then use the ideas and procedures from this lab to test your hypothesis. Obtain your teacher's permission before trying your experiment.

SECTION
3 Hazardous Wastes

DISCOVER ••ACTIVITY••••

What's Hazardous?

1. Your teacher will give you labels from some common hazardous household products.

2. Read the information on each label. Identify the word or words that tell why the product is hazardous.

Think It Over

Forming Operational Definitions Based on your observations of the product labels, write a definition of the term *hazardous.*

GUIDE FOR READING

◆ **What are the categories of hazardous wastes?**

◆ **How can hazardous wastes affect human health?**

◆ **What techniques can be used to manage hazardous wastes?**

Reading Tip Before you read, rewrite the headings in each section as *how, what,* or *where* questions. As you read, look for answers to these questions.

Key Terms hazardous waste
• toxic • explosive • flammable
• corrosive • radioactive

Figure 15 This school in Love Canal was abandoned because of pollution.

In the early 1950s, the city of Niagara Falls, New York, bought an area of land around an old canal. The canal had been filled with chemical wastes from nearby industries. On top of this land, the city built a new neighborhood and elementary school. The neighborhood was named Love Canal.

Then strange things began to happen. Children playing in muddy fields developed skin rashes. Wooden fence posts rotted and turned black. People reported colored liquid seeping into their basements. Babies were born with birth defects. Adults developed epilepsy, liver disease, and nerve disorders. The neighborhood was finally declared a federal emergency disaster area. More than two hundred families were moved away.

What was behind these strange events at Love Canal? Building the neighborhood had caused the clay cover on the old canal dump site to crack. Rainwater seeped into the buried wastes through the cracks. The construction caused chemicals to leak from the underground storage containers. Over time, water mixed with the chemicals to form a dangerous leachate. This leachate polluted the soil and the groundwater and leaked into people's basements.

The Love Canal problem was the first time a federal emergency was declared in an area because of hazardous wastes. It helped people realize that certain chemicals can remain dangerous in soil and water for many years. As a result, new laws were passed to find and clean up other dangerous waste sites.

Types of Hazardous Wastes

Many people picture hazardous wastes as bubbling chemicals, thick fumes, or oozing slime. But even some harmless-looking, common materials such as window cleaner, house paint, radio batteries, and nail polish remover can become hazardous wastes. **Hazardous waste** is any material that can be harmful to human health or the environment if it is not properly disposed of.

Hazardous wastes are created during the manufacture of many household products. Many more are produced as a result of agriculture, industry, military operations, and research at hospitals and scientific laboratories.

Hazardous wastes are classified into four categories: toxic, explosive, flammable, and corrosive. Figure 16 gives some examples of these types of waste. **Toxic** wastes, or poisonous wastes, are wastes that can damage the health of humans and other organisms. **Explosive** wastes are wastes that react very quickly when exposed to air or water, or that explode when they are dropped. Explosive wastes are also called reactive wastes. **Flammable** wastes catch fire easily and can begin burning at fairly low temperatures. **Corrosive** wastes are wastes that dissolve or eat through many materials.

Other wastes that require special disposal are radioactive wastes. **Radioactive** wastes are wastes that contain unstable atoms. These unstable atoms give off radiation that can cause cancer and other diseases. There are two types of radioactive wastes: high-level waste and low-level waste. An example of high-level radioactive waste is the used fuel from nuclear reactors. Low-level radioactive wastes are produced when radioactive minerals such as uranium are mined. They are also produced at some medical and scientific research sites. Radioactive waste can remain dangerous for thousands of years.

Figure 16 Vehicles transporting dangerous materials must use signs like these to alert people of the potential dangers of their loads.

Category: Radioactive
Examples: Uranium, plutonium

Category: Flammable
Example: Kerosene

Category: Corrosive
Examples: Hydrochloric acid, sodium hydroxide

Category: Explosive
Example: Nitroglycerin

Category: Toxic
Examples: Chlorine, PCBs, mercury

Health Effects of Hazardous Wastes

INTEGRATING HEALTH A person can be exposed to hazardous wastes by breathing, eating or drinking, or touching them. Many factors determine the effects of a hazardous substance on a person. One factor is how harmful the substance is. Another factor is how much of the substance a person is exposed to. A third factor is how long the exposure lasts. A person may be exposed for a short time, such as a child accidentally drinking antifreeze. Or a person may be exposed for many years, as were the residents of Love Canal. Finally, a person's age, weight, and health all influence how a substance affects that person.

In general, short-term exposure to hazardous wastes may cause irritation or more severe health problems. These health problems can include breathing difficulties, internal bleeding, paralysis, coma, and even death. **Long-term exposure to hazardous wastes may cause diseases, such as cancer, and may damage body organs, including the brain, liver, kidneys, and lungs.** These effects may eventually be life threatening.

Disposal of Hazardous Wastes

It is hard to safely dispose of hazardous wastes. Burying them can pollute the soil or groundwater. Releasing wastes into lakes or rivers can pollute surface water. Burning hazardous wastes can pollute the air. You can see the problem!

Methods of hazardous waste disposal include burial in landfills, incineration, and breakdown by living organisms. Another method involves storing liquid wastes in deep rock layers.

Figure 17 Hazardous wastes can pollute the soil, water, and air. The chemical drums on the left were illegally dumped in a field. Below, environmental scientists in protective gear test the contents of an old storage tank.

440

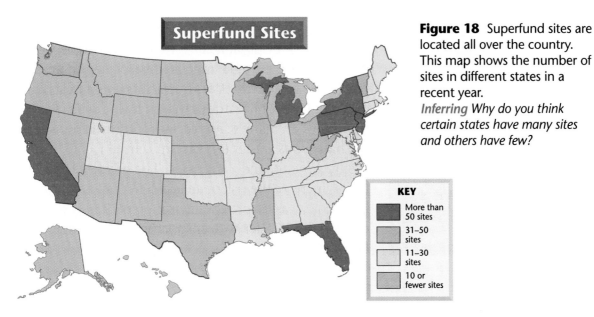

Superfund Sites

KEY
- More than 50 sites
- 31–50 sites
- 11–30 sites
- 10 or fewer sites

Figure 18 Superfund sites are located all over the country. This map shows the number of sites in different states in a recent year.
Inferring Why do you think certain states have many sites and others have few?

Hazardous wastes are most often disposed of in carefully designed landfills. These landfills are lined with clay and plastic to keep chemicals from leaking into the soil and groundwater. A clay and plastic cover prevents rainwater from seeping into the wastes.

Scientists have developed some other methods for disposing of hazardous waste. For example, wastes can be incinerated at very high temperatures. Incineration often breaks down harmful compounds into less harmful ones. Bacteria, algae, and fungi can break down some hazardous chemicals. Another disposal method involves pumping liquid wastes into a layer of sandstone or limestone thousands of meters underground. The wastes spread throughout this soft rock layer. But the wastes cannot move through the impermeable layers of rock above and below. An impermeable rock layer is one that water cannot easily pass through, such as clay or granite. A few types of hazardous waste, such as motor oil and lead-acid car batteries, can even be recycled.

Scientists have not been able to develop completely safe methods for disposing of radioactive waste. Some techniques used today are mixing the waste with concrete or sealing it in abandoned mine shafts. High-level radioactive wastes are currently stored in vaults dug hundreds of meters underground or in concrete and steel containers above ground. But these storage areas are temporary. Scientists are still searching for methods that will provide safe, permanent disposal of radioactive wastes.

✓ *Checkpoint* How are most hazardous wastes disposed of?

Locating Disposal Sites

Communities must also decide *where* to dispose of hazardous wastes. Should there be fewer, larger disposal sites, or many smaller ones? Each answer has costs and benefits.

Social Studies
CONNECTION

In 1980, Congress passed a law creating a hazardous waste site cleanup program called the Superfund. The law determines who should pay for the cleanup. This can include any businesses or people that have ever owned or operated the property, or have ever contributed wastes to it.

In Your Journal

Most industries did not purposely pollute the air, land, and water. In the past, people were largely unaware that some industrial wastes were hazardous, and that these substances could have serious effects many years later. Should these industries still be responsible for paying for the cleanup? If not, where should this money come from? Write a paragraph explaining your opinion.

Figure 19 The scent of these citronella candles naturally repels insects and creates less hazardous waste than bug spray.

Most people don't want to live or work near a hazardous waste disposal facility. In general, people would prefer to have a single large facility located in an area where few people live. A central facility could treat many different types of hazardous wastes. It would be easier to monitor than many scattered sites. However, transporting hazardous wastes to a distant central facility can be costly, difficult, and dangerous. The greater travel distances increase the risk of an accident that could release hazardous wastes into the environment. It may be safer, cheaper, and easier to transport wastes to small local facilities instead.

Reducing Hazardous Waste

The best way to manage hazardous wastes is to produce less of them in the first place. Industries are eager to develop safe alternatives to harmful chemicals. For example, some brands of furniture polishes are now made from lemon oil and beeswax instead of petroleum oils. Many products such as air fresheners, plastic dishes and countertops, carpets, and curtains used to be made with the chemical formaldehyde, which gradually leaked out of these products into the air. Companies have developed alternatives to formaldehyde to use in their products. For instance, the next time you are in a supermarket or hardware store, look for air fresheners that are labeled "formaldehyde-free."

At home, you can find substitutes for some hazardous household chemicals. For example, instead of using insect spray, use harmless materials that naturally repel insects, such as the citronella candles shown in Figure 19. Many household cleaners also now come in biodegradable forms.

Section 3 Review

1. List and define the four categories of hazardous waste.
2. Describe the short-term and long-term effects of hazardous substances on human health.
3. Describe one method used to dispose of hazardous wastes.
4. What was the significance of the events at Love Canal?
5. Explain why radioactive wastes are particularly difficult to manage.
6. **Thinking Critically** **Making Judgments** Do you think hazardous wastes should be treated and disposed of at one central facility or at many small local facilities? Give reasons for your answer.

Check Your Progress
CHAPTER PROJECT

By now you should be investigating what happens to the different materials in your package when it is thrown away. You will need to find out what types of waste your community recycles, and how it handles other solid waste. (*Hint:* The town engineer or Department of Public Works may be a good source of this information. Be sure to check with your teacher before contacting anyone.)

SECTION 1 How Land is Used

Key Ideas

◆ Land is a nonrenewable resource that people use for agriculture, development, mining, and other uses.

◆ Soil is a complex system that takes a very long time to form.

◆ Poor soil management can cause erosion, nutrient depletion, and desertification.

◆ In the nitrogen cycle, free nitrogen in the air is converted into nitrogen compounds by bacteria in soil. The nitrogen compounds then become part of plants and other living things, which eventually die and decay, releasing nitrogen gas and continuing the cycle.

Key Terms

development
land reclamation
litter
topsoil
subsoil
bedrock

erosion
desertification
nutrient depletion
fallow
crop rotation
nitrogen cycle

SECTION 2 Solid Waste

Key Ideas

◆ Wastes are produced in the making and using of many products.

◆ Three ways of handling solid waste are to bury it, to burn it, or to recycle it.

◆ Most municipal solid waste in the United States is buried in sanitary landfills.

◆ Municipal solid wastes such as metal, glass, paper, and plastic can be recycled.

◆ One way to help solve the solid waste problem is to practice the "three R's"—reduce, reuse, and recycle.

Key Terms

municipal solid waste
leachate
sanitary landfill
incineration

recycling
biodegradable
resins
composting

SECTION 3 Hazardous Wastes

Key Ideas

◆ Hazardous wastes are materials that can threaten human health and safety or can be harmful to the environment if they are not properly disposed of.

◆ Hazardous wastes include toxic, explosive, flammable, and corrosive wastes. Radioactive wastes also require special disposal.

◆ How a person is affected by a hazardous substance depends on several factors, including the amount of the substance, the length of time the person is exposed, and how the substance enters the person's body.

◆ It is very difficult to find safe ways to dispose of hazardous wastes and good places to store them. A good way to manage hazardous wastes is to produce less of them.

Key Terms

hazardous waste
toxic
explosive

flammable
corrosive
radioactive

Organizing Information

Compare/Contrast Table On a separate sheet of paper, copy the table below about ways to dispose of municipal solid waste. Then complete it and add a title. (For more on compare/contrast tables, see the Skills Handbook.)

	Landfill	Incinerator
Cost		
Pollution		
Attractiveness		
Usefulness to community		

Reviewing Content

Review key concepts online using iText at www.phschool.com

Multiple Choice
Choose the letter of the best answer.

1. The advance of desertlike conditions into areas that previously were fertile is called
   a. desertification.
   b. crop rotation.
   c. nutrient depletion.
   d. land reclamation.
2. Water containing dissolved chemicals from a landfill is called
   a. resin.
   b. litter.
   c. leachate.
   d. compost.
3. Solid wastes are burned in the process of
   a. incineration.
   b. composting.
   c. erosion.
   d. recycling.
4. Which of the following is a biodegradable waste?
   a. a glass jar   b. a metal can
   c. an apple core   d. a plastic bag
5. Wastes that contain unstable atoms are called
   a. corrosive.   b. flammable.
   c. radioactive.   d. explosive.

True and False
If the statement is true, write true. If it is false, change the underlined word or words to make the statement true.

6. Three major types of land use are agriculture, development, and <u>mining</u>.
7. <u>Development</u> is the process of restoring land to a more natural state.
8. Fields that are left unplanted with crops are called <u>fallow</u>.
9. Most of the municipal solid waste generated in the United States is disposed of in <u>landfills</u>.
10. Liners prevent the waste in landfills from polluting the <u>air</u>.

Checking Concepts

11. List two living things and two nonliving things that are found in topsoil.
12. Choose one of the following techniques and explain how it can reduce soil erosion: contour plowing, terracing, conservation plowing, or windbreaks.
13. What role does bacteria play in the nitrogen cycle?
14. What does the number on a plastic container indicate?
15. Describe one way communities can encourage residents to produce less solid waste.
16. What is composting? What kinds of materials can be composted?
17. Explain how a person might be exposed to a hazardous substance that was buried underground many years ago.
18. **Writing to Learn** Write a public service announcement to inform people about household hazardous wastes. Begin with a "hook" to catch your listener's attention. Be sure to explain what makes a waste hazardous. Also give examples of household hazardous wastes, and tell people what to do with these substances.

Thinking Critically

19. **Relating Cause and Effect** Every few years, a farmer plants clover in a wheat field. Explain this practice.
20. **Applying Concepts** If you owned a large farm on a hill, how would you prevent soil erosion? Explain your answer.
21. **Problem Solving** In strip mining, a layer of soil is removed to expose a resource, such as coal, underneath. What methods could be used to restore this damaged land?
22. **Making Judgments** Suppose you go to the store to buy some juice. You can choose from juice sold in an aluminum, glass, or plastic container, all for the same price. Which would you choose? Explain your answer.

Applying Skills

Use the following data on municipal solid waste in the United States to answer Questions 23–25.

Type of Waste	Percent of Total
Paper and cardboard	38%
Food wastes	10%
Yard wastes	13%
Metals	8%
Plastics	9%
Glass	6%
Other wastes	16%

23. **Graphing** Use the data to create a circle graph. (To review circle graphs, see the Skills Handbook.)
24. **Classifying** Which of the types of waste shown are recyclable? Which include wastes that can be composted?

25. **Developing Hypotheses** Why do you think paper makes up the largest percent of solid waste?

Performance CHAPTER PROJECT **Assessment**

Present Your Project As you finish work on your project, share it with one or more classmates. Ask: Does the display clearly explain what the package is made of? Are the benefits of the package identified? Does the display describe what happens to each material? If you need to make any revisions to your display, do so now.

Reflect and Record In your project notebook, describe the most surprising information you learned during this project. What questions might you ask before purchasing a product like the one you studied?

Test Preparation

Use these questions to prepare for standardized tests.

Study the information below. Then answer Questions 26–28.

The graph shows how rain can wash away certain compounds that plants need.

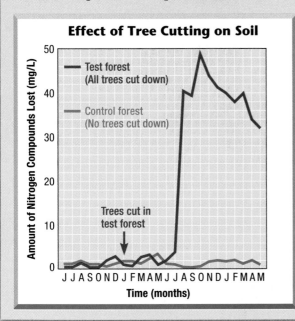

26. Before trees were cut down, the loss of nitrogen compounds was
    A unknown.
    B about the same in both forests.
    C greater in the test forest.
    D greater in the control forest.

27. During the second year, the amount of nitrogen compounds lost in the test forest was
    F about the same as in the first year.
    G about 2 times greater than in the first year.
    H about 20 times greater than in the first year.
    J about 20 times less than in the first year.

28. According to the graph, cutting down trees
    A caused the death of other trees.
    B had no effect on the loss of nitrogen compounds.
    C caused more nitrogen compounds to be lost.
    D caused nitrogen compounds to increase.

CHAPTER

13 Air and Water Resources

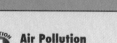

www.phschool.com

SECTION 1 **Air Pollution**
Discover How Does the Scent Spread?
Real-World Lab How Does the Garden Grow?

SECTION 2 **The Water Supply**
Discover How Does the Water Change?
Skills Lab Concentrate on This!

SECTION 3 **Finding Pollution Solutions**
Discover Can You Remove the Tea?

Pollution vs. Purity

Pollution is a change to the environment that has a harmful effect on humans and other living things. Pollution can come from a single smokestack or from many different sources all over the world.

As you study this chapter, your project is to help communicate the importance of preventing pollution and protecting air or water quality.

Your Goal To create a book, game, or video that educates younger students about air or water quality.

Your product should

◆ present facts about the causes and effects of a form of pollution

◆ engage your audience while informing them about the topic

◆ include steps that the students can take to be part of the "pollution solution"

Get Started Survey the chapter to see what types of pollution are discussed. Begin thinking about which topic you would like to explore. Discuss with your teacher what age group your product should be designed for. Decide which form your product will take.

Check Your Progress You'll be working on the project as you study this chapter. To keep your project on track, look for Check Your Progress boxes at the following points.

Section 2 Review, page 461: Gather information on your topic and organize it.

Section 3 Review, page 466: Design and create your product.

Wrap Up At the end of the chapter (page 469), you will present your product to younger students and get their feedback.

Smoke billows from a row of smokestacks at an automobile plant.

TEKS

In addition to process TEKS, this chapter addresses these concept TEKS as they relate to the chapter's topics.

(8.12) The student knows that cycles exist in Earth systems. The student is expected to:
(C) predict the results of modifying the Earth's nitrogen, water, and carbon cycles.

(8.14) The student knows that natural events and human activity can alter Earth systems. The student is expected to:
(A) predict land features resulting from gradual changes such as mountain building, beach erosion, land subsidence, and continental drift;
(C) describe how human activities have modified soil, water, and air quality.

SECTION 1 Air Pollution

DISCOVER • ACTIVITY

How Does the Scent Spread?

1. Choose a place to stand so that you and your classmates are evenly spaced around the room.

2. Your teacher will open a bottle of perfume in one corner of the room.

3. Raise your hand when you first smell the perfume.

Think It Over

Inferring Describe the pattern you observed as people raised their hands. How do you think the smell traveled across the room?

GUIDE FOR READING

◆ What causes photochemical smog?

◆ How is the ozone layer important?

Reading Tip As you read, make a list of different types of air pollution. Write a sentence about the effect of each type.

Key Terms air pollution
• emissions • ozone
• photochemical smog
• temperature inversion
• acid rain • ozone layer
• chlorofluorocarbons

J une 25, 1997, began as an ordinary day aboard the Russian space station *Mir*. The three crew members were busy with their usual tasks. One checked on the various scientific experiments. Another was exercising. The third cosmonaut was skillfully guiding a supply ship as it docked with *Mir*.

Suddenly, the crew members heard a frightening sound—the crumpling of collapsing metal. The space station jolted from side to side. The pressure gauges indicated an air leak! One crew member hurried to prepare the emergency evacuation vehicle. Meanwhile, the other two managed to close the airtight door between the damaged area and the rest of the space station. Fortunately, the air pressure soon returned to normal. A disaster had been avoided. There was no need to abandon ship.

Closing the door preserved the most valuable resource on *Mir*—the air. Although you probably don't think about the air very often, it is just as important on Earth as it is on a space station. Air is a resource you use every minute of your life.

What's in the Air?

Though you can't see, taste, or smell it, you are surrounded by air. Air is a mixture of nitrogen, oxygen, carbon dioxide, water vapor, and other gases. Almost all living things depend on these gases to carry out their life processes.

Nitrogen, oxygen, and carbon dioxide cycle between the atmosphere and living things. These cycles ensure that the air supply on Earth will not run out. But they don't guarantee that the air will always be clean. A change to the atmosphere that has harmful effects is called **air pollution.** Substances that cause pollution are called pollutants. Pollutants can be solid particles,

Figure 1 The air supply aboard the space station *Mir* was threatened by a collision during docking.

such as ash, or gases, such as chlorine. Air pollution can affect the health of humans and other living things. Pollution can even impact the climate of the whole planet.

What causes air pollution? If you're like many people, you probably picture a factory smokestack, belching thick black smoke into the sky. Until the mid-1900s, factories and power plants that burned coal produced most of the air pollution in the United States. Solid particles and gases that are released into the air are called **emissions.** Today, there is an even larger source of emissions that cause air pollution: motor vehicles such as cars, trucks, and airplanes. The engines of these vehicles release gases such as carbon monoxide, an invisible toxic gas.

Though most air pollution is the result of human activities, there are some natural causes as well. For example, an erupting volcano sends an enormous load of soot, ash, sulfur, and nitrogen oxide gases into the atmosphere.

☑ *Checkpoint* *What are some examples of air pollutants?*

Smog

Have you ever heard a weather forecaster talk about a "smog alert"? A smog alert is a warning about a type of air pollution called photochemical smog. **Photochemical smog** is a thick, brownish haze formed when certain gases in the air react with sunlight. When the smog level is high, it settles as a haze over a city. Smog can make people's eyes burn and irritate their throats.

The major sources of photochemical smog are the gases emitted by automobiles and trucks. Burning gasoline in a car engine releases some gases into the air. These gases include hydrocarbons (compounds containing hydrogen and carbon) and nitrogen oxides. The gases react in the sunlight and produce a form of oxygen called **ozone.** Ozone, which is toxic, is the major chemical found in smog.

Figure 2 A haze of photochemical smog hangs over this city's skyline. *Interpreting Photographs What is the source of the smog?*

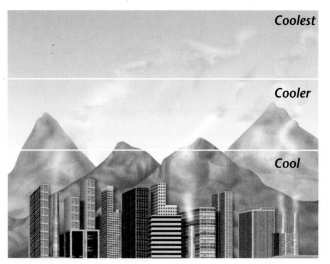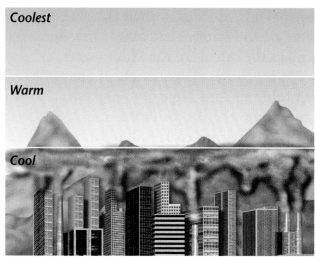

Coolest

Coolest

Cooler

Warm

Cool

Cool

Figure 3 Normally, pollutants rise high in the air and blow away (left). But during a temperature inversion, a layer of warm air traps pollutants close to the ground (right).

Temperature Inversion Pollutants usually blow away from the place where they are produced. Normally, air close to the ground is heated by Earth's surface. As the air warms, it rises into the cooler air above it. The pollutants are carried higher into the atmosphere where they blow away. But certain weather conditions can cause a temperature inversion. A layer of warm air prevents rising air from escaping during a **temperature inversion.** The polluted air is trapped and held close to Earth's surface. The smog becomes more concentrated and dangerous.

Health Effects of Smog The effects of smog can be more

INTEGRATING HEALTH serious than itchy, watery eyes and a scratchy throat. The ozone in smog can cause lung problems and harm the body's defenses against infection. When smog levels reach a certain point, a city issues a smog alert. During a smog alert, you should avoid exercising outdoors. People who have asthma or other conditions that affect their breathing should be particularly careful.

☑ *Checkpoint* *What happens during a temperature inversion?*

Acid Rain

Another type of air pollution is caused by power plants and factories that burn coal and oil. These fuels produce nitrogen oxides and sulfur oxides when they are burned. These gases react with water vapor in the air, forming nitric acid and sulfuric acid. The acids return to Earth's surface dissolved in precipitation. Precipitation that is more acidic than normal is called **acid rain.** Snow, sleet, or fog can also be acidic.

When acid rain falls into a pond or lake, it changes the conditions there. Many fish, and their eggs, cannot survive in more acidic water. Acid rain that falls on the ground can damage plants by affecting the nutrient levels in the soil. Whole forests have been destroyed by acid rain. Fortunately, some of the effects of acid rain are reversible. Badly damaged lakes have been restored by adding lime to neutralize the acid.

Indoor Air Pollution

The air inside buildings can also become polluted. Some indoor pollutants such as dust, pet hair, and air fresheners, bother only those people who are allergic to them. Asbestos, a building material common in older buildings, can cause lung disease. Products such as oil-based paints, glues, and cleaning supplies may give off toxic fumes. Read the label whenever you use any of these products. You may need to open a window or use the chemical outdoors.

Another indoor pollutant is cigarette smoke. Smoke reaches your lungs every time you inhale near a smoking person. Research has shown that cigarette smoke can damage the lungs and heart. Now smoking is banned in many public places such as restaurants, airports, and stadiums.

Radon Another type of pollution that is difficult to detect is radon. Radon is a colorless, odorless gas that is radioactive. It is formed naturally by certain types of rocks underground. Radon can enter homes through cracks in basement walls or floors. Research indicates that breathing radon gas over many years may cause lung cancer and other health problems. But the level of radon necessary to cause these effects is unknown. To be safe, many homeowners have installed ventilation systems to prevent radon from building up in their homes.

How Acid Is Your Rain?

In this activity you will test **ACTIVITY** whether rain in your area is more or less acidic than lemon juice (citric acid).

1. Collect some rainwater in a clean plastic cup.

2. Indoors, dip a piece of pH paper into the cup. Compare the color of the paper to the chart on the package to find the pH. (The lower the pH of a substance, the more acidic it is.)

3. 🥽 Put on your goggles.

4. Pour a little lemon juice into a plastic cup. Repeat Step 2 with the lemon juice.

Measuring What is the pH of the rainwater? How does it compare to the pH of the lemon juice?

Figure 4 Air inside buildings can be polluted, too. *Observing How many sources of pollution can you spot in this room?*

Figure 5 Installing a carbon monoxide detector in a home can save lives. Because carbon monoxide has no color or odor, it cannot be detected by sight or smell.

Carbon Monoxide One particularly dangerous type of indoor air pollution is carbon monoxide. Carbon monoxide is a colorless, odorless gas that forms when wood, coal, oil, or gas are incompletely burned. When carbon monoxide builds up in an enclosed space such as a basement, apartment, or house, it can be deadly. Because carbon monoxide cannot be detected by sight or smell, its victims have no warning that the level is dangerously high. Any home heated by wood, coal, oil, or gas should have a carbon monoxide detector. The detector sounds a warning alarm when the gas is present.

☑ *Checkpoint* *Why is it important to install carbon monoxide detectors in homes?*

The Ozone Layer

If you have ever had a sunburn, you have experienced the painful effects of the sun's ultraviolet radiation. But did you know that such burns would be even worse without the protection of the ozone layer? The **ozone layer** is a layer of the upper atmosphere about 30 kilometers above Earth's surface. Actually, the concentration of ozone in this layer is very low—only a few parts per million. **Yet even the small amount of ozone in the ozone layer protects people from the effects of too much ultraviolet radiation.** These effects include sunburn, eye diseases, and skin cancer.

Since you read earlier that ozone is a pollutant, the fact that ozone can be helpful may sound confusing. The difference between ozone as a pollutant and ozone as a helpful gas is its location. Ozone close to Earth's surface in the form of smog is harmful. Higher in the atmosphere, where people cannot breathe it, ozone protects us.

Sharpen your Skills

Communicating

Using a computer, write a radio public service announcement that informs people about either carbon monoxide or radon. Think about how the announcement could catch your listeners' attention. Describe the source and effects of the pollutant. Suggest how listeners can protect themselves.

ACTIVITY

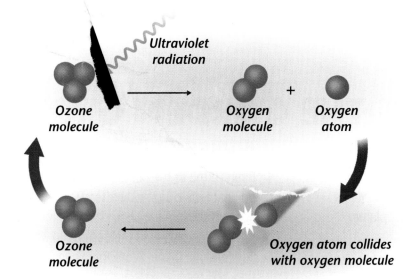

Figure 6 When ultraviolet radiation from the sun strikes an ozone molecule, some energy is absorbed by the ozone molecule. This energy causes the ozone molecule to split into an oxygen molecule and a free oxygen atom. *Interpreting Diagrams What happens when the free oxygen atom collides with an oxygen molecule?*

The Source of Ozone   Ozone is constantly being made and destroyed. When sunlight strikes an ozone molecule, the energy of the ultraviolet radiation is partly absorbed. This energy causes the molecule to break apart into an oxygen molecule and an oxygen atom, as shown in Figure 6. The oxygen atom soon collides with another oxygen molecule. They react to form a new ozone molecule. Each time this cycle occurs, some ultraviolet energy is absorbed. That energy does not reach Earth's surface.

The Ozone Hole   In the late 1970s, scientists observed that the amount of ozone in the ozone layer seemed to be decreasing. One problem was a group of gases containing chlorine and fluorine, called **chlorofluorocarbons,** or "CFCs." CFCs had been used in refrigerators, air conditioners, and aerosol spray cans. Then scientists discovered that CFCs react with ozone molecules. The CFCs block the cycle that absorbs ultraviolet radiation. In 1990, many nations signed an agreement to ban the use of almost all CFCs by the year 2000. Scientists predict that if the ban is maintained, the ozone layer will gradually recover.

Section 1 Review

1. How does photochemical smog form?
2. What is acid rain? How does acid rain affect the environment?
3. How does the ozone layer protect people?
4. Give three examples of indoor air pollutants and list their sources.
5. **Thinking Critically** **Predicting** If a city did nothing to reduce photochemical smog, how could this affect the health of city residents?

Science at Home

It's in the Air What solid particles are in your air? With a family member, set up two particle collectors. Smear petroleum jelly on the inside of two clean, empty glass jars. Place one inside your home and the other outside in locations where they will not be disturbed. Predict what you will find if you leave the jars in place for a few days. Compare the solid particles in each jar. How similar are they? Can you identify any of the particles?

HOW DOES THE GARDEN GROW?

Air pollution can affect rain, which then falls on the land, harming organisms living there. In this lab you will investigate how pollutants affect plants.

Problem

How do pollutants affect seed growth?

Skills Focus

controlling variables, measuring, interpreting data

Materials

2 plastic petri dishes with lids	metric ruler
	wax pencil
potting soil	acid solution
20 radish seeds	oil solution
masking tape	salt solution
day-old tap water	detergent solution

Procedure

1. Read all the steps of the lab. Choose a pollutant to investigate. Write a hypothesis about the effect of this pollutant. Make a data chart to organize your data so that you can examine and evaluate your data later. Write the name of the pollutant in the data chart.

2. Write your initials on the lids of the petri dishes. Then write "Control" on one lid. Label the other lid with the name of your pollutant.

3. Fill each dish with potting soil. Do not pack down the soil.

4. Pour 10 mL of water into the control dish. Pour 10 mL of the pollutant solution into the pollutant dish. Lightly scatter 10 seeds on the soil surface in each dish.

5. Cover each dish with the correct lid. Tape the lids firmly in place. Store the dishes where they will receive light and will not be moved. Wash your hands with soap.

6. Once a day for the next five days, observe the seeds (do not open the lids). Record your observations in the data chart. Use a metric ruler to measure the length of any roots or shoots that develop. If you do not observe any change, record that observation.

Analyze and Conclude

1. How many seeds germinated each day in the control dish? In the pollutant dish? How many seeds total germinated in each dish?

2. Did the seedlings grown under the two conditions differ? If so, how?

3. Did your results support your hypothesis? Explain.

4. **Apply** Predict what the effect would be if the pollutant you investigated reached a vegetable garden or farm.

Design an Experiment

Do you think the pollutant you studied has the same effect on all types of plants? Write a hypothesis, and design an experiment to test it. With your teacher's approval, carry out your plan.

DATA CHART

Date	Number of Seeds That Germinated		Condition of Seedlings	
	Control	Pollutant	Control	Pollutant

2 The Water Supply

DISCOVER ··· ACTIVITY····

How Does the Water Change?

1. Shine a flashlight through a clear plastic cup of water.

2. Add 6 drops of milk to the water and stir.

3. Shine the flashlight through the cup again. Note any differences.

Think It Over

Observing Where in the cup of water is the milk located? Could you easily separate the milk from the water?

How could you determine whether life has ever existed on another planet in the solar system? One piece of evidence scientists look for is the presence of water. This is because water is the most common compound in all living cells on Earth. Water is necessary for life as we know it.

Most of Earth's surface is covered by some form of water. From space you cannot even see many parts of Earth because they are hidden behind clouds of tiny water droplets. Around the poles are vast sheets of ice. Oceans cover nearly three fourths of Earth's surface.

The Water Cycle

Water in Earth's oceans does not remain there indefinitely. Water is constantly recycled through the water cycle. **The water cycle is the continuous process through which water moves from Earth's oceans to the atmosphere, to the land surface, and then returns to the oceans.** The processes of evaporation, condensation, and precipitation make up the **water cycle.** As you read about these processes, follow the water cycle in Figure 8.

GUIDE FOR READING

◆ What is the water cycle?

◆ Why is fresh water a limited resource?

◆ What are the major sources of water pollution?

Reading Tip As you read, identify sentences that support this statement: *Water is a scarce resource that must be protected.*

Key Terms water cycle
• evaporaton • condensation
• precipitation • groundwater
• drought • water pollution
• sewage • fertilizer • pesticide
• sediment • land subsidence

Figure 7 A view from space shows the abundance of water on Earth and in the atmosphere.

Figure 8 In the water cycle, water moves continuously from Earth's surface to the atmosphere and back. *Interpreting Diagrams In which step of the water cycle does water return to Earth's surface?*

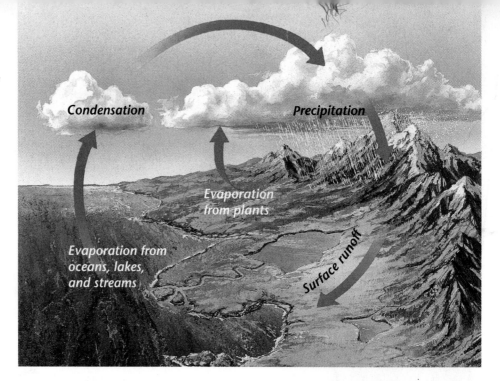

Condensation

Precipitation

Evaporation from plants

Evaporation from oceans, lakes, and streams

Surface runoff

Getting Clean

In this activity **ACTIVITY** you will see how Earth's fresh water is purified in the water cycle.

1. Pour 15 mL of water into a plastic cup.

2. Add a few drops of food coloring and half a teaspoon of sugar. Stir until the sugar is dissolved.

3. Put the cup in the sunlight in a place where it will not be disturbed.

4. Check on the cup twice a day until all the water has evaporated. Observe what remains in the cup.

Making Models What do the sugar and food coloring represent? What happens to the water in this activity?

Evaporation The process by which molecules of liquid water absorb energy and change to the gas state is called **evaporation.** In the water cycle, liquid water evaporates from Earth's surface and forms water vapor, a gas, in the atmosphere. Most water evaporates from the surfaces of oceans and lakes. The energy for evaporation comes from the sun.

Some water is also given off by living things. For example, plants take in water through their roots and release water vapor from their leaves. You take in water when you drink and eat. You release liquid water in your wastes and water vapor when you exhale.

Condensation What happens next to the water vapor in the atmosphere? As the water vapor rises higher in the atmosphere, it cools down. When it cools to a certain temperature, the vapor turns back into tiny drops of liquid water. The process by which a gas changes to a liquid is called **condensation.** The water droplets collect around particles of dust in the air, eventually forming clouds.

Precipitation As more water vapor condenses, the drops of water in the cloud grow larger and heavier. Eventually the heavy drops fall back to Earth as a form of precipitation—rain, snow, sleet, or hail. Most precipitation falls back into oceans or lakes. The **precipitation** that falls on land may soak into the soil and become groundwater. Or the precipitation may run off the land, ultimately flowing into a river or ocean once again.

☑ *Checkpoint* What change of state occurs when water from the surface of the ocean enters the atmosphere as water vapor?

Figure 9 The water cycle constantly moves water between Earth's surface and the atmosphere. As water vapor evaporates from this pond, it condenses in the cool air, forming mist.

The Water Cycle as a System

The water cycle is a complex system driven by energy from the sun and by gravity. The sun's energy is the source of the thermal energy that causes evaporation and lifts water vapor into the atmosphere. Gravity pulls precipitation to the surface and causes runoff to flow downhill.

Presently, the water cycle is in balance worldwide. This means that total precipitation and runoff are about equal to the total amount of evaporation.

A change in one part of the water cycle, however, could affect other parts of the cycle. For example, scientists think that 20,000 years ago, during the last ice age, sea level was about 100 meters lower than at present. Where did this huge volume of water go? Much of it had become frozen in the vast continental glaciers that existed during the ice age. The change in the volume of ocean water affected evaporation and precipitation worldwide.

Human actions can have a local effect on the water cycle. When a forest is cut down, for example, the water that trees would have released as water vapor becomes groundwater or runoff. This increases the flow of streams or rivers in the area. A change in the water cycle thus affects other Earth systems.

A Limited Supply

How can water be scarce when there is so much of it on Earth's surface? **The reason is that most of the water on Earth—about 97 percent—is salt water. Salt water cannot be used for drinking or watering crops.** People need fresh water for these purposes.

In addition, about three quarters of the fresh water on Earth is in the form of ice. This water is not available for people to use. Finally, the supplies of liquid fresh water that do exist are not always close to where people live. For example, many cities in the southwestern United States draw their drinking water from rivers hundreds of kilometers away. About half the people in the United States use **groundwater,** water stored in layers of soil and rock beneath Earth's surface.

Figure 10 People obtain and store water in many ways. At left, a tower holds the water supply of a community in Bucks County, Pennsylvania. At right, women in the Yucatán in Mexico draw water from a well.

Renewing the Supply Fortunately, Earth's supply of fresh water is renewable. Water continually moves between the atmosphere and Earth's surface in the water cycle. Water evaporates from oceans, lakes, and rivers, becoming water vapor in the atmosphere. As the water evaporates, any dissolved substances are left behind. The pure water vapor condenses into tiny droplets which form clouds. When the droplets become large and heavy enough, they fall as precipitation.

Water Shortages Water shortages occur when people use water in an area faster than the water cycle can replace it. This is more likely to happen during a **drought,** a period when less rain than normal falls in an area. During a drought, people have to limit their water use. All unnecessary water uses may be banned. If the drought is severe, crops may die from lack of water.

Due to growing populations, many places in the world never receive enough rain to meet their water needs. They must obtain water from distant sources or by other means. For example, the desert nation of Saudi Arabia obtains more than half its fresh water by removing salt from ocean water.

✓ *Checkpoint* *What is a drought?*

Water Pollution

When fresh water supplies are scarce, pollution can be devastating. Any change to water that has a harmful effect on people or other living things is called **water pollution.** Some pollutants, such as iron and copper, make water unpleasant to drink or wash in. Other pollutants, such as mercury or benzene, can cause sickness or even death.

Most pollution is the result of human activities. Many activities—including agriculture, industry, construction, and mining—produce wastes that can end up in water.

If you did the Discover activity, you saw that a few drops of milk quickly spread throughout a cup of water. You could not tell where the milk first entered the water. In the same way, pollutants dissolve and move throughout a body of water. This is how pollution can affect areas far from its source.

Sewage The water and human wastes that are washed down sinks, toilets, and showers are called **sewage.** If sewage is not treated to kill disease-causing organisms, the organisms quickly multiply. If untreated sewage mixes with water used for drinking or swimming, these organisms can make people very ill.

Even treated sewage can pollute. Any remaining wastes in the sewage can feed bacteria living in the water. As the bacteria multiply, they use up the oxygen in the water. Other organisms that need the oxygen, such as fish, cannot survive.

Agricultural Wastes Animal wastes and farm chemicals are also sources of pollution. Two examples are fertilizers and pesticides. **Fertilizers** are chemicals that provide nutrients to help crops grow better. But rain can wash fertilizers into ponds, where they cause algae to grow quickly. The algae soon cover the pond, blocking light from reaching plants in the pond. **Pesticides** are chemicals that kill crop-destroying organisms such as beetles or worms. However, pesticides can also harm other animals such as birds that feed in the sprayed fields.

Because agricultural chemicals are usually spread over a large, open area, it is hard to keep them from polluting nearby water. Even low levels of chemicals in the water can build up to harmful concentrations as they move through the food chain.

Figure 11 This plane is spraying crops with pesticides.
Relating Cause and Effect How might pesticides sprayed on a field affect fish that live in a nearby pond?

Figure 12 Industrial processes and mining are two sources of chemical pollutants. At left, a chemical plant spills wastes into a river. At right, dissolved copper from a mine turns a stream turquoise.

Industry and Mining Chemical plants, paper and textile mills, and factories that use metals produce wastes that can pollute water. Mining sites are another source of metal wastes. Chemicals and metals can harm the living things in the polluted bodies of water. In addition, humans who drink the water or feed on these organisms are exposed to the pollution.

Sediments When water runs off bare ground, it turns a muddy brown color. This color is due to particles of rock, silt, and sand called **sediments.** Water that flows through places where the ground is disturbed, such as building sites and mines, can pick up large loads of sediments.

As sediments wash into bodies of water, the particles cover up the food sources, nesting sites, and eggs of organisms. By blocking sunlight in the water, the sediments prevent algae and plants from growing. This affects other organisms that rely on the algae and plants for food.

Oil and Gasoline One of the most dramatic forms of water pollution is an oil spill. You may have seen news reports showing beaches covered with tarry black oil, or of volunteers cleaning globs of oil from the feathers of birds. It can take many years for an area to recover from such a spill.

Another pollution problem is caused by oil and gasoline that leak out of underground storage tanks. Think of how many gas stations there are in your area. Each one has storage tanks below the street level to hold the gasoline. In the past, these tanks were often made of steel. Over time, they rusted and developed small holes.

As the gasoline leaked out, it soaked into the soil and polluted the groundwater. The pollution was sometimes carried very far away from the leaking tank. Controlling this type of pollution has been difficult because the sources are hidden underground.

Land Subsidence and Groundwater Withdrawal

Water pollution is not the only environmental problem that can result from people's use of water. As groundwater is pumped out of the ground, land subsidence can occur. The sinking of the land surface that results when water is lost from spaces between loose particles of soil and rock underground is called **land subsidence.** As the water is removed, the particles of soil and rock settle closer together and occupy less space. This causes the land surface above to sink or subside.

Land subsidence due to groundwater withdrawal is a problem in many parts of the United States. In parts of Houston and Galveston, Texas, land subsidence due to groundwater withdrawal has made some neighborhoods more likely to be flooded. To prevent further subsidence, the region has placed limits on the pumping of groundwater.

Figure 13 In California's San Joaquin valley, large amounts of water were pumped out of the ground for use in irrigating crops. In parts of the valley, the land subsided by as much as 8 meters.

Section 2 Review

1. Describe the steps in the water cycle.
2. Why isn't most of the water on Earth's surface available for people to use?
3. Name four types of human activities that can be sources of water pollution.
4. Explain why finding the source of water pollution can be difficult.
5. What is land subsidence?
6. **Thinking Critically Relating Cause and Effect** Why should sewage be treated before being released to the environment?

Check Your Progress CHAPTER PROJECT
By now you should be gathering information to include in your product. Consider including the story of a historical event related to your topic in order to get your audience's interest. As you collect information, begin putting it in a logical order. Using an outline or a storyboard can help you organize your thoughts. (*Hint:* Be sure to keep your topic well focused. Air and water quality are very broad topics! Focusing your topic will help you stay on task and manage your time.)

Concentrate on This!

Many pollutants have harmful effects even at very low concentrations. In this lab you will compare different concentrations of a pollutant in water.

Problem

Can you detect a pollutant in water at a very low concentration?

Materials

9 small test tubes   test tube rack
marker   food coloring
plastic dropper   water

Procedure

1. Read through the entire procedure. Write a prediction of the results you expect. Then copy the data table into your notebook.
2. Label 9 test tubes 1 through 9.
3. Use a plastic dropper to add 9 drops of water to each test tube. Try to make all the drops about the same size.
4. Add 1 drop of food coloring to Test Tube 1. Record the total number of drops now in the test tube. Swirl the test tube gently to mix.
5. The concentration of food coloring in Test Tube 1 is 1 drop in 10 drops, or 1 part per 10. Record that concentration in the data table.
6. Now use the dropper to transfer 1 drop of the mixture from Test Tube 1 into Test Tube 2. Swirl Test Tube 2 to mix its contents.

7. Record the concentration in Test Tube 2. [*Hint:* The drop you just added had a concentration of 1 part per 10. When you dilute (water down) that drop to 1/10 of its strength, the new concentration is 1 part per (10 × 10).]
8. For test tubes 3 through 9, add 1 drop from the previous test tube. Record each new concentration in the data table.
9. Observe the water in each test tube. Record your observation. If you do not observe any color in a test tube, write "colorless."

Analyze and Conclude

1. How does the appearance of the water change from test tubes 1 through 9?
2. Food coloring consists of molecules of dye. Are there any food coloring molecules remaining in Test Tube 9? Explain.
3. What is meant by a "part" in this lab?
4. Which test tube has a concentration of 1 part per million? Which test tube has a concentration of 1 part per billion?
5. **Think About It** Why is parts per million a useful form of measurement when discussing environmental issues?

Design an Experiment

Which is more concentrated, a mixture with 5 parts per million, or 10 parts per 10 million? How different do the two mixtures appear? Use the ideas from this lab to design a plan to find out. Check your plan with your teacher before beginning your experiment.

DATA TABLE

Test Tube	Total Drops Added	Concentration of Food Coloring	Color
1			
2			

SECTION 3 Finding Pollution Solutions

DISCOVER  · ACTIVITY · · ·

Can You Remove the Tea?

1. Pour some cooled herbal tea into a plastic cup. Observe the color of the tea.

2. Place a paper filter in a funnel. Fill it halfway with crushed charcoal. Put the funnel on top of another plastic cup.

3. Slowly pour the tea through the funnel so that it collects in the cup.

4. Observe the filtered liquid.

Think It Over

Developing Hypotheses Suggest an explanation for any changes you observe in the tea after pouring it through the funnel.

Only 50 years ago, the French Broad River in North Carolina was a river to avoid. Its color changed daily, depending on the dyes being used at a nearby blanket factory. Towns dumped raw sewage into the water. Sediment and fertilizers from farms washed into the river with every rainfall. The few fish were unhealthy and covered with sores. Mostly, the river was a home for wastes and bacteria—certainly not a place for people to play. Today, however, the river is a popular whitewater rafting spot. Fish thrive in the clear water. The blanket factory and other plants have stopped releasing wastes into the river. The towns have sewage treatment plants. And ponds catch the runoff from farm fields before it reaches the river.

This story shows that pollution problems can be solved. People near the river still carry out the same activities—farming, building houses, and even making blankets. But by changing the way they do these things, they have stopped the pollution.

In the United States, laws regulate the amount of certain pollutants that can be released into the environment. Laws also state how these pollutants must be handled. The major federal laws that control air and water quality are the Clean Air Act and the Clean Water Act. These laws also encourage the development of new technology to reduce pollution.

Rafters enjoying the clean water of the French Broad River

GUIDE FOR READING

◆ How can technology help control air pollution?

◆ How can technology help control water pollution?

Reading Tip Before you read, use the section headings to make an outline. Leave space in your outline to take notes.

Key Terms scrubber
• catalytic converter
• primary treatment
• secondary treatment

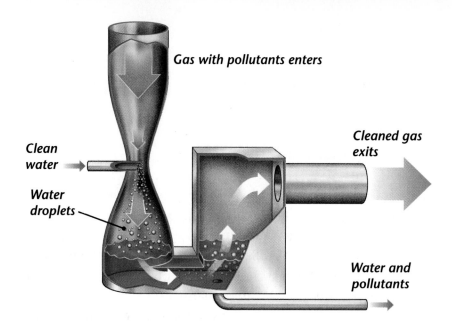

Figure 14 A smokestack scrubber removes pollutants such as sulfur dioxide from emissions. The dirty gas passes through a tube containing water droplets. Pollutants dissolve in the water, leaving clean gas to flow out of the chamber. The dirty water still must be properly disposed of.

Gas with pollutants enters

Clean water

Water droplets

Cleaned gas exits

Water and pollutants

Reducing Air Pollution

The Clean Air Act has resulted in the development of technology to control air pollution. **The major role of technology in controlling air pollution is to reduce emissions.**

Emissions Controls At one time, industries dealt with emissions by building tall smokestacks. The stacks released wastes high in the air, where they could blow away. But the pollutants still ended up somewhere. Now factories place devices in the stacks to treat emissions. For example, a filter can trap particles of ash. The device in Figure 14, called a **scrubber,** removes pollutants from emissions using a stream of water droplets. Pollutants dissolve in the water and fall into a container.

Cars and trucks now contain pollution control devices. For example, a **catalytic converter** is a device that reduces emissions of carbon monoxide, hydrocarbons, and nitrogen oxides. This device causes the gases to react, forming less harmful carbon dioxide and water.

Laws can ensure that people use pollution-control devices. For example, in many states, cars must pass emissions tests. The state of California's strict emissions-testing laws have helped reduce the smog problem in Los Angeles in recent years.

CFC Substitutes When a pollutant is banned by law, people must find substitutes for the banned substance. For example, in 1990 many nations agreed to stop using most CFCs by the year 2000. Scientists immediately began to search for substitutes for these chemicals. Refrigerators and air conditioners were redesigned to use less harmful substances. Researchers developed new ways to make products such as plastic foam without using CFCs. As a result of this work, fewer CFCs should enter the atmosphere after 2000 than in the past.

Sharpen your Skills

Graphing ACTIVITY

The table below shows a scientist's predictions of chlorine levels in the atmosphere with and without the ban on CFCs. Make a line graph of the data, using two different colors. Write a short paragraph describing the results.

| Year | Chlorine Level (parts per billion) | |
	With Ban	Without Ban
1985	2.5	2.5
1990	3.5	4.0
1995	3.8	5.0
2000	3.6	7.5
2005	3.4	10.0

Cleaning Up the Water

Technology can also help control water pollution. **Two ways to reduce water pollution are to treat wastes so that they are less harmful, and to find substitutes for pollutants.**

Sewage Treatment Most communities treat wastewater before returning it to the environment. A typical sewage plant handles the waste in several steps. **Primary treatment** removes solid materials from the wastewater. During primary treatment, the water passes through filters. Then it is held in tanks where heavy particles settle out. **Secondary treatment** involves using bacteria to break down wastes. Finally, the water is treated with chlorine to kill disease-causing organisms.

The town of Arcata, California, treats sewage in a creative way. Wastewater flows into ponds containing algae that begin to break down the sewage. Then the water flows into artificial marshes lined with cattails and bulrushes. These plants and the bacteria in the marsh filter and clean the water. These marshes are also habitats for many mollusks, fish, and birds. Trails for walking and biking encourage people to enjoy the marshes as well. After two months in this system, the wastewater is cleaner than the bay into which it is released!

Oil and Gasoline Oil is a pollutant that nature can handle in small amounts. Bacteria that break down oil live in the ocean. When oil is present, the bacteria multiply quickly as they feed on it. As the oil disappears, the bacteria population dies down. But in the case of a very large spill, many organisms are affected before the balance in the ecosystem is restored.

Gasoline or oil that leaks from an underground tank is hard to clean up. If the pollution has not spread far, the soil around the tank can be removed. But pollution that reaches groundwater may be carried far away. Groundwater can be pumped to the surface, treated, and then returned underground. This can take many years.

Figure 15 A bicyclist in Arcata, California, may not even be aware that this peaceful marsh is also a sewage treatment system.
Applying Concepts What are the two major sewage treatment steps?

Figure 16 Workers struggle to clean oil from a rocky beach.

Figure 17 These teens are planting trees in a park in Austin, Texas. Planting trees is one way to improve air quality. Trees absorb carbon dioxide from the air and produce oxygen.

Industrial and Agricultural Chemicals Instead of releasing wastes to the environment, industries can recycle their wastes to recover useful materials. Once such programs are underway, companies often find they save money as well as reduce pollution. Others change their processes to produce less waste or less harmful waste. For example, some industries use natural fruit acids as cleaning agents rather than toxic solvents. Likewise, many farmers are finding alternatives to toxic pesticides and fertilizers for their crops.

What Can You Do?

You may not think there is much you can do to reduce air and water pollution. But in fact, some small changes in people's behavior can make a big difference.

You can help reduce air pollution by reducing certain types of energy use. Much air pollution is a result of fuels that are burned to provide electricity and transportation. Using less energy conserves fuel resources and also reduces pollution. When you take public transportation, walk, or ride a bicycle, there is one fewer car on the road. This means there are fewer emissions that contribute to smog and the greenhouse effect. In the next chapter, you will read how you can use less energy for these purposes.

It is also easy to prevent water pollution at home. Some common household water pollutants are paint and paint thinner, motor oil, and garden chemicals. You can avoid causing water pollution by never pouring these chemicals down the drain. Instead, save these materials for your community's next hazardous household waste collection day.

Section 3 Review

1. What role does technology usually play in controlling air pollution?
2. In what two basic ways can technology help control water pollution?
3. Describe one smokestack device that can help reduce emissions from factories.
4. Explain how small oil spills can be cleaned up naturally.
5. **Thinking Critically** **Making Generalizations** Explain how laws can play a part in reducing pollution.

Check Your Progress CHAPTER PROJECT

Now you are ready to make your finished product using the information you have gathered. Keep in mind the age group of your audience when you are considering word choice, number and style of pictures, music, and other parts of your product. (*Hint:* Don't forget to include steps that members of your audience can take to be part of the solution. Make sure these suggestions are appropriate for their age.)

SECTION 1 Air Pollution

Key Ideas

◆ Air pollutants can be in the form of particles or gases.

◆ The major sources of photochemical smog are the gases emitted by motor vehicles.

◆ Sources of indoor air pollution include smoke, dust, pet hair, asbestos, and other substances. Two dangerous pollutants that are very difficult to detect are carbon monoxide and radon.

◆ The ozone layer protects people and other living things from the effects of too much ultraviolet radiation.

Key Terms

air pollution
emissions
photochemical smog
ozone

temperature inversion
acid rain
ozone layer
chlorofluorocarbons

SECTION 3 Finding Pollution Solutions

 INTEGRATING TECHNOLOGY

Key Ideas

◆ The major role of technology in controlling air pollution is to reduce emissions.

◆ Two basic ways to reduce water pollution are to treat wastes so that they are less harmful and to find substitutes for pollutants.

Key Terms

scrubber
catalytic converter

primary treatment
secondary treatment

SECTION 2 The Water Supply

Key Ideas

◆ The water cycle is the continuous process through which water moves from Earth's oceans to the atmosphere, to the land surface, and back to the oceans.

◆ Most of Earth's water—about 97 percent— is salt water.

◆ People and many other organisms require fresh water to carry out their life processes.

◆ Although there are some natural sources of water pollution, most pollution is the result of human activities. Agriculture, industry, construction, and mining all produce wastes that can end up in water.

Key Terms

water cycle
evaporation
condensation
precipitation
groundwater
drought

water pollution
sewage
fertilizer
pesticide
sediment
land subsidence

Organizing Information

Concept Map Copy the concept map below onto a sheet of paper. Then complete it and add a title.

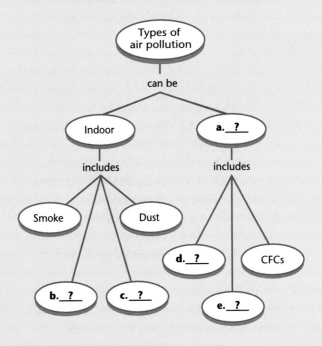

Reviewing Content

 Review key concepts online using iText at www.phschool.com

Multiple Choice

Choose the letter of the best answer.

1. Solid particles and gases released into the air are
   - **a.** sewage.
   - **b.** emissions.
   - **c.** scrubbers.
   - **d.** acid rain.

2. A deadly gas formed when fuels are incompletely burned is
   - **a.** ozone.
   - **b.** carbon monoxide.
   - **c.** photochemical smog.
   - **d.** CFCs.

3. The process of a gas changing into a liquid is called
   - **a.** evaporation.
   - **b.** condensation.
   - **c.** precipitation.
   - **d.** runoff.

4. The water and waste materials washed down toilets and sinks are called
   - **a.** pesticides.
   - **b.** sewage.
   - **c.** industrial chemicals.
   - **d.** fertilizers.

5. A technology that reduces carbon monoxide emissions from vehicles is a
   - **a.** scrubber.
   - **b.** catalytic converter.
   - **c.** filter.
   - **d.** CFC substitute.

True or False

If the statement is true, write true. If it is false, change the underlined word or words to make the statement true.

6. Most photochemical smog is produced by <u>motor vehicles</u>.

7. The presence of a layer of warm air that traps pollutants close to Earth's surface is called a <u>temperature inversion</u>.

8. As part of the <u>water cycle</u>, solar energy evaporates water from the oceans.

9. About 97 percent of Earth's water is <u>fresh</u> water.

10. <u>Air pollution</u> occurs because the pumping of groundwater causes particles of soil and rock to compact together underground.

Checking Concepts

11. Describe some possible health effects of photochemical smog.

12. How does acid rain form?

13. How do the sun and gravity drive the water cycle?

14. What is a drought? What effects could a drought have on people?

15. Explain how fertilizers from a farm might pollute a nearby river.

16. Why must limits be placed on the pumping of groundwater in some places?

17. What is one way to reduce emissions from cars and trucks?

18. **Writing to Learn** Suppose there was an oil spill near your home. Write a television newscast explaining how the spill will impact the ecosystem.

Thinking Critically

19. **Comparing and Contrasting** How are radon and carbon monoxide alike? How are they different?

20. **Predicting** What effect might a sudden increase in the amount of ozone in the ozone layer have?

21. **Making Generalizations** Would you expect the levels of photochemical smog to be worse in cities or in rural areas? Explain your answer.

22. **Applying Concepts** Suppose someone says that the heat cannot cause water pollution because heat is not a substance. What could you say to show that the person is wrong? Include examples of the possible effects of heat pollution in your response.

23. **Problem Solving** Write a summary of a plan you could follow to evaluate your school's air quality.

24. **Predicting** Your town wants to cut down a small forest to build a new shopping mall with a large parking lot. What impact could this development have on the water cycle?

Applying Skills

Use the graph to answer Questions 25–27.

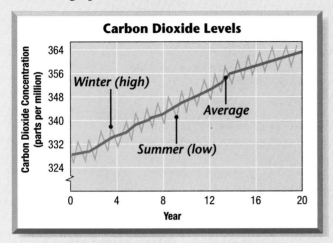

Carbon Dioxide Levels

Carbon Dioxide Concentration (parts per million)

364 356 348 340 332 324

Winter (high)

Average

Summer (low)

Year — 0 4 8 12 16 20

25. Interpreting Data What was the average level of carbon dioxide in the atmosphere at the beginning of the study? What was the average level of carbon dioxide in Year 20 of the study?

26. Calculating How much did the average level of carbon dioxide increase during the study period?

27. Developing Hypotheses In each year of the study, the winter level of carbon dioxide was higher than the summer level. Suggest an explanation for this.

Performance ▼ Assessment
CHAPTER PROJECT

Present Your Project Share your finished project with a group of younger students. As the children view or play with the product, notice what parts they find most interesting. After they are finished, ask them what they liked and didn't like about the product. What do they remember most?

Reflect and Record In your project notebook, write a short evaluation of your product. What parts of the product do you feel worked best? Which ones were most difficult? What challenges did you face in trying to communicate information in the form you chose to work with?

Test Preparation
Use these questions to prepare for standardized tests.

The map below shows one prediction of the possible effects of global warming. Use the map to answer Questions 28–30.

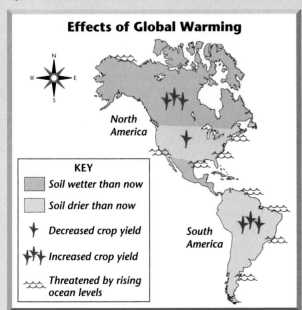

Effects of Global Warming

North America

South America

KEY

- Soil wetter than now
- Soil drier than now
- Decreased crop yield
- Increased crop yield
- Threatened by rising ocean levels

28. According to the map, global warming might cause wetter soils in
   A farming regions. **B** deserts.
   C South America. **D** North America.

29. The map shows that the land areas most threatened by rising ocean levels are
   F restricted to North America.
   G located under the ozone hole.
   H mainly on the east coasts of North America and South America.
   J mainly on the west coasts of North America and South America.

30. The map shows that global warming will cause crop yields to
   A be unaffected.
   B be affected the same way everywhere.
   C increase in some areas and decrease in other areas.
   D decrease everywhere.

The many residents of this
New Guinea coral reef include golden
fairy basslets, a red gorgonian sea
fan, and a vibrant blue sea star.

WEB
ACTIVITY
www.phschool.com

At Home in the Sea

A coral reef is a beautiful home for the organisms who dart, crawl, and hide within its lacy structure. But the reef is also a fragile place. Slight changes in water temperature and other conditions can threaten the delicate coral and the other organisms that inhabit the reef.

A coral reef is one of many different ocean habitats. From sandy tropical beaches to the cold depths of the ocean floor, organisms are able to thrive in all of them. In this chapter you will learn about the conditions in different parts of the ocean and the organisms that live there. Throughout the chapter you will work in a group to create your own model of one of the habitats.

Your Goal To build a three-dimensional model of a marine habitat and include some of the organisms that live there.

To complete the project successfully, you will need to

◆ include the significant physical features of the habitat
◆ create a life-size model of one organism that lives in the habitat
◆ write an explanation of how the organism is adapted to its habitat
◆ follow the safety guidelines in Appendix A

Get Started Begin now by previewing the visuals in the chapter to identify different ocean habitats. With your group, discuss which habitat you would like to learn more about. Begin a list of questions you have about the habitat. Also start to think about the materials you will need to build your model.

Check Your Progress You'll be working on this project as you study this chapter. To keep your project on track, look for Check Your Progress boxes at the following points.

Section 3 Review, page 493: Draw a scale diagram of your model.
Section 4 Review, page 500: Research your organism and build your model.

Present Your Project At the end of the chapter (page 511), you will display your model organism in its habitat.

TEKS

In addition to process TEKS, this chapter addresses these concept TEKS as they relate to the chapter's topics.

(8.6) The student knows that interdependence occurs among living systems. The student is expected to:
(C) Describe interactions within ecosystems.

(8.12) The student knows that cycles exist in Earth systems. The student is expected to:
(A) analyze and predict the sequence of events in the lunar and rock cycles;

(8.14) The student knows that natural events and human activities can alter Earth systems. The student is expected to:
(A) predict land features resulting from gradual changes such as mountain building, beach erosion, land subsidence, and continental drift; and
(C) describe how human activities had modified soil, water, and air quality.

① Exploring the Ocean

DISCOVER •••••••••••••••••••••••••••••••••••••ACTIVITY•••

What Can You Learn Without Seeing?

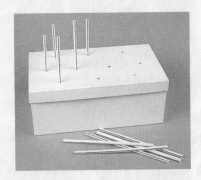

1. Your teacher will provide your group with ten plastic drinking straws and a covered box containing a mystery object. The top of the box has several holes punched in it. Using the straws as probes, try to determine the size, shape, and location of the object inside the box.

2. Based on the information you gathered, describe your object. What can you say about its length, shape, and position? Write down your hypothesis about the identity of the object.

3. Remove the box top to reveal the object.

Think It Over

Inferring Explain how you used the method of indirect observation in this activity to learn about the object.

GUIDE FOR READING

◆ What factors make ocean-floor research difficult?

◆ What are some features of the ocean floor?

Reading Tip As you read, make a list of features found on the ocean floor. Write one sentence about each feature.

Key Terms sonar
• continental shelf
• continental slope
• seamount • abyssal plain
• mid-ocean ridge • trench

Figure 1 This engraving shows HMS *Challenger* in the Indian Ocean in 1874, two years into its journey around the world.

Imagine going on a voyage around the world lasting three and a half years. Your assignment: to investigate "everything about the sea." Your vessel: a former warship, powered by sails and a steam engine. Its guns have been removed to make room for scientific gear. On board there are thermometers for measuring the temperature of ocean water and hundreds of kilometers of cable for lowering dredges to the bottom of the ocean. With the dredges, you scrape sand, muck, and rock from the ocean floor. You drag trawl nets behind the ship to collect ocean organisms.

The crew of a British ship, HMS *Challenger*, began such a voyage in 1872. By the end of the journey, the scientists had gathered enough data to fill 50 volumes and had collected more than 4,000 new organisms! It took 23 years to publish all the information they learned about oceanwater chemistry, currents, ocean life, and the shape of the ocean floor. The voyage of the *Challenger* was so successful that it became the model for many later ocean expeditions.

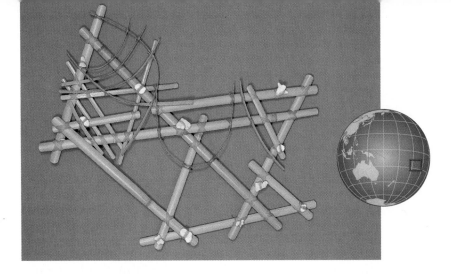

Voyages of Discovery

For thousands of years before the *Challenger* expedition, people explored the oceans. Knowledge of the oceans has always been important to the people living along their coasts. The oceans have provided food and routes for trade and travel.

The Phoenicians, who lived along the Mediterranean Sea, were one of the earliest cultures to explore the oceans. By 1200 B.C., they had established sea routes for trade with the other nations around the Mediterranean. After the Phoenicians, people of many European, African, and Asian cultures sailed along the coasts to trade with distant lands.

In the Pacific Ocean, around 2,000 years ago, the Polynesians boldly sailed into the open ocean. They settled the islands of Hawaii, Tahiti, and New Zealand. To find their way, they used maps, called stick charts, like the one in Figure 2.

As modern science developed and trade increased, ocean exploration resulted in accurate maps of the oceans and continents and also new scientific discoveries. For example, in the late 1700s, Captain James Cook led three voyages of exploration. Cook's crew included scientists who studied the stars and collected new species of plants and animals.

After all of Earth's coastlines had been mapped, scientists began to explore the unknown ocean depths. The *Challenger* expedition marked the beginning of the modern science of oceanography.

☑ *Checkpoint* *What are two reasons why people have explored the oceans?*

Exploring the Ocean Floor

INTEGRATING TECHNOLOGY Following the *Challenger*'s example, governments and universities sponsored many other major ocean research expeditions. Until recently, however, the ocean floor was unexplored, and much of the life in the oceans was unknown. Why did it take so long to reach this part of the ocean? Studying the ocean floor is extremely difficult.

Sharpen your Skills

Communicating

ACTIVITY

Obtain or construct a map of your school's floor plan. Show the route from the front door of your school to your desk in your science classroom. Use a compass and record the direction of each leg of the route. Also note the approximate distance of each part of your route and any major "landmarks." Have a classmate use your map and a compass to navigate from the front door to your desk.

For one thing, the ocean is very deep—3.8 kilometers deep on average, more than twice as deep as the Grand Canyon. Conditions are very harsh at such depths. First, because sunlight does not penetrate far below the surface, the deep ocean is in total darkness. Second, the water is very cold—only a few degrees above freezing. Finally, there is tremendous pressure due to the mass of water pushing down from above.

Because of the darkness, cold, and extreme pressure, scientists have had to develop new technology to enable them to study the deep ocean floor. Since humans cannot survive these conditions, many of the inventions have involved indirect methods of gathering information. One of the simplest methods, used by the *Challenger*'s crew, was to lower a weight on a long line into the water until the weight touched the bottom. The length of line

SCIENCE & History

Technology and Ocean Exploration

The time line includes several inventions that have helped scientists overcome the challenges of studying the ocean world.

1943 SCUBA

Jacques Cousteau and Emile Gagnan invented SCUBA, which stands for "**s**elf-**c**ontained **u**nderwater **b**reathing **a**pparatus." A tank containing compressed air is strapped to the diver's back and connected by a tube to a mouthpiece. SCUBA enables divers to explore to a depth of 40 meters.

| 1915 | 1930 | 1945 | 1960 |

1925 Sonar

Scientists aboard the German ship *Meteor* used sonar to map the ocean floor. They used a device called an echo sounder to produce pulses of sound. The ship's crew then timed the return of the echoes.

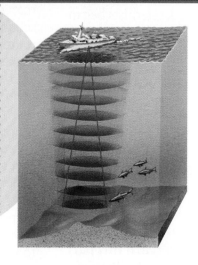

1960 Submersibles

Vehicles with very thick metal hulls protect explorers from extreme pressure and temperature, while enabling them to directly observe the ocean depths.

that got wet was approximately equal to the water's depth at that location. This method was slow and often inaccurate, as the line would descend at an angle. Nevertheless, these depth readings produced the first rough maps of the floor of the North Atlantic.

A major advance in ocean-floor mapping was sonar, a technology invented during World War I to detect submarines. **Sonar**, which stands for "sound navigation and ranging," is a system that uses sound waves to calculate the distance to an object. The sonar equipment on a ship sends out pulses of sound that bounce off the ocean floor. The equipment then measures how quickly the sound waves return to the ship. Sound waves return quickly if the ocean floor is close. Sound waves take longer to return if the ocean floor is farther away.

☑ *Checkpoint* *How is sonar an indirect way of gathering data?*

In Your Journal

Each of the inventions shown on these two pages helped solve a problem of ocean exploration. Find out more about one of these inventions. Write a short newspaper article telling the story of its development. Include details about the people who invented it and how it added to people's knowledge of the oceans.

1986

Remote Underwater Manipulator

The Remote Underwater Manipulator, or RUM III, is about the size of a small car. It is controlled by a computer aboard a ship at the surface. Without a crew, the RUM III can collect samples, take photographs, and map the ocean floor.

1975	1990	2005	2020

1978 **Satellites**

Seasat A was the first satellite in Earth's orbit to study the oceans. Since satellites make millions of observations a day, they provide data on rapidly changing and widespread ocean conditions. Such data include temperatures, algae growth patterns, and even the movement of large schools of fish.

1995

Gravity Mapping

The United States Navy used advanced satellite data to create a new map of the ocean floor. The satellite detected slight changes in gravity related to the shape of the ocean floor, providing accurate measurements within a few centimeters.

Features of the Ocean Floor

Once scientists were able to map the ocean floor, they discovered something surprising. The bottom of the ocean was not a flat, sandy plain. The deep waters hid mountain ranges and deep canyons.

If you could take a submarine voyage along the ocean floor, what would you see? **Features of the ocean floor include the continental shelf, continental slope, seamounts, abyssal plains, and the mid-ocean ridge.** Trace your journey from the edge of one continent to another in *Exploring the Ocean Floor*.

As you leave the harbor, your submarine first passes over the **continental shelf,** a gently sloping, shallow area of the ocean floor that extends outward from the edge of a continent. At a depth of about 130 meters, the ocean floor begins to slope more steeply. This incline at the edge of the continental shelf is called the **continental slope.** Here, the rock that makes up the continent stops and the rock of the ocean floor begins.

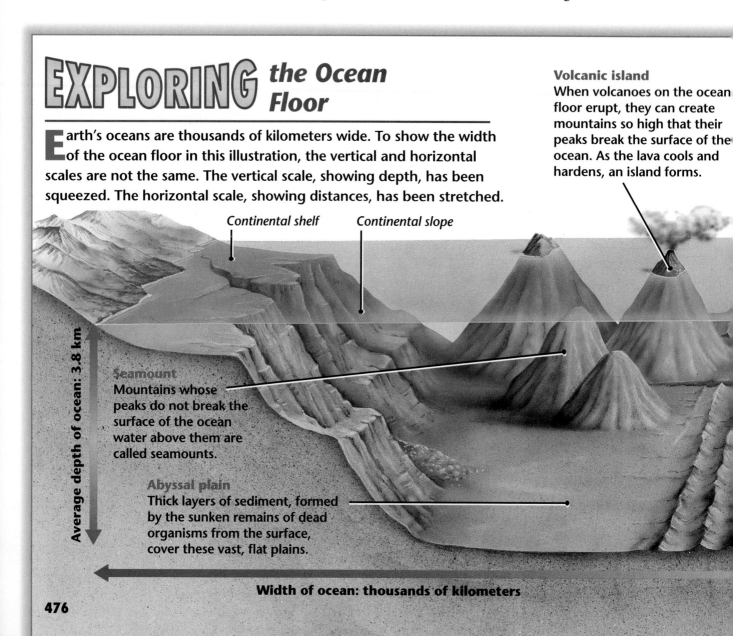

EXPLORING *the Ocean Floor*

Earth's oceans are thousands of kilometers wide. To show the width of the ocean floor in this illustration, the vertical and horizontal scales are not the same. The vertical scale, showing depth, has been squeezed. The horizontal scale, showing distances, has been stretched.

Volcanic island
When volcanoes on the ocean floor erupt, they can create mountains so high that their peaks break the surface of the ocean. As the lava cools and hardens, an island forms.

Continental shelf

Continental slope

Average depth of ocean: 3.8 km

Seamount
Mountains whose peaks do not break the surface of the ocean water above them are called seamounts.

Abyssal plain
Thick layers of sediment, formed by the sunken remains of dead organisms from the surface, cover these vast, flat plains.

Width of ocean: thousands of kilometers

Your submarine descends more gradually now, following the ocean floor as it slopes toward the deep ocean. After some distance, you encounter a group of mountains. Some are tall enough to break the ocean's surface, forming islands. Others, called **seamounts,** are mountains that are completely underwater. Some seamounts have flat tops because their peaks have eroded away.

Next you cross a broad area covered with thick layers of mud and silt. This smooth, nearly flat region of the ocean floor is called the **abyssal plain** (uh BIHS uhl plain). After gliding over the abyssal plain for many kilometers, you need to steer the submarine sharply upward to avoid a mountain range ahead. The **mid-ocean ridge** is a continuous range of mountains that winds around Earth, much as a line of stitches winds around a baseball. The mid-ocean ridge passes through all of Earth's oceans. Nearly 80,000 kilometers long, it is the longest mountain range on Earth.

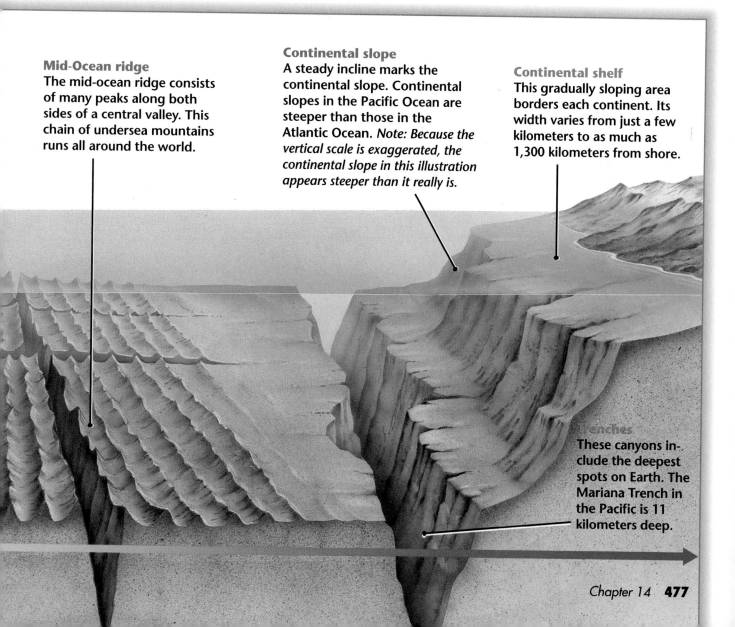

Mid-Ocean ridge
The mid-ocean ridge consists of many peaks along both sides of a central valley. This chain of undersea mountains runs all around the world.

Continental slope
A steady incline marks the continental slope. Continental slopes in the Pacific Ocean are steeper than those in the Atlantic Ocean. *Note: Because the vertical scale is exaggerated, the continental slope in this illustration appears steeper than it really is.*

Continental shelf
This gradually sloping area borders each continent. Its width varies from just a few kilometers to as much as 1,300 kilometers from shore.

Trenches
These canyons include the deepest spots on Earth. The Mariana Trench in the Pacific is 11 kilometers deep.

Sharpen your Skills

Interpreting Data

ACTIVITY

What is Earth's largest mountain? Use the following data to answer the question. Mauna Kea projects about 4,200 meters above sea level. Its base is on the floor of the Pacific Ocean, approximately 9,600 meters deep. Mt. Everest rises 8,850 meters from base to summit. Its base is located 100 meters above sea level. (*Hint:* Drawing a diagram may be helpful. Start with a line that represents sea level.)

Figure 3 When an undersea volcano reaches above the surface of the water, it forms an island. This peak is Mauna Kea in Hawaii.

At the top of the mid-ocean ridge, your submarine is about two kilometers above the abyssal plain, but you are still at least one kilometer below the surface. From this vantage you can see that the mid-ocean ridge actually consists of two parallel chains of mountains separated by a central valley.

You descend from the mid-ocean ridge to another abyssal plain. Soon your submarine's lights reveal a dark gash in the ocean floor ahead of you. As you pass over it, you look down into a steep-sided canyon in the ocean floor called a **trench.** The trench is so deep you cannot see the bottom.

Your journey is nearly over as your submarine slowly climbs the continental slope. Finally you cross the continental shelf and maneuver the submarine into harbor.

Section 1 Review

1. List three factors that make exploring the deep ocean and the ocean floor difficult.
2. Which ocean floor feature makes up the deepest parts of the ocean?
3. Explain how sonar can be used to determine the depth of the ocean.
4. Describe one technique or expedition that has added to knowledge of the oceans.
5. **Thinking Critically** **Inferring** Newly formed volcanic islands have a rich supply of minerals. Explain why this is so.

Science at Home

Make a "Room-Floor" Map With a family member, choose a room in your house and make a "room-floor" map based on depth readings. Imagine that the ceiling is the ocean surface and the floor is the bottom of the ocean. Follow a straight path across the middle of the room from one wall to another. At regular intervals, use a carpenter's measuring tape to take a depth reading from the ceiling to the floor or to the top of any furniture in that spot. Plot the depths on a graph. Then challenge another family member to identify the room by looking at the graph.

478

THE SHAPE OF THE OCEAN FLOOR

Suppose you are an oceanographer traveling across the Atlantic along the 45° N latitude line marked on the map. You and your crew are using sonar to gather data on the depth of the ocean between Canada and France. In this lab, you will interpret the data to create a profile of the ocean floor.

Halifax, Canada

Soulac, France

Problem

How can you use data about ocean depths to determine the shape of the ocean floor?

Materials

pencil   graph paper   computer (optional)

Procedure

1. Using pencil and paper or the computer, draw the axes of a graph. Label the horizontal axis Longitude. Mark from 65° W to 0° from left to right. Label the vertical axis Ocean Depth. Mark 0 meters at the top of the vertical axis to represent sea level. Mark –5,000 meters at the bottom to represent the depth of 5,000 meters below sea level. Mark depths at equal intervals along the vertical axis.

2. Examine the data in the table. The numbers in the Longitude column give the ship's location at 19 points in the Atlantic Ocean. Location 1 is Halifax, and Location 19 is Soulac. The numbers in the Ocean Depth column give the depth measurements recorded at each location. Plot each measurement on your graph. Remember that the depths are represented on your graph as numbers below 0, or sea level.

3. Connect the points you have plotted with a line to create a profile of the ocean floor.

Analyze and Conclude

1. On your graph, identify and label the continental shelf and continental slope.
2. Label the abyssal plain on your graph. How would you expect the ocean floor to look there?
3. Label the mid-ocean ridge on your graph. Describe the process that is occurring there.
4. What might the feature at 10° W be? Explain.
5. **Think About It** How is it helpful to organize data into a data table or graph?

More to Explore

Use the depth measurements in the table to calculate the average depth of the Atlantic Ocean between Canada and France.

Ocean Depth Sonar Data	
Longitude	Ocean Depth (m)
1. 64° W	0
2. 60° W	91
3. 55° W	132
4. 50° W	73
5. 48° W	3512
6. 45° W	4024
7. 40° W	3805
8. 35° W	4171
9. 33° W	3439
10. 30° W	3073
11. 28° W	1756
12. 27° W	2195
13. 25° W	3146
14. 20° W	4244
15. 15° W	4610
16. 10° W	4976
17. 05° W	4317
18. 04° W	146
19. 01° W	0

② Tides and the Lunar Cycle

DISCOVER • ACTIVITY

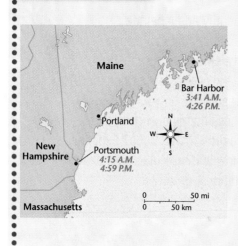

When Is High Tide?

Twice a day, the ocean rises and falls on the New England coast. These daily changes in water level are called tides. The map shows the times of the two high tides in each city on a particular day.

1. Calculate the length of time between the two high tides for each city. Remember to consider both hours and minutes.

2. Look at the times of the high tides in Bar Harbor and in Portsmouth. Is there a pattern in the times of the high tides?

Think It Over

Predicting Notice that the high tides for Portland are not shown. Based on the times of the other high tides on the map, predict when the high tides will occur in Portland.

GUIDE FOR READING

◆ What causes tides?

◆ What is the lunar cycle?

Reading Tip As you read, use the headings to make an outline about tides.

Key Terms tides • new moon • first quarter • full moon • third quarter • spring tide • neap tide

The Bay of Fundy in Canada is famous for its dramatic daily tides. When the tide comes in, fishing boats float on the water near the piers. But once the tide goes out, so much water flows back to sea that the boats are stranded on the muddy harbor bottom.

The daily rise and fall of Earth's waters on its coastlines are called **tides.** As the tide comes in, the level of the water on the beach rises gradually. When the water reaches its highest point, it is high tide. Then the tide goes out, flowing back toward the sea. When the water reaches its lowest point, it is low tide. Tides occur in all bodies of water, but they are most noticeable in the ocean and large lakes.

Figure 4 In the Bay of Fundy there is a great difference in water level between high tide **(A)** and low tide **(B)**.

What Causes Tides?

Tides are caused by the interaction of Earth, the moon, and the sun. How can distant objects like the moon and sun influence water on Earth? The answer is gravity. Gravity is the force exerted by an object that pulls other objects toward it. Gravity keeps you and everything around you on Earth's surface. As the distance between objects increases, however, gravity's pull grows weaker.

Figure 5 shows the effect of the moon's gravity on the water on Earth's surface. The moon pulls on the water on the side closest to it (point A) more strongly than it pulls on the center of the Earth. This pull creates a bulge of water, called a tidal bulge, on the side of Earth facing the moon. The water at point C is pulled toward the moon less strongly than is Earth as a whole. This water is "left behind," forming a second bulge.

In the places in Figure 5 where there are tidal bulges (points A and C), high tide is occurring along the coastlines. In the places between the bulges (points B and D), low tide is occurring. As Earth rotates, different places on the planet's surface pass through the areas of the tidal bulges and experience the change in water levels.

☑ *Checkpoint* *What force causes the tides to occur on Earth's surface?*

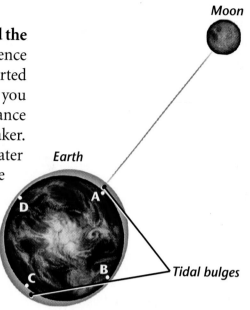

Figure 5 The moon's pull on Earth's water causes tidal bulges to form on the side closest to the moon and the side farthest from the moon. *Comparing and Contrasting Where is the level of the water higher, at point C or point D?*

The Lunar Cycle

For thousands of years, people have been fascinated by the relationship between tides and the phases of the moon. Before learning about this relationship, though, it's important to know something about the moon's phases. You already know that over several weeks the moon's appearance as viewed from Earth gradually changes. These changes in appearance are called the phases of the moon.

A regular cycle in the Earth-moon system produces the phases of the moon. This cycle is called the lunar cycle. In the lunar cycle, the moon takes 29.5 days to move through its phases. During the lunar cycle, the moon itself does not change. But its position relative to Earth and the sun does change. You can follow these changes through the lunar cycle in Figure 6 on page 482.

Waxing Phases The lunar cycle begins with the new moon. At the **new moon,** the side of the moon facing Earth also faces directly away from the sun. The moon therefore is not visible from Earth's surface during the new moon phase.

Waxing Gibbous
The moon continues to wax.

First Quarter
You see half of the lighted side of the moon.

Waxing Crescent
You begin to see more of the lighted side of the moon.

New Moon
The dark side of the moon faces earth.

Full Moon
You see the whole lighted side of the moon.

Waning Crescent
You see a crescent again.

Waning Gibbous
The moon begins to wane.

Third Quarter
You see half of the moon's lighted side.

Figure 6 The diagram in the center shows a view of Earth and the moon phases. The sun is shining from the right. The outer ring of photos shows the different amounts of the sunlit side of the moon that an observer on Earth sees as the moon revolves around Earth. *Interpreting Diagrams How can an observer on Earth tell if a crescent moon is waxing or waning?*

Then, each night, the moon turns in relation to the sun. A person on Earth begins to see sunlight reflected from more and more of the moon's surface. The moon is said to "wax," or grow. What grows is the amount of the moon's Earth-facing side that is lit by the sun. At first, people see only a thin sliver of the moon, called the crescent moon. When half of the moon's Earth-facing side is lit by the sun, the moon is said to be in its **first quarter.** When the moon's Earth-facing side directly faces the sun, the moon's face is completely lit, and a **full moon** occurs. Look at Figure 6 to observe the relative positions of Earth, the sun, and the moon during a full moon.

Waning Phases After the full moon, the moon begins to wane, or decrease gradually in size. Again, it's not the moon's size that changes, just the size of the sunlit area that can be seen from Earth. When just half of the moon is visible, the moon is in its **third quarter.**

The moon continues to wane until only a crescent moon is visible. Then, 29.5 days after the last new moon, the moon can no longer be seen from Earth. The lunar cycle completes itself with another new moon. As you will see, new moons, quarter moons, and full moons have important effects on tides.

☑ *Checkpoint* *What is the difference between a new moon and a full moon?*

The Daily Tide Cycle

As Earth turns completely around once each day, people on or near the shore observe the rise and fall of the tides as they reach the area of each tidal bulge. The high tides occur about 12 hours and 25 minutes apart in each location. As Earth rotates, eastern-most points pass through the area of the tidal bulge before points farther to the west. Therefore, high tide occurs later the farther west you go along a coastline.

In some places, the two high tides and two low tides are easy to observe each day. But in other places, the range between the water levels is less dramatic. One set of tides may even be so minimal that there appears to be only one high tide and one low tide per day. This situation is common along the coasts of Texas and western Florida, due to the gradual slope of the ocean floor in the Gulf of Mexico.

Several factors affect the height of the tide in any particular location. For example, high tide on a certain day in southern California is not necessarily the same height as high tide farther up the Pacific coast in Oregon. Landforms such as capes, peninsulas, and islands interrupt the water's movements.

The Monthly Tide Cycle

Even though the sun is 150 million kilometers from Earth, it is so massive that its gravity also affects the tides. The sun pulls the water on Earth's surface toward it. In Figure 7 on the next page, you can follow the positions of Earth, the moon, and the sun at different times during a month. Notice that sometimes the moon and sun pull together on Earth's waters. At other times, they pull in different directions. Changes in the positions of Earth, the moon, and the sun affect the height of the tides during a month.

Spring Tides Twice a month, at the new moon and the full moon, the sun and moon are lined up. Their combined gravitational pull produces the greatest range between high and low tide, called a **spring tide.** These tides get their name not because they occur during the season spring, but from an Old English word, *springen,* which means "to jump."

Sharpen your Skills

Graphing

ACTIVITY

This table lists the highest high tides and lowest low tides at the mouth of the Savannah River at the Atlantic Ocean in Georgia for one week. Use the data to make a graph.

Day	Highest High Tide (m)	Lowest Low Tide (m)
1	1.9	0.2
2	2.1	0.1
3	2.3	0.0
4	2.4	−0.2
5	2.5	−0.2
6	2.6	−0.3
7	1.9	0.3

1. On the horizontal axis, mark the days.

2. On the vertical axis, mark tide heights ranging from 3.0 to −1.0 meters. (*Hint:* Mark the negative numbers below the horizontal axis.)

3. Plot the tide heights for each day on the graph. Connect the high tide points with one line and the low tide points with another line.

How do the high and low tides change during the week? What type of tide might be occurring on Day 6? Explain.

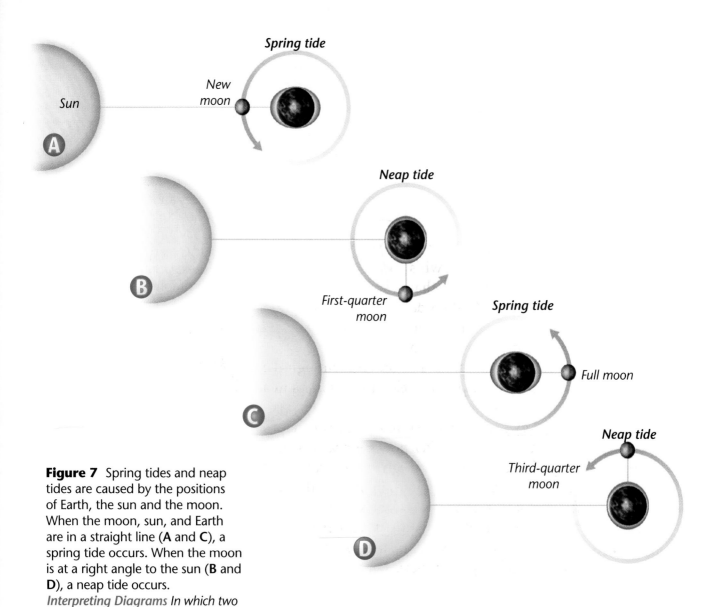

Figure 7 Spring tides and neap tides are caused by the positions of Earth, the sun and the moon. When the moon, sun, and Earth are in a straight line (**A** and **C**), a spring tide occurs. When the moon is at a right angle to the sun (**B** and **D**), a neap tide occurs.
Interpreting Diagrams In which two alignments is there the greatest difference between high and low tide?

Labels in figure: Spring tide, Sun, New moon, **A**, Neap tide, **B**, First-quarter moon, Spring tide, **C**, Full moon, Neap tide, Third-quarter moon, **D**

Neap Tides In between spring tides, at the first and third quarters of the moon, the sun and moon pull at right angles to each other. This line-up produces a **neap tide,** a tide with the least difference between low and high tide. During a neap tide, the sun's gravity pulls some of the water away from the tidal bulge facing the moon. This acts to "even out" the water level over Earth's surface, reducing the difference between high and low tides.

Monthly Tide Tables Despite the complex factors affecting the tides, scientists can predict tides quite accurately for various locations. They combine knowledge of the movements of the moon and Earth with information about the shape of the coastline and other local conditions. If you live near the coast, your local newspaper probably publishes a tide table. Knowing the times and heights of tides is important to sailors, marine scientists, people who fish, and others who live along a coast.

Energy From Tides

INTEGRATING TECHNOLOGY The movement of huge amounts of water between high and low tide is a source of potential energy—energy that is stored and waiting to be used. Engineers have designed tidal power plants that capture some of this energy as the tide moves in and out.

The first large-scale tidal power plant was built in 1967 on the Rance River in northwestern France. As high tide swirls up the river, the plant's gates open so that the water flows into a basin. As the tide retreats, the gates shut to trap the water. Gravity pulls the water back to sea through tunnels. The energy of the water moving through the tunnels powers generators that produce electricity, just as in a hydroelectric dam on a river.

Although tidal energy is a clean, renewable source of energy, it has several limitations. Harnessing tidal power is practical only where there is a large difference between high and low tides—at least 4 or 5 meters. There are very few places in the world where such a large difference occurs. Daily tides also may not occur at the time when there is a demand for electricity. However, tidal power can be a useful part of an overall plan to generate electricity that also includes other power sources between tides.

Figure 8 Pulled by the tide, water rushes through this tidal power plant in France.

Section 2 Review

1. Explain how the moon causes a tidal bulge to form on the side of Earth closest to it.
2. Describe the changes that occur in the moon's appearance as seen from Earth. Explain your answer.
3. How can tides be used to generate electricity?
4. Describe the positions of the sun and the moon in relation to Earth when spring tides occur.
5. **Thinking Critically Applying Concepts** Imagine that you are the captain of a fishing boat. Why would it be helpful to know the times of the tides?

Science at Home

Moonwatch Consult an almanac or newspaper weather section to determine the time of moonrise and moonset. Make a note of how many days it has been since the last new moon. With an adult family member, go outside after dark when the moon can be seen above the horizon. Explain the current phase of the moon. Also explain where that phase falls in the lunar cycle. Predict how the phase of the moon will have changed if you observe the moon several days later.

SECTION 3 Life at the Ocean's Edge

DISCOVER ··· ACTIVITY ····

Can Your Animal Hold On?

1. Your teacher will give you a ping-pong ball, a rock, and a box containing some materials. The ping-pong ball represents an ocean animal. Use some of the materials to design a way for the animal to cling to the rock.

2. Attach the ping-pong ball to the rock.

3. Place the rock in a sink or deep pan. Run water over the rock from a faucet or pitcher. Observe how well your animal stays in place on the rock.

Think About It

Inferring How might the ability to "hold on" be important to an animal that lives on the shore?

GUIDE FOR READING

◆ What factors affect where ocean organisms live?

◆ What are the major types of coastal wetlands?

◆ How do waves cause beach erosion?

Reading Tip As you read, make a list of the habitats described in this section. Write a sentence or two describing each habitat.

Key Terms plankton • nekton • benthos • food web • intertidal zone • longshore drift • sandbar • dune • barrier beach

At first glance, a sandy ocean beach may seem lifeless. As you walk along the water's edge in the soft, wet sand, you may notice some dark, tangled seaweed that has washed up on the shore. A crab scuttles away from the pile as you walk by. Seagulls screech and swoop overhead. But for the most part, the beach appears deserted.

If you look more closely at the wet sand, you will see evidence of living things right beneath your feet. Tiny, round holes are signs of burrowing clams. These clams dig down into the sand for protection and to prevent being washed away in the waves. If you wade into the water, you may be able to spot a sand crab taking advantage of the surf to feed. The bottom half of its body buried in the sand, the crab waits for the waves to carry in a fresh supply of food for its next meal.

The organisms on this beach are well suited to the conditions there. In this section, you will learn how marine organisms have adapted to other areas where the land and ocean meet.

Living Conditions

A sandy beach is one type of marine, or ocean, habitat. Remember that an organism's habitat provides the things the organism needs to survive. An organism also must be suited to the physical conditions of the environment it lives in. **Some physical factors that determine where marine organisms can live include salinity, water temperature, light, dissolved gases, nutrients, and wave action.**

Conditions vary in different parts of the ocean. For example, salinity is lower where rivers flow into the ocean, bringing a stream of fresh water. Salinity is higher in

shallow, warm seas, where more evaporation takes place. Because cold water holds more dissolved gas than warm water, cold ocean waters contain more oxygen than tropical waters. Different organisms are suited to live in these different conditions. As a result, the same organisms do not live in every part of the ocean.

On land, most organisms live on or near the surface. The ocean, on the other hand, is a three-dimensional environment. It is inhabited by organisms at every depth. Scientists classify marine organisms according to where they live and how they move.

Plankton are tiny algae and animals that float in the water and are carried by waves and currents. Algae plankton include geometrically shaped diatoms like those shown in Figure 9. Animal plankton include microscopic crustaceans and fish larvae. **Nekton** are free-swimming animals that can move throughout the water column. Octopus and squid, most fishes, and marine mammals such as whales and dolphins are nekton. **Benthos** are organisms that inhabit the ocean floor. Some benthos, like crabs, sea stars, and lobsters, move from place to place. Others, like sponges and sea anemones, stay in one location.

Plankton, nekton, and benthos are all found in most marine habitats. Many plankton and benthos are algae which, like plants, use sunlight to produce their own food through photosynthesis. Other plankton and benthos, as well as all nekton, are consumers. They eat either the algae or other consumers. Finally, some organisms, including many benthos, are decomposers. They break down wastes and remains of other organisms. These feeding relationships in a habitat make up a **food web.**

Figure 9 Marine organisms can be classified as plankton, nekton, or benthos. **(A)** Intricate diatoms, one type of algae plankton, float on the ocean surface. **(B)** These microscopic crustaceans, called copepods, are animal plankton. **(C)** Free-swimming animals, such as this school of sweetlip fish, are nekton. **(D)** Benthos live on the ocean floor. The sea stars and sea anemones in this colorful array are benthos.

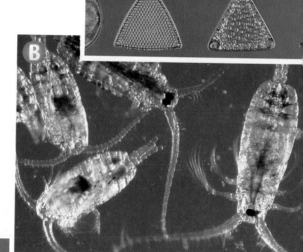

About 350 years ago, a form of poetry called *haiku* grew popular in Japan. Here is an example of a haiku about a beach.

Shining air bubbles
pushing up the hardpacked sand:
a shy clam revealed.

This poem may appear simple, but it follows a strict structure. A haiku is a 17-syllable poem written in 3 lines. There are 5 syllables in the first line, 7 syllables in the second line, and 5 syllables in the third line. A haiku should capture a moment in nature and suggest a mood or feeling.

In Your Journal

Prepare to write your own haiku about the edge of the ocean. Work with a partner to think of what you might see, hear, and feel. Review the habitats in this section for ideas. Then choose one simple, specific subject to write about. Write a draft and exchange it with your partner. After making revisions, illustrate your poem.

The first group of ocean habitats you will learn about are those found at the very edge of the ocean. The sandy beach you read about earlier is one example. Two habitats with a richer variety of life are rocky shores and salt marshes. As you read, think about how conditions in these habitats are similar, and how they are different.

☑ *Checkpoint* *Are sharks plankton, nekton, or benthos? Why?*

Rocky Shores

Imagine if your home had no walls or roof. Twice a day, a huge storm passes through, bringing a drenching downpour and winds so strong you can hardly keep your balance. At other times, the hot sun beats down, leaving you parched and dry. This is what life is like for organisms that live on rocky shores in the intertidal zone. The **intertidal zone** stretches from the highest high-tide line on land out to the point on the continental shelf exposed by the lowest low tide.

Organisms that live in the rocky intertidal zone must be able to tolerate the pounding of the waves and changes in salinity and temperature. They must also withstand periods of being underwater and periods of being exposed to the air. They must avoid drying out, hide from predators, and find food in this harsh setting. How are these organisms able to survive?

Along the Rocks Rocky shores are found along much of both coasts of the United States. Figure 10 shows some of the colorful organisms that typically live along the rocky California coast.

The highest rocks, above the highest high-tide line, make up the spray zone. The spray zone is never completely covered with water, but it gets wet as the waves break against the rocks. A stripe of black algae indicates the highest high-tide line. The rocks below this level are encrusted with barnacles. Barnacles can close up their hard shells, trapping a drop of water inside to carry

Sea urchin

Sea anemones

Sea lettuce

Abalone

Brittle star

them through the dry period until the next high tide. Lower down, clumps of blue and black mussels stick out amidst the algae. The mussels produce sticky threads that harden on contact with the water, attaching the mussels to the rock. The threads are so strong that scientists are studying them as a model for new glues. The rocks are also home to flat mollusks called limpets. Limpets have a large, muscular foot to hold on tightly. They secrete drops of mucus around the edges of their shells to form a tight seal.

Algae that live in the intertidal zone are also adapted to withstand the physical conditions. Rootlike structures anchor the strands of algae firmly to the rocks. Some algae are covered with a thick layer of slime. The slime keeps the algae from drying out during low tide.

In Tide Pools When the tide goes out, some water remains in depressions among the rocks called tide pools. As the water in a tide pool is warmed by the sun, it begins to evaporate. The remaining water becomes saltier. If it rains, however, the salinity quickly decreases. Organisms in the tide pool must be able to withstand these changes in temperature and salinity, as well as the force of the waves when the tide comes in again.

Sea stars cling to the rocks with rows of tiny suction cups on their undersides. Spiny purple sea urchins crawl slowly along the bottom of the tide pool. If the bottom is sandy, sea urchins can use their spines to dig a hole in which to bury themselves during heavy surf. Under shady rock ledges, sponges and sea anemones wait for the incoming tide to bring a fresh supply of plankton and other food particles. A sea anemone may look delicate, but some can survive out of water for over two weeks. When out of the water, the anemone pulls its tentacles inside. It folds up into a round blob, resembling a rolled-up sock.

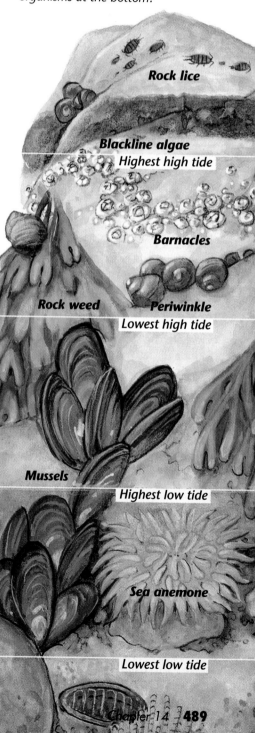

Figure 10 The constantly changing water level in the intertidal zone creates different habitats along a rocky coast. *Comparing and Contrasting How are conditions different for organisms near the top of the rocks compared to organisms at the bottom?*

Rock lice

Blackline algae
Highest high tide

Barnacles

Rock weed

Periwinkle

Lowest high tide

Chitons

Mussels

Highest low tide

Sea star

Sea anemone

Limpets

Lowest low tide

Hermit crab

Where River Meets Ocean

Other important environments along the ocean's edge are estuaries. Estuaries are coastal inlets or bays where fresh water from rivers mixes with the salty ocean water. Water that is partly salty and partly fresh is brackish.

Coastal wetlands are habitats found in and around estuaries. **Along the United States coasts, most coastal wetlands are either salt marshes or mangrove forests.** Salt marshes are especially abundant along the east coast from Massachusetts to Florida. Mangrove forests are found in the tropical waters along the southern coast of Florida and the Gulf of Mexico.

Salt Marshes A salt marsh oozes with smelly mud. Mosquitoes swarm over the water as it flows slowly through the tall, green grasses. The fresh water and tides contribute sediments, animal and plant matter, and other nutrients to the salt marsh, forming a soft, rich mud bottom.

A single plant, cord grass, dominates the marsh. Unlike most plants, cordgrass can survive in salt water. The plant releases salt through small openings in its long, narrow leaves. The cord grass that is not eaten by animals breaks down and is decomposed by bacteria and fungi in the water. The decomposed material supplies nutrients to organisms in the marsh.

Tidal channels run through the cord grass. Waves break up as they enter the channels, so that organisms in the marsh are protected from the surf. Within the shelter of the marsh, fish, crabs, shrimp, and oysters hatch and feed before entering the harsher ocean environment offshore. As the tide retreats, mud flats are exposed. Hordes of crabs search for food in the rich mud. Herons, stilts, and egrets stalk across the mud to prey on the crabs and other benthos exposed by the low tide.

Mangrove Forests Mangroves—short, gnarled trees that grow well in brackish water—fringe the coastline of southern Florida. The mangroves'

Figure 11 Salt marshes and mangrove forests are two types of coastal wetlands. **(A)** Salt water flows through tidal channels in a salt marsh. **(B)** Arching prop roots anchor these black mangrove trees firmly in the soft, sandy soil around Florida Bay. *Making Generalizations How does the plant life in each of these habitats provide shelter for marine organisms?*

prop roots anchor the trees to the land. Mangroves can withstand all but the strongest hurricane winds. Without the mangroves to break the action of winds and waves, the coastline would change dramatically each hurricane season. The prop roots also trap sediment from the land. They create a protected nursery rich in nutrients for many young animals.

Protecting Estuaries The rivers that flow into estuaries can carry harmful substances as well as nutrients. When pollutants such as pesticides, sewage, and industrial waste get into the river water, they end up in the estuary. The pollutants change the water quality in the estuary. In turn, organisms that live in the estuary are affected. It can take many years for ocean tides to flush a heavy load of pollutants out of an estuary.

For example, Chesapeake Bay is a huge estuary located on the mid-Atlantic coast. It has been a rich source of oysters, clams, and blue crabs. However, pollutants from inland sources accumulated in the bay for many years. Their effect was to greatly reduce the number and kinds of organisms in the Chesapeake. When people realized the threat to the estuary, they took action. The water quality of rivers that empty into Chesapeake Bay is now regulated by law. Cleanup efforts have reduced much of the pollution in the bay. Today, organisms like the blue crab are making a comeback.

Figure 12 A crabber in Chesapeake Bay pulls up the last trap of the day. As the health of the estuary improves, the blue crab population is growing again.

Waves and Beach Erosion

Recall from Chapter 4 that a wave is the movement of energy through a body of water. Because of the energy in ocean waves, the boundary between land and ocean is always changing shape. If you walk on the same beach every day, you might not notice that it is changing. From day to day, waves remove sand and bring new sand at about the same rate. But if you visit a beach just once each year, you might be startled by the changes that you see. **Waves shape a beach by eroding the shore in some places and building it up in others. Natural events and human activities can affect beach erosion.**

As you learned in Chapter 11, erosion is the process of breaking up rock and carrying it away. How do waves cause erosion?

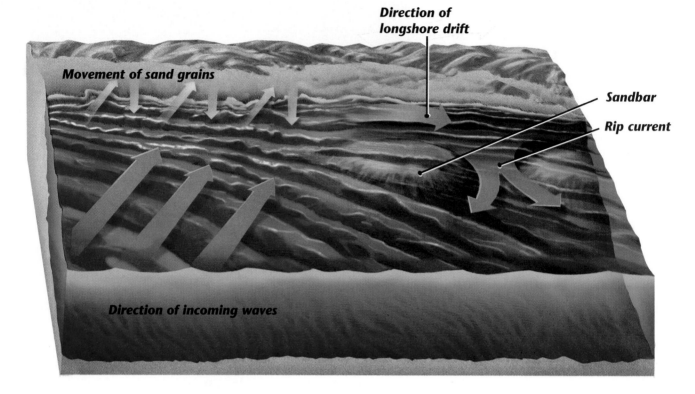

Direction of longshore drift

Movement of sand grains

Sandbar

Rip current

Direction of incoming waves

Figure 13 Waves approach the shore at an angle. This results in a gradual movement of sand along the beach. *Interpreting Diagrams In which direction is longshore drift moving the sand along this beach?*

Figure 14 To reduce beach erosion, people have built a series of groins along the North Carolina coast.

At first, waves striking a rocky shoreline erode the rocks into tall cliffs and arches. Over many thousands of years, waves break the rocks into pebbles and grains of sand. A wide, sandy beach forms. Then the waves begin to eat away at the exposed beach. The shoreline slowly moves farther inland.

A process called longshore drift carries the sand along the coast and deposits it elsewhere. As waves come into shore, water washes up the beach at an angle, carrying sand grains with it. The water and some of the sand then run straight back down the beach. **Longshore drift** is this movement of sand along the beach. As the waves slow down, they deposit the sand they are carrying on the shallow, underwater slope. The result is a long, underwater ridge called a **sandbar.** As a sandbar grows, it can trap the water flowing along the shore. In some places, water breaks through the sand bar and begins to flow back down the sloping ocean bottom. This process creates a rip current, a rush of water that flows rapidly back to sea through a narrow opening in the sandbar.

Reducing Erosion

Over time, erosion can wear away a beach. Storms can bring high waves and higher-than-normal tides that cause severe beach erosion. This threatens homes and other buildings. To avoid losing their property, people look for ways to reduce erosion.

Groins One method of reducing erosion along a stretch of beach is to build a wall of rocks or concrete, called a groin, seaward from the beach. The sand carried by the water piles up against the groins instead of moving along the shore. However, the groins increase the amount of erosion farther down the beach.

Dunes Some natural landforms protect beaches and reduce erosion, although they can't completely stop the movement of sand. **Dunes** are hills of wind-blown sand. The strong roots of dune plants, such as beach grass and sea oats, hold the sand in place. These plants help to slow erosion of dunes by both wind and water. But if the dune plants are destroyed by cars, bicycles, or people walking, the rate at which the dune erodes will increase.

Barrier Beaches Another natural landform that protects shorelines from wave action is the barrier beach. **Barrier beaches** are long, low-lying sand deposits that form parallel to the shore. The beaches are separated from the mainland by a shallow lagoon. Waves break against the barrier beach instead of against the land inside. For this reason, people are working to preserve natural barrier beaches along the Atlantic and Gulf coasts of the United States.

Figure 15 Barrier beaches line much of the Gulf coast of Texas.

Section 3 Review

1. Name five physical factors that affect organisms in marine habitats.
2. List two ways that salt marshes and mangrove forests are alike and two ways they are different.
3. Describe conditions in the rocky intertidal zone.
4. Describe how longshore drift causes beach erosion.
5. **Thinking Critically Making Judgments** A builder has proposed building a seaside resort on grass-covered sand dunes that are part of a barrier beach. Would you support the proposal? Why or why not?

Check Your Progress
Your group should now select the marine environment you will create. Measure the space where you will build your model. Make a list of the physical features you will need to represent. Draw a scale diagram of your model and show it to your teacher. Label the different features and note the materials you will use. (*Hint:* Draw your sketch on graph paper to plan its size to fit the space.)

CHAPTER PROJECT

SECTION 4 The Neritic Zone and Open Ocean

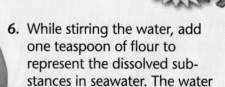

DISCOVER

How Deep Can You See?

1. With a permanent marker, divide a white plastic lid into four quarters. Shade in two quarters as shown.

2. ✂ Use a pair of scissors to carefully poke a small hole in the center of the lid.

3. Tie a piece of string to a paper clip. Place the clip underneath the lid and thread the string up through the hole.

4. Tape the string tightly to a meter stick so that the lid presses against the bottom of the meter stick.

5. Fill a large, deep bucket with tap water.

6. While stirring the water, add one teaspoon of flour to represent the dissolved substances in seawater. The water should be slightly cloudy.

7. Lower the lid into the water so that it is 5 cm below the surface. Note whether the lid is still visible in the water.

8. Lower the lid 10 cm below the surface, then 15 cm, and so on until the lid is no longer visible.

Think It Over

Observing At what depth could you no longer see the lid? Based on your results, how do you think visibility changes with depth in the ocean?

GUIDE FOR READING

◆ What conditions in the neritic zone support organisms?

◆ Where do algae live in the open ocean?

◆ How do hydrothermal vents support organisms?

Reading Tip Before you read, preview Figure 16 on the facing page. Write some predictions about how the neritic zone and open ocean are similar and how they are different.

Key Terms neritic zone
• open-ocean zone • holdfast
• atoll • bioluminescence
• hydrothermal vent

Floating mats of golden-brown, leaflike fronds on the ocean surface mark the location of a kelp forest. Diving below the surface, you find yourself surrounded by tall, swaying stalks of giant kelp. Sunlight filters through the water, producing a greenish light. As you pull yourself hand over hand down one of the kelp strands, you notice small bulbs at the base of each frond. You pinch one of the bulbs, and a bubble of gas escapes. These bulbs keep the heavy kelp fronds upright in the water.

The kelp forest is full of life. Bright-orange sheephead fish dart past you. Young sea lions chase one another around the kelp stalks. A sea otter, surrounded by a stream of bubbles, dives past you, down to the rocky bottom.

◀ Sea otter eating a sea star

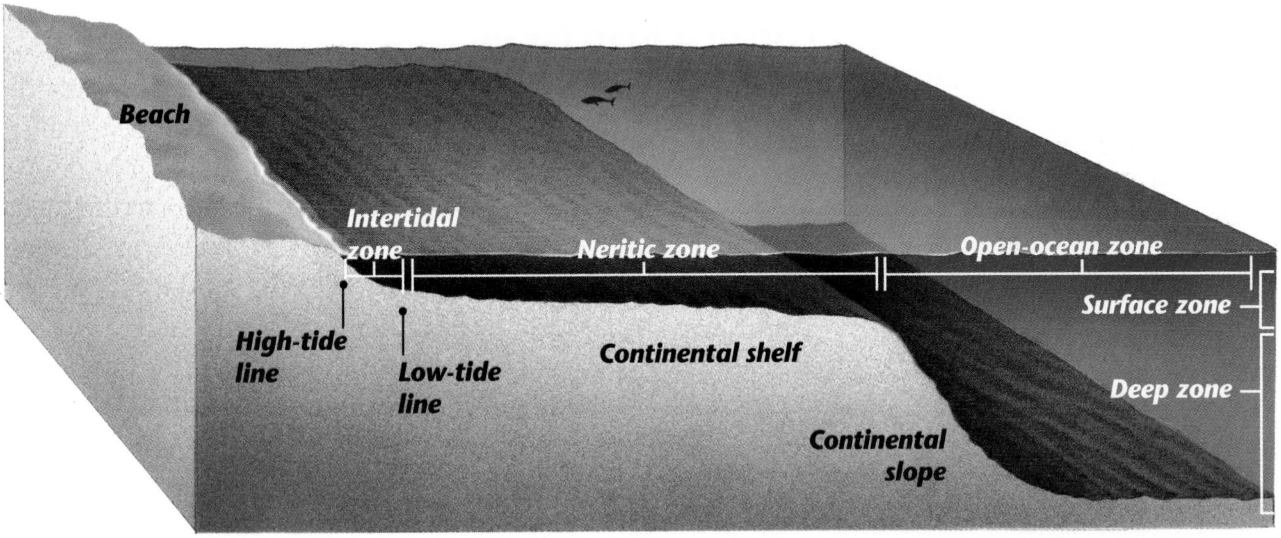

Figure 16 The ocean zone closest to land is the intertidal zone, which is bounded by the high-tide and low-tide lines. Next is the neritic zone, followed by the open-ocean zone, which makes up most of the world's oceans. The open ocean is divided by depth into the surface zone and the deep zone. *Interpreting Diagrams Which zones lie over the continental shelf?*

A kelp forest is one habitat found in the neritic zone. The **neritic zone** is the part of the ocean that extends from the low-tide line out to the edge of the continental shelf. Beyond the edge of the continental shelf lies the **open-ocean zone.** Locate the neritic and open-ocean zones in Figure 16. In this section you will learn how organisms are adapted to the conditions in these zones, from the sunlit surface waters to the coldest depths.

Conditions in the Neritic Zone

A huge variety of organisms are found in the neritic zone, more than in any other area of the ocean. Most of the world's major fishing grounds are found in this zone. What makes the neritic zone home to so many living things? The answer has to do with its location over the continental shelf. **The shallow water over the continental shelf receives sunlight and a steady supply of nutrients washed from the land into the ocean.** The light and nutrients enable large, plantlike algae, such as the giant kelp, to grow. These algae serve as a food source and shelter for other organisms.

In many parts of the neritic zone, upwelling currents bring additional nutrients from the bottom to the surface. These nutrients support large numbers of plankton, which form the base of ocean food webs. Schools of fish such as sardines and anchovies feed on the plankton. Major fisheries in upwelling areas include Monterey Canyon off the California coast, Newfoundland's Grand Banks, and Georges Bank off the New England coast.

Two diverse habitats typically found within the neritic zone are kelp forests and coral reefs. As you read about each, think about how they are similar and how they are different.

☑ *Checkpoint* *What are two ways that nutrients may be supplied to the neritic zone?*

Life in a Kelp Forest

Kelp forests grow in cold neritic waters, such as those along the Pacific coast from Alaska to Mexico. These large, heavy algae require a solid, rocky bottom to anchor their stalks. A bundle of rootlike strands called a **holdfast** attaches the algae to the rocks. A stalk of giant kelp can grow to 30 meters in length. The gas-

Figure 17 Light streams through a forest of giant kelp and shadowy rockfish near Monterey, California. The closeup shows the gas-filled bulbs that keep the kelp upright in the water.

filled bulbs shown in the closeup to the left keep the heavy kelp stalk upright in the water.

The kelp use the sunlight and dissolved gases in the neritic zone to produce their own food. The kelp also provide a habitat for many other organisms. The curtains of kelp hide young gray whales from predators while their mothers are feeding. Sea slugs and snails live amid the tangle of the holdfasts.

Sea otters play a particularly important role in the kelp forest. In addition to eating abalone, sea otters feed on sea urchins, which eat the kelp. In areas where sea otters have disappeared, armies of sea urchins have devoured the kelp. The once-thriving forest has become a barren rocky zone.

Coral Reefs

Although a coral reef may look as if it is made of rock, it is actually made of living things. Coral reefs are created by colonies of tiny coral animals, each of which is not much larger than a pencil eraser. The coral animals produce a hard structure that surrounds their soft bodies. After the coral dies, the empty structure remains. New coral animals attach and grow on top of it. Over many years, a reef is built. Most of the coral reefs that exist today were begun about 5,000 to 10,000 years ago.

Microscopic algae live within the bodies of the coral animals and provide food for them. Because the algae require warm temperatures and sunlight, coral reefs can only form in shallow, tropical ocean waters. The reefs grow above continental shelves or around volcanic islands, where the water is shallow.

In areas where the seafloor is sinking, a reef may develop over time into an atoll. An **atoll** is a ring-shaped reef surrounding a shallow lagoon. Figure 18 shows the development of an atoll. It begins as a fringing reef that closely surrounds the edges of the island. As the reef grows upward, the island sinks, and a barrier reef forms. Water separates the top of the barrier reef from the land. The island continues to sink until it is eventually underwater, forming the atoll.

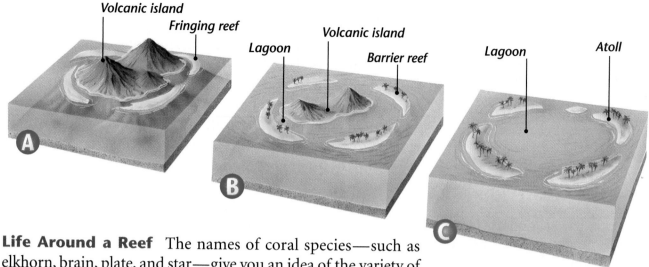

Volcanic island
Fringing reef

A

Lagoon   Volcanic island
              Barrier reef

B

Lagoon   Atoll

C

Life Around a Reef The names of coral species—such as elkhorn, brain, plate, and star—give you an idea of the variety of shapes coral can form. Many animals live in and around the crevices of the reef, including octopuses, spiny lobsters, shrimp, toothy moray eels, and fish in all colors and sizes. Parrotfish like the one in Figure 19 scrape coral off the reef to eat. The parrotfish grind up the broken coral inside their bodies, producing the fine, soft sand commonly found around the reef.

Coral Reefs and Humans Coral reefs are natural aquarium exhibits, displaying a colorful diversity of life to be enjoyed and studied. Reefs also protect coastlines during violent storms. The reefs break up the surf, preventing waves from severely eroding the land. However, human activities can harm the fragile reefs. Boat anchors dragging across a reef can damage it. Divers can accidentally break off pieces of the reef. Even brushing against the reef can harm some of the coral animals. Because coral only grows a few millimeters a year, a reef cannot quickly recover.

Changes in water temperature and clarity also affect coral reefs. For example, if the water becomes too warm, the corals release the algae that live inside them. Cloudy water endangers the algae by reducing the amount of light that reaches them. If sediments produced by storms or human activities bury a reef, the algae in the living coral cannot survive. Without the algae, the coral animals do not grow well and eventually die.

Today many people understand the importance of coral reefs and try to protect them. Many reef areas have been designated as marine sanctuaries, which limits the amount of diving and other activity allowed near the reef. Scientists worldwide are also studying the effects of temperature change and pollution on the reefs to better protect them.

✓ *Checkpoint* How can human activities affect a coral reef?

Figure 18 An atoll develops in stages. **(A)** A fringing reef closely surrounds an island. **(B)** As the island sinks, a lagoon forms inside the barrier reef. **(C)** Finally, the island sinks below the surface, leaving a ring-shaped atoll. *Interpreting Diagrams In which stage is the reef the youngest?*

Figure 19 A parrotfish delicately nibbles away at a coral reef in the Red Sea. Reefs provide a habitat for many fish and other marine organisms.

Inferring

ACTIVITY

To keep from sinking, many plankton rely on the friction between their bodies and the surrounding water. More friction is needed to stay afloat in warm water than in denser cold water. One of the copepods below is found in tropical ocean waters, while the other is found near the poles. Which do you think is which? Explain your reasoning. (*Hint:* More streamlined shapes create less friction with their surroundings.)

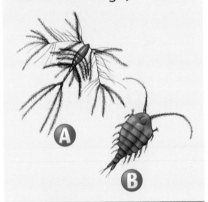

Conditions in the Open Ocean

The open ocean begins where the neritic zone ends, at the edge of the continental shelf. Diving into the open ocean is like descending a long staircase with a light only at the very top. Light from the sun only penetrates a short distance into the water, typically to a depth of less than 200 meters. If the water is cloudy with sediment, sunlight does not reach as deep. In clear tropical waters, on the other hand, some light may reach as deep as a few hundred meters.

The fact that only a small portion of the open ocean receives sunlight is one way it differs from the neritic zone. Another difference is the amount of dissolved nutrients in the water. While the neritic zone receives a constant supply of nutrients from shore, dissolved nutrients are less abundant in the open ocean. As a result, the open ocean zone supports fewer organisms.

The Surface Zone The surface zone extends as far as sunlight reaches below the surface. **The surface zone is the only part of the open ocean that receives enough sunlight to support the growth of algae.** These microscopic algae are the base of open-ocean food webs. Animal plankton that feed on algae include tiny crustaceans called copepods, shrimp-like krill, and the young of many ocean animals such as crabs, mollusks, and fishes.

Figure 21 on the facing page shows an Arctic food web. Each organism in this food web depends either directly or indirectly on the plankton. Throughout the ocean, plankton are a source of food for other organisms of all sizes. If you think of sharks as sharp-toothed, meat-eating hunters, you might be surprised to learn that the biggest sharks of all feed entirely on tiny plankton! Whale sharks, which can grow to more than 10 meters long, strain plankton from the water. Many whales feed only on plankton as well, including Earth's largest animal, the blue whale.

The Deep Zone If you could descend into the deep ocean, you would find that the ocean becomes darker and colder as you descend. Because of its harsh conditions, the deep ocean is often compared to a desert. Compared to other land and ocean environments, few organisms live in the deep zone. But unlike a desert baking under the bright sun, the deep ocean is cold, dark, and wet.

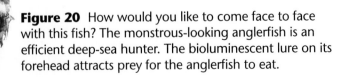

Figure 20 How would you like to come face to face with this fish? The monstrous-looking anglerfish is an efficient deep-sea hunter. The bioluminescent lure on its forehead attracts prey for the anglerfish to eat.

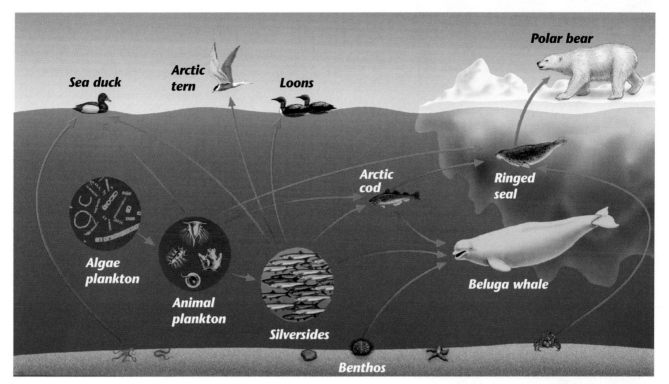

Sea duck

Arctic tern

Loons

Polar bear

Algae plankton

Animal plankton

Silversides

Arctic cod

Ringed seal

Beluga whale

Benthos

Figure 21 This marine food web includes typical organisms found in the Arctic Ocean. The arrows indicate what each organism eats. *Interpreting Diagrams Which organisms feed directly on the Arctic cod? Which organisms depend indirectly on the cod?*

Finding food in the darkness is a challenge. Many deep-sea fishes produce their own light. The production of light by living things is called **bioluminescence.** Some fishes use chemical reactions to produce their own light, like fireflies on land. Other fishes have colonies of bioluminescent bacteria living in pockets on their bodies. Still others have light-producing organs. The anglerfish, for example, has a light organ on its head. The fish lurks in the shadows below the pool of light. Shrimp and fishes that are attracted to the light become the anglerfish's prey.

Because the food supply in most of the deep ocean is much more limited than in shallower water, animals in this zone must be good hunters to survive. The gaping mouths of many deep-sea fishes are filled with fang-like teeth. Rows of sharp teeth stick out at angles, ensuring that any animal it bites cannot escape.

☑ *Checkpoint Why do very few organisms live in the deep zone?*

Hydrothermal Vents

As the submersible *Alvin* descended to a depth of 2,500 meters into the Galápagos Rift in the Pacific Ocean one day in 1977, the scientists aboard could hardly believe their eyes. Outside the submersible, the headlights revealed a bizarre scene. Clouds of black water billowed up from chimney-shaped structures on the ocean floor. Meter-long tubes with gaping, lipstick-red ends swayed in the water. White crabs scuttled over the rocks, crawling around clams as big as dinner plates.

Figure 22 Giant tube worms cluster around a hydrothermal vent on the deep ocean floor.

The scientists were surprised not only by the strange appearance of these deep-sea creatures, but also by the fact that they were so abundant. In the deepest parts of the ocean, organisms tend to be very small and slow-moving because food is so rare. The number, size, and variety of organisms were unusually large for such a deep part of the ocean. What could these organisms find to eat so far from sunlight?

The strange community the scientists in *Alvin* observed was located around a hydrothermal vent. A **hydrothermal vent** is an area where ocean water sinks through cracks in the ocean floor, is heated by the underlying magma, and rises again through the cracks. These vents are located along ocean ridges, where the plates are moving apart and new ocean floor is forming.

The heated water coming from a vent carries gases and minerals from Earth's interior. **The chemical nutrients in the heated water support the unique group of organisms that are found around hydrothermal vents.** Bacteria feed directly on the chemical nutrients that are spewed out of the vents. Like the algae in the surface zone that use sunlight to produce food, these bacteria use the chemicals to produce food. They form the base of the food web at a hydrothermal vent.

Other organisms, like the giant clams, feed on the bacteria. The red-tipped tube worms are supplied with food by bacteria living within their tissues. Meanwhile, the scuttling crabs feed on the remains of the other inhabitants in their unusual habitat.

Section 4 Review

1. Describe the physical conditions in the neritic zone.
2. What factor limits where algae are found in the open ocean?
3. What is the source of nutrients for organisms around a hydrothermal vent?
4. Explain how bioluminescence is important to some fish that live in the deep ocean.
5. **Thinking Critically** **Relating Cause and Effect** When forests on a tropical island are cut down, the soil is more easily eroded. Explain how this could affect a coral reef near the island.

Check Your Progress CHAPTER PROJECT

By now you should have selected an organism to model. Research your organism to determine its size and other physical characteristics. How does the organism survive in its marine habitat? Check your plan for constructing the organism with your teacher. Your group should also begin building your model habitat. Make sure you have collected all the necessary materials before you begin building.

⑤ Resources From the Ocean

When European explorers began sailing to North America, they were astounded by the huge number of codfish that lived off its eastern coast. One traveler reported that this area was so "swarming with fish that they could be taken not only with a net but in baskets let down and weighted with a stone." Others reported sailing through schools of cod so thick they slowed the boats down!

This cod fishery stretched from Newfoundland to a hook of land appropriately named Cape Cod. For more than 400 years, the seemingly endless supply of "King Cod" supported a thriving fishing industry. But beginning in the early 1900s, fishing crews had to work harder to catch the same amount of cod. As the fishing grew more difficult each year, it became clear that the cod were disappearing. With the price of cod rising, there was more competition to catch the fewer fish available. In 1992, the Canadian government had to declare the fishery closed.

No one knows for sure how long it will take the cod population to fully recover. Scientists are studying cod and other fisheries to learn how to preserve them for future generations.

Living Resources

Cod are just one example of a living resource from the ocean. How many other kinds of seafood

Figure 23 Big catches of cod like this one from Georges Bank, off the New England coast, have become less common since the early 1900s.

have you tasted: tuna, shrimp, flounder, lobster, clams, squid, oysters, seaweed, or mussels? These foods and the many others that come from the ocean make up about five percent of the world's total food supply.

Harvesting Fish Just six species make up the majority of fishes harvested for eating: herring, sardine, anchovy, cod, pollock, and mackerel. Locate the world's major fisheries in Figure 24. You can see that they are all located close to coasts. Nearly all fishes caught are harvested from coastal waters or areas of upwelling. These waters contain nutrients and plankton on which they feed.

If used wisely, fisheries naturally renew themselves each year. **New fish are born, replacing those that are caught, but only as long as the fishery is not overfished. Overfishing causes the supply of fish to decrease.** Overfishing has become a problem as better technology has enabled people to catch large numbers of fish very quickly. For example, some fishing fleets have electronic equipment that allows them to locate schools of fish precisely. They can be caught faster than they can reproduce. Once this occurs, it begins a cycle that leads to fewer and fewer fish each season. Eventually, the fishery may be depleted, like the cod fishery you read about earlier.

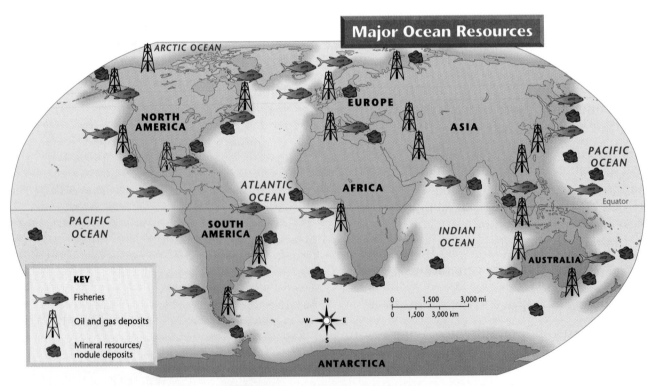

Figure 24 All over the world, the oceans are an important source of food, oil and gas, and minerals. *Interpreting Maps* Where are Africa's major fisheries located?

Aquaculture As fish stocks become depleted, **aquaculture,** the farming of saltwater and freshwater organisms, is likely to become more common. Aquaculture has been practiced in some Asian countries for centuries. This process involves creating an environment for the organisms and controlling nutrient levels, water temperature, light, and other factors to help them thrive. Oysters, abalone, and shrimp have successfully been farmed in artificial saltwater ponds and protected bays. Even landlocked regions can produce seafood using aquaculture. For example, salmon are now being raised in Nebraska fields that once were cattle ranches.

INTEGRATING TECHNOLOGY

Other Ocean Products People harvest ocean organisms for many purposes besides food. For example, algae is an ingredient in many household products. Its gelatin-like texture makes it an ideal base for detergents, shampoos, cosmetics, paints, and even ice cream! Sediments containing the hard fragments of diatoms are used for abrasives and polishes. Many researchers believe that other marine organisms may be important sources of chemicals for medicines in the future.

✓ *Checkpoint* *How are fisheries naturally renewed each year?*

Mineral Resources

In addition to living organisms, the ocean contains valuable non-living resources. Some of these are found within ocean water itself. Today, fresh water can be extracted from ocean water in the process of desalination. Desalination provides fresh water for many dry areas and islands. When the fresh water is removed from ocean water, the salts that are left behind are also a valuable resource. Over half of the world's supply of magnesium, a strong, light metal, is obtained from seawater in this way.

A second source of nonliving resources is the ocean floor. From the layer of sediments covering the continental shelves, gravel and sand are mined for use in building construction. In some areas of the world diamonds and gold are mined from sand deposits. Metals such as manganese also accumulate on the ocean floor. The metals concentrate around pieces of shell, forming black lumps called **nodules** (NAHJ oolz). Because they sometimes occur in waters as deep as 5,000 meters, recovering the nodules is a difficult process. The technology to gather them is still being developed.

Not all nations have agreed on who owns the rights to nodules and other resources on the deep ocean floor. Some feel the nations who find and recover the minerals should own them.

TRY THIS

Seaweed Candy

Make this Asian dessert **ACTIVITY** to discover one way to eat algae. Remember to prepare food only in a non-science classroom. Be sure to get permission before using a stove.

2 blocks of agar (one 0.5-ounce package)
1 cup sugar
4 cups guava juice or other fruit juice
food coloring

1. Rinse the agar, a substance obtained from algae.

2. Break agar into cubes and place them in a saucepan.

3. Put on your goggles. Add the sugar and juice to the pan. Bring the mixture to a boil. Turn down the heat and cook, stirring, until the agar dissolves.

4. Remove pan from heat and stir in a few drops of food coloring. Pour the mixture into a shallow pan. Let cool.

5. Refrigerate candy until firm.

6. Cut into blocks and serve.

Inferring What purpose does the agar serve in this recipe? What purposes do the sugar and juice serve?

Figure 25 Lit up like a city at night, this Norwegian oil-drilling platform rises above the icy waters of the North Sea. Hundreds of people may live and work aboard such an oil rig.

Others feel that this is unfair to nations that cannot yet afford the technology to obtain a share of these resources.

Fuels From the Ocean Floor

Another type of nonliving resource forms from the remains of dead marine organisms. These remains sink to the bottom of the ocean, where they are buried by sediments. As more sediments accumulate, the buried remains decompose. Over hundreds of thousands of years, the heat and pressure from the overlying layers gradually transform the remains into oil and natural gas.

As you know, many organisms live in the part of the ocean above the continental shelf. The thick sediments on the continental shelves bury the remains of living things. As a result, the richest deposits of oil and gas are often located on the continental shelves.

Oil rigs like the one in Figure 25 drill the rocky ocean floor as much as 300 meters below the surface. Imagine trying to dig a hole in the concrete bottom of a swimming pool, while standing on a raft floating on the surface of the water. You can see why drilling the ocean floor is very difficult! Ocean drilling is made even harder by strong currents, winds, and violent storms.

✓ *Checkpoint* **What is the source of the oil and gas deposits on the ocean floor?**

Ocean Pollution and Water Quality

It was once thought that the ocean was so vast that people could not damage it by throwing wastes into it. This is partially true—the ocean is a self-cleaning system that can absorb some wastes without permanent damage. But dumping large amounts of wastes into the ocean threatens many marine organisms.

Sharpen your Skills

Observing

ACTIVITY

Refer back to the map of ocean resources in Figure 24. Which resources are located close to land? Which are located throughout the ocean? Can you suggest an explanation for any patterns you observe?

504

Recall that water pollution is the addition of any substance that has a negative effect on the living things that depend on the water. Most ocean pollution comes from the land. Although some is the result of natural occurrences, most pollution that threatens the oceans' water quality is related to human activities.

Natural Sources Some pollution is the result of weather. For example, heavy rains wash fresh water into estuaries and out into the water offshore. This surge of fresh water pollutes the ocean by lowering its salinity. A sudden change in salinity may kill ocean animals that are unable to adjust to it.

Human Sources Pollutants related to human activities include sewage, chemicals, and trash dumped into coastal waters. Chemicals that run off fields and roads often end up in the ocean. These substances can harm ocean organisms directly. The pollutants can also build up in their bodies and poison other animals, including people, that feed on them. Trash can cause serious problems, too. Seals, otters, and other marine mammals that need to breathe air can get tangled in old fishing lines or nets and drown. Other animals are harmed when they swallow plastic bags that block their stomachs.

Oil Spills One major threat to ocean life is oil pollution. When an oil tanker or drilling platform is damaged, oil leaks into the surrounding ocean. Oil is harmful to many organisms. It coats the bodies of marine mammals and birds. This destroys their natural insulation and affects their ability to float. The oil is also harmful to animals that swallow it.

Figure 26 Removing oil from a beach is a difficult, messy chore. This cleanup worker is using absorbent mops to remove oil from the sand. In the closeup, two more workers try to clean oil from a bird's beak and feathers. *Inferring What might have caused this oil pollution?*

Figure 27 Flags fly outside the United Nations headquarters in New York City. The United Nations develops policies on the use of the oceans by countries. *Applying Concepts Why can't each nation make its own laws regarding ocean resources?*

Interestingly, there is a natural cleaning process that slowly takes place after oil spills. Certain bacteria that live in the ocean feed on the oil and multiply. It takes many years, but eventually an oil-covered beach can become clean again. This has happened even in the portions of the Prince William Sound in Alaska that were blanketed with oil from the 1989 wreck of the oil tanker *Exxon Valdez*.

Protecting Earth's Oceans

Who owns the ocean and its resources? Who has the responsibility of protecting them? These are questions that nations have been struggling to answer for hundreds of years. **Because the world ocean is a continuous body of water that has no boundaries, it is difficult to determine who, if anyone, should control portions of it. Nations must cooperate to manage and protect the oceans.**

The United Nations has established different boundaries in the oceans. According to one treaty, a nation now controls the first 22 kilometers out from its coasts. The nation also controls resources in the waters or on the continental shelf that lie within 370 kilometers of shore. This treaty leaves approximately half of the ocean's surface waters as "high seas," owned by no nation. Ownership of the ocean floor beneath the high seas is still under debate.

Other international efforts have resulted in cooperation aimed at reducing ocean pollution. Examples include the establishment of marine refuges and regulations for building safer oil tankers.

Section 5 Review

1. How can overfishing affect a fishery?
2. Explain why international cooperation is necessary to solve many problems related to ocean resources.
3. Name a nonliving resource found in the ocean. Where is it located? How is it obtained and used?
4. **Thinking Critically Making Judgments** Should mineral resources on the ocean floor belong to whoever finds them, or to the closest nation? Consider each position and write a short paragraph stating your opinion.

Science at Home

Ocean Escape Have a family member hook one end of a rubber band around his or her wrist. Stretch the rubber band across the back of the hand and hook the free end over three fingers as shown. Now ask the person to try to remove the rubber band without using the other hand. Explain that this shows how difficult it is for seals or dolphins to free themselves from a plastic beverage ring or piece of net. Can you propose any ways to reduce this threat to marine mammals?

Shrimp Farms—At What Cost to the Environment?

About one quarter of the world's shrimp are raised on shrimp farms. Many shrimp farms are created by clearing trees from mangrove forests and digging shallow, fenced-in ponds. Farmers then fill the ponds with ocean water and shrimp larvae. After about six months, when the shrimp are big enough to sell, the farmers drain the pond water back into the ocean.

To grow healthy shrimp, farmers often add fertilizers, medicines, and pesticides to the ponds. When the pond water is released to the ocean, these chemicals can harm other animals. The United Nations has estimated that 25 percent of the world's mangrove forests have been destroyed as a result of shrimp farming. As awareness of the environmental impact of shrimp farms has grown, the industry has come under attack.

▲ Shrimp farmer in Malaysia

The Issues

How Important Is Shrimp Farming? For many people in the world, shrimp is more than luxury food: It is a staple of their diet and their main source of animal protein. The demand for shrimp currently is greater than the natural supply in Earth's oceans. To meet the demand, many countries, including the United States, have turned to shrimp farming. Shrimp farms provide needed food and jobs that some people believe are worth a certain amount of damage to the environment. They feel it is not possible to have shrimp farms that are both highly productive and environmentally safe.

Can the Pollution Be Reduced? Shrimp farmers are exploring ways to reduce the impact of their farms on the coastal environment. Better pond construction can help stop chemicals from leaking into the surrounding waters. Some governments recognize the importance of mangrove forests in providing a habitat for many species and in protecting the shoreline. These

governments have passed laws regulating where shrimp farms may be built. Farmers must investigate the impact their ponds will have on nearby mangrove forests and get approval before choosing a location. These methods of reducing environmental damage, however, are expensive and time-consuming for the shrimp farmers.

Should Farmers Use Alternative Methods? In some parts of Asia, a less-destructive method of shrimp farming has been practiced for centuries. Raising shrimp in ditches dug around clusters of mangroves provides the young shrimp with a natural nutrient supply that includes debris from the trees. A gate keeps the shrimp from escaping into the ocean and also allows the motion of the tides to replenish the water in the ditches. The disadvantage of this method is that it is much less profitable than the constructed shrimp ponds. Many shrimp farmers could not afford to switch to this method. If they did, the price of shrimp worldwide would rise.

You Decide

1. Identify the Problem

In your own words, summarize the problem facing shrimp farmers.

2. Analyze the Options

Make a list of the solutions mentioned. List the advantages and drawbacks of each. Who would benefit from each plan? Who might suffer?

3. Find a Solution

Write a brochure or pamphlet for shrimp farmers that states your proposed solution to their problem. After you have written the text, illustrate your brochure.

CLEANING UP AN OIL SPILL

Oil Spill in Bay

An oil tanker hit a reef yesterday, spilling thousands of barrels of crude oil into the water. Cleanup efforts will begin today. Workers must race against time to save birds and sea otters. With stormy weather forecasted, however, scientists expect considerable damage. Volunteers are needed to help clean up.

Imagine that you are a volunteer helping to clean up an oil spill. In this activity, you will use a variety of materials to remove as much oil as possible from the water and to keep oil from reaching the beach. You will also see how oil affects animals that are exposed to a spill.

Problem

How can an oil spill be cleaned up?

Skills Focus

making models, forming operational definitions

Materials

water	shallow pan	vegetable oil
feather	paper cup	plastic dropper
paper towels	cotton balls	wooden sticks
marking pen	graduated cylinder, 100 mL	

Procedure

1. Place a pan on a table or desk covered with newspaper. Label one end of the pan "Beach" and the other end "Open Ocean."
2. Pour water into the pan to a depth of 2 cm.
3. Gently pour 20 mL of vegetable oil into the center of the pan. Record your observations.
4. Dip a feather and your finger into the oil. Observe how each is affected by the oil.

5. Try to wipe oil off the feather and your finger using paper towels. Record whether any oil is left on the feather or your skin.
6. Now try to clean up the spill. Record your observations with each step. First, using the wooden sticks, try to keep the oil from reaching the "beach." Next, gently blow across the surface of the water from the "open ocean" side to simulate wind and waves. Then use the cotton balls, paper towels, and dropper to recover as much of the oil as possible.
7. When you are finished, dispose of the oil and used items in the paper cup. Wash your hands.

Analyze and Conclude

1. How successful were you in cleaning up the oil? Is the water as clean as it was at the start?
2. How well were you able to keep the oil from reaching the beach? Describe how useful the different materials were in cleaning up the oil.
3. Describe what happened when you cleaned the feather and your finger. What might happen to fish, birds, and other animals if they were coated with oil as a result of an oil spill?
4. Predict how storms with strong winds and waves would affect the cleanup of an oil spill.
5. **Apply** Look at the used cleanup materials in the paper cup. What additional problems for cleanup crews does this suggest?

Getting Involved

One way to reduce the threat of oil spills is to transport less oil across the oceans. To make that possible, people would need to use less oil in their daily lives. Oil is used to heat homes, to produce gasoline, and to make products such as plastics and textiles. List at least three ways to reduce the amount of oil you and your family use.

SECTION 1 — Exploring the Ocean

Key Ideas

◆ Technology such as sonar enables scientists to study the deep ocean floor despite the darkness, cold, and extreme pressure there.

◆ The ocean floor has features similar to those found on the continents, including plains, mountain ranges, volcanoes, and trenches.

Key Terms

sonar   abyssal plain
continental shelf   mid-ocean ridge
continental slope   trench
seamount

SECTION 2 — Tides and the Lunar Cycle

Key Ideas

◆ Tides are caused by the interaction of Earth, the moon and the sun.

◆ The lunar cycle is a cycle in the Earth-moon system that produces the phases of the moon.

◆ The height of tides during a month varies with changes in the positions of Earth, the moon, and the sun.

Key Terms

tides   full moon   spring tide
new moon   third quarter   neap tide
first quarter

SECTION 3 — Life at the Ocean's Edge

INTEGRATING LIFE SCIENCE

Key Ideas

◆ Physical factors that affect marine organisms include salinity, water temperature, light, dissolved gases, nutrients, and wave action.

◆ Organisms in the rocky intertidal zone must tolerate the pounding of the waves, as well as being both underwater and exposed to the air.

Key Terms

plankton   food web   sandbar
nekton   intertidal zone dune
benthos   longshore drift barrier beach

SECTION 4 — The Neritic Zone and Open Ocean

INTEGRATING LIFE SCIENCE

Key Ideas

◆ The neritic zone receives sunlight and nutrients washed from the land. Habitats in this zone include kelp forests and coral reefs.

◆ The thin layer of sunlit water at the surface is the only part of the open ocean that can support algae, which need the sunlight to produce food. Other marine organisms depend on the food made by algae.

◆ The chemical nutrients in the hot water around a hydrothermal vent support the organisms that live around the vent.

Key Terms

neritic zone   atoll
open-ocean zone   bioluminescence
holdfast   hydrothermal vent

SECTION 5 — Resources From the Ocean

Key Ideas

◆ If used wisely, fisheries are a renewable resource. New fish will replace those that are caught, but only if overfishing does not reduce the population too severely.

◆ Nonliving resources from the ocean include dissolved substances in seawater and minerals and fuels from the ocean floor.

Key Terms

aquaculture   nodules

Organizing Information

Compare/Contrast Table Make a table about ocean habitats on a separate sheet of paper. Include rows for the following habitats: tide pool, coral reef, surface zone, and hydrothermal vent. For each habitat, fill in the ocean zone where it is found, the conditions (such as sunlight, pressure, and temperature) that exist there, and the types of organisms typically found there. (See the Skills Handbook for more on compare/contrast tables.)

Reviewing Content

 Review key concepts online using iText at **www.phschool.com**

Multiple Choice
Choose the letter of the best answer.

1. A smooth, nearly flat region of the ocean floor is called a(n)
   a. trench.　　　　**b.** mid-ocean ridge.
   c. abyssal plain.　**d.** sea mount.

2. At the full moon, the combined gravitational pulls of the sun and moon produce the biggest difference between low and high tide, called
   a. surface current.　**b.** neap tide.
   c. spring tide.　　　**d.** rip current.

3. A tropical ocean community made by tiny animals that have algae growing in their tissues is a(n)
   a. mangrove forest.　**b.** salt marsh.
   c. intertidal zone.　　**d.** coral reef.

4. In the open-ocean zone, organisms depend directly or indirectly on food that is made by
   a. marine mammals.
   b. nekton in the water column.
   c. plants growing on the deep ocean floor.
   d. algae near the surface.

5. Most ocean pollutants come from
   a. marine organisms.　**b.** the land.
   c. the atmosphere.　　**d.** Earth's core.

True or False
If the statement is true, write true. If it is false, change the underlined word or words to make the statement true.

6. The phase of the moon in which the moon can't be seen from Earth is the <u>new moon</u>.

7. The area between the high and low tide lines is the <u>neritic</u> zone.

8. <u>Benthos</u> are free-swimming animals that can move throughout the water column.

9. A ring-shaped coral reef surrounding a lagoon is called a(n) <u>seamount</u>.

10. Many deep-sea fishes use their <u>bioluminescence</u> to attract prey.

Checking Concepts

11. Describe one method that has been used to study the ocean floor.

12. How can sonar be used to measure the depth of the ocean?

13. Describe the phases of the moon in relation to the lunar cycle.

14. Describe a typical marine food web.

15. Describe three physical factors that organisms in the rocky intertidal zone must overcome.

16. What is an atoll? How is it formed?

17. Explain why scientists were surprised to discover the variety of organisms living around hydrothermal vents.

18. **Writing to Learn** Imagine that you are an "aquanaut" on a voyage of discovery across the ocean floor. Write a logbook entry that summarizes your observations as you travel from one continent to another. Include details about the shape of the ocean floor, as well as some organisms you encounter along your journey.

Thinking Critically

19. **Classifying** Classify each of the following organisms as plankton, nekton, or benthos: squid, sea stars, microscopic algae, whales, sea otters, anglerfish, and giant clams.

20. **Making Generalizations** Explain why many of the world's fisheries are located in the neritic zone.

21. **Predicting** Suppose the number of plankton in the ocean suddenly decreased to half their current number. Predict how this would affect other marine organisms.

22. **Relating Cause and Effect** How might fertilizers used on farmland result in ocean pollution near shore?

23. **Predicting** A storm occurs along a seacoast when the moon is in the phase called the "third quarter." Is it likely that the high tides during the storm will be much higher than usual? Explain your answer.

Applying Skills

Use the diagram of a portion of the ocean floor to answer Questions 24–26.

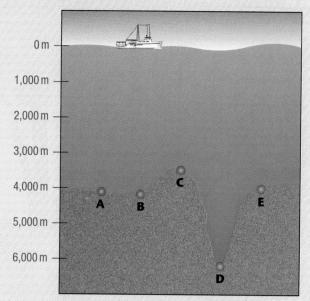

24. Interpreting Diagrams What is the approximate depth of the ocean floor at point A? At point C?

25. Inferring What might the feature between locations A and B be? The feature at point D?

26. Posing Questions What other information would help you determine whether point A or point E is closer to the mid-ocean ridge? Explain.

Performance ▽ CHAPTER PROJECT **Assessment**

Present Your Project With your group, rehearse the guided tour of the environment you will give. As you rehearse, check to see that your marine environment is complete. Make any final changes now.

Reflect and Record In your notebook, write a paragraph summarizing how each organism your group modeled belongs in the habitat you built. What was the most difficult element of the environment to model?

Test Preparation

Use these questions to prepare for standardized tests.

Study the diagram. Then answer Questions 27–30.

27. Which part of the ocean supports the greatest variety of organisms?
A neritic zone
B intertidal zone
C open-ocean deep zone
D open-ocean surface zone

28. Which part of the ocean is in constant darkness and cold, with few organisms?
F neritic zone
G intertidal zone
H open-ocean deep zone
J open-ocean surface zone

29. Organisms in this area must be able to survive severe changes in salinity, temperature, and exposure to air.
A neritic zone
B intertidal zone
C open-ocean surface zone
D open-ocean deep zone

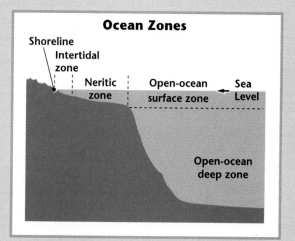

30. The edge of the continental shelf forms the boundary between which parts of the ocean?
F high tide and low tide lines
G intertidal zone and neritic zone
H neritic zone and open ocean
J open-ocean deep zone and hydrothermal vents

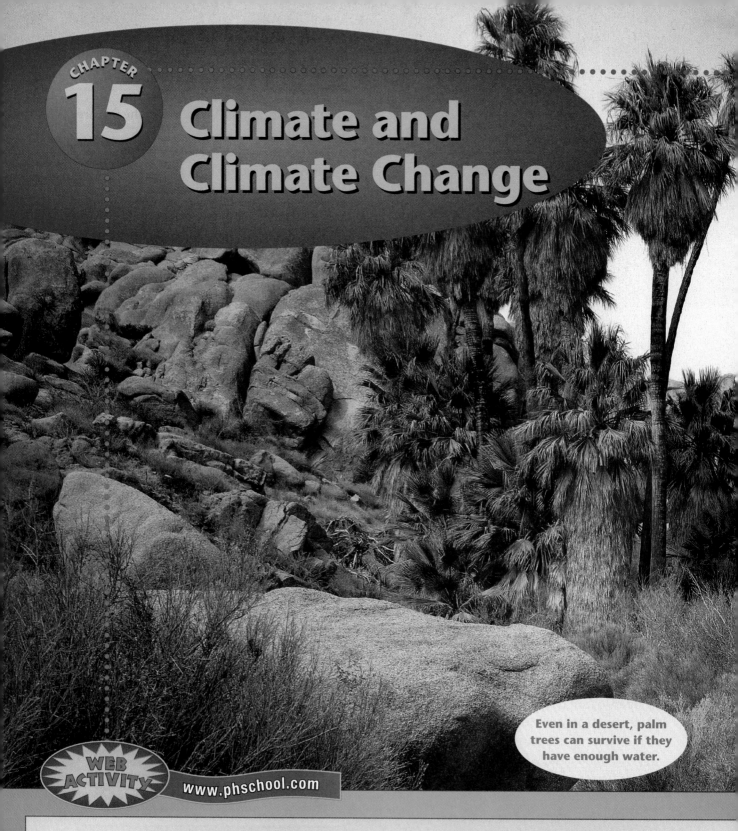

Even in a desert, palm
trees can survive if they
have enough water.

WEB
ACTIVITY
www.phschool.com

Investigating Microclimates

Most of the Mojave Desert is too dry for trees. Only cactus, shrubs, and other hardy plants are able to survive in the parched land. So if you see palm trees there, you know there must be water nearby. Palm trees in the desert grow only in a small area with a climate different from that of the area around it—a microclimate. As you work through this chapter, you will investigate microclimates in your community.

Your Goal To compare weather conditions from at least three microclimates.

To complete your project, you must

◆ hypothesize how the microclimates in three areas will differ from one another

◆ collect data at the same places and times each day

◆ relate each microclimate to the plants and animals found there

◆ follow the safety guidelines in Appendix A

Get Started Begin by brainstorming a list of nearby places that may have different microclimates. How are the places different? Keep in mind weather factors such as temperature, precipitation, humidity, wind direction, and wind speed. Consider areas that are grassy, sandy, sunny, or shaded. Start thinking about what instruments you will need to do your investigation.

Check Your Progress You'll be working on this project as you study this chapter. To keep your project on track, look for Check Your Progress boxes at the following points.

Section 1 Review, page 521: Measure and record weather data.
Section 3 Review, page 540: Graph your data and look for patterns.

Present Your Project At the end of the chapter (page 549), you will present the data you collected about your microclimates. Include any patterns you observed.

TEKS

In addition to process TEKS, this chapter addresses these concept TEKS as they relate to the chapter's topics.

(8.10) The student knows that complex interactions occur between matter and energy. The student is expected to:
(B) describe interactions among solar, weather, and ocean systems.

(8.12) The student knows that cycles exist in Earth systems. The student is expected to:
(B) relate the role of oceans to climatic changes; and
(C) predict the results of modifying the Earth's nitrogen, water, and carbon cycles.

(8.14) The student knows that natural events and human activities can alter Earth systems. The student is expected to:
(C) describe how human activities have modified soil, water, and air quality.

What Causes Climate?

DISCOVER ••

How Does Earth's Shape Affect Climate Zones?

1. On a globe, tape a strip of cash register paper from the equator to the North Pole. Divide the tape into three equal parts. Label the section near the North Pole *poles*, the section near the equator *equator*, and the middle section *mid-latitudes*.

2. Tape the end of an empty toilet paper roll to the end of a flashlight. Hold the flashlight about 30 cm from the equator. Turn on the flashlight to represent the sun. On the paper strip, have a partner draw the shape of the area the light shines on.

3. Move the flashlight up slightly to aim at the section of the paper marked "mid-latitudes." Keep the flashlight horizontal and at the same distance from the globe. Again have a partner draw the shape of the area that the light shines on.

4. Move the flashlight up again to shine on the section of the paper marked "poles." Keep the flashlight horizontal and at the same distance from the globe. Draw the shape of the area that the light shines on.

Think It Over

Observing How does the shape of the area that is illuminated change? Do you think the sun's rays heat Earth's surface evenly?

GUIDE FOR READING

◆ What are the factors that influence precipitation and temperature?

◆ What causes the seasons?

Reading Tip As you read, use the headings to make an outline of the factors that affect climate.

Key Terms climate
• windward • leeward
• tropical zone • polar zone
• temperate zone
• marine climate
• continental climate • El Niño
• microclimate

If you telephone a friend in another state and ask, "What's the weather there today?" she might answer: "It's gray, cool, and rainy. It's usually like that this time of year." Your friend has told you something about both weather and climate.

Weather is day-to-day events. The weather may be cloudy and rainy one day and clear and sunny the next. Weather refers to the condition of the atmosphere at a particular place and time. **Climate,** on the other hand, refers to the average, year-after-year conditions of temperature, precipitation, winds, and clouds in an area. How would you describe the climate where you live?

Two main factors—precipitation and temperature—determine the climate of a region. A climate region is a large area with similar climate conditions throughout. For example, the climate in the southeastern United States is humid, with moderate temperatures.

Factors Affecting Precipitation

The amount of rain and snow that falls in an area each year determines how wet or dry its climate is. But what determines how much precipitation an area gets? **The main factors that affect precipitation are prevailing winds and the presence of mountains.**

Prevailing Winds As you know, weather patterns depend on the movement of huge air masses. Air masses are moved from place to place by prevailing winds, the directional winds that usually blow in a region. Air masses can be warm or cool, dry or humid. The amount of water vapor in the air mass influences how much rain or snow will fall.

Warm air can carry more water vapor than cold air can. When warm air rises and cools, water comes out of the air as precipitation. For example, surface air near the equator is generally hot and humid. As the air rises and cools, heavy rains fall, nourishing thick tropical forests. In contrast, sinking cold air is usually dry. Because the air becomes warmer as it sinks, it can hold more water vapor. The water vapor stays in the air and little or no rain falls. The result may be a desert.

The amount of water vapor in prevailing winds also depends on where the winds come from. Winds that blow inland from oceans carry more water vapor than winds that blow from over land. For example, the Sahara in Africa is near both the Atlantic Ocean and the Mediterranean Sea. Yet the Sahara is very dry. This is because few winds blow from the oceans toward this area. Instead, the prevailing winds are the dry northeast trade winds. The source of these winds is cool, sinking air from southwest Asia.

Mountain Ranges A mountain range in the path of prevailing winds can also influence where precipitation falls. As you have learned, when humid winds blow from the ocean toward coastal mountains, they are forced to rise up to pass over the mountains. The rising warm air cools and its water vapor condenses, forming clouds. Rain or snow falls on the **windward** side of the mountains, the side the oncoming wind hits.

By the time the air reaches the other side of the mountains, it has lost much of its water vapor, so it is cool and dry. The land on the **leeward** side of the mountains—downwind—is in a rain shadow.

Figure 1 The prevailing winds that blow across the Sahara begin far inland. Since the air is dry, the Sahara gets very little rain.
Inferring Why are the winds that blow toward the Sahara dry?

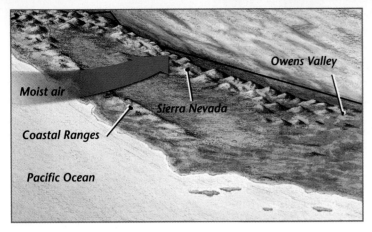

The Owens Valley in California, shown in Figure 2, is in the rain shadow of the Sierra Nevada. Humid winds blow eastward from the Pacific Ocean. Then the air flows down the leeward side of the mountains. As it moves downward, the air becomes warmer. The desert in the Owens Valley, on the eastern side of the Sierra Nevada, was formed by this hot, dry air.

Figure 2 The Sierra Nevada runs through eastern California, parallel to the Pacific coast. To the east of the Sierras is the Owens Valley, shown above. *Inferring Is the Owens Valley on the windward or leeward side of the mountains?*

Factors Affecting Temperature

Tropical countries, such as Panama, are usually hot. Northern countries, such as Finland, are usually cold. **The main factors that influence temperature are latitude, altitude, distance from large bodies of water, and ocean currents.**

Latitude In general, climates of locations farther from the equator are cooler than climates of areas closer to the equator. Why is this? The reason is that the sun's rays hit Earth's surface most directly at the equator. At the poles, the same amount of solar radiation is spread out over a larger area, and therefore brings less warmth.

Recall that latitude is the distance from the equator, measured in degrees. Based on latitude, Earth's surface can be divided into the three temperature zones shown in Figure 3. The **tropical zone** is the area near the equator, between about 23.5° north latitude and 23.5° south latitude. The tropical zone receives direct or nearly direct sunlight all year round, making climates there warm.

Figure 3 Earth has three main temperature zones. *Interpreting Maps In which temperature zone is most of the United States located?*

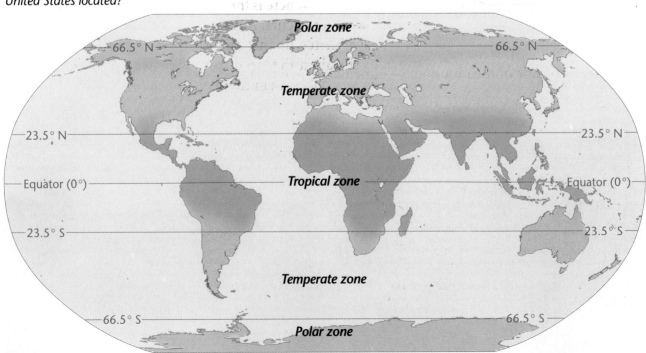

Figure 4 Mount Kilimanjaro in Tanzania, Africa, is near the equator.

In contrast, the sun's rays always strike at a lower angle near the North and South poles. As a result, the areas near both poles have cold climates. These **polar zones** extend from about 66.5° to 90° north and 66.5° to 90° south latitudes.

The **temperate zones** are between the tropical and the polar zones—from about 23.5° to 66.5° north and 23.5° to 66.5° south latitudes. In summer, the sun's rays strike the temperate zones more directly. In winter, the sun's rays strike at a lower angle. As a result, the weather in the temperate zones ranges from warm or hot in summer to cool or cold in winter.

Altitude The peak of Mount Kilimanjaro towers high above the African plains. At nearly 6 kilometers above sea level, Kilimanjaro is covered in snow all year round. Yet it is located near the equator, at 3° south latitude. Why is Mount Kilimanjaro so cold?

In the case of high mountains, altitude is a more important climate factor than latitude. Scientists have found that the temperature of the troposphere decreases about 6.5 Celsius degrees for every 1-kilometer increase in altitude. The troposphere is the lowest level of the atmosphere, in which weather occurs. As a result, highland areas everywhere have cool climates, no matter what their latitude. At nearly 6 kilometers, the air at the top of Mount Kilimanjaro is about 39 Celsius degrees colder than the air at sea level at the same latitude.

☑ *Checkpoint* *Why is there snow on Mount Kilimanjaro?*

Distance From Large Bodies of Water Oceans or large lakes can also affect temperatures. Oceans greatly moderate, or make less extreme, the temperatures of nearby land. Water heats up more slowly than land; it also cools down more slowly. Therefore, winds from the ocean keep coastal regions from reaching extremes of hot and cold. Much of the west coasts of North America, South America, and Europe have mild **marine climates,** with relatively warm winters and cool summers.

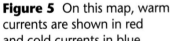
The centers of North America and Asia are too far inland to be warmed or cooled by the oceans. Most of Canada and Russia, as well as the central United States, have **continental climates.** Continental climates have more extreme temperatures than marine climates. Winters are cold, while summers are warm or hot.

Ocean Currents Many marine climates are influenced by ocean currents, streams of water within the oceans that move in regular patterns. In general, warm ocean currents carry warm water from the tropics toward the poles. Cold currents bring cold water from the polar zones toward the equator. The surface of the water warms or cools the air above it. The warmed or cooled air then moves over the nearby land. So a warm current brings warm air to the land it touches. A cold current brings cool air.

The best-known warm-water current is the Gulf Stream, shown on the map in Figure 5. When the Gulf Stream crosses the North Atlantic, it becomes the North Atlantic Drift. This warm current gives Ireland and southern England a mild, wet climate despite their relatively high latitude.

In contrast, the cool California Current flows from Alaska southward down the West Coast. The California Current makes climates of places along the West Coast cooler than you would expect at their latitudes.

☑ *Checkpoint* *What effect do oceans have on the temperatures of nearby land areas?*

Figure 5 On this map, warm currents are shown in red and cold currents in blue.

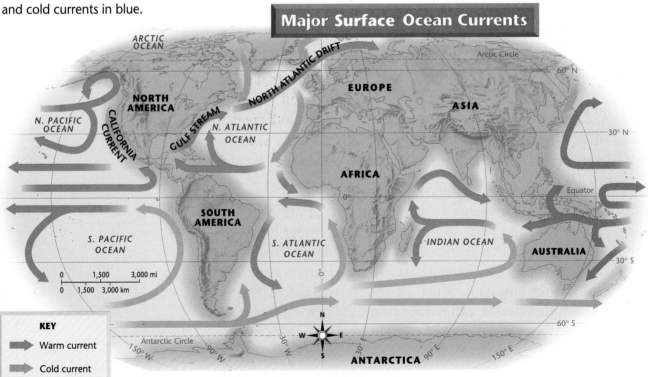

Oceans and Climate Changes

Changes in ocean currents and winds can greatly affect climate. One example is **El Niño,** an abnormal climate event that occurs every two to seven years in the Pacific Ocean. El Niño begins when an unusual pattern of winds forms over the western Pacific. This causes a vast sheet of warm water to move eastward toward the South American coast. El Niño conditions can last for one to two years before the usual winds and currents return.

The arrival of El Niño's warm surface water disrupts the cold ocean current along the western coast of South America and changes weather patterns there. But El Niño also causes shifts in weather patterns around the world, bringing unusual and often severe conditions to different areas. For example, El Niño of 1997 and 1998 caused heavy rains to fall in normally dry coastal parts of Peru and Ecuador. In the United States, El Niño brought an unusually warm winter to the Northeast and heavy rains, flooding, and mudslides to California.

Other events can disrupt ocean currents and change climate. For example, scientists have found evidence that the Gulf Stream's flow of warm water was disrupted about 11,000 years ago. The causes of this event were complex. One factor may have been the flow into the North Atlantic of very cold, fresh water from melting glaciers in North America. The cold water changed the usual currents in the North Atlantic and greatly weakened the Gulf Stream. Without the warmth from the Gulf Stream, Europe's climate became markedly colder for hundreds of years.

☑ *Checkpoint* *What is El Niño?*

Microclimates

Have you ever noticed that it is cooler and more humid in a grove of trees than in an open field? The same factors that affect large climate regions also affect smaller areas. A small area with specific climate conditions different from surrounding areas is said to have its own **microclimate.** Inland mountains, lakes, forests, and other natural features can influence climate nearby, resulting in a microclimate.

You might find a microclimate in a downtown area with tall buildings, or on a windy peninsula jutting into the ocean. Even a small park, if it is usually sunnier or windier than nearby areas, may have its own microclimate. The grass on a lawn can be covered in dew and produce conditions like a rain forest, while the pavement in the parking lot is dry, like a desert.

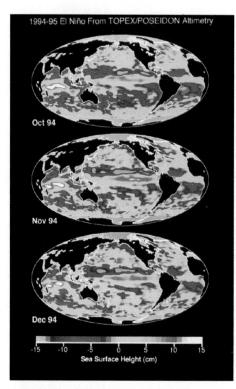

Figure 6 When El Niño occurs, warm surface water from the western Pacific moves east toward the coast of South America. In these maps based on satellite data, the red areas represent the warmer water.

Angles

Light from the sun strikes Earth's surface at different angles. An angle is made up of two lines that meet at a point. Angles are measured in degrees. A full circle has 360 degrees.

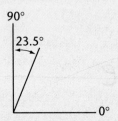

When the sun is directly overhead near the equator, it is at an angle of 90° to Earth's surface. A 90° angle is called a right angle. It is one fourth of a circle.

When the sun is near the horizon, it is at an angle of close to 0° to Earth's surface.

Earth's axis is tilted at an angle of 23.5°. About what fraction of a right angle is this?

The Seasons

 INTEGRATING SPACE SCIENCE Although you can describe the average weather conditions of a climate region, these conditions are not constant all year long. Instead, most places on Earth outside the tropics have four seasons: winter, spring, summer, and autumn.

You might think that Earth is closer to the sun during the summer and farther away during winter. If this were true, every place on Earth would have summer at the same time. Actually, when it is summer in the Northern Hemisphere it is winter in the Southern Hemisphere. So the seasons are *not* a result of changes in the distance between Earth and the sun.

Tilted Axis *Exploring the Seasons* on page 521 shows how Earth's axis is tilted in relation to the sun. **The seasons are caused by the tilt of Earth's axis as Earth travels around the sun.** The axis is an imaginary line through Earth's center that passes through both poles. Earth turns, or rotates, around this axis once each day. Earth's axis is not straight up and down, but is tilted at an angle of 23.5°. The axis always points in the same direction—toward the North Star. As Earth travels around the sun, the north end of the axis is pointed away from the sun for part of the year and toward the sun for part of the year.

Winter or Summer Look at *Exploring the Seasons* on the next page. Which way is the north end of Earth's axis tilted in June? Notice that the Northern Hemisphere receives more direct rays from the sun. Also, in June the days in the Northern Hemisphere are longer than the nights. The combination of more direct rays and longer days makes Earth's surface warmer in the Northern Hemisphere than at any other time of the year. It is summer.

In June, when the north end of Earth's axis is tilted toward the sun, the south end of the axis is tilted away from the sun. The Southern Hemisphere receives fewer direct rays from the sun. The days are shorter than the nights. As a result, the Southern Hemisphere is experiencing winter.

Now look at the situation in December, six months later. Which way is the north end of Earth's axis tilted now? The Northern Hemisphere receives fewer direct rays from the sun and has shorter days. It is winter in the Northern Hemisphere and summer in the Southern Hemisphere.

Twice during the year, in March and September, neither end of Earth's axis is tilted toward the sun. At both of these times, one hemisphere has spring while the other has autumn.

EXPLORING the Seasons

The seasons are a result of Earth's tilted axis. The seasons change as the amount of energy each hemisphere receives from the sun changes.

December
The south end of Earth's axis is tilted toward the sun. The Southern Hemisphere receives more energy from the sun. It is summer in the Southern Hemisphere and winter in the Northern Hemisphere.

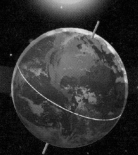

June
As the north end of Earth's axis is tilted toward the sun, the Northern Hemisphere receives more energy. It is summer in the Northern Hemisphere and winter in the Southern Hemisphere.

March and September
Neither end of Earth's axis is tilted toward the sun. Both hemispheres receive the same amounts of energy.

Section 1 Review

1. Name the four main factors that influence the temperature of an area.
2. How do prevailing winds affect the amount of precipitation an area receives?
3. On which side of mountains—leeward or windward—does precipitation fall?
4. Describe El Niño and how it affects weather and climate.
5. How does the tilt of Earth's axis cause the seasons?
6. **Thinking Critically Developing Hypotheses** How might Earth's climates be different if Earth were not tilted on its axis?

CHAPTER PROJECT

Check Your Progress
Have you chosen your microclimate study sites? If your sites are on private property, get permission. Set up a logbook so that you can record your data. How do you think the conditions in these sites will differ? Write down your hypotheses. Now you are ready to measure daily weather conditions for your microclimates. (*Hint:* Be sure to take your measurements at the same time each day.)

Designing Experiments

Sunny Rays and Angles

In this lab, you will investigate how the angle of the sun's rays affects the amount of energy absorbed by different parts of Earth's surface.

Problem

How does the angle of a light source affect the rate of temperature change of a surface?

Materials

books   graph paper   pencil
scissors   ruler   clear tape
watch or clock protractor
100-W incandescent lamp
black construction paper
3 thermometers or temperature probes (optional)

Procedure

1. Cut a strip of black construction paper 5 cm by 10 cm. Fold the paper in half and tape two sides to form a pocket.
2. Repeat Step 1 to make two more pockets.
3. Place the bulb of a thermometer or a temperature probe inside each pocket.
4. Place the pockets with thermometers close together, as shown in the photo. Place one thermometer in a vertical position (90° angle), one at a 45° angle, and the third one in a horizontal position (0° angle). Use a protractor to measure the angles. Support the thermometers with books.
5. Position the lamp so that it is 30 cm from each of the thermometer bulbs. Make sure the lamp will not move during the activity.

6. Copy a data table like the one below into your notebook.
7. In your data table, record the temperature on all three thermometers. (All three temperatures should be the same.)
8. Switch on the lamp. In your data table, record the temperature on each thermometer every minute for 15 minutes. **CAUTION:** *Be careful not to touch the hot lampshade.*
9. After 15 minutes, switch off the lamp.

Analyze and Conclude

1. In this experiment, what was the manipulated variable? What was the responding variable? How do you know which is which?
2. Graph your data. Label the horizontal axis and vertical axis of your graph as shown on the sample graph. Use solid, dashed, and dotted lines to show the results from each thermometer, as shown in the key.
3. Based on your data, at which angle did the temperature increase the most?
4. At which angle did the temperature increase the least?

DATA TABLE

Time (min.)	Temperature (°C)		
	0° Angle	45° Angle	90° Angle
Start			
1			
2			
3			
4			
5			

5. What part of Earth's surface does each thermometer represent?

6. Why is air at the North Pole still very cold in the summer even though the Northern Hemisphere is tilted toward the sun?

7. **Think About It** In this experiment, what variables were held constant?

Design an Experiment

Design an experiment to find out how the results of this investigation would change if the lamp were placed farther from the thermometers. Then design another experiment to find out what would happen if the lamp were placed closer to the thermometers.

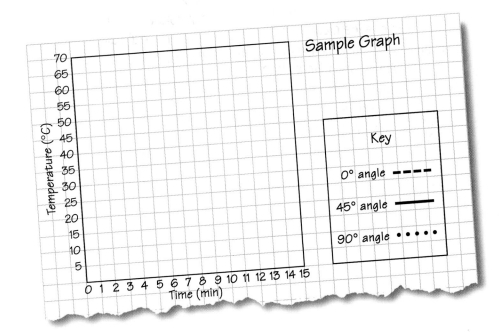

Sample Graph

Temperature (°C)

70
65
60
55
50
45
40
35
30
25
20
15
10
5

0 1 2 3 4 5 6 7 8 9 10 11 12 13 14 15
Time (min)

Key

0° angle – – – –

45° angle ———

90° angle • • • • •

What Are Different Climate Types?

1. Collect pictures from magazines and newspapers of a variety of land areas around the world.
2. Sort the pictures into categories according to common weather characteristics.

Think It Over
Forming Operational Definitions Choose several words that describe the typical weather for each of your categories. What words would you use to describe the typical weather where you live?

GUIDE FOR READING

◆ What factors are used to classify climates?

◆ What are the five main types of climate regions?

Reading Tip Before you read, preview *Exploring Climate Regions*. Write a list of any questions you have about climate regions.

Key Terms rain forest
• savanna • desert • steppe
• humid subtropical • subarctic
• tundra • permafrost

When the Spanish settlers came to California in the 1700s, they brought with them plants from home. The padres, or priests, who established missions planted vineyards and orchards. They found that grapes, figs, and olives grew as well in California as they had in Spain. What do Spain and California have in common? They have similar climates.

Classifying Climates

The Spanish padres traveled a long distance but found a familiar climate. Suppose you traveled from your home to a place where the weather, the sunlight, and even the plants and trees were very different from what you are used to. Would you know what caused those differences?

Scientists classify climates according to two major factors: temperature and precipitation. They use a system developed around 1900 by Wladimir Köppen (KEP un). This system identifies broad climate regions, each of which has smaller subdivisions.

There are five main types of climate regions: tropical rainy, dry, temperate marine, temperate continental, and polar. Note that there is only one category of dry climates, whether hot or cold. These climate regions are shown in *Exploring Climate Regions* on pages 526–527.

◀ Olive trees

Exploring Climate Regions also shows a sixth type of climate: highlands. Recall that temperatures are cooler at the tops of mountains than in the surrounding areas. So a highland climate can occur within any of the other zones.

Maps show boundaries between the climate regions. In the real world, of course, no clear boundaries mark where one climate region ends and another begins. Each region blends gradually into the next.

☑ *Checkpoint* **What are the five main climate regions?**

Tropical Rainy Climates

The tropics have two types of rainy climates: tropical wet and tropical wet-and-dry. Trace the equator on *Exploring Climate Regions* with your finger. Tropical wet climates are found in low-lying lands near the equator. If you look north and south of tropical wet climates on the map, you can see two bands of tropical wet-and-dry climates.

Tropical Wet In areas that have a tropical wet climate, many days are rainy, often with afternoon thunderstorms. With year-round heat and heavy rainfall, vegetation grows lush and green. Dense rain forests grow in these rainy climates. **Rain forests** are forests in which plenty of rain falls all year-round. Tall trees such as teak and mahogany form the top layer, or canopy, while smaller bushes and vines grow near the ground. There are also many animals in the rain forest, including colorful parrots and toucans, bats, insects, frogs, and snakes.

In the United States, only the windward sides of the Hawaiian islands have a tropical wet climate. Rainfall is very heavy—over 10 meters per year on the windward side of the Hawaiian island of Kauai. The rain forests in Hawaii have a large variety of plants, including ferns, orchids, and many types of vines and trees.

Figure 7 Lush tropical rain forests grow in the tropical wet climate. *Relating Cause and Effect* What climate factors encourage this growth?

EXPLORING Climate Regions

Climate regions are classified according to a combination of temperature and precipitation. Climates in highland regions change rapidly as altitude changes.

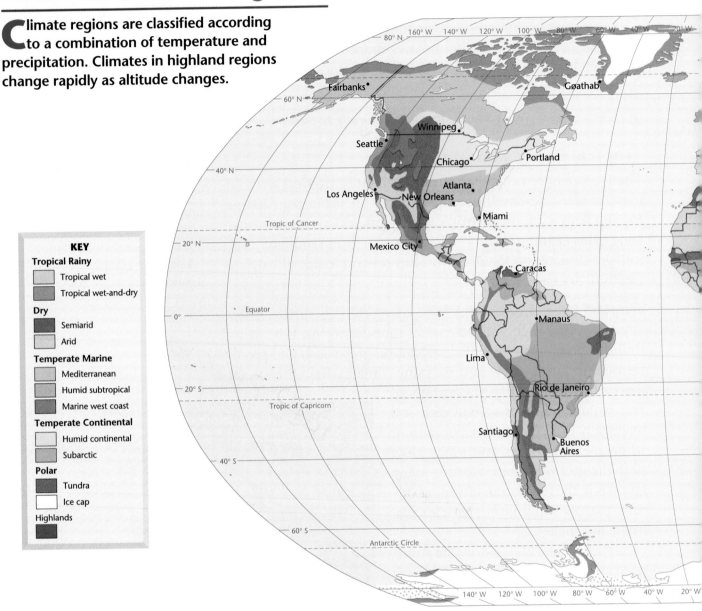

KEY

Tropical Rainy
- Tropical wet
- Tropical wet-and-dry

Dry
- Semiarid
- Arid

Temperate Marine
- Mediterranean
- Humid subtropical
- Marine west coast

Temperate Continental
- Humid continental
- Subarctic

Polar
- Tundra
- Ice cap

Highlands

Tropical Rainy
Temperature always 18°C or above.

Tropical wet *Always hot and humid, with heavy rainfall (at least 6 centimeters a month) year-round.*
Tropical wet-and-dry *Always hot, with alternating wet and dry seasons; heavy rainfall in the wet season.*

Dry
Occurs wherever potential evaporation is greater than precipitation. May be hot or cold.

Arid *Desert, with little precipitation, usually less than 25 centimeters a year.*
Semiarid *Dry but receives about 25 to 50 centimeters of precipitation a year.*

Temperate Marine
Average temperature 10°C or above in the warmest month, between −3°C and 18°C in the coldest month.

Mediterranean *Warm, dry summers and rainy winters.*
Humid subtropical *Hot summers and cool winters.*
Marine west coast *Mild winters and cool summers, with moderate precipitation year-round.*

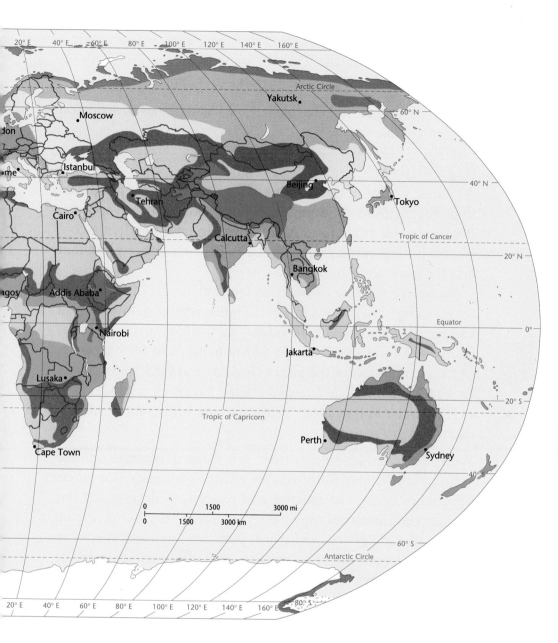

Temperate Continental

Average temperature 10°C or above in the warmest month, −3°C or below in the coldest month.

Humid continental *Hot, humid summers and cold winters, with moderate precipitation year-round.*
Subarctic *Short, cool summers and long, cold winters. Light precipitation, mainly in summer.*

Polar

Average temperature below 10°C in the warmest month.

Tundra *Always cold with a short, cool summer—warmest temperature about 10°C.*
Ice cap *Always cold, average temperature at or below 0°C.*

Highlands

Generally cooler and wetter than nearby lowlands, temperature decreasing with altitude.

Figure 8 A reticulated giraffe gazes across the grasses and shrubby trees of the African savanna. Savannas are found in tropical wet-and-dry climates.

Tropical Wet-and-Dry Tropical wet-and-dry climates get slightly less rain than tropical climates and have distinct dry and rainy seasons. Instead of rain forests, there are tropical grasslands called **savannas.** Scattered clumps of trees that can survive the dry season dot the coarse grasses. Only a small part of the United States—the southern tip of Florida—has a tropical wet-and-dry climate.

✓ *Checkpoint* *What parts of the United States have tropical rainy climates?*

Dry Climates

A climate is "dry" if the amount of precipitation that falls is less than the amount of water that could potentially evaporate. Because water evaporates more slowly in cool weather, a cool place with low rainfall may not be as dry as a hotter place that gets the same amount of rain.

Look at *Exploring Climate Regions.* What part of the United States is dry? Why is precipitation in this region so low? As you can see, dry regions often lie inland, far from oceans that are the source of humid air masses. In addition, much of the region lies in the rain shadow of the Sierra Nevadas and Rocky Mountains to the west. Humid air masses from the Pacific Ocean lose much of their water as they cross the mountains. Little rain or snow is carried to dry regions.

Arid The word *desert* may make you think of blazing heat and drifting sand dunes. Some deserts are hot and sandy, but others are cold or rocky. On average, arid regions, or **deserts,** get less than 25 centimeters of rain every year. Some years may bring no rain at all. Only specialized plants such as cactus and yucca can survive the desert's dryness and extremes of hot and cold. In the United States there are arid climates in portions of California, the Great Basin, and the southwest.

Figure 9 Dry-land wheat farming is common in the steppe region of the Great Plains. *Comparing and Contrasting How are steppes similar to savannas, shown in Figure 8? How are they different?*

Semiarid Locate the semiarid regions on *Exploring Climate Regions*. As you can see, large semiarid areas are usually located on the edges of deserts. A steppe is dry but gets enough rainfall for short grasses and low bushes to grow. For this reason, a **steppe** may also be called a prairie or grassland.

The Great Plains are the steppe region of the United States. Many kinds of short grasses and wildflowers grow here, along with scattered forests. Livestock grazing is an important part of the economy of the Great Plains. Beef cattle, sheep, and goats graze on the short grasses of the region. Farm crops include grains, such as wheat and oats, and sunflowers.

Temperate Marine Climates

Look at *Exploring Climate Regions,* along the coasts of continents in the temperate zones. You will find the third main climate region, temperate marine. There are three kinds of temperate marine climates. Because of the moderating influence of oceans, all three are humid and have mild winters.

Marine West Coast The coolest temperate marine climates are found on the west coasts of continents north of 40° north latitude and south of 40° south latitude. Humid ocean air brings cool, rainy summers and mild, rainy winters.

In North America, the marine west coast climate extends from northern California to southern Alaska. In the Pacific Northwest of the United States, humid air from the Pacific Ocean rises as it hits the western slopes of the Coastal Ranges. As the air cools, large amounts of rain or snow fall on the western slopes.

Because of the heavy precipitation, thick forests of tall trees grow in this region, including coniferous, or cone-bearing, trees such as Sitka spruce, Douglas fir, redwoods, and Western red cedar. One of the main industries of this region is harvesting and processing wood for lumber, paper, and furniture.

TRY THIS

Modeling a Humid Climate

ACTIVITY

Here's how you can create humidity.

1. Put the same amount of water in each of two small plastic bowls.
2. Place a sheet of transparent plastic wrap over each bowl. Secure each sheet with a rubber band.
3. Place one bowl on a warm, sunny windowsill or near a radiator. Put the other bowl in a cool location.
4. Wait a day and then look at the two bowls. What do you see on the plastic wrap over each bowl?

Inferring Would you expect to find more water vapor in the air in a warm climate or in a cool one? Why? Explain your results in terms of solar energy.

Figure 10 Seattle, Washington, is in the marine west coast climate region. Here the summers are cool and rainy, and winters are wet and mild.

Figure 11 Much of Italy (above) has a Mediterranean climate, with warm, dry summers and cool, rainy winters. Rice is a major food crop in places with a humid subtropical climate, as in parts of China (below). *Comparing and Contrasting How are Mediterranean and humid subtropical climates similar? How do they differ?*

Mediterranean A coastal climate that is drier and warmer than west coast marine is known as Mediterranean. Find the Mediterranean climates in *Exploring Climate Regions*. In the United States, the southern coast of California has a Mediterranean climate. This climate is mild, with two seasons. In winter, marine air masses bring cool, rainy weather. Summers are somewhat warmer, with little rain.

Mediterranean climates have two main vegetation types. One is made up of dense shrubs and small trees, called chaparral (chap uh RAL). The other vegetation type includes grasses with a few oak trees.

Agriculture is an important part of the economy of California's Mediterranean climate region. Some crops, including olives and grapes, were originally introduced by Spanish settlers. With the help of irrigation, farmers grow many different crops, including rice, oranges, and many vegetables, fruits, and nuts.

Humid Subtropical The warmest temperate marine climates are on the edges of the tropics. **Humid subtropical** climates are wet and warm, but not as constantly hot as the tropics. Locate the humid subtropical climates in *Exploring Climate Regions*.

The southeastern United States has a humid subtropical climate. Summers are hot, with much more rainfall than in winter. Maritime tropical air masses move inland, bringing tropical weather conditions, including thunderstorms and occasional hurricanes, to southern cities such as Houston, New Orleans, and Atlanta. Winters are cool to mild, with more rain than snow. However, polar air masses moving in from the north can bring freezing temperatures and severe frosts.

Mixed forests of oak, ash, hickory, and pines grow in the humid subtropical region of the United States. Cotton was once the most important crop grown in this region. Other crops, including oranges, grapefruits, peaches, peanuts, sugar cane, and rice, are now more important to the economy.

✓ *Checkpoint What is the main difference between a humid subtropical climate and a tropical climate?*

Temperate Continental Climates

Temperate continental climates are found on continents in the Northern Hemisphere. Because they are not influenced very much by oceans, temperate continental climates have extremes of temperature. Why do continental climates occur only in the Northern Hemisphere? The parts of continents in the Southern Hemisphere south of 40° south latitude are not far enough from oceans for dry continental air masses to form.

Humid Continental Shifting tropical and polar air masses bring constantly changing weather to humid continental climates. In winter, continental polar air masses move south, bringing bitterly cold weather. In summer, tropical air masses move north, bringing heat and high humidity. Humid continental climates receive moderate amounts of rain in the summer. Smaller amounts of rain or snow fall in winter.

What parts of the United States have a humid continental climate? The eastern part of the region—the Northeast—has a range of forest types, from mixed forests in the south to coniferous forests in the north. Much of the western part of this region—the Midwest—was once tall grasslands, but is now farmland. Farmers in the Midwest grow wheat, corn, other grains, and soybeans. These crops are used as food for people and for hogs, poultry, and beef cattle.

Subarctic The **subarctic** climates lie north of the humid continental climates. The world's largest subarctic regions are in Russia, Canada, and Alaska. Summers in the subarctic are short and cool. Winters are long and bitterly cold.

In North America, coniferous trees such as spruce and fir make up a huge northern forest that stretches from Alaska to Canada's east coast. Many large mammals, including bears, wolves, and moose, live in the forest. Small mammals such as beavers, porcupines, and red squirrels, and birds such as grouse and owls also live in the forest. Wood products from the northern forest are an important part of the economy.

Figure 12 Subarctic climates have cool summers and cold winters. Parts of this region are called "spruce-moose belts."

Figure 13 Emperor penguins live on the ice cap of Antarctica.

Polar Climates

The polar climate is the coldest climate region. Ice cap and tundra climates are found only in the far north and south, near the North and South poles.

Ice Cap As you can see in *Exploring Climate Regions,* ice cap climates are found mainly on Greenland and in Antarctica. With average temperatures always at or below freezing, the land in ice cap climate regions is covered with ice and snow. Intense cold makes the air dry. Lichens and a few low plants may grow on the rocks.

Tundra The **tundra** climate region stretches across northern Alaska, Canada, and Russia. Short, cool summers follow bitterly cold winters. Because of the cold, some layers of the tundra soil are always frozen. This permanently frozen tundra soil is called **permafrost.** Because of the permafrost, water cannot drain away, so the soil is wet and boggy in summer.

It is too cold on the tundra for trees to grow. Despite the harsh climate, during the short summers the tundra is filled with life. Mosquitoes and other insects hatch in the ponds and marshes above the frozen permafrost. Mosses, grasses, lichens, wildflowers, and shrubs grow quickly during the short summers. Herds of caribou and musk oxen eat the vegetation and are in turn preyed upon by wolves. Some birds, such as the white-tailed ptarmigan, live on the tundra year-round. Others, such as the arctic tern and many waterfowl, spend only the summer there.

✓ *Checkpoint* *What type of vegetation is found on the tundra?*

Figure 14 The tundra is often very cold, but still many plants and animals live there. *Observing How are these musk oxen adapted to the cold climate?*

Highlands

Why are highlands a distinct climate region? Remember that temperature falls as altitude increases, so highland regions are colder than the regions that surround them. Increasing altitude produces climate changes similar to the climate changes you would expect with increasing latitude. In the tropics, highlands are like cold islands overlooking the warm lowlands.

The climate on the lower slopes of a mountain range is like that of the surrounding countryside. The foothills of the Rocky Mountains, for instance, share the semiarid climate of the Great Plains. But as you go higher up into the mountains, temperatures become lower. Climbing 1,000 meters up in elevation is like traveling 1,200 kilometers north. The climate higher in the mountains is like that of the subarctic: cool with coniferous trees. Animals typical of the subarctic zone—such as moose and porcupines—live in the mountain forest.

Above a certain elevation—the tree line—no trees can grow. The climate above the tree line is like that of the tundra. Only low plants, mosses, and lichens can grow there.

Figure 15 The top of this mountain is too cold and windy for trees to grow. *Classifying What climate zone does this mountaintop resemble?*

Section 2 Review

1. What two factors are used to classify climates?
2. Briefly describe each of the five main climate types.
3. Give three examples of how the climate of a region affects what plants and animals can live there.
4. **Thinking Critically** **Applying Concepts** Which of these two places has more severe winters—central Russia or the west coast of France? Why?
5. **Thinking Critically** **Classifying** Classify the main climate regions according to whether or not trees usually grow in each one.

Science at Home

Climate Regions Describe to your family the characteristics of each of the climate regions found in the United States. Which climate region does your family live in? What plants and animals live in your climate region? What characteristics do these plants and animals have that make them well adapted to living in your climate region?

Cool Climate Graphs

You are a land-use planner who has been hired by a company that builds recreational facilities. Your company is considering buying land near at least one of four cities, all at about the same latitude. Your job is to decide which of the cities would be the best place to build a water park and which is the best place to build a ski-touring center.

Problem

Based on climate data, which city is the best place for each type of recreational facility?

Skills Focus

graphing, interpreting data, drawing conclusions

Materials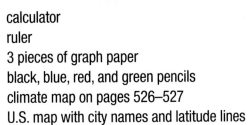

calculator
ruler
3 pieces of graph paper
black, blue, red, and green pencils
climate map on pages 526–527
U.S. map with city names and latitude lines

Procedure

1. 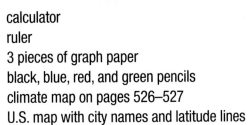 Work in groups of three. Each person should graph the data for a different city, A, B, or C. You may construct your graphs using paper and pencil or on the computer.

2. On graph paper, use a black pencil to label the axes as on the climate graph below. Title your climate graph City A, City B, or City C.

3. Use your green pencil to make a bar graph of the monthly average amount of precipitation. Place a star below the name of each month that has more than a trace of snow.

4. Use a red pencil to plot the average monthly maximum temperature. Make a dot for the temperature in the middle of each space for the month. When you have plotted data for all 12 months, connect the points into a smooth curved line.

5. Use a blue pencil to plot the average monthly minimum temperature for your city. Use the same procedure as in Step 4.

6. Calculate the total average annual precipitation for this city. Include it in your observations by adding its average precipitation for each month.

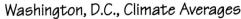

Washington, D.C., Climate Averages

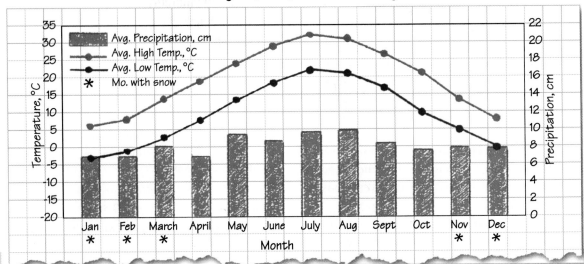

Climate Data

Washington, D.C.	Jan	Feb	Mar	April	May	June	July	Aug	Sept	Oct	Nov	Dec
Average High Temp. (°C)	6	8	14	19	24	29	32	31	27	21	14	8
Average Low Temp. (°C)	-3	-2	3	8	14	19	22	21	17	10	5	0
Average Precipitation (cm)	6.9	6.9	8.1	6.9	9.4	8.6	9.7	9.9	8.4	7.6	7.9	7.9
Months With Snow	*	*	*	trace	—	—	—	—	—	trace	*	*

City A	Jan	Feb	Mar	Apr	May	Jun	July	Aug	Sept	Oct	Nov	Dec
Average High Temp. (°C)	13	16	16	17	17	18	18	19	21	21	17	13
Average Low Temp. (°C)	8	9	9	10	11	12	12	13	13	13	11	8
Average Precipitation (cm)	10.4	7.6	7.9	3.3	0.8	0.5	0.3	0.3	0.8	3.3	8.1	7.9
Months With Snow	trace	trace	trace	—	—	—	—	—	—	—	—	trace

City B	Jan	Feb	Mar	Apr	May	Jun	July	Aug	Sept	Oct	Nov	Dec
Average High Temp. (°C)	5	7	10	16	21	26	29	27	23	18	11	6
Average Low Temp. (°C)	–9	–7	–4	1	6	11	14	13	8	2	–4	–8
Average Precipitation (cm)	0.8	1.0	2.3	3.0	5.6	5.8	7.4	7.6	3.3	2.0	1.3	1.3
Months With Snow	*	*	*	*	*	—	—	—	trace	*	*	*

City C	Jan	Feb	Mar	Apr	May	Jun	July	Aug	Sept	Oct	Nov	Dec
Average High Temp. (°C)	7	11	13	18	23	28	33	32	27	21	12	8
Average Low Temp. (°C)	–6	–4	–2	1	4	8	11	10	5	1	–3	–7
Average Precipitation (cm)	2.5	2.3	1.8	1.3	1.8	1	0.8	0.5	0.8	1	2	2.5
Months With Snow	*	*	*	*	*	trace	—	—	trace	trace	*	*

Analyze and Conclude

Compare your climate graphs and observations. Use all three climate graphs, plus the graph for Washington, D.C., to answer these questions.

1. Which of the four cities has the least change in average temperatures during the year?
2. In which climate region is each city located?
3. Which of the cities listed below matches each climate graph?

Colorado Springs, Colorado	latitude 39° N
San Francisco, California	latitude 38° N
Reno, Nevada	latitude 40° N
Washington, D.C.	latitude 39° N

4. Even though these cities are at approximately the same latitude, why are their climate graphs so different?
5. **Apply** Which city would be the best location for a water slide park? For a cross-country ski touring center? What other factors should you consider when deciding where to build each type of recreational facility? Explain.

More to Explore

What type of climate does the area where you live have? Find out what outdoor recreational facilities your community has. How is each one particularly suited to the climate of *your* area?

DISCOVER ACTIVITY

What Story Can Tree Rings Tell?

1. Look at the photo of tree rings on page 537. Tree rings are the layers of new wood that form as a tree grows each year.

2. Look closely at the tree rings. Note whether they are all the same thickness.

3. What weather conditions might cause a tree to form thicker or thinner tree rings?

Think It Over

Inferring How could you use tree rings to tell you about weather in the past?

GUIDE FOR READING

◆ What principle do scientists follow in studying ancient climates?

◆ What changes occur on Earth's surface during an ice age?

◆ What theories have been proposed to explain natural climate change?

Reading Tip Before you read, preview the art and photos and read the captions. Write a prediction about how Earth's climate has changed through time.

Key Terms ice age • sunspot

One of the greatest Native American cultures in the American Southwest was the Ancestral Pueblos. These farming people built great pueblos, or "apartment houses," of stone and sun-baked clay, with hundreds of rooms. By about the year 1000, the Ancestral Pueblos were flourishing. They grew crops of corn, beans, and squash and traded extensively with other groups of people. But in the late 1200s, the climate became drier, reducing the size of their crops. After a long period of drought, the Ancestral Pueblos migrated to other areas.

Although weather can vary from day to day, climates usually change more slowly. But climates do change, both in small areas and throughout the world. Although climate change is usually slow, its consequences are great. Climate changes have affected many civilizations, including the Ancestral Pueblos.

Figure 16 The Ancestral Pueblos lived in these buildings, now in Mesa Verde National Park in southwestern Colorado, about 1,000 years ago.

Studying Climate Change

In studying ancient climates, scientists follow an important principle: If plants or animals today need certain conditions to live, then similar plants and animals in the past also required those conditions. For example, today magnolia and palm trees grow only in warm, moist climates. Scientists assume that the ancestors of these trees required similar conditions. Thus, 80-million-year-old fossils of these trees in Greenland are good evidence that the climate of Greenland was warm and moist 80 million years ago.

Tree rings can also be used to learn about ancient climates. Every summer, a tree grows a new layer of wood under its bark. These layers form rings when seen in a cross section, as shown in Figure 17. In cool climates, the amount the tree grows—the thickness of a ring—depends on the length of the warm growing season. In dry climates, the thickness of each ring depends on the amount of rainfall. By looking at cross sections of trees, scientists can count backward from the outer ring to see whether previous years were warm or cool, wet or dry. A thin ring indicates that the year was cool or dry. A thick ring indicates that the year was warm or wet.

A third source of information about ancient climates is pollen records. Each type of plant has a particular type of pollen. The bottoms of some lakes are covered with thick layers of mud and plant material, including pollen, that fell to the bottom of the lake over thousands of years. Scientists can drill down into these layers and bring up cores to examine. By looking at the pollen present in each layer, scientists can tell what types of plants lived in the area. The scientists can then infer that the climate that existed when the pollen was deposited was similar to the climate where the same plants grow today.

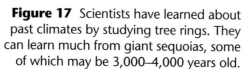

Figure 17 Scientists have learned about past climates by studying tree rings. They can learn much from giant sequoias, some of which may be 3,000–4,000 years old.

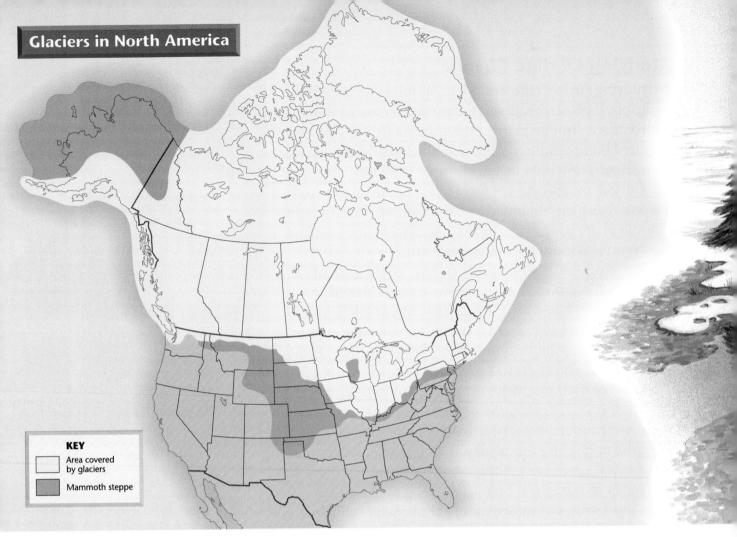

KEY

☐ Area covered by glaciers

▨ Mammoth steppe

Figure 18 The map shows the parts of North America that were covered by glaciers 18,000 years ago. On the steppe near the glaciers lived many mammals that are now extinct, including woolly mammoths and scimitar-toothed cats.

Ice Ages

Throughout Earth's history, climates have gradually changed. Over millions of years, warm periods have alternated with cold periods known as **ice ages,** or glacial episodes. **During each ice age, huge sheets of ice called glaciers covered large parts of Earth's surface.**

From fossils and other evidence, scientists have concluded that in the past two million years there have been at least four major ice ages. Each one lasted 100,000 years or longer. Long, warmer periods known as interglacials occurred between the ice ages. Some scientists think that we are now in a warm period between ice ages.

The most recent major ice age ended only about 10,500 years ago. Ice sheets covered much of northern Europe and North America, reaching as far south as present-day Iowa and Nebraska. In some places, the ice was more than 3 kilometers thick. So much water was frozen in the ice sheets that the average sea level was much lower than it is today. When the ice sheets melted, the rising oceans flooded coastal areas. Inland, large lakes formed.

☑ *Checkpoint* *Why were the oceans lower during the ice ages than they are now?*

Causes of Climate Change

Why do climates change? Scientists have formed several hypotheses. **Possible explanations for major climate changes include variations in the position of Earth relative to the sun, changes in the sun's energy output, and the movement of continents.**

Earth's Position Changes in Earth's position relative to the sun may have affected climates. According to one hypothesis, as Earth revolves around the sun, the time of year when Earth is closest to the sun shifts from January to July and back again over a period of about 26,000 years.

    The angle at which Earth's axis tilts and the shape of Earth's orbit around the sun also change slightly over long periods of time. The combined effects of these changes in Earth's movements may be the main cause of ice ages.

 **INTEGRATING SPACE SCIENCE** **Solar Energy** Short-term changes in climate have been linked to changes in the number of **sunspots**—dark, cooler regions on the surface of the sun. Sunspots increase and decrease in regular 11-year cycles. Sunspot cycles could in turn be caused by changes in the sun's energy output.

Social Studies
CONNECTION

Prehistoric people who lived during the last ice age faced a harsh environment. To endure the cold, they learned to make clothing from animal skins. They also used fires for warmth and cooking.

In Your Journal

Make a list of five ways your life would change if the climate suddenly became colder.

225 million years ago

180–200 million years ago

Figure 19 The continents have moved over millions of years. *Interpreting Maps Which present-day continents broke away from Gondwanaland? Which broke away from Laurasia?*

Recently, satellite measurements have shown that the amount of energy the sun produces increases and decreases slightly from year to year. These changes may cause Earth's temperature to increase and decrease. More observations are needed to test this hypothesis.

Movement of Continents Earth's continents have not always been located where they are now. About 225 million years ago, most of the land on Earth was part of a single continent called Pangaea (pan JEE uh).

As Figure 19 shows, most continents were far from their present positions. Continents that are now in the polar zones were once near the equator. This movement explains how tropical plants such as magnolias and palm trees could once have grown in Greenland.

Over millions of years, the continents broke away and gradually moved to their present positions. The movements of continents over time changed the locations of land and sea. These changes affected the global patterns of winds and ocean currents, which in turn slowly changed climates. And as the continents continue to move, climates will continue to change.

Section 3 Review

1. How do modern plants and animals help explain ancient climates?
2. How is the climate during an ice age different from the climate today?
3. List three factors that could be responsible for changing Earth's climates.
4. **Thinking Critically Predicting** What kinds of climate changes might be caused by a volcanic eruption? Would these changes be permanent? Explain.

CHAPTER PROJECT

Check Your Progress
What types of weather conditions have you measured at each site? Have you been recording all the data in your logbook? You should now be ready to graph and analyze your data. Are the weather conditions at all of your test areas similar, or do you see differences? What do you think causes the different conditions? What organisms did you observe at your sites?

SECTION 4 Global Changes in the Atmosphere

DISCOVER .... ACTIVITY

What Is the Greenhouse Effect?

1. ✂ Cut two pieces of black construction paper to fit the bottoms of two shoe boxes.

2. 🧤 Place a thermometer in one end of each box. Read the temperatures on the thermometers. (They should be the same.) Cover one box with plastic wrap.

3. Place the boxes together where sunlight or a light bulb can shine on them equally. **CAUTION:** *Avoid touching the lampshade. The light bulb will cause it to heat up.* Make sure the

thermometers are shaded by the sides of the boxes.

4. What do you think will happen to the temperatures on the thermometers? Wait 15 minutes and read the thermometers again. Record the temperatures.

Think It Over

Inferring How can you explain the temperature difference between the box with the plastic wrap and the open box? Why does the inside of a car left in direct sunlight get so warm?

Scientists have measured the gases in air bubbles trapped in ice from glaciers in Antarctica. These data show that the amount of carbon dioxide in Earth's atmosphere remained relatively stable during much of the past 1,000 years. That is, carbon dioxide was roughly in balance, or equilibrium.

Natural processes, such as volcanic activity and ice ages, and human activities can disturb this equilibrium. Scientists have data showing that the amount of carbon dioxide in the atmosphere is increasing today. Increased carbon dioxide causes changes in an Earth system called the carbon cycle.

The Carbon Cycle

In the **carbon cycle,** carbon is transferred from Earth's interior to the atmosphere, oceans, crust, and to living things. Eventually, carbon is returned to Earth's interior to begin the cycle again. **The carbon cycle is a system that transfers matter from one part of the environment to another. This system consists of nonliving matter in the crust, oceans, and atmosphere as well as living organisms.** The sun and the heat of Earth's interior provide the energy that drives the carbon cycle.

GUIDE FOR READING

◆ What is the carbon cycle?

◆ How might human activities be affecting the temperature of Earth's atmosphere?

◆ How have human activities affected the ozone layer?

Reading Tip As you read, draw a concept map showing how human activities can cause changes in the atmosphere and climate.

Key Terms carbon cycle
• photosynthesis
• greenhouse gas
• global warming • ozone
• ozone layer
• chlorofluorocarbons

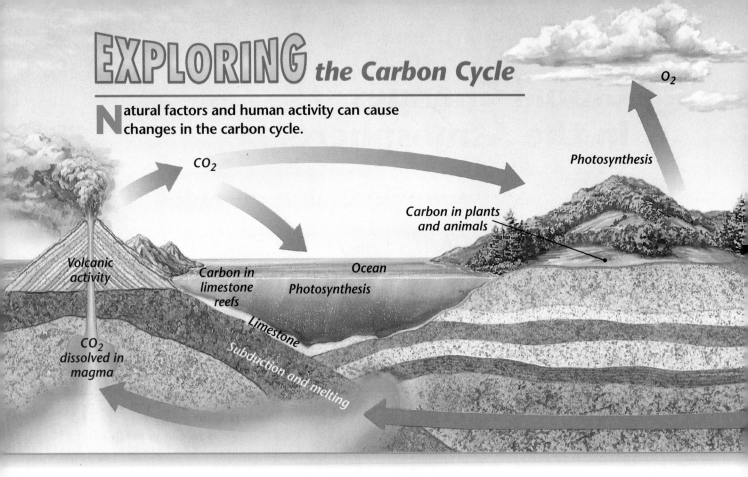

EXPLORING *the Carbon Cycle*

Natural factors and human activity can cause changes in the carbon cycle.

O_2

Photosynthesis

CO_2

Carbon in plants and animals

Volcanic activity

Carbon in limestone reefs

Ocean Photosynthesis

Limestone

CO_2 dissolved in magma

Subduction and melting

Beginning the Carbon Cycle As you can see in *Exploring the Carbon Cycle,* the carbon cycle begins with volcanic activity. Carbon dioxide is one of the gases dissolved in magma in Earth's mantle. When a volcano erupts, carbon dioxide gas is released into the atmosphere. Some carbon dioxide mixes with rain and snow. When this precipitation falls to the surface, the carbon dioxide dissolves in Earth's oceans and other bodies of water.

The Carbon Cycle and Living Things The carbon cycle continues in the atmosphere and oceans. Plants and other organisms that carry out photosynthesis take in carbon dioxide. **Photosynthesis** is the process by which plants use the energy of sunlight to change carbon dioxide and water into food and oxygen. The carbon from the carbon dioxide thus becomes part of the structure of plants and other living things. For example, the trees that make up Earth's forests contain a huge amount of carbon. As wood and other plant materials decay, the carbon is slowly converted to carbon dioxide and returned to the atmosphere.

Ocean organisms such as corals and diatoms are also part of the carbon cycle. As these organisms grow, they build skeletons made of a carbon compound called calcite (calcium carbonate). Calcite is the mineral that makes up the sedimentary rock limestone. Over hundreds of millions of years, the skeletons of ocean organisms have formed huge reefs made of limestone.

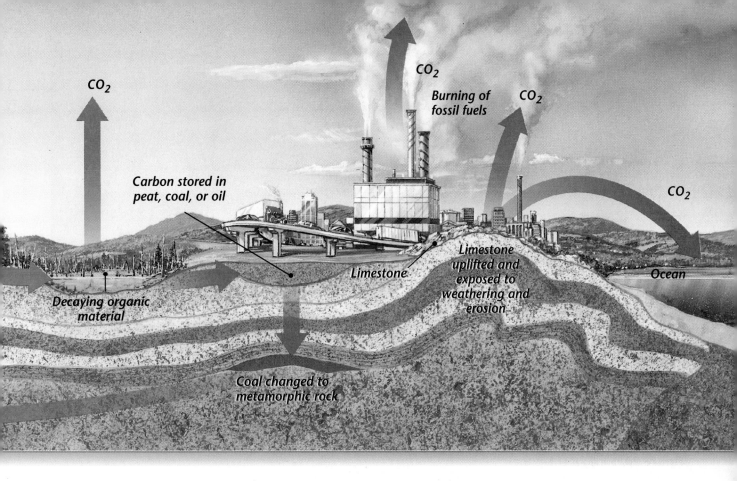

CO₂

Carbon stored in
peat, coal, or oil

Burning of
fossil fuels

CO₂

CO₂

CO₂

Limestone
uplifted and
exposed to
weathering and
erosion

Limestone

Ocean

Decaying organic
material

Coal changed to
metamorphic rock

The Carbon Cycle and Earth's Crust Much of Earth's carbon is stored in limestone in the crust. Although this rock may store carbon for millions of years, geologic processes continue the carbon cycle. For example, limestone formed in the oceans may eventually become deposits of sedimentary rock on land. Uplift raises the rock above sea level. Then erosion exposes the limestone at the surface. Weathering by rain that is slightly acidic causes a chemical change in the limestone, releasing carbon dioxide. The carbon dioxide may be dissolved in water and carried to the oceans, or released into the atmosphere.

As Earth's plates collide, some of the rocks containing carbon are subducted. When these rocks return to the mantle, they will melt and form magma. Melting breaks down the carbon compounds of limestone, allowing carbon dioxide to form. Volcanic eruptions return this carbon dioxide to the atmosphere, continuing the carbon cycle.

The Carbon Cycle and Human Activity Large amounts of carbon are stored in deposits of peat, coal, and oil. These substances, called fossil fuels, generally would remain in the ground for millions of years. But human activity—the burning of fossil fuels—releases carbon dioxide into the atmosphere. Many scientists think increased carbon dioxide in the atmosphere from the burning of fossil fuels could be responsible for a change in Earth's climate.

Sunlight

Infrared radiation cannot pass through greenhouse roof

Figure 20 Sunlight enters the greenhouse and is absorbed. The interior of the greenhouse radiates back energy in the form of infrared radiation, or heat. The heat is trapped and held inside the greenhouse, warming it.
Applying Concepts What gases in Earth's atmosphere can trap heat like a greenhouse?

Global Warming

Over the last 120 years, the average temperature of the troposphere has risen by about 0.5 Celsius degree. Was this increase part of natural variations, or was it caused by human activities? What effects could higher temperatures have? Scientists have done a great deal of research to try to answer these questions.

The Greenhouse Effect Gases in Earth's atmosphere hold in heat from the sun, keeping the atmosphere at a comfortable temperature for living things. The process by which gases in Earth's atmosphere trap solar energy is called the greenhouse effect.

Gases in the atmosphere that trap solar energy are called **greenhouse gases.** Water vapor, carbon dioxide, and methane are some of the greenhouse gases. **Human activities that add greenhouse gases to the atmosphere may be warming Earth's atmosphere.** For example, the burning of wood, coal, oil, and natural gas adds carbon dioxide to the air. If the increased carbon dioxide traps more heat, the result could be global warming. **Global warming** is a gradual increase in the temperature of Earth's atmosphere.

The amount of carbon dioxide in the atmosphere has been steadily increasing. Some scientists predict that if the level of carbon dioxide doubles by the year 2100, the average global temperature could go up by 1.5 to 3.5 Celsius degrees.

Another Hypothesis Not everyone agrees about the causes of global warming. Some scientists think that the 0.5 Celsius degree rise in global temperatures over the past 120 years may be part of natural variations in climate rather than a result of increases in carbon dioxide.

Satellite measurements have shown that the amount of energy the sun produces increases and decreases from year to year. These changes in solar energy could be causing periods of warmer and cooler climates. Or climate change could be a result of changes in both carbon dioxide levels and amounts of solar energy.

Possible Effects Global warming has some potential advantages. For example, places that are too cold for farming today could become farmland. But many effects of global warming are likely to be negative.

A rise in temperatures of even a few degrees could warm up water in the oceans. As ocean surface temperatures increased, the number of hurricanes might increase.

Glaciers and polar ice caps might partially melt, which would also increase sea levels. Sea levels have already risen by 10 to 20 centimeters over the last 100 years, and could rise another 25 to 80 centimeters by the year 2100. Even such a small rise in sea levels would flood low-lying coastal areas.

☑ *Checkpoint* *What are three possible effects of global warming?*

Ozone Depletion

Another global change in the atmosphere involves the ozone layer. **Ozone** is a form of oxygen that has three oxygen atoms in each molecule instead of the usual two. The **ozone layer** is a region nearly 50 kilometers above Earth's surface where ozone is concentrated.

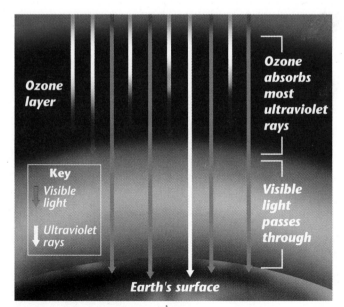

Ozone layer

Ozone absorbs most ultraviolet rays

Key
Visible light

Ultraviolet rays

Visible light passes through

Earth's surface

Figure 21 The ozone layer blocks much of the ultraviolet radiation coming from the sun. Visible light can pass through the ozone layer.

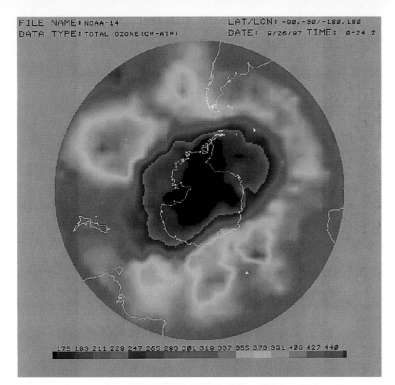

FILE NAME: NOAA-14   LAT/LON: -90,-30/-180,180
DATA TYPE: TOTAL OZONE (CM-ATM)   DATE: 9/26/97 TIME: 0-24 Z

175 193 211 229 247 265 283 301 319 337 355 373 391 409 427 440

Figure 22 This satellite image shows the concentration of ozone in the air over the South Pole. The dark area shows where the ozone layer is the thinnest.

Processes high in the atmosphere produce the ozone layer. Ozone in the ozone layer filters out much of the harmful ultraviolet radiation from the sun.

In the 1970s, scientists noticed that the ozone layer over Antarctica was growing thinner each spring. By 1992, the area of thinner ozone was more than twice as large as the continental United States. What created the ozone hole? **Scientists think that chemicals produced by humans have been damaging the ozone layer.**

The main cause of ozone depletion is a group of chlorine compounds called **chlorofluorocarbons,** or CFCs. CFCs were used in air conditioners and refrigerators, as cleaners for electronic parts, and in spray cans. Most chemical compounds released into the air eventually break down. CFCs, however, can last for decades and rise all the way to the stratosphere. In the stratosphere, ultraviolet radiation breaks down the CFC molecules into atoms, including chlorine. The chlorine atoms then break ozone down into oxygen atoms.

Because ozone blocks ultraviolet radiation, a decrease in ozone means an increase in the amount of ultraviolet radiation that reaches Earth's surface. If you have ever been sunburned, you can understand one effect of stronger ultraviolet radiation! Ultraviolet radiation can also cause eye damage and several kinds of skin cancer.

Section 4 Review

1. Beginning with volcanic activity, describe the steps in the carbon cycle.
2. What human actions increase the amount of carbon dioxide in Earth's atmosphere?
3. How could increases in carbon dioxide in the air affect world temperatures?
4. What chemicals are the major cause of ozone depletion in the stratosphere?
5. **Thinking Critically Predicting** How might global warming change conditions where you live? How would this affect your life?

Science at Home

Compare Sunscreens Visit a drugstore with your family. Compare the SPF (sun protection factor) of the various sunscreens for sale. Explain why it is important to protect your skin from ultraviolet radiation. Ask your family members to determine the best value for their money in terms of SPF rating and price.

SECTION 1 — What Causes Climate?

Key Ideas

◆ The main factors that affect precipitation are prevailing winds and the presence of mountains.
◆ The main factors that influence temperature are latitude, altitude, distance from large bodies of water, and ocean currents.
◆ The different seasons are a result of the tilt of Earth's axis as Earth travels around the sun.

Key Terms

climate
windward
leeward
tropical zone
polar zone

temperate zone
marine climate
continental climate
El Niño
microclimate

SECTION 2 — Climate Regions

Key Ideas

◆ Climates are classified according to temperature and precipitation.
◆ There are five main types of climate regions.

Key Terms

rain forest
savanna
desert

steppe
humid subtropical
subarctic

tundra
permafrost

SECTION 3 — Long-Term Changes in Climate

Key Ideas

◆ Scientists who study ancient climates follow the principle that plants and animals of the past needed the same living conditions as similar modern plants and animals.
◆ During an ice age, huge sheets of ice cover much of Earth's surface.
◆ Possible explanations for major climate changes include movement of continents, variations in the position of Earth relative to the sun, and changes in the sun's energy output.

Key Terms

ice age   sunspot

SECTION 4 — Global Changes in the Atmosphere

INTEGRATING ENVIRONMENTAL SCIENCE

Key Ideas

◆ In the carbon cycle, carbon is transferred from Earth's interior to the atmosphere, oceans, and crust, and to living things.
◆ Human activities that add greenhouse gases to the atmosphere may be warming Earth's atmosphere.
◆ Chemicals produced by humans have been damaging the ozone layer.

Key Terms

carbon cycle
photosynthesis
greenhouse gas
global warming
ozone
ozone layer
chlorofluorocarbons

Organizing Information

Concept Map Copy the concept map about climate onto a separate sheet of paper. Then complete it and add a title. (For more on concept maps, see the Skills Handbook.)

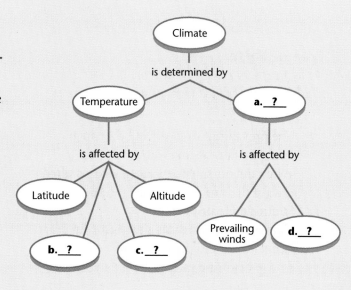

Reviewing Content

Review key concepts online using
iText at www.phschool.com

Multiple Choice
Choose the letter of the best answer.

1. Temperatures are highest in the tropical zone because
   a. the land is flat.
   b. the sun's rays strike most directly.
   c. Earth's axis is tilted toward the sun.
   d. ocean currents warm the region.

2. Continental climates are found
   a. on every continent.
   b. only near the equator.
   c. only in the Northern Hemisphere.
   d. only in the Southern Hemisphere.

3. In a wet-and-dry tropical climate, the most common vegetation is
   a. coniferous forests.
   b. savanna grasslands.
   c. tropical rain forest.
   d. steppe grasslands.

4. As part of the carbon cycle, plants use carbon dioxide to make food in the process of
   a. global warming.   b. photosynthesis.
   c. climate change.   d. ozone formation.

5. Chlorofluorocarbons, or CFCs, are the main cause of
   a. ozone depletion.   b. global warming.
   c. the carbon cycle.   d. ice ages.

True or False
If the statement is true, write true. If it is false, change the underlined word or words to make it true.

6. The prevailing winds affect how much <u>sunlight</u> falls on an area.

7. When the north end of Earth's axis is tilted toward the sun, it is <u>summer</u> in the Southern Hemisphere.

8. Climate regions are classified according to temperature and <u>precipitation</u>.

9. A <u>thin</u> tree ring indicates that a year was cool or dry.

10. An increase in atmospheric <u>nitrogen</u> may be the cause of global warming.

Checking Concepts

11. Explain how distance from large bodies of water can affect the temperatures of nearby land areas.

12. Give an example of how changes in the oceans can affect climate. Explain.

13. Identify the parts of the United States that are located in each of the three temperature zones.

14. What causes Earth's seasons?

15. How are "dry" climates defined? How do the two types of dry climate differ?

16. How does the movement of continents explain major changes in climate over time?

17. To be effective, why must agreements aimed at preventing or reducing ozone depletion be international?

18. **Writing to Learn** In what climate region do you live? Write a description of your local climate and identify some of the things—such as latitude, bodies of water, or wind patterns—that affect the climate.

Thinking Critically

19. **Predicting** Suppose that volcanic activity greatly increased, releasing large amounts of carbon dioxide into the atmosphere. How would increased carbon dioxide affect the carbon cycle?

20. **Relating Cause and Effect** Describe three ways in which water influences climate.

21. **Comparing and Contrasting** How is global warming different from earlier changes in Earth's climate?

22. **Making Judgments** What is the most important thing that needs to be done about global warming?

23. **Relating Cause and Effect** Why do parts of the United States have a semiarid climate while neighboring areas have a humid continental climate?

Applying Skills

Use the map of world temperature zones to answer Questions 24–26.

24. Interpreting Maps Name each of the five zones shown on the map.

25. Measuring What is the name of the temperature zone that includes the equator? How many degrees of latitude does this zone cover?

26. Interpreting Data Which of the five zones shown on the map has the greatest amount of land area suitable for people to live?

Performance ▼ CHAPTER PROJECT Assessment

Present Your Project Decide how to present your project. You could use a written report, oral presentation, or a bulletin board. Do your graphs compare the conditions in the different microclimates? What conditions favor plants or animals in some areas? After you present your project to the class, discuss what you think causes different microclimates.

Reflect and Record In your journal, describe how you could improve your investigation. Are there factors you did not study? Did you notice any organisms that live only in certain microclimates? What additional information about microclimates would you like to find?

Test Preparation

Use these questions to prepare for standardized tests.

Study the graph. Then answer Questions 27–32.

27. Which of the following months has the widest range of temperatures during the year?
A September   B June
C May   D April

28. Which month shown on the graph is the warmest on average?
F August   G June
H July   J May

29. Which month is the coldest on average?
A January   B December
C March   D February

30. What is the average temperature in April?
F about −21°C   G about −17°C
H about 0°C   J about −30°C

31. What is the average temperature in December?
A about −20°C   B about −26°C
C about 0°C   D about −30°C

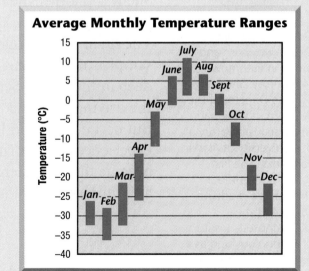

Average Monthly Temperature Ranges

32. What kind of climate is indicated by the graph?
F polar
G temperate continental
H temperate marine
J tropical rainy

Life in a Sunless World

Dr. Cindy Lee Van Dover was born and raised in Eatontown, New Jersey. She is now Science Director of the West Coast National Undersea Laboratory at the University of Alaska, Fairbanks. She first studied ocean-floor shrimp as a graduate student at the Massachusetts Institute of Technology and as a researcher at the Woods Hole Oceanographic Institution in Massachusetts.

Oceanographer Cindy Lee Van Dover never thought that her childhood curiosity would lead her to this moment. But there she was, heading toward the cold, dark depths of the ocean floor. She was piloting the famous *Alvin*, a tiny research submarine known as a submersible. The *Alvin* would collect data and gather samples of rocks and delicate animals living deep in the ocean. Scientists usually leave the driving to trained submersible pilots. But because Dr. Van Dover wanted the full experience of exploring the ocean, she became the first scientist ever to qualify as a submersible pilot.

Light from the *Alvin* illuminates the dark sea floor where crabs and huge masses of shrimp feed around black smoker vents. ▶

Life on the Ocean Floor

Slowly, the *Alvin* entered the sunless world far beneath the surface of the Atlantic Ocean — one of the strangest and most remote places on Earth. As the *Alvin* approached an underwater mountain range, Dr. Van Dover could see colonies of animals swarming around undersea hot springs called "black smokers."

The black clouds that give these areas their name are not smoke at all. Rather they are streams of very hot water packed with minerals flowing from openings in the sea floor. Some microorganisms are able to use the minerals as their food source. Dr. Van Dover's special interest was in some very unusual shrimp that feed on these microorganisms.

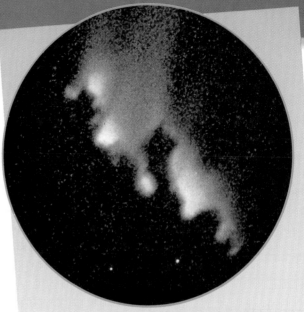

▲ Black smoker vents are hot enough to glow. Water as hot as 350°C pours up from these hot springs. When the hot water mixes with the cold sea water, it quickly cools.

Endless Questions

How did Dr. Van Dover reach this moment in her life? As a child she was full of questions about everything in nature. "I had my bug period; I had my frog-and-tadpole period; I had my flower period and tree period and bird period. But I settled pretty firmly and quickly on marine invertebrates, sea animals without backbones," she explains. "That's because they were so unusual. I just loved all the odd structures they had, each with a function. Why does a crustacean have ten legs — or whatever number it might have? What does it use them all for?"

Could These Shrimp Have Eyes?

As she steered the *Alvin,* Dr. Van Dover thought about the shrimp she planned to observe. She knew that these shrimp live in the dark depths of the ocean. They lack eyestalks and the black, beady eyes of their better known relatives. She also knew that eyeless animals are common

at depths too far beneath the surface for sunlight to reach.

Dr. Van Dover had made an interesting discovery about the shrimp in the lab. Her discovery

> **Other people told me I was crazy. There's no light on the sea floor. Why do they need eyes?**

came after she noticed odd, shiny patches on their backs. She asked herself what the function of the patches might be. "I dissected a shrimp in the laboratory," she recounts. "I found this pair of organs and pulled it out. It was very recognizable, and to my surprise, it was attached to what I took to be the brain of the shrimp.

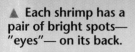

▲ Each shrimp has a pair of bright spots— "eyes"— on its back.

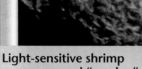

Light-sensitive shrimp swarm around "smoker" vents deep in the Atlantic Ocean. ▶

I looked at it and said, 'Looks like an eye!' Other people told me I was crazy. There's no light on the sea floor. Why do they need eyes?"

Dr. Van Dover kept an open mind and showed the structure to crustacean eye experts. They confirmed that it was not only an eye, but a very unusual one. It was able to detect very dim light. Immediately that raised another question: What could the shrimp be looking at?

"We thought about alternatives," Dr. Van Dover says. "The obvious thing is that these shrimp are only found around high-temperature black smokers. We all know that hot things glow. Did these vents glow?" The answer turned out to be yes. Those unusual eyes were just right for spotting undersea hot spots. Scientists hypothesize that the shrimp use these eyes to guide them toward the dim light in order to feed on the microorganisms. As the shrimp approach the vent, the light gets brighter. That signals the shrimp to keep a distance from the hottest water just emerging from the vent.

Looking Ahead

From time to time now, Dr. Van Dover thinks about the submersible that scientists plan to send to watery Europa, a moon of Jupiter. Scientists in a control room will pilot a robot version of *Alvin* under the oceans of Europa. "I'm delighted that I'm young enough that I'm going to see that," she says. When asked if she would like to be one of those scientists, she doesn't hesitate.

"Wouldn't that be sweet!" she says — and smiles.

▲ A surface ship lifts the *Alvin* from the ocean after a deep-sea expedition.

In Your Journal

Cindy Lee Van Dover's discoveries usually begin with her paying attention to details and then asking questions about what she finds. Think of a familiar place outdoors that you like to visit. Describe the place from memory. Jot down details. Then visit the place again to observe and record questions.

Predicting Inherited Characteristics

CHAPTER 16 PROJECT

All in the Family

Did you ever wonder why some offspring resemble their parents while others do not? In this chapter, you'll learn how offspring come to have characteristics similar to those of their parents. In this project, you'll create a family of "paper pets" and predict how some characteristics are inherited.

Your Goal To create a "paper pet" that will be crossed with a pet belonging to a classmate, and to determine what inherited characteristics the offspring will have.

To complete this project successfully, you must

◆ create your own unique paper pet with five different traits
◆ cross your pet with another pet to produce six offspring
◆ predict the inherited characteristics of the offspring, and explain how they came to have those characteristics

Get Started Cut out your pet from either blue or yellow construction paper. Choose other inherited characteristics for your pet from this list: female or male; square eyes or round eyes; oval nose or triangular nose; pointed teeth or square teeth. Then create your pet using materials of your choice.

Check Your Progress You'll be working on this project as you study this chapter. To keep your project on track, look for Check Your Progress boxes at the following points.

Section 1 Review, page 561: Identify your pet's genotype.
Section 3 Review, page 576: Predict the inherited characteristics of your pet's offspring.
Section 4 Review, page 582: Make a display of your pet's family.

Present Your Project At the end of the chapter (page 585), you and your partner will display your pet's family and analyze the inherited characteristics of the family members.

TEKS

In addition to process TEKS, this chapter addresses these concept TEKS as they relate to the chapter's topics.

(8.11) The student knows that traits of species can change through generations and that the instructions for traits are contained in the genetic material of the organisms. The student is expected to:
(C) make predictions about possible outcomes of various genetic combinations of inherited characteristics.

1 Mendel's Work

DISCOVER ·········· ACTIVITY

What Does the Father Look Like?

1. Observe the colors of each kitten in the photo. Record each kitten's coat colors and patterns. Include as many details as you can.

2. Observe the mother cat in the photo. Record her coat color and pattern.

Think It Over

Inferring Based on your observations, predict what you think the kittens' father looks like. Identify the evidence on which you based your inference.

GUIDE FOR READING

◆ What controls the inherited characteristics of organisms?

Reading Tip Before you read, list the boldfaced terms. As you read, write a definition for each term in your own words.

Key Terms trait • heredity • genetics • purebred • gene • allele • dominant allele • recessive allele • hybrid

Gregor Mendel in the monastery garden ▼

The year was 1851. Gregor Mendel, a young priest from a monastery in Central Europe, entered the University of Vienna to study mathematics and science. Two years later, Mendel returned to the monastery and began teaching at a nearby high school.

Mendel also cared for the monastery's garden, where he grew hundreds of pea plants. He became curious about why some of the plants had different physical characteristics, or **traits.** Some pea plants grew tall while others were short. Some plants produced green seeds, while others had yellow seeds.

Mendel observed that the pea plants' traits were often similar to those of their parents. Sometimes, however, the pea plants had different traits than their parents. The passing of traits from parents to offspring is called **heredity.** For more than ten years, Mendel experimented with thousands of pea plants to understand the process of heredity. Mendel's work formed the foundation of **genetics,** the scientific study of heredity.

Mendel's Peas

Mendel made a wise decision when he chose to study peas rather than other plants in the monastery garden. Pea plants are easy to study because they have many traits that exist in only two forms. For example, pea plant stems are either tall or short, but not medium height. Also, garden peas produce a large number of offspring in one generation. Thus, it is easy to collect large amounts of data to analyze.

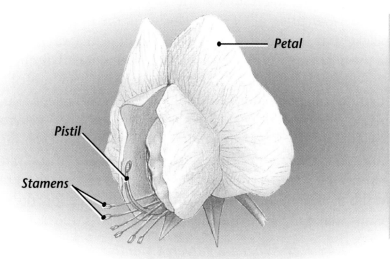

Petal

Pistil

Stamens

Figure 1 Garden peas usually reproduce by self-pollination. Pollen from a flower's stamens lands on the pistil of the same flower. Plants that result from self-pollination inherit all of their characteristics from the same parent plant.
Relating Cause and Effect Why was it important for Mendel to prevent his pea plants from self-pollinating?

Figure 1 shows a flowering pea plant. Notice that the flower's petals surround the pistil and the stamens. The pistil produces female sex cells, or eggs, while the stamens produce pollen, which contains the male sex cells.

In nature, pea plants usually self-pollinate. This means that pollen from one flower lands on the pistil of the same flower. Mendel developed a method by which he could cross-pollinate, or "cross," pea plants. To cross two plants, he removed pollen from a flower on one plant and brushed it onto a flower on a second plant. To prevent the pea plants from self-pollinating, he carefully removed the stamens from the flowers on the second plant.

Mendel's Experiments

Suppose you had some pea plants, and wanted to study their inherited characteristics. What would you do? Mendel decided to cross plants with opposite forms of a trait. For example, he crossed tall plants with short plants to study the trait of height. He started with purebred plants. A **purebred** plant is one that always produces offspring with the same form of a trait as the parent. For example, purebred short pea plants always produce short offspring. To produce purebred plants, Mendel allowed peas with one specific trait to self-pollinate for many generations. By using purebred plants, Mendel knew that the offspring's trait would always be identical to that of the parents.

In his first experiment, Mendel crossed purebred tall plants with purebred short plants. He called these parent plants the parental generation, or P generation. He called the offspring from this cross the first filial (FIL ee ul) generation, or the F_1 generation. The word *filial* means "son" or "daughter" in Latin.

Gregor Mendel presented a detailed description of his observations in a scientific paper in 1866. In the excerpt that follows, notice how clearly he describes his observations of the two different seed shapes in peas.

"These are either round or roundish, the depressions, if any, occur on the surface, being always only shallow; or they are irregularly angular and deeply wrinkled."

In Your Journal

Choose an everyday object, such as a piece of fruit or a pen. Make a list of the object's features. Then write a short paragraph describing the object. Use clear, precise language in your description.

You can see the results of Mendel's first cross in Figure 2. To Mendel's surprise, all of the offspring in the F_1 generation were tall. Despite the fact that one of the parent plants was short, none of the offspring were short. The shortness trait had disappeared!

Mendel let the plants in the F_1 generation grow and allowed them to self-pollinate. The results of this experiment also surprised Mendel. The plants in the F_2 (second filial) generation were a mix of tall and short plants. This occurred even though none of the F_1 parent plants were short. The shortness trait had reappeared. Mendel counted the number of tall and short plants in the F_2 generation. He found that about three fourths of the plants were tall, while one fourth of the plants were short.

Checkpoint **What is a purebred plant?**

Other Inherited Characteristics

In addition to stem height, Mendel studied six other traits in garden peas: seed shape, seed color, seed coat color, pod shape, pod color, and flower position. Compare the two forms of each trait in Figure 3. Mendel crossed plants with these traits in the same manner as he did for stem height. The results in each experiment were similar to those that he observed with stem height. Only one form of the trait appeared in the F_1 generation. However, in the F_2 generation the "lost" form of the trait always reappeared in about one fourth of the plants.

Figure 2 When Mendel crossed purebred tall and short pea plants, all the offspring in the F_1 generation were tall. In the F_2 generation, three fourths of the plants were tall, while one fourth were short.

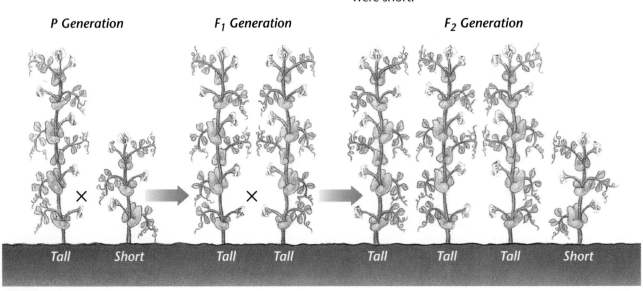

P Generation		F₁ Generation		F₂ Generation			
Tall	Short	Tall	Tall	Tall	Tall	Tall	Short

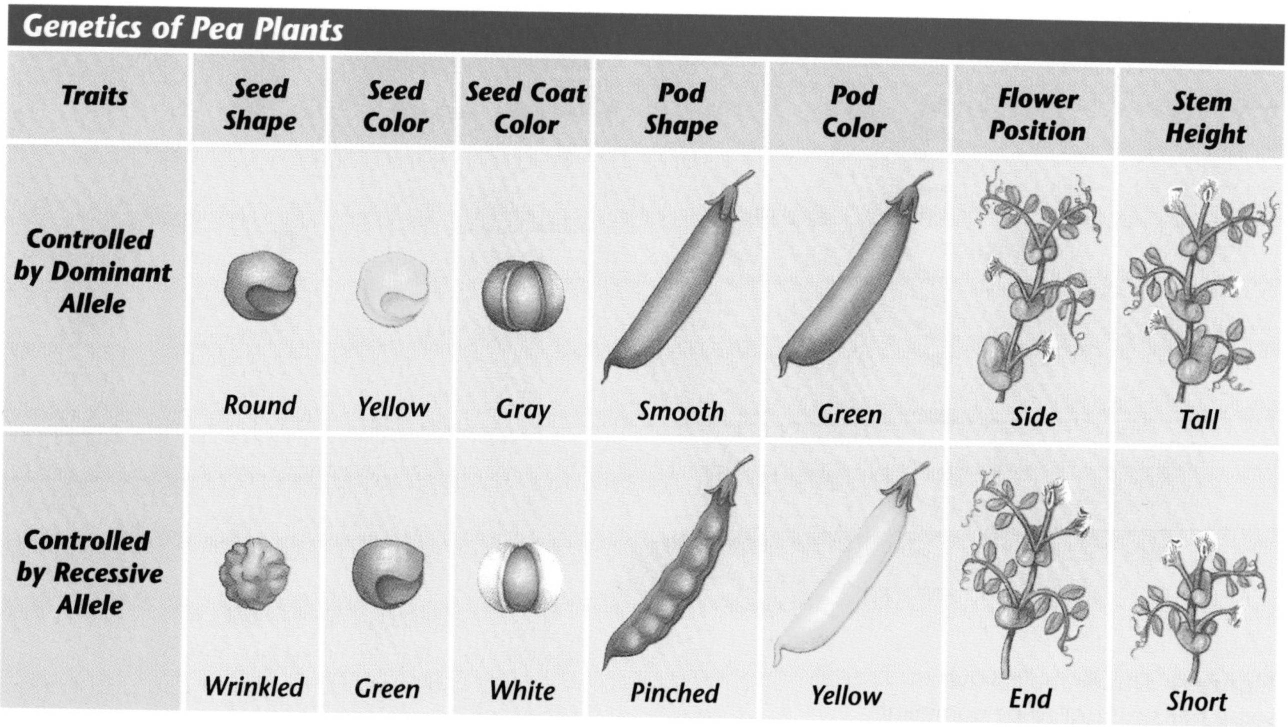

Genetics of Pea Plants

Traits	Seed Shape	Seed Color	Seed Coat Color	Pod Shape	Pod Color	Flower Position	Stem Height
Controlled by Dominant Allele	Round	Yellow	Gray	Smooth	Green	Side	Tall
Controlled by Recessive Allele	Wrinkled	Green	White	Pinched	Yellow	End	Short

Dominant and Recessive Alleles

From his results, Mendel reasoned that individual factors must control the inheritance of traits in peas. The factors that control each trait exist in pairs. The female parent contributes one factor, while the male parent contributes the other factor.

Mendel went on to reason that one factor in a pair can mask, or hide, the other factor. The tallness factor, for example, masked the shortness factor in the F_1 generation.

Today, scientists call the factors that control traits **genes.** They call the different forms of a gene **alleles** (uh LEELZ). The gene that controls stem height in peas, for example, has two forms: one allele for tall stems and one allele for short stems. Each pea plant inherits two height alleles from its parents—either two alleles for tall stems, two alleles for short stems, or one for each.

Individual alleles control the inheritance of traits. Some alleles are dominant, while other alleles are recessive. A **dominant allele** is one whose trait always shows up in the organism when the allele is present. A **recessive allele,** on the other hand, is masked, or covered up, whenever the dominant allele is present. A trait controlled by a recessive allele will only show up if the organism does not have the dominant allele.

In pea plants, the allele for tall stems is dominant over the allele for short stems. Therefore, pea plants with one allele for tall stems and one allele for short stems will be tall. The allele for tall stems masks the allele for short stems. Only pea plants that inherit two recessive alleles for short stems will be short.

Figure 3 Mendel studied seven inherited characteristics in pea plants. Each trait has two different forms. *Interpreting Diagrams* Is yellow seed color controlled by a dominant allele or a recessive allele? What type of allele controls pinched pod shape?

Figure 4 These rabbits have some traits controlled by dominant alleles and other traits controlled by recessive alleles. For example, the allele for black fur is dominant over the allele for white fur.
Inferring What combination of alleles must the white rabbit have?

Understanding Mendel's Crosses

You can understand Mendel's results by following the inheritance of alleles in his experiments. Each of the purebred plants in the P generation had two identical alleles for stem height. The purebred tall plants had two alleles for tall stems. The purebred short plants had two alleles for short stems. In the F_1 generation, all of the plants received one allele for tall stems from the tall parent. They received one allele for short stems from the short parent. The F_1 plants are called **hybrids** (HY bridz) because they have two different alleles for the trait. All the F_1 plants are tall because the dominant allele for tall stems masks the recessive allele for short stems.

When Mendel crossed the hybrid plants in the F_1 generation, some of the plants inherited two dominant alleles for tall stems. These plants were tall. Other plants inherited one dominant allele for tall stems and one recessive allele for short stems. These plants were also tall. Other plants inherited two recessive alleles for short stems. These plants were short.

Checkpoint If a pea plant has a tall stem, what possible combinations of alleles could it have?

Using Symbols in Genetics

Geneticists today use a standard shorthand method to write about the alleles in genetic crosses. Instead of using words such as "tall stems" to represent alleles, they simply use letters.

A dominant allele is represented by a capital letter. For example, the allele for tall stems is represented by *T*. A recessive allele is represented by the lowercase version of the letter. So the allele for short stems would be represented by *t*. When a plant inherits two dominant alleles for tall stems, its alleles are written as *TT*. When a plant inherits two recessive alleles for short stems, its alleles are written as *tt*. When a plant inherits one allele for tall stems and one allele for short stems, its alleles are written as *Tt*.

Mendel's Contribution

In 1866, Mendel presented his results to a scientific society that met regularly near the monastery. In his paper, Mendel described the principles of heredity he had discovered. Unfortunately, other scientists did not understand the importance of Mendel's work. Some scientists thought that Mendel had oversimplified the process of inheritance. Others never read his paper, or even heard about his work. Remember, at that time there were no telephones or other types of electronic communication. Scientists in different parts of the world were isolated from each other. Mendel was especially isolated because he wasn't at a university.

Mendel's work was forgotten for 34 years. In 1900, three different scientists rediscovered Mendel's work. They had made many of the same observations as Mendel had. The scientists quickly recognized the importance of Mendel's work. Many of the genetic principles that Mendel discovered still stand to this day. Because of his work, Mendel is often called the Father of Genetics.

Figure 5 The dominant allele for yellow skin color in summer squash is represented by the letter *Y*. The recessive allele for green skin color is represented by the letter *y*.

Section 1 Review

1. Explain how the inheritance of traits is determined in organisms. Use the terms *genes* and *alleles* in your explanation.
2. What is a dominant allele? What is a recessive allele? Give an example of each.
3. The allele for round seeds is represented by *R*. Suppose that a pea plant inherited two recessive alleles for wrinkled seeds. How would you write the symbols for its alleles?
4. **Thinking Critically Applying Concepts** Can a short pea plant ever be a hybrid? Why or why not?

Check Your Progress   CHAPTER PROJECT

By now you should have constructed your paper pet. On the back, write what alleles your pet has for each trait. Use XX for a female, and XY for a male. The dominant alleles for the other four traits are: *B* (blue skin), *R* (round eyes), *T* (triangular nose), and *P* (pointed teeth). (*Hint:* If your pet has a trait controlled by a dominant allele, you can choose which of the possible combinations of alleles your pet has.)

Take a Class Survey

In this lab, you'll explore how traits can vary greatly in a group of people—your classmates.

Problem

Are traits controlled by dominant alleles more common than traits controlled by recessive alleles?

Materials

mirror (optional)   PTC paper
computer (optional)

Procedure

Part 1 Alleles

1. Write a hypothesis about the problem question. Use the computer or pencil and paper to make the data table shown here.

2. Determine which of traits A, B, C, D, and E you have. Circle those traits in your data table.

3. For trait F, wash and dry your hands. Taste the PTC paper your teacher gives you. Circle either "can taste PTC" or "cannot taste PTC" in your data table. **CAUTION:** *Never taste any substance in the lab unless directed to by your teacher.*

4. Count the number of students who have each trait. Record that number in your data table. Also record the total number of students.

DATA TABLE

Total Number _____

	Trait 1	Number	Trait 2	Number
A	Free ear lobes		Attached ear lobes	
B	Hair on fingers		No hair on fingers	
C	Widow's peak		No widow's peak	
D	Curly hair		Straight hair	
E	Cleft chin		Smooth chin	
F	Can taste PTC*		Cannot taste PTC*	

*PTC stands for phenylthiocarbamide.

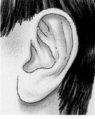

Free ear lobe

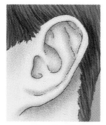

Attached ear lobe

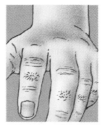

Hair on fingers

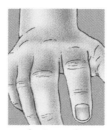

No hair on fingers

Widow's peak

No widow's peak

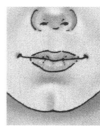

Cleft chin

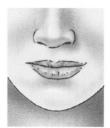

No cleft chin

Part 2 Are Your Traits Unique?

5. Look at the circle of traits below. All the traits in your data table appear in the circle. Place the eraser end of your pencil on the trait in the small central circle that applies to you—either free ear lobes or attached ear lobes.

6. Look at the two traits touching the space your eraser is on. Move your eraser to the next description that applies to you. Continue using your eraser to trace your traits until you reach a number on the outside rim of the circle. Share that number with your classmates.

Analyze and Conclude

1. The traits listed under Trait 1 in the data table are controlled by dominant alleles. The traits listed under Trait 2 are controlled by recessive alleles. Which traits controlled by dominant alleles were shown by a majority of students? Which traits controlled by recessive alleles were shown by a majority of students?

2. How many students shared numbers on the circle of traits? How many students were the only ones to have their number? What do the results suggest about each person's combination of inherited characteristics?

3. **Think About It** Do your data support the hypothesis you proposed in Step 1? Explain your answer with examples.

Design an Experiment

Do people who are related to each other show more genetic similarity than unrelated people? Write a hypothesis. Then design an experiment to test your hypothesis.

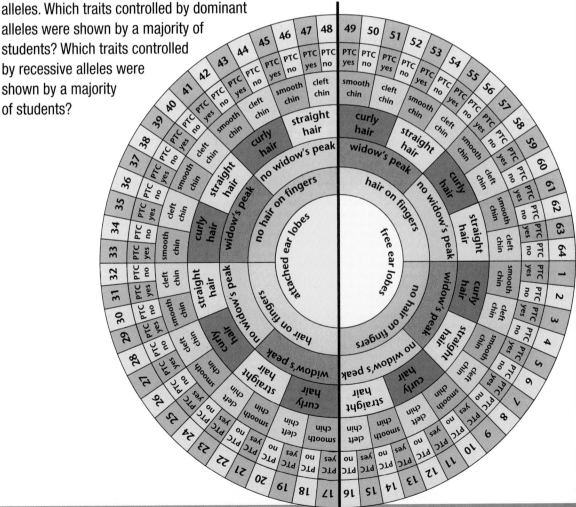

SECTION

2 Probability and Genetics

DISCOVER

What's the Chance?

1. Suppose you were to toss a coin 20 times. Predict how many times the coin would land "heads up" and how many times it would land "tails up."

2. Now test your prediction by tossing a coin 20 times. Record the number of times the coin lands heads up and the number of times it lands tails up.

3. Combine the data from the entire class. Record the total number of tosses, the number of heads, and the number of tails.

Think It Over

Predicting How did your results in Step 2 compare to your prediction? How can you account for any differences between your results and the class results?

GUIDE FOR READING

◆ How do the principles of probability help explain Mendel's results?

◆ How do geneticists use Punnett squares?

Reading Tip Before you read, rewrite the headings in the section as questions that begin with *how, what,* or *why.* As you read, look for answers to these questions.

Key Terms probability
• Punnett square • phenotype
• genotype • homozygous
• heterozygous • codominance

The city of Portland, Oregon, was founded in the mid-1800s. Two men, Asa L. Lovejoy and Francis W. Pettygrove, owned the land on which the new city was built. Lovejoy, who was from Massachusetts, wanted to name the new town Boston. Pettygrove, however, thought the town should be named after his hometown, Portland, Maine. To settle the dispute, they decided to toss a coin. Pettygrove won, and the new town was named Portland.

What was the chance that Pettygrove would win the coin toss? To answer this question, you need to understand the principles of probability. **Probability** is the likelihood that a particular event will occur.

Principles of Probability

If you did the Discover activity, you used the principles of probability to predict the results of a particular event. Each time you toss a coin, there are two possible ways that the coin can land—heads up or tails up. Each of these two events is equally likely to occur. In mathematical terms, you can say that the probability that a tossed coin will land heads up is 1 in 2. There is also a 1 in 2 probability that the coin will land tails up. A 1 in 2 probability can also be expressed as the fraction $\frac{1}{2}$ or as a percent—50 percent.

If you tossed a coin 20 times, you might expect it to land heads up 10 times and tails up 10 times. However, you might not actually get these results. You might get 11 heads and 9 tails, or 8 heads and 12 tails. Remember that the laws of probability predict what is likely to occur, not necessarily what will occur. However, the more tosses you make, the closer your actual results will be to the results predicted by probability.

When you toss a coin more than once, the results of one toss do not affect the results of the next toss. Each event occurs independently. For example, suppose you toss a coin five times and it lands heads up each time. What is the probability that it will land heads up on the next toss? Because the coin landed heads up on the previous five tosses, you might think that it would be likely to land heads up on the next toss. However, this is not the case. The probability of the coin landing heads up on the next toss is still 1 in 2, or 50 percent. The results of the first five tosses do not affect the results of the sixth toss.

☑ *Checkpoint* Why is there a 1 in 2 probability that a tossed coin will land heads up?

Calculating Probability

When the probability of an event is 1, the event is *certain* to happen. When the probability of an event is 0, the event is *impossible*. Events with probabilities between 0 and 1 are *possible*.

Suppose that 6 out of 10 marbles in a bag are red. Here's how you can calculate the probability of pulling out a red marble from the bag.

1. There are 10 marbles in the bag, and 6 of them are red.

2. Write this comparison as a fraction.

$$\frac{6 \text{ red marbles}}{10 \text{ marbles total}} = \frac{6}{10} = \frac{3}{5}$$

The probability of choosing a red marble is $\frac{3}{5}$, or 3 out of 5.

If the other 4 marbles in the bag are blue, what is the probability of pulling out a blue marble? What is the probability of pulling out a green marble?

Figure 6 According to the laws of probability, there is a 50 percent probability that the coin will land heads up. *Calculating* What is the probability that the coin will land tails up?

Mendel and Probability

How is probability related to genetics? To answer this question, think back to Mendel's experiments with peas. Remember that Mendel carefully counted the offspring from every cross that he carried out. When Mendel crossed two plants that were hybrid for stem height (Tt), three fourths of the F_1 plants had tall stems. One fourth of the plants had short stems.

Each time Mendel repeated the cross, he obtained similar results. Mendel realized that the mathematical principles of probability applied to his work. He could say that the probability of such a cross producing a tall plant was 3 in 4. The probability of producing a short plant was 1 in 4. **Mendel was the first scientist to recognize that the principles of probability can be used to predict the results of genetic crosses.**

Predicting Genetic Outcomes

A tool that can help you apply the laws of probability to genetics is called a Punnett square. A **Punnett square** is a chart that shows all the possible combinations of alleles that can result from a genetic cross. **Geneticists use Punnett squares to show all the possible outcomes of various genetic combinations of inherited traits and to determine the probability of a particular outcome.**

The Punnett square in Figure 7 shows a cross between two hybrid tall pea plants (Tt). Each parent can pass either of its alleles, T or t, to its offspring. The possible alleles that one parent can pass on are written across the top of the Punnett square. The possible alleles that the other parent can pass on are written down the left side of the Punnett square. The boxes in the Punnett square represent the possible combinations of alleles among the offspring. The boxes are filled in like a multiplication problem, with one allele contributed by each parent.

Using a Punnett Square You can use a Punnett square to calculate the probability that offspring will have a certain combination of alleles. The allele that each parent will pass on is based on chance, just like the toss of a coin. Thus, there are four possible combinations of alleles. The probability that an offspring will

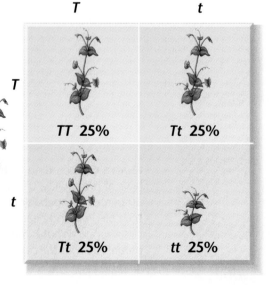

Figure 7 This Punnett square shows a cross between two hybrid tall pea plants. *Interpreting Charts Which allele combinations will result in tall offspring?*

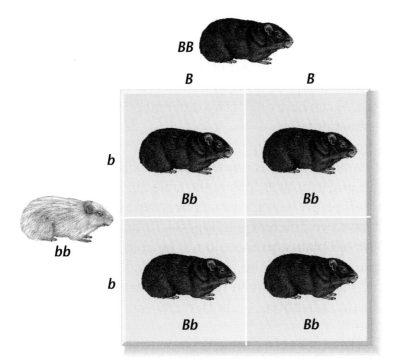

BB

B   B

b   **Bb**   **Bb**

bb

b   **Bb**   **Bb**

Figure 8 This Punnett square shows a cross between a black guinea pig (*BB*) and a white guinea pig (*bb*). *Calculating* What is the probability that an offspring will have white fur?

be *TT* is 1 in 4, or 25 percent. The probability that an offspring will be *tt* is also 1 in 4, or 25 percent. Notice, however, that the *Tt* allele combination appears in two boxes in the Punnett square. This is because there are two possible ways in which this combination can occur. The probability, then, that an offspring will be *Tt* is 2 in 4, or 50 percent.

Recall that when Mendel performed this cross, he discovered that about three fourths of the plants (75%) had tall stems. The remaining one fourth of the plants (25%) had short stems. Now you can understand why that was true. Plants with the *TT* allele combination would be tall. So too would those plants with the *Tt* allele combination. Remember that the dominant allele masks the recessive allele. Only those plants with the *tt* allele combination would be short.

Predicting Probabilities You can also use a Punnett square to predict probabilities. For example, Figure 8 shows a cross between a purebred black guinea pig and a purebred white guinea pig. The allele for black fur is dominant over the allele for white fur. Notice that only one allele combination is possible in the offspring—*Bb*. All of the offspring will inherit the dominant allele for black fur. Because of this, all of the offspring will have black fur. You can predict that there is a 100% probability that the offspring will have black fur.

Checkpoint *If two guinea pigs with the alleles Bb are crossed, what is the probability that an offspring will have white fur?*

Coin Crosses

ACTIVITY

Here's how you can use coins to model Mendel's cross between two *Tt* pea plants.

1. Place a small piece of masking tape on each side of two coins.

2. Write a *T* (for tall) on one side of each coin and a *t* (for short) on the other.

3. Toss both coins together 20 times. Record the letter combinations that you obtain from each toss.

Interpreting Data How many of the offspring would be tall plants? (*Hint:* What different letter combinations would result in a tall plant?) How many would be short? Convert your results to percents. Then compare your results to Mendel's.

Phenotypes and Genotypes	
Phenotype	**Genotype**
Tall	*TT*
Tall	*Tt*
Short	*tt*

Figure 9 The phenotype of an organism is its physical appearance. Its genotype is its genetic makeup.

Phenotypes and Genotypes

Two useful terms that geneticists use to describe organisms are phenotype and genotype. An organism's **phenotype** (FEE noh typ) is its physical appearance, or its observable traits. For example, pea plants can have one of two different phenotypes for stem height—short or tall.

An organism's **genotype** (JEN uh typ) is its genetic makeup, or allele combinations. To understand the difference between phenotype and genotype, look at the table in Figure 9. Although all of the tall plants have the same phenotype (they are all tall), they can have two different genotypes—*TT* or *Tt*. If you were to look at the tall plants, you would not be able to tell the difference between those with the *TT* genotype and those with the *Tt* genotype. The short pea plants, on the other hand, would all have the same phenotype—short stems—as well as the same genotype—*tt*.

Geneticists use two additional terms to describe an organism's genotype. An organism that has two identical alleles for a trait is said to be **homozygous** (hoh moh ZY gus) for that trait. A tall pea plant that has the alleles *TT* and a short pea plant with the alleles *tt* are both homozygous. An organism that has two different alleles for a trait is said to be **heterozygous** (het ur oh ZY gus) for that trait. A tall pea plant with the alleles *Tt* is heterozygous. Mendel used the term *hybrid* to describe heterozygous pea plants.

☑ *Checkpoint* *If a pea plant's genotype is* Tt, *what is its phenotype?*

Codominance

For all of the traits that Mendel studied, one allele was dominant while the other was recessive. This is not always the case. For some alleles, an inheritance pattern called codominance exists. In **codominance,** the alleles are neither dominant nor recessive. As a result, neither allele is masked in the offspring.

Look at the Punnett square in Figure 11. Mendel's principle of dominant and recessive alleles does not explain why the heterozygous chickens have both black and white feathers. The alleles for feather color are

Figure 10 In Erminette chickens, the alleles for black feathers and white feathers are codominant.

Figure 11 The offspring from the cross in this Punnett square will have both black and white feathers. *Classifying* Predict whether the offspring will be heterozygous or homozygous. Explain your answer.

codominant—neither dominant nor recessive. As you can see, neither allele is masked in the heterozygous chickens. Notice also that the codominant alleles are written as capital letters with superscripts—F^B for black feathers and F^W for white feathers. As the Punnett square shows, heterozygous chickens have the $F^B F^W$ allele combination.

Another example of codominance can be found in cattle. Red hair and white hair are codominant. Heterozygous cattle have coats with both white hairs and red hairs. From a distance, heterozygous cattle look pinkish brown, a color called roan.

Section 2 Review

1. What is meant by the term *probability*? How is probability related to genetics?
2. How are Punnett squares useful to geneticists?
3. What is the difference between a phenotype and a genotype? Give an example of each.
4. A white cow is crossed with a red bull. The calf is neither white nor red, but roan. Explain how this happens.
5. **Thinking Critically Problem Solving** In pea plants, the allele for round seeds (*R*) is dominant over the allele for wrinkled seeds (*r*). Construct a Punnett square that shows a cross between a heterozygous plant with round seeds (*Rr*) and a homozygous plant with wrinkled seeds (*rr*). Predict the probability that an offspring will have wrinkled seeds.

Science at Home

The Guessing Game Have a family member think of a number between 1 and 5. Then try to guess the number. Discuss the probability of guessing the correct number. Then repeat the guessing activity four more times. How did your success rate compare to the probability of guessing correctly? How can you account for any difference between your success rate and the results predicted by probability?

MAKE THE RIGHT CALL!

You know that making predictions is an important part of science. An accurate prediction can be a sign that you understand the event you are studying. In this lab, you will make predictions as you model the events involved in genetic crosses.

Problem

How can you predict the possible results of genetic crosses?

Materials

2 small paper bags
marking pen
3 blue marbles
3 white marbles

Procedure

1. Label one bag "Bag 1, Female Parent." Label the other bag "Bag 2, Male Parent." Then read over Part 1, Part 2, and Part 3 of this lab. Write a prediction about the kinds of offspring you expect from each cross.

Part 1 Crossing Two Homozygous Parents

2. Copy the data table and label it *Data Table Number 1*. Then place two blue marbles in Bag 1. This pair of marbles represents the female parent's alleles. Use the letter *B* to represent the dominant allele for blue color.

3. Place two white marbles in Bag 2. Use the letter *b* to represent the recessive allele for white color.

4. For Trial 1, remove one marble from Bag 1 without looking in the bag. Record the result in your data table. Return the marble to the bag. Again, without looking in the bag, remove one marble from Bag 2. Record the result in your data table. Return the marble to the bag.

5. In the column labeled *Offspring's Alleles,* write *BB* if you removed two blue marbles, *bb* if you removed two white marbles, or *Bb* if you removed one blue marble and one white marble.

6. Repeat Steps 4 and 5 nine more times.

DATA TABLE

Number _____

Trial	Allele From Bag 1 (Female Parent)	Allele From Bag 2 (Male Parent)	Offspring's Alleles
1			
2			
3			
4			
5			
6			

Part 2 Crossing a Homozygous Parent With a Heterozygous Parent

7. Place two blue marbles in Bag 1. Place one white marble and one blue marble in Bag 2. Copy the data table again, and label it *Data Table Number 2.*
8. Repeat Steps 4 and 5 ten times.

Part 3 Crossing Two Heterozygous Parents

9. Place one blue marble and one white marble in Bag 1. Place one blue marble and one white marble in Bag 2. Copy the data table again and label it *Data Table Number 3.*
10. Repeat Steps 4 and 5 ten times.

Analyze and Conclude

1. Make a Punnett square for each of the crosses you modeled in Part 1, Part 2, and Part 3.
2. According to your results in Part 1, how many different kinds of offspring are possible when the homozygous parents (*BB* and *bb*) are crossed? Do the results you obtained using the marble model agree with the results shown by a Punnett square?

3. According to your results in Part 2, what percent of offspring are likely to be homozygous when a homozygous parent (*BB*) and a heterozygous parent (*Bb*) are crossed? What percent of offspring are likely to be heterozygous? Does the model agree with the results shown by a Punnett square?
4. According to your results in Part 3, what different kinds of offspring are possible when two heterozygous parents (*Bb* × *Bb*) are crossed? What percent of each type of offspring are likely to be produced? Does the model agree with the results of a Punnett square?
5. For Part 3, if you did 100 trials instead of 10 trials, would your results be closer to the results shown in a Punnett square? Explain.
6. **Think About It** How does the marble model compare with a Punnett square? How are the two methods alike? How are they different?

Design an Experiment

In peas, the allele for yellow seeds (*Y*) is dominant over the allele for green seeds (*y*). What possible crosses do you think could produce a heterozygous plant with yellow seeds (*Yy*)? Use the marble model and Punnett squares to test your hypothesis.

SECTION 3 The Cell and Inheritance

DISCOVER ······························ ACTIVITY ····

Which Chromosome Is Which?

Mendel did not know that chromosomes play a role in genetics. Today we know that genes are located on chromosomes.

1. Label two craft sticks with the letter *A*. The craft sticks represent a pair of chromosomes in the female parent. Turn the sticks face down on a piece of paper.

2. Label two more craft sticks with the letter *a*. These represent a pair of chromosomes in the male parent. Turn the sticks face down on another piece of paper.

3. Turn over one craft stick "chromosome" from each piece of paper. Move both sticks to a third piece of paper. These represent a pair of chromosomes in the offspring. Note the allele combination that the offspring received.

Think It Over

Inferring Use this model to explain how chromosomes are involved in the inheritance of alleles.

GUIDE FOR READING

◆ What role do chromosomes play in inheritance?

◆ What events occur during meiosis?

Reading Tip As you read, write a sentence that states the main idea of each paragraph.

Key Terms sperm • egg • meiosis

Sperm cells ▼

When Mendel's results were rediscovered in 1900, scientists became excited about his principles of inheritance. They were eager to identify the structures that carried Mendel's hereditary factors, or genes.

In 1903, Walter Sutton, an American geneticist, added an important piece of information to the understanding of genetics. Sutton was studying the cells of grasshoppers. He was trying to understand how sex cells—sperm and egg—form. A **sperm** is the male sex cell. An **egg** is the female sex cell. During his studies, Sutton examined sex cells in many different stages of formation. He became particularly interested in the movement of chromosomes during the formation of sex cells. Sutton hypothesized that chromosomes were the key to understanding how offspring come to have traits similar to those of their parents.

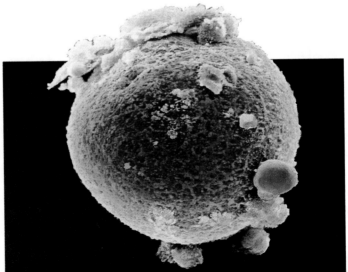

◄ Egg cell

Figure 12 Grasshoppers have 24 chromosomes in each of their body cells. *Applying Concepts How many chromosomes did Sutton observe in the sperm cells and egg cells of grasshoppers?*

Chromosomes and Inherited Characteristics

Sutton knew that structures inside cells must be responsible for the inheritance of genes. He needed evidence to support his hypothesis that chromosomes were those structures. Sutton compared the number of chromosomes in a grasshopper's sex cells with the number of chromosomes in the other cells in the grasshopper's body. As you can see in Figure 12, the body cells of grasshoppers have 24 chromosomes. To his surprise, Sutton found that the grasshopper's sex cells have only 12 chromosomes. In other words, a grasshopper's sex cells have exactly half the number of chromosomes found in its body cells.

Sutton knew that he had discovered something important. He observed what happened when a sperm cell (with 12 chromosomes) and an egg cell (with 12 chromosomes) joined. The fertilized egg that formed had 24 chromosomes—the original number. As a result, the grasshopper offspring had exactly the same number of chromosomes in its cells as did each of its parents. The 24 chromosomes existed in 12 pairs. One chromosome in each pair came from the male parent, while the other chromosome came from the female parent.

Sutton concluded that the chromosomes carried Mendel's hereditary factors, or genes, from one generation to the next. In other words, genes are located on chromosomes. Sutton's idea came to be known as the chromosome theory of inheritance. **According to the chromosome theory of inheritance, genes are carried from parents to their offspring on chromosomes.**

✓ *Checkpoint How does the number of chromosomes in a grasshopper's sex cells compare to the number in its body cells?*

Meiosis

How do sex cells end up with half the number of chromosomes as body cells? To answer this question, you need to understand the events that occur during meiosis. **Meiosis** (my OH sis) is the process by which the number of chromosomes is reduced by half to form sex cells—sperm and eggs.

You can trace the events of meiosis in *Exploring Meiosis.* In this example, each parent cell has four chromosomes arranged in two pairs. **During meiosis, the chromosome pairs separate and are distributed to two different cells. The resulting sex cells have only half as many chromosomes as the other cells in the organism.** In *Exploring Meiosis,* notice that the sex cells end up with only two chromosomes each—half the number found in the parent cell. Only one chromosome from each chromosome pair ends up in each sex cell.

When sex cells combine to produce offspring, each sex cell will contribute half the normal number of chromosomes. Thus, the offspring gets the normal number of chromosomes—half from each parent.

☑ *Checkpoint* *What types of cells form by meiosis?*

Meiosis and Punnett Squares

The Punnett squares that you learned about earlier in this chapter are actually a shorthand way to show the events that occur at meiosis. When the chromosome pairs separate into two different sex cells, so do the alleles carried on each chromosome. One allele from each pair goes to each sex cell. In Figure 13, you can see how the Punnett square accounts for the separation of alleles during meiosis.

As shown across the top of the Punnett square, half of the sperm cells from the male parent will receive the chromosome with the *T* allele. The other half of the sperm cells will receive the chromosome with the *t* allele. In this example, the same is true for the egg cells from the female parent, as shown down the left side of the Punnett square. Depending on which sperm cell combines with which egg cell, one of the allele combinations shown in the boxes will result.

Figure 13 This Punnett square shows how alleles separate when sex cells form during meiosis. It also shows the possible allele combinations that can result after fertilization occurs. *Interpreting Charts* *What is the probability that a sperm cell will contain a T allele?*

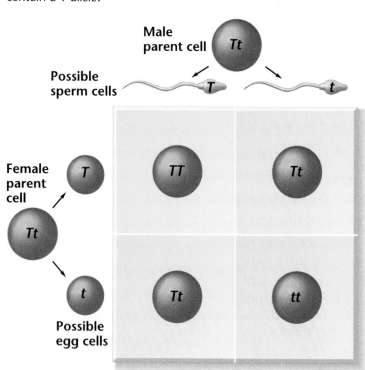

Male parent cell Tt

Possible sperm cells   T   t

Female parent cell   T

Tt

t

Possible egg cells

TT   Tt

Tt   tt

EXPLORING Meiosis

During meiosis, a cell undergoes two divisions to produce sex cells that have half the number of chromosomes.

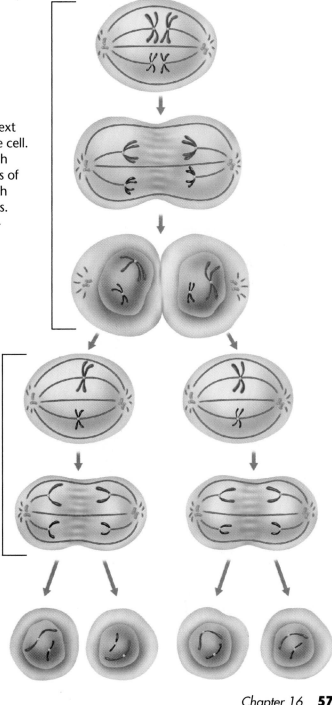

1 Beginning of meiosis
Before meiosis begins, every chromosome in the cell is copied. As in mitosis, centromeres hold the double-stranded chromosomes together.

2 Meiosis I
The chromosome pairs line up next to each other in the center of the cell. The pairs then separate from each other and move to opposite ends of the cell. Two cells form, each with half the number of chromosomes. Each chromosome is still double-stranded.

3 Meiosis II
The double-stranded chromosomes move to the center of the cell. The centromeres split and the two strands of each chromosome separate. The two strands move to opposite ends of the cell.

4 End of meiosis
Four sex cells have been produced. Each cell has only half the number of chromosomes that the parent cell had at the beginning of meiosis. Each cell has only one chromosome from each original pair.

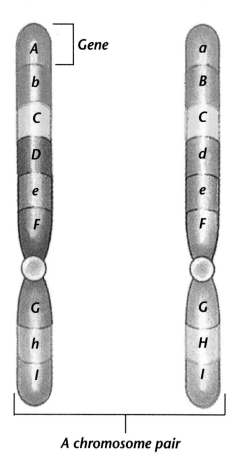

Gene

A chromosome pair

Figure 14 Genes are located on chromosomes. The chromosomes in a pair may have different alleles for some genes and the same alleles for others. *Classifying For which genes is this organism homozygous? For which genes is it heterozygous?*

Chromosomes

Since Sutton's time, scientists have studied the chromosomes of many different organisms. The body cells of humans, for example, contain 23 pairs, or 46 chromosomes. The body cells of dogs have 78 chromosomes, while the body cells of silkworms have 56 chromosomes. As you can see, larger organisms don't always have more chromosomes.

Chromosomes are made up of many genes joined together like beads on a string. Sutton reasoned that chromosomes must contain a large number of genes because organisms have so many traits. Although you have only 23 pairs of chromosomes, your body cells contain more than 60,000 genes. Each of the genes controls a particular trait.

Look at the pair of chromosomes in Figure 14. One chromosome in the pair came from the female parent. The other chromosome came from the male parent. Notice that each chromosome in the pair has the same genes. The genes are lined up in the same order from one end of the chromosome to the other. However, the alleles for some of the genes might be different. For example, the organism has the *A* allele on one chromosome and the *a* allele on the other. As you can see, this organism is heterozygous for some traits and homozygous for others.

Section 3 Review

1. Explain the role that chromosomes play in inheritance.
2. Briefly describe what happens to chromosomes during meiosis.
3. On what structures in a cell are genes located?
4. How is a Punnett square a model for what happens during meiosis?
5. **Thinking Critically** **Inferring** The body cells of hamsters have 44 chromosomes. How many chromosomes would the sex cells of a hamster have?

Check Your Progress

CHAPTER PROJECT

At this point, you should find a classmate with a paper pet of the opposite sex. Suppose the two pets were crossed and produced six offspring. For each trait, use coin tosses to determine which allele the offspring will inherit from each parent. Construct a paper pet for each offspring, showing the traits each one has inherited. Write the genotype for each trait on their backs.

SECTION 4 The DNA Connection

A •–	N –•
B –•••	O –––
C –•–•	P •––•
D –••	Q ––•–
E •	R •–•
F ••–•	S •••
G ––•	T –
H ••••	U ••–
I ••	V •••–
J •–––	W •––
K –•–	X –••–
L •–••	Y –•––
M ––	Z ––••

Can You Crack the Code?

1. Use the Morse code in the chart to decode the question in the message below. The letters are separated by slash marks.

   •––/••••/•/•–•/•/•–/•–•/•/––•/•/–•/
   •/•••/•–••/–––/–•–•/•–/–/•/–••/

2. Write your answer to the question in Morse code.

3. Exchange your coded answer with a partner. Then decode your partner's answer.

Think It Over

Forming Operational Definitions Based on your results from this activity, write a definition of the word *code*. Then compare your definition to one in a dictionary.

A white buffalo calf was born on Childs Place Farm near Hanover, Michigan, in 1998. White buffaloes are extremely rare, occurring only once in every 10 million births. Why was this calf born with such an uncommon phenotype? To answer this question, you need to know how the genes on a chromosome control an organism's traits.

The Genetic Code

Today scientists know that the main function of genes is to control the production of proteins in the organism's cells. Proteins help to determine the size, shape, and many other traits of an organism.

GUIDE FOR READING

◆ What is meant by the term "genetic code"?

◆ How does a cell produce proteins?

◆ How do mutations affect an organism?

Reading Tip As you read, create a flowchart that shows how a cell produces proteins.

Key Terms messenger RNA • transfer RNA • mutation

Figure 15 The white color of this buffalo calf is very unusual. Both of the calf's parents had brown coats.

DNA is a major component of chromosomes. In Figure 16, notice that a DNA molecule is made up of four different nitrogen bases—adenine (A), thymine (T), guanine (G), and cytosine (C). These bases form the rungs of the DNA "ladder." The bases on one side of a DNA molecule pair with those on the other side. Adenine always pairs with thymine, and guanine with cytosine. A single gene on a chromosome may contain anywhere from several hundred to a million or more of these bases. The bases are arranged in a specific order—for example, ATGACGTAC. This order determines the structure of proteins.

Protein molecules are made up of amino acids. There are only 20 common amino acids, but they can be combined in different ways to form thousands of different proteins. **The order of the nitrogen bases along a gene forms a genetic code that specifies what type of protein will be produced.** In the genetic code, a group of three bases codes for the attachment of a specific amino acid. The order of the bases determines the order in which amino acids are put together to form a protein. You can think of the bases as three-letter code words. The code words tell the cell which amino acid to add to the growing protein chain.

How Cells Make Proteins

The production of proteins is called protein synthesis. **During protein synthesis, the cell uses information from a gene on a chromosome to produce a specific protein.** Protein synthesis takes place on the ribosomes in the cytoplasm of the cell. The cytoplasm is outside the nucleus, but the chromosomes are inside the nucleus.

Figure 16 A chromosome contains thousands of genes along its length. The sequence of bases along a gene forms a code that tells the cell what protein to produce. *Interpreting Diagrams Where in the cell are the chromosomes located?*

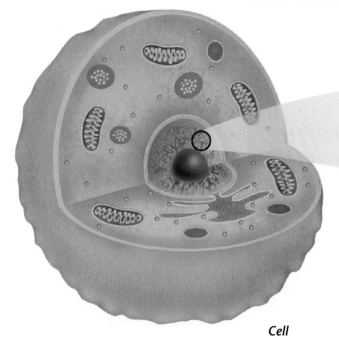

Cell

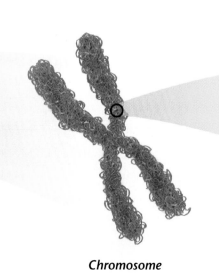

Chromosome

The Role of RNA Before protein synthesis can take place, a "messenger" must first carry the genetic code from the DNA inside the nucleus into the cytoplasm. This genetic messenger is called ribonucleic acid, or RNA.

Although RNA is similar to DNA, the two molecules differ in some important ways. Unlike DNA, which looks like a twisted ladder, an RNA molecule almost always looks like only one side, or strand, of the ladder. RNA also contains a different sugar molecule from the sugar found in DNA. Another difference between DNA and RNA is in their nitrogen bases. Like DNA, RNA contains adenine, guanine, and cytosine. However, instead of thymine, RNA contains uracil (YOOR uh sil).

There are several types of RNA involved in protein synthesis. **Messenger RNA** copies the coded message from the DNA in the nucleus, and carries the message into the cytoplasm. Another type of RNA, called **transfer RNA,** carries amino acids and adds them to the growing protein.

Translating the Code The process of protein synthesis is shown in *Exploring Protein Synthesis* on the next page. The first step is for a DNA molecule to "unzip" between its base pairs. Then one of the strands of DNA directs the production of a strand of messenger RNA. To form the RNA strand, RNA bases pair up with the DNA bases. Instead of thymine, however, uracil pairs with adenine. The messenger RNA then leaves the nucleus and attaches to a ribosome in the cytoplasm. There, molecules of transfer RNA pick up the amino acids specified by each three-letter code word. Each transfer RNA molecule puts the amino acid it is carrying in the correct order along the growing protein chain.

☑ *Checkpoint* *What is the function of transfer RNA?*

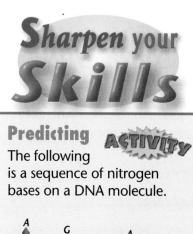
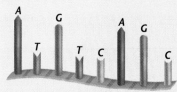
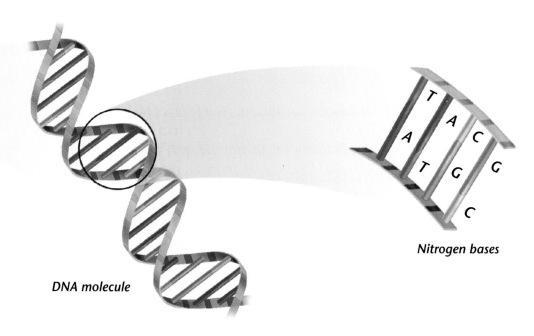

DNA molecule

Nitrogen bases

EXPLORING *Protein Synthesis*

To make proteins, messenger RNA copies information from DNA in the nucleus. Transfer RNA then uses this information to produce proteins in the ribosomes.

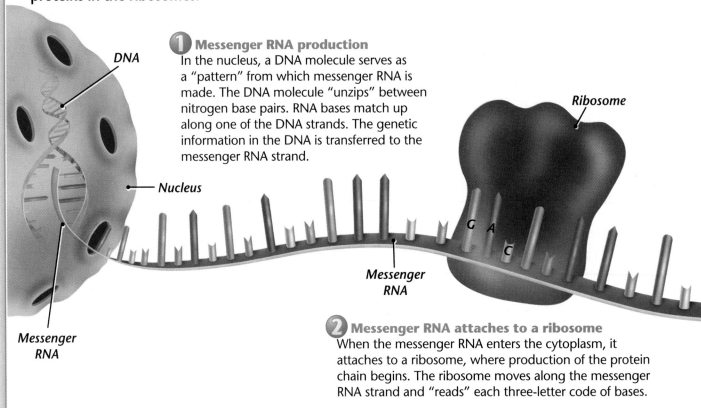

1 Messenger RNA production
In the nucleus, a DNA molecule serves as a "pattern" from which messenger RNA is made. The DNA molecule "unzips" between nitrogen base pairs. RNA bases match up along one of the DNA strands. The genetic information in the DNA is transferred to the messenger RNA strand.

DNA

Ribosome

Nucleus

Messenger RNA

Messenger RNA

2 Messenger RNA attaches to a ribosome
When the messenger RNA enters the cytoplasm, it attaches to a ribosome, where production of the protein chain begins. The ribosome moves along the messenger RNA strand and "reads" each three-letter code of bases.

Mutations

Suppose that a mistake occurred in one gene of a chromosome. Instead of the base A, for example, the DNA molecule might have the base G. This is one type of mistake that can occur in a cell's hereditary material. Any change that occurs in a gene or chromosome is called a **mutation.** Mutations can cause a cell to produce an incorrect protein during protein synthesis. As a result, the organism's traits, or phenotype, will be different from what it normally would have been. In fact, the term *mutation* comes from a Latin word that means "change."

Types of Mutations Some mutations are the result of small changes in an organism's hereditary material, such as the substitution of a single base for another. This type of mutation can occur during the DNA replication process. The white coat on the

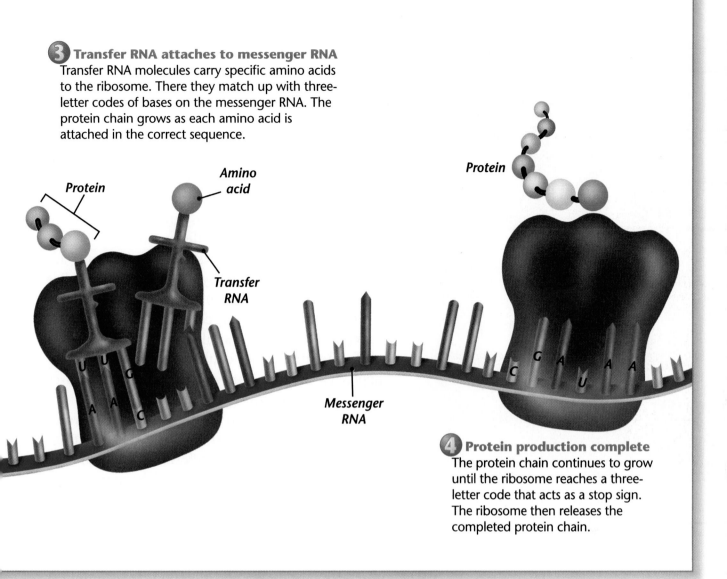

3 **Transfer RNA attaches to messenger RNA**
Transfer RNA molecules carry specific amino acids to the ribosome. There they match up with three-letter codes of bases on the messenger RNA. The protein chain grows as each amino acid is attached in the correct sequence.

Protein

Amino acid

Protein

Transfer RNA

Messenger RNA

4 **Protein production complete**
The protein chain continues to grow until the ribosome reaches a three-letter code that acts as a stop sign. The ribosome then releases the completed protein chain.

buffalo calf you read about at the start of this section might have resulted from this type of mutation. Other mutations may occur when chromosomes don't separate correctly during meiosis. When this type of mutation occurs, a cell can end up with too many or too few chromosomes.

If a mutation occurs in a body cell, such as a skin cell, the mutation will affect only the cell that carries it. If, however, a mutation occurs in a sex cell, the mutation can be passed on to an offspring and affect the offspring's phenotype.

The Effects of Mutations Because mutations can introduce changes in an organism, they can be a source of genetic variety. **Many changes brought about by mutations in an organism are harmful to the organism. Some mutations, however, are helpful, and still others are neither harmful nor helpful.**

Figure 17 Mutations can affect an organism's traits, or phenotype. The unusually large strawberries on the left are the result of a mutation. The cells of these strawberries have extra sets of chromosomes.

A mutation harms an organism if it reduces the organism's chance to survive and reproduce.

Whether a mutation is harmful or not depends partly on the organism's environment. The mutation that led to the production of a white buffalo calf would probably be harmful to an organism in the wild. Its white color would make it more visible, and thus easier for predators to find. However, a white buffalo calf raised on a farm probably has the same chance for survival as a brown buffalo. On the farm, the mutation does not harm the buffalo.

 INTEGRATING HEALTH Some diseases in humans are caused by harmful mutations. For example, some forms of cancer are caused by mutations in an organism's body cells. Overexposure to the ultraviolet radiation in sunlight, for example, may lead to mutations that could cause skin cancer. In Chapter 17, you will learn more about other diseases that result from harmful mutations.

Helpful mutations, on the other hand, improve an organism's chances for survival and reproduction. Antibiotic resistance in bacteria is an example. Antibiotics are chemicals that kill bacteria. Gene mutations have enabled some kinds of bacteria to become resistant to certain antiobiotics—that is, the antibiotics do not kill the bacteria that have the mutations. Since the antibiotic-resistant bacteria are not killed by the antibiotics, the mutations have improved the bacteria's ability to survive and reproduce.

Section 4 Review

1. How do the nitrogen bases along a gene serve as a genetic code?
2. Briefly describe the process by which a cell makes proteins.
3. What possible effects can a mutation have on an organism?
4. Where in a cell does protein synthesis take place?
5. **Thinking Critically Relating Cause and Effect** Why are mutations that occur in an organism's body cells not passed on to its offspring?

Check Your Progress CHAPTER PROJECT

With your partner, plan a display of your pet's family. Label the parents the P generation. Label the offspring the F_1 generation. Construct a Punnett square for each trait to help explain the inheritance pattern in your pet's family. (Hint: Attach your pets to the display in a way that lets viewers turn the pets over to read their genotypes.)

SECTION 1 — Mendel's Work

Key Ideas

◆ Gregor Mendel's work was the foundation for understanding why offspring have traits similar to those of their parents.

◆ Alleles control inherited characteristics. Organisms inherit one allele from each parent.

◆ Some alleles are dominant and some alleles are recessive.

Key Terms

trait	purebred	dominant allele
heredity	gene	recessive allele
genetics	allele	hybrid

SECTION 2 — Probability and Genetics

INTEGRATING **MATHEMATICS**

Key Ideas

◆ Probability is the likelihood that a certain event will happen.

◆ Mendel used the principles of probability to predict the results of genetic crosses.

◆ Geneticists use Punnett squares to show all the possible outcomes of a genetic cross.

Key Terms

probability	homozygous
Punnett square	heterozygous
phenotype	codominance
genotype	

SECTION 3 — The Cell and Inheritance

Key Ideas

◆ According to the chromosome theory of inheritance, chromosomes carry genes from parent to offspring.

◆ During meiosis, chromosome pairs separate to form sex cells. Only one chromosome from each pair ends up in each sex cell. The sex cells have half the number of chromosomes as the body cells.

Key Term

sperm	egg	meiosis

SECTION 4 — The DNA Connection

Key Ideas

◆ The nitrogen bases along a gene form a code that specifies the order in which amino acids will be put together to produce a protein.

◆ During protein synthesis, messenger RNA copies the coded message from the DNA in the nucleus and carries the message into the cytoplasm. Transfer RNA adds amino acids to the growing protein.

◆ A mutation is a change in a gene or chromosome. Many mutations are harmful, some are helpful, and some are neutral.

Key Terms

messenger RNA
transfer RNA
mutation

Organizing Information

Compare/Contrast Table Copy the table comparing DNA and messenger RNA onto a separate sheet of paper. Then complete the table. (For more about compare/contrast tables, see the Skills Handbook.)

Characteristic	DNA	Messenger RNA
Nitrogen bases	a. ? b. ? c. ? d. ?	Adenine, uracil, guanine, cytosine
Structure	Twisted ladder	e. ?
Function	Forms a genetic code that specifies what type of protein will be produced	f. ?

Reviewing Content

Review key concepts online using iText at www.phschool.com

Multiple Choice

Choose the letter of the best answer.

1. The different forms of a gene are called
   a. alleles.   b. chromosomes.
   c. phenotypes.   d. genotypes.
2. In a coin toss, the probability of the coin landing heads up is
   a. 100 percent.   b. 75 percent.
   c. 50 percent.   d. 25 percent.
3. An organism with two identical alleles for a trait is
   a. heterozygous.
   b. homozygous.
   c. recessive.
   d. dominant.
4. If the body cells of an organism have 10 chromosomes, then its sex cells would have
   a. 5 chromosomes.
   b. 10 chromosomes.
   c. 15 chromosomes.
   d. 20 chromosomes.
5. During protein synthesis, messenger RNA
   a. "reads" each three-letter code of bases.
   b. releases the completed protein chain.
   c. copies information from DNA in the nucleus.
   d. carries amino acids to the ribosome.

True or False

If the statement is true, write true. If it is false, change the underlined word or words to make the statement true.

6. The scientific study of heredity is called <u>genetics</u>.
7. An organism's physical appearance is its <u>genotype</u>.
8. In <u>codominance</u>, neither of the alleles is dominant or recessive.
9. <u>Heredity</u> is the process by which sex cells form.
10. Proteins are made in the <u>nucleus</u> of the cell.

Checking Concepts

11. Describe what happened when Mendel crossed purebred tall pea plants with purebred short pea plants.
12. You toss a coin five times and it lands heads up each time. What is the probability that it will land heads up on the sixth toss? Explain your answer.
13. In guinea pigs, the allele for black fur (*B*) is dominant over the allele for white fur (*b*). In a cross between a heterozygous black guinea pig (*Bb*) and a homozygous white guinea pig (*bb*), what is the probability that an offspring will have white fur? Use a Punnett square to answer the question.
14. In your own words, describe the sequence of steps in the process of meiosis.
15. Describe the role of transfer RNA in protein synthesis.
16. **Writing to Learn** Imagine that you are a student in the 1860s visiting Gregor Mendel in his garden. Write a letter to a friend describing Mendel's experiments.

Thinking Critically

17. **Applying Concepts** In rabbits, the allele for a spotted coat is dominant over the allele for a solid-colored coat. A spotted rabbit was crossed with a solid-colored rabbit. The offspring all had spotted coats. What probably were the genotypes of the parents? Explain.
18. **Problem Solving** Suppose you are growing purebred green-skinned watermelons. One day you find a mutant striped watermelon. You cross the striped watermelon with a purebred green watermelon. Fifty percent of the offspring are striped, while fifty percent are green. Is the allele for the striped trait dominant or recessive? Explain.
19. **Predicting** A new mutation in mice causes the coat to be twice as thick as normal. In what environments would this mutation be helpful?

Applying Skills

In peas, the allele for green pods (G) is dominant over the allele for yellow pods (g). The table shows the phenotypes of the offspring produced from a cross of two plants with green pods. Use the data to answer Questions 20–22.

Phenotype	Number of Offspring
Green pods	9
Yellow pods	3

20. Calculating Calculate what percent of the offspring have green pods. Calculate what percent have yellow pods.

21. Inferring What is the genotype of the offspring with yellow pods? What are the possible genotypes of the offspring with green pods?

22. Drawing Conclusions What are the genotypes of the parents? How do you know?

CHAPTER PROJECT

Performance Assessment

Present Your Project Finalize your display of your pet's family. Be prepared to discuss the inheritance patterns in your pet's family. Examine your classmates' exhibits, and see which offspring look most like, and least like, their parents. Can you find any offspring that "break the laws" of inheritance?

Reflect and Record How did your paper pets help you learn about genetics? How do the inheritance patterns in your pet's family resemble real-life patterns? How could you use paper pets to help you understand other topics in genetics?

Test Preparation

Use these questions to prepare for standardized tests.

Use the information to answer Questions 23–26.

A pet store's customers prefer pet mice with black fur over mice with white fur. With this in mind, the owner crossed a female with black fur and a male with black fur. When the mice were born, she was surprised that three of the ten offspring had white fur. She did not know that the parents were heterozygous for fur color.

23. Which letters represent the genotype of the female parent?

  A BB   **B** Bb

  C B   **D** bb

24. Which letters represent the genotype of the male parent?

  F BB   **G** Bb

  H B   **J** bb

25. How could the pet store owner breed a litter of only white mice?

  A by making sure that either the mother or the father has white fur

  B by making sure that both the mother and the father have white fur

  C by making sure that at least one of the grandparents has white fur

  D She could not breed a litter of only white mice.

26. If the pet store owner were to cross one homozygous black mouse with a heterozygous black mouse, what percentage of the mice would you expect to have white fur?

  F 0%   **G** 25%

  H 50%   **J** 75%

WEB ACTIVITY
www.phschool.com

 Human Inheritance
SECTION 1
Discover How Tall Is Tall?

 Human Genetic Disorders
SECTION 2
Discover How Many Chromosomes?
Real-World Lab Family Puzzles

 Advances in Genetics
SECTION 3
Discover What Do Fingerprints Reveal?
Real-World Lab Guilty or Innocent?

A Family Portrait

A pedigree, or family tree, is a branched drawing that shows many generations of a family. In some cases, a pedigree may show centuries of a family's history.

In genetics, pedigrees are used to show how inherited characteristics are passed from one generation to the next. In this project, you will create a genetic pedigree for an imaginary family. Although the family will be imaginary, your pedigree must show how real human traits are passed from parents to children.

The children in this family have some traits like their mother's and some traits like their father's.

Your Goal To create a pedigree for an imaginary family that shows the transfer of genetic traits from one generation to the next.

To complete the project you will

◆ choose two different genetic traits, and identify all the possible genotypes and phenotypes
◆ create pedigrees that trace each trait through three generations of your imaginary family
◆ prepare a family "photo" album to show what each family member looks like

Get Started With a partner, review the human traits described on page 562 in Chapter 16. List what you already know about human inheritance. For example, which human traits are controlled by dominant alleles? Which are controlled by recessive alleles? Then preview Section 1 of this chapter, and list the traits you'll be studying. Choose two traits that you would like to focus on in your project.

Check Your Progress You'll be working on this project as you study this chapter. To keep your project on track, look for Check Your Progress boxes at the following points.

Section 1 Review, page 594: Create a pedigree for the first trait you chose.
Section 2 Review, page 599: Create the second pedigree, and begin your family album.

Present Your Project At the end of the chapter (page 613), you will present your family's pedigrees and "photo" album to the class.

TEKS

In addition to process TEKS, this chapter addresses these concept TEKS as they relate to the chapter's topics.

(8.11) The student knows that traits of species can change through generations and that the instructions for traits are contained in the genetic material of the organisms. The student is expected to:
(B) distinguish between inherited traits and other characteristics that result from interactions with the environment;
(C) make predictions about possible outcomes of various genetic combinations of inherited characteristics.

1 Human Inheritance

How Tall Is Tall?

1. Choose a partner. Measure each other's height to the nearest 5 centimeters. Record your measurements on the chalkboard.

2. Create a bar graph showing the number of students at each height. Plot the heights on the horizontal axis and the number of students on the vertical axis.

Think It Over

Inferring If Gregor Mendel had graphed the heights of his pea plants, the graph would have had two bars—one for tall stems and one for short stems. Do you think height in humans is controlled by a single gene, as it is in peas? Explain your answer.

GUIDE FOR READING

◆ Why do some human traits show a large variety of phenotypes?

◆ How does the environment affect an organism's characteristics?

◆ Why are some sex-linked traits more common in males than in females?

Reading Tip Before you read, rewrite the headings in this section as *how, why,* or *what* questions. As you read, write answers to the questions.

Key Terms multiple alleles • sex-linked gene • carrier • pedigree

---

Have you ever heard someone say "He's the spitting image of his dad" or "She has her mother's eyes"? Children often resemble their parents. The reason for this is that alleles for eye color, hair color, and thousands of other traits are passed from parents to their children. People inherit some alleles from their mother and some from their father. This is why most people look a little like their mother and a little like their father.

Traits Controlled by Single Genes

In Chapter 16, you learned that many traits in peas and other organisms are controlled by a single gene with two alleles. Often one allele is dominant, while the other is recessive. Many human traits are also controlled by a single gene with one dominant allele and one recessive allele. As with tall and short pea plants, these human traits have two distinctly different phenotypes, or physical appearances.

For example, a widow's peak is a hairline that comes to a point in the middle of the forehead. The allele for a widow's peak is dominant over the allele for a straight hairline. The Punnett square in Figure 1 illustrates a cross between two parents who are heterozygous for a widow's peak. Trace the possible combinations of alleles that a child may inherit. Notice that each child has a 3 in 4, or 75 percent, probability of having a widow's peak. There is only a 1 in 4, or 25 percent, probability that a child will have a straight hairline. Recall from Chapter 16 that when Mendel crossed peas that were heterozygous for a trait, he obtained similar percentages in the offspring.

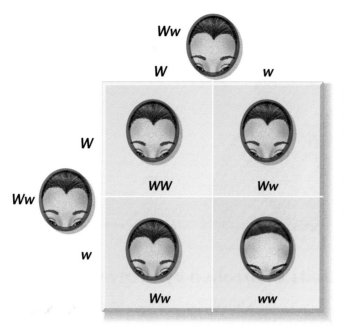

Figure 1 This Punnett square shows a cross between two parents with widow's peaks. *Interpreting Diagrams* Predict the possible genotypes of the offspring. What percentage of the offspring will probably have each genotype?

Do you have dimples when you smile? If so, then you have the dominant allele for this trait. Like having a widow's peak, having smile dimples is controlled by a single gene. People who have two recessive alleles do not have smile dimples.

Multiple Alleles

Some human traits are controlled by a single gene that has more than two alleles. Such a gene is said to have **multiple alleles**—three or more forms of a gene that code for a single trait. You can think of multiple alleles as being like flavors of pudding. Pudding usually comes in more flavors than just chocolate and vanilla!

Even though a gene may have multiple alleles, a person can carry only two of those alleles. This is because chromosomes exist in pairs. Each chromosome in a pair carries only one allele for each gene.

One human trait that is controlled by a gene with multiple alleles is blood type. There are four main blood types—A, B, AB, and O. Three alleles control the inheritance of blood types. The allele for blood type A and the allele for blood type B are codominant. The codominant alleles are written as capital letters with superscripts—I^A for blood type A and I^B for blood type B. The allele for blood type O—written i—is recessive. Recall that when two codominant alleles are inherited, neither allele is masked. A person who inherits an I^A allele from one parent and an I^B allele from the other parent will have type AB blood. Figure 2 shows the allele combinations that result in each blood type. Notice that only people who inherit two i alleles have type O blood.

☑ *Checkpoint* If a gene has multiple alleles, why can a person only have two of the alleles for the gene?

Blood Types	
Blood Type	**Combination of Alleles**
A	$I^A I^A$ or $I^A i$
B	$I^B I^B$ or $I^B i$
AB	$I^A I^B$
O	ii

Figure 2 Blood type is determined by a single gene with three alleles. This chart shows which combinations of alleles result in each blood type.

Figure 3 Skin color in humans is determined by three or more genes. Different combinations of alleles at each of the genes result in a wide range of possible skin colors.

Traits Controlled by Many Genes

There is an enormous variety of phenotypes for height in humans. What causes this wide range of phenotypes? **Some human traits show a large number of phenotypes because the traits are controlled by many genes. The genes act together as a group to produce a single trait.** At least four genes control height in humans, so there are many possible combinations of genes and alleles.

Like height, skin color is determined by many genes. Human skin color ranges from almost white to nearly black, with many shades in between. Skin color is controlled by at least three genes. Each gene, in turn, has at least two possible alleles. Various combinations of alleles at each of the genes determine the amount of pigment that a person's skin cells produce. Thus, a wide variety of skin colors is possible.

The Effect of Environment

The effects of genes are often altered by the environment—the organism's surroundings. **Many of an organism's characteristics are determined by an interaction between genes and the environment.** For example, people's diets can affect their height. A diet lacking in protein, minerals, and vitamins can prevent a person from growing to his or her potential maximum height. Since the late 1800s, the average height of adults in the United States has increased by almost 10 centimeters. During that time, American diets have become more healthful.

Height is determined by both genes and the environment. **In contrast, some characteristics of organisms are not determined by genes at all. Instead, these characteristics result entirely from interactions with the environment.** For example, suppose a person becomes blind as the result of an accident. The blindness was caused by the environment, not by alleles that the person inherited from his or her parents.

The Eyes Have It

ACTIVITY

One inherited trait is eye dominance—using one eye more than the other. Test yourself for this trait.

1. Hold your hand out in front of you at arm's length. Point your finger at an object across the room.

2. Close your right eye only and observe how far your finger appears to move.

3. Repeat Step 2 with the left eye closed. With which eye did your finger seem to remain closer to the object? That eye is dominant.

Designing Experiments Is eye dominance related to hand dominance—whether a person is right-handed or left-handed? Design an experiment to find out. Obtain your teacher's permission before carrying out your experiment.

Male or Female?

What determines whether a baby is a boy or a girl? As with other traits, the sex of a baby is determined by genes on chromosomes. Among the 23 pairs of chromosomes in each body cell is a single pair of chromosomes called the sex chromosomes. The sex chromosomes determine whether a person is male or female.

The sex chromosomes are the only pair of chromosomes that do not always match. If you are female, your two sex chromosomes match. The two chromosomes are called X chromosomes. If you are male, your sex chromosomes do not match. One of your sex chromosomes is an X chromosome. The other sex chromosome is a Y chromosome. The Y chromosome is much smaller than the X chromosome.

What happens to the sex chromosomes when egg and sperm cells form? As you know, each egg and sperm cell has only one chromosome from each pair. Since both of a female's sex chromosomes are X chromosomes, all eggs carry one X chromosome. Males, however, have two different sex chromosomes. This means that half of a male's sperm cells carry an X chromosome, while half carry a Y chromosome.

When a sperm cell with an X chromosome fertilizes an egg, the egg has two X chromosomes. The fertilized egg will develop into a girl. When a sperm with a Y chromosome fertilizes an egg, the egg has one X chromosome and one Y chromosome. The fertilized egg will develop into a boy. Thus it is the sperm that determines the sex of the child, as you can see in Figure 4.

☑ *Checkpoint* *What pair of chromosomes do not always match?*

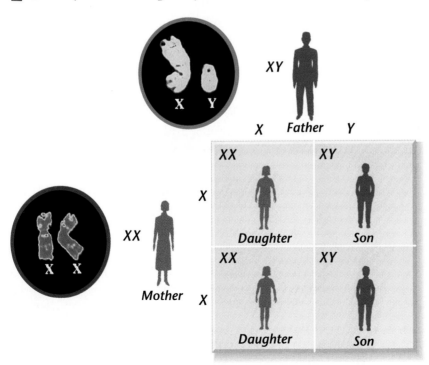

Figure 4 As this Punnett square shows, there is a 50 percent probability that a child will be a girl and a 50 percent probability that a child will be a boy. *Interpreting Diagrams Predict the sex of the child if a sperm with a Y chromosome fertilizes an egg.*

You can model **ACTIVITY** how the sex of an offspring is determined.

1. Label one paper bag "female." Label another paper bag "male."

2. Place two red marbles in the bag labeled "female." The red marbles represent X chromosomes.

3. Place one red marble and one white marble in the bag labeled "male." The white marble represents a Y chromosome.

4. Without looking, pick one marble from each bag. Two red marbles represent a female offspring. One red marble and one white marble represent a male offspring. Record the sex of the "offspring."

5. Put the marbles back in the correct bags. Repeat Step 4 nine more times.

Making Models How many males were produced? How many females? How close were your results to the expected probabilities for male and female offspring?

Sex-Linked Genes

Some human traits occur more often in one sex than the other. The genes for these traits are often carried on the sex chromosomes. Genes on the X and Y chromosomes are often called **sex-linked genes** because their alleles are passed from parent to child on a sex chromosome. Traits controlled by sex-linked genes are called sex-linked traits.

Like other genes, sex-linked genes can have dominant and recessive alleles. Recall that females have two X chromosomes, whereas males have one X chromosome and one Y chromosome. In females, a dominant allele on one X chromosome will mask a recessive allele on the other X chromosome. The situation is not the same in males, however. In males, there is no matching allele on the Y chromosome to cover up the allele on the X chromosome. As a result, any allele on the X chromosome—even a recessive allele—will produce the trait in a male who inherits it. **Because males have only one X chromosome, males are more likely than females to have a sex-linked trait that is controlled by a recessive allele.**

One example of a sex-linked trait that is controlled by a recessive allele is red-green colorblindness. A person with red-green colorblindness cannot distinguish between red and green.

Many more males than females have red-green colorblindness. You can understand why this is the case by examining the Punnett square in Figure 6. Both parents in this example have normal color vision. Notice, however, that the mother is a carrier of colorblindness. A **carrier** is a person who has one recessive allele for a trait and one dominant allele. Although a carrier does not have the trait, the carrier can pass the recessive allele on to his or her offspring. In the case of sex-linked traits, only females can be carriers.

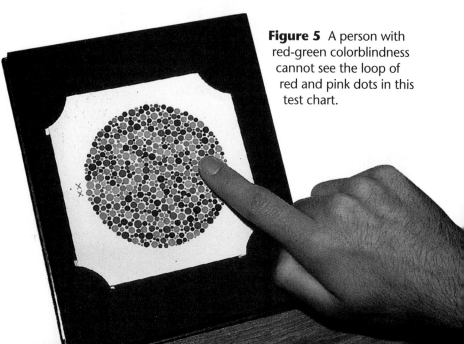

Figure 5 A person with red-green colorblindness cannot see the loop of red and pink dots in this test chart.

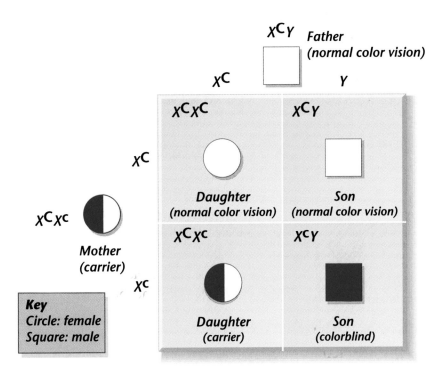

Figure 6 Red-green colorblindness is a sex-linked trait. A girl who receives only one recessive allele (written X^c) for red-green colorblindness will not have the trait. However, a boy who receives one recessive allele will be colorblind. *Applying Concepts What allele combination would a daughter need to inherit to be colorblind?*

As you can see in Figure 6, there is a 25 percent probability that this couple will have a colorblind child. Notice that none of the couple's daughters will be colorblind. On the other hand, the sons have a 50 percent probability of being colorblind. For a female to be colorblind, she must inherit two recessive alleles for colorblindness, one from each parent. A male needs to inherit only one recessive allele. This is because there is no gene for color vision on the Y chromosome. Thus, there is no allele that could cover up the recessive allele on the X chromosome.

Pedigrees

Imagine that you are a geneticist studying inheritance patterns in humans. What would you do? You can't set up crosses with people as Mendel did with peas. Instead, you would need to trace the inheritance of traits through many generations in a number of families.

One tool that geneticists use to trace the inheritance of traits in humans is a pedigree. A **pedigree** is a chart or "family tree" that tracks which members of a family have a particular trait. The trait recorded in a pedigree can be an ordinary trait such as the widow's peak, or it could be a sex-linked trait such as colorblindness. In *Exploring a Pedigree* on page 594, you can trace the inheritance of colorblindness through three generations of a family.

☑ *Checkpoint* How is a pedigree like a "family tree"?

EXPLORING *a Pedigree*

This pedigree traces the occurrence of colorblindness in three generations of a family. Colorblindness is a sex-linked trait that is controlled by a recessive allele. Notice that specific symbols are used in pedigrees to communicate genetic information.

A circle represents a female.

A square represents a male.

A horizontal line connecting a male and female represents a marriage.

A vertical line and a bracket connect the parents to their children.

A half-shaded circle or square indicates that a person is a carrier of the trait.

A completely shaded circle or square indicates that a person has the trait.

A circle or square that is not shaded indicates that a person neither has the trait nor is a carrier of the trait.

Section 1 Review

1. Why do human traits such as height and skin color have many different phenotypes?
2. Explain how a person's height is determined by both genes and the environment.
3. Explain why red-green colorblindness is more common in males than in females.
4. **Thinking Critically** **Predicting** Could two people with widow's peaks have a child with a straight hairline? Could two people with straight hairlines have a child with a widow's peak? Explain.

Check Your Progress

CHAPTER PROJECT

By now, you should be creating your pedigree for the first trait you chose. Start with one couple, and show two generations of offspring. The couple should have five children. It is up to you to decide how many children each of those children has. Use Punnett squares to make sure that your imaginary family's inheritance pattern follows the laws of genetics.

...

Human Genetic Disorders

DISCOVER

ACTIVITY

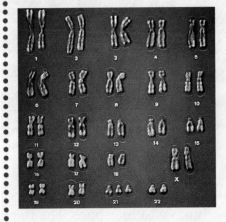

How Many Chromosomes?

The photo at the left shows the chromosomes from a cell of a person with Down syndrome, a genetic disorder. The chromosomes have been sorted into pairs.

1. Count the number of chromosomes in the photo.

2. How does the number of chromosomes compare to the usual number of chromosomes in human cells?

Think It Over

Inferring How do you think a cell could have ended up with this number of chromosomes? (*Hint:* Think about the events that occur during meiosis.)

he air inside the stadium was hot and still. The crowd cheered loudly as eight runners approached the starting blocks. The runners shook out their arms and legs to loosen up their muscles and calm their jitters. When the starter raised the gun, all eyes focused on the runners. At the crack of the starter's gun, the runners leaped into motion and sprinted down the track.

Seconds later, the race was over. The runners, bursting with pride, hugged each other and their coaches. It didn't matter where each of the runners placed. All that mattered was that they had finished the race and done their best. These athletes were running in the Special Olympics, a competition for people with disabilities.

Many of the athletes who compete in the Special Olympics have disabilities that result from genetic disorders. A **genetic disorder** is an abnormal condition that a person inherits through genes or chromosomes. **Genetic disorders are caused by mutations, or changes in a person's DNA.** In some cases, a mutation occurs when sex cells form during meiosis. In other cases, a mutation that is already present in a parent's cells is passed on to the offspring. In this section, you will learn about some common genetic disorders.

GUIDE FOR READING

◆ What causes genetic disorders?

◆ How are genetic disorders diagnosed?

Reading Tip As you read, make a list of different types of genetic disorders. Write a sentence about each disorder.

Key Terms genetic disorder • amniocentesis • karyotype

A runner at the Special Olympics ▶

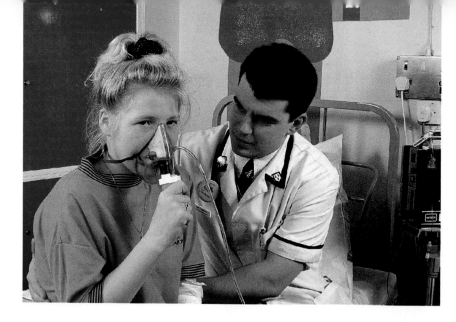

Figure 7 Cystic fibrosis is a genetic disorder that causes thick mucus to build up in a person's lungs and intestines. This patient is inhaling a fine mist that will help loosen the mucus in her lungs.

Cystic Fibrosis

Cystic fibrosis is a genetic disorder in which the body produces abnormally thick mucus in the lungs and intestines. The thick mucus fills the lungs, making it hard for the affected person to breathe. Bacteria that grow in the mucus can cause infections and, eventually, lung damage. In the intestines, the mucus makes it difficult for digestion to occur.

The mutation that leads to cystic fibrosis is carried on a recessive allele. The cystic fibrosis allele is most common among people whose ancestors are from Northern Europe. Every day in this country, four babies are born with cystic fibrosis.

Currently there is no cure for cystic fibrosis. Medical treatments include drugs to prevent infections and physical therapy to break up mucus in the lungs. Recent advances in scientists' understanding of the disease may lead to better treatments and longer lifespans for people with cystic fibrosis.

✓ *Checkpoint* *What are some symptoms of cystic fibrosis?*

Figure 8 Normally, red blood cells are shaped like round disks (top). In a person with sickle-cell disease, red blood cells can become sickle-shaped (bottom). *Relating Cause and Effect What combination of alleles leads to sickle-cell disease?*

Sickle-Cell Disease

Sickle-cell disease is a genetic disorder that affects the blood. The mutation that causes the disorder affects the production of an important protein called hemoglobin. Hemoglobin is the protein in red blood cells that carries oxygen. People with sickle-cell disease produce an abnormal form of hemoglobin. When oxygen concentrations are low, their red blood cells have an unusual sickle shape, as you can see in Figure 8.

Sickle-shaped red blood cells cannot carry as much oxygen as normal-shaped cells. Because of their shape, the cells become stuck in narrow blood vessels, blocking them. People with sickle-cell disease suffer from lack of oxygen in the blood and experience pain and weakness.

The allele for the sickle-cell trait is most common in people of African ancestry. About 9 percent of African Americans carry the sickle-cell allele. The allele for the sickle-cell trait is codominant with the normal allele. A person with two sickle-cell alleles will have the disease. A person with one sickle-cell allele will produce both normal hemoglobin and abnormal hemoglobin. This person usually will not have symptoms of the disease.

Currently, there is no cure for sickle-cell disease. People with sickle-cell disease are given drugs to relieve their painful symptoms and to prevent blockages in blood vessels. As with cystic fibrosis, scientists are hopeful that new, successful treatments will soon be found.

Hemophilia

Hemophilia is a genetic disorder in which a person's blood clots very slowly or not at all. People with the disorder do not produce one of the proteins needed for normal blood clotting. A person with hemophilia can bleed to death from a minor cut or scrape. The danger of internal bleeding from small bumps and bruises is also very high.

Hemophilia is an example of a disorder that is caused by a recessive allele on the X chromosome. Because hemophilia is a sex-linked disorder, it occurs more frequently in males than in females. **INTEGRATING HEALTH** People with hemophilia must get regular doses of the missing clotting protein. In general, people with hemophilia can lead normal lives. However, they are advised to avoid contact sports and other activities that could cause internal injuries.

Social Studies CONNECTION

Hemophilia has affected European history. Queen Victoria of England had a son and three grandsons with hemophilia. Victoria, at least two of her daughters, and four of her granddaughters were carriers of the disease.

As Victoria's descendants passed the hemophilia allele to their offspring, hemophilia spread through the royal families of Europe. For example, Empress Alexandra, Queen Victoria's granddaughter, married the Russian Czar Nicholas II in 1894. Alexandra, a carrier of hemophilia, passed the disease to her son Alexis, who was heir to the throne.

A monk named Rasputin convinced Alexandra that he could cure Alexis. As a result of his control over Alexandra, Rasputin was able to control the Czar as well. The people's anger at Rasputin's influence may have played a part in the Russian Revolution of 1917, in which the Czar was overthrown.

In Your Journal

Imagine that you are Empress Alexandra. Write a diary entry expressing your feelings and unanswered questions about Alexis's condition.

Figure 9 Empress Alexandra of Russia (center row, left) passed the allele for hemophilia to her son Alexis (front).

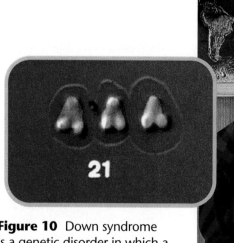

Figure 10 Down syndrome is a genetic disorder in which a person's cells have an extra copy of chromosome 21. Although people with Down syndrome have some mental and physical limitations, they can lead active, productive lives.

Down Syndrome

Some genetic disorders are the result of too many or too few chromosomes. In one such disorder, called Down syndrome, a person's cells have an extra copy of chromosome 21. The extra chromosome is the result of an error during meiosis. Recall that in meiosis, cells divide and chromosomes separate to produce sex cells with half the normal chromosome number. Down syndrome most often occurs when chromosomes fail to separate properly during meiosis.

People with Down syndrome have a distinctive physical appearance, and have some degree of mental retardation. Heart defects are also common, but can be treated. Despite their limitations, many people with Down syndrome lead full, active lives.

Diagnosing Genetic Disorders

INTEGRATING TECHNOLOGY Years ago, doctors had only Punnett squares and pedigrees to help them predict whether a child might have a genetic disorder. **Today doctors use tools such as amniocentesis and karyotypes to help detect genetic disorders.**

Before a baby is born, doctors can use a procedure called **amniocentesis** (am nee oh sen TEE sis) to determine whether the baby will have some genetic disorders. During amniocentesis, a doctor uses a very long needle to remove a small amount of the fluid that surrounds the developing baby. The fluid contains cells from the baby.

The doctor then examines the chromosomes from the cells. To do this, the doctor creates a karyotype. A **karyotype** (KA ree uh typ) is a picture of all the chromosomes in a cell. The chromosomes in a karyotype are arranged in pairs. A karyotype can reveal whether a developing baby has the correct number of chromosomes in its cells and whether it is a boy or a girl. If you did the Discover activity, you saw a karyotype from a girl with Down syndrome.

Genetic Counseling

A couple that has a family history or concern about a genetic disorder may turn to a genetic counselor for advice. Genetic counselors help couples understand their chances of having a child with a particular genetic disorder. Genetic counselors use tools such as karyotypes, pedigree charts, and Punnett squares to help them in their work.

Suppose, for example, that a husband and wife both have a history of cystic fibrosis in their families. If they are considering having children, they might seek the advice of a genetic counselor. The genetic counselor might order a test to determine whether they are carriers of the allele for cystic fibrosis. The genetic counselor would then apply the same principles of probability that you learned about in Chapter 16 to calculate the couple's chances of having a child with cystic fibrosis.

Figure 11 Couples may meet with a genetic counselor and their doctor in order to understand their chances of having a child with a genetic disorder.

Section 2 Review

1. Explain how genetic disorders occur in humans. Give two examples of genetic disorders.
2. Describe two tools that doctors use to detect genetic disorders.
3. How do the cells of people with Down syndrome differ from those of others? How might this difference arise?
4. **Thinking Critically** **Problem Solving** A couple with a family history of hemophilia is about to have a baby girl. What information about the parents would you want to know? How would this information help you determine whether the baby will have hemophilia?

Check Your Progress

CHAPTER PROJECT

At this point, you should begin to trace the inheritance of another trait through the same family members that are in your first pedigree. Also, start making your family "photo" album. Will you use drawings or some other method to show what the family members look like? (*Hint:* Photo albums show phenotypes. Remember that more than one genotype can have the same phenotype.)

Family Puzzles

Imagine that you are a genetic counselor. Two couples come to you for advice. Their family histories are summarized in the boxes labeled *Case Study 1* and *Case Study 2*. They want to understand more about certain genetic disorders that run in their families. In this lab, you will find answers to their questions.

Problem

How can you investigate inheritance patterns in families?

Materials

12 index cards
scissors
marker

Procedure

Part 1 Investigating Case Study 1

1. Read over Case Study 1. In your notebook, draw a pedigree that shows all the family members. Use circles to represent the females, and squares to represent the males. Shade in the circles or squares representing the individuals who have cystic fibrosis.

Case Study 1: Joshua and Bella

◆ Joshua and Bella have a son named Ian. Ian has been diagnosed with cystic fibrosis.
◆ Joshua and Bella are both healthy.
◆ Bella's parents are both healthy.
◆ Joshua's parents are both healthy.
◆ Joshua's sister, Sara, has cystic fibrosis.

2. You know that cystic fibrosis is controlled by a recessive allele. To help you figure out Joshua and Bella's family pattern, create a set of cards to represent the alleles. Cut each of six index cards into four smaller cards. On 12 of the small cards, write *N* to represent the dominant normal allele. On the other 12 small cards, write *n* for the recessive allele.

3. Begin by using the cards to represent Ian's alleles. Since he has cystic fibrosis, what alleles must he have? Write in this genotype next to the pedigree symbol for Ian.

4. Joshua's sister, Sara, also has cystic fibrosis. What alleles does she have? Write in this genotype next to the pedigree symbol that represents Sara.

Case Study 2: Li and Mai

- The father, Li, has a skin condition. The mother, Mai, has normal skin.
- Li and Mai's first child, a girl named Gemma, has the same skin condition as Li.
- Mai's sister has a similar skin condition, but Mai's parents do not.
- Li has one brother whose skin is normal, and one sister who has the skin condition.
- Li's mother has the skin condition. His father does not.
- Li's family lives in a heavily wooded area. His family has always thought the skin condition was a type of allergy.

5. Now use the cards to figure out what genotypes Joshua and Bella must have. Write their genotypes next to their symbols in the pedigree.

6. Work with the cards to figure out the genotypes of all other family members. Fill in each person's genotype next to his or her symbol in the pedigree. If more than one genotype is possible, write in both genotypes.

Part 2 Investigating Case Study 2

7. Read over Case Study 2.

8. You suspect that Gemma and Li's skin condition is caused by an inherited recessive allele. Begin to investigate this possibility by drawing a family pedigree in your notebook. Use shading to indicate which individuals have the skin condition.

9. Fill in the genotype *ss* beside each individual who has the skin condition. Then use cards as you did in Case Study 1 to figure out each family member's genotype. If more than one genotype is possible, fill in both genotypes.

Analyze and Conclude

1. In Case Study 1, what were the genotypes of Joshua's parents? What were the genotypes of Bella's parents?

2. In Case Study 1, Joshua also has a brother. What is the probability that he has cystic fibrosis? Explain.

3. Can you conclude that the skin condition in Case Study 2 is most likely an inherited trait controlled by a recessive allele? Explain.

4. What is the probability that Mai and Li's next child will have the skin condition? Explain.

5. **Apply** Why do genetic counselors need information about many generations of a family in order to draw conclusions about a hereditary condition?

More to Explore

Review the two pedigrees that you just studied. What data suggest that the traits are not sex-linked? Explain.

SECTION 3 Advances in Genetics

GUIDE FOR READING

◆ What are three ways in which an organism's traits can be altered?

◆ What is the goal of the Human Genome Project?

Reading Tip As you read, make a concept map of the methods used to produce organisms with desirable traits. Include at least one example of each technique.

Key Terms selective breeding • inbreeding • hybridization • clone • genetic engineering • gene therapy • genome

▼ Dolly

In the summer of 1996, a lamb named Dolly was born in Scotland. Dolly was an ordinary lamb in every way except one. The fertilized cell that developed into Dolly was produced in a laboratory by geneticists using experimental techniques. You will learn more about the techniques used by the geneticists later in the section.

Although the techniques used to create Dolly are new, the idea of producing organisms with specific traits is not. For thousands of years, people have tried to produce plants and animals with desirable traits. **Three methods that people have used to develop organisms with desirable traits are selective breeding, cloning, and genetic engineering.**

Selective Breeding

More than 5,000 years ago, people living in what is now central Mexico discovered that a type of wild grass could be used as food. They saved the seeds from those plants that produced the best food, and planted them to grow new plants. By repeating this process over many generations of plants, they developed an early variety of the food crop we now call corn. The process of selecting a few organisms with desired traits to serve as parents of the next generation is called **selective breeding.**

People have used selective breeding with many different plants and animals. Breeding programs usually focus on increasing the value of the plant or animal to people.

For example, dairy cows are bred to produce larger quantities of milk. Many varieties of fruits and vegetables are bred to resist diseases and insect pests.

Inbreeding One useful selective breeding technique is called inbreeding. **Inbreeding** involves crossing two individuals that have identical or similar sets of alleles. The organisms that result from inbreeding have alleles that are very similar to those of their parents. Mendel used inbreeding to produce purebred pea plants for his experiments.

One goal of inbreeding is to produce breeds of animals with specific traits. For example, by only crossing horses with exceptional speed, breeders can produce purebred horses that can run very fast. Purebred dogs, such as Labrador retrievers and German shepherds, were produced by inbreeding.

Unfortunately, because inbred organisms are genetically very similar, inbreeding reduces an offspring's chances of inheriting new allele combinations. Inbreeding also increases the probability that organisms may be homozygous for alleles that lead to genetic disorders. For example, inherited hip problems are common in many breeds of dogs.

Hybridization Another selective breeding technique is called hybridization. In **hybridization** (hy brid ih ZAY shun), breeders cross two genetically different individuals. The hybrid organism that results is bred to have the best traits from both parents. For example, a farmer might cross corn that produces many kernels with corn that is resistant to disease. The result might be a hybrid corn plant with both of the desired traits. Today, most crops grown on farms and in gardens were produced by hybridization.

Figure 13 Plants can be easily cloned by making a cutting. Once the cutting has grown roots, it can be planted and will grow into a new plant. *Applying Concepts Why is the new plant considered to be a clone of the original plant?*

Cloning

One problem with selective breeding is that the breeder cannot control whether the desired allele will be passed from the parent to its offspring. This is because the transmission of alleles is determined by probability, as you learned in Chapter 16. For some organisms, another technique, called cloning, can be used to produce offspring with desired traits. A **clone** is an organism that is genetically identical to the organism from which it was produced. This means that a clone has exactly the same genes as the organism it came from. Cloning can be done in plants and animals, as well as other organisms.

Cloning Plants One way to produce a clone of a plant is through a cutting. A cutting is a small part of a plant, such as a leaf or a stem, that is cut from the plant. The cutting can grow into an entire new plant. The new plant is genetically identical to the plant from which the cutting was taken.

Cloning Animals Remember Dolly, the lamb described at the beginning of this section? Dolly was the first clone of an adult mammal. To create Dolly, researchers first removed an egg cell from one sheep. The cell's nucleus was replaced with the nucleus from a cell of a six-year-old sheep. The egg was then implanted into the uterus of a third sheep. Five months later, Dolly was born. Dolly is genetically identical to the six-year-old sheep that supplied the cell nucleus. Dolly is a clone of that sheep.

Since scientists first cloned Dolly, pigs and calves have also been cloned. Scientists hope that cloning animals will allow humans to live healthier lives. For example, pigs are being cloned that have special genes, which will make their organs suitable for organ transplants into humans.

✓ *Checkpoint* How can a clone of a plant be produced?

Genetic Engineering

In the past few decades, geneticists have developed another powerful technique for producing organisms with desired traits. In this technique, called **genetic engineering,** genes from one organism are transferred into the DNA of another organism. Genetic engineering is sometimes called "gene splicing" because a DNA molecule is cut open and a gene from another organism is spliced into it. Genetic engineering can produce medicines and improve food crops, and may cure human genetic disorders.

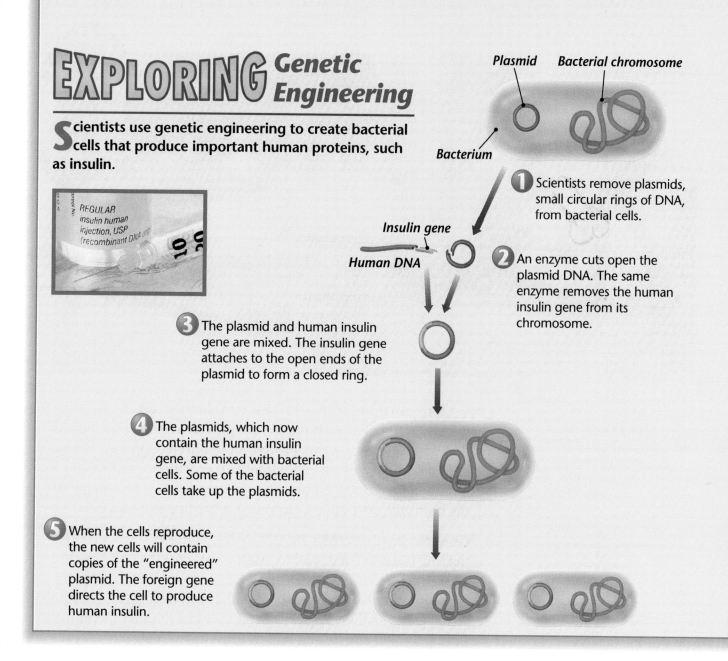

EXPLORING Genetic Engineering

Scientists use genetic engineering to create bacterial cells that produce important human proteins, such as insulin.

Plasmid   **Bacterial chromosome**

Bacterium

REGULAR
insulin human
injection, USP
(recombinant DNA

① Scientists remove plasmids, small circular rings of DNA, from bacterial cells.

Insulin gene

Human DNA

② An enzyme cuts open the plasmid DNA. The same enzyme removes the human insulin gene from its chromosome.

③ The plasmid and human insulin gene are mixed. The insulin gene attaches to the open ends of the plasmid to form a closed ring.

④ The plasmids, which now contain the human insulin gene, are mixed with bacterial cells. Some of the bacterial cells take up the plasmids.

⑤ When the cells reproduce, the new cells will contain copies of the "engineered" plasmid. The foreign gene directs the cell to produce human insulin.

Genetic Engineering in Bacteria Researchers had their first successes with genetic engineering when they inserted DNA from other organisms into bacteria. Bacterial cells have a major DNA molecule, or chromosome, in the cytoplasm. Some bacterial cells also contain small circular pieces of DNA called plasmids.

In *Exploring Genetic Engineering,* you can see how scientists insert a human gene into the plasmid of a bacterium. Once the DNA is spliced into the plasmid, the bacterial cell and all its offspring will contain this human gene. As a result, the bacteria produce the protein that the human gene codes for, in this case insulin. Because bacteria reproduce quickly, large amounts of insulin can be produced in a short time. The insulin can be collected and used to treat people with diabetes, a disorder in which the body does not produce enough of this protein.

Figure 14 Scientists created this new variety of tomatoes using genetic engineering. The tomatoes taste better and keep longer than other varieties.
Making Judgments What other traits would be desirable in tomatoes?

Today, many human proteins are produced in genetically engineered bacteria. For example, human growth hormone is a protein that controls the growth process in children. Children whose bodies do not produce enough human growth hormone can be given injections of the hormone. Today, an unlimited supply of the hormone exists, thanks to genetically engineered bacteria.

Genetic Engineering in Other Organisms Genetic engineering has also been used to insert genes into the cells of other organisms. Scientists have inserted genes from bacteria into the cells of tomatoes, wheat, rice, and other important crops. Some of the genes enable the plants to survive in colder temperatures or in poor soil conditions, and to resist insect pests.

Genetic engineering techniques can also be used to insert genes into animals, which then produce important medicines for humans. For example, scientists can insert human genes into the cells of cows. The cows then produce the human protein for which the gene codes. Scientists have used this technique to produce the blood-clotting protein needed by people with hemophilia. The protein is produced in the cows' milk, and can easily be extracted and used to treat people with the disorder.

Gene Therapy Researchers are also using genetic engineering to try to correct some genetic disorders. This process, called **gene therapy,** involves inserting working copies of a gene directly into the cells of a person with a genetic disorder. For example, people with cystic fibrosis do not produce a protein that is needed for proper lung function. Both copies of the gene that codes for the protein are defective in these people.

Scientists can insert working copies of the gene into harmless viruses. The "engineered" viruses can then be sprayed into the lungs of patients with cystic fibrosis. The researchers hope that the working copies of the gene in the viruses will function in the patient to produce the protein. Gene therapy is still an experimental method for treating genetic disorders. Researchers are working hard to improve this promising technique.

DNA Fingerprinting

In courtrooms across the country, a genetic technique called DNA fingerprinting is being used to help solve crimes. If you did the Discover activity, you know that fingerprints can help to identify people. No two people have the same fingerprints. Detectives routinely use fingerprints found at a crime scene to help identify the person who committed the crime. In a similar way, DNA from samples of hair, skin, and blood can also be used to identify a person. No two people, except for identical twins, have the same DNA.

In DNA fingerprinting, chemicals called enzymes are used to cut some DNA found at a crime scene into fragments. An electrical current then separates the fragments by size to form a pattern of bands, like the ones you see in Figure 15. Each person's pattern of DNA bands is unique. The DNA pattern can then be compared to the pattern produced by DNA taken from people suspected of committing the crime.

☑ *Checkpoint* **In what way is DNA like fingerprints?**

Figure 15 This scientist is explaining how DNA finger-printing can be used to help solve crimes. DNA from blood or other substances collected at a crime scene can be compared to DNA from a suspect's blood.

Figure 16 The goal of the Human Genome Project is to identify the sequence of every DNA base pair in the human genome.

The Human Genome Project

Imagine trying to crack a code that is 3 billion characters long. Then imagine working with people all over the world to accomplish this task. That's exactly what scientists working on the Human Genome Project are doing. A **genome** is all the DNA in one cell of an organism. Researchers estimate that the 23 pairs of chromosomes that make up the human genome contain about 60,000 to 80,000 genes—or about 3 billion DNA base pairs.

The main goal of the Human Genome Project is to identify the DNA sequence of every gene in the human genome. The Human Genome Project will provide scientists with an encyclopedia of genetic information about humans. Scientists will know the DNA sequence of every human gene, and thus the amino acid sequence of every protein.

With the information from the Human Genome Project, researchers may gain a better understanding of how humans develop from a fertilized egg to an adult. They may also learn what makes the body work, and what causes things to go wrong. New understandings may lead to new treatments and prevention strategies for many genetic disorders and for diseases such as cancer.

Section 3 Review

1. Name three techniques that people have used to produce organisms with desired traits.
2. Why do scientists want to identify the DNA sequence of every human gene?
3. What is genetic engineering? Describe three possible benefits of this technique.
4. Explain how a DNA fingerprint is produced. What information can a DNA fingerprint reveal?
5. **Thinking Critically Making Judgments** Do you think there should be any limitations on genetic engineering? Give reasons to support your position.

Science at Home

Grocery Genetics With a parent or other adult family member, go to a grocery store. Look at the different varieties of potatoes, apples, and other fruits and vegetables. Discuss how these varieties were created by selective breeding. Then choose one type of fruit or vegetable and make a list of different varieties. If possible, find out what traits each variety was bred for.

Who Should Have Access to Genetic Test Results?

Scientists working on the Human Genome Project have identified many alleles that put people at risk for certain diseases, such as breast cancer and Alzheimer's disease. Through techniques known as genetic testing, people can have their DNA analyzed to find out whether they have any of these alleles. If they do, they may be able to take steps to prevent the illness or to seek early treatment.

Some health insurance companies and employers want access to this type of genetic information. However, many people believe that genetic testing results should be kept private.

The Issues

Why Do Insurance Companies Want Genetic Information? Health insurance companies set their rates based on a person's risk of health problems. To determine a person's insurance rate, insurance companies often require that a person have a physical examination. If the examination reveals a condition such as high blood pressure, the company may charge that person more for an insurance policy. This is because he or she would be more likely to need expensive medical care.

Insurance companies view genetic testing as an additional way to gather information about a person's health status. Insurers argue that if they were unable to gather this information, they would need to raise rates for everyone. This would be unfair to people who are in good health.

Why Do Employers Want Genetic Information? Federal laws forbid employers with 15 or more workers from choosing job applicants based on their health status. These laws

do not apply to smaller companies, however. Employers may not want to hire employees with health problems because they often miss more work time than other employees. In addition, employers who hire people with health problems may be charged higher health insurance rates. Many small companies cannot afford to pay these higher rates.

Should Genetic Information Be Kept Private? Some people think that the government should prohibit all access to genetic information. Today, some people fear that they will be discriminated against as a result of genetic test results. Because of this fear, some people avoid genetic testing—even though testing might allow them to seek early treatment for a disorder. These people want tighter control of genetic information. They want to be sure that insurers and employers will not have access to genetic test results.

You Decide

1. Identify the Problem

In your own words, explain the problem of deciding who should have access to genetic test results.

2. Analyze the Options

Examine the pros and cons of keeping genetic test results private. List some reasons to maintain privacy. List some important reasons why test results should be shared.

3. Find a Solution

Create a list of rules to control access to genetic information. Who should have access, and under what circumstances? Explain your reasoning.

Guilty or Innocent?

In this lab, you will investigate how DNA fingerprinting can be used to provide evidence related to a crime.

Problem

How can DNA be used to identify individuals?

Skills Focus

observing, making models, drawing conclusions

Materials

4–6 bar codes   magnifying glass

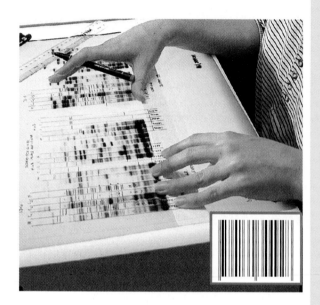

Procedure

1. Look at the photograph of DNA band patterns shown at right. Each person's DNA produces a unique pattern of these bands.
2. Now look at the Universal Product Code, also called a bar code, shown below the DNA bands. A bar code can be used as a model of a DNA band pattern. Compare the bar code with the DNA bands to see what they have in common. Record your observations.
3. Suppose that a burglary has taken place, and you're the detective leading the investigation. Your teacher will give you a bar code that represents DNA from blood found at the crime scene. You arrange to have DNA samples taken from several suspects. Write a sentence describing what you will look for as you try to match each suspect's DNA to the DNA sample from the crime scene.
4. You will now be given bar codes representing DNA samples taken from the suspects. Compare those bar codes with the bar code that represents DNA from the crime scene.

5. Use your comparisons to determine whether any of the suspects was present at the crime scene.

Analyze and Conclude

1. Based on your findings, were any of the suspects present at the crime scene? Support your conclusion with specific evidence.
2. Why do people's DNA patterns differ so greatly?
3. How would your conclusions be affected if you learned that the suspect whose DNA matched the evidence had an identical twin?
4. **Apply** In everyday life, do you think that DNA evidence is enough to determine that a suspect committed the crime? Explain.

More to Explore

Do you think the DNA fingerprints of a parent and a child would show any similarities? Draw what you think they would look like. Then explain your thinking.

SECTION 1 Human Inheritance

Key Ideas

◆ Some human traits are controlled by a single gene that has multiple alleles—three or more forms.

◆ Some human traits show a wide range of phenotypes because these traits are controlled by many genes. The genes act together as a group to produce a single trait.

◆ Traits are often influenced by the organism's environment.

◆ Males have one X chromosome and one Y chromosome. Females have two X chromosomes. Males are more likely than females to have a sex-linked trait controlled by a recessive allele.

◆ Geneticists use pedigrees to trace the inheritance pattern of a particular trait through a number of generations of a family.

Key Terms

multiple alleles   carrier
sex-linked gene   pedigree

 SECTION 2 Human Genetic Disorders

Key Ideas

◆ Genetic disorders are abnormal conditions that are caused by mutations, or DNA changes, in genes or chromosomes.

◆ Common genetic disorders include cystic fibrosis, sickle-cell disease, hemophilia, and Down syndrome.

◆ Amniocentesis and karyotypes are tools used to diagnose genetic disorders.

◆ Genetic counselors help couples understand their chances of having a child with a genetic disorder.

Key Terms

genetic disorder   karyotype
amniocentesis

 SECTION 3 Advances in Genetics

INTEGRATING TECHNOLOGY

Key Ideas

◆ Selective breeding is the process of selecting a few organisms with desired traits to serve as parents of the next generation.

◆ Cloning is a technique used to produce genetically identical organisms.

◆ Genetic engineering can be used to produce medicines and to improve food crops. Researchers are also using genetic engineering to try to cure human genetic disorders.

◆ DNA fingerprinting can be used to help determine whether material found at a crime scene came from a particular suspect.

◆ The goal of the Human Genome Project is to identify the DNA sequence of every gene in the human genome.

Key Terms

selective breeding   genetic engineering
inbreeding   gene therapy
hybridization   genome
clone

Organizing Information

Concept Map Copy the concept map about human traits onto a separate sheet of paper. Then complete it and add a title. (For more on concept maps, see the Skills Handbook.)

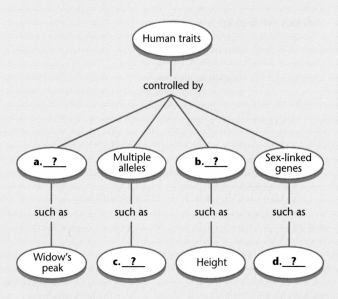

Reviewing Content

Review key concepts online using iText at www.phschool.com

Multiple Choice

Choose the letter of the best answer.

1. A human trait that is controlled by multiple alleles is
   a. dimples.
   b. blood type.
   c. height.
   d. skin color.

2. A genetic disorder caused by a sex-linked gene is
   a. cystic fibrosis.
   b. sickle-cell disease.
   c. hemophilia.
   d. Down syndrome.

3. Sickle-cell disease is characterized by
   a. abnormally shaped red blood cells.
   b. abnormally thick body fluids.
   c. abnormal blood clotting.
   d. an extra copy of chromosome 21.

4. Inserting a human gene into a bacterial plasmid is an example of
   a. inbreeding.
   b. selective breeding.
   c. DNA fingerprinting.
   d. genetic engineering.

5. DNA fingerprinting is a way to
   a. clone organisms.
   b. breed organisms with desirable traits.
   c. identify people.
   d. map and sequence human genes.

True or False

If the statement is true, write true. If it is false, change the underlined word or words to make the statement true.

6. A widow's peak is a human trait that is controlled by a single gene.

7. A person who inherits two X chromosomes will be male.

8. A karyotype is a chart that shows the relationships between the generations of a family.

9. Hybridization is the crossing of two genetically similar organisms.

10. A clone is an organism that is genetically identical to another organism.

Checking Concepts

11. Is a person's health determined by genes, the environment, or interaction between genes and the environment? Explain.

12. Explain why traits controlled by recessive alleles on the X chromosome are more common in males than in females.

13. What is sickle-cell disease? How is this disorder inherited?

14. How can amniocentesis be used to detect a disorder such as Down syndrome?

15. Explain how a horse breeder might use selective breeding to produce horses that have golden coats.

16. Describe how gene therapy might be used in the future to treat a person with hemophilia.

17. **Writing to Learn** As the webmaster for a national genetics foundation, you must create a Web site to inform the public about genetic disorders. Choose one human genetic disorder discussed in this chapter. Write a description of the disorder that you will use for the Web site.

Thinking Critically

18. **Applying Concepts** Why can a person be a carrier of a trait caused by a recessive allele but not of a trait caused by a dominant allele?

19. **Problem Solving** A woman with normal color vision has a colorblind daughter. What are the genotypes and phenotypes of both parents?

20. **Calculating** If a mother is a carrier of hemophilia, what is the probability that her son will have the trait? Explain your answer.

21. **Inferring** How could ancient people selectively breed corn if they didn't know about genes and inheritance?

22. **Comparing and Contrasting** How are selective breeding and genetic engineering different? How are they similar?

Applying Skills

Use the information below to answer Questions 23–25.

◆ Bob and Helen have three children.

◆ Bob and Helen have one son who has albinism, an inherited condition in which the skin does not have brown pigments.

◆ Bob and Helen have two daughters who do not have albinism.

◆ Neither Bob nor Helen has albinism.

◆ Albinism is neither sex-linked nor codominant.

23. Interpreting Data Use the information to construct a pedigree. If you don't know whether people are carriers, leave their symbols empty. If you decide later that a person is a carrier, change your pedigree.

24. Drawing Conclusions Is albinism controlled by a dominant allele or by a recessive allele? Explain your answer.

25. Predicting Suppose Bob and Helen were to have another child. What is the probability that the child will have albinism? Explain.

Performance ▽CHAPTER PROJECT Assessment

Present Your Project Before displaying your project, exchange it with another group to check each other's work. Make any necessary corrections, and then display your materials to the class. Be ready to explain the inheritance patterns shown in your pedigrees.

Reflect and Record In your journal, describe what you learned by creating the pedigrees. What questions do you have as a result of the project?

Test Preparation

Use these questions to prepare for standardized tests.

Use the information to answer Questions 26–29. The Punnett square below shows how muscular dystrophy, a sex-linked recessive disorder, is inherited.

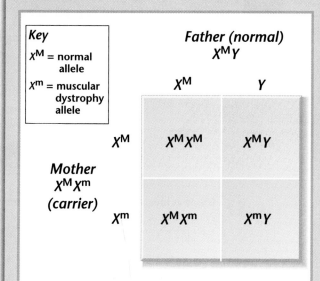

Key
X^M = normal allele
X^m = muscular dystrophy allele

Father (normal)
$X^M Y$

	X^M	Y
X^M	$X^M X^M$	$X^M Y$
X^m	$X^M X^m$	$X^m Y$

Mother $X^M X^m$ (carrier)

26. What is the probability that a daughter of these parents will have muscular dystrophy?
A 0%   B 25%
C 50%   D 100%

27. What is the probability that a son of these parents will have muscular dystrophy?
F 0%   G 25%
H 50%   J 100%

28. What is the probability that a daughter of these parents will be a carrier of the disease?
A 0%   B 25%
C 50%   D 100%

29. Which of the following statements is true?
F More males than females have muscular dystrophy.
G More females than males have muscular dystrophy.
H More males than females are carriers of muscular dystrophy.
J No females can have muscular dystrophy.

WEB ACTIVITY

www.phschool.com

614

Life's Long Calendar

How far back in your life can you remember? Think of how life has changed in the last 10, 50, or 100 years. This chapter looks back in time as well. But instead of looking back hundreds of years, you'll explore millions, hundreds of millions, and even billions of years.

The geologic evidence indicates that the time frame of Earth's history is so large that it can be overwhelming. This project will help you understand it. In this project, you'll find a way to convert enormous time periods into a more familiar scale.

Your Goal To use a familiar measurement scale to create two time lines for Earth's history.

To complete the project you will

- represent Earth's history using a familiar scale, such as hours on a clock, months on a calendar, or yards on a football field
- use your chosen scale twice, once to plot out 5 billion years of history, and then to focus on the past 600 million years
- include markers on both scales to show certain blocks of time in the history of life

Get Started Preview *Exploring Life's History* on pages 632–633 to see the time periods in Earth's geologic history. In a small group, discuss some familiar scales you might use for your time lines. You could select a time interval such as a year or a day. Alternatively, you could choose a distance interval such as the length of your schoolyard or the walls in your classroom. Decide on the kind of time lines you will make.

Check Your Progress You will be working on this project as you study this chapter. To keep your project on track, look for Check Your Progress boxes at the following points.

Section 1 Review, page 626: Plan your time lines.
Section 3 Review, page 639: Construct your time lines.

Present Your Project At the end of the chapter (page 643), you'll display your time lines for the class.

This *Triceratops* lived in western North America about 70 million years ago. It used its sharp horns to defend itself against predators.

TEKS

In addition to process TEKS, this chapter addresses these concept TEKS as they relate to the chapter's topics.

(8.11) The student knows that traits of species can change through generations and that the instructions for traits are contained in the genetic material of the organisms. The student is expected to:
(A) identify that change in environmental conditions can affect the survival of individuals and of species.

(8.14) The student knows that natural events and human activities can alter Earth systems. The student is expected to:
(B) analyze how natural or human events may have contributed to the extinction of some species.

1 Darwin's Voyage

DISCOVER

ACTIVITY

How Do Living Things Vary?

1. Use a metric ruler to measure the length and width of 10 sunflower seeds. Record each measurement.

2. Now use a hand lens to carefully examine each seed. Record each seed's shape, color, and number of stripes.

Think It Over

Classifying In what ways are the seeds in your sample different from one another? In what ways are they similar? How could you group the seeds based on their similarities and differences?

GUIDE FOR READING

◆ How did Darwin explain the differences between species on the Galapagos Islands and on mainland South America?

◆ How did Darwin explain the role of natural selection in evolution?

◆ How might new species form?

Reading Tip As you read, make a list of main ideas and supporting details about evolution.

Key Terms species
• adaptation • evolution
• natural selection • variation

In December 1831, the British naval ship HMS *Beagle* set sail from England on a five-year-long trip around the world. On board was a 22-year-old named Charles Darwin. Darwin eventually became the ship's naturalist—a person who studies the natural world. His job was to learn as much as he could about the living things he saw on the voyage.

During the voyage, Darwin observed plants and animals he had never seen before. He wondered why they were so different from those in England. Darwin's observations led him to develop a scientific theory that is known as the theory of evolution by natural selection.

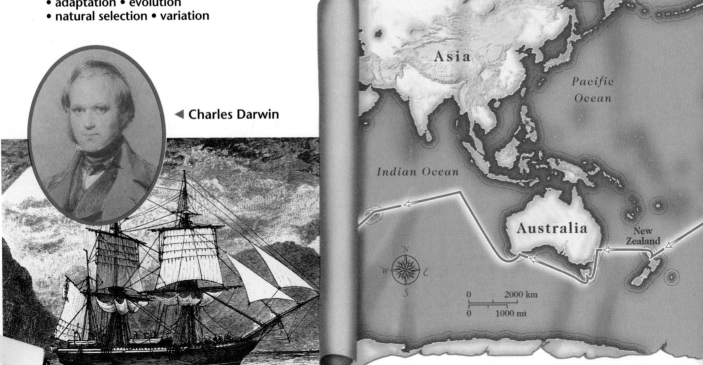

◀ Charles Darwin

Darwin's Observations

One of the *Beagle's* first stops was the coast of South America. In Brazil, Darwin saw insects that looked like flowers, and ants that marched across the forest floor like huge armies. In Argentina, he saw armadillos—burrowing animals covered with small, bony plates. He also saw sloths, animals that moved very slowly and spent much of their time hanging upside down in trees.

Darwin was amazed by the tremendous diversity, or variety, of living things. Today scientists know that living things are even more diverse than Darwin could ever have imagined. Scientists have identified more than 1.7 million species of organisms on Earth. A **species** is a group of similar organisms that can mate with each other and produce fertile offspring.

Darwin saw something else in Argentina that puzzled him: the bones of animals that had died long ago. From the bones, Darwin inferred that the animals had looked like the sloths he had seen. However, the bones were much larger than those of the living sloths. He wondered why only smaller sloths were alive today. What had happened to the giant sloths from the past?

In 1835, the *Beagle* reached the Galapagos Islands, a group of small islands in the Pacific Ocean off the west coast of South America. It was on the Galapagos Islands that Darwin observed many unusual life forms. For example, the giant tortoises, or land turtles, he saw were so tall that they could look him in the eye. He also saw seals covered with fur, and lizards that ate nothing but tough, prickly cactus plants.

Figure 1 Charles Darwin sailed on HMS *Beagle* from England to South America and then to the Galapagos Islands. He saw many unusual organisms on the Galapagos Islands.

Galapagos hawk ▼

▲ **Giant tortoise**

▲ **Sally lightfoot crab**

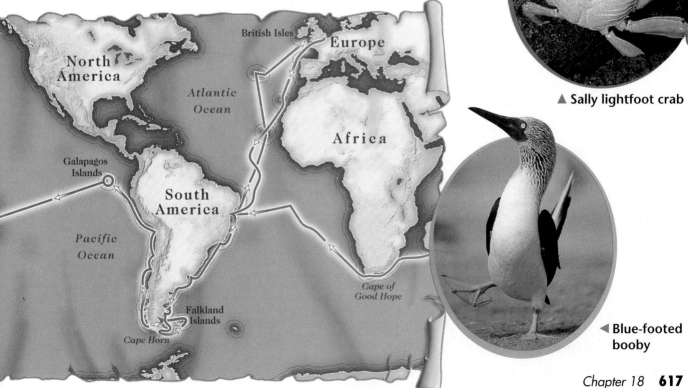

◄ **Blue-footed booby**

Similarities and Differences

Darwin was surprised that many of the plants and animals on the Galapagos Islands were similar to organisms on mainland South America. For example, many of the birds on the islands, including hawks, mockingbirds, and finches, resembled those on the mainland. Many of the plants were also similar to plants Darwin had collected on the mainland.

However, there were also important differences between the organisms on the islands and those on the mainland. Large sea birds called cormorants, for example, lived in both places. The cormorants on the mainland were able to fly, while those on the Galapagos Islands were unable to fly. The iguanas on the Galapagos Islands had large claws that allowed them to keep their grip on slippery rocks, where they fed on seaweed. The iguanas on the mainland had smaller claws. Smaller claws allowed the mainland iguanas to climb trees, where they ate leaves.

From his observations, Darwin inferred that a small number of different plant and animal species had come to the Galapagos Islands from the mainland. They might have been blown out to sea during a storm or set adrift on a fallen log. Once the plants and animals reached the islands, they reproduced. Eventually, their offspring became different from their mainland relatives.

Darwin also noticed many differences among similar organisms as he traveled from one Galapagos island to the next. For example, the tortoises on one island had dome-shaped shells. Those on another island had saddle-shaped shells. The governor of one of the islands told Darwin that he could tell which island a tortoise came from just by looking at its shell.

☑ *Checkpoint* *How did Darwin think plants and animals had originally come to the Galapagos Islands?*

Figure 2 Darwin observed many differences between organisms in South America and similar organisms on the Galapagos Islands. For example, green iguanas (left) live in South America. Marine iguanas (right) live on the Galapagos Islands. *Comparing and Contrasting How are the two species similar? How are they different?*

Figure 3 Darwin made these drawings of four species of Galapagos finches. The beak of each finch is adapted to the type of food it eats.

Adaptations

Like the tortoises, birds called finches on the Galapagos Islands were noticeably different from one island to another. The most obvious differences were the varied sizes and shapes of their beaks. As Darwin studied the different finches, he noticed that each species was well suited to the life it led. Finches that ate insects had sharp, needlelike beaks. Finches that ate seeds had strong, wide beaks. Beak shape is an example of an **adaptation,** a genetic trait that helps an organism survive and reproduce.

Evolution

After he returned to England, Darwin continued to think about what he had seen during his voyage on the *Beagle.* Darwin spent the next 20 years consulting with other scientists, gathering more information, and thinking through his ideas. He especially wanted to understand how the variety of similar organisms with different adaptations came to exist on the Galapagos Islands.

Darwin reasoned that plants and animals that arrived on one of the Galapagos Islands faced conditions that were different from those on the mainland. **Perhaps, Darwin thought, the species gradually changed over many generations and became better adapted to the new environment.** Scientists call the change in a species over long periods of time **evolution.**

Darwin's ideas are often referred to as the theory of evolution. Recall that a scientific theory is a well-tested concept that explains a wide range of observations. From the evidence and information he collected, Darwin concluded that organisms had changed over time on the Galapagos Islands. He did not know how this process took place. Darwin studied other examples of changes in living things to help him understand how evolution might occur.

Bird Beak Adaptations

Use this activity to explore adaptations in birds.

1. Scatter a small amount of birdseed into a petri dish. Scatter 20 raisins on the plate to represent insects.
2. Obtain a variety of objects such as tweezers, hair clips, clothes pins, and hairpins. Pick one object to use as a "beak."
3. See how many seeds you can pick up and drop into a cup in 10 seconds.
4. Now see how many "insects" you can pick up and drop into a cup in 10 seconds.
5. Use a different "beak" and repeat Steps 3 and 4.

Inferring What type of beak worked well for seeds? For insects? How are different-shaped beaks useful for eating different foods?

One example of change that Darwin studied was the offspring of animals produced by selective breeding. English farmers in Darwin's time used selective breeding to produce sheep with fine wool. Darwin himself had bred pigeons with large, fan-shaped tails. By repeatedly mating only those pigeons with many tail feathers, Darwin produced pigeons with two or three times the usual number of tail feathers. Darwin thought that a process similar to selective breeding happens in nature. But he wondered why certain traits were selected for, and how.

☑ *Checkpoint* **What observations led Darwin to propose his theory of evolution?**

Natural Selection

In 1858, Darwin and another British biologist, Alfred Russel Wallace, each proposed an explanation for how evolution could occur in nature. The next year, Darwin described this mechanism in a book entitled *The Origin of Species.* In his book, Darwin proposed that evolution occurs by means of natural selection. **Natural selection** is the process by which individuals that are better adapted to their environment are more likely to survive and reproduce than other members of the same species. Darwin identified factors that affect the process of natural selection: overproduction, competition, and variations.

Overproduction Darwin knew that most species produce far more offspring than can possibly survive. In many species, so many offspring are produced that there are not enough resources—food, water, and living space—for all of them. For example, each year a female sea turtle may lay more than 100 eggs. If all the young turtles survived, the sea would soon be full of turtles. Darwin knew that this doesn't happen. Why not?

Figure 4 Most young loggerhead sea turtles will not survive to adulthood.
Making Generalizations
What factors limit the number of young that survive?

Competition Since food and other resources are limited, the members of a species must compete with each other to survive. Competition does not usually involve direct physical fights. Instead, competition is usually indirect. For example, some turtles may not find enough to eat. Others may not escape from predators. Only a few turtles will survive long enough to reproduce.

Variations As you learned in your study of genetics, members of a species differ from one another in many of their traits. Any difference between individuals of the same species is called a **variation.** For example, some newly hatched turtles are able to swim faster than other turtles.

Selection Darwin observed that some variations make individuals better adapted to their environment. Those individuals are more likely to survive and reproduce. When they do reproduce, their offspring may inherit the allele for the helpful trait. The offspring, in turn, will be more likely to survive and reproduce, and thus pass on the allele to their offspring. After many generations, more members of the species will have the helpful trait. In effect, the environment has "selected" organisms with helpful traits to be the parents of the next generation—hence the term "natural selection." **Darwin proposed that over a long period of time, natural selection can lead to change. Helpful variations gradually accumulate in a species, while unfavorable ones disappear.**

A change in environmental conditions can affect an organism's ability to survive, and therefore lead to selection. For example, suppose a new predator moves into the turtles' habitat. Turtles that are fast swimmers would be more likely to escape from the new predator. The faster turtles are thus more likely to survive and reproduce. Over time, more and more turtles in the species would have the "fast-swimmer" trait.

Figure 5 The walruses lying on this rocky beach in Alaska must compete for resources. All organisms compete for limited resources such as food.

Inferring

Scatter 15 black buttons and 15 white buttons on a sheet of white paper. Have a partner time you to see how many buttons you can pick up in 10 seconds. Pick up the buttons one at a time.

Did you collect more buttons of one color than the other? Why? How can a variation such as color affect the process of natural selection?

Nature at Work

In this lab, you will investigate how natural selection might affect a species over time. You'll explore the interaction between genetic and environmental factors.

Problem

How might species change over time?

Materials

scissors   marking pen
construction paper, 2 colors
computer (optional)

Procedure

1. Work with two other students. One student should choose construction paper of one color and make the team's 50 "mouse" cards, as described in Table 1. The second student should choose a different color construction paper and make the team's 25 "event" cards, as described in Table 2. The third student should use the computer or pencil and paper to copy the data table and record all the data.

Part 1 A White Sand Environment

2. Mix up the mouse cards.
3. Begin by using the cards to model what might happen to a group of mice in an environment of white sand dunes. Choose two mouse cards. Allele pairs *WW* and *Ww* produce a white mouse. Allele pair *ww* produces a brown mouse. Record the color of the mouse with a tally mark in the data table.

4. Choose an event card. An "S" card means the mouse survives. A "D" or a "P" card means the mouse dies. A "C" card means the mouse dies if its color contrasts with the white sand dunes. (Only brown mice will die when a "C" card is drawn.) Record each death with a tally mark in the data table.
5. If the mouse lives, put the two mouse cards in a "live mice" pile. If the mouse dies, put the cards in a "dead mice" pile. Put the event card at the bottom of its pack.
6. Repeat Steps 3 through 5 with the remaining mouse cards to study the first generation of mice. Record your results.
7. Leave the dead mice cards untouched. Mix up the cards from the live mice pile. Mix up the events cards.
8. Repeat Steps 3 through 7 for the second generation. Then repeat Steps 3 through 6 for the third generation.

Table 1: "Mouse" Cards

Number	Label	Meaning
25	W	Dominant allele for white fur
25	w	Recessive allele for brown fur

Table 2: "Event" Cards

Number	Label	Meaning
5	S	Mouse survives.
1	D	Disease kills mouse.
1	P	Predator kills mice of all colors.
18	C	Predator kills mice that contrast with the environment.

DATA TABLE

Type of Environment: _____

Generation	White Mice	Brown Mice	Deaths	
			White Mice	Brown Mice
1				
2				
3				

Part 2 A Forest Floor Environment

9. How would the data differ if the mice in this model lived on a dark brown forest floor? Record your prediction in your notebook.

10. Make a new copy of the data table. Then use the cards to test your prediction. Remember that a "C" card now means that any mouse with white fur will die.

Analyze and Conclude

1. In Part 1, how many white mice were there in each generation? How many brown mice? In each generation, which color mouse had the higher death rate? (*Hint:* Death rate is expressed as a percentage. To calculate the death rate for white mice, divide the number of white mice that died by the total number of white mice, then multiply by 100%.)

2. If the events in Part 1 occurred in nature, how might the group of mice change over time?

3. How did the results in Part 2 differ from those in Part 1?

4. What are some ways in which this investigation models natural selection? What are some ways in which natural selection differs from this model?

5. **Think About It** How would it affect your model if you increased the number of "C" cards? If you decreased the number?

Design an Experiment

Choose a different species with a trait that interests you. Make a set of cards similar to these cards to investigate how natural selection might affect that trait over time.

The Role of Genes in Natural Selection

Without variations, all the members of a species would have the same traits. Natural selection would not occur because all individuals would have an equal chance of surviving and reproducing. But where do variations come from? How are they passed on from parents to offspring? Darwin could not answer these questions.

Darwin did not know anything about genes or chromosomes. It is not surprising that he could not explain what caused variations or how they were passed on. As scientists later learned, variations can result from the shuffling of alleles during meiosis. Only genes are passed from parents to their offspring. Because of this, only traits that are inherited, or controlled by genes, can be acted upon by natural selection.

Natural Selection in Action

Since Darwin published his book, scientists have observed many examples of natural selection in action. In a 1977 study of the finches on Daphne Major, one of the Galapagos Islands, scientists observed that beak size could change very quickly by natural selection. That year, little rain fell on the island—only 25 millimeters instead of the usual 130 millimeters or so. Because of the lack of rain, many plants died. Fewer of the seeds that the finches usually ate were available. Instead, the birds had to eat large seeds that were enclosed in tough, thorny seed pods.

Finches with larger and stronger beaks were better able to open the tough pods than were finches with smaller, weaker beaks. Many of the finches with smaller beaks did not survive the drought. The next year, more finches on the island had larger and stronger beaks. Natural selection had affected a group of organisms in just one year.

Figure 6 Light-gray peppered moths are easy to see on a dark background, while black moths can be seen on a light background. *Predicting Suppose all the buildings and trees in an area were black. Which kind of moth—light gray or black—might be better able to avoid the birds that feed on it?*

How Might New Species Form?

Natural selection explains how variations can lead to changes in a species. But how could an entirely new species form? Evidence collected since Darwin's time supports the idea that geographic isolation is one of the main ways that new species could form. Isolation, or complete separation, occurs when some members of a species become cut off from the rest of the species.

Sometimes a group is separated from the rest of its species by a river, volcano, or mountain range. Even an ocean wave can separate a few individuals from the rest of their species by sweeping them out to sea and later washing them ashore on an island. This may have happened on the Galapagos Islands. Once a group becomes isolated, members of the isolated group can no longer mate with members of the rest of the species.

A new species might form when a group of individuals remains separated from the rest of its species long enough to accumulate different traits. The longer the group remains isolated from the rest of the species, the more likely it is to develop into a new species. For example, Abert's squirrel and the Kaibab squirrel live in forests in the Southwest. Evidence indicates that about 10,000 years ago both types of squirrels were members of the same species. About that time, however, a small group of squirrels became isolated in a forest on the north side of the Grand Canyon in Arizona. Over time, this group developed into the Kaibab squirrel, which has a distinctive black belly. Scientists are not sure whether the Kaibab squirrel has become different enough from Abert's squirrel to be considered a separate species.

☑ *Checkpoint* *How did geographic isolation affect the Kaibab squirrel?*

Figure 7 About 10,000 years ago, a group of squirrels became isolated from the rest of the species. Since then, the Kaibab squirrel (left) has become different from Abert's squirrel (right).
Interpreting Maps *What geographic feature separates the range of the Kaibab squirrel from that of Abert's squirrel?*

Continental Drift

Geographic isolation may also have occurred on a worldwide scale. For example, evidence indicates that hundreds of millions of years ago all of Earth's land-masses were connected as one landmass. It formed a supercontinent called Pangaea. Organisms could migrate from one part of the supercontinent to another. Scientists hypothesize that over millions of years, Pangaea gradually split apart in a process called continental drift. As the continents separated, their environments changed and species became isolated from one another. Natural selection occurred.

Perhaps the most striking example of how continental drift might have affected species is on the continent of Australia. The organisms living in Australia have been isolated from all other organisms on Earth for millions of years. Many kinds of unique organisms live in Australia today. For example, most mammals in Australia belong to the group known as marsupials. Unlike other mammals, a marsupial gives birth to very small young that continue to develop in a pouch on the mother's body. Figure 8 shows two of the many marsupial species that exist in Australia. In contrast, few species of marsupials exist on other continents.

Figure 8 Many species of marsupials thrive in Australia. Australian marsupials include the numbat (top) and the spotted cuscus (bottom).

Section 1 Review

1. How did Darwin account for the differences between species on the Galapagos Islands and those in South America?
2. Explain why variations are needed for natural selection to occur.
3. Describe how geographic isolation might result in the formation of a new species.
4. **Thinking Critically Applying Concepts** Some insects look just like sticks. How could this be an advantage to the insects? How could this trait have developed through natural selection?

Check Your Progress

CHAPTER PROJECT

You should now be ready to submit your plans for your time lines to your teacher. Include a detailed list of the major time periods you will include on your time lines. Remember, you want to emphasize the life forms that were present at each period. When your plans are approved, begin to construct your time lines. (*Hint:* You will need to divide your time lines into equal-sized intervals. For example, if you use a 12-month calendar to represent 5 billion years, calculate how many months will represent 1 billion years.)

SECTION
2 The Fossil Record

What Can Fossils Tell You?

1. Look at the fossil in the photograph. Describe the fossil's characteristics in as much detail as you can.

2. From your description in Step 1, try to figure out how the organism lived. How did it move? Where did it live?

Think It Over

Inferring What type of present-day organism do you think is related to the fossil? Why?

A crime has been committed. You and another detective arrive at the crime scene after the burglar has fled. To piece together what happened, you begin searching for clues. First you notice a broken first-floor window. Leading up to the window are footprints in the mud. From the prints, you can infer the size and type of shoes the burglar wore. As you gather these and other clues, you slowly piece together a picture of what happened and who the burglar might be.

To understand events that occurred long ago, scientists act like detectives. Some of the most important clues to Earth's past are fossils. A **fossil** is the preserved remains or traces of an organism that lived in the past. A fossil can be formed from a bone, tooth, shell, or other part of an organism. Other fossils can be traces of the organism, such as footprints or worm burrows left in mud that later turned to stone.

How Do Fossils Form?

Very few fossils are of complete organisms. When an animal dies, the soft parts of its body generally either decay or are eaten within a short time. Usually only the hard parts of the animal, such as the bones or shells, remain. Plants also form fossils. The parts of plants that are most often preserved as fossils include leaves, stems, roots, and seeds.

The formation of any fossil is a rare event. The conditions must be just right for a fossil to form. **Most fossils form when organisms become buried under sediments after they die.**

GUIDE FOR READING

◆ How do most fossils form?

◆ How can scientists determine a fossil's age?

◆ What events contribute to the extinction of species?

Reading Tip As you read, write four multiple-choice questions about the content in this section. Exchange questions with a partner and answer each other's questions.

Key Terms fossil
• petrified fossil • mold • cast
• relative dating
• absolute dating
• radioactive element • half-life
• fossil record • extinct
• gradualism
• punctuated equilibria

A fossilized shark tooth ▶

1. Two dinosaurs are buried by ash from an erupting volcano.

2. Minerals gradually replace the remains. Over millions of years, the fossils become buried by sediments.

Figure 9 Fossils are the preserved remains or traces of organisms that lived in the past. Most fossils form when organisms that die become buried in sediments.
Interpreting Diagrams What is one way in which a buried fossil can be uncovered?

Sediments are particles of soil and rock. When a river flows into a lake or ocean, the sediments in the river settle to the bottom. Layers of sediments build up over the dead organisms. Over millions of years, the layers harden to become sedimentary rock.

Petrified Fossils Some remains that become buried in sediments are actually changed to rock. Minerals dissolved in the water soak into the buried remains. Gradually, the minerals replace the remains, changing them into rock. Fossils that form in this way are called **petrified fossils.**

Molds and Casts Sometimes shells or other hard parts of organisms buried by sediments are gradually dissolved. An empty space remains in the place the part once occupied. A hollow space in sediment in the shape of an organism or part of an organism is called a **mold.**

Sometimes a mold becomes filled in with hardened minerals, forming a **cast.** A cast is a copy of the shape of the organism that made the mold. If you have ever made a gelatin dessert in a plastic mold, then you can understand how a cast forms.

Preserved Remains Organisms can also be preserved in substances other than sediments. Entire organisms, such as the huge elephant-like mammoths that lived thousands of years ago, have been preserved in ice. The low temperatures preserved the mammoths' soft parts.

The bones and teeth of other ancient animals have been preserved in tar pits. Tar is a dark, sticky form of oil. Tar pits formed when tar seeped up from under the ground to the surface. The tar pits were often covered with water. Animals that came to drink the water became stuck in the tar.

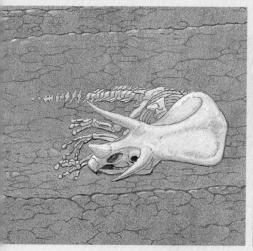
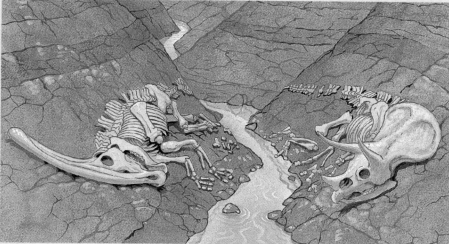

3. Running water cuts through the sedimentary rock layers, exposing the fossils.

Insects and some other organisms can become stuck in the sticky sap that some evergreen trees produce. The sap then hardens, forming a substance called amber. The amber protects the organism's body from decay.

Determining a Fossil's Age

To understand when different organisms lived on Earth, scientists need to be able to determine the ages of fossils. They can then determine when the organisms lived. This information can be used to reconstruct the history of life on Earth. **Scientists can determine a fossil's age in two ways: relative dating and absolute dating.**

Relative Dating Scientists use **relative dating** to determine which of two fossils is older. To understand how relative dating works, imagine that a river has cut down through layers of sedimentary rock to form a canyon. If you look at the canyon walls, you can see the layers of sedimentary rock piled up one on top of another. The layers near the top of the canyon were formed most recently. These layers are the youngest rock layers. The lower down the canyon wall you go, the older the layers are. Therefore, fossils found in layers near the top of the canyon are younger than fossils found near the bottom of the canyon.

Relative dating can only be used when the rock layers have been preserved in their original sequence. Relative dating can help scientists determine whether one fossil is older than another. However, relative dating cannot tell scientists the fossil's actual age.

✓ *Checkpoint* *Which rock layers contain younger fossils?*

Preservation in Ice

1. Place fresh **ACTIVITY** fruit, such as apple slices, strawberries, and blueberries, in an open plastic container.

2. Completely cover the fruit with water. Put the container in a freezer.

3. Place the same type and amount of fresh fruit in another open container. Leave it somewhere where no one will disturb it.

4. After three days, observe the fruit in both containers.

Inferring Use your observations to explain why fossils preserved in ice are more likely to include soft, fleshy body parts.

Figure 10 The half-life of potassium-40, a radioactive element, is 1.3 billion years. This means that half of the potassium-40 in a sample will break down into argon-40 every 1.3 billion years. *Interpreting Charts If a sample contains one fourth of the original amount of potassium-40, how old is the sample?*

	Decay of Potassium-40 (Half-life = 1.3 billion years)		
Time	**Amount of Potassium-40**		**Amount of Argon-40**
2.6 billion years ago		4 g	0 g
1.3 billion years ago		2 g	2 g
Present		1 g	3 g

Absolute Dating   Scientists use another technique, called

INTEGRATING CHEMISTRY **absolute dating,** to determine the actual age of a fossil. The rocks that fossils are found near contain **radioactive elements,** unstable elements that decay, or break down, into different elements. The **half-life** of a radioactive element is the time it takes for half of the atoms in a sample to decay. Figure 10 shows how a sample of potassium-40, a radioactive element, breaks down into argon-40 over time.

Scientists can compare the amount of a radioactive element in a sample to the amount of the element into which it breaks down. As you can see in Figure 10, this information can be used to calculate the age of the rock, and thus the age of the fossil.

☑ *Checkpoint What is a half-life?*

What Do Fossils Reveal?

Like pieces in a jigsaw puzzle, fossils help scientists piece together information about Earth's past. The millions of fossils that scientists have collected are called the **fossil record.**

Almost all of the species preserved as fossils are now extinct. A species is **extinct** if no members of that species are still alive. Most of what scientists know about extinct species is based on the fossil record. Scientists use fossils of bones and teeth to build models of extinct animals. Fossil footprints provide clues about how fast an animal could move and how tall it was.

The fossil record also provides evidence about when different kinds of organisms may have lived on Earth. Using absolute dating, scientists have estimated the ages of many fossils and rocks.

Sharpen your Skills

Calculating

ACTIVITY

A radioactive element has a half-life of 713 million years. After 2,139 million years, how many half-lives will have gone by?

Calculate how much of a 16-gram sample of the element will remain after 2,139 million years.

From this information, scientists have created a "calendar" of Earth's history that spans more than 4.6 billion years. Scientists have divided this large time period into smaller units called eras and periods. This calendar of Earth's history is sometimes called the Geologic Time Scale.

The largest span of time in the Geologic Time Scale is Precambrian Time. This span of time is sometimes referred to simply as the Precambrian (pree KAM bree un). It covers the first 4 billion years of Earth's history. Scientists know very little about the Precambrian because there are few fossils from these ancient times. After the Precambrian, the Geologic Time Scale is divided into three major blocks of time, or eras. Each era is further divided into shorter periods. In *Exploring Life's History* on pages 632 and 633, you can see what information the fossil record provides about each time period.

The Incomplete Fossil Record

The fossil record has provided scientists with a lot of important information about past life on Earth. The fossil record, however, is incomplete, because most organisms died without leaving fossils behind. These gaps in the fossil record have left many questions about evolution unanswered. For example, scientists are not sure how rapidly species change.

One idea, called **gradualism,** proposes that evolution occurs slowly but steadily. According to gradualism, tiny changes in a species gradually add up to major changes over very long periods of time. This is how Darwin thought evolution occurred.

Another idea, called **punctuated equilibria,** is that species change a lot during short periods of time. These periods of rapid change are separated by long periods of little or no change. According to punctuated equilibria, species change quickly when groups become isolated and adapt to new environments.

Most scientists today think that species change gradually at some times and fairly rapidly at others. But because the fossil record is incomplete, no one can know for sure how rapidly species change.

Figure 11 Complete skeletons of animals that scientists estimate lived thousands of years ago have been found in the Rancho La Brea tar pits in Los Angeles, California. The photo shows a model of an elephant-like animal. Scientists created the model based on information learned from the fossils.

EXPLORING Life's History

Take a trip through geologic history, which is based on evidence from the fossil record.

PRECAMBRIAN TIME The Precambrian covers about 87 percent of Earth's history.

4.6 billion years ago

PRE-CAMBRIAN	PALEOZOIC ERA

Millions of years ago

544   505   438   408   360

PRE-CAMBRIAN

Early bacteria

Algae

Jellyfish-like animal

The formation of Earth marks the beginning of Precambrian Time. Bacteria are living in seas 3.5 billion years ago. Algae and fungi are living on Earth 1 billion years ago. Animals live in the seas 640 million years ago.

Cambrian Period

Opabinia

Sponges

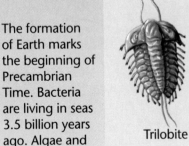

Trilobite

Many invertebrate animals such as sponges, snails, clams, and worms live in the seas.

Ordovician Period

Eumorphocystis

Jawless fish

Fishes, the first vertebrates, live in the ocean. Although many new species of animals live at this time, many become extinct by the end of the period.

Silurian Period

Eurypterid

Arachnid

Land plants

Some plants and animals now live on land. The plants are similar to today's mosses. The animals resemble today's insects and spiders.

Devonian Period

Shark

Pterichthyodes

Many types of fishes live in the seas. Amphibians, fishlike animals that have legs and can breathe air, exist. The first ferns and cone-bearing plants grow on land.

Carboniferous Period

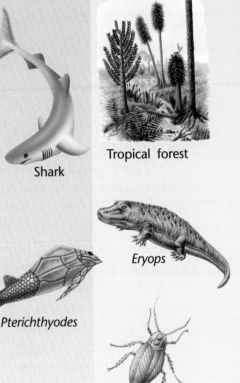

Tropical forest

Eryops

Cockroach

Tropical forests become widespread. Many different insects and amphibians thrive. Reptiles roam land.

632

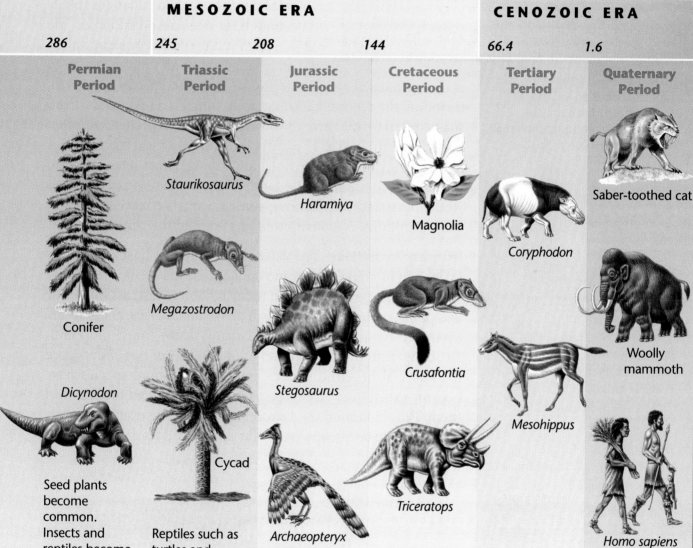

PALEOZOIC		**CENOZOIC** **MESOZOIC**		
544 million years ago	245 million years ago	66.4 million years ago		

MESOZOIC ERA

CENOZOIC ERA

286	245	208	144	66.4	1.6
Permian Period	Triassic Period	Jurassic Period	Cretaceous Period	Tertiary Period	Quaternary Period

Staurikosaurus

Haramiya

Magnolia

Saber-toothed cat

Conifer

Megazostrodon

Coryphodon

Dicynodon

Stegosaurus

Crusafontia

Woolly
mammoth

Cycad

Mesohippus

Triceratops

Archaeopteryx

Homo sapiens

Seed plants
become
common.
Insects and
reptiles become
widespread.
Reptile-like
mammals
appear. At the
end of the
period, most sea
animals and
amphibians
become extinct.

Reptiles such as
turtles and
crocodiles are
common.
Dinosaurs and
reptile-like
mammals live on
land. Conifers
and palmlike
trees dominate
forests.

Large dinosaurs
roam the world.
Mammals
become more
common and
varied. The first
birds live on
Earth.

Flowering plants
first live on land.
There are more
kinds of
mammals than
before. At the
end of the
period, dinosaurs
become extinct.

New groups of
mammals,
including the
first primates,
roam Earth.
Flowering plants
become the
most common
kind of plant.

Humans live on
Earth. Later in
the period, many
large mammals,
including woolly
mammoths,
become extinct.

Figure 12 When trees in a rainforest are cut down, the habitats of organisms may be destroyed. Habitat destruction may lead to the extinction of species.

Causes of Extinction

Most of the organisms in *Exploring Life's History* are extinct. Extinction of species continues to occur in the present time. **Change in environmental conditions can affect the survival of species. Natural events cause some species to become extinct, while human activities are responsible for other extinctions.**

Natural Events Major changes in climate may have been responsible for the extinction of many species. For example, a climate change about 65 million years ago probably caused the extinction of half the species on Earth, including the dinosaurs. An asteroid, which is a rocky mass from space, may have hit Earth, throwing huge clouds of dust and other materials into the air. The dust clouds would have blocked sunlight, making the climate cooler and killing plants, which depend on sunlight to manufacture food. Without plants, many animals would have starved. However, some scientists believe it was volcanic eruptions, not an asteroid, that caused the climate change.

Human Activities The activities of humans have caused the extinction of many species and endangered the survival of others. The major cause of extinction today is habitat destruction, or the loss of the environment in which an organism lives. Habitats are destroyed by activities such as cutting down forests and constructing buildings in wetland areas. Pollution has endangered the survival of some species. And some animal species have become extinct because humans hunted and killed too many of them. People hunted the Carolina parakeet, for example, partly because it ate crops, and partly for its colorful feathers.

Section 2 Review

1. Describe how fossils form in sedimentary rock.
2. Explain the process of absolute dating.
3. What are two causes of species extinction? Describe an example of each.
4. **Thinking Critically Comparing and Contrasting** How are gradualism and punctuated equilibria similar? How are they different?

Science at Home

Make Your Mark With a family member, spread some mud in a shallow, flat-bottomed pan. Smooth the surface of the mud. Use your fingertips to make "footprints" across the mud. Let the mud dry and harden, so that the footprints become permanent. Explain to your family how this is similar to the way some fossils form.

SECTION 3 Other Evidence of Change

DISCOVER **ACTIVITY**

How Can You Classify Species?

1. Collect six to eight different pens. Each pen will represent a different species of similar organisms.

2. Choose a trait that varies among your pen species, such as size or ink color. Using this trait, try to divide the pen species into two groups.

3. Now choose another trait. Divide each group into two smaller groups.

Think It Over

Classifying Which of the pen species share the most characteristics? Which of the pen species share the fewest characteristics?

Do you know anyone who has had his or her appendix out? The appendix is a tiny organ attached to the large intestine. You might think that having a part of the body removed would cause a problem. However, this is not the case with the appendix. In humans, the appendix does not seem to have much function. In some other species of mammals, though, the appendix is much larger and plays an important role in digestion. To most scientists, the existence of appendices in different species is evidence of a relationship among the organisms.

The appendix is just one example of how scientists use modern-day organisms as evidence to support Darwin's theory of evolution. When scientists compare organisms, they may infer how closely related the organisms are in an evolutionary sense. **Scientists use comparisons of body structures, development before birth, and DNA sequences to infer evolutionary relationships among organisms.**

Similarities in Body Structure

Scientists long ago began to compare the body structures of living species to better understand organisms. In fact, Darwin compared body structures of the organisms he observed during his travels. An organism's body structure is its basic body plan, such as how its bones are arranged. Fishes, amphibians, reptiles, birds, and mammals, for example, all have a similar body

GUIDE FOR READING

◆ What evidence from modern-day organisms do scientists use to infer evolutionary relationships among groups?

Reading Tip As you read, use the headings to make an outline about the different types of evidence for evolution.

Key Terms branching tree • homologous structure

Sharpen your Skills

Inferring

ACTIVITY

Look at the drawing below of the bones in a crocodile's leg. Compare this drawing to the drawings in Figure 13. Can you infer that crocodiles share a common ancestor with birds, dolphins, and dogs? Support your answer with evidence.

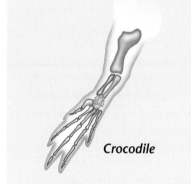

Crocodile

structure—an internal skeleton with a backbone. This is why scientists classify all five groups of animals together as vertebrates. Most scientists think these groups probably inherited the similar structures from a common ancestor.

Look closely at Figure 13. Notice that the bones in the forelimbs of these three animals are arranged in a similar way. The arrangement of the bones forms a 3-part pattern: upper forelimb, middle forelimb, and lower forelimb. Scientists use the similar structure of the forelimbs as evidence that these three organisms share a common ancestor. Body parts that are structurally similar in related species are called **homologous structures** (hoh MAHL uh gus).

Sometimes the fossil record supports the evidence provided by homologous structures. For example, scientists have found fossils of ancient whale-like creatures. The fossils show that these creatures had legs. This evidence supports evidence from homologuous structures and leads scientists to propose that whales and humans share a common ancestor.

☑ *Checkpoint* *What are homologous structures?*

Similarities in Early Development

Scientists also make inferences about evolutionary relationships by comparing the early development of different organisms. Suppose you were asked to compare an adult turtle, a chicken, and a rat. You would probably say they look quite different from each other. However, during their early development, these organisms have some similarities. For example, during the early stages of development all three organisms have a tail and tiny slits in their throats.

Figure 13 A bird's wing, dolphin's flipper, and dog's leg perform different kinds of movements. However, the arrangement of the bones in each forelimb is similar. *Observing What similarities in structure do the three forelimbs share?*

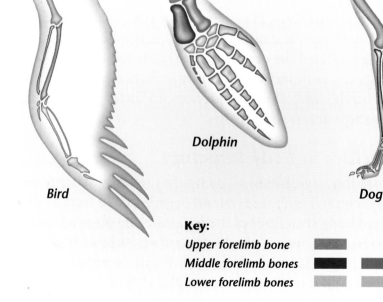

Bird

Dolphin

Dog

Key:
Upper forelimb bone
Middle forelimb bones
Lower forelimb bones

636

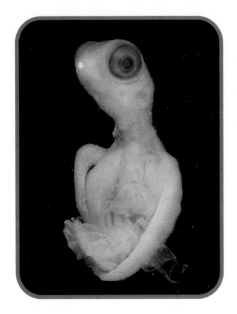
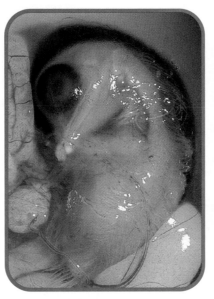
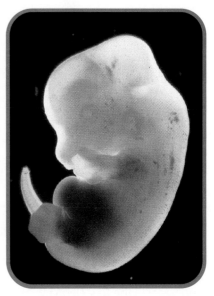

Figure 14 Turtles (left), chickens (center), and rats (right) look similar during the earliest stages of development. Scientists use such similarities as evidence that these three animals developed from a common ancestor.

In Figure 14, you can see that the developing animals are similar. Scientists infer from such similarities that these three vertebrate species are related and share a common ancestor.

When scientists study early development more closely, they notice that the turtle appears more similar to the chicken than it does to the rat. Therefore, scientists infer that turtles are more closely related to chickens than they are to rats.

Similarities in DNA

Why do some species have similar body structures and development patterns? Scientists infer that the species inherited many of the same genes from a common ancestor. Recently, scientists have begun to compare the genes of different species to determine possible relationships among species.

Recall that genes are made of DNA. By comparing the sequence of nitrogen bases in the DNA of different species, scientists can observe how similar their DNA is. The scientists then infer that the more similar the sequences of nitrogen bases, the more closely related the species are.

Recall also that the DNA bases along a gene specify what type of protein will be produced. Thus, scientists also use comparisons of the orders of amino acids in a protein to infer how closely related two species are.

Sometimes DNA evidence does not confirm other inferences about relationships between species. For example, aside from its long nose, the tiny elephant shrew looks very similar to rodents such as mice. Because of this, biologists once inferred that the elephant shrew was closely related to rodents. But when scientists compared DNA from elephant shrews to that of both rodents and elephants, they got a surprise. The elephant shrew's DNA

Figure 15 Because of its appearance, the tiny elephant shrew was thought to be closely related to mice and other rodents. Surprisingly, DNA comparisons showed that the elephant shrew's DNA is more similar to the DNA of elephants than the DNA of rodents.

was more similar to the elephant's DNA than it was to the rodent's DNA. Scientists now think that elephant shrews are more closely related to elephants than to rodents.

INTEGRATING TECHNOLOGY Recently, scientists have developed techniques that allow them to extract, or remove, DNA from fossils. Using these techniques, scientists have now extracted DNA from fossils of bones, teeth, and plants, and from insects trapped in amber. The DNA from fossils has provided scientists with new information about DNA similarities among fossils and today's organisms.

Combining the Evidence

Scientists have combined evidence from fossils, body structures, early development, and DNA and protein sequences to infer evolutionary relationships among species. In most cases, DNA and protein sequences have confirmed conclusions based on other evidence. For example, recent DNA comparisons show that dog DNA is more similar to the DNA of wolves than to the DNA of coyotes. Scientists had already inferred that dogs were more closely related to wolves than to coyotes based on similarities in body structure and development.

Another example of how scientists combined evidence from different sources is shown in the branching tree in Figure 16. A **branching tree** is a diagram that shows how scientists think different groups of organisms are related. Based on similar body structures, lesser pandas were thought to be closely related to giant pandas. But the two panda species also resemble both bears and raccoons. How are these four groups related? Recently DNA analysis and other methods have shown that giant pandas have DNA that is more similar to bears than to lesser pandas. Therefore, scientists infer that giant pandas are more closely related to bears, while lesser pandas are more closely related to raccoons.

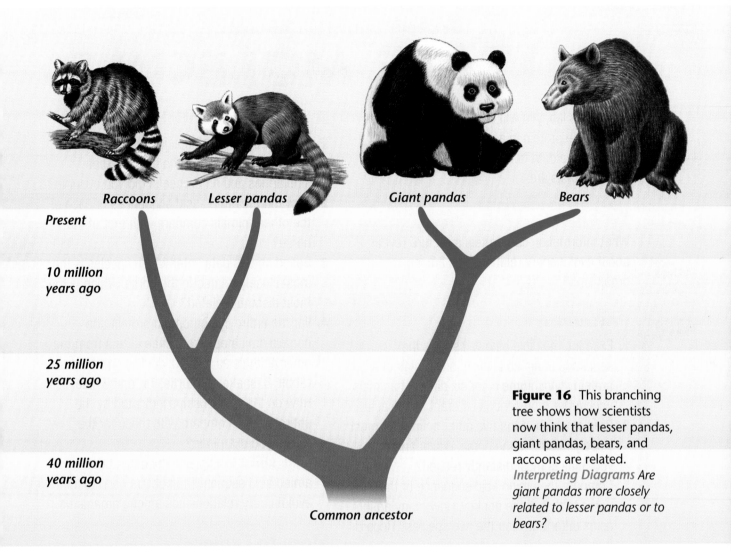

Raccoons Lesser pandas Giant pandas Bears

Present

10 million
years ago

25 million
years ago

40 million
years ago

Common ancestor

Figure 16 This branching
tree shows how scientists
now think that lesser pandas,
giant pandas, bears, and
raccoons are related.
*Interpreting Diagrams Are
giant pandas more closely
related to lesser pandas or to
bears?*

Section 3 Review

1. Name three types of evidence from modern-day
organisms that scientists use to infer evolutionary
relationships.
2. Why are homologous structures important?
3. What did scientists infer by comparing the early
developmental stages of turtles, chickens, and rats?
4. If scientists state that two species are closely
related, what would you expect a comparison
of their DNA base sequences to reveal?
5. **Thinking Critically** **Making Judgments**
Most scientists today consider similarities in DNA,
not body structure or early development, to be
the best indicator of how closely two species are
related. Why do you think this is the case?

Check Your Progress

CHAPTER
PROJECT

You should be completing
construction of the time line
that covers 5 billion years. Now
begin work on the time line showing
600 million years. This version is a
magnified view of one part of the first
time line. It will give you additional
space to show what has happened in
the more recent years of Earth's
history. (*Hint:* Prepare drawings to
show the life forms on Earth during
each period. Also try to include more
information than was mentioned in
the text.)

TELLTALE MOLECULES

In this lab, you will compare the structure of one protein in a variety of animals. You'll use the data to infer how closely related those animals are.

Problem

What information can protein structure reveal about evolutionary relationships among organisms?

Procedure

1. Examine the table below. It shows the sequence of amino acids in one region of a protein, cytochrome c, for six different animals. Each letter represents a different amino acid.
2. Predict which of the five other animals is most closely related to the horse. Which animal do you think is most distantly related?
3. Compare the amino acid sequence of the horse to that of the donkey. How many amino acids differ between the two species? Record that number in your notebook.
4. Compare the amino acid sequences of each of the other animals to that of the horse. Record the number of differences in your notebook.

Analyze and Conclude

1. Which animal's amino acid sequence was most similar to that of the horse? What similarities and difference(s) did you observe?
2. How did the amino acid sequences of each of the other animals compare with that of the horse?
3. Based on this data, infer which species is the most closely related to the horse. Which is the most distantly related?
4. For the entire cytochrome c protein, the horse's amino acid sequence differs from the other animals as follows: donkey, 1 difference; rabbit, 6; snake, 22; turtle, 11; and whale, 5. How do the relationships indicated by the entire protein compare with those for the region you examined?
5. **Think About It** Explain why data about amino acid sequences might be used to infer evolutionary relationships among organisms.

More to Explore

Use the amino acid data to construct a branching tree that includes horses, donkeys, and snakes. The tree should show one way that scientists might infer how the three species are related.

Section of Cytochrome c Protein in Animals														
Amino Acid Position														
Animal	39	40	41	42	43	44	45	46	47	48	49	50	51	52	53
Horse	A	B	C	D	E	F	G	H	I	J	K	L	M	N	O
Donkey	A	B	C	D	E	F	G	H	Z	J	K	L	M	N	O
Rabbit	A	B	C	D	E	Y	G	H	Z	J	K	L	M	N	O
Snake	A	B	C	D	E	Y	G	H	Z	J	K	W	M	N	O
Turtle	A	B	C	D	E	V	G	H	Z	J	K	U	M	N	O
Whale	A	B	C	D	E	Y	G	H	Z	J	K	L	M	N	O

Darwin's Voyage

Key Ideas

◆ Darwin thought that species gradually changed over many generations as they became better adapted to new conditions. This process is called evolution.

◆ Darwin's observations led him to propose that evolution occurs through natural selection. Natural selection occurs due to overproduction, competition, and variations.

◆ Only traits controlled by genes can change over time as a result of natural selection.

◆ Darwin thought that if a group of individuals remains separated from the rest of its species long enough to develop different traits, a new species could form.

Key Terms

species	evolution	variation
adaptation	natural selection	

 The Fossil Record

INTEGRATING EARTH SCIENCE

Key Ideas

◆ Most fossils form when organisms die and sediments bury them.

◆ Relative dating determines which of two fossils is older and which is younger. Absolute dating determines the actual age of a fossil.

◆ Fossils help scientists infer how extinct organisms looked.

◆ The Geologic Time Scale shows when during Earth's history major groups of organisms lived.

◆ Species may have changed gradually at some times and fairly rapidly at other times.

◆ Both natural events and human activities have caused extinction of organisms.

Key Terms

fossil	radioactive element
petrified fossil	half-life
mold	fossil record
cast	extinct
relative dating	gradualism
absolute dating	punctuated equilibria

 Other Evidence of Change

Key Ideas

◆ By comparing modern-day organisms, scientists can infer how closely related they are in an evolutionary sense.

◆ Scientists use homologous structures to infer how species are related and whether they might share a common ancestor.

◆ Scientists use similarities in early developmental stages to infer how species are related.

◆ Scientists can compare DNA and protein sequences to infer how species are related.

◆ A branching tree is a diagram that shows how scientists think different groups of organisms are related.

Key Terms
homologous structure
branching tree

Organizing Information

Flowchart Copy the flowchart about natural selection onto a separate sheet of paper. Complete the flowchart by writing a sentence describing each factor that leads to natural selection. Then add a title. (For more on flowcharts, see the Skills Handbook.)

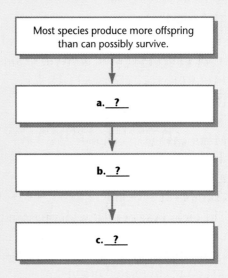

Reviewing Content

 Review key concepts online using iText at www.phschool.com

Multiple Choice

Choose the letter of the best answer.

1. Changes that may occur in a species over long periods of time are called
   a. relative dating.
   b. evolution.
   c. homologous structures.
   d. developmental stages.

2. A trait that helps an organism survive and reproduce is called a(n)
   a. variation.   b. adaptation.
   c. species.   d. selection.

3. The type of fossil formed when an organism dissolves and leaves an empty space in a rock is called a
   a. cast.   b. mold.
   c. trace.   d. petrified fossil.

4. The rate of decay of a radioactive element is measured by its
   a. year.   b. era.
   c. half-life.   d. period.

5. Which of these is *not* used as evidence for evolution?
   a. DNA sequences
   b. stages of development
   c. body size
   d. body structures

True or False

If the statement is true, write true. If it is false, change the underlined word or words to make the statement true.

6. Darwin's idea about how evolution occurs is called <u>punctuated equilibria</u>.

7. Major changes in <u>climate</u> may have caused the extinction of species.

8. A footprint of an extinct dinosaur is an example of a <u>fossil</u>.

9. The technique of <u>relative dating</u> can be used to determine the actual age of a fossil.

10. <u>Homologous structures</u> are similar structures in related organisms.

Checking Concepts

11. What role does the overproduction of offspring play in the process of natural selection?

12. Use an example to explain how natural selection might lead to evolution.

13. What human activities have contributed to the extinction of species?

14. How are rock layers used to determine the relative ages of fossils?

15. Explain why scientists think that similarities in the early development of different species suggest that the species are related.

16. **Writing to Learn** You are a reporter for a local newspaper near the home of Charles Darwin. You have been asked to interview Darwin about his theory of evolution. Write three questions that you would ask Darwin. Then choose one question and answer it as Darwin might have.

Thinking Critically

17. **Applying Concepts** Why did Darwin's visit to the Galapagos Islands have such an important influence on his development of the theory of evolution by natural selection?

18. **Predicting** Suppose most members of a species eat only one kind of food. Predict how natural selection might work if that food suddenly became unavailable.

19. **Relating Cause and Effect** What is the role of geographic isolation in the change of a species?

20. **Comparing and Contrasting** How does relative dating differ from absolute dating?

21. **Applying Concepts** A seal's flipper and a human arm have very different functions. What evidence might scientists look for to determine whether the structures are homologous?

Applying Skills

Radioactive carbon-14 decays to nitrogen with a half-life of 5,730 years. Use this information and the table below to answer Questions 22–24.

Fossil	Amount of Carbon-14 in Fossil	Amount of Nitrogen in Fossil	Position of Fossil in Rock Layers
A	1 gram	7 grams	bottom layer
B	4 grams	4 grams	top layer
C	2 grams	6 grams	middle layer

22. Inferring Use the positions of the fossils in the rock layers to put the fossils in order from youngest to oldest.

23. Calculating Calculate the age of each fossil using the data about carbon-14 and nitrogen.

24. Drawing Conclusions Do your answers to Questions 22 and 23 agree or disagree with each other? Explain.

Performance CHAPTER PROJECT **Assessment**

Present Your Project Display your completed time lines for the class. Be prepared to explain why you chose the scale that you did. Also, describe how your time lines are related to each other.

Reflect and Record In your notebook, describe how the time lines helped you understand the long periods of time in Earth's history. What surprised you the most? In what way was making two time lines more useful than making only one?

Test Preparation

Use these questions to prepare for standardized tests.

Use the illustration to answer Questions 25–28.

25. What is the best title for this illustration?
A Plant Growth Over Time
B Branching Tree of Plant Evolution
C Mosses and Ferns, the Oldest Plants
D Flowering Plants, the Youngest Plants

26. About how long ago did mosses first live on Earth?
F 100 million years ago
G 150 million years ago
H 350 million years ago
J 450 million years ago

27. Which group of plants would have DNA that is most similar to the DNA of flowering plants?
A mosses
B ferns
C conifers
D They would all be equally alike.

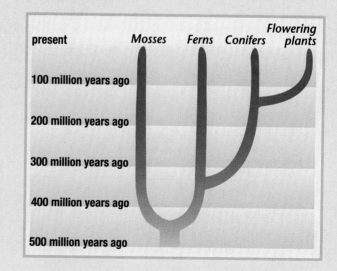

28. Which group of plants would have DNA that is least similar to the DNA of flowering plants?
F mosses
G ferns
H conifers
J They would all be equally alike.

CHAPTER

19 Interdependence in Living Systems

This broad-tailed hummingbird enjoys a sip of nectar from a beardtongue flower. Feeding relationships are one of the ways in which organisms interact.

WEB ACTIVITY
www.phschool.com

Interaction at a Bird Feeder

One of the best ways to learn about interdependence among organisms is to watch how animals feed and how they interact with one another. In this project, you'll watch birds and other animals that visit a bird feeder. What do birds eat? How do different birds interact? Do birds compete with other kinds of animals for food? Careful observation and record keeping will reveal answers to these questions.

Your Goal To make detailed observations of the interactions that occur at a bird feeder.

To complete this project successfully, you must
- observe the feeder regularly for at least two weeks, and identify the birds and other animals that visit the feeder
- make detailed observations of how the birds at your feeder eat
- describe how the birds interact with one another and with other animals
- follow the safety guidelines in Appendix A

Get Started Begin by meeting with some of your classmates to share your knowledge about interactions at a bird feeder. Do birds compete with one another for food? What other animals might visit a feeder? How do animals interact with one another?

Check Your Progress You'll be working on this project as you study this chapter. To keep your project on track, look for Check Your Progress boxes at the following points.

Section 2 Review, page 660: Identify birds and other animals that come to the feeder. Observe how the animals interact.

Section 3 Review, page 670: Interpret your observations and plan your presentation.

Present Your Project At the end of this chapter (page 673), you will share what you have learned about birds and their interactions.

TEKS

In addition to process TEKS, this chapter addresses these concept TEKS as they relate to the chapter's topic

(8.6) The student knows that interdependence occurs among living systems. The student is expected to:
(A) describe interaction among systems in the human organism;
(B) identify feedback mechanisms that maintain equilibrium of systems such as body temperature, turgor pressure, and chemical reactions; and
(C) describe interactions within ecosystems.

Interactions in the Human Body

How Do Body Systems Depend on One Another?

1. Stand on one foot for a few seconds. Pay close attention to how your body enables you to keep your balance.

2. Close your eyes. Again try to stand on one foot for a few seconds. Compare your reactions this time to your reactions when you had your eyes open.

Think It Over

Inferring Is it easier to keep your balance when your eyes are open than when they are closed? What body systems are working together to enable you to maintain your balance?

GUIDE FOR READING

◆ What are the levels of organization in many-celled organisms?

◆ What are some ways in which human body systems interact?

Reading Tip As you read this section, write one or two sentences summarizing the information under each heading.

Key Terms system • tissue • organ • organ system • trachea • alveolus • diaphragm • villus

At the Cinco de Mayo festival, performers in brightly colored costumes dance swiftly and gracefully in time to the lively music. As they tap their feet, leap, and twirl, the dancers are celebrating Mexican American culture. They are also expressing their joyful mood.

Many parts of the body work together to produce the smooth, rhythmic movement of a dance. Bones support the body, and muscles make the body move. The brain directs the body motions, coordinates them, and makes them smooth. The lungs provide the oxygen that the dancers need. The dancers' energy comes from food supplied by the mouth, stomach, and other organs involved in digestion.

◄ Dancers at a Cinco de Mayo festival

646

What Is a System?

Your body is a system composed of many parts. A **system** is any group of parts that work together as a unit. For example, your school is a system made up of things such as the school building, students, teachers, books, and the athletic fields.

Many systems involve living things. An ecosystem is a system made up of all the living and nonliving things in an area. You will learn more about interaction in an ecosystem in Section 3. And your body is made up of several systems, such as the digestive, cardiovascular, and respiratory systems.

☑ *Checkpoint* *What is a system?*

How the Body Is Organized

The bodies of all complex organisms, including humans, have several levels of organization. **The levels of organization in a many-celled organism begin with cells. Cells combine to form tissues, organs, and organ systems.** The least complex level is a cell. The most complex level is an organ system.

Cells The first level of organization in the body is the cell. Cells are the basic unit of structure and function in a living organism. Each of the trillions of cells in your body has its own job. For example, some cells are involved in sensing external conditions for your body. Other cells absorb food molecules into your body.

Tissues After cells, the next level of organization is tissues. A **tissue** is a group of cells that perform the same function. There are four basic types of tissue in the human body: muscle, connective, nerve, and epithelial. Muscle tissue enables the body to move. The muscles that make you throw a baseball and those that pump blood through your body are made of muscle tissue.

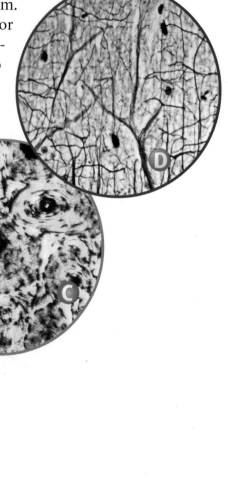

Figure 1 Muscle tissue **(A)** makes the body move. Epithelial tissue **(B)** covers body surfaces. Connective tissue, such as bone **(C)**, supports and connects parts of the body. Nerve tissue **(D)** conveys messages. *Applying Concepts* *What type of tissue is blood?*

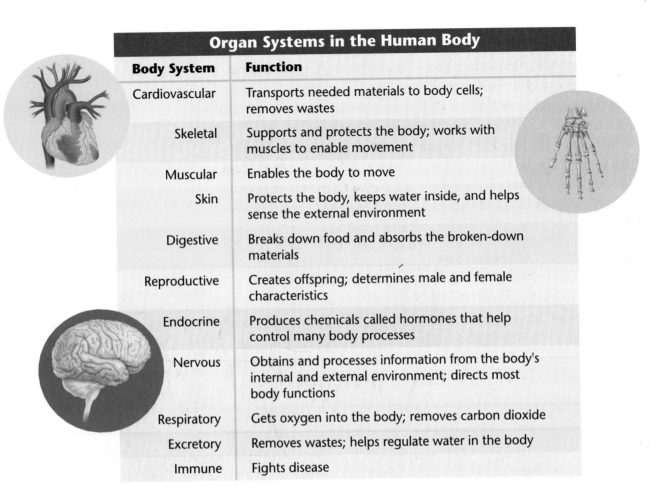

Organ Systems in the Human Body	
Body System	**Function**
Cardiovascular	Transports needed materials to body cells; removes wastes
Skeletal	Supports and protects the body; works with muscles to enable movement
Muscular	Enables the body to move
Skin	Protects the body, keeps water inside, and helps sense the external environment
Digestive	Breaks down food and absorbs the broken-down materials
Reproductive	Creates offspring; determines male and female characteristics
Endocrine	Produces chemicals called hormones that help control many body processes
Nervous	Obtains and processes information from the body's internal and external environment; directs most body functions
Respiratory	Gets oxygen into the body; removes carbon dioxide
Excretory	Removes wastes; helps regulate water in the body
Immune	Fights disease

Figure 2 The human body is made up of several organ systems, whose functions are indicated in this table.
Interpreting Charts Which system removes wastes?

Connective tissue provides support for the body and connects its parts. Bone tissue, fat, and blood are all connective tissues. Messages travel back and forth between your brain and the rest of your body through nerve tissue. Epithelial tissue covers external and internal surfaces of your body, such as your skin and the lining of your stomach.

Organs Just as cells join together to form tissues, different types of tissue combine to form organs. An **organ** is a group of tissues that performs a specific function. For example, the heart is an organ that pumps blood. The heart is made mostly of muscle tissue, but it also contains other kinds of tissue, such as nerve tissue and connective tissue.

Organ Systems The highest level of organization in the body is the organ system. An **organ system** is a group of organs that work together to perform a specific function. For example, the cardiovascular system performs the function of carrying blood to all parts of your body. Figure 2 identifies the body's organ systems and describes the functions of each.

☑ *Checkpoint* *What are tissues?*

Interactions Within the Human Body

In order to carry out their jobs, most systems are dependent on other systems. Your school system, for example, obtains the money it needs mainly from taxes raised by your local government. Systems in the living world work together too. Each organ system in the human body is dependent on other body systems. *Exploring Interaction Among Body Systems* shows you how organ systems work together to enable a musician to play a musical instrument.

Interdependence among body systems is necessary for the processes that keep humans alive and enable them to reproduce. The examples that follow show how different body systems affect one another and depend on one another.

EXPLORING *Interaction Among Body Systems*

As the musician plays a lively tune, several body systems work together to enable him to perform this complex task.

Nervous system
The musician's ears enable him to hear the music and to keep in harmony with the other musicians. The ears are part of the nervous system. The nervous system directs the actions of the musician's muscles.

Respiratory system
Oxygen enters the musician's body through the respiratory system. To blow the horn, the musician uses air exhaled from the respiratory system.

Cardiovascular system
Blood delivers oxygen and nutrients to the musician's cells, including muscle cells.

Muscular and skeletal systems
Muscles make the musician's fingers move. These muscles attach to bones in the skeletal system.

Digestive system
The muscles involved in playing an instrument need energy. That energy comes from food that is broken down and absorbed into the body by the digestive system.

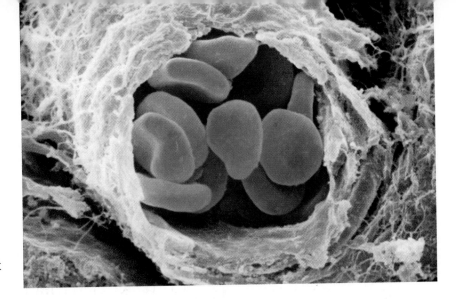

Figure 3 The cardiovascular system carries materials to all parts of your body. These red blood cells, which are one component of blood, transport oxygen to body cells.

Blood—The Link to All Body Systems

Cars, trucks, trains, and airplanes carry people and materials all over the world. Similarly, blood carries materials throughout your body. The main task of the cardiovascular system, or circulatory system, is transportation. The cardiovascular system delivers needed materials to body cells and carries waste products away from body cells. These substances all travel in blood. The heart pumps blood through blood vessels that reach all parts of the body. **Since every cell in the body depends on the cardiovascular system to deliver needed materials to it and to remove wastes, all body systems interact with the cardiovascular system.**

☑ *Checkpoint* *What substance carries materials throughout the body?*

Interactions in Transporting Oxygen

Every minute, you breathe in and out, over and over, without even thinking about it. If you didn't breathe, your cells would not obtain the oxygen they need. The organ system responsible for delivering oxygen to your cells is the respiratory system, which is shown in Figure 4. The respiratory system also removes carbon dioxide. **The respiratory system could not deliver oxygen to your body cells or remove carbon dioxide without the cardiovascular and muscular systems.**

The Role of the Respiratory System Air enters the body through the nostrils. It travels to the lungs through a tube called the **trachea** (TRAY kee uh), or windpipe. The lungs, which are the main organs of the respiratory system, contain hundreds of round sacs called **alveoli** (al VEE uh ly) (singular *alveolus*). The alveoli are the structures through which oxygen moves from the air into the blood. Carbon dioxide moves through alveoli in the opposite direction: from the blood into the air.

The Role of the Cardiovascular System Each alveolus is surrounded by capillaries. Capillaries are the smallest blood vessels in the cardiovascular system. Inside each lung, oxygen in the air moves through the walls of the alveoli and into the capillaries. In the capillaries, the oxygen binds to red blood cells, which are carried in the bloodstream through the rest of the body. As the oxygen-rich red blood cells move through the cardiovascular system, they release the oxygen to body cells.

As oxygen in the alveoli passes into the bloodstream, carbon dioxide is moving in the opposite direction. Carbon dioxide passes from the blood, through the walls of the alveoli, and into the air inside the alveoli. From the alveoli, carbon dioxide leaves your body. When you breathe out, you expel this waste carbon dioxide from your body.

The Role of the Muscular System The muscular system enables air to enter your lungs. When you are about to inhale, or breathe in, muscles attached to your ribs lift the rib cage outward. At the same time, a dome-shaped muscle called the **diaphragm** (DIGH uh fram) flattens out. The actions of these muscles make your chest expand. The expansion of your chest

Blood and Oxygen

ACTIVITY

Work with other students to construct a model that demonstrates how the circulatory and respiratory systems work together to deliver oxygen to cells. Your model might show both systems as a whole, or you might focus on what happens in an alveolus and the capillaries that surround it.

Making Models Have another team examine your model and evaluate it. What does it show accurately about the interaction between the two body systems? What aspects of this interaction doesn't it show?

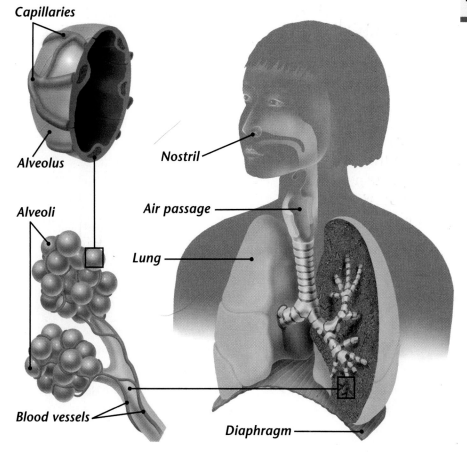

Capillaries

Alveolus

Alveoli

Nostril

Air passage

Lung

Blood vessels

Diaphragm

Figure 4 The respiratory system brings oxygen into your body and eliminates carbon dioxide from your body. *Applying Concepts How does oxygen in the lungs pass into the bloodstream?*

pulls air into your lungs. When you exhale, or breathe out, the rib muscles lower the rib cage and the diaphragm returns to its normal dome-shaped position. These muscular actions work together to make the space inside the chest decrease. This forces air out of your lungs.

Interactions in Digesting Food

Most foods that you eat cannot be used immediately by your body. They must first be digested, or broken down into small molecules, called nutrients, that can be absorbed into your body. **The digestive, muscular, and cardiovascular systems interact to digest and absorb the food you eat and deliver nutrients to your cells.**

The Role of the Digestive System
The digestive system breaks down food into simpler substances that can be absorbed into the body and used by body cells. Food enters the digestive system through the mouth and then travels to the stomach. Both the mouth and the stomach begin to break down food. From the stomach, food passes into the small intestine. The small intestine completes the breakdown of food and absorbs the nutrients into the body. Figure 6 shows that the small intestine is lined with tiny finger-shaped projections called **villi** (VIL eye) (singular *villus*), which absorb nutrients into the body. After the nutrients have been absorbed, undigested food then passes into the large intestine and is eliminated from the body as wastes.

Figure 5 The diaphragm is a muscle involved in breathing. When the diaphragm flattens, air rushes into the lungs.
Relating Cause and Effect What happens when the diaphragm becomes dome-shaped?

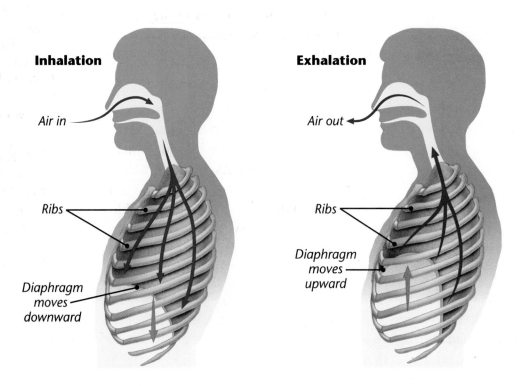

Inhalation

Air in

Ribs

Diaphragm moves downward

Exhalation

Air out

Ribs

Diaphragm moves upward

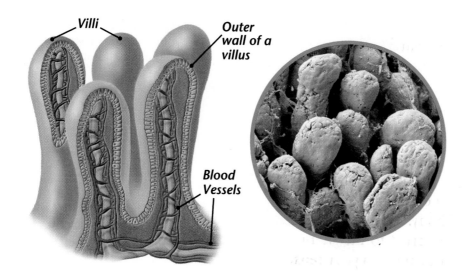

Figure 6 Villi are tiny, finger-shaped projections that line the wall of the small intestine and absorb nutrients.

The Role of the Muscular System By itself, the digestive system could not carry out the breakdown of food and the absorption of nutrients. The muscles that move your jaws enable your teeth to chew your food. The muscular system also enables you to swallow food. After you swallow, waves of muscle contractions push food through your digestive system. In the stomach, three layers of muscle churn and squeeze food, breaking it down into smaller particles.

The Role of the Cardiovascular System The small intestine absorbs nutrients, but it is the cardiovascular system that carries those nutrients to cells. Each villus contains tiny capillaries. After nutrients are absorbed by the villi, the nutrients pass into the blood that flows through the capillaries. The blood carries the absorbed nutrients to cells in the body. Without the cardiovascular system, cells could not obtain the nutrients they need for growth and energy.

Movement: Muscles, Bones, and Nerves

The muscular system makes your body move. Your body uses muscles for automatic processes such as the movement of food through your digestive system and the beating of your heart. Muscles also carry out voluntary movements, or movements that you control, such as getting up from your chair and walking to the front of the classroom. **The muscular, skeletal, and nervous systems are all involved in voluntary movements.**

The Role of the Muscular System Muscles produce movement by contracting, or shortening. When you open your mouth, for example, muscles contract to pull your jaw downward. Contracting muscles act something like a stretched rubber band that is shrinking back to its normal size.

TRY THIS

Soak It Up

The villi provide a large **ACTIVITY** surface area. You can determine the effect of surface area on absorption.

1. Obtain two identical paper cups. Pour 10 mL of water into each.

2. Cut a square of paper towel that is 1 cm × 1 cm. Then cut a long strip of paper towel that is 1 cm × 30 cm.

3. Put the small square of paper towel into one cup.

4. Carefully remove the piece of paper towel. Measure the volume of water that remains in the cup.

5. Fold the long strip of paper towel like an accordion. The folds model the villi. Put the folded strip in the water in the second cup. Repeat Step 4.

Inferring Does a large surface area increase absorption?

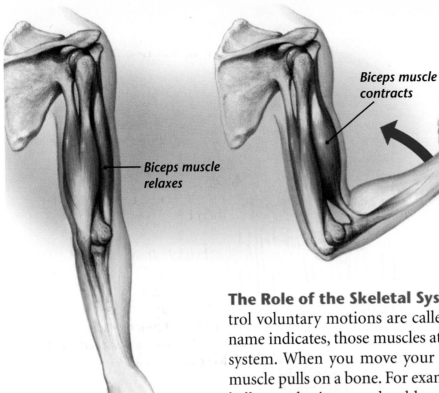

Figure 7 When you bend your arm, the biceps muscle pulls a bone to produce movement.

Biceps muscle contracts

Biceps muscle relaxes

The Role of the Skeletal System The muscles that control voluntary motions are called skeletal muscles. As their name indicates, those muscles attach to bones in the skeletal system. When you move your body, you do so because a muscle pulls on a bone. For example, when you pitch a baseball, muscles in your shoulders, arms, and hands carry out the movement by pulling on bones in your arms, wrists, and fingers. Figure 7 shows how a muscle contracts to make you bend your arm.

The Role of the Nervous System Your nervous system is involved in the process of movement, too. Your brain and nerves direct muscles to contract. Consider what happens when you decide to move your leg, for example. A message "telling" your leg to move begins in your brain. The message travels down your back through your spinal cord, and eventually reaches nerves in your leg. These nerves then stimulate the leg muscles to contract.

Section 1 Review

1. What are the levels of organization in the body?
2. Why do all body systems interact with the cardiovascular system?
3. Describe how body systems interact during the process of respiration.
4. How is the muscular system involved in digestion?
5. **Thinking Critically** Relating Cause and Effect Suppose a nerve leading to an arm muscle became damaged. How would this affect the arm's ability to move? Explain your answer.

Science at Home

Systems Interacting Explain to your family that body systems interact with one another. Then, with family members, perform some simple activity such as playing a board game or taking a bicycle ride. Work with your family to identify the body systems that are involved in this activity.

② Equilibrium and Feedback

What Happens When You Are Startled?

1. Read this activity, and then close your eyes.

2. Your teacher is behind you and will pop a balloon at any moment.

3. Pay attention to how your body reacts when you hear the balloon pop. Observe whether you jump and whether your heart rate and breathing rate change.

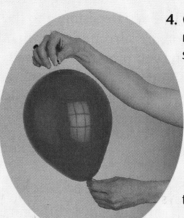

4. Observe how your body returns to normal after it responds to the sound.

Think It Over
Predicting How might your body respond if you suddenly saw a huge, threatening animal rushing toward you? How might your response be an advantage to you?

I t is one o'clock on a Sunday morning. Suddenly, you find yourself face to face with a horrible-looking creature. You let out a scream and wake yourself out of a deep sleep. As you become more awake, you realize that it was all just a dream. The creature was not real. But your reaction to confronting the creature certainly was! Your heart pounded thunderously in your chest. Your breathing rate almost doubled, and your body was covered with perspiration.

A nightmare—or any frightening or startling event—disrupts your body's internal stability. When you wake up after a nightmare, gradually your heart stops pounding, and your breathing rate slows down. Eventually, your body returns to its stable, normal state.

Stability of Living Systems

In its stable state, the human body is something like a well-balanced mobile. To make a mobile hang evenly, you need to adjust the positions of the various objects so that they balance one another. All systems, including mobiles and the human body, need a way of maintaining **equilibrium,** or balance. **When a system is in equilibrium, it is stable, and all its parts function smoothly.**

GUIDE FOR READING

◆ What are the characteristics of a system in equilibrium?

◆ What role do feedback mechanisms play in maintaining equilibrium?

Reading Tip As you read, write a definition, in your own words, of each boldfaced term.

Key Terms equilibrium
• homeostasis
• negative feedback
• hormone • diffusion
• osmosis • turgor pressure

Figure 8 A mobile is in equilibrium when all its parts are balanced. Like a mobile, an organism needs to maintain equilibrium.

All organisms, whether they are humans, bacteria, or plants, must maintain internal equilibrium no matter what happens in their environment. The process by which the body's internal environment is kept stable in spite of changes in the external environment is called **homeostasis** (hoh mee oh STAY sis).

Homeostasis is at work when your body returns to its normal state after a startling or frightening event, such as a nightmare. The body's resistance to disease also demonstrates homeostasis. You are surrounded by microorganisms that can make you sick, but you probably stay well most of the time. And when people become ill, they usually recover quickly. The immune system helps maintain homeostasis by killing disease-causing organisms before they can do much harm.

☑ *Checkpoint* What is homeostasis?

Negative Feedback

Organisms have different ways of keeping internal stability. **Negative feedback is one way in which living systems maintain internal equilibrium, or homeostasis.** In **negative feedback,** a process is turned off by the condition it produces.

To understand how negative feedback works, consider how a thermostat regulates the temperature in a room. When the room becomes cool, the thermostat "senses" the drop in temperature. The thermostat then turns the heater on. Later, when the heater has made the room warmer, the thermostat "senses" the rise in temperature and turns the heater off. Negative feedback is a cycle, as you can see in Figure 9. In humans, negative feedback helps regulate many functions. For example, negative feedback helps control the temperature of your body and the level of the sugar glucose in your blood.

Figure 9 The operation of a thermostat is an example of negative feedback. In negative feedback, a process, such as heating a room, is turned off by the condition it produces.
Interpreting Diagrams What happens when a room becomes too cool?

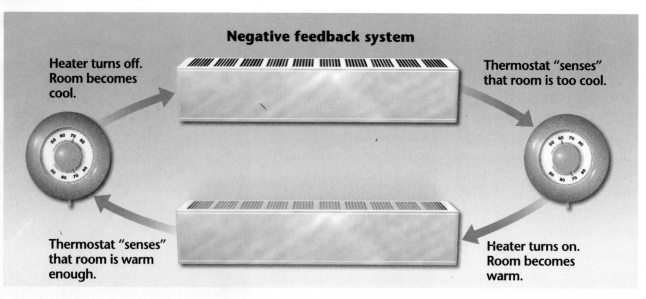

Negative feedback system

Heater turns off. Room becomes cool.

Thermostat "senses" that room is too cool.

Thermostat "senses" that room is warm enough.

Heater turns on. Room becomes warm.

Keeping Body Temperature Constant

Whether the air is cold or hot, the internal body temperature of birds and mammals is always about the same. A healthy human, for example, always has a temperature that is close to 37°C. Several processes keep body temperatures stable.

Staying Cool Sweating is one thing that helps keep the human body at a stable temperature. When you become warm, you perspire. Perspiration, which is mostly water, then evaporates from your skin. Heat is needed to make water evaporate. That heat comes from your body. Therefore, the process of evaporation cools your body by removing heat. Some animals, such as dogs, get rid of excess heat by panting. When an animal pants, some of the saliva in its mouth evaporates. The evaporation of saliva, like the evaporation of perspiration, helps cool the body.

Negative feedback is at work in both perspiration and panting. That is because excessive body heat leads to perspiration or panting, which in turn results in a reduction in body heat.

Figure 10 Running generates a lot of body heat. Perspiration helps maintain temperature equilibrium by cooling the body.
Applying Concepts How does perspiration remove excess heat?

Shivering While perspiration helps the body cool off, shivering helps keep it warm. If you become chilled, you shiver. When you shiver, muscles in your body contract involuntarily. These muscle contractions require energy, and the production of energy generates heat. Therefore, shivering has the effect of warming the body. This method of temperature regulation, like perspiration and panting, is an example of negative feedback. When the body becomes uncomfortably cool, shivering results. Then shivering makes the body warmer.

✓ *Checkpoint How does shivering help maintain homeostasis?*

Maintaining Glucose Levels in the Blood

INTEGRATING CHEMISTRY The energy your body needs to function comes from the breakdown of the sugar glucose in chemical reactions inside your cells. Glucose comes from the food you eat. After glucose is absorbed by the digestive system, blood transports the glucose and delivers it to cells.

Droopy Plants

Learn what role roots play in plants.

1. Dig up two plants of the same kind and approximately the same size. Include the soil around them, and avoid damaging the roots. Use field equipment such as trowels, spades, and flowerpots.

2. Put each plant and its soil in a flowerpot. Take the plants back to the classroom.

3. Spread newspapers beneath one of the flowerpots. Carefully take the plant out of the flowerpot. Cut the roots off at the base of the stem. Put the plant back in the soil in the flowerpot.

4. Water both plants. Add the same amount of water to each flowerpot.

5. Put the plants in a sunny place. Observe them for three days.

6. With your teacher, devise a plan for recycling the materials in this activity or returning them to their natural environment.

Inferring What role do roots play in maintaining homeostasis?

The level of glucose in the blood is regulated by chemical reactions. The chemical reactions are controlled by hormones of the endocrine system. A **hormone** is a chemical produced by an endocrine gland that affects the activity of a tissue or organ.

One hormone that helps regulate glucose levels is **insulin,** which is produced by an organ called the pancreas. When the level of glucose in the blood is high, the pancreas releases insulin. Insulin stimulates body cells to take up glucose from the blood. This lowers the level of glucose in the blood. Low levels of glucose in the blood, in turn, "turn off" the production of insulin. This is a negative feedback process because high levels of glucose eventually lead to the reduction of glucose levels in the blood.

☑ *Checkpoint* *What is the function of insulin?*

Maintaining Water Equilibrium in Plant Cells

To maintain homeostasis, living things need some way of regulating the amount of water in their cells and tissues. Like all organisms, plants need to maintain water equilibrium in spite of changing conditions.

Diffusion Many plants obtain water through roots. Water *INTEGRATING* enters these plants through root cells. The *CHEMISTRY* cells in a plant's roots, like all cells, are bound by a thin, flexible structure called the cell membrane. The cell membrane is selectively permeable—that is, some substances can pass through, while others cannot. Substances move back and forth through the cell membrane by a process called **diffusion.** In diffusion, molecules move from an area in which they are highly concentrated into one in which their concentration is lower.

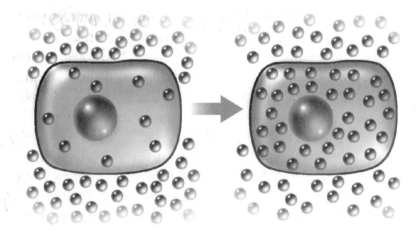

Figure 11 Molecules move from an area of higher concentration to an area of lower concentration. **(A)** There is a lower concentration of molecules inside the cell than outside. **(B)** Molecules from the outside diffuse into the cell. Eventually, there is an equal concentration of molecules inside and outside the cell.

The Movement of Water in Cells Water enters and leaves a cell through osmosis. **Osmosis** is the diffusion of water molecules through a selectively permeable membrane. The concentration of water molecules inside and outside the cell helps determine whether water enters a cell or leaves it. Suppose the concentration of water molecules is higher outside a cell than inside. Water molecules then move into the cell. The cell membrane expands because of all the water molecules that have moved inside the cell. The cell swells in much the same way that a balloon expands when you blow air into it.

Turgor Pressure The structure of plant cells contributes to a plant's ability to maintain water balance. A plant cell is surrounded by a rigid structure called the cell wall, which is located outside the cell membrane. Since cell walls are rigid, they limit the ability of plant cells to expand. As water molecules move into a plant cell, the expanding cell membrane presses against the rigid cell wall. The pressure of water against the cell wall of a plant cell is called **turgor pressure.** Turgor pressure helps give shape and firmness to plant stems and leaves.

If the environment outside a plant cell is dry, more water leaves the plant cell than enters it. As a result, turgor pressure inside cells is reduced. The cell membranes no longer press against the cell walls. The plant then loses its stiffness and wilts.

Figure 12 When a plant receives enough water, turgor pressure enables the stem and leaves to hold their shapes. When a plant does not receive enough water, the stem and leaves wilt. *Relating Cause and Effect* If someone watered the wilted plant, what would probably happen?

The Role of Negative Feedback in Turgor Pressure Turgor pressure contributes to a plant's ability to maintain water balance. After a heavy rain, the roots of a plant may be surrounded by water. However, turgor pressure helps keep excess water from entering the plant, even if the concentration of water molecules is very high outside the plant's cells. As water molecules enter the cell, the pressure of water molecules against the cell wall increases. Because of this increase in turgor pressure, the movement of water molecules into the cell slows down. Equilibrium is reached when the number of water molecules that enter the cell is equal to the number of water molecules that leave the cell. This is a negative feedback system because an increase in water molecules entering the cell eventually causes fewer water molecules to move into the cell.

✔ Checkpoint **What is turgor pressure?**

Figure 13 When you drink fluids, you are helping to maintain homeostasis by supplying your body with the water it needs.

Water Equilibrium in Animals

Animals, like plants, need to maintain water balance. When your body needs water, you become thirsty, and you drink fluids. This action enables your body to obtain the water it needs.

Many animals have excretory systems that help maintain water balance in the body. Your kidneys, which are part of your excretory system, remove wastes produced by your cells. Another role of the kidneys is to adjust the amount of water in your blood. They do this by changing the concentration of water in the urine they produce.

Suppose, for example, that you drink a lot of water—too much for your body to use right away. When that happens, the kidneys produce urine in which the concentration of water molecules is high. When the urine is eliminated from the body, the excess water is eliminated too.

In contrast, on a hot day, you might lose a lot of water through perspiration. In that case, the urine that the kidneys produce will have relatively little water. This helps keep water inside the body, where it is needed.

Section 2 Review

1. What does it mean for a system to be in equilibrium?
2. What is negative feedback?
3. Describe how the human body regulates the level of glucose in the blood.
4. How does turgor pressure help control the amount of water in plant cells?
5. **Thinking Critically** Applying Concepts Explain why the regulation of the amount of water in urine is a negative feedback process.

Check Your Progress CHAPTER PROJECT
By now you should have set up the bird feeder and begun observations. Use field guides to identify the birds and other animals. Pay careful attention to the way in which the birds interact with one another and with other animals. Do different birds compete for food? How do the birds react if another bird or other animal visits the feeder? Can you see any repeated patterns of interaction? Look for signs that some birds are trying to dominate others.

DISCOVER •••**ACTIVITY**••••

How Well Can You Hide a Butterfly?

1. Using the outline at the right, trace a butterfly onto a piece of paper.

2. Look around the classroom and pick a spot where you will place your butterfly. The butterfly must be placed completely in the open. Color your butterfly so it will blend in with the spot you choose.

3. Tape your butterfly to its spot. Someone will now enter the room to look for the butterflies. This person will have one minute to find all the butterflies he or she can. Will your butterfly be found?

Think It Over
Predicting How might a butterfly's appearance affect its ability to survive in its environment?

Imagine giving a big hug to the plant in the photo. Ouch! The sharp spines on its trunk would make you think twice before hugging—or even touching—the saguaro (suh GWAHR oh) cactus. But if you could spend a day hidden inside a saguaro, you would see that many species do interact with this spiky plant.

As the day breaks, you hear a twittering noise coming from a nest tucked in one of the saguaro's arms. Two young red-tailed hawks are preparing to fly for the first time. Farther down the trunk, a tiny elf owl peeks out of its nest in a small hole. The elf owl is so small it could fit in your palm! A rattlesnake slithers around the base of the saguaro, looking for lunch. Spying a nearby shrew, the snake moves in for the kill. With a sudden movement, it strikes the shrew with its sharp fangs.

The activity around the saguaro doesn't stop after the sun goes down. At night, long-nosed bats feed on the nectar from the saguaro's blossoms. They stick their faces into the flowers to feed, covering their long snouts with a dusting of white pollen in the process. As the bats move from plant to plant, they carry the pollen along. This enables the cactuses to reproduce.

GUIDE FOR READING

◆ How do adaptations help an organism survive?

◆ What are the major types of interactions among organisms in an ecosystem?

◆ What are the three forms of symbiotic relationships?

Reading Tip As you read, use the section headings to make an outline. Fill in details under each heading.

Key Terms ecosystem
• niche • competition
• predation • predator • prey
• symbiosis • mutualism
• commensalism • parasitism
• parasite • host

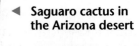
◀ Saguaro cactus in the Arizona desert

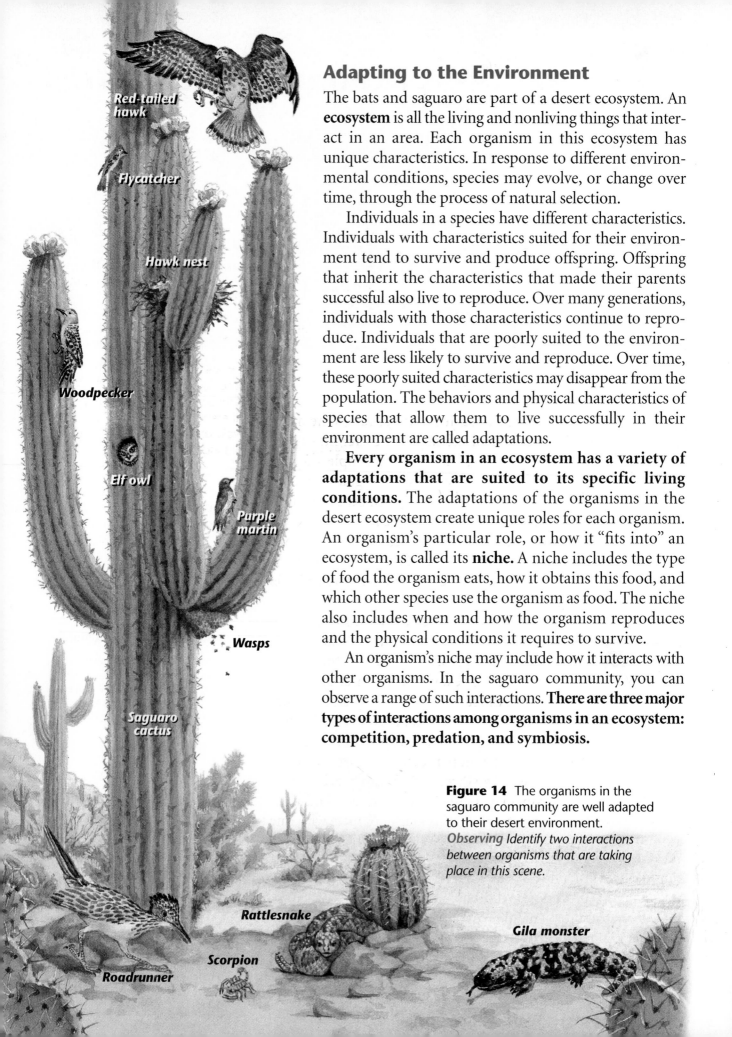

Adapting to the Environment

The bats and saguaro are part of a desert ecosystem. An **ecosystem** is all the living and nonliving things that interact in an area. Each organism in this ecosystem has unique characteristics. In response to different environmental conditions, species may evolve, or change over time, through the process of natural selection.

Individuals in a species have different characteristics. Individuals with characteristics suited for their environment tend to survive and produce offspring. Offspring that inherit the characteristics that made their parents successful also live to reproduce. Over many generations, individuals with those characteristics continue to reproduce. Individuals that are poorly suited to the environment are less likely to survive and reproduce. Over time, these poorly suited characteristics may disappear from the population. The behaviors and physical characteristics of species that allow them to live successfully in their environment are called adaptations.

Every organism in an ecosystem has a variety of adaptations that are suited to its specific living conditions. The adaptations of the organisms in the desert ecosystem create unique roles for each organism. An organism's particular role, or how it "fits into" an ecosystem, is called its **niche.** A niche includes the type of food the organism eats, how it obtains this food, and which other species use the organism as food. The niche also includes when and how the organism reproduces and the physical conditions it requires to survive.

An organism's niche may include how it interacts with other organisms. In the saguaro community, you can observe a range of such interactions. **There are three major types of interactions among organisms in an ecosystem: competition, predation, and symbiosis.**

Red-tailed hawk

Flycatcher

Hawk nest

Woodpecker

Elf owl

Purple martin

Wasps

Saguaro cactus

Figure 14 The organisms in the saguaro community are well adapted to their desert environment.
Observing Identify two interactions between organisms that are taking place in this scene.

Rattlesnake

Gila monster

Scorpion

Roadrunner

The bay-breasted warbler *feeds in the middle part of the tree.*

The Cape May warbler *feeds at the tips of branches near the top of the tree.*

The yellow-rumped warbler *feeds in the lower part of the tree and at the bases of the middle branches.*

Figure 15 Each of these warblers occupies a different niche in its spruce tree habitat. By feeding in different areas of the tree, the birds avoid competing with one another for food.

Competition

Different species can share the same habitat, such as the many animals that live in and around the saguaro. Different species can also share similar food requirements. For example, the red-tailed hawk and the elf owl both live on the saguaro and eat similar food. However, these two species do not occupy exactly the same niche. The hawk is active during the day, while the owl is active mostly at night. If two species occupy the same niche, one of the species will eventually die off. The reason for this is **competition,** the struggle between organisms to survive in a habitat with limited resources.

An ecosystem cannot satisfy the needs of all the living things in a particular habitat. There is a limited amount of food, water, and shelter. Organisms that survive have adaptations that enable them to reduce competition. For example, the three species of warblers in Figure 15 live in the same spruce forest habitat. They all eat insects that live in the spruce trees. How do these birds avoid competing for the limited insect supply? Each warbler "specializes" in feeding in a certain part of a spruce tree. By finding their own places to feed, the three species can coexist.

INTEGRATING CHEMISTRY Many plants use chemicals to ward off their competition. Plants often compete with one another for growing space and water. Some shrubs release toxic, or poisonous, chemicals into the ground around them. These chemicals keep grass and weeds from growing around the shrubs, sometimes forming a ring of bare ground a meter or two wide.

✓ *Checkpoint* *Why can't two species occupy the same niche?*

Predation

A tiger shark lurks beneath the surface of the clear blue water, looking for shadows of young albatrosses floating above it. The shark sees a chick and silently swims closer. Suddenly, the shark bursts through the water and seizes the albatross with one snap of its powerful jaw. This interaction between two organisms has an unfortunate ending for the albatross.

An interaction in which one organism hunts and kills another for food is called **predation.** The organism that does the killing, in this case the tiger shark, is the **predator.** The organism that is caught, the albatross, is the **prey.**

Predator Adaptations Predators have adaptations that help them catch and kill their prey. For example, a cheetah can run very fast for a short time, enabling it to catch its prey. A jellyfish's tentacles contain a poisonous substance that paralyzes tiny water

EXPLORING *Defense Strategies*

Organisms display a wide array of adaptations that help them avoid becoming prey.

Protective coverings
This sea urchin sends a clear message to predators: "Don't touch!" Porcupines, hedgehogs, and cactuses all use the same spiny strategy. After a few painful encounters, a predator will look for less-prickly prey. ▼

Camouflage ▲
These delicate spiny bugs are a perfect match for their branch habitat. The more an organism resembles its surroundings, the less likely it is that a predator will notice it. Some animals, such as flounder, can even change their colors to match a variety of settings.

animals. You can probably think of many predators that have claws, sharp teeth, or stingers. Some plants, too, have adaptations for catching prey. The sundew plant is covered with sticky bulbs on stalks—when a fly lands on the plant, it remains snared in the sticky goo while the plant digests it.

Some predators have adaptations that enable them to hunt at night. For example, the big eyes of an owl let in as much light as possible to help it see in the dark. Bats can hunt without seeing at all. Instead, they locate their prey by producing pulses of sound and listening for the echoes. This precise method enables a bat to catch a flying moth in complete darkness.

Prey Adaptations How do prey organisms manage to avoid being caught by such effective predators? In *Exploring Defense Strategies*, below, you can see some examples of how an organism's physical characteristics can help protect it.

Warning coloring ▲
A frog this bright certainly can't hide. How could such a color be an advantage? The bright red and blue of this poison arrow frog warn predators not to eat it— glands on the frog's back that release toxic chemicals make it a bad choice for a meal.

Mimicry
If you've ever been stung by a bee, you'd probably keep your distance from this insect. But actually this "bee" is a harmless fly. The fly's resemblance to a stinging bee protects it from birds and other predators, who are fooled into staying away. ▼

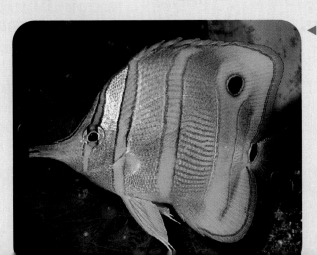

◄ False coloring
Which way is this butterfly fish swimming? The black dot on its tail is a false eye. A predator may bite this end of the fish, allowing the fish to escape with only part of its tail missing.

LOOKING AT
AN OWL'S LEFTOVERS

Predator-prey relationships are one way in which organisms interact in an ecosystem. All owls are predators. They feed on various kinds of prey. In this lab you will gather evidence and draw conclusions about an owl's diet.

Problem

What can you learn about owls' diets from studying the material in the pellets that they cough up?

Materials

owl pellet   hand lens
dissecting needle   metric ruler
forceps   computer (optional)

Procedure

1. An owl pellet is a collection of undigested materials that an owl coughs up after a meal. Write a hypothesis describing what items you expect an owl pellet to contain. List the reasons for your hypothesis.

2. Use a hand lens to observe the outside of an owl pellet. Use a pencil and paper or a computer to record your observations.

3. Use one hand to grasp the owl pellet with forceps. Hold a dissecting needle in your other hand, and use it to gently separate the pellet into pieces. **CAUTION:** *Dissecting needles are sharp. Never cut material toward you; always cut away from your body.*

4. Using the forceps and dissecting needle, carefully separate the bones from the rest of the pellet. Remove any fur that might be attached to bones.

Shrew	House mouse	Meadow vole	Mole	Rat

Upper jaw has at least 18 teeth; teeth are brown. Skull length is 23 mm or less.	Upper jaw has 2 biting teeth and extends past lower jaw. Skull length is 22 mm or less.	Upper jaw has 2 biting teeth that are smooth, not grooved. Skull length is more than 23 mm.	Upper jaw has at least 18 teeth. Skull length is 23 mm or more.	Upper jaw has 2 biting teeth. Upper jaw extends past lower jaw. Skull length is 22 mm or more.

5. Group similar bones together in separate piles. Observe the skulls, and draw them. Record the number of skulls, their length, and the number, shape, and color of the teeth.

6. Use the chart on this page to determine what kinds of skulls you found. If any skulls do not match the chart exactly, record which animal each skull resembles most.

7. Try to fit together any of the remaining bones to form complete or partial skeletons. Sketch your results.

8. Wash your hands thoroughly with soap when you are finished.

Analyze and Conclude

1. How many animals' remains were in the pellet? What data led you to that conclusion?

2. Combine your results with those of your classmates. Which three animals were eaten most frequently? How do these results compare to your hypothesis?

3. Owls cough up about two pellets a day. Based on your class's data, what can you predict about the number of animals an owl might eat in one month?

4. **Think About It** In this lab, you were able to examine only the part of the owl's diet that it did not digest. How might this fact affect your confidence in the conclusions you reached?

Design an Experiment

Design a study that might tell you how an owl's diet varies at different times of the year. Give an example of a conclusion you might expect to draw from such a study.

Figure 16 The populations of wolves and moose on Isle Royale are related. The predator wolf population depends on the size of the prey moose population, and vice versa.
Predicting How might a disease in the wolf population one year affect the moose population the next year?

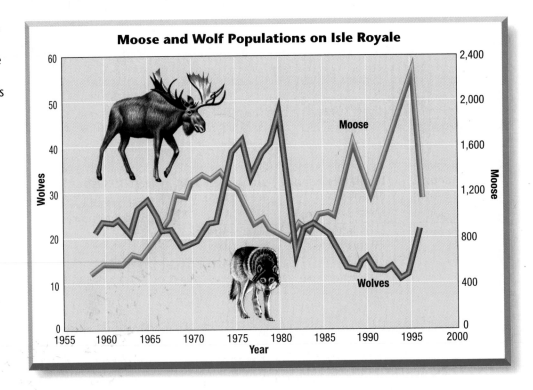

Moose and Wolf Populations on Isle Royale

The Effect of Predation on Population Size

Predation can have a major effect on the size of a population, or all the members of one species in a particular area. When the death rate exceeds the birth rate in a population, the size of the population usually decreases. If predators are very effective at hunting their prey, the result is often a decrease in the size of the prey population. But a decrease in the prey population in turn affects the predator population.

To see how predator and prey populations can affect each other, look at the graph above. The graph shows the number of moose and wolves living on Isle Royale, an island in Lake Superior. From 1965 to 1975, the number of prey moose increased. The wolves now had enough to eat, so more of them survived. Within a few years, the wolf population began to increase. The growing number of wolves killed more and more moose. The moose population decreased. By 1980, the lack of moose had greatly affected the wolves. Some wolves starved, and others could not raise as many young. Soon the moose population began to climb again. This cycle for the two species has continued.

Of course, other factors also affect the populations on Isle Royale. For instance, cold winters and disease can also reduce the size of one or both of the populations.

✓ *Checkpoint* *If predation removes more members of a population than are born, how will the population change?*

Symbiosis

Many of the interactions in the saguaro community you read about earlier are examples of symbiosis. **Symbiosis** (sim bee OH sis) is a close relationship between two species that benefits at least one of the species. **The three types of symbiotic relationships are mutualism, commensalism, and parasitism.**

Mutualism A relationship in which both species benefit is called **mutualism** (MYOO choo uh liz um). The relationship between the saguaro and the long-eared bats is an example of mutualism. The bat benefits because the cactus flowers provide it with food. The saguaro benefits as its pollen is carried on the bat's nose to another plant.

INTEGRATING HEALTH At this very moment, you are participating in a mutualistic relationship with a population of bacteria in your large intestine. These bacteria, called *Escherichia coli*, live in the intestines of most mammals. These bacteria break down some foods that the mammal cannot digest. The bacteria benefit by receiving food and a place to live. You also benefit from the relationship because the bacteria provide you with vitamin K, a nutrient that is needed to make your blood clot.

Commensalism A relationship in which one species benefits and the other species is neither helped nor harmed is called **commensalism** (kuh MEN suh liz um). The red-tailed hawks' interaction with the saguaro is an example of commensalism. The hawks are helped by having a place to build their nest, while the cactus is not affected by the birds.

Commensalism is not very common in nature because two species are usually either helped or harmed a little by any interaction. For example, by creating a small hole for its nest in the cactus trunk, the elf owl slightly damages the cactus.

Figure 17 Three yellow-billed oxpeckers get a cruise and a snack aboard an obliging hippopotamus. The oxpeckers eat ticks living on the hippo's skin. Since both the birds and the hippo benefit from this interaction, it is an example of mutualism.

Figure 18 The white objects on this sphinx moth larva are wasp cocoons. When the wasps emerge, they will feed on the larva. *Applying Concepts Which organism in this interaction is the parasite? Which organism is the host?*

Parasitism The third type of symbiosis is called parasitism. **Parasitism** (PA ruh sit iz um) involves one organism living on or inside another organism and harming it. The organism that benefits is called a **parasite.** The organism the parasite lives on or in is called a **host.** The parasite is usually smaller than the host. In a parasitic relationship, the parasite benefits from the interaction while the host is harmed.

Some common parasites you may be familiar with are fleas, ticks, and leeches. These parasites have adaptations that enable them to attach to their host and feed on its blood. Other parasites live inside the host's body, such as tapeworms that live inside the digestive systems of many mammals, including dogs and wolves.

Unlike a predator, a parasite does not usually kill the organism it feeds on. If the host dies, the parasite loses its source of food. An interesting example of this rule is shown by a species of mite that lives in the ears of moths. The mites almost always live in just one of the moth's ears. If they live in both ears, the moth's hearing is so badly affected that it is likely to be quickly caught and eaten by its predator, a bat.

Section 3 Review

1. How do an organism's adaptations help it to survive?
2. Name and define the three major types of interactions among organisms in ecosystems.
3. List the three types of symbiosis. For each one, explain how the two organisms are affected.
4. A walking stick is an insect that resembles a small twig. How do you think this insect avoids predators?
5. **Thinking Critically Comparing and Contrasting** How are parasitism and predation similar? How are they different?

Check Your Progress CHAPTER PROJECT
Continue to observe interactions among animals at your bird feeder. Record your observations in your notebook. Now is the time to plan your presentation. You may want to include the following information in your presentation: drawings of the different animals you have observed, detailed descriptions of their interactions, and other interesting observations you have made.

SECTION 1 Interactions in the Human Body

Key Ideas

◆ A system is any group of parts that work together as a unit.
◆ Interdependence among organ systems is necessary for the processes that keep humans alive and enable them to reproduce.
◆ All body systems interact with the cardiovascular system.
◆ The respiratory system interacts with the cardiovascular and muscular systems to deliver oxygen to cells and remove carbon dioxide.
◆ The digestive, muscular, and cardiovascular systems interact to digest the food you eat and deliver nutrients to cells.
◆ The muscular, skeletal, and nervous system are all involved in voluntary movements.

Key Terms

system	trachea
tissue	alveolus
organ	diaphragm
organ system	villus

SECTION 2 Equilibrium and Feedback

Key Ideas

◆ When a system is in equilibrium, it is stable, and all its parts function smoothly.
◆ Negative feedback is one way in which living systems maintain homeostasis. In negative feedback, a process is turned off by the condition it produces.
◆ Negative feedback mechanisms are involved in maintaining body temperature and regulating glucose levels in the blood.
◆ Through negative feedback, turgor pressure helps keep excess water from entering plants.

Key Terms

equilibrium	diffusion
homeostasis	osmosis
negative feedback	turgor pressure
hormone	

SECTION 3 Interactions Among Living Things

Key Ideas

◆ Over time, species of organisms develop specialized adaptations and behaviors that help them succeed in their environments.
◆ The major types of interactions among organisms are competition, predation, and symbiosis.
◆ Symbiosis is a close relationship between two species. The three types of symbiotic relationships are mutualism, commensalism, and parasitism.

Key Terms

ecosystem	predator	commensalism
niche	prey	parasitism
competition	symbiosis	parasite
predation	mutualism	host

Organizing Information

Concept Map Copy the concept map about interactions among organisms onto a sheet of paper. Complete it and add a title. (For more on concept maps, see the Skills Handbook.)

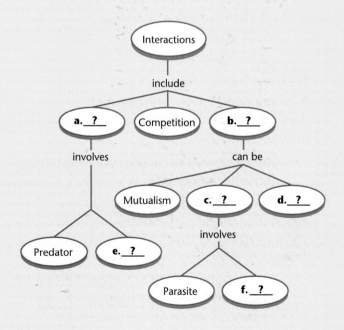

Reviewing Content

 Review key concepts online using iText at www.phschool.com

Multiple Choice

Choose the letter of the best answer.

1. A group of parts that work together is called a
   a. system. **b.** cell.
   c. tissue. **d.** stability.

2. The body system that fights disease is the
   a. cardiovascular system.
   b. digestive system.
   c. immune system.
   d. skeletal system.

3. The process by which the body's internal environment is kept stable in spite of changes in the external environment is called
   a. circulation. **b.** homeostasis.
   c. mutualism. **d.** diffusion.

4. In which type of interaction do both species benefit?
   a. predation **b.** mutualism
   c. commensalism **d.** parasitism

5. Which of these relationships is an example of parasitism?
   a. a bird building a nest on a tree branch
   b. a bat pollinating a saguaro cactus
   c. a flea living on a cat's blood
   d. *Escherichia coli* bacteria making vitamin K in your intestine

True or False

If the statement is true, write true. If it is false, change the underlined word or words to make the statement true.

6. The <u>excretory</u> system transports absorbed nutrients to body cells.

7. When a system is in <u>equilibrium</u>, it is stable, and all parts function smoothly.

8. In <u>negative feedback</u>, a process is turned on by the condition it produces.

9. The struggle between organisms for limited resources is called <u>mutualism</u>.

10. A parasite lives on or inside its <u>predator</u>.

Checking Concepts

11. Describe how the muscular, skeletal, and nervous systems work together to move the bones in your arm.

12. Why is the cardiovascular system so important to interactions within the human body?

13. Why would it be impossible for your body to use oxygen without your muscular system?

14. Explain what turgor pressure is and what causes turgor pressure.

15. Explain how negative feedback helps regulate the level of glucose in the blood.

16. What are two adaptations that prey organisms have developed to protect themselves? Describe how each adaptation protects the organism.

17. **Writing to Learn** Write a description of your niche in the environment. Include details about both living and nonliving things. Be sure to describe your feeding habits as well as any interactions you have with members of other species.

Thinking Critically

18. **Relating Cause and Effect** Suppose disease damaged the muscles involved in breathing. How would this affect the functioning of the respiratory system?

19. **Applying Concepts** Explain how eating food helps the body maintain homeostasis.

20. **Applying Concepts** In general, the more athletes practice, the better they become at their sport and the more they want to play it. Is this situation an example of negative feedback? Explain.

21. **Relating Cause and Effect** Competition for resources in an area is usually more intense within a single species than between two different species. Can you suggest an explanation for this observation? *(Hint: Consider how niches help organisms avoid competition.)*

22. **Comparing and Contrasting** Explain how parasitism and mutualism are similar and how they are different.

Applying Skills

A scientist fed a strong sugar solution to an animal. The scientist then checked the concentration of sugar in the animal's blood every 30 minutes. The table below shows the results of the experiment.

Time After Eating Sugar (minutes)	Sugar Concentration (milligrams/100 milliliters)
0	75
30	125
60	110
90	90
120	75
150	75

23. What was the concentration of sugar in the animal's blood after 90 minutes?
24. At what point was the concentration of sugar highest?

25. How do the data in the experiment show homeostasis at work? (*Hint:* Compare the concentrations of glucose at the beginning and the end of the experiment.)

Performance ▼ CHAPTER PROJECT Assessment

Present Your Project When you present your project, display the drawings that you made and the notebook in which you recorded your observations. Be sure to describe the type of interactions that you observed among animals at the bird feeder and other interesting animal behaviors that you observed.

Reflect and Record In your journal, analyze how successful the project was. Did many birds and other animals come to the feeder? If not, why might this have happened? What are the advantages and limitations for using field guides to identify birds and other animals?

Test Preparation

Use these questions to prepare for standardized tests.

Use the information to answer Questions 26–28.

The crown of thorns is a species of sea star, or starfish. Like all sea stars, the crown of thorns lives in the ocean. Specifically, the crown of thorns lives among the corals that make up the Great Barrier Reef off the coast of Australia. The crown of thorns feeds on the tiny coral animals that make up the coral reef. In turn, several kinds of fishes feed on the crown of thorns. In recent years, however, fishing by humans has caused the populations of those fishes to decrease. The crown of thorns population has recently grown much larger.

26. The coral animals are the crown of thorns'
    A prey.   **B** predators.
    C parasites.   **D** hosts.

27. What is the most likely explanation for the increase in the crown of thorns' population?
    F The crown of thorns' food supply has increased.
    G There are fewer predators that kill the crown of thorns.
    H The crown of thorns has changed its feeding habits.
    J The fishes have found new prey.

28. Predict what has happened to the coral animals as the result of the increase in the numbers of crown of thorns.
    A The coral animals have found new prey.
    B The population of coral animals has increased.
    C The population of coral animals has decreased.
    D There has been no significant change in the population of coral animals.

DOGS

LOYAL COMPANIONS

WHAT'S YOUR IMAGE OF A **DOG?**

+ A small, floppy-eared spaniel?

+ A large, powerful Great Dane?

+ A protective German shepherd guide dog?

+ A shaggy sheepdog?

+ A tiny, lively Chihuahua?

+ A friendly, lovable mutt?

The gray wolf is the ancestor of most modern breeds of dogs.

More than 3,000 years ago, an artist in ancient Egypt drew three dogs chasing a hyena.

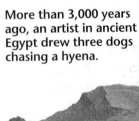

Most dogs are descendants of the gray wolf, which was originally found throughout Europe, Asia, and North America. Dogs were the first animals to be domesticated, or tamed. As far back as 9,000 years ago, farmers who raised sheep, cattle, and goats tamed dogs to herd and guard the livestock.

After taming dogs, people began to breed them for traits that people valued. Early herding dogs helped shepherds. Speedy hunting dogs learned to chase deer and other game. Strong, sturdy working dogs pulled sleds and even rescued people. Small, quick terriers hunted animals, such as rats. "Toy" dogs were companions to people of wealth and leisure. More recently, sporting dogs were trained to flush out and retrieve birds. Still others were bred to be guard dogs. But perhaps the real reason people bred dogs was for their loyalty and companionship.

From Wolf to Purebred

About ten thousand years ago, some wolves may have been attracted to human settlements. They may have found it easier to feed on food scraps than to hunt for themselves. Gradually the wolves came to depend on people for food. The wolves, in turn, kept the campsites clean and safe. They ate the garbage and barked to warn of approaching strangers. These wolves were the ancestors of the dogs you know today.

Over time dogs became more and more a part of human society. People began to breed dogs for the traits needed for tasks such as herding sheep and hunting. Large, aggressive dogs, for example, were bred to be herding dogs, while fast dogs with a keen sense of smell were bred to be hunting dogs. Today there are hundreds of breeds. They range from the tiny Chihuahua to the massive Saint Bernard, one of which can weigh as much as fifty Chihuahuas.

Today, people breed dogs mostly for their appearance and personality. Physical features such as long ears or a narrow snout are valued in particular breeds of dogs. To create "pure" breeds of dogs, breeders use a method known as inbreeding. Inbreeding involves mating dogs that are genetically very similar. Inbreeding is the surest way to produce dogs with a uniform physical appearance.

One undesirable result of inbreeding is an increase in genetic disorders. Experts estimate that 25 percent of all purebred dogs have a genetic disorder. Dalmatians, for example, often inherit deafness. German shepherds may develop severe hip problems. Mixed-breed dogs, in contrast, are less likely to inherit genetic disorders.

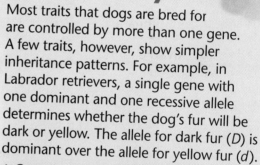

Science Activity

Most traits that dogs are bred for are controlled by more than one gene. A few traits, however, show simpler inheritance patterns. For example, in Labrador retrievers, a single gene with one dominant and one recessive allele determines whether the dog's fur will be dark or yellow. The allele for dark fur (*D*) is dominant over the allele for yellow fur (*d*).

◆ Construct a Punnett square for a cross between 2 Labrador retrievers that are both heterozygous for dark fur (*Dd*).

◆ Suppose there were 8 puppies in the litter. Predict how many would have dark fur and how many would have yellow fur.

◆ Construct a second Punnett square for a cross between a Labrador retriever with yellow fur (*dd*) and one with dark fur (*Dd*). In a litter with 6 puppies, predict how many would have dark fur and how many would have yellow fur.

In Labrador retrievers, the allele for dark-colored fur is dominant over the allele for yellow fur.

Golden retriever
Great Britain, A.D. 1870s
Lord Tweedsmouth developed this breed to help hunters retrieve waterfowl and other small animals.

Border collie
Great Britain, after A.D. 1100
This breed was developed in the counties near the border of England and Scotland for herding sheep. The Border collie's ancestors were cross-breeds of local sheepdogs and dogs brought to Scotland by the Vikings.

Dachshund
Germany, A.D. 1700s
These dogs were bred to catch badgers or rats. Their short legs and long body can fit into a badger's burrow. In fact, in German the word *dachshund* means "badger dog."

Basset hound
France, A.D. 1600s
Second only to the bloodhound at following a scent, the basset hound has short legs and a compact body that help it run through underbrush.

Greyhound
Egypt, 3500 B.C.
These speedy, slender hounds were bred for chasing prey. Today, greyhounds are famous as racers.

Dogs and People

Over thousands of years, people have developed many different breeds of dogs. Each of the dogs shown on the map was bred for a purpose—hunting, herding, guarding, pulling sleds—as well as companionship. Every breed has its own story.

Siberian husky
Siberia, 1000 B.C.
The Chukchi people of northeastern Siberia used these strong working dogs to pull sleds long distances across the snow.

Pekingese
China, A.D. 700s
These lapdogs were bred as pets in ancient China. One Chinese name for a Pekingese means "lion dog," which refers to the dog's long, golden mane.

Chow chow
China, 150 B.C.
Chow chows, the working dogs of ancient China, worked as hunters, herders, and guard dogs.

Akita
Japan, A.D. 1600s
This breed was developed in the cold mountains of northern Japan as a guard dog and hunting dog. The Akita is able to hunt in deep snow and is also a powerful swimmer.

Lhasa apso
Tibet, A.D. 1100
This breed has a long, thick coat to protect it from the cold air of the high Tibetan plateau. In spite of its small size, the Lhasa apso guarded homes and temples.

Social Studies Activity

Draw a time line that shows the approximate date of origin of different breeds of domestic dogs from 7000 B.C. to the present. Use the information on the map to fill out your time line. Include information about where each breed was developed.

Picking a Puppy

People look for different traits in the dogs they choose. Here is how one expert selected his dog based on good breeding and personality.

James Herriot, a veterinarian in England, had owned several dogs during his lifetime. But he had always wanted a Border terrier. These small, sturdy dogs are descendants of working terrier breeds that lived on the border of England and Scotland. For centuries they were used to hunt foxes, rats, and other small animals. In this story, Herriot and his wife Helen follow up on an advertisement for Border terrier puppies.

Language Arts Activity

James Herriot describes this scene using dialog and first-person narrative. The narrative describes Herriot's feelings about a memorable event—finally finding the dog he had wanted for so long. Write a first-person narrative describing a memorable event in your life. You might choose a childhood memory or a personal achievement at school. What emotions did you feel? How did you make your decision? If possible, use dialog in your writing.

Border terrier ▶

S he [Helen, his wife] turned to me and spoke agitatedly, "I've got Mrs. Mason on the line now. There's only one pup left out of the litter and there are people coming from as far as eighty miles away to see it. We'll have to hurry. What a long time you've been out there!"

We bolted our lunch and Helen, Rosie, granddaughter Emma and I drove out to Bedale. Mrs. Mason led us into the kitchen and pointed to a tiny brindle creature twisting and writhing under the table.

"That's him," she said.

I reached down and lifted the puppy as he curled his little body round, apparently trying to touch his tail with his nose. But that tail wagged furiously and the pink tongue was busy at my hand. I knew he was ours before my quick examination for hernia and overshot jaw.

The deal was quickly struck and we went outside to inspect the puppy's relations. His mother and grandmother were out there. They lived in little barrels which served as kennels and both of them darted out and stood up at our legs, tails lashing, mouths panting in delight. I felt vastly reassured. With happy, healthy ancestors like those I knew we had every chance of a first rate dog.

As we drove home with the puppy in Emma's arms, the warm thought came to me. The wheel had indeed turned. After nearly fifty years I had my Border terrier.

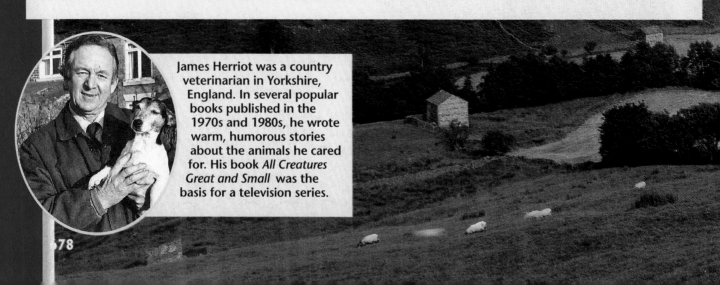

James Herriot was a country veterinarian in Yorkshire, England. In several popular books published in the 1970s and 1980s, he wrote warm, humorous stories about the animals he cared for. His book *All Creatures Great and Small* was the basis for a television series.

Breed	1970	1980	1990	1997
Poodle	265,879	92,250	71,757	54,773
Labrador Retriever	25,667	52,398	99,776	158,366
Cocker Spaniel	21,811	76,113	105,642	41,439

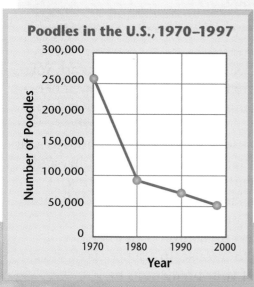

Poodles in the U.S., 1970–1997

(Line graph: Number of Poodles vs. Year. Y-axis from 0 to 300,000 in increments of 50,000; X-axis years 1970, 1980, 1990, 2000. Points showing approximately 250,000 at 1970, declining to about 90,000 at 1980, 70,000 at 1990, and 50,000 at 1997.)

Math Activity

The popularity of different breeds of dogs changes over time. For example, the line graph shows how the number of poodles registered with the American Kennel Club changed between 1970 and 1997. Use the table to create your own line graph for Labrador retrievers and cocker spaniels.

Which breed was more popular in 1980, Labrador retrievers or cocker spaniels? How has the number of Labrador retrievers changed from 1970 to 1997? How has the number of cocker spaniels changed over the same time?

Tie It Together

Best of Breed Show

In many places proud dog owners of all ages bring their animals to compete in dog shows. Organize your own dog show. With a partner, choose one specific breed of dog. Pick a breed shown on the map on pages 176–177, or use library resources to research another breed.

◆ Find out what the breed looks like, the time and place where it originated, and what traits it was first bred for.

◆ List your breed's characteristics, height, weight, and coloring.

◆ Research the breed's personality and behavior.

◆ Find out your breed's strengths. Learn what weakness may develop as a result of inbreeding.

◆ Make a poster for your breed. Include a drawing or photo and the information that you researched.

◆ With your class, organize the dog displays into categories of breeds, such as hunting dogs, herding dogs, and toy dogs.

Think Like a Scientist

Although you may not know it, you think like a scientist every day. Whenever you ask a question and explore possible answers, you use many of the same skills that scientists do. Some of these skills are described on this page.

Observing

When you use one or more of your five senses to gather information about the world, you are **observing.** Hearing a dog bark, counting twelve green seeds, and smelling smoke are all observations. To increase the power of their senses, scientists sometimes use microscopes, telescopes, or other instruments that help them make more detailed observations.

An observation must be an accurate report of what your senses detect. It is important to keep careful records of your observations in science class by writing or drawing in a notebook. The information collected through observations is called evidence, or data. Evidence can be either direct or indirect.

Inferring

When you interpret an observation, you are **inferring,** or drawing an inference. For example, if you hear your dog barking, you may infer that someone is at your front door. To draw this inference, you combine the evidence—the barking dog—and your experience or knowledge—you know that your dog barks when strangers approach—to reach a logical conclusion.

Notice that an inference is not a fact; it is only one of many possible interpretations of an observation. For example, your dog may be barking because it wants to go for a walk. An inference may turn out to be incorrect even if it is based on accurate observations and logical reasoning. The only way to find out if an inference is correct is to investigate further.

Predicting

When you listen to the weather forecast, you may hear predictions about future weather— what the temperature will be, whether it will rain, and how windy it will be. Weather forecasters use observations and knowledge of weather patterns to predict the weather and weather trends. The skill of **predicting** involves making an inference about a future event based on current evidence.

Because a prediction is an inference, it may prove to be false. In science class, you can test some of your predictions by doing experiments. For example, suppose you predict that larger paper airplanes can fly farther than smaller airplanes. How could you test your prediction?

ACTIVITY Use the photograph to answer the questions below.

Observing Look closely at the photograph. List at least three observations.

Inferring Use your observations to make an inference about what has happened. What experience or knowledge did you use to make the inference?

Predicting Predict what will happen next. On what evidence or experience do you base your prediction?

Classifying

Could you imagine searching for a book in the library if the books were shelved in no particular order? Your trip to the library would be an all-day event! Luckily, librarians group together books on similar topics or by the same author. Grouping together items that are alike in some way is called **classifying.** You can classify items in many ways: by size, by shape, by use, and by other important characteristics.

Like librarians, scientists use the skill of classifying to organize information and objects. When things are sorted into groups, the relationships among them become easier to understand.

 ACTIVITY
Classify the objects in the photograph into two groups based on any characteristic you choose. Then use another characteristic to classify the objects into three groups.

Making Models

Have you ever drawn a picture to help someone understand what you were saying? Such a drawing is one type of model. A model is a picture, diagram, computer image, or other representation of a complex object or process. **Making models** helps people understand things that they cannot observe directly.

Scientists use models to represent very large or very small things, such as the planets in the solar system, or the parts of a cell. Such models are physical models—drawings or three-dimensional structures that look like the real thing. Other models are mental models—mathematical equations or words that describe how something works. All models have limitations.

ACTIVITY
This student is using a model to demonstrate what causes day and night on Earth. What do the flashlight and the tennis ball in the model represent? What are the model's limitations?

Communicating

Whenever you talk on the phone, write a letter, or listen to your teacher at school, you are communicating. **Communicating** is the process of sharing ideas and information with other people. Communicating effectively requires many skills, including writing, reading, speaking, listening, and making models.

Scientists communicate to share results, information, and opinions. Scientists often communicate about their work in journals, over the telephone, in

letters, and on the Internet. They also attend scientific meetings where they share their ideas with one another in person.

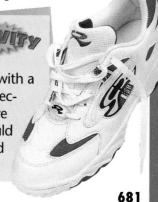

ACTIVITY
On a sheet of paper, write out clear, detailed directions for tying your shoe. Then exchange directions with a partner. Follow your partner's directions exactly. How successful were you at tying your shoe? How could your partner have communicated more clearly?

Making Measurements

When scientists make observations, it is not sufficient to say that something is "big" or "heavy." Instead, scientists use instruments to measure just how big or heavy an object is. By measuring, scientists can express their observations more precisely and communicate more information about what they observe.

Measuring in SI

The standard system of measurement used by scientists around the world is known as the International System of Units, which is abbreviated as SI (in French, *Système International d'Unités*). SI units are easy to use because they are based on multiples of 10. Each unit is ten times larger than the next smallest unit and one tenth the size of the next largest unit. The table lists the prefixes used to name the most common SI units.

Common SI Prefixes

Prefix	Symbol	Meaning
kilo-	k	1,000
hecto-	h	100
deka-	da	10
deci-	d	0.1 (one tenth)
centi-	c	0.01 (one hundredth)
milli-	m	0.001 (one thousandth)

Length To measure length, or the distance between two points, the unit of measure is the **meter (m)**. The distance from the floor to a doorknob is approximately one meter. Long distances, such as the distance between two cities, are measured in kilometers (km). Small lengths are measured in centimeters (cm) or millimeters (mm). Scientists use metric rulers and meter sticks to measure length.

Common Conversions

1 km = 1,000 m
1 m = 100 cm
1 m = 1,000 mm
1 cm = 10 mm

The larger lines on the metric ruler in the picture show centimeter divisions, while the smaller, unnumbered lines show millimeter divisions. How many centimeters long is the shell? How many millimeters long is it?   **ACTIVITY**

Liquid Volume To measure the volume of a liquid, or the amount of space it takes up, you will use a unit of measure known as the **liter (L)**. One liter is the approximate volume of a medium-sized carton of milk. Smaller volumes are measured in milliliters (mL). Scientists use graduated cylinders to measure liquid volume.

Common Conversion

1 L = 1,000 mL

The graduated cylinder in the picture is marked in milliliter divisions. Notice that the water in the cylinder has a curved surface. This curved surface is called the *meniscus*. To measure the volume, you must read the level at the lowest point of the meniscus. What is the volume of water in this graduated cylinder?   **ACTIVITY**

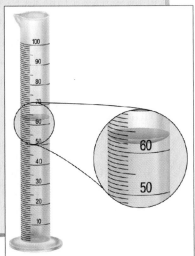

Mass To measure mass, or the amount of matter in an object, you will use a unit of measure known as the **gram (g).** One gram is approximately the mass of a paper clip. Larger masses are measured in kilograms (kg). Scientists use a balance to find the mass of an object.

Common Conversion

1 kg = 1,000 g

The mass of the apple in the picture is measured in kilograms. What is the mass of the apple? Suppose a recipe for applesauce called for one kilogram of apples. About how many apples would you need?

ACTIVITY

Temperature
To measure the temperature of a substance, you will use the **Celsius scale.** Temperature is measured in degrees Celsius (°C) using a Celsius thermometer. Water freezes at 0°C and boils at 100°C.

ACTIVITY

What is the temperature of the liquid in degrees Celsius?

Converting SI Units

To use the SI system, you must know how to convert between units. Converting from one unit to another involves the skill of **calculating,** or using mathematical operations. Converting between SI units is similar to converting between dollars and dimes because both systems are based on multiples of ten.

Suppose you want to convert a length of 80 centimeters to meters. Follow these steps to convert between units.

1. Begin by writing down the measurement you want to convert—in this example, 80 centimeters.
2. Write a conversion factor that represents the relationship between the two units you are converting. In this example, the relationship is *1 meter = 100 centimeters.* Write this conversion factor as a fraction, making sure to place the units you are converting from (centimeters, in this example) in the denominator.

3. Multiply the measurement you want to convert by the fraction. When you do this, the units in the first measurement will cancel out with the units in the denominator. Your answer will be in the units you are converting to (meters, in this example).

Example

80 centimeters = ___?___ meters

$$80 \text{ centimeters} \times \frac{1 \text{ meter}}{100 \text{ centimeters}} = \frac{80 \text{ meters}}{100}$$

$$= 0.8 \text{ meters}$$

Convert between the following units.

ACTIVITY

1. 600 millimeters = _?_ meters
2. 0.35 liters = _?_ milliliters
3. 1,050 grams = _?_ kilograms

Conducting a Scientific Investigation

In some ways, scientists are like detectives, piecing together clues to learn about a process or event. One way that scientists gather clues is by carrying out experiments. In an experiment, scientists test an idea in a careful, orderly manner. Although experiments do not all follow the same steps in the same order, many follow a pattern similar to the one described here.

Asking Questions

Experiments begin by asking a scientific question. A scientific question is one that can be answered by gathering evidence. For example, the question "Which freezes faster—fresh water or salt water?" is a scientific question because you can carry out an investigation and gather information to answer the question.

Formulating a Hypothesis

The next step is to form a hypothesis. A **hypothesis** is a possible explanation for a set of observations or answer to a scientific question. In science, a hypothesis must be something that can be tested. A hypothesis can be worded as an *If ... then ...* statement. For example, a hypothesis might be "*If I add salt to fresh water, then the water will take longer to freeze.*" A hypothesis worded this way serves as a rough outline of the experiment you should perform.

Designing an Experiment

Next you need to plan a way to test your hypothesis. Your plan should be written out as a step-by-step procedure and should describe the observations or measurements you will make.

Two important steps involved in designing an experiment are controlling variables and forming operational definitions.

Controlling Variables

In a well-designed experiment, you need to keep all variables the same except for one. A **variable** is any factor that can change in an experiment. The factor that you change is called the **manipulated variable.** In this experiment, the manipulated variable is the amount of salt added to the water. Other factors, such as the amount of water or the starting temperature, are kept constant.

The factor that changes as a result of the manipulated variable is called the responding variable. The **responding variable** is what you measure or observe to obtain your results. In this experiment, the responding variable is how long the water takes to freeze.

An experiment in which all factors except one are kept constant is a **controlled experiment.** Most controlled experiments include a test called the control. In this experiment, Container 3 is the control. Because no salt is added to Container 3, you can compare the results from the other containers to it. Any difference in results must be due to the addition of salt alone.

Forming Operational Definitions

Another important aspect of a well-designed experiment is having clear operational definitions. An **operational definition** is a statement that describes how a particular variable is to be measured or how a term is to be defined. For example, in this experiment, how will you determine if the water has frozen? You might decide to insert a stick in each container at the start of the experiment. Your operational definition of "frozen" would be that the stick can no longer move.

EXPERIMENTAL PROCEDURE

1. Fill 3 containers with 300 milliliters of cold tap water.

2. Add 10 grams of salt to Container 1; stir. Add 20 grams of salt to Container 2; stir. Add no salt to Container 3.

3. Place the 3 containers in a freezer.

4. Check the containers every 15 minutes. Record your observations.

Interpreting Data

The observations and measurements you make in an experiment are called data. At the end of an experiment, you need to analyze the data to look for any patterns or trends. Patterns often become clear if you organize your data in a data table, chart, or graph. Then think about what the data might reveal. Do they support your hypothesis? Do they point out a flaw in your experiment? Do you need to collect more data?

Drawing Conclusions

A conclusion is a statement that sums up what you have learned from an experiment. When you draw a conclusion, you need to decide whether the data you collected support your hypothesis. You may need to repeat an experiment several times before you can draw any conclusions from it. Conclusions often lead you to ask new questions and plan new experiments to answer them.

Is a ball's bounce affected by the height from which it is dropped? Using the steps just described, plan a controlled experiment to investigate this problem. **ACTIVITY**

Thinking Critically

Has a friend ever asked for your advice about a problem? If so, you may have helped your friend think through the problem in a logical way. Without knowing it, you used critical-thinking skills to help your friend. Critical thinking involves the use of reasoning and logic to solve problems or make decisions. Some critical-thinking skills are described below.

Comparing and Contrasting

When you examine two objects for similarities and differences, you are using the skill of **comparing and contrasting.** Comparing involves identifying similarities, or common characteristics. Contrasting involves identifying differences. Analyzing objects in this way can help you discover details that you might otherwise overlook.

ACTIVITY
Compare and contrast the two animals in the photo. First list all the similarities that you see. Then list all the differences.

Applying Concepts

When you use your knowledge about one situation to make sense of a similar situation, you are using the skill of **applying concepts.** Being able to transfer your knowledge from one situation to another shows that you truly understand a concept. You may use this skill in answering test questions that present different problems from the ones you've reviewed in class.

ACTIVITY
You have just learned that water takes longer to freeze when other substances are mixed into it. Use this knowledge to explain why people need a substance called antifreeze in their car's radiator in the winter.

Interpreting Illustrations

Diagrams, photographs, and maps are included in textbooks to help clarify what you read. These illustrations show processes, places, and ideas in a visual manner. The skill called **interpreting illustrations** can help you learn from these visual elements. To understand an illustration, take the time to study the illustration along with all the written information that accompanies it. Captions identify the key concepts shown in the illustration. Labels point out the important parts of a diagram or map, while keys identify the symbols used in a map.

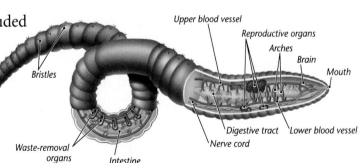

Upper blood vessel
Reproductive organs
Arches
Brain
Mouth
Bristles
Digestive tract
Lower blood vessel
Nerve cord
Waste-removal organs
Intestine

▲ **Internal anatomy of an earthworm**

ACTIVITY
Study the diagram above. Then write a short paragraph explaining what you have learned.

Relating Cause and Effect

If one event causes another event to occur, the two events are said to have a cause-and-effect relationship. When you determine that such a relationship exists between two events, you use a skill called **relating cause and effect.** For example, if you notice an itchy, red bump on your skin, you might infer that a mosquito bit you. The mosquito bite is the cause, and the bump is the effect.

It is important to note that two events do not necessarily have a cause-and-effect relationship just because they occur together. Scientists carry out experiments or use past experience to determine whether a cause-and-effect relationship exists.

ACTIVITY

You are on a camping trip and your flashlight has stopped working. List some possible causes for the flashlight malfunction. How could you determine which cause-and-effect relationship has left you in the dark?

Making Generalizations

When you draw a conclusion about an entire group based on information about only some of the group's members, you are using a skill called **making generalizations.** For a generalization to be valid, the sample you choose must be large enough and representative of the entire group. You might, for example, put this skill to work at a farm stand if you see a sign that says, "Sample some grapes before you buy." If you sample a few sweet grapes, you may conclude that all the grapes are sweet—and purchase a large bunch.

ACTIVITY

A team of scientists needs to determine whether the water in a large reservoir is safe to drink. How could they use the skill of making generalizations to help them? What should they do?

Making Judgments

When you evaluate something to decide whether it is good or bad, or right or wrong, you are using a skill called **making judgments.** For example, you make judgments when you decide to eat healthful foods or to pick up litter in a park. Before you make a judgment, you need to think through the pros and cons of a situation, and identify the values or standards that you hold.

ACTIVITY

Should children and teens be required to wear helmets when bicycling? Explain why you feel the way you do.

Problem Solving

When you use critical-thinking skills to resolve an issue or decide on a course of action, you are using a skill called **problem solving.** Some problems, such as how to convert a fraction into a decimal, are straightforward. Other problems, such as figuring out why your computer has stopped working, are complex. Some complex problems can be solved using the trial and error method—try out one solution first, and if that doesn't work, try another. Other useful problem-solving strategies include making models and brainstorming possible solutions with a partner.

687

Organizing Information

As you read this textbook, how can you make sense of all the information it contains? Some useful tools to help you organize information are shown on this page. These tools are called *graphic organizers* because they give you a visual picture of a topic, showing at a glance how key concepts are related.

Concept Maps

Concept maps are useful tools for organizing information on broad topics. A concept map begins with a general concept and shows how it can be broken down into more specific concepts. In that way, relationships between concepts become easier to understand.

A concept map is constructed by placing concept words (usually nouns) in ovals and connecting them with linking words. Often, the most general concept word is placed at the top, and the words become more specific as you move downward. Often the linking words, which are written on a line extending between two ovals, describe the relationship between the two concepts they connect. If you follow any string of concepts and linking words down the map, it should read like a sentence.

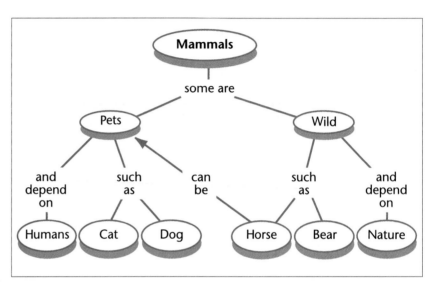

Some concept maps include linking words that connect a concept on one branch of the map to a concept on another branch. These linking words, called cross-linkages, show more complex interrelationships among concepts.

Compare/Contrast Tables

Compare/contrast tables are useful tools for sorting out the similarities and differences between two or more items. A table provides an organized framework in which to compare items based on specific characteristics that you identify.

To create a compare/contrast table, list the items to be compared across the top of a table. Then list the characteristics that will form the basis of your comparison in the left-hand column. Complete the table by filling in information about each characteristic, first for one item and then for the other.

Characteristic	Baseball	Basketball
Number of Players	9	5
Playing Field	Baseball diamond	Basketball court
Equipment	Bat, baseball, mitts	Basket, basketball

Venn Diagrams

Another way to show similarities and differences between items is with a Venn diagram. A Venn diagram consists of two or more circles that partially overlap. Each circle represents a particular concept or idea. Common characteristics, or similarities, are written within the area of overlap between the two circles. Unique characteristics, or differences, are written in the parts of the circles outside the area of overlap.

To create a Venn diagram, draw two overlapping circles. Label the circles with the names of the items being compared. Write the

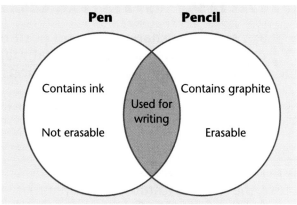

unique characteristics in each circle outside the area of overlap. Then write the shared characteristics within the area of overlap.

Flowcharts

A flowchart can help you understand the order in which certain events have occurred or should occur. Flowcharts are useful for outlining the stages in a process or the steps in a procedure.

To make a flowchart, write a brief description of each event in a box. Place the first event at the top of the page, followed by the second event, the third event, and so on. Then draw an arrow to connect each event to the one that occurs next.

Preparing Pasta

Boil water
↓
Cook pasta
↓
Drain water
↓
Add sauce

Cycle Diagrams

A cycle diagram can be used to show a sequence of events that is continuous, or cyclical. A continuous sequence does not have an end because, when the final event is over, the first event begins again. Like a flowchart, a cycle diagram can help you understand the order of events.

To create a cycle diagram, write a brief description of each event in a box. Place one event at the top of the page in the center. Then, moving in a clockwise direction around an imaginary circle, write each event in its proper sequence. Draw arrows that connect each event to the one that occurs next, forming a continuous circle.

Steps in Scientific Inquiry

Pose a question → Develop a hypothesis → Design an experiment → Interpret data → Draw conclusions → (back to Pose a question)

Making and Reading Maps

Maps show the shape, size, and position of Earth's features. To understand the information that maps convey, you must learn about the symbols and other conventions that mapmakers use.

A Map's Scale

A map is a flat model that shows all or part of Earth's surface as it looks from above. Of course, the size of a feature on a map differs from the real size of the feature on Earth. The same is true of a globe, which is a sphere that represents Earth's entire surface. Both maps and globes include a **scale**, which relates distances on the map to the corresponding distances on Earth's surface.

A scale is sometimes given as a ratio. For example, one unit on a map may equal 100,000 units on the ground. This means that 1 centimeter on the map represents 100,000 centimeters, or 1 kilometer, on Earth. Similarly, 1 inch on the map represents 100,000 inches, or 1.58 miles, on Earth.

This scale, "one to one-hundred thousand" is written "1 : 100,000." The three types of map scales are shown below.

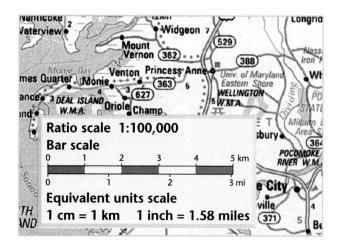

Ratio scale 1:100,000
Bar scale
Equivalent units scale
1 cm = 1 km   1 inch = 1.58 miles

Compass Rose

Maps also include a compass rose. The compass rose relates directions on the map to directions on Earth. North is usually located at the top of a map.

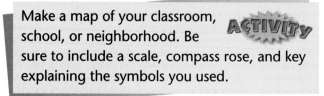

Make a map of your classroom, school, or neighborhood. Be sure to include a scale, compass rose, and key explaining the symbols you used. **ACTIVITY**

Map Symbols

Mapmakers use a variety of symbols to show where important landmarks and other features are located. The symbols are explained in a section of the map called the key, or legend. The table below shows some of the most common symbols often found on maps.

Commonly Used Map Symbols

Building	■ □ ▨ ▨	Primary highway	━━━━	Airport	✈
School; church	⚑ ✝	Secondary highway	━ ━ ━	Body of water	〜
Campground; picnic area	⛺ ⛱	Divided highway	═══	Waterfall or rapids	≋
Cemetery	⌐Cem¬	Railroad tracks	┼─┼─┼	Woods or parks	▨

Latitude and Longitude

To find a point on Earth's surface, mapmakers use a reference system similar to the grid of squares on a checkerboard. The grid is made up of two types of imaginary lines. Lines of **latitude** run east-to-west around the globe, while lines of **longitude** run north-to-south.

Lines of latitude are sometimes called parallels because they run parallel to each other. In the middle of the globe is a parallel known as the equator. The **equator** divides Earth into two halves—the Northern and Southern hemispheres.

The equator is the starting line for measuring distances north or south. Distances are measured in units called degrees. The equator is 0° latitude. The farthest distance north of the equator is 90° north latitude, the location of the North Pole. The farthest distance south of the equator is 90° south latitude, the location of the South Pole.

If you look on a globe, you see that, unlike lines of latitude, lines of longitude are not parallel. Lines of longitude run north-to-south and meet at the poles. The **prime meridian** is a line of longitude that passes through Greenwich, England. Places east of the prime meridian are in the Eastern hemisphere. Places west of the prime meridian are in the Western hemisphere.

The prime meridian is at 0° longitude, the starting line for measuring longitude. Longitude lines in each hemisphere are numbered up to 180°. At 180° east or 180° west lies a single longitude line that is directly opposite the prime meridian.

Every point on Earth's surface has a particular latitude and longitude. By finding the point where a latitude line crosses a longitude line, you can determine where a given place is located.

Where in the World? ACTIVITY

Using a globe, determine what city is found at each of the following points:

a. 2° S, 79° W   **d.** 34° S, 58° W
b. 38° N, 9° W   **e.** 55° N, 3° W
c. 34° N, 135° E   **f.** 1° N, 103° E

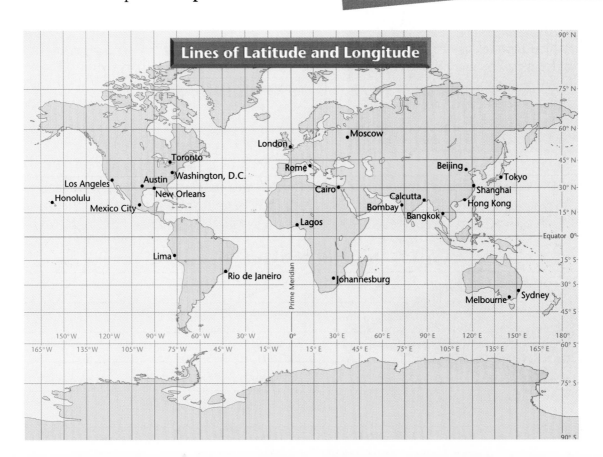

Lines of Latitude and Longitude

Topographic Maps

Some maps include information about a region's **topography,** or its physical features, such as mountains, hills, and valleys. These maps use symbols to show the land's elevation, or height above sea level.

A topographic map is a map that uses symbols known as contour lines to show the physical features of a region. On a topographic map, a **contour line** connects points of equal elevation. The change in elevation from one contour line to the next is called the **contour interval.** The contour interval for a given map is always the same. For example, the map below has a contour interval of 200 feet. If you start at one contour line and count up 5 contour lines, you have reached an elevation 1,000 feet above where you started. Usually every fifth contour line is darker and heavier than the others. This contour line is called the index contour. This line is labeled with the elevation in round units, such as 1,600 or 2,000 feet above sea level.

ACTIVITY

You are planning to hike up Mt. Monadnock. Use the topographic map to find the difference in elevation between the park headquarters and the summit. Also, determine which route is steeper: the White Arrow Trail or the Pumpelly Trail. How do you know?

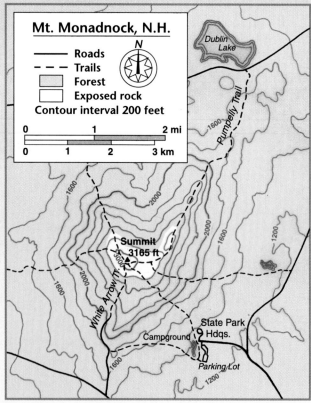

In addition to showing elevation, contour maps also show other features, such as bodies of water, roads, and buildings. The topographic map below, which shows part of Tennessee, was made by the United States Geological Survey (USGS). Note that contour maps, like all maps, include a scale. You can use the scale to figure out the size of the whole area or the distance between any two points on the map.

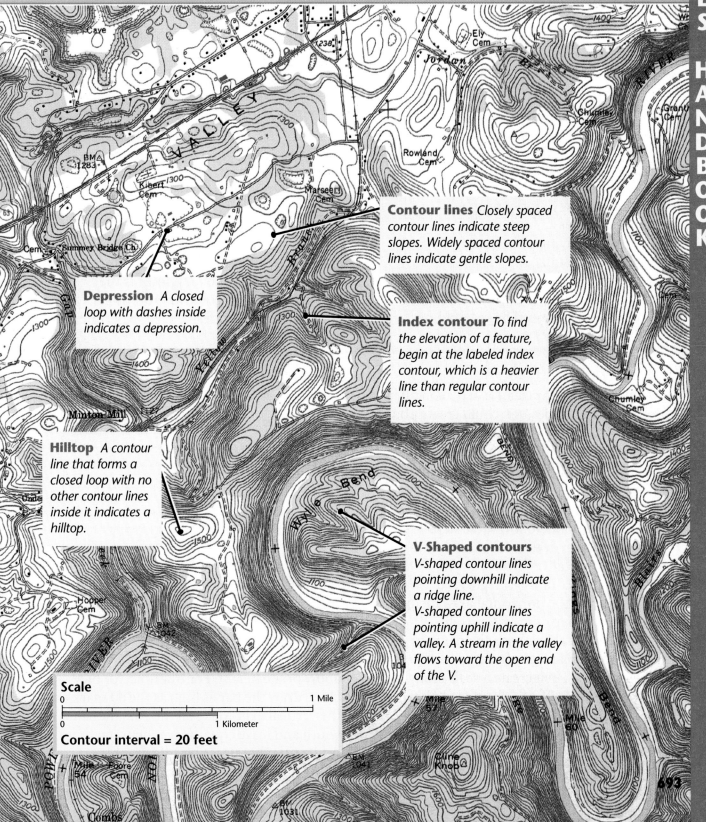

Contour lines *Closely spaced contour lines indicate steep slopes. Widely spaced contour lines indicate gentle slopes.*

Depression *A closed loop with dashes inside indicates a depression.*

Index contour *To find the elevation of a feature, begin at the labeled index contour, which is a heavier line than regular contour lines.*

Hilltop *A contour line that forms a closed loop with no other contour lines inside it indicates a hilltop.*

V-Shaped contours *V-shaped contour lines pointing downhill indicate a ridge line. V-shaped contour lines pointing uphill indicate a valley. A stream in the valley flows toward the open end of the V.*

Scale

0   1 Mile

0   1 Kilometer

Contour interval = 20 feet

693

Creating Data Tables and Graphs

How can you make sense of the data in a science experiment? The first step is to organize the data to help you understand them. Data tables and graphs are helpful tools for organizing data.

Data Tables

You have gathered your materials and set up your experiment. But before you start, you need to plan a way to record what happens during the experiment. By creating a data table, you can record your observations and measurements in an orderly way.

Suppose, for example, that a scientist conducted an experiment to find out how many Calories people of different body masses burn while doing various activities. The data table shows the results.

Notice in this data table that the manipulated variable (body mass) is the heading of one column. The responding

CALORIES BURNED IN 30 MINUTES OF ACTIVITY			
Body Mass	Experiment 1 Bicycling	Experiment 2 Playing Basketball	Experiment 3 Watching Television
30 kg	60 Calories	120 Calories	21 Calories
40 kg	77 Calories	164 Calories	27 Calories
50 kg	95 Calories	206 Calories	33 Calories
60 kg	114 Calories	248 Calories	38 Calories

variable (for Experiment 1, the number of Calories burned while bicycling) is the heading of the next column. Additional columns were added for related experiments.

Bar Graphs

To compare how many Calories a person burns doing various activities, you could create a bar graph. A bar graph is used to display data in a number of separate, or distinct, categories. In this example, bicycling, playing basketball, and watching television are three separate categories.

To create a bar graph, follow these steps.

1. On graph paper, draw a horizontal, or *x*-, axis and a vertical, or *y*-, axis.
2. Write the names of the categories to be graphed along the horizontal axis. Include an overall label for the axis as well.
3. Label the vertical axis with the name of the responding variable. Include units of measurement. Then create a scale along the axis by marking off equally spaced numbers that cover the range of the data collected.
4. For each category, draw a solid bar using the scale on the vertical axis to determine the

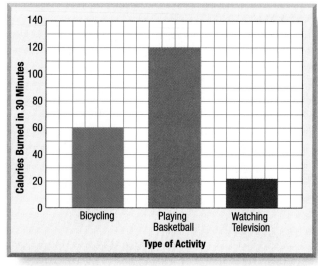

Calories Burned by a 30-kilogram Person in Various Activities

appropriate height. For example, for bicycling, draw the bar as high as the 60 mark on the vertical axis. Make all the bars the same width and leave equal spaces between them.
5. Add a title that describes the graph.

Line Graphs

To see whether a relationship exists between body mass and the number of Calories burned while bicycling, you could create a line graph. A line graph is used to display data that show how one variable (the responding variable) changes in response to another variable (the manipulated variable). You can use a line graph when your manipulated variable is *continuous*, that is, when there are other points between the ones that you tested. In this example, body mass is a continuous variable because there are other body masses between 30 and 40 kilograms (for example, 31 kilograms). Time is another example of a continuous variable.

Line graphs are powerful tools because they allow you to estimate values for conditions that you did not test in the experiment. For example, you can use the line graph to estimate that a 35-kilogram person would burn 68 Calories while bicycling.

To create a line graph, follow these steps.

1. On graph paper, draw a horizontal, or *x*-, axis and a vertical, or *y*-, axis.
2. Label the horizontal axis with the name of the manipulated variable. Label the vertical axis with the name of the responding variable. Include units of measurement.
3. Create a scale on each axis by marking off equally spaced numbers that cover the range of the data collected.
4. Plot a point on the graph for each piece of data. In the line graph above, the dotted lines show how to plot the first data point (30 kilograms and 60 Calories). Draw an imaginary vertical line extending up from the horizontal axis at the 30-kilogram mark. Then draw an imaginary horizontal line extending across from the vertical axis at the 60-Calorie mark. Plot the point where the two lines intersect.

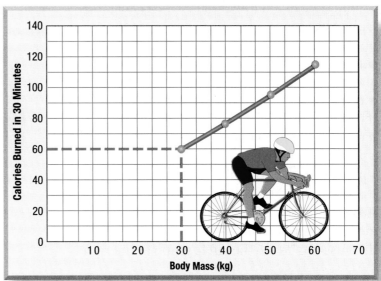

Effect of Body Mass on Calories Burned While Bicycling

5. Connect the plotted points with a solid line. (In some cases, it may be more appropriate to draw a line that shows the general trend of the plotted points. In those cases, some of the points may fall above or below the line. Also, not all graphs are linear. It may be more appropriate to draw a curve to connect the points.)
6. Add a title that identifies the variables or relationship in the graph.

Create line graphs to display the data from Experiment 2 and Experiment 3 in the data table. **ACTIVITY**

You read in the newspaper that a total of 4 centimeters of rain fell in your area in June, 2.5 centimeters fell in July, and 1.5 centimeters fell in August. What type of graph would you use to display these data? Use graph paper to create the graph. **ACTIVITY**

Circle Graphs

Like bar graphs, circle graphs can be used to display data in a number of separate categories. Unlike bar graphs, however, circle graphs can only be used when you have data for *all* the categories that make up a given topic. A circle graph is sometimes called a pie chart because it resembles a pie cut into slices. The pie represents the entire topic, while the slices represent the individual categories. The size of a slice indicates what percentage of the whole a particular category makes up.

The data table below shows the results of a survey in which 24 teenagers were asked to identify their favorite sport. The data were then used to create the circle graph at the right.

Sports That Teens Prefer

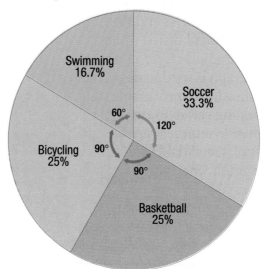

FAVORITE SPORTS	
Sport	*Number of Students*
Soccer	8
Basketball	6
Bicycling	6
Swimming	4

To create a circle graph, follow these steps.
1. Use a compass to draw a circle. Mark the center of the circle with a point. Then draw a line from the center point to the top of the circle.
2. Determine the size of each "slice" by setting up a proportion where x equals the number of degrees in a slice. (NOTE: A circle contains 360 degrees.) For example, to find the number of degrees in the "soccer" slice, set up the following proportion:

$$\frac{\text{students who prefer soccer}}{\text{total number of students}} = \frac{x}{\text{total number of degrees in a circle}}$$

$$\frac{8}{24} = \frac{x}{360}$$

Cross-multiply and solve for x.

$$24x = 8 \times 360$$
$$x = 120$$

The "soccer" slice should contain 120 degrees.

3. Use a protractor to measure the angle of the first slice, using the line you drew to the top of the circle as the 0° line. Draw a line from the center of the circle to the edge for the angle you measured.
4. Continue around the circle by measuring the size of each slice with the protractor. Start measuring from the edge of the previous slice so the wedges do not overlap. When you are done, the entire circle should be filled in.
5. Determine the percentage of the whole circle that each slice represents. To do this, divide the number of degrees in a slice by the total number of degrees in a circle (360), and multiply by 100%. For the "soccer" slice, you can find the percentage as follows:

$$\frac{120}{360} \times 100\% = 33.3\%$$

6. Use a different color to shade in each slice. Label each slice with the name of the category and with the percentage of the whole it represents.
7. Add a title to the circle graph.

ACTIVITY

In a class of 28 students, 12 students take the bus to school, 10 students walk, and 6 students ride their bicycles. Create a circle graph to display these data.

Laboratory Safety

Safety Symbols

These symbols alert you to possible dangers in the laboratory and remind you to work carefully.

Safety Goggles Always wear safety goggles to protect your eyes in any activity involving chemicals, flames or heating, or the possibility of broken glassware.

Lab Apron Wear a laboratory apron to protect your skin and clothing from damage.

Breakage You are working with materials that may be breakable, such as glass containers, glass tubing, thermometers, or funnels. Handle breakable materials with care. Do not touch broken glassware.

Heat-resistant Gloves Use an oven mitt or other hand protection when handling hot materials. Hot plates, hot glassware, or hot water can cause burns. Do not touch hot objects with your bare hands.

Heating Use a clamp or tongs to pick up hot glassware. Do not touch hot objects with your bare hands.

Sharp Object Pointed-tip scissors, scalpels, knives, needles, pins, or tacks are sharp. They can cut or puncture your skin. Always direct a sharp edge or point away from yourself and others. Use sharp instruments only as instructed.

Electric Shock Avoid the possibility of electric shock. Never use electrical equipment around water, or when the equipment is wet or your hands are wet. Be sure cords are untangled and cannot trip anyone. Disconnect the equipment when it is not in use.

Corrosive Chemical You are working with an acid or another corrosive chemical. Avoid getting it on your skin or clothing, or in your eyes. Do not inhale the vapors. Wash your hands when you are finished with the activity.

Poison Do not let any poisonous chemical come in contact with your skin, and do not inhale its vapors. Wash your hands when you are finished with the activity.

Physical Safety When an experiment involves physical activity, take precautions to avoid injuring yourself or others. Follow instructions from your teacher. Alert your teacher if there is any reason you should not participate in the activity.

Animal Safety Treat live animals with care to avoid harming the animals or yourself. Working with animal parts or preserved animals also may require caution. Wash your hands when you are finished with the activity.

Plant Safety Handle plants in the laboratory or during field work only as directed by your teacher. If you are allergic to certain plants, tell your teacher before doing an activity in which those plants are used. Avoid touching harmful plants such as poison ivy, poison oak, or poison sumac, or plants with thorns. Wash your hands when you are finished with the activity.

Flames You may be working with flames from a lab burner, candle, or matches. Tie back loose hair and clothing. Follow instructions from your teacher about lighting and extinguishing flames.

No Flames Flammable materials may be present. Make sure there are no flames, sparks, or other exposed heat sources present.

Fumes When poisonous or unpleasant vapors may be involved, work in a ventilated area. Avoid inhaling vapors directly. Only test an odor when directed to do so by your teacher, and use a wafting motion to direct the vapor toward your nose.

Disposal Chemicals and other laboratory materials used in the activity must be disposed of safely. Follow the instructions from your teacher.

Hand Washing Wash your hands thoroughly when finished with the activity. Use antibacterial soap and warm water. Lather both sides of your hands and between your fingers. Rinse well.

General Safety Awareness You may see this symbol when none of the symbols described earlier appears. In this case, follow the specific instructions provided. You may also see this symbol when you are asked to develop your own procedure in a lab. Have your teacher approve your plan before you go further.

Science Safety Rules

To prepare yourself to work safely in the laboratory, read over the following safety rules. Then read them a second time. Make sure you understand and follow each rule. Ask your teacher to explain any rules you do not understand.

Dress Code

1. To protect yourself from injuring your eyes, wear safety goggles whenever you work with chemicals, burners, glassware, or any substance that might get into your eyes. If you wear contact lenses, notify your teacher.
2. Wear a lab apron or coat whenever you work with corrosive chemicals or substances that can stain.
3. Tie back long hair to keep it away from any chemicals, flames, or equipment.
4. Remove or tie back any article of clothing or jewelry that can hang down and touch chemicals, flames, or equipment. Roll up or secure long sleeves.
5. Never wear open shoes or sandals.

General Precautions

6. Read all directions for an experiment several times before beginning the activity. Carefully follow all written and oral instructions. If you are in doubt about any part of the experiment, ask your teacher for assistance.
7. Never perform activities that are not assigned or authorized by your teacher. Obtain permission before "experimenting" on your own. Never handle any equipment unless you have specific permission.
8. Never perform lab activities without direct supervision.
9. Never eat or drink in the laboratory.
10. Keep work areas clean and tidy at all times. Bring only notebooks and lab manuals or written lab procedures to the work area. All other items, such as purses and backpacks, should be left in a designated area.
11. Do not engage in horseplay.

First Aid

12. Always report all accidents or injuries to your teacher, no matter how minor. Notify your teacher immediately of any fires.
13. Learn what to do in case of specific accidents, such as getting acid in your eyes or on your skin. (Rinse acids from your body with lots of water.)
14. Be aware of the location of the first-aid kit, but do not use it unless instructed by your teacher. In case of injury, your teacher should administer first aid. Your teacher may also send you to the school nurse or call a physician.
15. Know the location of emergency equipment, such as the fire extinguisher and fire blanket, and know how to use it.
16. Know the location of the nearest telephone and whom to contact in an emergency.

Heating and Fire Safety

17. Never use a heat source, such as a candle, burner, or hot plate, without wearing safety goggles.
18. Never heat anything unless instructed to do so. A chemical that is harmless when cool may be dangerous when heated.
19. Keep all combustible materials away from flames. Never use a flame or spark near a combustible chemical.
20. Never reach across a flame.
21. Before using a laboratory burner, make sure you know proper procedures for lighting and adjusting the burner, as demonstrated by your teacher. Do not touch the burner. It may be hot. And never leave a lighted burner unattended!
22. Chemicals can splash or boil out of a heated test tube. When heating a substance in a test tube, make sure that the mouth of the tube is not pointed at you or anyone else.
23. Never heat a liquid in a closed container. The expanding gases produced may blow the container apart.
24. Before picking up a container that has been heated, hold the back of your hand near it. If you can feel heat on the back of your hand, the container is too hot to handle. Use an oven mitt to pick up a container that has been heated.

Using Chemicals Safely

25. Never mix chemicals "for the fun of it." You might produce a dangerous, possibly explosive, substance.

26. Never put your face near the mouth of a container that holds chemicals. Never touch, taste, or smell a chemical unless you are instructed by your teacher to do so. Many chemicals are poisonous.

27. Use only those chemicals needed in the activity. Read and double-check labels on supply bottles before removing any chemicals. Take only as much as you need. Keep all containers closed when chemicals are not being used.

28. Dispose of all chemicals as instructed by your teacher. To avoid contamination, never return chemicals to their original containers. Never simply pour chemicals or other substances into the sink or trash containers.

29. Be extra careful when working with acids or bases. Pour all chemicals over the sink or a container, not over your work surface.

30. If you are instructed to test for odors, use a wafting motion to direct the odors to your nose. Do not inhale the fumes directly from the container.

31. When mixing an acid and water, always pour the water into the container first, and then add the acid to the water. Never pour water into an acid.

32. Take extreme care not to spill any material in the laboratory. Wash chemical spills and splashes immediately with plenty of water. Immediately begin rinsing with water any acids that get on your skin or clothing, and notify your teacher of any acid spill at the same time.

Using Glassware Safely

33. Never force glass tubing or thermometers into a rubber stopper or rubber tubing. Have your teacher insert the glass tubing or thermometer if required for an activity.

34. If you are using a laboratory burner, use a wire screen to protect glassware from any flame. Never heat glassware that is not thoroughly dry on the outside.

35. Keep in mind that hot glassware looks cool. Never pick up glassware without first checking to see if it is hot. Use an oven mitt. See rule 24.

36. Never use broken or chipped glassware. If glassware breaks, notify your teacher and dispose of the glassware in the proper broken-glassware container. Never handle broken glass with your bare hands.

37. Never eat or drink from lab glassware.

38. Thoroughly clean glassware before putting it away.

Using Sharp Instruments

39. Handle scalpels or other sharp instruments with extreme care. Never cut material toward you; cut away from you.

40. Immediately notify your teacher if you cut your skin when working in the laboratory.

Animal and Plant Safety

41. Never perform experiments that cause pain, discomfort, or harm to mammals, birds, reptiles, fishes, or amphibians. This rule applies at home as well as in the classroom.

42. Animals should be handled only if absolutely necessary. Your teacher will instruct you as to how to handle each animal species brought into the classroom.

43. If you know that you are allergic to certain plants, molds, or animals, tell your teacher before doing an activity in which these are used.

44. During field work, protect your skin by wearing long pants, long sleeves, socks, and closed shoes. Know how to recognize the poisonous plants and fungi in your area, as well as plants with thorns, and avoid contact with them.

45. Never eat any part of an unidentified plant or fungus.

46. Wash your hands thoroughly after handling animals or the cage containing animals. Wash your hands when you are finished with any activity involving animal parts, plants, or soil.

End-of-Experiment Rules

47. After an experiment has been completed, clean up your work area and return all equipment to its proper place.

48. Dispose of waste materials as instructed by your teacher.

49. Wash your hands after every experiment.

50. Always turn off all burners or hot plates when they are not in use. Unplug hot plates and other electrical equipment. If you used a burner, check that the gas-line valve to the burner is off as well.

Using a Laboratory Balance

The laboratory balance is an important tool in scientific investigations. You can use a balance to determine the masses of materials that you study or experiment with in the laboratory.

Different kinds of balances are used in the laboratory. One kind of balance is the triple-beam balance. The balance that you may use in your science class is probably similar to the balance illustrated in this Appendix. To use the balance properly, you should learn the name, location, and function of each part of the balance you are using. What kind of balance do you have in your science class?

The Triple-Beam Balance

The triple-beam balance is a single-pan balance with three beams calibrated in grams. The back, or 100-gram, beam is divided into ten units of 10 grams each. The middle, or 500-gram, beam is divided into five units of 100 grams each.

The front, or 10-gram, beam is divided into ten major units of 1 gram each. Each of these units is further divided into units of 0.1 gram. What is the largest mass you could find with a triple-beam balance?

The following procedure can be used to find the mass of an object with a triple-beam balance:

1. Place the object on the pan.
2. Move the rider on the middle beam notch by notch until the horizontal pointer drops below zero. Move the rider back one notch.
3. Move the rider on the back beam notch by notch until the pointer again drops below zero. Move the rider back one notch.
4. Slowly slide the rider along the front beam until the pointer stops at the zero point.
5. The mass of the object is equal to the sum of the readings on the three beams.

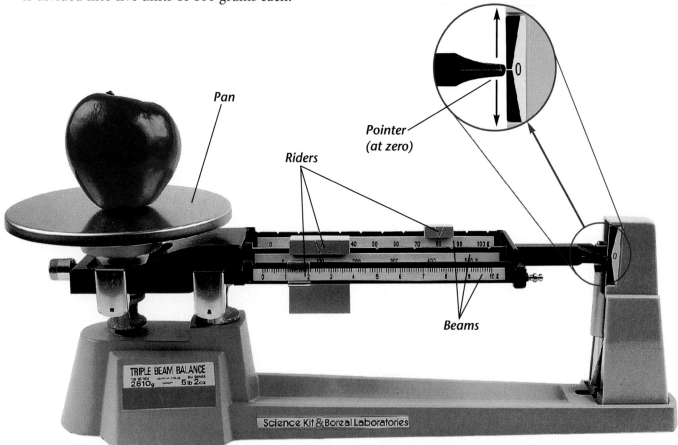

Triple-Beam Balance

List of Chemical Elements

Name	Symbol	Atomic Number	Atomic Mass[†]
Actinium	Ac	89	227.028
Aluminum	Al	13	26.982
Americium	Am	95	(243)
Antimony	Sb	51	121.75
Argon	Ar	18	39.948
Arsenic	As	33	74.922
Astatine	At	85	(210)
Barium	Ba	56	137.327
Berkelium	Bk	97	(247)
Beryllium	Be	4	9.012
Bismuth	Bi	83	208.980
Bohrium	Bh	107	(262)
Boron	B	5	10.811
Bromine	Br	35	79.904
Cadmium	Cd	48	112.411
Calcium	Ca	20	40.078
Californium	Cf	98	(251)
Carbon	C	6	12.011
Cerium	Ce	58	140.115
Cesium	Cs	55	132.905
Chlorine	Cl	17	35.453
Chromium	Cr	24	51.996
Cobalt	Co	27	58.933
Copper	Cu	29	63.546
Curium	Cm	96	(247)
Dubnium	Db	105	(262)
Dysprosium	Dy	66	162.50
Einsteinium	Es	99	(252)
Erbium	Er	68	167.26
Europium	Eu	63	151.965
Fermium	Fm	100	(257)
Fluorine	F	9	18.998
Francium	Fr	87	(223)
Gadolinium	Gd	64	157.25
Gallium	Ga	31	69.723
Germanium	Ge	32	72.61
Gold	Au	79	196.967
Hafnium	Hf	72	178.49
Hassium	Hs	108	(265)
Helium	He	2	4.003
Holmium	Ho	67	164.930
Hydrogen	H	1	1.008
Indium	In	49	114.818
Iodine	I	53	126.904
Iridium	Ir	77	192.22
Iron	Fe	26	55.847
Krypton	Kr	36	83.80
Lanthanum	La	57	138.906
Lawrencium	Lr	103	(260)
Lead	Pb	82	207.2
Lithium	Li	3	6.941
Lutetium	Lu	71	174.967
Magnesium	Mg	12	24.305
Manganese	Mn	25	54.938
Meitnerium	Mt	109	(266)
Mendelevium	Md	101	(258)
Mercury	Hg	80	200.659
Molybdenum	Mo	42	95.94

Name	Symbol	Atomic Number	Atomic Mass[†]
Neodymium	Nd	60	144.2
Neon	Ne	10	20.180
Neptunium	Np	93	237.048
Nickel	Ni	28	58.69
Niobium	Nb	41	92.906
Nitrogen	N	7	14.007
Nobelium	No	102	(259)
Osmium	Os	76	190.23
Oxygen	O	8	15.999
Palladium	Pd	46	106.42
Phosphorus	P	15	30.974
Platinum	Pt	78	195.08
Plutonium	Pu	94	(244)
Polonium	Po	84	(209)
Potassium	K	19	39.098
Praseodymium	Pr	59	140.908
Promethium	Pm	61	(145)
Protactinium	Pa	91	231.036
Radium	Ra	88	226.025
Radon	Rn	86	(222)
Rhenium	Re	75	186.207
Rhodium	Rh	45	102.906
Rubidium	Rb	37	85.468
Ruthenium	Ru	44	101.07
Rutherfordium	Rf	104	(261)
Samarium	Sm	62	150.36
Scandium	Sc	21	44.956
Seaborgium	Sg	106	(263)
Selenium	Se	34	78.96
Silicon	Si	14	28.086
Silver	Ag	47	107.868
Sodium	Na	11	22.990
Strontium	Sr	38	87.62
Sulfur	S	16	32.066
Tantalum	Ta	73	180.948
Technetium	Tc	43	(98)
Tellurium	Te	52	127.60
Terbium	Tb	65	158.925
Thallium	Tl	81	204.383
Thorium	Th	90	232.038
Thulium	Tm	69	168.934
Tin	Sn	50	118.710
Titanium	Ti	22	47.88
Tungsten	W	74	183.85
Ununbium	Uub	112	(272)
Ununhexium	Uuh	116	*
Ununnilium	Uun	110	(269)
Unununium	Uuu	111	(272)
Ununoctium	Uuo	118	*
Ununquadium	Uuq	114	*
Uranium	U	92	238.029
Vanadium	V	23	50.942
Xenon	Xe	54	131.29
Ytterbium	Yb	70	173.04
Yttrium	Y	39	88.906
Zinc	Zn	30	65.39
Zirconium	Zr	40	91.224

[†]Numbers in parentheses give the mass number of the most stable or common isotope.

*Newly discovered

Periodic Table of the Elements

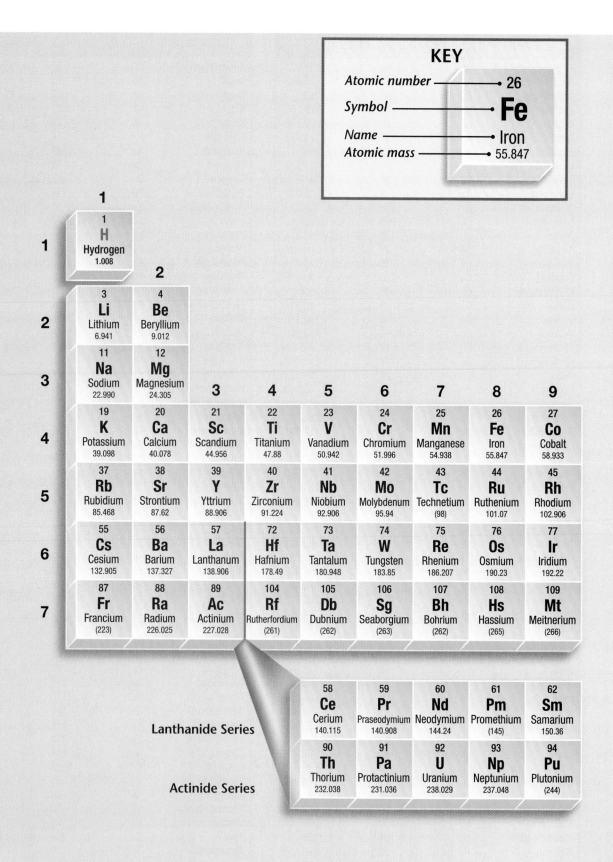

KEY

Atomic number —————— 26
Symbol —————— **Fe**
Name —————— Iron
Atomic mass —————— 55.847

1

1
H
Hydrogen
1.008

2

3	4
Li	**Be**
Lithium	Beryllium
6.941	9.012

11	12
Na	**Mg**
Sodium	Magnesium
22.990	24.305

3 4 5 6 7 8 9

19	20	21	22	23	24	25	26	27
K	**Ca**	**Sc**	**Ti**	**V**	**Cr**	**Mn**	**Fe**	**Co**
Potassium	Calcium	Scandium	Titanium	Vanadium	Chromium	Manganese	Iron	Cobalt
39.098	40.078	44.956	47.88	50.942	51.996	54.938	55.847	58.933

37	38	39	40	41	42	43	44	45
Rb	**Sr**	**Y**	**Zr**	**Nb**	**Mo**	**Tc**	**Ru**	**Rh**
Rubidium	Strontium	Yttrium	Zirconium	Niobium	Molybdenum	Technetium	Ruthenium	Rhodium
85.468	87.62	88.906	91.224	92.906	95.94	(98)	101.07	102.906

55	56	57	72	73	74	75	76	77
Cs	**Ba**	**La**	**Hf**	**Ta**	**W**	**Re**	**Os**	**Ir**
Cesium	Barium	Lanthanum	Hafnium	Tantalum	Tungsten	Rhenium	Osmium	Iridium
132.905	137.327	138.906	178.49	180.948	183.85	186.207	190.23	192.22

87	88	89	104	105	106	107	108	109
Fr	**Ra**	**Ac**	**Rf**	**Db**	**Sg**	**Bh**	**Hs**	**Mt**
Francium	Radium	Actinium	Rutherfordium	Dubnium	Seaborgium	Bohrium	Hassium	Meitnerium
(223)	226.025	227.028	(261)	(262)	(263)	(262)	(265)	(266)

Lanthanide Series

58	59	60	61	62
Ce	**Pr**	**Nd**	**Pm**	**Sm**
Cerium	Praseodymium	Neodymium	Promethium	Samarium
140.115	140.908	144.24	(145)	150.36

Actinide Series

90	91	92	93	94
Th	**Pa**	**U**	**Np**	**Pu**
Thorium	Protactinium	Uranium	Neptunium	Plutonium
232.038	231.036	238.029	237.048	(244)

Mass numbers in parentheses are those of the most stable or common isotope.

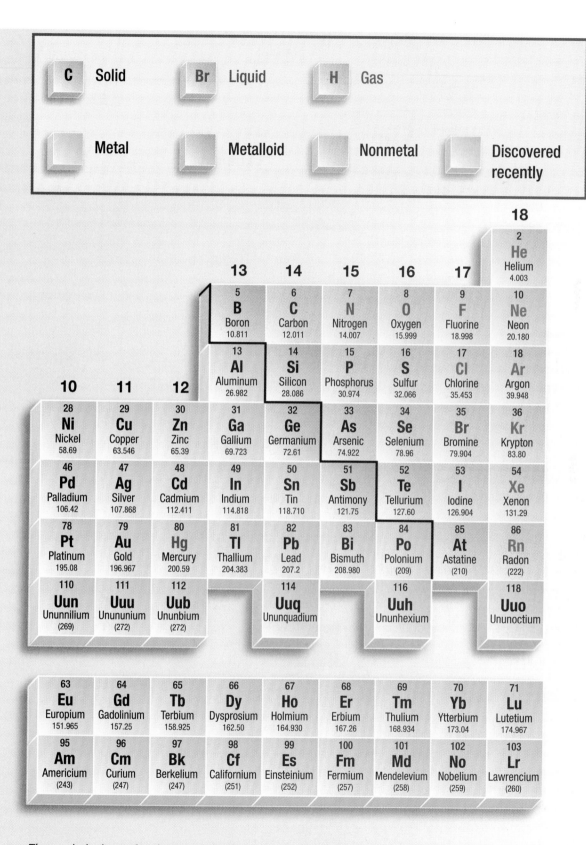

							18
							2 **He** Helium 4.003

Solid C · **Liquid** Br · **Gas** H

Metal · **Metalloid** · **Nonmetal** · **Discovered recently**

13	14	15	16	17
5 **B** Boron 10.811	6 **C** Carbon 12.011	7 **N** Nitrogen 14.007	8 **O** Oxygen 15.999	9 **F** Fluorine 18.998	10 **Ne** Neon 20.180
13 **Al** Aluminum 26.982	14 **Si** Silicon 28.086	15 **P** Phosphorus 30.974	16 **S** Sulfur 32.066	17 **Cl** Chlorine 35.453	18 **Ar** Argon 39.948

10	11	12					
28 **Ni** Nickel 58.69	29 **Cu** Copper 63.546	30 **Zn** Zinc 65.39	31 **Ga** Gallium 69.723	32 **Ge** Germanium 72.61	33 **As** Arsenic 74.922	34 **Se** Selenium 78.96	35 **Br** Bromine 79.904 · 36 **Kr** Krypton 83.80
46 **Pd** Palladium 106.42	47 **Ag** Silver 107.868	48 **Cd** Cadmium 112.411	49 **In** Indium 114.818	50 **Sn** Tin 118.710	51 **Sb** Antimony 121.75	52 **Te** Tellurium 127.60	53 **I** Iodine 126.904 · 54 **Xe** Xenon 131.29
78 **Pt** Platinum 195.08	79 **Au** Gold 196.967	80 **Hg** Mercury 200.59	81 **Tl** Thallium 204.383	82 **Pb** Lead 207.2	83 **Bi** Bismuth 208.980	84 **Po** Polonium (209)	85 **At** Astatine (210) · 86 **Rn** Radon (222)
110 **Uun** Ununnilium (269)	111 **Uuu** Unununium (272)	112 **Uub** Ununbium (272)		114 **Uuq** Ununquadium		116 **Uuh** Ununhexium	118 **Uuo** Ununoctium

63 **Eu** Europium 151.965	64 **Gd** Gadolinium 157.25	65 **Tb** Terbium 158.925	66 **Dy** Dysprosium 162.50	67 **Ho** Holmium 164.930	68 **Er** Erbium 167.26	69 **Tm** Thulium 168.934	70 **Yb** Ytterbium 173.04	71 **Lu** Lutetium 174.967
95 **Am** Americium (243)	96 **Cm** Curium (247)	97 **Bk** Berkelium (247)	98 **Cf** Californium (251)	99 **Es** Einsteinium (252)	100 **Fm** Fermium (257)	101 **Md** Mendelevium (258)	102 **No** Nobelium (259)	103 **Lr** Lawrencium (260)

The symbols shown for elements 110–118 are being used temporarily until names for these elements can be agreed upon.

Physical Map: Texas

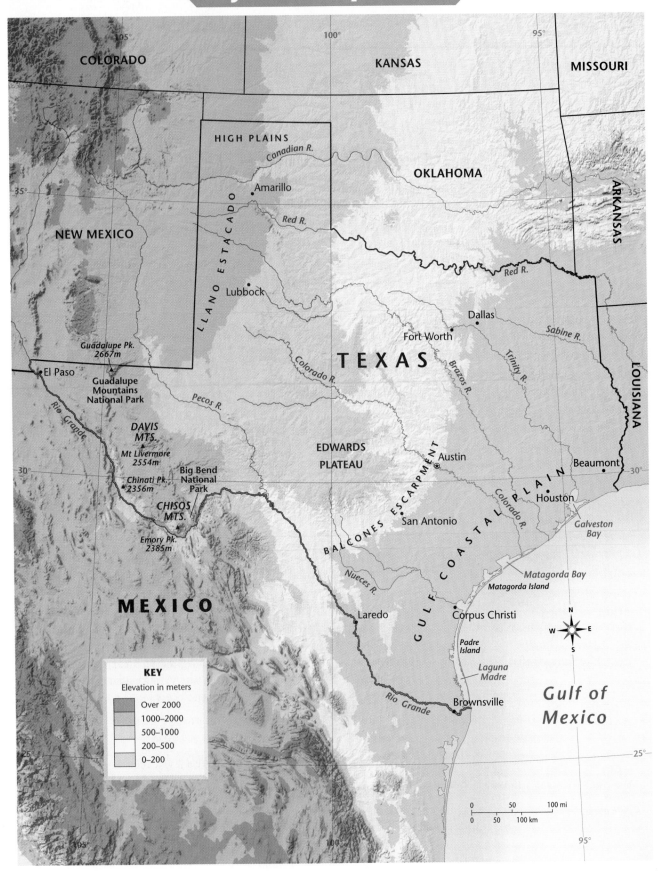

COLORADO

KANSAS

MISSOURI

HIGH PLAINS

Canadian R.

OKLAHOMA

ARKANSAS

NEW MEXICO

Amarillo

Red R.

L L A N O   E S T A C A D O

Lubbock

Red R.

Dallas

Guadalupe Pk.
2667m

Fort Worth

Sabine R.

El Paso

Guadalupe
Mountains
National Park

TEXAS

Trinity R.

Brazos R.

LOUISIANA

Rio Grande

Pecos R.

Colorado R.

DAVIS
MTS.

Mt Livermore
2554m

EDWARDS
PLATEAU

Austin

Beaumont

Chinati Pk.
2356m

Big Bend
National
Park

BALCONES ESCARPMENT

Houston

Colorado R.

CHISOS
MTS.

San Antonio

Galveston
Bay

Emory Pk.
2385m

G U L F   C O A S T A L   P L A I N

MEXICO

Nueces R.

Matagorda Bay

Matagorda Island

Laredo

Corpus Christi

N
W   E
S

Padre
Island

Laguna
Madre

KEY

Elevation in meters

Over 2000
1000–2000
500–1000
200–500
0–200

Rio Grande

Brownsville

*Gulf of
Mexico*

0   50   100 mi

0   50   100 km

Identifying Common Minerals

GROUP 1
Metallic Luster, Mostly Dark-Colored

Mineral/ Formula	Hardness	Density (g/cm³)	Luster	Streak	Color	Other Properties/Remarks
Pyrite FeS_2	6–6.5	5.0	Metallic	Greenish, brownish black	Light yellow	Harder than chalcopyrite and pyrrhotite; called "fool's gold," but harder than gold and very brittle
Magnetite Fe_3O_4	6	5.2	Metallic	Black	Iron black	Very magnetic; important iron ore; some varieties known as "lodestone"
Hematite Fe_2O_3	5.5–6.5	4.9–5.3	Metallic or earthy	Red or red brown	Reddish brown to black; also steel gray crystals	Most important ore of iron; known as "red ocher"; often used as red pigment in paint.
Pyrrhotite FeS	4	4.6	Metallic	Gray black	Brownish bronze	Less hard than pyrite: slightly magnetic
Sphalerite ZnS	3.5–4	3.9–4.1	Resinous	Brown to light yellow	Brown to yellow	Most important zinc ore
Chalcopyrite $CuFeS_2$	3.5–4	4.1–4.3	Metallic	Greenish black	Golden yellow, often tarnished	Most important copper ore; softer than pyrite and more yellow; more brittle than gold
Bornite Cu_5FeS_4	3	4.9–5.4	Metallic	Gray black	Copper, brown; turns to purple and black	Important copper ore; known as "peacock ore" because of iridescent purple color when exposed to air for a time
Copper Cu	2.5–3	8.9	Metallic	Copper red	Copper red to black	Can be pounded into various shapes and drawn into wires; used in making electrical wires, coins, pipes
Gold Au	2.5–3	19.3	Metallic	Yellow	Rich yellow	Can be pounded into various shapes and drawn into wires; does not tarnish; used in jewelry, coins, dental fillings
Silver Ag	2.5–3	10.0–11.0	Metallic	Silver to light gray	Silver white, tarnishes to black	Can be pounded into various shapes and drawn into wires; used in jewelry, coins, electrical wire
Galena PbS	2.5	7.4–7.6	Metallic	Lead gray	Lead gray	Main ore of lead; used in shields against radiation
Graphite C	1–2	2.3	Metallic to dull	Black	Black	Feels greasy; very soft; used as pencil "lead" and as a lubricant

GROUP 2
Nonmetallic Luster, Mostly Dark-Colored

Mineral/ Formula	Hardness	Density (g/cm³)	Luster	Streak	Color	Other Properties/Remarks
Corundum Al_2O_3	9	3.9–4.1	Brilliant to glassy	White	Usually brown	Very hard; used as an abrasive; transparent crystals used as gems called "ruby" (red) and "sapphire" (blue and other colors)
Garnet $(Ca,Mg,Fe)_3$ $(Al,Fe,Cr)_2(SiO_4)_3$	7–7.5	3.5–4.3	Glassy to resinous	White, light brown	Red, brown, black, green	A group of minerals used in jewelry, as a birthstone, and as an abrasive
Olivine $(Mg,Fe)_2SiO_4$	6.5–7	3.3–3.4	Glassy	White or gray	Olive green	Found in igneous rocks; sometimes used as a gem
Augite $Ca(Mg,Fe,Al)$ $(AlSi)_2O_6$	5–6	3.2–3.4	Glassy	Greenish gray	Dark green to black	Found in igneous rocks
Hornblende $NaCa_2(Mg,Fe,Al)_5$ $(Si,Al)_8O_{22}(OH)_2$	5–6	3.0–3.4	Glassy, silky	White to gray	Dark green to brown, black	Found in igneous and metamorphic rocks
Apatite $Ca_5(PO_4)_3F$	5	3.1–3.2	Glassy	White	Green, brown, red, blue, violet, yellow	Sometimes used as a gem; source of the phosphorus needed by plants
Azurite $Cu_3(CO_3)_2(OH)_2$	3.5–4	3.8	Glassy to dull	Pale blue	Intense blue	Ore of copper; used as a gem
Biotite $K(Mg,Fe)_3AlSiO_{10}$ $(OH)_2$	2.5–3	2.8–3.4	Glassy or pearly	White to gray	Dark green, brown, or black	A type of mica, sometimes used as a lubricant
Serpentine $Mg_6Si_4O_{10}(OH)_8$	2–5	2.2–2.6	Greasy, waxy, silky	White	Usually green	Once used in insulation but found to cause cancer; used in fireproofing; can be in the form of asbestos
Limonite Mixture of hydrous iron oxides	1–5.5	2.8–4.3	Glassy to dull	Yellow brown	Brown black to brownish yellow	Ore of iron, also known as "yellow ocher," a pigment; a mixture that is not strictly a mineral
Bauxite Mixture of hydrous aluminum oxides	1–3	2.0–2.5	Dull to earthy	Colorless to gray	Brown, yellow, gray, white	Ore of aluminum, smells like clay when wet; a mixture that is not strictly a mineral

GROUP 3
Nonmetallic Luster, Mostly Light-Colored

Mineral/ Formula	Hardness	Density (g/cm³)	Luster	Streak	Color	Other Properties/Remarks
Diamond C	10	3.5	Brilliant	White	Colorless and varied	Hardest known substance; used in jewelry; as an abrasive; in cutting instruments
Topaz $Al_2SiO_4(F,OH)_2$	8	3.5–3.6	Glassy	White	Straw yellow, pink, bluish, greenish	Valuable gem
Quartz SiO_2	7	2.6	Glassy, greasy	White	Colorless, white; any color when not pure	The second most abundant mineral; many varieties are gems (amethyst, cat's-eye, bloodstone, agate, jasper, onyx); used in making glass
Feldspar (K,Na,Ca) $(AlSi_3O_8)$	6	2.6	Glassy	Colorless, white	Colorless, white, various colors	As a family, the most abundant of all minerals; the different types of feldspar make up over 60 percent of Earth's crust
Fluorite CaF_2	4	3.0–3.3	Glassy	Colorless	Purple, light, green, yellow, bluish green, other colors	Some types are fluorescent (glow when exposed to ultraviolet light); used in making steel
Dolomite $CaMg(CO_3)_2$	3.5–4	2.8	Glassy or pearly	White	Colorless, white, pinkish, or light tints	Used in making concrete and cement; fizzes slowly in dilute hydrochloric acid
Calcite $CaCO_3$	3	2.7	Glassy	White to grayish	Colorless, white, pale tints	Easily scratched; bubbles in dilute hydrochloric acid; frequently fluorescent
Halite $NaCl$	2.5	2.1–2.6	Glassy	White	Colorless or white	Occurs as perfect cubic crystals; has salty taste
Gypsum $CaSO_4 \cdot 2H_2O$	2	2.3	Glassy, pearly, silky	White	Colorless, white, light tints	Very soft; used in manufacture of plaster of Paris; form known as alabaster used for statues
Sulfur S	2	2.0–2.1	Resinous to greasy	White	Yellow to yellowish brown	Used in making many medicines, in production of sulfuric acid, and in vulcanizing rubber
Talc $Mg_3Si_4O_{10}(OH)_2$	1	2.7–2.8	Pearly to greasy	White	Gray, white, greenish	Very soft; used in talcum powder; found mostly in metamorphic rocks; also called "soapstone"

Star Charts

Autumn Sky

To use this chart, hold it up in front of you and turn it so that the direction you are facing is at the bottom of the chart. This chart works best at 34° north latitude, but can be used at other times and latitudes within the continental United States. It works best at the following times: 10:00 P.M. on September 1; 9:00 P.M. on September 15; 8:00 P.M. on September 30.

NORTHERN HORIZON

EASTERN HORIZON

WESTERN HORIZON

SOUTHERN HORIZON

Winter Sky

To use this chart, hold it up in front of you and turn it so that the direction you are facing is at the bottom of the chart. This chart works best at 34° north latitude, but can be used at other times and latitudes within the continental United States. It works best at the following times: 10:00 P.M. on December 1; 9:00 P.M. on December 15; 8:00 P.M. on December 30.

NORTHERN HORIZON

EASTERN HORIZON

WESTERN HORIZON

SOUTHERN HORIZON

Spring Sky

To use this chart, hold it up in front of you and turn it so that the direction you are facing is at the bottom of the chart. This chart works best at 34° north latitude, but can be used at other times and latitudes within the continental United States. It works best at the following times: 10:00 P.M. on March 1; 9:00 P.M. on March 15; 8:00 P.M. on March 30.

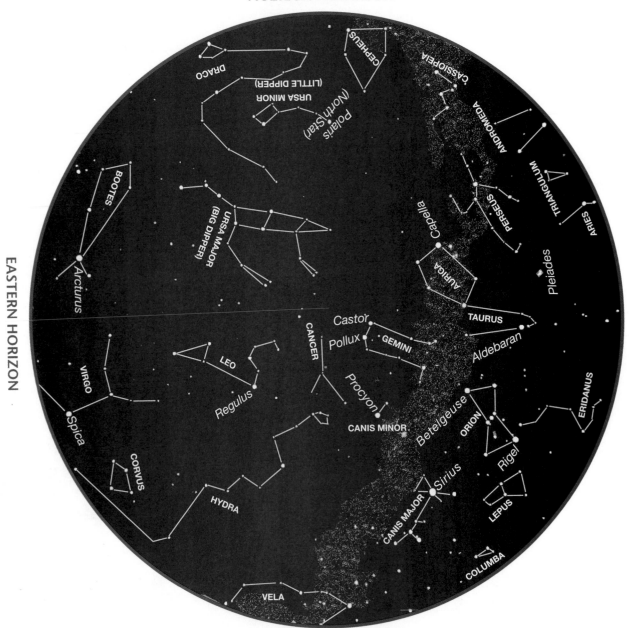

Summer Sky

To use this chart, hold it up in front of you and turn it so that the direction you are facing is at the bottom of the chart. This chart works best at 34° north latitude, but can be used at other times and latitudes within the continental United States. It works best at the following times: 10:00 P.M. on June 1; 9:00 P.M. on June 15; 8:00 P.M. on June 30.

Glossary

A

absolute dating A technique used to determine the absolute age of a fossil. (p. 630)

absolute magnitude The brightness of a star if it were a standard distance from Earth. (p. 288)

absolute zero The temperature at which no more energy can be removed from matter. (p. 114)

abyssal plain The smooth, nearly flat region of the deep ocean floor. (p. 477)

acceleration The rate at which velocity changes. (p. 104)

acid rain Rain that is more acidic than normal, caused by the release of molecules of sulfur dioxide and nitrogen oxide into the air. (p. 450)

acoustics The study of how well sounds can be heard in a particular room or hall. (p. 180)

activation energy The minimum amount of energy needed to start a chemical reaction. (p. 55)

adaptation A characteristic that helps an organism survive in its environment or reproduce. (p. 619)

air pollution A change to the atmosphere that has harmful effects. (p. 448)

alleles The different forms of a gene. (p. 559)

alloy A mixture made of two or more elements, at least one of which is a metal, that has the properties of a metal. (pp. 79, 380)

alpha particle A form of nuclear radiation consisting of two protons and two neutrons. (p. 91)

alveoli Tiny sacs of lung tissue specialized for the movement of gases between the air and the blood. (p. 650)

amniocentesis A technique by which a small amount of the fluid that surrounds a developing baby is removed; the fluid is analyzed to determine whether the baby will have a genetic disorder. (p. 598)

amplitude The maximum distance the particles of a medium move away from their rest positions as a wave passes through the medium. (p. 141)

amplitude modulation (AM) The method of transmitting radio signals by changing the amplitude of the waves. (p. 223)

angle of incidence The angle between the incoming wave and an imaginary line drawn perpendicular to the surface of the barrier or new medium. (p. 146)

angle of reflection The angle between a reflected wave and an imaginary line drawn perpendicular to the surface of the barrier. (p. 146)

antinode A point of maximum amplitude on a standing wave. (p. 150)

apparent magnitude The brightness of a star as seen from Earth. (p. 287)

aquaculture The farming of saltwater and freshwater organisms. (p. 503)

asthenosphere The soft layer of the mantle on which the lithosphere floats. (p. 319)

atoll A ring-shaped coral island found far from land. (pp. 401, 496)

atom The smallest particle of an element. (p. 24)

atomic mass unit A unit of measurement for the mass of particles in atoms. (p. 25)

atomic mass The average mass of one atom of an element. (p. 30)

atomic number The number of protons in the nucleus of an atom. (p. 25)

B

balanced forces Equal forces acting on an object in opposite directions. (p. 106)

barrier beach A long, low-lying sand deposit that forms parallel to the shore. (p. 493)

basalt A dark, dense igneous rock with a fine texture, found in oceanic crust. (p. 318)

beats The regular changes in loudness of a sound when two sounds of different frequencies are played together. (p. 181)

bedrock The solid layer of rock beneath the soil. (p. 423)

benthos Organisms that live on the bottom of the ocean or another body of water. (p. 487)

beta particle An electron that is given off by its nucleus during radioactive decay. (p. 91)

big bang The initial explosion that, according to theory, resulted in the formation and expansion of the universe. (p. 302)

bimetallic strip A strip made of two different metals that expand at different rates. (p. 130)

binary star A star system that contains two stars. (p. 297)

biodegradable A substance that can be broken down and recycled by bacteria and other decomposers. (p. 432)

bioluminescence The production of light by living things that occurs as a result of a chemical reaction among proteins and oxygen in the organism. (pp. 219, 499)

black hole The remains of an extremely massive star pulled into a small volume by the force of gravity. (p. 295)

branching tree A diagram that shows how scientists think different groups of organisms are related. (p. 638)

camera An optical instrument that uses lenses to focus light and record an image of an object. (pp. 261–262)

carbon cycle The system in which carbon is transferred from Earth's interior to the atmosphere, oceans, crust, and living things. (p. 541)

carrier A person who has one recessive allele for a trait and one dominant allele, but does not have that trait. (p. 592)

cast A fossil that is a copy of an organism's shape, formed when minerals seep into a mold. (p. 628)

catalyst A material that increases the rate of a chemical reaction by lowering the activation energy. (p. 58)

catalytic converter A device that reduces emissions of carbon monoxide, hydrocarbons, and nitrogen oxides. (p. 464)

Celsius scale The temperature scale on which 0 and 100 are the temperatures at which water freezes and boils, respectively. (pp. 113, 683)

cementation The process by which dissolved minerals crystallize and glue particles of sediment together into one mass. (p. 397)

ceramic A hard, crystalline solid made by heating clay and other materials to high temperatures. (p. 84)

change of state The physical change of matter from one state to another. (p. 126)

chemical bond The force that holds two atoms together. (p. 27)

chemical equation A short, easy way to show a chemical reaction, using symbols instead of words. (p. 46)

chemical reaction A process in which substances undergo chemical changes. (p. 38)

chemical rock Sedimentary rock that forms when minerals crystallize from a solution. (p. 400)

chemical symbol The set of characters that is used to identify an element. (p. 34)

chlorofluorocarbon One of a group of chlorine compounds formerly used in air conditioners and refrigerators. (pp. 453, 546)

classifying Grouping together items that are alike in some way. (p. 681)

clastic rock Sedimentary rock that forms when rock fragments are squeezed together under high pressure. (p. 398)

cleavage A mineral's ability to split evenly along flat surfaces. (p. 367)

climate The average conditions of temperature, precipitation, winds, and clouds in an area over time. (p. 514)

clone An organism that is genetically identical to the organism from which it was produced. (p. 604)

cochlea A snail-shaped tube in the inner ear lined with sound receptors; nerve impulses are sent from the cochlea to the brain. (p. 185)

codominance A condition in which neither of two alleles of a gene is dominant or recessive. (p. 568)

coefficient A number placed in front of a chemical formula in an equation, that indicates how many atoms or molecules of each reactant and product take part in the reaction. (p. 50)

commensalism A relationship between two species in which one species benefits and the other is neither helped nor harmed. (p. 669)

communication The process of sharing ideas and information with other people. (p. 681)

compaction The process by which sediments are pressed together under their own weight. (p. 397)

competition The struggle between organisms for the limited resources in a habitat. (p. 663)

complementary colors Any two colors that combine to form white light or black pigment. (p. 252)

composite A combination of two or more substances that creates a new material. (p. 72)

composting The process of helping the natural decomposition process break down many forms of waste. (p. 435)

compound A substance made of two or more elements chemically combined in a set ratio. (p. 362)

compression Stress that squeezes rock until it folds or breaks; also, the part of a longitudinal wave where the particles of the medium are close together. (p. 139)

concave lens A lens that is thinner in the center than at the edges. (p. 246)

concave mirror A mirror with a surface that curves inward like the inside of a bowl. (p. 241)

concentration The amount of one material dissolved in a given amount of another material. (p. 57)

condensation The change from the gaseous to the liquid state of matter. (p. 456)

conduction The transfer of thermal energy through direct contact between particles of matter. (pp. 116, 324)

cone A cell in the retina that responds to color. (p. 257)

conservation of mass The principle stating that matter is neither created nor destroyed during a chemical reaction. (p. 49)

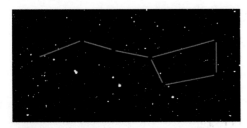

constellation A pattern of stars in the sky. (p. 275)

constructive interference The interference that occurs when two waves combine to make a wave with a larger amplitude. (p. 148)

continental climate The climate of the centers of continents with cold winters and warm or hot summers. (p. 516)

continental drift The hypothesis that the continents slowly move across Earth's surface. (p. 327)

continental shelf A gently sloping, shallow area of the ocean floor that extends outward from the edge of a continent. (p. 476)

continental slope An incline leading down from the edge of the continental shelf. (p. 476)

controlled experiment An investigation in which all variables except one remain the same. (p. 12)

convection The transfer of thermal energy by movements of a fluid. (pp. 117, 324)

convection current The movement of a fluid, caused by differences in temperature, that transfers thermal energy from one part of the fluid to another. (p. 324)

convergent boundary A plate boundary where two plates move toward each other. (p. 344)

convex lens A lens curved so that it is thicker in the center than at the edges. (pp. 246, 276)

convex mirror A mirror with a surface that curves outward. (p. 242)

coral reef A structure of calcite skeletons built up by coral animals in warm, shallow ocean water. (p. 400)

cornea The transparent front surface of the eye. (p. 256)

corrosive wastes Materials that dissolve or eat through many materials. (p. 439)

crest The highest point of a transverse wave. (p. 138)

crop rotation The planting of different crops in a field each year. (p. 426)

crust The layer of rock that forms Earth's outer surface. (p. 318)

crystal A solid in which the particles form a repeating pattern. (p. 362)

data The facts, figures, and other evidence collected in an experiment. (p.12)

decibels (dB) The unit of measurement of loudness. (p. 169)

decomposition A chemical reaction that breaks down a compound into simpler products. (p. 52)

deep-ocean trench A deep valley along the ocean floor through which oceanic crust slowly sinks towards the mantle. (p. 336)

deformation A change in the volume or shape of the Earth's crust. (p. 346)

density The measurement of how much mass is contained in a given volume of a substance. (p. 324)

deposition The process by which sediment settles out of the water or wind that is carrying it and is deposited in a new location. (p. 397)

desert A desert is an arid region that gets less than 25 centimeters of rain every year. (p. 528)

desertification The advance of desert-like conditions into areas that previously were fertile. (p. 425)

destructive interference The interference that occurs when two waves combine to make a wave with a smaller amplitude. (p. 148)

development The construction of buildings, roads, bridges, dams, and other structures. (p. 421)

diaphragm A large, dome-shaped muscle that has an important function in breathing. (p. 651)

diffraction The bending of waves around the edge of a barrier. (p. 147)

diffuse reflection Reflection that occurs when parallel rays of light hit a rough surface and reflect at different angles. (p. 239)

diffusion The process by which molecules move from an area in which they are highly concentrated to an area in which they are less concentrated. (p. 658)

dissonance The sound produced when notes that have no musical relationship are played together. (p. 177)

divergent boundary A plate boundary where two plates move away from each other. (p. 343)

dominant allele An allele whose trait always shows up in the organism when the allele is present. (p. 559)

Doppler effect The apparent change in frequency of sound as the source moves in relation to the listener. (p. 110)

drought A water shortage caused by long periods of low precipitation in a particular area. (p. 458)

dune A hill of wind-blown sand. (p. 493)

ear canal The narrow region leading from the outside of the human ear to the eardrum. (p. 184)

eardrum The membrane that separates the outer ear from the middle ear and that vibrates when sound waves strike it. (p. 185)

earthquake The shaking that results from the movement of rock beneath Earth's surface. (p. 347)

echolocation The use of reflection of sound waves to navigate and to locate prey. (p. 190)

eclipsing binary A star system in which one star periodically blocks the light from another. (p. 298)

ecosystem All the living and nonliving things that interact in an area. (p. 662)

egg A female sex cell. (p. 572)

elasticity The ability of a material to bounce back after being disturbed. (p. 165)

electromagnetic radiation Energy that travels through space in the form of waves. (p. 203)

electromagnetic spectrum The range of electromagnetic waves placed in a certain order. (p. 207)

electromagnetic wave A transverse wave that transfers electric and magnetic energy. (p. 203)

electron A tiny, negatively charged, high-energy particle that moves in the space outside the nucleus of an atom. (p. 24)

electron dot diagram A representation of the number of valence electrons in an atom, using dots placed around the symbol of an element. (p. 28)

element A substance that cannot be broken down into any other substances by chemical or physical means. (pp. 24, 362)

elliptical galaxy A galaxy shaped like a flattened ball that can contain only old stars. (p. 300)

emissions Solid particles and gases from motor vehicles that are released into the air. (p. 449)

endothermic reaction A reaction that absorbs energy in the form of heat. (p. 41)

energy The ability to do work or cause change, such as moving one object some distance. (p. 108)

enzyme A biological catalyst that lowers the activation energy of reactions in cells. (p. 59)

equilibrium A state in which opposing forces in a system are equally balanced or stable. (p. 655)

erosion The process by which water, ice, wind, or gravity moves fragments of rock and soil. (pp. 397, 424)

evaporation The process by which molecules of liquid water absorb energy and change to the gas state. (p. 456)

evolution The gradual change in a species over time. (p. 619)

exothermic reaction A reaction that releases energy in the form of heat. (p. 41)

explosive waste A waste material that reacts quickly when exposed to air or water or that explodes when dropped. (p. 439)

extinct A species that has disappeared from Earth. (p. 630)

extrusive rock Igneous rock that forms from lava on Earth's surface. (p. 393)

eyepiece lens A lens that magnifies the image formed by the objective lens. (p. 260)

Fahrenheit scale The temperature scale on which 32 and 212 are the temperatures at which water freezes and boils. (p.18)

fallow An area of land left unplanted with crops. (p. 425)

farsighted The condition in which distant objects can be seen clearly but nearby objects look blurry. (p. 258)

fault A break or crack in the Earth's lithosphere along which rocks move. (p. 342)

fault-block mountain A mountain that forms where a normal fault uplifts a block of rock. (p. 350)

fertilizer Chemicals that provide nutrients that help crops grow better. (p. 459)

first quarter The phase of the moon in which the moon's Earth-facing side is lit by the sun. (p. 482)

flammable waste A waste material that can catch fire easily at a fairly low temperature. (p. 439)

fluorescence The property of a mineral in which the mineral glows under ultraviolet light. (p. 368)

fluorescent light Lights that glow when an electric current causes ultraviolet waves to strike a coating inside a tube. (p. 217)

focal point The point at which rays of light meet, or appear to meet, after being reflected (or refracted) by a mirror (or a lens). (pp. 241, 242)

foliated Metamorphic rocks whose grains are arranged in parallel layers or bands. (p. 403)

food web The pattern of overlapping food chains in an ecosystem. (p. 487)

footwall The block of rock that forms the lower half of a fault. (p. 348)

force A push or pull exerted on an object. (p. 104)

formula A combination of symbols that shows the ratio of the elements in a compound. (p. 47)

fossil The preserved remains or traces of living things that lived in the past. (pp. 328, 627)

fossil record The millions of fossils that scientists have collected. (p. 630)

fracture The way a mineral looks when it breaks apart in an irregular way. (p. 367)

frequency The number of complete waves that pass a given point in a certain amount of time. (p. 144)

frequency modulation (FM) The method of transmitting radio signals by changing the frequency of the waves. (p. 224)

full moon A phase of the moon in which the moon's Earth-facing side is completely lit by the sun. (p. 482)

galaxy A giant structure that contains hundreds of billions of stars. (p. 283)

gamma radiation A form of nuclear radiation consisting of high-energy waves. (p. 91)

gamma rays Electromagnetic waves with the shortest wavelengths and highest frequencies. (p. 214)

gemstone A hard, colorful mineral that has a brilliant or glassy luster. (p. 377)

gene A segment of DNA on a chromosome that codes for a specific trait. (p. 559)

genetic disorder An abnormal condition that a person inherits through genes or chromosomes. (p. 595)

gene therapy The insertion of working copies of a gene into the cells of a person with a genetic disorder in an attempt to correct the disorder. (p. 606)

genetic engineering The transfer of a gene from the DNA of one organism into another organism, in order to produce an organism with desired traits. (p. 604)

genotype An organism's genetic makeup, or allele combinations. (p. 568)

geologist A scientist who studies the forces that make and shape Earth. (p. 315)

geology The study of the solid Earth. (p. 315)

giant star A very large star, much larger than the sun. (p. 286)

glass A clear, solid material with no crystal structure, created by heating sand to a very high temperature. (p. 86)

global warming A gradual increase in the temperature of Earth's atmosphere. (p. 544)

gradualism The theory that evolution occurs slowly but steadily. (p. 634)

grain A particle of mineral or other rock that gives a rock its texture. (p. 389)

gram A unit of measure for measuring mass, or the amount of matter in an object. (p. 683)

granite A usually light-colored rock that is found in continental crust. (p. 318)

greenhouse gases Gases in the atmosphere that trap heat. (p. 544)

groundwater Water that fills the cracks and pores in underground soil and rock layers. (p. 457)

group Elements in the same vertical column of the periodic table; also called a family. (p. 34)

half-life The length of time needed for half the atoms of a radioactive isotope to decay. (pp. 92, 630)

hanging wall The block of rock that forms the upper half of a fault. (p. 348)

hazardous waste A material that can be harmful if it is not disposed of properly. (p. 439)

heat transfer The movement of energy from a warmer object to a cooler object. (p. 323)

heat The movement of thermal energy from one substance to another. (p. 115)

heredity The passing of traits from parents to offspring. (p. 556)

hertz (Hz) Unit of measure for frequency. (p. 144)

Hertzsprung–Russell diagram A graph relating the temperature and brightness of stars. (p. 288)

heterozygous Having two different alleles for a trait. (p. 568)

holdfast A bundle of rootlike strands that attaches algae to rocks. (p. 496)

hologram A three-dimensional photograph formed by the interference between two laser beams. (p. 266)

homeostasis The process by which the body's internal environment is kept stable in spite of changes in the external environment. (p. 656)

homologous structure An homologous structure is a body part that is structurally similar in two or more related species. (p. 636)

homozygous Having two identical alleles for a trait. (p. 568)

host An organism that provides a source of energy or a suitable environment for a virus or for another organism to live. (p. 670)

hot spot An area where magma from deep within the mantle melts through the crust above it. (p. 353)

humid subtropical A warm, wet climate area bordering the tropics. (p. 530)

hybrid An organism that has two different alleles for a trait; an organism that is heterozygous for a particular trait. (p. 560)

hybridization A selective breeding method in which two genetically different individuals are crossed. (p. 603)

hydrothermal vent An area where ocean water sinks through cracks in the ocean floor, is heated by the underlying magma, and rises again through the cracks. (p. 500)

hypothesis A possible explanation for a set of observations or an answer to a scientific question; must be testable. (p. 110)

ice ages Cold time periods in Earth's history, during which glaciers covered large parts of the surface. (p. 538)

igneous rock A type of rock that forms from the cooling of molten rock at or below the surface. (p. 391)

illuminated A word used to describe an object that can be seen because it reflects light. (p. 216)

image a copy of an object formed by reflected or refracted rays of light. (p. 240)

inbreeding A selective breeding method in which two individuals with identical or similar sets of alleles are crossed. (p. 603)

incandescent light A lights that glows when a filament inside it gets hot. (p. 216)

incineration The burning of solid waste. (p. 431)

index of refraction The measure of how much a ray of light bends when it enters a new medium. (p. 244)

inference An interpretation of an observation based on evidence and prior knowledge. (pp. 11, 680)

infrared rays Electromagnetic waves with shorter wavelengths and higher frequencies than radio waves. (p. 210)

infrasound Sound waves with frequencies below 20 Hz. (p. 170)

inhibitor A material that decreases the rate of a reaction. (p. 59)

inner core A dense ball of solid metal at the center of Earth. (p. 319)

inorganic Not formed from living things or the remains of living things. (p. 361)

insulator A material that does not easily transfer thermal energy or electric current between its particles. (p. 119)

insulin A chemical produced in the pancreas that enables the body's cells to take in glucose from the blood and use it for energy. (p. 658)

intensity The amount of energy per second carried through a unit area by a wave. (p. 168)

interference The interaction between waves that meet. (p. 148)

intertidal zone The area that stretches from the highest high-tide line on land to the point on the continental shelf exposed by the lowest tide. (p. 488)

intrusive rock Igneous rock that forms when magma hardens beneath Earth's surface. (p. 393)

iris A ring of muscle that contracts and expands to change the amount of light that enters the eye. (p. 256)

irregular galaxy A galaxy that does not have a regular shape. (p. 300)

isotope An atom with the same number of protons and different number of neutrons from other atoms of the same element. (p. 90)

karyotype A picture of all the chromosomes in a cell arranged in pairs. (p. 599)

Kelvin scale The temperature scale on which zero is the temperature at which no more energy can be removed from matter. (p. 114)

kinetic energy Energy that an object has because of its motion. (p. 109)

land reclamation The process of restoring land to a more natural state. (p. 422)

land subsidence A sinking or subsiding of a land surface as a result of geologic processes or of human activities. (pp. 350, 461)

larynx Two folds of tissue that make up the human voicebox. (p. 163)

laser A device that produces coherent light. (p. 263)

lava Magma that reaches the surface; also, the rock formed when liquid lava hardens. (p. 351)

leachate Water that has passed through buried wastes in a landfill. (p. 431)

leeward The downwind side of mountains. (p. 519)

lens The flexible structure that focuses light that has entered the eye; also, a curved piece of glass or other transparent material that is used to refract light. (p. 246)

light-year The distance that light travels in one year. (p. 284)

lithosphere A rigid layer made up of the uppermost part of the mantle and the crust. (p. 318)

liter a unit used for measuring volume. (p. 682)

litter The loose layer of dead plant leaves and stems on the surface of the soil. (p. 423)

longitudinal wave A wave that moves the particles of the medium parallel to the direction in which the waves are traveling. (p. 138)

longshore drift The movement of water and sediment along a beach caused by waves coming into shore at an angle. (p. 492)

loudness Perception of the intensity of a sound. (p. 169)

luminous The term used to describe an object that can be seen because it emits light. (p. 216)

luster The way a mineral reflects light from its surface. (p. 365)

magma The molten mixture of rock-forming substances, gases, and water that make up part of Earth's mantle. (p. 351)

magnetic resonance imaging A process that uses radio waves to form pictures of the inside of the human body. (p. 209)

main sequence An area on the Hertzsprung-Russell diagram that runs from the upper left to the lower right and includes more than 90 percent of all stars. (p. 288)

manipulated variable The one factor that a scientist changes during an experiment. (p. 685)

mantle The layer of hot, solid materials between Earth's crust and core. (p. 318)

marine climate The climate of some coastal regions, with relatively warm winters and cool summers. (p. 516)

mass number The sum of the protons and the neutrons in the nucleus of an atom. (p. 90)

mechanical wave A wave that requires a medium through which to travel. (p. 137)

medium Material through which a mechanical wave travels. (p. 137)

meiosis The process that occurs in sex cells (sperm and egg) by which the number of chromosomes is reduced by half. (p. 574)

messenger RNA Substance that copies the coded message from the DNA in the nucleus and carries the message into the cytoplasm. (p. 579)

metalloid An element that has some of the characteristics of metals and some of the characteristics of nonmetals. (p. 36)

metal An element that easily gives up its valence electron in a chemical reaction and that can be classified based on physical properties (such as hardness, shininess, ease of malleability, and ductility). (p. 35)

metamorphic rock A type of rock that forms from an existing rock that is changed by heat, pressure, or chemical reactions. (p. 391)

meter A unit of length, or the distance between two points.

microclimate The climate characteristic of a small specific area; it may be different from the climate of the surrounding area. (p. 519)

microscope An instrument that makes small objects look larger. (p. 261)

microwaves Radio waves with the shortest wavelengths and the highest frequencies. (p. 207)

middle ear The area behind the eardrum that contains the hammer, the anvil, and the stirrup. (p. 185)

mid-ocean ridge The undersea mountain chain where new ocean floor is produced; a divergent plate boundary. (pp. 332, 477)

mineral A naturally occurring, inorganic solid that has a crystal structure and a definite chemical composition. (p. 361)

mirage An image of a distant object caused by refraction of light as it travels through air of varying temperatures. (p. 245)

Mohs hardness scale A scale ranking ten minerals from softest to hardest; used in testing the hardness of minerals. (p. 364)

mold A fossil formed when an organism buried in sediment dissolves, leaving a hollow area. (p. 628)

molecule A combination of two or more atoms that are bonded together. (p. 42)

monomers Small, carbon-based molecules that make up the links in a polymer chain. (p. 69)

motion The state in which one object's distance from another is changing. (p. 102)

multiple alleles Three or more forms of a gene that code for a single trait. (p. 589)

municipal solid waste Waste produced in homes, businesses, and schools. (p. 430)

music A set of tones and overtones combined in ways that are pleasing to the ear. (p. 176)

mutation A change in a gene or chromosome. (p. 580)

mutualism A type of symbiosis in which both partners benefit from living together. (p. 669)

natural selection The process by which individuals that are better adapted to their environment are more likely to survive and reproduce than other members of the same species. (p. 620)

neap tide A tide with the least difference between low and high tide that occurs when the sun and moon pull at right angles to each other. (p. 484)

nearsighted The condition in which a person can see nearby objects clearly but distant objects look blurry. (p. 258)

nebula A large amount of gas and dust in space spread out in an immense volume. (p. 293)

negative feedback A process in which a system is turned off by the condition it produces; examples of negative feedback systems include regulation of temperature by a thermostat and the regulation of the levels of many hormones in the blood. (p. 656)

nekton Free-swimming animals that can move throughout the water column. (p. 487)

neon light A glass tube filled with neon that produces light. (p. 218)

neritic zone The region of shallow water in the ocean that extends from the low-tide line out to the edge of the continental shelf. (p. 495)

neutron star A tiny star that remains after a supernova explosion. (p. 294)

neutron Small, uncharged particle in the nucleus of an atom. (p. 24)

new moon The phase of the moon in which the side of the moon facing Earth is the side facing directly away from the sun. The new moon, therefore, is not visible from Earth. (p. 481)

niche An organism's particular role in an ecosystem, or how it lives. (p. 662)

nitrogen cycle The process by which nitrogen is removed from the atmosphere, fixed in the soil by bacteria, incorporated into other living things, and then released back into the atmosphere. (p. 426)

node A point of zero amplitude on a standing wave. (p. 149)

nodules Bumps on the roots of certain plants that house nitrogen-fixing bacteria. (p. 503)

noise A mixture of sound waves with no pleasing timbre and no identifiable pitch. (p. 177)

nonmetal An element that lacks most of the properties of metals. (p. 35)

normal fault A type of fault where the hanging wall slides downward; caused by tension in the crust. (p. 348)

nuclear radiation Particles and energy produced during radioactive decay. (p. 91)

nuclear reaction A reaction involving the particles in the nucleus of an atom that can change one element into another element. (p. 90)

nucleus The control center of the cell that directs the cell's activities and determines the cell's characteristics; also, the central core of an atom containing protons and usually neutrons. (p. 24)

nutrient depletion The process in which plants use more nutrients than decomposers can replace and that makes the soil less fertile. (p. 425)

objective lens Lens that gathers light from an object and forms a real image. (p. 260)

observatory A building that contains one or more telescopes. (p. 277)

observation The process of using one of more of the five senses to gather information about the world. (pp. 11, 680)

opaque Term used to describe a material that reflects or absorbs all light that strikes it. (p. 238)

open-ocean zone The area of the ocean beyond the edge of the continental shelf. (p. 495)

operational definition A statement that describes how a particular variable is measured. (p. 685)

optic nerve Short, thick nerve that carries signals from the eye to the brain. (p. 257)

optical fiber Long, thin strand of glass or plastic that can carry light for long distances without allowing the light to fade out; can be used for transmitting messages. (pp. 87, 266)

ore A rock that contains a metal or economically useful mineral. (p. 377)

organ A structure in the body that is composed of different kinds of tissue. (p. 648)

organ system A group of organs that work together to perform a major function in the body of an organism. (p. 648)

organic rock A sedimentary rock that forms where remains of organisms are deposited in thick layers. (p. 399)

osmosis The diffusion of water molecules through a selectively permeable membrane. (p. 659)

outer core A layer of molten iron and nickel that surrounds the inner core of Earth. (p. 319)

ozone A form of oxygen that has three oxygen atoms in each molecule instead of the usual two. (pp. 449, 545)

ozone layer The layer of the upper atmosphere about 30 kilometers above Earth's surface where ozone is concentrated. (pp. 452, 545)

Pangaea The name of the single landmass that broke apart 225 million years ago and gave rise to today's continents. (p. 327)

parallax The apparent change in position of an object when seen from different places. (p. 284)

parasite An organism that lives on or in a host and causes harm to the host. (p. 670)

parasitism A relationship in which one organism lives on or in another and harms it. (p. 670)

pedigree A chart, or family tree, that tracks which members of a family have a particular trait. (p. 593)

period A horizontal row of elements in the periodic table. (p. 34)

periodic table An arrangement of the elements in order of atomic number, in which elements with similar properties are grouped in columns. (p. 31)

permafrost Permanently frozen soil found in tundra climate regions. (p. 532)

pesticide A chemical intended to kill insects and other organisms that damage crops. (p. 459)

petrified fossil A fossil in which minerals replace all or part of an organism. (p. 628)

phenotype An organism's physical appearance, or visible traits. (p. 568)

photochemical smog A brownish haze that is a mixture of ozone and other chemicals that is formed when nitrogen oxides, hydrocarbons, and other pollutants react with one another in the presence of sunlight. (p. 449)

photoelectric effect The movement of electrons in a substance when light is shined on it. (p. 205)

photon A tiny particle or packet of light energy. (p. 205)

photosynthesis The process by which plants and some other organisms capture light energy and use it to make food from carbon dioxide and water. (p. 542)

pigments Opaque substances used to color other materials. (p. 252)

pitch Perception of the frequency of a sound. (p. 170)

plane mirror A flat mirror that produces an upright, virtual image the same size as the object. (p. 240)

plankton Tiny algae and animals that float in water and are carried by waves and currents. (p. 487)

plastic A synthetic polymer that can be molded or shaped. (p. 71)

plate tectonics The theory that pieces of Earth's lithosphere are in constant motion, driven by convection currents in the mantle. (p. 341)

plate A section of the lithosphere that slowly moves over the asthenosphere, carrying pieces of continental and oceanic crust. (p. 340)

polar zones The areas near both poles, from about 66.5° to 90° north and 66.5° to 90° south latitudes. (p. 515)

polarized light Light that vibrates in only one direction. (p. 204)

polymer A large, complex molecule built from smaller molecules bonded together. (p. 69)

porphyritic texture An igneous rock texture in which large crystals are scattered on a background of much smaller crystals. (p. 393)

potential energy Energy that is stored and available to be used later. (p. 108)

precipitate A solid that forms from a solution during a chemical reaction. (p. 39)

precipitation Forms of water such as rain, snow, sleet, or hail that fall from clouds and reach Earth's surface. (p. 456)

predation An interaction in which one organism hunts and kills another animal for food. (p. 664)

predator A carnivore that hunts and kills other animals for food and has adaptations that help it capture the animals it preys upon. (p. 664)

predicting making an inference about a future event based on current evidence or past experience. (p. 680)

pressure The force exerted on a surface divided by the total area over which the force is exerted; also the force of a gas's outward push divided by the area of the walls of the container. (p. 317)

prey An animal that a predator feeds upon. (p. 664)

primary colors Three colors that can be used to make any other color. (p. 251)

primary treatment The removal of solid materials from waste water. (p. 465)

primary wave A longitudinal seismic wave. (p. 155)

probability The likelihood that a particular event will occur. (p. 564)

product A substance formed as a result of a chemical reaction. (p. 48)

proton A small, positively charged particle in the nucleus of an atom. (p. 24)

protostar A contracting cloud of gas and dust; the earliest stage of a star's life. (p. 293)

pulsar A neutron star that produces radio waves. (p. 292)

punctuated equilibria The theory that species evolve during short periods of rapid change. (p. 634)

Punnett square A chart that shows all the possible combinations of alleles that can result from a genetic cross. (p. 566)

pupil The opening through which light enters the eye. (p. 256)

purebred An organism that always produces offspring with the same form of a trait as itself. (p. 557)

quasar A distant galaxy with a black hole at its center. (p. 296)

radar A system of detecting reflected radio waves. (p. 208)

radiation The transfer of energy by electromagnetic waves. (pp. 118, 323)

radiation therapy A process in which radioactive elements are used to destroy unhealthy cells. (p. 94)

radio telescope A device used to detect radio waves given off by objects in space. (p. 276)

radio wave Electromagnetic wave with the longest wavelengths and lowest frequencies. (p. 207)

radioactive dating The process of determining the age of an object using the half-life of one or more radioactive isotopes. (p. 92)

radioactive decay The process in which the atomic nuclei of unstable isotopes release fast-moving particles and energy. (p. 90)

radioactive element An unstable chemical element that decays, or breaks down, into a different element or elements. (p. 630)

radioactive wastes A waste substance that contains unstable atoms. (p. 439)

rain forest A forest in the tropical wet climate zone that gets plenty of rain all year. (p. 525)

rarefaction The part of a longitudinal wave where the particles of the medium are far apart. (p. 139)

ray A straight line used to represent a light wave. (p. 239)

reactant A substance that enters into a chemical reaction. (p. 48)

real image An inverted image formed where rays of light meet. (p. 241)

recessive allele An allele that is masked when a dominant allele is present. (p. 559)

recycling The process of reclaiming raw materials and reusing them. (p. 432)

reference point A place or object used for comparison to determine if an object is in motion. (p. 102)

reflecting telescope A telescope that uses one or more mirrors to gather light from distant objects. (pp. 260, 276)

reflection The bouncing back of a wave when it hits a surface through which it cannot pass. (p. 146)

refracting telescope A telescope that uses convex lenses to gather and focus light. (pp. 260, 276)

refraction The bending of waves as they enter a different medium. (p. 147)

regular reflection The image that occurs when parallel rays of light hit a smooth surface and all reflect at the same angle. (p. 239)

relative dating A technique used to determine which of two fossils is older. (p. 629)

replacement A reaction in which one element replaces another in a compound, or in which two elements in different compounds trade places. (p. 53)

resin The solid material left over when oil is refined to make gasoline and other petroleum products. (p. 433)

resonance The increase in the amplitude of vibration that occurs when external vibrations match the object's natural frequency. (p. 150)

responding variable The variable that is expected to change in response to the manipulated variable. (p. 10)

retina The layer of cells that lines the inside of the eyeball. (p. 257)

reverse fault A type of fault where the hanging wall slides upward; caused by compression in the crust. (p. 349)

rift valley A deep valley that forms where two plates move apart. (p. 343)

rock The material that forms Earth's hard surface. (p. 315)

rock cycle A series of processes on the surface and inside Earth that slowly changes rocks from one kind to another. (p. 406)

rod Cells in the retina that detect dim light and distinguish among black, white, and shades of gray. (p. 257)

sandbar A ridge of sand deposited by waves as they slow down near shore. (p. 492)

sanitary landfill A landfill that holds nonhazardous waste such as municipal solid waste and construction debris. (p. 431)

savanna A tropical grassland with scattered clumps of trees; found in the tropical wet-and-dry climate zone close to the equator. (p. 528)

science A way of learning about the natural world through observations and logical reasoning; leads to a body of knowledge. (p. 10)

scientific inquiry The diverse ways in which scientists study the natural world. (p. 10)

scientific law A statement that describes what scientists expect to happen every time under a particular set of conditions. (p. 16)

scientific theory A well-tested concept that explains a wide range of observations. (p. 341)

scrubber A device that removes pollutants from emissions using a stream of water droplets. (p. 464)

sea-floor spreading The process by which molten material adds new oceanic crust to the ocean floor. (p. 333)

seamount A mountain on the ocean floor that is completely under water. (p. 477)

secondary color Any color that is produced by combining equal amounts of any two primary colors. (p. 251)

secondary treatment A treatment that involves using bacteria to break down wastes. (p. 465)

secondary wave A transverse seismic wave. (p. 155)

sediment Small, solid particles of material from rocks or organisms that are moved by water or wind, resulting in erosion and deposition. (pp. 396, 460)

sedimentary rock A type of rock that forms when particles of other rocks or the remains of plants and animals are pressed and cemented together. (p. 391)

seismic wave A vibration that travels through Earth carrying the energy released during an earthquake. (pp. 155, 316)

seismograph A device that records ground movements caused by seismic waves as they move through Earth. (p. 156)

selective breeding The process of selecting a few organisms with desired traits to serve as parents of the next generation. (p. 602)

sewage Water containing human wastes. (p. 459)

sex-linked gene A gene carried on the X or Y chromosome. (p. 592)

smelting The process by which ore is melted to separate the useful metal from other elements. (p. 380)

sodium vapor light A light bulb containing solid sodium plus neon and argon gas. (p. 218)

solution A well-mixed mixture having the same properties throughout. (p. 372)

sonar A system of detecting reflected sound waves. (pp. 189, 332, 475)

sonogram An image formed by an ultrasound machine. (p. 191)

species A group of similar organisms whose members can mate with one another and produce fertile offspring. (p. 617)

specific heat The amount of thermal energy required to raise the temperature of one kilogram of a substance by one Kelvin. (p. 120)

spectrograph An instrument that breaks the light from an object into colors and photographs the resulting spectrum. (p. 279)

spectroscope An instrument used to view the different colors of light produced by different sources. (p. 216)

speed The distance an object travels in one unit of time. (p. 103)

sperm A male sex cell. (p. 572)

spiral galaxy A galaxy whose arms curve outward in a pinwheel pattern. (p. 300)

spring tide A tide with the greatest difference between high and low tide that occurs when the sun and the moon are aligned with Earth. (p. 483)

standing wave A wave that appears to stand in one place, even though it is really two waves interfering as they pass through each other. (p. 149)

state The physical form of matter, for example, solid or liquid or gas. (p. 126)

steppe A prairie or grassland found in the semiarid climate region. (p. 529)

streak The color of a mineral's powder. (p. 364)

stress A force that acts on rock to change its shape or volume. (p. 346)

strike-slip fault A type of fault where rocks on either side move past each other sideways with little up-and-down motion. (p. 348)

subarctic A climate zone that lies north of the humid continental climate zone, with short, cool summers and long, bitterly cold winters. (p. 531)

subduction The process by which oceanic crust sinks beneath a deep-ocean trench and back into the mantle at a convergent plate boundary. (p. 336)

subscript A number in a chemical formula that tells the number of atoms in a molecule or the ratio of elements in a compound. (p. 47)

subsoil The layer of soil beneath the topsoil that contains mostly clay and other minerals. (p. 423)

sunspots Dark, cooler regions on the surface of the sun. (p. 539)

supernova The explosion of a dying giant or supergiant star. (p. 294)

surface wave A type of seismic wave that forms when P waves and S waves reach Earth's surface. (p. 139)

symbiosis A close relationship between two organisms in which at least one of the organisms benefits. (p. 669)

synthesis A chemical reaction in which two or more simple substances combine to form a new, more complex substance. (p. 51)

telescope An optical instrument that forms enlarged images of distant objects. (p. 260)

temperate zones The area between the tropical and polar zones, from about 23.5° to 66.5° north and 23.5° to 66.5° south latitudes. (p. 515)

temperature inversion A condition in which a layer of warm air prevents the rising air from escaping. (p. 450)

texture The size, shape, and pattern of a rock's grains. (p. 389)

thermal expansion The expansion of matter when it is heated. (p. 129)

thermogram An image that shows regions of different temperatures in different colors. (p. 211)

thermostat A device that regulates temperature. (p. 130)

third quarter The phase of the moon in which half of the moon's Earth-facing side is again lit by the sun. (p. 482)

tides The daily rise and fall of Earth's waters on shores. (p. 480)

timbre The overall quality of a sound. (p. 175)

tissue A group of similar cells that perform a specific function in an organism. (p. 647)

topsoil The mixture of humus, clay, and other minerals that forms the crumbly, topmost layer of soil. (p. 423)

total internal reflection The complete reflection of light by the inside surface of a medium. (p. 268)

toxic waste A waste material that can harm an organism. (p. 439)

tracer A radioactive isotope that can be followed through the steps of a chemical reaction or industrial process. (p. 93)

trait A characteristic that an organism can pass on to its offspring through its genes. (p. 556)

transfer RNA RNA in the cytoplasm that carries an amino acid to the ribosome and adds it to the growing protein chain. (p. 579)

transform boundary A plate boundary where two plates move past each other in opposite directions. (p. 342)

translucent Term used to describe a material that scatters light as it passes through. (p. 238)

transparent Term used to describe a material that transmits light. (p. 238)

transverse wave A wave that moves the medium in a direction perpendicular to the direction in which the wave travels. (p. 138)

trench A deep canyon in the ocean floor. (p. 478)

tropical zone The area near the equator, between about 23.5° north latitude and 23.5° south latitude. (p. 515)

trough The lowest part of a transverse wave. (p. 138)

tsunami A giant wave caused by an earthquake on the ocean floor. (p. 155)

tundra A polar climate region, found across northern Alaska, Canada, and Russia, with short, cool summers and bitterly cold winters. (p. 532)

tungsten–halogen light A light bulb containing a tungsten filament and a halogen gas that produce light. (p. 219)

turgor pressure The force of water against the cell wall of a plant cell. (p. 659)

ultrasound Sound waves with frequencies above 20,000 Hz. (pp. 170, 212)

unbalanced force A net force that causes a change in an object's motion. (p. 105)

universe All of space and everything in it. (p. 283)

valence electrons The electrons that are farthest away from the nucleus of an atom and are involved in chemical reactions. (p. 27)

variable Any factor that can change an experiment. (pp. 11, 685)

variation Any difference between individuals of the same species. (p. 621)

vein A blood vessel that carries blood back to the heart; also, a narrow slab of a mineral that is sharply different from the surrounding rock. (p. 372)

velocity Speed in a given direction. (p. 103)

vibration A repeated back-and-forth or up-and-down motion. (p. 137)

villi Tiny finger-shaped structures that cover the inner surface of the small intestine and provide a large surface area through which digested food is absorbed. (p. 652)

virtual image An upright image formed where rays of light appear to meet or come from. (p. 240)

visible light Electromagnetic radiation that can be seen with the unaided eye. (p. 212)

volcano A weak spot in the crust where magma has come to the surface. (p. 351)

water cycle The continuous process by which water moves from Earth's surface to the atmosphere and back, passing through the living and nonliving parts of the environment. (p. 455)

water pollution The addition of any substance that has a negative effect on water or the living things that depend on the water. (p. 458)

wave A disturbance that transfers energy from place to place. (p. 136)

wavelength The distance between the crest of one wave and the crest of the next. (p. 143)

white dwarf The remaining hot core of a star after its outer layers have expanded and drifted out into space. (p. 294)

windward The side of a mountain that faces the oncoming wind. (p. 519)

work The product of force and distance when a force is used to move an object. (p. 107)

X-rays Electromagnetic waves with higher frequencies than ultraviolet rays but lower frequnecies than gamma rays. (p. 213)

Spanish Glossary

A

absolute dating/datación absoluta Técnica empleada para determinar la edad absoluta de un fósil. (pág. 630)

absolute magnitude/magnitud absoluta Luminosidad que poseería una estrella si estuviera a una distancia establecida de la Tierra. (pág. 288)

absolute zero/cero absoluto Temperatura a la que no puede extraerse más energía de la materia. (pág. 114)

abyssal plain/llanura abisal Región lisa y casi plana en las profundidades del fondo oceánico. (pág. 477)

acceleration/aceleración Ritmo de cambio de velocidad. (pág. 104)

acid rain/lluvia ácida La que es más ácida de lo normal; está provocada por la liberación en el aire de moléculas de dióxido de azufre y óxido de nitrógeno. (pág. 450)

acoustics/acústica Estudio de la calidad de los sonidos percibidos en un cuarto o sala específicos. (pág. 180)

activation energy/energía de activación Cantidad mínima de energía necesaria para iniciar una reacción química. (pág. 55)

adaptation/adaptación Rasgo que ayuda a un organismo a sobrevivir en su entorno o a reproducirse. (pág. 619)

air pollution/contaminación del aire Cambio en la atmósfera que tiene efectos nocivos. (pág. 448)

alleles/alelos Diferentes formas de un gen. (pág. 559)

alloy/aleación Sustancia formada por dos o más elementos, de los cuales por lo menos uno es un metal, y que presenta las propiedades de un metal. (págs. 79, 380)

alpha particle/partícula alfa Tipo de radiación nuclear que consiste en dos protones y dos neutrones. (pág. 91)

alveoli/alveolos Sacos minúsculos de tejido pulmonar especializados en el intercambio de gases entre el aire y la sangre. (pág. 650)

amniocentesis/amniocentesis Técnica en la que se extrae una pequeña cantidad del líquido que rodea al bebé en desarrollo; el líquido se analiza para determinar si el bebé tendrá algún trastorno genético. (pág. 598)

amplitude/amplitud Distancia máxima a la que las partículas de un medio se alejan desde la posición de reposo mientras pasa una onda por el medio. (pág. 141)

amplitude modulation (AM)/amplitud modulada (AM) Método de transmisión radiofónica en el que varía la amplitud de las ondas. (pág. 223)

angle of incidence/ángulo de incidencia El formado entre la onda incidente y una línea imaginaria trazada perpendicularmente a la superficie de la barrera o del nuevo medio. (pág. 146)

angle of reflection/ángulo de reflexión El formado entre una onda reflejada y una línea imaginaria trazada perpendicularmente a la superficie de la barrera. (pág. 146)

antinode/antinodo Punto de máxima amplitud de una onda estacionaria. (pág. 150)

apparent magnitude/magnitud aparente Luminosidad de una estrella tal como se observa desde la Tierra. (pág. 287)

aquaculture/acuicultura Cría de organismos de agua salada y agua dulce. (pág. 503)

asthenosphere/astenosfera Capa blanda del manto sobre la que flota la litosfera. (pág. 319)

atoll/atolón Isla coralina con forma de anillo situada a mucha distancia de la tierra. (págs. 401, 496)

atom/átomo Partícula más pequeña de un elemento. (pág. 24)

atomic mass/masa atómica Masa media de un átomo de un elemento. (pág. 30)

atomic mass unit/unidad de masa atómica La empleada para medir la masa de las partículas de los átomos. (pág. 25)

atomic number/número atómico El de protones que hay en el núcleo de un átomo. (pág. 25)

B

balanced forces/fuerzas equilibradas Aquellas iguales que actúan sobre un objeto en sentidos opuestos. (pág. 106)

barrier beach/cordón litoral Depósito de arena extenso y de baja altura que se forma paralelo a la costa. (pág. 493)

basalt/basalto Roca ígnea oscura, densa y de textura fina que se encuentra en la corteza oceánica. (pág. 318)

beats/pulsos Cambios regulares en el volumen de un sonido cuando se tocan simultáneamente dos sonidos de distinta frecuencia. (pág. 181)

bedrock/lecho de roca Capa de roca sólida situada bajo el suelo. (pág. 423)

benthos/bentos Organismos que habitan el fondo del océano o de otra masa de agua. (pág. 487)

beta particle/partícula beta Electrón liberado de su núcleo durante la desintegración radiactiva. (pág. 91)

big bang/big bang Explosión inicial que según la teoría dio origen a la formación y expansión del universo. (pág. 302)

bimetallic strip/barra bimetálica La formada por dos metales diferentes que se expanden a ritmos distintos. (pág. 130)

binary star/estrella binaria Sistema compuesto por dos estrellas. (pág. 297)

biodegradable/biodegradable Sustancia que se descompone y recicla por bacterias y otros descomponedores. (pág. 432)

bioluminescence/bioluminiscencia Luz producida por seres vivos a raíz de una reacción química entre las proteínas y el oxígeno de los mismos. (págs. 219, 499)

black hole/agujero negro Restos de una estrella extremadamente masiva reunidos en un volumen pequeño por la fuerza de gravedad. (pág. 295)

branching tree/diagrama de árbol Esquema que muestra el parentesco que según los científicos existe entre diferentes grupos de organismos. (pág. 638)

camera/cámara Instrumento óptico que usa lentes para concentrar la luz y registrar la imagen de un objeto. (págs. 261 a 262)

carbon cycle/ciclo del carbono Sistema en el que se traslada el carbono del interior de la Tierra hasta la atmósfera, los océanos, la corteza y a todos los seres vivos. (pág. 541)

carrier/portador Persona que tiene para un rasgo un alelo recesivo y otro dominante pero sin manifestarlo. (pág. 592)

cast/vaciado Fósil que es una copia de la forma de un organismo; se origina tras introducirse minerales en un molde. (pág. 628)

catalyst/catalizador Material que acelera una reacción química al reducir la energía de activación. (pág. 58)

catalytic converter/convertidor catalítico Dispositivo que reduce las emisiones de monóxido de carbono, hidrocarburos y óxidos de nitrógeno. (pág. 464)

Celsius scale/escala Celsius La de temperaturas donde 0 y 100 son las temperaturas a las que el agua se congela o hierve. (págs. 113, 683)

cementation/cementación Proceso mediante el cual los minerales disueltos se cristalizan, aglutinando en una sola masa las partículas de sedimentos. (pág. 397)

ceramic/cerámica Sólido duro y cristalino que se forma al calentar a temperaturas altas arcilla y otros materiales minerales. (pág. 84)

change of state/cambio de estado Transformación física de la materia de un estado al otro. (pág. 126)

chemical bond/enlace químico Fuerza que une dos átomos. (pág. 27)

chemical equation/ecuación química Forma breve y sencilla de mostrar una reacción química, usando símbolos en lugar de palabras. (pág. 46)

chemical reaction/reacción química Proceso en el cual las sustancias sufren cambios químicos. (pág. 38)

chemical rock/roca química La sedimentaria que se forma al cristalizarse minerales de una solución. (pág. 400)

chemical symbol/símbolo químico Conjunto compuesto normalmente por una o dos letras que sirve para identificar un elemento. (pág. 34)

chlorofluorocarbon/clorofluorocarbono Uno de un grupo de compuestos de cloro que antes se utilizaban en los acondicionador del aire refrigeradores. (págs. 453, 546)

classifying/clasificar Agrupar objetos que presentan entre sí alguna semejanza. (pág. 681)

clastic rock/roca clástica La sedimentaria que se forma al comprimirse a alta presión fragmentos rocosos. (pág. 398)

cleavage/exfoliación Capacidad de un mineral para fragmentarse de forma regular por sus caras planas. (pág. 367)

climate/clima Condiciones típicas de temperaturas, precipitaciones, vientos y nubes dadas en una zona a lo largo del tiempo. (pág. 514)

clone/clon Organismo genéticamente idéntico al del que proviene. (pág. 604)

cochlea/cóclea Conducto del oído interno con forma de caracol, recubierto de receptores de sonido; los impulsos nerviosos se transmiten desde la cóclea al cerebro. (pág. 185)

codominance/codominancia Estado en que ninguno de los dos alelos de un gen es dominante ni recesivo. (pág. 568)

coefficient/coeficiente Número que colocado delante de una fórmula química de una ecuación indica cuántos átomos o moléculas de cada reactivo y producto intervienen en la reacción. (pág. 50)

commensalism/comensalismo Relación entre dos especies donde una se beneficia y la otra no obtiene ni beneficios ni perjuicios. (pág. 669)

communication/comunicación Proceso de compartir ideas e informaciones con otras personas. (pág. 681)

compaction/compactación Proceso por el que los sedimentos se comprimen entre sí por su propio peso. (pág. 397)

competition/competición Lucha entre organismos por los recursos limitados de un hábitat. (pág. 663)

complementary colors/colores complementarios Dos cualesquiera que al combinarse producen luz blanca o pigmento negro. (pág. 252)

composite/materiales compuestos Combinación de dos o más sustancias que crean un material nuevo. (pág. 72)

composting/hacer compost Proceso de colaborar con los sistemas naturales de descomposicion para desintegrar gran variedad de desechos. (pág. 435)

compound/compuesto Sustancia formada por dos o más elementos combinados químicamente según una razón establecida. (pág. 362)

compression/compresión Esfuerzo que oprime las rocas hasta doblarlas o fragmentarlas; además, aquella parte de una onda longitudinal donde las partículas del medio están próximas unas a otras. (pág. 139)

concave lens/lente cóncava La que tiene más delgado el centro que los bordes. (pág. 246)

concave mirror/espejo cóncavo El que tiene su superficie curvada hacia dentro como las paredes interiores de una taza. (pág. 241)

concentration/concentración Cantidad de un material disuelto en un determinado volumen de otro. (pág. 57)

condensation/condensación Paso de la materia del estado gaseoso al líquido. (pág. 456)

conduction/conducción Transferencia de energía térmica mediante el contacto directo entre partículas de materia. (págs. 116, 324)

cone/cono Célula de la retina que reacciona ante el color. (pág. 257)

conservation of mass/conservación de la masa Principio que establece que durante una reacción química la materia ni se crea ni se destruye. (pág. 49)

constellation/constelación Patrón de estrellas en el cielo. (pág. 275)

constructive interference/interferencia constructiva La que ocurre cuando dos ondas se combinan y producen otra de mayor amplitud. (pág. 148)

continental climate/clima continental El del centro de los continentes, con inviernos fríos y veranos templados o calientes. (pág. 516)

continental drift/deriva continental Hipótesis según la cual los continentes se desplazan lentamente por la superficie terrestre. (pág. 327)

continental shelf/plataforma continental Zona del fondo oceánico poco profunda y ligeramente inclinada que se extiende desde el borde de cada continente. (pág. 476)

continental slope/talud continental Pendiente que desciende desde el borde de la plataforma continental. (pág. 476)

controlled experiment/experimento controlado Investigación en que todas las variables menos una se mantienen iguales. (pág. 12)

convection/convección Transferencia de energía térmica mediante los movimientos de un fluido. (págs. 117, 324)

convection current/corriente de convección Movimiento de un fluido debido a las diferencias de temperatura, transfiriéndose energía térmica de una parte del fluido a otra. (pág. 324)

convergent boundary/borde destructivo Aquel donde dos placas se aproximan una a otra. (pág. 344)

convex lens/lente convexa La curvada que tiene el centro más grueso que los bordes. (págs. 246, 276)

convex mirror/espejo convexo El que tiene su superficie curvada hacia fuera. (pág. 242)

coral reef/arrecife coralino Estructura de esqueletos calcáreos construida por animales coralinos en aguas oceánicas cálidas y poco profundas. (pág. 400)

cornea/córnea Superficie anterior transparente del ojo. (pág. 256)

corrosive wastes/residuos corrosivos Materiales que disuelven o desgastan a otros muchos. (pág. 439)

crest/cresta Punto más alto de una onda transversal. (pág. 138)

crop rotation/rotación de cultivos Sistema en el que cada año se plantan en un campo cultivos diferentes. (pág. 426)

crust/corteza Capa de rocas que forma la superficie externa de la Tierra. (pág. 318)

crystal/cristal Sólido cuyas partículas forman un patrón que se repite. (pág. 362)

data/datos Hechos, cifras y otras evidencias recogidos en un experimento. (pág. 12)

decibels (dB)/decibeles (dB) Unidad de medida del volumen. (pág. 169)

decomposition/descomposición Reacción química que separa los compuestos en productos más simples. (pág. 52)

deep-ocean trench/fosa oceánica Valle profundo situado en el fondo oceánico por el que la corteza se hunde lentamente hacia el manto. (pág. 336)

deformation/deformación Cambio en el volumen o la forma de la corteza terrestre. (pág. 346)

density/densidad Medida de la cantidad de masa que contiene un volumen determinado de una sustancia. (pág. 324)

deposition/sedimentación Proceso mediante el cual los sedimentos dejan el agua o viento que los traslada, depositándose en un nuevo lugar. (pág. 397)

desert/desierto Región árida que recibe menos de 25 centímetros de lluvia al año. (pág. 528)

desertification/desertificación Avance de condiciones semejantes a las del desierto en zonas que anteriormente fueron fértiles. (pág. 425)

destructive interference/interferencia destructiva La que ocurre cuando dos ondas se combinan y producen otra de menor amplitud. (pág. 148)

development/desarrollo Construcción de edificios, carreteras, puentes, presas y otras estructuras. (pág. 421)

diaphragm/diafragma Músculo grande con forma de bóveda que tiene una función importante en la respiración. (pág. 651)

diffraction/difracción Desviación de las ondas por el borde de una barrera. (pág. 147)

diffuse reflection/reflexión difusa La producida cuando los rayos de luz paralelos chocan contra una superficie áspera, reflejándose todos en ángulos diferentes. (pág. 239)

diffusion/difusión Proceso por el que las moléculas pasan de una zona de alta concentración a otra de menos concentración. (pág. 658)

dissonance/disonancia Sonido producido cuando se tocan al mismo tiempo notas que no tienen relación musical. (pág. 177)

divergent boundary/borde constructivo Aquel donde dos placas se separan una de otra. (pág. 343)

dominant allele/alelo dominante Aquel cuyo rasgo siempre se manifiesta en el organismo cuando ese alelo está presente. (pág. 559)

Doppler effect/efecto Doppler Cambio aparente en la frecuencia de un sonido cuya fuente se mueve en relación con el observador. (pág. 110)

drought/sequía Escasez de agua ocasionada por períodos prolongados de bajas precipitaciones en una zona determinada. (pág. 458)

dune/duna Colina de arena formada por el viento. (pág. 493)

ear canal/conducto auditivo Canal estrecho que va desde la parte externa del oído humano hasta el tímpano. (pág. 184)

eardrum/tímpano Membrana que separa el oído externo del oído medio y que vibra cuando las ondas sonoras lo golpean. (pág. 185)

earthquake/terremoto Sacudidas producidas por los movimientos de las rocas debajo de la superficie terrestre. (pág. 347)

echolocation/localización por eco Uso de la reflexión de las ondas sonoras para navegar y para localizar las presas. (pág. 190)

eclipsing binary/eclipse binario Sistema estelar en el que una estrella periódicamente intercepta la luz de la otra. (pág. 298)

ecosystem/ecosistema Todos los seres vivos o no que interactúan en una zona. (pág. 662)

egg/óvulo Célula sexual femenina. (pág. 572)

elasticity/elasticidad Facultad de un material para recuperar su forma original tras sufrir alteraciones. (pág. 165)

electromagnetic radiation/radiación electromagnética Energía que se propaga a través del espacio en forma de ondas. (pág. 203)

electromagnetic spectrum/espectro electromagnético Gama de ondas electromagnéticas colocadas en cierto orden. (pág. 207)

electromagnetic wave/onda electromagnética La transversal que transfiere energía eléctrica y magnética. (pág. 203)

electron/electrón Partícula diminuta con carga negativa y de alta energía que se mueve por el exterior del núcleo de un átomo. (pág. 24)

electron dot diagram/esquema de puntos de electrones Representación del número de electrones de valencia de un átomo en la cual el símbolo del elemento está rodeado de puntos. (pág. 28)

element/elemento Sustancia que no se puede descomponer en otras por medios físicos o químicos. (págs. 24, 362)

elliptical galaxy/galaxia elíptica La que tiene forma de pelota aplastada y contiene sólo estrellas viejas. (pág. 300)

emissions/emisiones Partículas sólidas y gases liberados al aire por vehículos de motor. (pág. 449)

endothermic reaction/reacción endotérmica Aquella que absorbe energía en forma de calor. (pág. 41)

energy/energía Capacidad para realizar un trabajo o producir cambios como, por ejemplo, trasladar un objeto a cierta distancia. (pág. 108)

enzyme/enzima Catalizador biológico que reduce la energía de activación de las reacciones en las células. (pág. 59)

equilibrium/equilibrio Estado en el cual las fuerzas opuestas de un sistema están balanceadas o estables. (pág. 655)

erosion/erosión Proceso por el cual el agua, el hielo, el viento o la gravedad desplazan fragmentos de roca y suelo. (págs. 397, 424)

evaporation/evaporación Proceso por el cual las moléculas de agua líquida absorben energía y pasan al estado gaseoso. (pág. 456)

evolution/evolución Cambio gradual en una especie a lo largo del tiempo. (pág. 619)

exothermic reaction/reacción exotérmica La que libera energía en forma de calor. (pág. 41)

explosive waste/residuos explosivos Materiales de desecho que reaccionan con rapidez al entrar en contacto con el aire o el agua o que explotan al caer. (pág. 439)

extinct/extinto Se dice del miembro de una especie que ya no existe en el planeta. (pág. 630)

extrusive rock/roca efusiva La ígnea que se forma a partir de la lava de la superficie terrestre. (pág. 393)

eyepiece lens/lente ocular La que amplifica la imagen formada por el objetivo. (pág. 260)

Fahrenheit scale/escala Fahrenheit La de temperaturas donde 32 y 212 son las temperaturas a las que el agua se congela o hierve. (pág. 18)

fallow/barbecho Tierra que se deja sin cultivar. (pág. 425)

farsighted/hipermetropía Condición en la cual los objetos lejanos se ven con claridad y los cercanos borrosos. (pág. 258)

fault/falla Fractura o grieta en la litosfera terrestre a lo largo de la cual se desplazan las rocas. (pág. 342)

fault-block mountain/montaña de bloques fallados La formada en el lugar donde una falla normal levanta un bloque rocoso. (pág. 350)

fertilizer/fertilizante Sustancias químicas que aportan nutrientes para mejorar los cultivos. (pág. 459)

first quarter/cuarto creciente Fase en la que el lado lunar que se dirige hacia la Tierra queda iluminado por el Sol. (pág. 482)

flammable waste/residuos inflamables Materiales de desecho capaces de encenderse fácilmente y arder a temperaturas bastante bajas. (pág. 439)

fluorescence/fluorescencia Propiedad de un mineral de brillar bajo la luz ultravioleta. (pág. 368)

fluorescent light/lámpara fluorescente La que brilla cuando la corriente eléctrica hace que las ondas ultravioleta choquen contra un revestimiento interior del tubo. (pág. 217)

focal point/punto focal Sitio donde los rayos de luz se juntan o parecen juntarse tras ser reflejados (o refractados) por un espejo (o una lente). (págs. 241, 242)

foliated/foliadas Se dice de las rocas metamórficas cuyos granos están dispuestos en capas o bandas paralelas. (pág. 403)

food web/red alimenticia Patrón de cadenas alimenticias superpuestas de un ecosistema. (pág. 487)

footwall/labio inferior Bloque rocoso que compone la mitad inferior de una falla. (pág. 348)

force/fuerza Impulso o atracción ejercido sobre un objeto. (pág. 104)

formula/fórmula Combinación de símbolos que muestra la razón entre los elementos de un compuesto. (pág. 47)

fossil/fósil Restos conservados o rastros de seres que vivieron en el pasado. (págs. 328, 627)

fossil record/registro fósil Conjunto de los millones de fósiles que han recogido los científicos. (pág. 630)

fracture/fractura Aspecto de un mineral al fragmentarse de forma irregular. (pág. 367)

frequency/frecuencia La de una ola es el número de olas completas que pasan por un punto dado durante un tiempo determinado. (pág. 144)

frequency modulation (FM)/frecuencia modulada (FM) Método de transmisión radiofónica en el que varía la frecuencia de las ondas. (pág. 224)

full moon/luna llena Fase en la que el lado lunar que se dirige hacia la Tierra está completamente iluminado por el Sol. (pág. 482)

galaxy/galaxia Estructura gigante que contiene cientos de miles de millones de estrellas. (pág. 283)

gamma radiation/radiación gamma Tipo de radiación nuclear formada por ondas de alta energía. (pág. 91)

gamma rays/rayos gamma Las ondas electromagnéticas de menor longitud y mayor frecuencia. (pág. 214)

gemstone/gema Mineral duro y colorido de brillo intenso o vítreo. (pág. 377)

gene/gen Segmento de ADN de un cromosoma que lleva codificado un rasgo específico. (pág. 559)

gene therapy/terapia con genes Inserción de copias funcionales de un gen en las células de una persona afectada de algún padecimiento genético, en un intento de corregir el trastorno. (pág. 606)

genetic disorder/trastorno genético Estado anormal que una persona hereda a través de los genes o cromosomas. (pág. 595)

genetic engineering/ingeniería genética Transferencia de un gen desde el ADN de un organismo al de otro, para producir un ser con rasgos deseados. (pág. 604)

genotype/genotipo Composición genética de un organismo o sus combinaciones de alelos. (pág. 568)

geologist/geólogo Científico que estudia las fuerzas que forman y configuran el planeta Tierra. (pág. 315)

geology/geología Estudio de la masa terrestre. (pág. 315)

giant star/estrella gigante La de tamaño enorme mucho más grande que el Sol. (pág. 286)

glass/vidrio Material sólido y transparente sin estructura cristalina; se produce al calentar arena a temperaturas muy altas. (pág. 86)

global warming/calentamiento global Aumento gradual de la temperatura de la atmósfera terrestre. (pág. 544)

gradualism/gradualismo Teoría que sostiene que la evolución ocurre lentamente pero constantemente. (pág. 634)

grain/grano Partícula de un mineral u otra roca que caracteriza su textura. (pág. 389)

gram/gramo Unidad que mide la masa o la cantidad de materia de un objeto. (pág. 683)

granite/granito Roca de la corteza continental que suele ser de color claro. (pág. 318)

greenhouse gases/gases de invernadero Los de la atmósfera que captan el calor. (pág. 544)

groundwater/agua subterránea La que llena las grietas y los poros de las capas de tierra y roca del subsuelo. (pág. 457)

group/grupo Elementos de una misma columna vertical de la tabla periódica; se llama también familia. (pág. 34)

half-life/vida media Tiempo necesario para que se desintegren la mitad de los átomos de un isótopo radiactivo. (págs. 92, 630)

hanging wall/labio superior Bloque rocoso que compone la mitad superior de una falla. (pág. 348)

hazardous waste/residuos peligrosos Materiales que pueden ser dañinos si no se eliminan adecuadamente. (pág. 439)

heat/calor Traslado de energía térmica de una sustancia a otra. (pág. 115)

heat transfer/transferencia de calor Traslado de energía de un objeto con más temperatura a otro con menos. (pág. 323)

heredity/herencia Transmisión de rasgos de padres a hijos. (pág. 556)

hertz (Hz)/hertzio (Hz) Unidad de medida de la frecuencia. (pág. 144)

Hertzsprung-Russell diagram/diagrama de Hertzsprung-Russell Gráfica que relaciona la temperatura y el brillo de las estrellas. (pág. 288)

heterozygous/heterocigoto Que tiene dos alelos diferentes para un mismo rasgo. (pág. 568)

holdfast/rizoides Masa de filamentos con aspecto de raíces con la cual las algas se sujetan a las rocas. (pág. 496)

hologram/holograma Fotografía tridimensional formada por la interferencia de dos haces de láser. (pág. 266)

homeostasis/homeostasis Proceso mediante el cual el entorno interno del cuerpo se mantiene estable a pesar de los cambios producidos en el ambiente externo. (pág. 656)

homologous structure/estructura homóloga Parte corporal estructuralmente similar en dos o más especies emparentadas. (pág. 636)

homozygous/homocigoto Que tiene dos alelos idénticos para un mismo rasgo. (pág. 568)

host/huésped Organismo que proporciona una fuente de energía o un ambiente adecuado para la vida de un virus u otro organismo. (pág. 670)

hot spot/punto caliente Sitio por el que el magma procedente de zonas profundas del manto atraviesa a altas temperaturas la corteza situada encima. (pág. 353)

humid subtropical/subtropical húmedo Zona climática húmeda y templada situada en el borde de los trópicos. (pág. 530)

hybrid/híbrido Organismo que tiene dos alelos diferentes para un rasgo; organismo que es heterocigoto para un rasgo determinado. (pág. 560)

hybridization/hibridación Método de apareamiento dirigido en el que se cruzan dos individuos genéticamente distintos. (pág. 603)

hydrothermal vent/abertura hidrotermal Lugar donde el agua desciende por las grietas del fondo oceánico, es calentada por el magma subterráneo y vuelve a ascender por las grietas. (pág. 500)

hypothesis/hipótesis Explicación posible a una serie de observaciones o respuesta a una pregunta científica; capaz de ser verificada. (pág. 110)

ice ages/glaciaciones Períodos fríos de la historia de la Tierra durante los cuales los glaciares cubrieron grandes extensiones de la superficie. (pág. 538)

igneous rock/roca ígnea Tipo de roca que se forma al enfriarse las rocas fundidas en o debajo de la superficie. (pág. 391)

illuminated/iluminado Palabra con que se describe un objeto que es visible por reflejar la luz. (pág. 216)

image/imagen Copia de un objeto formada por la reflexión o refracción de los rayos de luz. (pág. 240)

inbreeding/endogamia Método de apareamiento dirigido en el que se cruzan dos individuos con juegos idénticos o similares de alelos. (pág. 603)

incandescent light/lámpara incandescente La que brilla al calentarse un filamento interior. (pág. 216)

incineration/incineración Quema de residuos sólidos. (pág. 431)

index of refraction/índice de refracción Medida de la inclinación de un rayo de luz al pasar a un nuevo medio. (pág. 244)

inference/inferencia Interpretación de una observación basándose en evidencias y conocimientos previos. (págs. 11, 680)

infrared rays/rayos infrarrojos Ondas electromagnéticas de menor longitud y mayor frecuencia que las ondas de radio. (pág. 210)

infrasound/infrasonido Ondas sonoras de frecuencia inferior a 20 Hz. (pág. 170)

inhibitor/inhibidor Material que desacelera una reacción. (pág. 59)

inner core/núcleo interior Se aplica al de la Tierra; densa bola de metal sólido. (pág. 319)

inorganic/inorgánico Que no está formado por seres vivos o los restos de éstos. (pág. 361)

insulator/aislante Material que no transmite fácilmente entre sus partículas energía térmica o corriente eléctrica. (pág. 119)

insulin/insulina Sustancia química producida en el páncreas que permite a las células del cuerpo tomar glucosa de la sangre y utilizarla como energía. (pág. 658)

intensity/intensidad Cantidad de energía que cada segundo es conducida por una onda a través de una unidad de superficie. (pág. 168)

interference/interferencia Interacción entre ondas que se cruzan. (pág. 148)

intertidal zone/zona intermareal Espacio comprendido entre la línea de la marea alta más elevada de la tierra y el lugar de la plataforma continental expuesto a la marea más baja. (pág. 488)

intrusive rock/roca intrusiva La ígnea que se forma al solidificarse el magma bajo la superficie terrestre. (pág. 393)

iris/iris Disco musculado que al contraerse y expandirse cambia la cantidad de luz que entra en el ojo. (pág. 256)

irregular galaxy/galaxia irregular Galaxia la que no tiene forma regular. (pág. 300)

isotope/isótopo Átomo con igual número de protones y distinto número de neutrones que otros átomos del mismo elemento. (pág. 90)

karyotype/cariotipo Imagen de todos los cromosomas de una célula organizados en parejas. (pág. 599)

Kelvin scale/escala Kelvin La de temperaturas donde cero es la temperatura a la que no puede extraerse más energía de la materia. (pág. 114)

kinetic energy/energía cinética La que posee un objeto debido a su movimiento. (pág. 109)

land reclamation/recuperación de la tierra Proceso de restituir la tierra a un estado más natural. (pág. 422)

land subsidence/subsidencia de la tierra Hundimiento o descenso de parte de la superficie terrestre debido a procesos geológicos o actividades humanas. (págs. 350, 461)

larynx/laringe Dos capas de tejido que constituyen la caja de la voz humana. (pág. 163)

laser/láser Aparato que produce luz coherente. (pág. 263)

lava/lava Magma que llega a la superficie; además, rocas formadas al solidificarse lava líquida. (pág. 351)

leachate/lixiviado Agua que ha atravesado los desechos enterrados en un relleno sanitario. (pág. 431)

leeward/sotovento Se aplica a la ladera de las montañas resguardada del viento. (pág. 519)

lens/lente Estructura flexible que concentra la luz que entra en el ojo; además, pieza curvada de vidrio u otro material transparente empleado para refractar la luz. (pág. 246)

light-year/año luz Distancia que recorre la luz en un año. (pág. 284)

lithosphere/litosfera Capa rígida formada por la parte superior del manto y la corteza. (pág. 318)

liter/litro Unidad empleada para medir el volumen. (pág. 682)

litter/mantillo Capa suelta de hojas y tallos de plantas secas de la superficie del suelo. (pág. 423)

longitudinal wave/onda longitudinal La que mueve las partículas del medio paralelamente al sentido del recorrido de las ondas. (pág. 138)

longshore drift/deriva longitudinal Movimiento del agua y los sedimentos a lo largo de una playa, provocado por las olas que llegan en cierto ángulo. (pág. 492)

loudness/volumen Percepción de la intensidad de un sonido. (pág. 169)

luminous/luminoso Palabra con que se describe un objeto que es visible por la luz que emite. (pág. 216)

luster/brillo Forma en que un mineral refleja la luz que recibe sobre su superficie. (pág. 365)

magma/magma Mezcla fundida de las sustancias que forman las rocas, los gases y el agua que componen parte del manto terrestre. (pág. 351)

magnetic resonance imaging/imágenes por resonancia magnética Proceso en el que se emplean ondas de radio para formar imágenes del interior del cuerpo humano. (pág. 209)

main sequence/secuencia principal Sección del diagrama de Hertzsprung-Russell que va desde la parte superior izquierda hasta la parte inferior derecha, abarcando más del 90 por ciento de todas las estrellas. (pág. 288)

manipulated variable/variable manipulada Único factor que un científico cambia durante un experimento. (pág. 685)

mantle/manto Capa de materiales sólidos y calientes situada entre la corteza y el núcleo de la Tierra. (pág. 318)

marine climate/clima marítimo El de ciertas regiones costeras, con inviernos relativamente cálidos y veranos frescos. (pág. 516)

mass number/número de masa Suma de los protones y neutrones del núcleo de un átomo. (pág. 90)

mechanical wave/onda mecánica La que requiere de un medio para trasladarse. (pág. 137)

medium/medio Material por el que se propaga una onda. (pág. 137)

meiosis/meiosis Proceso ocurrido en las células sexuales (espermatozoide y óvulo) en el que se reduce a la mitad el número de cromosomas. (pág. 574)

messenger RNA/ARN mensajero El que copia el mensaje codificado del ADN del núcleo y lo traslada al citoplasma. (pág. 579)

metal/metal Elemento que en una reacción química cede fácilmente su electrón de valencia; puede clasificarse basándose en sus propiedades físicas (como dureza, brillo, maleabilidad o ductilidad). (pág. 35)

metalloid/metaloide Elemento que presenta algunas de las características de los metales y otras de los no metales. (pág. 36)

metamorphic rock/roca metamórfica Tipo de roca que se forma a partir de otra roca preexistente modificada por el calor, la presión o las reacciones químicas. (pág. 391)

meter/metro Unidad que mide la longitud o distancia entre los puntos. (pág. 682)

microclimate/microclima El característico de una pequeña zona determinada; puede ser diferente del de las zonas circundantes. (pág. 519)

microscope/microscopio Instrumento que amplifica la imagen de objetos pequeños. (pág. 261)

microwaves/microondas Las ondas de radio de menor longitud y mayor frecuencia. (pág. 207)

middle ear/oído medio Espacio posterior al tímpano que contiene el martillo, el yunque y el estribo. (pág. 185)

mid-ocean ridge/dorsal medioceánica Cordillera subacuática donde se producen nuevos fondos oceánicos; borde de placas constructivo. (págs. 332, 477)

mineral/mineral Sólido inorgánico de origen natural, estructura de cristal y composición química definida. (pág. 361)

mirage/espejismo Imagen de un objeto lejano causada por la refracción de la luz al propagarse ésta por el aire a temperaturas variadas. (pág. 245)

Mohs hardness scale/escala de dureza Mohs La que clasifica diez minerales del más blando al más duro; se emplea para averiguar la dureza de los minerales. (pág. 364)

mold/molde Fósil formado al disolverse un organismo enterrado en sedimentos, dejando un espacio vacío. (pág. 628)

molecule/molécula Combinación de dos o más átomos unidos entre sí. (pág. 42)

monomers/monómeros Moléculas pequeñas con base de carbono que constituyen los eslabones de una cadena de polímeros. (pág. 69)

motion/movimiento Estado en el que varía la distancia entre un objeto y otro. (pág. 102)

multiple alleles/alelos múltiples Tres o más formas de un gen que llevan codificado un rasgo específico. (pág. 589)

municipal solid waste/residuos sólidos urbanos Los producidos en hogares, oficinas y escuelas. (pág. 430)

music/música Conjunto de tonos y semitonos combinados para producir efectos placenteros al oído. (pág. 176)

mutation/mutación Cambio en un gen o cromosoma. (pág. 580)

mutualism/mutualismo Forma de simbiosis en la que ambos organismos se benefician de su mutua convivencia. (pág. 669)

natural selection/selección natural Proceso por el cual los individuos mejor adaptados al medio ambiente tienen más probabilidades de sobrevivir y reproducirse que otros miembros de la misma especie. (pág. 620)

neap tide/marea muerta Marea con la diferencia mínima entre la marea baja y la marea alta; ocurre cuando el Sol y la Luna se encuentran en ángulo recto. (pág. 484)

nearsighted/miopía Condición en la cual los objetos cercanos se ven con claridad y los lejanos borrosos. (pág. 258)

nebula/nebulosa Concentración enorme de gas y polvo en el espacio, con un volumen muy extenso. (pág. 293)

negative feedback/reacción negativa Proceso en el cual un sistema se para debido a su propia condición; ejemplos de sistemas de reacción negativa son la regulación de la temperatura por el termostato y la regulación de los niveles de muchas hormonas en la sangre. (pág. 656)

nekton/necton Animales que flotan libremente y pueden moverse por toda la columna del agua. (pág. 487)

neon light/lámpara de neón Tubo de vidrio lleno de neón para producir luz. (pág. 218)

neritic zone/zona nerítica Región de aguas poco profundas del océano que se extiende desde la línea de la marea baja hasta el borde de la plataforma continental. (pág. 495)

neutron/neutrón Pequeña partícula sin carga eléctrica del núcleo de un átomo. (pág. 24)

neutron star/estrella de neutrones Estrella muy pequeña que permanece tras la explosión de una supernova. (pág. 294)

new moon/luna nueva Fase en la que el lado lunar que se dirige hacia la Tierra es el opuesto al Sol. Por eso, la Luna no se observa desde la Tierra. (pág. 481)

niche/nicholas Papel propio de un organismo en un ecosistema o funciones que realiza. (pág. 662)

nitrogen cycle/ciclo del nitrógeno Proceso mediante el cual el nitrógeno se elimina de la atmósfera, es fijado en el suelo por las bacterias, se incorpora a otros seres vivos y se libera de nuevo en la atmósfera. (pág. 426)

node/nodo Punto de amplitud cero en una onda estacionaria. (pág. 149)

nodules/nódulos Abultamientos en las raíces de ciertas plantas que alojan bacterias fijadoras del nitrógeno. (pág. 503)

noise/ruido Mezcla de ondas sonoras sin tono identificable y desagradables al oído. (pág. 177)

nonmetal/no metal Elemento que carece de la mayoría de las propiedades de los metales. (pág. 35)

normal fault/falla normal Tipo de falla donde el labio superior se desliza hacia abajo; está provocada por la tensión en la corteza. (pág. 348)

nuclear radiation/radiación nuclear Partículas y energía producidas durante la desintegración radiactiva. (pág. 91)

nuclear reaction/reacción nuclear Aquella en que intervienen las partículas del núcleo de un átomo y que puede transformar un elemento en otro. (pág. 90)

nucleus/núcleo Centro de control que dirige las actividades de la célula y determina las características de ésta; además, parte central del átomo que contiene protones y generalmente neutrones. (pág. 24)

nutrient depletion/agotamiento de nutrientes Proceso en el cual las plantas consumen más nutrientes de los que los descomponedores pueden restituir, haciendo menos fértil el suelo. (pág. 425)

objective lens/objetivo Lente que recoge la luz procedente de un objeto, formando una imagen real. (pág. 260)

observation/observación Uso de al menos uno de los cinco sentidos para recoger información sobre el mundo. (págs. 11, 680)

observatory/observatorio Edificio que alberga uno o más telescopios. (pág. 277)

opaque/opaco Palabra que describe un material que refleja o absorbe toda la luz que choca contra él. (pág. 238)

open-ocean zone/zona de mar abierto Parte del océano más allá del borde de la plataforma continental. (pág. 495)

operational definition/definición operativa Enunciado que describe cómo se mide una variable determinada. (pág. 685)

optic nerve/nervio óptico Aquel grueso y corto que transmite los impulsos del ojo al cerebro. (pág. 257)

optical fiber/fibra óptica Filamento largo y delgado de vidrio o plástico que puede trasladar la luz a través de largas distancias sin decaer; sirve también para transmitir mensajes. (págs. 87, 266)

ore/mena Roca que contiene un metal o mineral con utilidad económica. (pág. 377)

organ/órgano Estructura del cuerpo compuesta de diferentes clases de tejidos. (pág. 648)

organ system/sistema de órganos Grupo de órganos que realizan conjuntamente una función principal en el cuerpo de un organismo. (pág. 648)

organic rock/roca organógena La sedimentaria originada en lugares donde los restos de organismos se depositan formando gruesas capas. (pág. 399)

osmosis/ósmosis Difusión de moléculas del agua a través de una membrana selectivamente permeable. (pág. 659)

outer core/núcleo exterior Capa de hierro y níquel fundidos que rodea el núcleo interior de la Tierra. (pág. 319)

ozone/ozono Forma de oxígeno que tiene tres átomos en cada molécula en lugar de los dos habituales. (págs. 449, 545)

ozone layer/capa de ozono La de la atmósfera superior, situada a unos 30 kilómetros sobre la superficie terrestre, donde se encuentra concentrado el ozono. (págs. 452, 545)

Pangaea/Pangea Nombre de una única masa continental que se fragmentó hace 225 millones de años, dando origen a los continentes actuales. (pág. 327)

parallax/paralaje Cambio aparente en la posición de un objeto cuando se observa desde lugares diferentes. (pág. 284)

parasite/parásito Organismo que vive en la superficie o en el interior de un huésped, provocándole daños. (pág. 670)

parasitism/parasitismo Relación en la cual un organismo vive en la superficie o en el interior de otro, provocándole daños. (pág. 670)

pedigree/genealogía Cuadro o árbol genealógico que muestra qué miembros de una familia poseen un rasgo determinado. (pág. 593)

period/período Fila horizontal de elementos en la tabla periódica. (pág. 34)

periodic table/tabla periódica Disposición de los elementos ordenados según su número atómico y en la que los elementos de propiedades similares están agrupados en columnas. (pág. 31)

permafrost/permafrost Suelo permanentemente helado de las regiones climáticas de tundra. (pág. 532)

pesticide/pesticida Sustancia química para matar insectos y otros organismos que dañan los cultivos. (pág. 459)

petrified fossil/fósil petrificado El formado cuando todo o parte de un organismo queda reemplazado por minerales. (pág. 628)

phenotype/fenotipo Aspecto físico o rasgos visibles de un organismo. (pág. 568)

photochemical smog/smog fotoquímico Bruma pardusca, mezcla de ozono y otras sustancias químicas, que se forma cuando los óxidos de nitrógeno, los hidrocarburos y otros contaminantes reaccionan entre sí en presencia de luz solar. (pág. 449)

photoelectric effect/efecto fotoeléctrico Movimiento de los electrones a través de una sustancia cuando ésta queda iluminada por la luz. (pág. 205)

photon/fotón Partícula o paquete minúsculos de energía luminosa. (pág. 205)

photosynthesis/fotosíntesis Proceso por el cual las plantas y algunos otros organismos captan la energía de la luz y la utilizan para elaborar su alimento a partir del agua y del dióxido de carbono. (pág. 542)

pigments/pigmentos Sustancias opacas que sirven para colorear otros materiales. (pág. 252)

pitch/tono Percepción de la frecuencia de un sonido. (pág. 170)

plane mirror/espejo plano El que produce una imagen vertical virtual del mismo tamaño que el objeto. (pág. 240)

plankton/plancton Algas y animales diminutos que flotan en el agua y son transportados por las olas y las corrientes. (pág. 487)

plastic/plástico Polímero sintético maleable. (pág. 71)

plate/placa Sección de la litosfera que se desplaza lentamente por la astenosfera, llevando consigo fragmentos de la corteza continental y oceánica. (pág. 340)

plate tectonics/tectónica de placas Teoría según la cual fragmentos de la litosfera terrestre se desplazan de forma constante, impulsados por las corrientes de convección del manto. (pág. 341)

polar zones/zonas polares Las cercanas a los polos, aproximadamente entre 66.5° y 90° en las latitudes norte y sur. (pág. 515)

polarized light/luz polarizada La que vibra en un solo sentido. (pág. 204)

polymer/polímero Molécula grande y compleja constituida por la unión de moléculas más pequeñas. (pág. 69)

porphyritic texture/textura porfídica Aquella de las rocas ígneas en la que los cristales gruesos están esparcidos en una trama de cristales mucho más pequeños. (pág. 393)

potential energy/energía potencial La que se almacena para usarse posteriormente. (pág. 108)

precipitate/precipitado Sólido que se forma en una solución durante una reacción química. (pág. 39)

precipitation/precipitación Agua en forma como de lluvia, nieve, aguanieve o granizo, que procede de las nubes y llega a la superficie terrestre. (pág. 456)

predation/depredación Interacción en la cual un organismo caza y mata a otro para alimentarse de él. (pág. 664)

predator/depredador Carnívoro que caza y mata otros animales para alimentarse de ellos y que cuenta con adaptaciones que le ayudan a capturar sus presas. (pág. 664)

predicting/predecir Inferir acerca de un suceso futuro basándose en evidencias actuales o experiencias pasadas. (pág. 680)

pressure/presión Fuerza ejercida sobre una superficie dividida entre el área total sobre la que se ejerce la fuerza; además, fuerza del impulso de un gas hacia el exterior dividida entre el área de las paredes del recipiente. (pág. 317)

prey/presa Animal del que se alimenta un depredador. (pág. 664)

primary colors/colores primarios Los tres que pueden usarse para formar cualquier otro color. (pág. 251)

primary treatment/tratamiento primario Eliminación de los materiales sólidos de las aguas residuales. (pág. 465)

primary wave/onda primaria Onda sísmica longitudinal. (pág. 155)

probability/probabilidad Posibilidad de que ocurra un suceso determinado. (pág. 564)

product/producto Sustancia formada como resultado de una reacción química. (pág. 48)

proton/protón Partícula pequeña con carga positiva del núcleo de un átomo. (pág. 24)

protostar/protoestrella Nube condensada de gas y polvo; primera fase de la vida de una estrella. (pág. 293)

pulsar/púlsar Estrella de neutrones que produce ondas de radio. (pág. 292)

punctuated equilibria/equilibrio puntual Teoría que afirma que las especies evolucionan durante períodos breves de cambios rápidos. (pág. 634)

Punnett square/cuadro de Punnett Tabla que muestra todas las posibles combinaciones de alelos que puede producir un cruce genético. (pág. 566)

pupil/pupila Abertura a través de la cual la luz entra en el ojo. (pág. 256)

purebred/raza pura Se dice del organismo cuyos descendientes siempre tienen los mismos rasgos que el progenitor. (pág. 557)

quasar/quásar Galaxia distante con un agujero negro en su centro. (pág. 296)

radar/radar Sistema para detectar ondas de radio reflejadas. (pág. 208)

radiation/radiación Transferencia de energía mediante ondas electromagnéticas. (págs. 118, 323)

radiation therapy/radioterapia Proceso basado en el uso de elementos radiactivos para destruir células enfermas. (pág. 94)

radio telescope/radiotelescopio Aparato usado para detectar ondas de radio procedentes de objetos del espacio. (pág. 276)

radio wave/onda de radio La electromagnética de mayor longitud y menor frecuencia. (pág. 207)

radioactive dating/datación radiactiva Proceso para determinar la antigüedad de un objeto usando la vida media de uno o más isótopos radiactivos. (pág. 92)

radioactive decay/desintegración radiactiva Proceso en el cual los núcleos atómicos de los isótopos inestables liberan partículas y energía aceleradas. (pág. 90)

radioactive element/elemento radiactivo El elemento químico inestable que se desintegra para formar un elemento o elementos diferentes. (pág. 630)

radioactive wastes/residuos radiactivos Materiales de desecho que contienen átomos inestables. (pág. 439)

rain forest/bosque tropical El situado en zonas de clima tropical húmedo, con abundantes precipitaciones durante todo el año. (pág. 525)

rarefaction/rarefacción Parte de una onda longitudinal donde las partículas del medio están muy alejadas entre sí. (pág. 139)

ray/rayo Línea recta usada para representar una onda de luz. (pág. 239)

reactant/reactivo Sustancia que interviene en una reacción química. (pág. 48)

real image/imagen real La invertida que se forma donde se encuentran los rayos de luz. (pág. 241)

recessive allele/alelo recesivo El que no se manifiesta en presencia de un alelo dominante. (pág. 559)

recycling/reciclaje Proceso para recuperar y volver a usar materias primas. (pág. 432)

reference point/punto de referencia Objeto o lugar que se usa como punto de comparación para determinar si un objeto está en movimiento. (pág. 102)

reflecting telescope/telescopio de reflexión El que usa uno o más espejos para captar la luz de objetos lejanos. (págs. 260, 276)

reflection/reflexión Rebote de una onda cuando choca contra una superficie a través de la cual no puede pasar. (pág. 146)

refracting telescope/telescopio de refracción El que usa lentes convexas para captar y concentrar la luz. (págs. 260, 276)

refraction/refracción Desviación de las ondas al penetrar en un medio diferente. (pág. 147)

regular reflection/reflexión regular Imagen producida cuando los rayos paralelos de luz chocan contra una superficie lisa, reflejándose todos en el mismo ángulo. (pág. 239)

relative dating/datación relativa Técnica que sirve para determinar cuál de dos fósiles es más antiguo. (pág. 629)

replacement/sustitución Reacción en la que un elemento de un compuesto reemplaza otro o dos elementos de diferentes compuestos se intercambian. (pág. 53)

resin/resina Material sólido que permanece tras refinar el petróleo para obtener gasolina y otros productos petrolíferos. (pág. 433)

resonance/resonancia Aumento de amplitud de la vibración producido cuando las vibraciones externas se corresponden con la frecuencia natural del objeto. (pág. 150)

responding variable/variable de respuesta La que se espera varíe como reacción a la variable manipulada. (pág. 685)

retina/retina Capa de células que recubre el interior del globo ocular. (pág. 257)

reverse fault/falla inversa Tipo de falla donde el labio superior se desliza hacia arriba; está provocada por la compresión en la corteza. (pág. 349)

rift valley/valle rift El profundo que se forma en el lugar donde dos placas se separan. (pág. 343)

rock/roca Material que forma la superficie dura de la Tierra. (pág. 315)

rock cycle/ciclo de las rocas Serie de procesos ocurridos en la superficie y en el interior de la Tierra que transforman lentamente rocas de una clase en otra. (pág. 406)

rod/bastón Células de la retina que detectan la luz tenue y distinguen el negro, el blanco y los tonos grisáceos. (pág. 257)

sandbar/banco de arena Montículo de arena depositado por las olas al disminuir su velocidad cerca de la orilla. (pág. 492)

sanitary landfill/relleno sanitario El que contiene residuos no peligrosos como sólidos urbanos y escombros de construcciones. (pág. 431)

savanna/sabana Pastizal tropical con grupos esparcidos de árboles; se encuentra en zonas próximas al ecuador de clima tropical alternativamente húmedo y seco. (pág. 528)

science/ciencia Estudio del mundo natural a través de las observaciones y el razonamiento lógico; conduce a un conjunto de conocimientos. (pág. 10)

scientific inquiry/investigación científica Diversidad de métodos con los que los científicos estudian el mundo natural. (pág. 10)

scientific law/ley científica Afirmación que describe lo que los científicos esperan que ocurra cada vez que se dan una serie determinada de condiciones. (pág. 16)

scientific theory/teoría científica Concepto comprobado que explica una gran variedad de observaciones. (pág. 341)

scrubber/depurador Aparato que elimina los contaminantes de las emisiones mediante una fina cortina de agua. (pág. 464)

sea-floor spreading/expansión del fondo oceánico Proceso mediante el cual el material fundido aporta nueva corteza al fondo oceánico. (pág. 333)

seamount/monte marino Montaña en el fondo oceánico completamente sumergida. (pág. 477)

secondary color/color secundario El producido por la combinación a partes iguales de dos colores primarios cualesquiera. (pág. 251)

secondary treatment/tratamiento secundario El que usa bacterias para descomponer productos de desecho. (pág. 465)

secondary wave/onda secundaria Onda sísmica transversal. (pág. 155)

sediment/sedimentos Partículas pequeñas y sólidas de material procedente de rocas u organismos que son trasladadas por el agua o el viento, dando origen a la erosión y la sedimentación. (págs. 396, 460)

sedimentary rock/roca sedimentaria Tipo de roca que se forma cuando las partículas de otras rocas o los restos vegetales y animales se comprimen y cementan entre sí. (pág. 391)

seismic wave/onda sísmica Vibración que se propaga por la Tierra llevando consigo la energía liberada durante un terremoto. (págs. 155, 316)

seismograph/sismógrafo Aparato que registra los movimientos que producen en el suelo las ondas sísmicas al desplazarse por la Tierra. (pág. 156)

selective breeding/apareamiento dirigido Proceso de seleccionar algunos organismos con rasgos deseables para usarlos como progenitores de la siguiente generación. (pág. 602)

sewage/aguas residuales Las que contienen desechos humanos. (pág. 459)

sex-linked gene/gen ligado al sexo El portado por el cromosoma X o Y. (pág. 592)

smelting/fundición Proceso mediante el cual la mena se funde para separar el metal aprovechable de los demás elementos. (pág. 380)

sodium vapor light/lámpara de vapores de sodio Bombilla que contiene sodio sólido y gases de neón y argón. (pág. 218)

solution/solución Mezcla uniforme que presenta las mismas propiedades en su conjunto. (pág. 372)

sonar/sonar Sistema para detectar ondas sonoras reflejadas. (págs. 189, 332, 475)

sonogram/sonograma Imagen formada por un aparato de ultrasonido. (pág. 191)

species/especie Grupo de organismos parecidos cuyos miembros pueden aparearse entre sí y tener descendencia fértil. (pág. 617)

specific heat/calor específico Cantidad de energía térmica necesaria para incrementar en un grado Kelvin la temperatura de un kilogramo de una sustancia. (pág. 120)

spectrograph/espectógrafo Instrumento que separa en colores la luz procedente de un objeto y fotografía el espectro resultante. (pág. 279)

spectroscope/espectroscopio Instrumento que sirve para observar los distintos colores de la luz producidos por diferentes fuentes. (pág. 216)

speed/rapidez Distancia que recorre un objeto durante una unidad de tiempo. (pág. 103)

sperm/espermatozoide Célula sexual masculina. (pág. 572)

spiral galaxy/galaxia espiral Aquella cuyos brazos se curvan hacia fuera como un rehilete. (pág. 300)

spring tide/marea viva La que presenta la máxima diferencia entre la marea alta y la marea baja; ocurre cuando el Sol y la Luna coinciden en línea recta con la Tierra. (pág. 483)

standing wave/onda estacionaria Aquella que parece detenida en un sitio, aunque en realidad son dos ondas interfiriéndose al pasar una a través de la otra. (pág. 149)

state/estado Forma física de la materia como, por ejemplo, sólida, líquida o gaseosa. (pág. 126)

steppe/estepa Pradera o pastizal de una región de clima semiárido. (pág. 529)

streak/raya Se aplica al color del polvo de un mineral. (pág. 364)

stress/esfuerzo Fuerza que actúa sobre las rocas para modificar su forma o volumen. (pág. 346)

strike-slip fault/falla transcurrente Tipo de falla donde las rocas de cada lado se desplazan en sentido horizontal, sin apenas movimientos verticales. (pág. 348)

subarctic/subártico Zona climática situada al norte de la continental húmeda, con veranos cortos y frescos e inviernos largos y extremadamente fríos. (pág. 531)

subduction/subducción Proceso mediante el cual la corteza oceánica se hunde bajo una fosa y vuelve al manto en un borde de placas destructivo. (pág. 336)

subscripts/subíndices Número escrito en una fórmula química que indica la cantidad de átomos de una molécula o la razon entre los elementos de un compuesto. (pág. 47)

subsoil/subsuelo Capa compuesta mayormente por arcilla y otros minerales, situada bajo el suelo superficial. (pág. 423)

sunspots/manchas solares Regiones oscuras y menos calientes de la superficie del Sol. (pág. 539)

supernova/supernova Explosión de una estrella gigante o supergigante en la última fase de su vida. (pág. 294)

surface wave/onda superficial Tipo de onda sísmica que se forma cuando las ondas P y S llegan a la superficie terrestre. (pág. 139)

symbiosis/simbiosis Relación estrecha entre dos organismos de la cual se beneficia al menos uno de ellos. (pág. 669)

synthesis/síntesis Reacción química donde dos o más sustancias simples se combinan para formar otra nueva y más compleja. (pág. 51)

telescope/telescopio Instrumento óptico que amplifica la imagen de objetos lejanos. (pág. 260)

temperate zones/zonas templadas Las comprendidas entre las zonas tropicales y polares, aproximadamente de 23.5° a 66.5° en las latitudes norte y sur. (pág. 515)

temperature inversion/inversión térmica Estado en el que una capa de aire templado impide que escape el aire ascendente. (pág. 450)

texture/textura Tamaño, forma y patrón de los granos de una roca. (pág. 389)

thermal expansion/expansión térmica La que sufre la materia al calentarse. (pág. 129)

thermogram/termograma Imagen que muestra en diferentes colores regiones con distintas temperaturas. (pág. 211)

thermostat/termostato Instrumento que regula la temperatura. (pág. 130)

third quarter/cuarto menguante Fase en la que la mitad del lado lunar que se dirige hacia la Tierra vuelve a estar iluminada por el Sol. (pág. 482)

tides/mareas Ascenso y descenso diarios de las aguas terrestres en las costas. (pág. 480)

timbre/timbre Característica general de un sonido. (pág. 175)

tissue/tejido Grupo de células similares que desempeñan una función determinada en un organismo. (pág. 647)

topsoil/suelo superficial Mezcla de humus, arcilla y otros minerales que forman la capa superior suelta del suelo. (pág. 423)

total internal reflection/reflexión interna total Reflexión completa de la luz en la superficie interior de un medio. (pág. 268)

toxic waste/residuos tóxicos Materiales de desecho que pueden dañar a un organismo. (pág. 439)

tracer/trazador Isótopo radiactivo cuyo rastro puede seguirse a través de las etapas de una reacción química o un proceso industrial. (pág. 93)

trait/rasgo Característica que un organismo puede transmitir con sus genes a su descendencia. (pág. 556)

transfer RNA/ARN de transferencia ARN citoplásmico que transporta un aminoácido al ribosoma y lo agrega a la cadena proteica en desarrollo. (pág. 579)

transform boundary/borde conservativo Aquel donde dos placas se desplazan mutuamente en sentidos opuestos. (pág. 342)

translucent/translúcido Palabra para describir un material que dispersa la luz que lo atraviesa. (pág. 238)

transparent/transparente Palabra para describir un material que transmite la luz. (pág. 238)

transverse wave/onda transversal La que mueve el medio en dirección perpendicular al sentido en que se propaga. (pág. 138)

trench/fosa Cañón profundo en el fondo oceánico. (pág. 478)

tropical zone/zona tropical La cercana al ecuador situada aproximadamente entre 23.5° de latitud norte y 23.5° de latitud sur. (pág. 515)

trough/seno Parte inferior de una onda transversal. (pág. 138)

tsunami/tsunami Ola gigante provocada por un terremoto en el fondo oceánico. (pág. 155)

tundra/tundra Región de clima polar que abarca el norte de Alaska, Canadá y Rusia, con veranos cortos y frescos e inviernos extremadamente fríos. (pág. 532)

tungsten-halogen light/lámpara de tungsteno-halógeno Bombilla que contiene un filamento de tungsteno y un gas halógeno para producir luz. (pág. 219)

turgor pressure/presión hidrostática Fuerza que ejerce el agua contra la pared de una célula vegetal. (pág. 659)

ultrasound/ultrasonido Ondas sonoras de frecuencia superior a 20,000 Hz. (págs. 170, 212)

unbalanced force/fuerza desequilibrada La neta distinta a cero que cambia el movimiento de un objeto. (pág. 105)

universe/universo Todo el espacio y su contenido. (pág. 283)

valence electrons/electrones de valencia Los más alejados del núcleo atómico que intervienen en las reacciones químicas. (pág. 27)

variable/variable Cualquier factor que puede cambiar en un experimento. (págs. 11, 685)

variation/variación Cualquier diferencia entre individuos de una misma especie. (pág. 621)

vein/vena Vaso sanguíneo por donde vuelve la sangre al corazón; además, bloque estrecho de un mineral que se diferencia enormemente de las rocas circundantes. (pág. 372)

velocity/velocidad Rapidez en una dirección dada. (pág. 103)

vibration/vibración Movimiento repetido de "atrás hacia adelante" o de "arriba hacia abajo." (pág. 137)

villi/vellosidades Estructuras minúsculas con forma de dedos que cubren la pared interior del intestino delgado y proporcionan una gran superficie por la que se absorben los alimentos digeridos. (pág. 652)

virtual image/imagen virtual La vertical formada en el lugar donde los rayos de luz parecen encontrarse o en aquel de donde proceden. (pág. 240)

visible light/luz visible Radiación electromagnética que se observa a simple vista. (pág. 212)

volcano/volcán Debilidad en la corteza por la que el magma ha salido a la superficie. (pág. 351)

water cycle/ciclo del agua Proceso constante mediante el cual el agua va de la superficie terrestre a la atmósfera y viceversa, pasando por los componentes vivos o no del medio ambiente. (pág. 455)

water pollution/contaminación del agua Incorporación al agua de cualquier sustancia que tenga efectos negativos para ella o para los seres vivos que de ella dependen. (pág. 458)

wave/onda Alteración que transfiere energía de un lugar a otro. (pág. 136)

wavelength/longitud de onda Distancia entre la cresta de una onda y la de la siguiente. (pág. 143)

white dwarf/enana blanca Núcleo caliente de una estrella que permanece después de que sus capas externas se han expandido y disgregado por el espacio. (pág. 294)

windward/barlovento Se aplica a la ladera de una montaña donde pega el viento. (pág. 519)

work/trabajo Producto de la fuerza y la distancia cuando se utiliza una fuerza para mover un objeto. (pág. 107)

X-rays/rayos X Ondas electromagnéticas de frecuencia mayor que la de los rayos ultravioleta y menor que la de los rayos gamma. (pág. 213)

Index

Index

Index

Index

Index

Index

Acknowledgments

Staff Credits

The people who made up the *Texas Science Explorer* team—representing design services, editorial, editorial services, electronic publishing technology, manufacturing & inventory planning, market research, marketing services, online services & multimedia development, product planning, production services, project office, and publishing processes—are listed below. Bold type denotes the core team members.

Scott Andrews, **Carolyn Belanger,** Barbara A. Bertell, Suzanne Biron, **Peggy Bliss,** Kristen Braghi, Dan Breslin, Jonathan Cheney, **Lisa J. Clark,** Robin Clark, Ed Cordero, Bob Craton, Christine Cuccio, **Patricia Cully,** Gabriella Della Corte, Kathleen J. Dempsey, Emily Ellen, Barnard Gage, Jane P. Gardner, **Julie Gecha,** Adam Goldberg, Kerri Hoar, Joanne Hudson, Alan Hull, Anne Jones, Toby Klang, Suzanne Klein, Carolyn Langley, Carolyn Lock, Diahanne Lucas, Don Manning, Jeanne Y. Maurand, **Tim McDonald,** Carolyn McGuire, Karen McHugh, Natania Mlawer, Judi Pinkham, **Robin L. Santel,** Suzanne Schineller, **Diane Walsh,** Jane Willan, Pat Williams, Char Lyn Yeakley, Helen Young

Illustrations

Alexander & Turner: 648
Suzanne Biron: 562, 622, 640
Peter Brooks: 281, 290
Warren Cutler: 488
Kathleen Dempsey: 167, 182, 220, 230, 248, 254, 369, 405
John Edwards & Associates: 26, 105, 106, 137, 138, 139, 147, 148, 159, 163, 172, 173, 196, 230, 231, 232, 295, 302, 430, 464, 481, 482, 484, 492, 495, 544, 654, 658, 667
Irene Elios: 648
David Fuller: 616
Biruta Hansen: 662
Floyd E. Hosmer: 651
Jared D. Lee: 55, 164, 184, 202, 284, 451
MapQuest.com, Inc: 327, 332, 341, 351, 357, 374, 415, 425, 441, 502, 517, 519, 526, 538, 625
Martucci Studio: 28, 56, 65, 89, 99, 127, 421, 469, 534
Matt Mayerchak: 69, 131, 157, 193, 233, 366, 383, 411, 467, 547, 549, 671
Fran Milner: 256, 271
Paul Mirocha: 499
Morgan Cain & Associates: 25, 26, 27, 32, 33, 34, 35, 43, 46, 50, 59, 90, 91, 99, 113, 117, 120, 130, 133, 141, 142, 143, 146, 149, 150, 155, 159, 163, 169, 175, 181, 189, 210, 229, 235, 271, 281, 289, 291, 302, 320–321, 322, 324, 325, 332, 333, 334, 336, 342, 347, 353, 357, 413, 415, 417, 453, 474, 476, 497, 545, 575, 578, 580, 630
Ortelius Design, Inc: 103, 226, 227, 344, 378, 379, 479, 480, 515, 518, 540
Matthew Pippin: 150, 198, 352, 372, 381, 542–543
Precision Graphics: 203, 223, 224, 239, 240, 241, 242, 245, 246, 247, 257, 258, 260, 261, 262, 263, 266, 268
Sandra Sevigny: 648
Nancy Smith: 44, 96, 110
Walter Stuart: 628, 629, 538
Pat Williams: 666
J/B Woolsey Associates: 426, 594, 605, 611, 613, 632, 633, 634, 636, 639, 652, 656, 663, 668

Photography

Cover Design: Studio Montage

Cover Image: Zefa Germany/The Stock Market

Front Matter
Page i, ii, Zefa Germany/The Stock Market; **iii l,** Courtesy of Michael J. Padilla, Ph.D; **iii r,** Courtesy of Martha Cyr, Ph.D. and Ioannis Miaoulis, Ph.D.; **viii l,** Bachmann/PhotoEdit; **viii r,** Ted Horowitz/The Stock Market; **ix,** Fotopic/Omni-Photo Communications; **x tl,** Stone/Matthew McVay; **x tr,** Eric Miller/Liaison Agency; **x b,** UCO/Lick Observatory; **xi t,** Norbert Wu; **xi b,** David Hosking/Photo Reseachers, Inc.; **xii l,** Russ Lappa; **xii r,** Bob Daemmrich/Stock Boston; **xiii l,** D. Holden Bailey/Tom Stack & Associates; **xiii r,** J. Alcock/Visuals Unlimited; **xiv t, xiv bl,** Richard Haynes; **xiv m,** Russ Lappa; **xiv br,** Ron Kimball; **xv t,** Steve Elmore/The Stock Market; **xv b,** Christie's Images, London/SuperStock; **xvi t,** NOAA; **xvi b,** Stone/Camille Tokerud; **xvii t,** Stephen J. Krasemann/DRK Photo; **xvii b,** Tim Fitzharris/Minden Pictures; **xviii t,** John Kieffer/Peter Arnold, Inc.; **xviii b,** David Young-Wolff/PhotoEdit; **xix t,** Ray Pfortner/Peter Arnold, Inc.; **xix b,** Richard Haynes; **xx t,** Stone/Marc Pokempner; **xx b,** Richard Haynes; **xxi t,** Dan McCoy/Rainbow; **xxi bl,** Stanley Rowin/The Picture Cube/Index Stock Imagery; **xxi br,** Andy Martinez/Photo Researchers, Inc.

Texas Field Trip
Page 2 b, NASA; **2–3,** NASA/Roger Ressmeyer/Corbis; **3 both, 4 both,** NASA; **5,** Stone/World Perspective.

Nature of Science
Page 6 t, Stone/Jim Ballard; **6 b,** Courtesy of Boeing; **7 all,** NASA; **8,** NASA/Science Source/Photo Reseachers, Inc.; **9,** Courtesy of Boeing.

What Is Science?
Page 10, John Sanford/Science Photo Library/Photo Researchers; **11 t,** John Brooks/Liaison Agency; **11 bl,** Bruce Henderson/Stock Boston; **11 br,** Index Stock Imagery; **12,** David Howell/ The Image Works; **13,** Russ Lappa; **14,** D'Andrea/Index Stock Imagery; **15,** James Holmes/ Photo Researchers, Inc.; **16,** Richard Haynes; **17,** Russ Lappa; **18 l,** Stone/Ben Osborne; **18 r,** Nieto/Jerrican/Photo Researchers Inc.; **19 l,** Robin L. Sachs/PhotoEdit; **19 r,** Index Stock Imagery; **20,** John Brooks/Liaison Agency

Chapter 1
Pages 22–23, Kunio Owaki/The Stock Market; **25 both, 26 both, 27 t,** Russ Lappa; **27 b,** Frank Cezus/FPG International; **29,** Russ Lappa; **30 t,** Jo Prater/Visuals Unlimited; **30 inset,** Peter L. Chapman/Stock Boston; **31 both,** The Granger Collection, NY; **35, 36 l,** Russ Lappa; **36 m,** PhotoDisc, Inc.; **36 r,** Bob Daemmrich/Stock Boston; **38,** Steve Elmore/The Stock Market; **39,** Brian Sytnyk/Masterfile; **40 t,** Charles D. Winters/Photo Researchers, Inc.; **40 ml,** Wood Sabold/International Stock; **40 mr,** Ken O'Donaghue; **40 bl,** Russ Lappa; **40 br,** Steven Needham/Envision; **41 t,** Michael Newman/PhotoEdit; **41 b,** SuperStock; **42 l,** Russ Lappa; **42 r,** J. Sulley/The Image Works; **43 both,** Richard Megna/Fundamental Photographs; **45,** Richard Haynes; **46, 48 all,** Russ Lappa; **49,** John D. Cummingham/Visuals Unlimited; **51 both,** E. R. Degginger; **52,** Stone/Donald Johnston; **53 t,** Russ Lappa; **53 b,** Charles D. Winters/Photo Researchers, Inc.; **54 t,** Richard Haynes; **54 b,** Stone/Simon Norfolk; **57 tl, 57 tr,** Richard Megna/Fundamental Photographs; **57 b,** Russ Lappa; **58,** AP/Wide World Photos; **60,** Russ Lappa; **61,** Richard Haynes; **62,** Dede Gilman/Photo Network.

Chapter 2
Pages 66–67, Larry Ulrich/DRK Photo; **68,** John Terence Turner/FPG International; **69,** Russ Lappa; **70 tl,** Tom Tracey/The Stock Market; **70 tr,** Inga Spence/Visuals Unlimited; **70 b,** William Whitehurst/The Stock Market; **72 t,** Leonard Lessin/Peter Arnold, Inc.; **72 bl,** Corbis-Bettmann; **72 br,** Terry Wild Studio/Uniphoto; **73 tl,** David Young-Wolff/PhotoEdit; **73 tr,** Nick Colaneri/Uniax Corporation; **73 b,** Jeffry W. Myers/The Stock Market; **74 l,** Stone/Bob Torrez; **74 r,** Stone/David J. Sams; **75 l,** Stone/Dennis O'Clair; **75 r,** Richard Hutchings/Photo Researchers, Inc.; **76,** Daemmrich/Uniphoto; **77,** Richard Haynes; **78,** Tom Smith/Photo Researchers, Inc.; **79 t,** Russ Lappa; **79 b,** Bachmann/PhotoEdit; **80 l,** Richard Haynes; **80 r,** Diana Calder/The Stock Market; **81 tl,** Peter Gridley/FPG International; **81 bl,** De Malglaive E./Liaison Agency; **81 m,** AP Photo/Boeing handout/Wide World Photos; **81 br,** Pratt & Whitney/Liaison Agency; **83 l,** William Hopkins; **83 r,** Stone/Marc Pokempner; **84 t,** Russ Lappa; **84 b,** M. Borchi White Star/Photo Researchers, Inc.; **85 t,** Daniel Aubry/The Stock Market; **85 bl,** Mark Richards/PhotoEdit; **85 br,** Dan McCoy/Rainbow; **86 both,** James L. Amos/Peter Arnold, Inc.; **87,** Courtsey of Dacor; **88,** Ted Horowitz/The Stock Market; **89,** Jan Van Der Straet/The Granger Collection, NY; **92,** T. A. Wiewandt/DRK Photo; **94 l,** Jean-Perrin/CNRI/Science Photo Library/Photo Researchers, Inc.; **94 r,** Alfred Pasieka/Science Photo Library/Photo Researchers, Inc.; **95 both,** Pat Cunningham/Liaison Agency.

Chapter 3
Pages 100–101, Alfred Pasieka/Peter Arnold, Inc.; **102 t,** Richard Haynes; **102 b,** Paul A. Souders/Corbis; **104 l,** Fotopic/Omni-Photo Communications; **104 m,** Stone/Cosmo Condina; **104 r,** Jon Ferrey/All Sport; **106,** SuperStock; **107,** Corbis Digital Stock; **108 l,** Zefa Visual Media - German/Index Stock Imagery; **108 r,** Dave Rusk/Index Stock Imagery; **109,** Stone/Kevin Horan; **110,** Richard Haynes; **111,** Ken O'Donoghue; **112, 114, 115 t,** Russ Lappa; **115 b,** Michael Mancuso/Omni-Photo Communications; **116,** Stephen L. Saks/Photo Researchers, Inc.; **117,** Ken O'Donoghue; **118 t,** Tom Campbell/Liaison Agency; **118 b,** Richard Haynes; **119 l,** Wayne Lynch/DRK Photo; **119 r,** Stone/Gay Bumgarner; **121,** Mike Mazzaschi/Stock Boston; **123,** Richard Haynes; **124,** Stone/Andy Sacks; **125 t,** Richard Haynes; **125 b,** Stone/Wayne Eastep; **126 tl,** Runk/Schoenberger/Grant Heilman Photography; **126 tr,** Jack Reznicki/The Stock Market; **126 b,** Jan Halaska/Photo

Library/Photo Researchers, Inc.; **428,** Richard Haynes; **429,** Russ Lappa; **431,** Hank Morgan/Science Source/Photo Researchers, Inc.; **432 l,** Stone/David Joel; **432 r,** Hank Morgan/Science Source/Photo Researchers, Inc.; **433,** Russ Lappa; **434,** David Lassman/The Image Works; **435,** Ray Pfortner/Peter Arnold, Inc.; **436,** Photo Edit; **437,** Richard Haynes; **438 t,** Russ Lappa; **438 b,** Galen Rowell/Peter Arnold, Inc.; **439 all,** Russ Lappa; **440 l,** Stone/Fred Hirschmann; **440 r,** Stephen Agricola/The Image Works; **442,** Russ Lappa.

Chapter 13
Pages 446–447, G. Randall/FPG International; **448 t,** Russ Lappa; **448 b,** NASA/Liaison Agency; **449,** Conor Caffrey/SPL/Photo Researchers, Inc.; **452,** Russ Lappa; **455 t,** Richard Haynes; **455 b,** NASA/The Stock Market; **457,** Tim Brown/Index Stock Imagery; **458 l,** Ed Wheeler/The Stock Market; **458 r,** Robert Fried/Stock Boston; **459,** Bilderberg/The Stock Market; **460 l,** Suzi Moore/Woodfin Camp & Associates; **460 r,** Jeffrey Muir Hamilton/Stock Boston; **461,** U.S. Geological Survey/Geologic Inquiries Group; **463 t,** Richard Haynes; **463 b,** Mike Booher/Transparencies, Inc.; **465 t,** Courtesy of city of Arcata, CA; **465 b,** Stephen Rose/Rainbow; **466,** Bob Daemmrich/Stock Boston; **467,** Conor Caffrey/SPL/Photo Researchers, Inc.

Chapter 14
Pages 470–471, Fred Bavendam; **472 t,** Russ Lappa; **472 b,** The Granger Collection, NY; **473,** Courtesy, Peabody Essex Museum, Salem, MA; **474,** Norbert Wu/The Stock Market; **475 t,** SCRIPPS Oceanographic Institute; **475 b,** Scott Camanzine/Photo Researchers, Inc.; **478 t,** Ted Streshinsky/Corbis; **478 b,** Russ Lappa; **480 both,** Gene Ahrens/Bruce Coleman, Inc.; **485,** Maher Attar/Corbis Sygma; **486,** Richard Dunoff/The Stock Market; **487 tr,** E. R. Degginger/Photo Researchers, Inc.; **487 mr,** Tim Heller/Mo Yung Productions; **487 br,** Doug Perrine/Innerspace Visions; **487 bl,** F. Stuart Westmorland/Photo Researchers, Inc.; **490 l,** Maresa Pryor/Animals Animals/Earth Scenes; **490 r,** Peter Weiman/Animals Animals/Earth Scenes; **491 t,** Lynda Richardson/Corbis; **491 b,** Andy Martinez/Photo Researchers, Inc.; **492,** Eric Horan/Liaison Agency; **493,** Bob Daemmrich Photography; **494 t,** Richard Haynes; **494 b,** Jeff Foott/Tom Stack & Associates; **496 l,** Stone/Chuck Davis; **496 inset,** Randy Morse/Tom Stack & Associates; **497,** Mike Bacon/Tom Stack & Associates; **498,** Norbert Wu; **500,** D. Foster/WHOI/Visuals Unlimited; **501 t,** Richard Haynes; **501 b,** Nathan Benn/Stock Boston; **503,** Russ Lappa; **504,** Stone/Arnulf Husmo; **505 l,** Stone/Bob Torrez; **505 r,** Bill Nation/Corbis Sygma; **506 t,** Stone/Jake Evans; **506 b,** Richard Haynes; **507,** Tim Hauf/Visuals Unlimited.

Chapter 15
Pages 512–513, David Muench Photography; **514 t,** Richard Haynes; **514 b,** Thomas D. Mangelsen/Peter Arnold, Inc.; **516,** David Madison/Bruce Coleman, Inc.; **518,** Stone/Duncan Wherrett; **519,** Stone/Chris Cheadle; **523,** Richard Haynes; **524 t,** Russ Lappa; **524 b,** Stone/Charlie Waite; **525,** Geogory G. Dimigian/Photo Researchers, Inc.; **528 t,** Thomas D. Mangelsen/Peter Arnold, Inc.; **528 b,** Alex S. MacLean/Peter Arnold, Inc.; **529,** Stone/Stephen Johnson; **530 t,** Ann Duncan/Tom Stack & Associates; **530 b,** Stone/Margaret Gowan; **531,** Kennan Ward Photography/Corbis; **532 t,** Stone/Art Wolfe; **532 b,** Thomas Kitchin/Tom Stack & Associates; **533,** PhotoDisc, Inc.; **536,** 1996 Ira Block; **537 r,** Tony Craddock/Science Photo Library/Photo Researchers, Inc.; **537 inset,** George Godfrey/Animals Animals/Earth Scenes; **541,** Richard Haynes; **546,** NOAA.

Chapter 16
Pages 554–555, Ron Kimball; **556 t,** Stone/Mike Rothwell; **556 b,** Corbis-Bettmann; **557,** Barry Runk/Grant Heilman Photography; **560 both,** Meinrad Faltner/The Stock Market; **561,** Inga Spence/The Picture Cube/Index Stock Imagery; **564–565,** Image Stop/Phototake; **568,** Hans Reinhard/Bruce Coleman, Inc.; **571,** Richard Haynes; **572 l,** David M. Phillips/Photo Researchers, Inc.; **572 r,** University "La Sapienza", Rome/Science Photo Library/Photo Researchers, Inc.; **573 l,** Jonathan D. Speer/Visuals Unlimited; **573 r,** M. Abbey/Photo Researchers, Inc.; **577,** AP/Wide World Photos; **582,** William E. Ferguson; **583,** Stone/Mike Rothwell.

Chapter 17
Pages 586–587, Herb Snitzer/Stock Boston; **588,** Richard Haynes; **590,** Stone/Camille Tokerud; **592,** Andrew McClenaghan/Science Photo Library/Photo Researchers, Inc.; **594,** Kwame Zikoma/Superstock; **595 t,** CNRI/Science Photo Library/Photo Researchers, Inc.; **595 b,** Stone/Lawrence Migdale; **596 t,** Simon Fraser/RVI, Newcastle-upon-TYNE/Science Photo Library/Photo Researchers, Inc.; **596 b,** Stanley Flegler/Visuals Unlimited; **597,** Corbis-Bettmann; **598,** Mugshots/The Stock Market; **598 inset,** CNRI/Science Photo Library/Photo Researchers, Inc.; **599,** Will and Deni McIntyre/Photo Researchers Inc.; **600,** Richard Haynes; **602,** AP /Wide World Photos; **603,** Tim Barnwell/Stock Boston; **604,** Patricia J. Bruno/Positive Images; **605,** Stone/LeLand Bobbe; **606,** Gary Wagner/Stock Boston; **607,** AP /Wide World Photos; **608,** U.S. Department of Energy/Human Genome Managment Information System, Oak Ridge National Laboratory; **609,** Michael Newman/PhotoEdit; **610,** David Parker/Science Photo Library/Photo Researchers, Inc.

Chapter 18
Pages 614–615, Bill Varie/Corbis Westlight; **616 t,** Portrait by George Richmond/Down House, Downe/The Bridgeman Art Library; **616 b,** Corbis-Bettmann; **617 t,** Tui De Roy/Minden Pictures; **617 m,** Frans Lanting/Minden Pictures; **617 b,** Tui De Roy/Minden Pictures; **618 l,** Zig Leszczynski/Animals Animals; **618 r,** Tui De Roy/Minden Pictures; **619,** Dr. Jeremy Burgess/Science Photo Library/Photo Researchers, Inc.; **620,** Mitsuaki Iwago/Minden Pictures; **621,** Jeff Gnass Photography/The Stock Market; **623,** Richard Haynes; **624 both,** Breck P. Kent; **625 both,** Pat & Tom Leeson/Photo Researchers, Inc.; **626 t,** John Cancalosi/Tom Stack & Associates; **626 b,** Tom McHugh/Photo Researchers, Inc.; **627 t,** James L. Amos/Photo Researchers, Inc.; **627 b,** Sinclair Stammers/Science Photo Library/Photo Researchers, Inc.; **631,** Robert Landau/Corbis Westlight; **634,** Peter Frey/Image Bank; **635,** Richard Haynes; **637 l,** Keith Gillett/Animals Animals; **637 m,** George Whiteley/Photo Researchers, Inc.; **637 r,** David Spears Ltd./Science Photo Library/Photo Researchers, Inc.; **638 l,** Gary Milburn/Tom Stack & Associates; **638 r,** Stone/Daryl Balfour.

Chapter 19
Pages 644–645, Robert A. Tyrrell; **646 b,** Cliff Hollenbeck/International Stock; **646 t,** Richard Haynes; **647 bm,** Pearson Education/PH College; **647 b,** Lester V. Bergman/Corbis; **647 tm,** Lester V. Bergman/Corbis; **647 t,** Stone /Robert Brons/BOS; **649,** Gary Conner/Index Stock Imagery; **650,** Photo Researchers, Inc.; **653,** Meckes/Ottawa/Photo Researchers, Inc.; **655 t,** Richard Haynes; **655 b,** Christie's Images. London/SuperStock; **657,** Robert Finken/Index Stock Imagery; **659 t,** Leonard Lessin /Photo Researchers, Inc.; **659 b,** Leonard Lessin /Photo Researchers, Inc.; **660,** Lawrence Migdale/PIX; **661,** Alcock/Visuals Unlimited; **663 tr,** Wayne Lankinen/DRK Photo; **663 l,** Patti Murray/Animals Animals; **663 br,** Ron Willocks/Animals Animals; **664 l,** Michael Fogden/DRK Photo; **664 r,** D. Holden Bailey/Tom Stack & Associates; **665 tl,** Stephen J. Krasemann/DRK Photo; **665 tr,** Donald Specker/Animals Animals; **665 b,** Jeanne White/Photo Researchers, Inc.; **666,** Richard Haynes; **667,** Ralph Reinhold/Index Stock Imagery; **669,** Stone/Daryl Balfour; **670,** John Gerlach/DRK Photo; **674 m,** Tim Fitzharris/Minden Pictures; **674 b,** Bridgeman Art Library; **674 t,** Stone/Peter Cade; **675,** Ron Kimball; **676 br,** Stone/Jack Daniels; **676 tr,** Charles Philip/Westlight; **676 tl, 676 m, 676 bl, 677 mr, 677 ml, 677 m, 677 t,** Corel Corp.; **677 b,** C. Jeanne White/Photo Researchers Inc.; **678 t,** Stone/Peter Cade; **678 inset,** AP/ Wide World Photos; **678-679 b,** Nick Meers/Panoramic Images.

Skills Handbook
Page 680, Mike Moreland/Photo Network; **681 t,** FoodPix; **681 m,** Richard Haynes; **681 b,** Russ Lappa; **684,** Richard Haynes; **686,** Ron Kimball; **687,** Renee Lynn/Photo Researchers; **692,** Paul Rezendes.

Appendix
Page 700 both, Russ Lappa; **708, 709, 710, 711,** Griffith Observer, Griffith Observatory, Los Angeles.

Glossary
Page 712, Bob Daemmrich Photography; **713,** Grant Heilman/Grant Heilman Photography; **714,** John Sanford/Science Photo Library/Photo Researchers, Inc.; **715,** Laurence Parent; **716,** Breck P. Kent; **719,** McDonald Observatory photo by Martin Harris; **720,** Charles D. Winters/Photo Researchers, Inc.; **722,** Anglo-Australian Observatory.

Library/Photo Researchers, Inc.; **428,** Richard Haynes; **429,** Russ Lappa; **431,** Hank Morgan/Science Source/Photo Researchers, Inc.; **432 l,** Stone/David Joel; **432 r,** Hank Morgan/Science Source/Photo Researchers, Inc.; **433,** Russ Lappa; **434,** David Lassman/The Image Works; **435,** Ray Pfortner/Peter Arnold, Inc.; **436,** Photo Edit; **437,** Richard Haynes; **438 t,** Russ Lappa; **438 b,** Galen Rowell/Peter Arnold, Inc.; **439 all,** Russ Lappa; **440 l,** Stone/Fred Hirschmann; **440 r,** Stephen Agricola/The Image Works; **442,** Russ Lappa.

Chapter 13
Pages 446–447, G. Randall/FPG International; **448 t,** Russ Lappa; **448 b,** NASA/Liaison Agency; **449,** Conor Caffrey/SPL/Photo Researchers, Inc.; **452,** Russ Lappa; **455 t,** Richard Haynes; **455 b,** NASA/The Stock Market; **457,** Tim Brown/Index Stock Imagery; **458 l,** Ed Wheeler/The Stock Market; **458 r,** Robert Fried/Stock Boston; **459,** Bilderberg/The Stock Market; **460 l,** Suzi Moore/Woodfin Camp & Associates; **460 r,** Jeffrey Muir Hamilton/Stock Boston; **461,** U.S. Geological Survey/Geologic Inquiries Group; **463 t,** Richard Haynes; **463 b,** Mike Booher/Transparencies, Inc.; **465 t,** Courtesy of city of Arcata, CA; **465 b,** Stephen Rose/Rainbow; **466,** Bob Daemmrich/Stock Boston; **467,** Conor Caffrey/SPL/Photo Researchers, Inc.

Chapter 14
Pages 470–471, Fred Bavendam; **472 t,** Russ Lappa; **472 b,** The Granger Collection, NY; **473,** Courtesy, Peabody Essex Museum, Salem, MA; **474,** Norbert Wu/The Stock Market; **475 t,** SCRIPPS Oceanographic Institute; **475 b,** Scott Camanzine/Photo Researchers, Inc.; **478 t,** Ted Streshinsky/Corbis; **478 b,** Russ Lappa; **480 both,** Gene Ahrens/Bruce Coleman, Inc.; **485,** Maher Attar/Corbis Sygma; **486,** Richard Dunoff/The Stock Market; **487 tr,** E. R. Degginger/Photo Researchers, Inc.; **487 mr,** Tim Heller/Mo Yung Productions; **487 br,** Doug Perrine/Innerspace Visions; **487 bl,** F. Stuart Westmorland/Photo Researchers, Inc.; **490 l,** Maresa Pryor/Animals Animals/Earth Scenes; **490 r,** Peter Weiman/Animals Animals/Earth Scenes; **491 t,** Lynda Richardson/Corbis; **491 b,** Andy Martinez/Photo Researchers, Inc.; **492,** Eric Horan/Liaison Agency; **493,** Bob Daemmrich Photography; **494 t,** Richard Haynes; **494 b,** Jeff Foott/Tom Stack & Associates; **496 l,** Stone/Chuck Davis; **496 inset,** Randy Morse/Tom Stack & Associates; **497,** Mike Bacon/Tom Stack & Associates; **498,** Norbert Wu; **500,** D. Foster/WHOI/Visuals Unlimited; **501 t,** Richard Haynes; **501 b,** Nathan Benn/Stock Boston; **503,** Russ Lappa; **504,** Stone/Arnulf Husmo; **505 l,** Stone/Bob Torrez; **505 r,** Bill Nation/Corbis Sygma; **506 t,** Stone/Jake Evans; **506 b,** Richard Haynes; **507,** Tim Hauf/Visuals Unlimited.

Chapter 15
Pages 512–513, David Muench Photography; **514 t,** Richard Haynes; **514 b,** Thomas D. Mangelsen/Peter Arnold, Inc.; **516,** David Madison/Bruce Coleman, Inc.; **518,** Stone/Duncan Wherrett; **519,** Stone/Chris Cheadle; **523,** Richard Haynes; **524 t,** Russ Lappa; **524 b,** Stone/Charlie Waite; **525,** Geogory G. Dimigian/Photo Researchers, Inc.; **528 t,** Thomas D. Mangelsen/Peter Arnold, Inc.; **528 b,** Alex S. MacLean/Peter Arnold, Inc.; **529,** Stone/Stephen Johnson; **530 t,** Ann Duncan/Tom Stack & Associates; **530 b,** Stone/Margaret Gowan; **531,** Kennan Ward Photography/Corbis; **532 t,** Stone/Art Wolfe; **532 b,** Thomas Kitchin/Tom Stack & Associates; **533,** PhotoDisc, Inc.; **536,** 1996 Ira Block; **537 r,** Tony Craddock/Science Photo Library/Photo Researchers, Inc.; **537 inset,** George Godfrey/Animals Animals/Earth Scenes; **541,** Richard Haynes; **546,** NOAA.

Chapter 16
Pages 554–555, Ron Kimball; **556 t,** Stone/Mike Rothwell; **556 b,** Corbis-Bettmann; **557,** Barry Runk/Grant Heilman Photography; **560 both,** Meinrad Faltner/The Stock Market; **561,** Inga Spence/The Picture Cube/Index Stock Imagery; **564–565,** Image Stop/Phototake; **568,** Hans Reinhard/Bruce Coleman, Inc.; **571,** Richard Haynes; **572 l,** David M. Phillips/Photo Researchers, Inc.; **572 r,** University "La Sapienza", Rome/Science Photo Library/Photo Researchers, Inc.; **573 l,** Jonathan D. Speer/Visuals Unlimited; **573 r,** M. Abbey/Photo Researchers, Inc.; **577,** AP/Wide World Photos; **582,** William E. Ferguson; **583,** Stone/Mike Rothwell.

Chapter 17
Pages 586–587, Herb Snitzer/Stock Boston; **588,** Richard Haynes; **590,** Stone/Camille Tokerud; **592,** Andrew McClenaghan/Science Photo Library/Photo Researchers, Inc.; **594,** Kwame Zikoma/Superstock; **595 t,** CNRI/Science Photo Library/Photo Researchers, Inc.; **595 b,** Stone/Lawrence Migdale; **596 t,** Simon Fraser/RVI, Newcastle-upon-TYNE/Science Photo Library/Photo Researchers, Inc.; **596 b,** Stanley Flegler/Visuals Unlimited; **597,** Corbis-Bettmann; **598,** Mugshots/The Stock Market; **598 inset,** CNRI/Science Photo Library/Photo Researchers, Inc.; **599,** Will and Deni McIntyre/Photo Researchers Inc.; **600,** Richard Haynes; **602,** AP /Wide World Photos; **603,** Tim Barnwell/Stock Boston; **604,** Patricia J. Bruno/Positive Images; **605,** Stone/LeLand Bobbe; **606,** Gary Wagner/Stock Boston; **607,** AP /Wide World Photos; **608,** U.S. Department of Energy/Human Genome Managment Information System, Oak Ridge National Laboratory; **609,** Michael Newman/PhotoEdit; **610,** David Parker/Science Photo Library/Photo Researchers, Inc.

Chapter 18
Pages 614–615, Bill Varie/Corbis Westlight; **616 t,** Portrait by George Richmond/Down House, Downe/The Bridgeman Art Library; **616 b,** Corbis-Bettmann; **617 t,** Tui De Roy/Minden Pictures; **617 m,** Frans Lanting/Minden Pictures; **617 b,** Tui De Roy/Minden Pictures; **618 l,** Zig Leszczynski/Animals Animals; **618 r,** Tui De Roy/Minden Pictures; **619,** Dr. Jeremy Burgess/Science Photo Library/Photo Researchers, Inc.; **620,** Mitsuaki Iwago/Minden Pictures; **621,** Jeff Gnass Photography/The Stock Market; **623,** Richard Haynes; **624 both,** Breck P. Kent; **625 both,** Pat & Tom Leeson/Photo Researchers, Inc.; **626 t,** John Cancalosi/Tom Stack & Associates; **626 b,** Tom McHugh/Photo Researchers, Inc.; **627 t,** James L. Amos/Photo Researchers, Inc.; **627 b,** Sinclair Stammers/Science Photo Library/Photo Researchers, Inc.; **631,** Robert Landau/Corbis Westlight; **634,** Peter Frey/Image Bank; **635,** Richard Haynes; **637 l,** Keith Gillett/Animals Animals; **637 m,** George Whiteley/Photo Researchers, Inc.; **637 r,** David Spears Ltd./Science Photo Library/Photo Researchers, Inc.; **638 l,** Gary Milburn/Tom Stack & Associates; **638 r,** Stone/Daryl Balfour.

Chapter 19
Pages 644–645, Robert A. Tyrrell; **646 b,** Cliff Hollenbeck/International Stock; **646 t,** Richard Haynes; **647 bm,** Pearson Education/PH College; **647 b,** Lester V. Bergman/Corbis; **647 tm,** Lester V. Bergman/Corbis; **647 t,** Stone /Robert Brons/BOS; **649,** Gary Conner/Index Stock Imagery; **650,** Photo Researchers, Inc.; **653,** Meckes/Ottawa/Photo Researchers, Inc.; **655 t,** Richard Haynes; **655 b,** Christie's Images. London/SuperStock; **657,** Robert Finken/Index Stock Imagery; **659 t,** Leonard Lessin /Photo Researchers, Inc.; **659 b,** Leonard Lessin /Photo Researchers, Inc.; **660,** Lawrence Migdale/PIX; **661,** Alcock/Visuals Unlimited; **663 tr,** Wayne Lankinen/DRK Photo; **663 l,** Patti Murray/Animals Animals; **663 br,** Ron Willocks/Animals Animals; **664 l,** Michael Fogden/DRK Photo; **664 r,** D. Holden Bailey/Tom Stack & Associates; **665 tl,** Stephen J. Krasemann/DRK Photo; **665 tr,** Donald Specker/Animals Animals; **665 b,** Jeanne White/Photo Researchers, Inc.; **666,** Richard Haynes; **667,** Ralph Reinhold/Index Stock Imagery; **669,** Stone/Daryl Balfour; **670,** John Gerlach/DRK Photo; **674 m,** Tim Fitzharris/Minden Pictures; **674 b,** Bridgeman Art Library; **674 t,** Stone/Peter Cade; **675,** Ron Kimball; **676 br,** Stone/Jack Daniels; **676 tr,** Charles Philip/Westlight; **676 tl, 676 m, 676 bl, 677 mr, 677 ml, 677 m, 677 t,** Corel Corp.; **677 b,** C. Jeanne White/Photo Researchers Inc.; **678 t,** Stone/Peter Cade; **678 inset,** AP/ Wide World Photos; **678-679 b,** Nick Meers/Panoramic Images.

Skills Handbook
Page 680, Mike Moreland/Photo Network; **681 t,** FoodPix; **681 m,** Richard Haynes; **681 b;** Russ Lappa; **684,** Richard Haynes; **686,** Ron Kimball; **687,** Renee Lynn/Photo Researchers; **692,** Paul Rezendes.

Appendix
Page 700 both, Russ Lappa; **708, 709, 710, 711,** Griffith Observer, Griffith Observatory, Los Angeles.

Glossary
Page 712, Bob Daemmrich Photography; **713,** Grant Heilman/Grant Heilman Photography; **714,** John Sanford/Science Photo Library/Photo Researchers, Inc.; **715,** Laurence Parent; **716,** Breck P. Kent; **719,** McDonald Observatory photo by Martin Harris; **720,** Charles D. Winters/Photo Researchers, Inc.; **722,** Anglo-Australian Observatory.